INFORMATION MO...
Specification and Impl...

Telephone: Malv...

...ICS DIVISION

To Wendy, Chris, John and Maura

INFORMATION MODELING

Specification and Implementation

David Edmond

Prentice Hall

New York   London   Toronto   Sydney   Tokyo   Singapore

© 1992 by Prentice Hall of Australia Pty Ltd

All rights reserved. No part of this publication may be reproduced, stored in a retrieval system, or transmitted in any form or by any means, electronic, mechanical, photocopying, recording, or otherwise, without written permission of the publisher.

Acquisitions Editor: Andrew Binnie.
Production Editor: Fiona Marcar.
Cover design: The Modern Art Production Group, South Melbourne, Victoria

Printed in Australia by Impact Printing, Brunswick, Victoria.

1 2 3 4 5 96 95 94 93 92

ISBN 0 13 457748 5

National Library of Australia
Cataloguing-in-Publication Data

Edmond, David
 Information modeling: specification and information

 Includes index.
 ISBN 0 13 457748 5.

 1. System design. 2. System design - Problems, exercises, etc. 3. System analysis. 4. System analysis - Problems, exercises, etc. 5. Data base management. 6. Data base management - Problems, exercises, etc. I. Title

003

Library of Congress
Cataloging-in-Publication Data

Edmond, David, 1945-
 Information modeling : specification and implementation / David
 p.   cm.
 Includes index.
 ISBN 0-13-457748-5 : $39.95
 1. Data base design.   I. Title

QA76.9.D26E36   1992   92-27853
005.75'6--dc20   CIP

Prentice Hall, Inc., *Englewood Cliffs, New Jersey*
Prentice Hall Canada, Inc., *Toronto*
Prentice Hall Hispanoamericana, SA, *Mexico*
Prentice Hall of India Private Ltd, *New Delhi*
Prentice Hall International, Inc., *London*
Prentice Hall of Japan, Inc., *Tokyo*
Prentice Hall of Southeast Asia Pty Ltd, *Singapore*
Editora Prentice Hall do Brasil Ltda, *Rio de Janeiro*

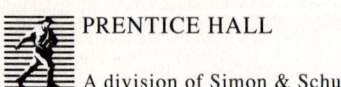 PRENTICE HALL
A division of Simon & Schuster

Contents

1 Introduction   **1**
   1.1 Why Compute? 1
   1.2 Facts and Knowledge 2
   1.3 Inside a Bank 4
   1.4 Next Please! 9
   1.5 The *NextPlease* Program 12
   1.6 Summary 15
        Exercises 17

2 Specific Facts   **18**
   2.1 Introduction 18
   2.2 The Plain Facts 19
   2.3 Facts as Relationships 20
   2.4 One-to-many Relationships 24
   2.5 One-to-one Relationships 27
   2.6 The Construction of Simple Sentences 29
   2.7 The Circle Database 35
   2.8 Compound Sentences 36
   2.9 Summary 42
        Exercises 43

3 Sets   **48**
   3.1 Introduction 48
   3.2 Sets and Everyday Language 48
   3.3 Set Extension 49
   3.4 A Sample Database 51
   3.5 Set Comprehension 52
   3.6 Set Operations 57
   3.7 Higher Order Sets 59
   3.8 Product sets 62
   3.9 Sets, Relations and Functions 63
   3.10 Set Terms 68
   3.11 Summary 69
        Exercises 70

4 Relations   **77**
   4.1 Introduction 77
   4.2 Merging Facts 77
   4.3 Relations 80
   4.4 Tuples 81
   4.5 Domains 85
   4.6 Problems with the Automatic 87

	4.7	The Cars Database	91
	4.8	Anatomy of a Database	92
	4.9	Relational Languages	94
	4.10	The Circle Database	102
	4.11	Summary	106
		Exercises	107
5	**Introducing SQL**		**111**
	5.1	Introduction	111
	5.2	SQL Databases	112
	5.3	Database Definition	113
	5.4	Database Retrieval	115
	5.5	Database Modification	117
	5.6	Database Security	119
	5.7	Using SQL	119
	5.8	Summary	120
		Exercises	121
6	**SQL Retrieval**		**124**
	6.1	Introduction	124
	6.2	Simple Queries	125
	6.3	Join Queries	126
	6.4	Statistical Queries	132
	6.5	"Group by" Queries	133
	6.6	Multi-table "Group by" Queries	136
	6.7	Product Queries	138
	6.8	Pattern Matching	139
	6.9	Summary	140
		Exercises	142
7	**SQL Modularization**		**149**
	7.1	Introduction	149
	7.2	Query Nesting	149
	7.3	Simple Nesting	151
	7.4	"In" Queries	152
	7.5	"All–Any" Queries	153
	7.6	Correlated Subqueries	155
	7.7	"Exists" Queries	156
	7.8	Subquery Usage	158
	7.9	The Union Operator	158
	7.10	Union Usage	161
	7.11	Views	162
	7.12	View Usage	164
	7.13	Summary	164
		Exercises	166

8	**Facts and Relations**	**170**
8.1	Introduction	170
8.2	Facts	171
8.3	A Simple Design	173
8.4	An Experiment	174
8.5	Another Experiment	176
8.6	Uniqueness Constraints	179
8.7	Single and Many-valued Fact Types	181
8.8	Irreducible Facts	183
8.9	Nested Fact Types	185
8.10	Aggregation	186
8.11	Establishing the Database	195
8.12	Summary	197
	Exercises	198
9	**Uncovering Facts**	**203**
9.1	Introduction	203
9.2	Defining Syntax	203
9.3	Analyzing a View	204
9.4	Another Analysis	206
9.5	A Summary of the Notation	206
9.6	Some More Examples	207
9.7	View Analysis	209
9.8	Deriving View Relations	209
9.9	Extracting Elementary Fact Types	211
9.10	Further Abstraction	213
9.11	Summary	216
	Exercises	217
10	**Fact-based Analysis**	**220**
10.1	Introduction	220
10.2	The Problem	222
10.3	Step 1: Uncover the fact types	222
10.4	Step 2: Look for uniqueness constraints	227
10.5	Step 3: Construct record types	229
10.6	Step 4: Decide which attributes may be null	233
10.7	Step 5: Define the database	234
10.8	Step 6: Review the design	236
10.9	Summary	237
	Exercises	238
11	**Entity-relationship Modeling**	**241**
11.1	Introduction	241
11.2	An Example	242
11.3	Database Design	252
11.4	The Conversion Process	253

11.5 Issues in ER Modeling	258
11.6 Summary	261
Exercises	263

12 Knowledge 267
12.1 Introduction	267
12.2 The Predicate Calculus	268
12.3 Quantification	271
12.4 Defining New Symbols	280
12.5 Generic Functions and Relations	287
12.6 Describing Change	291
12.7 Abbreviations	295
12.8 Sequences	298
12.9 Summary	302
Exercises	303

13 The Knowledge Base 309
13.1 Introduction	309
13.2 Information Systems Development	310
13.3 Knowledge	310
13.4 Representing Organizational Knowledge	311
13.5 A look at Z	312
13.6 Signatures	314
13.7 Predicates	321
13.8 Kinds of Schema	324
13.9 Summary	328
Exercises	330

14 From Specification to Implementation 331
14.1 Introduction	331
14.2 The State Schema	331
14.3 Schema Inclusion	332
14.4 Schema Decoration	333
14.5 State Transition	333
14.6 Operation Schemas	334
14.7 Read-only Transactions	339
14.8 Maintaining the State Invariant	339
14.9 Developing a State Schema	341
14.10 Implementation	343
14.11 Developing the Database	344
14.12 The State Schema and the Database	346
14.13 Implementing an Operation	348
14.14 From Operation to Program	349
14.15 Summary	350
Exercises	352

15 Database Definition in SQL — 358
- 15.1 Introduction — 358
- 15.2 Tables — 358
- 15.3 SQL Datatypes — 362
- 15.4 Referential Integrity and Other Constraints — 370
- 15.5 Views — 372
- 15.6 Indexes — 374
- 15.7 Summary — 380
- Exercises — 381

16 Database Manipulation in SQL — 386
- 16.1 Introduction — 386
- 16.2 Adding New Rows — 386
- 16.3 Modifying Existing Rows — 388
- 16.4 Removing Rows — 391
- 16.5 Transactions — 392
- 16.6 Referential Integrity — 393
- 16.7 View Update — 395
- 16.8 Controlling Database Access — 397
- 16.9 Summary — 399
- Exercises — 400

17 Application Programming — 405
- 17.1 Introduction — 405
- 17.2 Using SQL — 406
- 17.3 Host Language Interface — 407
- 17.4 Form-based Application Development — 420
- 17.5 Summary — 428
- Exercises — 429

18 Case Studies — 430
- 18.1 Introduction — 430
- 18.2 The League Table — 430
- 18.3 The Rocky Concrete Company — 443
- Exercises — 463
- Additional Cases — 464

19 Refinement — 470
- 19.1 Introduction — 470
- 19.2 The Abstract Specification — 471
- 19.3 Operations on Student Records — 474
- 19.4 The Concrete Specification — 478
- 19.5 A Review — 484
- 19.6 Verification — 485
- 19.7 Verifying the $Award_{EXE}$ Operation — 487
- 19.8 The External Interface — 491

19.9 Translating the $Award_{EXE}$ Schema into SQL 492
19.10 Summary 493

Appendices
A: Further Reading 494
B: SQL Syntax Summary 498
C: The Z Notation 503
D: Selected Answers 508

Index 580

Preface

The purpose of this book is to convey the essence of organizational computing, as seen by computing professionals. For this reason, the book attempts to show both the **specification** and the **implementation** of organizational information systems. Yet it avoids being too wide-ranging in describing all the potential problems associated with specifying the requirements of an information system. It also aims to avoid being too technical in its discussion of implementation.

The book is based on material taught in one of the four subjects that form the first year of the degree in information technology offered by the Queensland University of Technology. The subject attempts to straddle specification *and* implementation by providing a non procedurally-oriented view of both. It can be thought of as a combined introduction to both database systems and systems analysis.

Database material is included because it is too important to be left until the later stages of a computing degree. Material from systems analysis is included because it is important that students understand, from the beginning, the role of the computer in enabling an organization to model and understand its environment.

In later **database** subjects students are introduced to issues such as database recovery, concurrency, security, network and hierarchical databases, normalization and distributed databases. The first-year database material concentrates on the relational model, SQL, simple relational database design and database integrity.

In subsequent **systems analysis and design** subjects, students are introduced to some of the other tools of the analyst, such as data flow diagrams, systems flowcharts, structure charts, pseudocode and decision tables. Students are also introduced to other issues and concepts that are of major importance to the systems analyst, such as the systems life cycle, systems development methodologies, project management and interviewing techniques. The first-year systems analysis material concentrates on logical modeling or specification whereby a particular state of affairs is modelled and changes to that state (transactions) are specified.

The first-year material is presented in a fairly prescriptive manner. Only the relational model and only one style of specification are discussed.

The relational model is used for several reasons: it is the easiest to comprehend; SQL is the *current* means of implementation; and it fits, in a natural manner, the chosen specification style.

Deciding how to present a concise yet comprehensive discussion of specification was much more difficult. There are so many options. From the process school there are program flowcharts, pseudocode, structured English, Nassi-Shneiderman charts and data flow diagrams. Or, if you prefer the data school, there are ER diagrams, data structure and Bachman diagrams.

I decided to avoid all of these and to use instead a specification language called Z. This language is gaining increasing recognition, particularly in Europe and in Australia. However, its acceptance or otherwise is almost irrelevant because Z is really only a name for a standard way of writing set theory and predicate calculus. What is in question is whether mathematics is a useful way of specifying information systems. I believe that it is. It is worth outlining some of the advantages of using Z.

1. Z is a knowledge representation language. It is not just for data modeling or for process modeling. Z can model general facts (knowledge) as well as it can model specific facts (data).

2. Because it is based on logic, Z incorporates propositional calculus (Boolean algebra). In learning this, students learn how to form compound sentences or conditions. This is an important part of specification *and* is also the basis of the `where` clause of SQL.

3. Because Z is also based on set theory, set comprehension (the definition of a set through a property shared by its members) is an important part of the language. Learning how Z handles sets provides an invaluable theoretical introduction to SQL. This is further enhanced because Z uses **typed** sets.

4. Functions and relations which are essential to database design are also fundamental to Z. So by discussing how Z handles these, students are introduced to functional dependencies which lie behind relational database design, whether done by analysis (for example, normalization) or by synthesis (for example, NIAM).

5. Relational calculus is included in Z as part of its repertoire. Thus relational calculus is taught both as part of the specification language *and* as an introduction to SQL because SQL is based upon it. Hopefully, as a consequence, students will not only understand SQL, but they will also be better able to judge its shortcomings.

6. Complex user views, such as reports, can be formally described and incorporated into the specification where they may be related to other views.

7. A formal relationship may be established between these views and the underlying relational database from which they are to be constructed.

It should *not* be thought that the only reason for using Z is that it will help students to better understand relational database theory and practice. More importantly, experience in the use of Z will enable students to make precise and concise observations about situations and events, surely a priceless skill for a systems analyst.

A specification written in Z is simply a mathematical theory of the organization. Using logic, it should be possible to *prove* properties of the specification and hence of any verifiable implementation. It is my belief that, by improving their competence in mathematics, computing professionals can achieve a corresponding improvement in the status and standard of computing.

Why this Book?

Why do we need another textbook on database systems or on systems analysis and design? Such textbooks fall into two main categories.

The first category focuses on databases and database management. These books tend to be overly technical, making many assumptions about the background of the reader. They also tend to take a historical approach in describing and comparing the relational, hierarchical and network approaches to database construction. This is akin to an introductory book on Pascal that begins by describing the complexities of the language Algol-68 and how Pascal arose in reaction. This book aims to teach some of the fundamentals of computing most accessible through the database approach.

Preface   xiii

The second category focuses on systems analysis. These books introduce the concepts associated with the systems development life cycle. While laudably attempting to place systems development in its proper context, they discuss problems that young people find hard to become enthused about. They emphasize the top-down approach to problem solving. In my opinion, this technique is impossible to teach to beginners because it is founded upon knowledge, experience and self-confidence.

Facts, Knowledge and Computers

The major philosophy of the book is presented in the opening chapter. When we try to represent, in an information system, some aspects of an organization and its environment, there will be two kinds of statements that we want to make:

1. There will be **simple statements** that make connections between specific objects; these tend to be stored in a database of some kind. Let us call such statements **facts**.
2. There will be **more general statements** about the nature of the organization; these tend to end up in computer programs. Let us call such statements **knowledge**.

Systems analysis can be thought of as the uncovering and documenting of organizational knowledge or rules. These include:

- Rules concerning the kinds of things that are important to the organization, such as customers, products and orders; and the ways in which they are related – for example, a customer may make many orders but an order is made by only one customer.
- Rules specifying the ways in which calculations are to be performed – for example, the total value of an order is the sum of the values of each part of the order.
- Constraints regarding the necessary pre-conditions for an event to go ahead – for example, for an order of 10 units of product X to be valid, there must be at least 10 units currently in stock.
- Constraints regarding how a given situation must change in response to some event – for example, as a result of an order, the customer's current balance must be appropriately increased.

The task of the systems developer is to construct an information system that obeys and enforces all of these rules. The rules involving functional dependencies are used to develop the database structure and *that structure* will guarantee that these particular rules are enforced at all times. The rules in this category make up what is called the data model. The remainder of the rules will be implemented in various ways. This book will discuss how to implement them in SQL.

I believe that this book presents a coherent, consistent and modern approach to organizational systems analysis and design. It attempts to bridge the gap between systems analysis and database design. But it is not a compromise, rather, it is a unification achieved by using a *relational* specification language in conjunction with a *relational* database language.

By treating an information system as a combined fact and knowledge base, I aimed to provide a coverage of information systems that avoids the waffle of some texts on systems and analysis and the technicalities of texts on database management.

Structure of the Book

The material in this book may be partitioned in two ways:

1. It can be divided into chapters that deal with specification and those that deal with implementation.
2. Alternatively, it can be divided into chapters that deal with simple facts and those that deal with complex facts.

This two-way partitioning is the basis for the overall structure of the book.

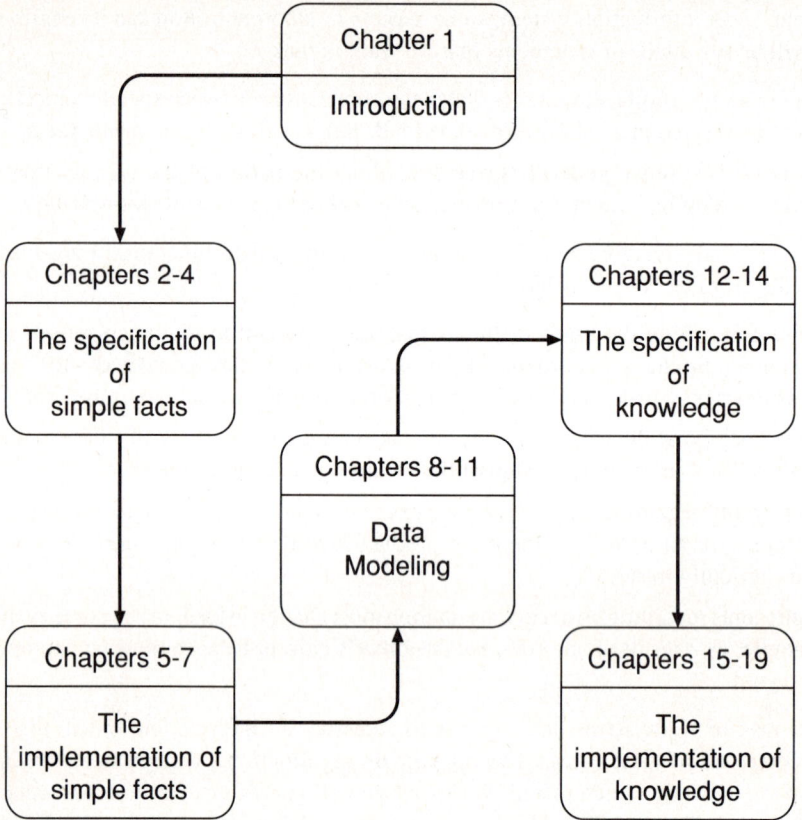

Chapter 2 introduces simple facts, how they are specified formally, and how they may be combined with other facts. Chapter 3 introduces sets and how they are specified and manipulated. It also shows that facts may themselves be considered as sets. Chapter 4 takes a step towards implementation by considering the special sets known as relations.

Chapters 5 to 7 continue the progression towards the implementation of simple facts by introducing one of the most important computing languages, SQL.

Chapters 8 to 11 introduce the basic concepts of data modeling using two contrasting notations – conceptual schema diagrams and entity-relationship diagrams. For each approach, enough material is presented to develop a good database design. This section of the book provides a link between data and knowledge because functional dependencies may be represented as relatively simple pieces of knowledge.

Chapters 12 to 14 discuss the concept of a knowledge base as the set of more general statements or rules about an organization. Some of these describe the organization's structure and some describe how it may change.

Chapters 15 to 18 re-present these rules as the programs that surround a database and discuss how best to implement these rules in SQL. Chapter 19 shows how we can establish a formally defined relationship between a specification and its implementation, and how we may verify the programs that implement the rules.

Answers are given to exercises marked ▶. Exercises marked ▷ have the odd-numbered components answered.

Acknowledgments

Nobody can write a textbook such as this without the help and advice of colleagues, family and friends. It is a pleasure to be able to thank people for their assistance. In particular, I would like to thank Alison Anderson, Peter Bancroft and Jim Reye. I would also like to thank Jason Aquilina, Denis Bridger, Judy Dionysius, Doug Grant, Ken Ling, Bob Smyth, Alan Tickle, Alan Underwood and Sylvia Willie for their support and encouragement. I must also thank the thousands of anonymous students who have shaped and been shaped by this material, and whose feedback has been essential. Finally, I would like to thank my family for their patience and support.

David Edmond
Brisbane
June 1992

CHAPTER 1

Introduction

1.1 Why Compute?

What *are* computers for? What is their purpose? Suppose your life depended upon coming up with a word or phrase that most accurately summed up what computing is all about. What would your answer be?

Would you say that computing is about . . .

> sex?
> drugs?
> rock'n'roll?

No, there's not too much of that in computing.

Well then, perhaps it's about . . .

> money?
> power?
> food?
> gambling?

No, these topics are hardly ever discussed in computing magazines.

This is surely most regrettable. Does this mean that, if we take out all the interesting things in life, computing is about what remains? Not quite, we hope!

Computing is concerned with taking the interesting things out of life and representing them somehow. It is all about **modeling**. Everything inside a computer is a representation of something else.

1.2 Facts and Knowledge

Suppose we got together and tried to describe all the things we know about some organization and its environment. The organization need not necessarily be a commercial or government organization. It could be the Great Barrier Reef, the town in which we live, or even one of us.

Our description might take any form, such as drawings, plans or photographs, but let us assume that it is a narrative written in English. That narrative might include many statements that are merely opinions, so we will try to restrict ourselves to ones that we collectively believe to be true. See Figure 1.1.

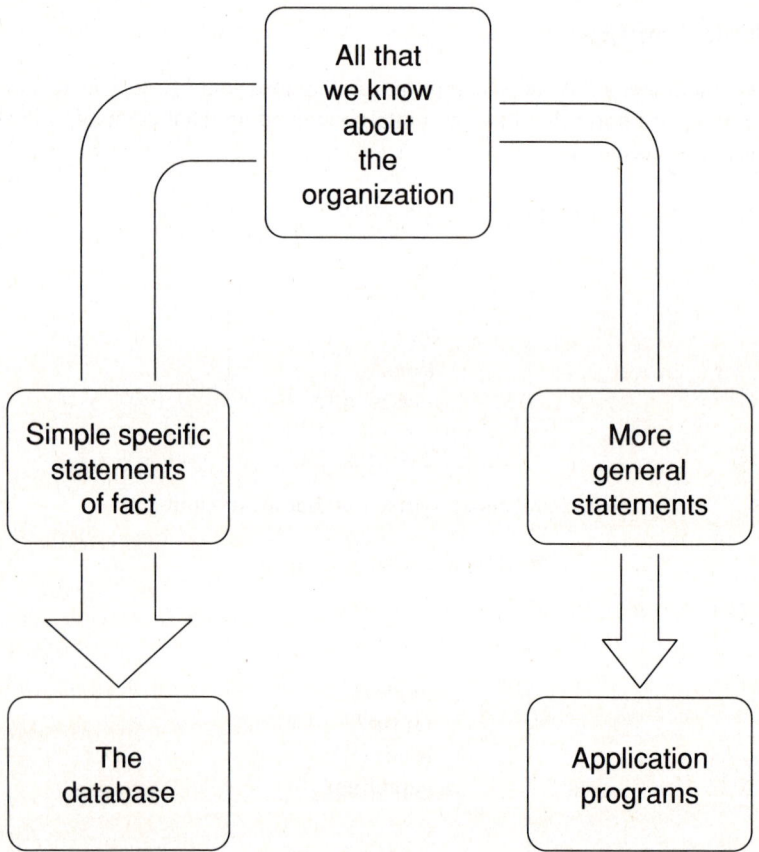

Figure 1.1 The Great Computing Divide

There will be two kinds of statements that we want to make.

1. Some will be simple facts, ones that make connections between specific objects; should we decide to represent these kinds of facts in a computer system they will be stored in a database of some kind.
2. Other facts will make more general statements about the nature of the organization; these tend to end up in computer programs.

Specific Statements

The vast majority of the things that we might write down will be relatively simple statements of fact. These will relate particular objects in some way. Some examples of such statements might be as follows.

- Bill Smith is a senior programmer.
- In the December quarter, the Jones family used 1600 kilowatt hours of electricity.
- F. Garcia owns the "River Breezes" property.
- The Accounts Department is located at Head Office.
- On Tuesday, 31 March, Ann Hampson spent two hours on the Fingle project.

These facts relate specific things – particular people, jobs, dates, quantities and locations, for example. There may be billions of facts of this kind. They constitute the *raw data* or database upon which all information systems are founded. As a consequence of these large numbers:

1. The facts are often partitioned in order to be more manageable, and so we have a Customer database, a Personnel database and so on.
2. Even then, a database may contain millions of facts. Yet a typical transaction might involve only two or three of these facts. Complex **access methods** are involved in enabling rapid access to the required information.

But it is considerations of *technology* and *volume* that drive these facts into a database to be controlled by a database management system, *not* anything intrinsic to the facts themselves. It is technological considerations that force us to make the division between simple facts and the more generalized ones.

General Statements

Of the things we might like to say, some will require more complex language, for example:

- Senior programmers and above are not paid overtime.
- A client may own several properties but a property is owned by only one client.
- The quarterly tariff for the use of electricity is 15 cents per kilowatt hour (kWh) for the first 300 kWh, 10 cents per kWh for the next 900 kWh, and 5 cents per kWh for the remainder.
- If two successive electricity meter readings are such that the second is *less* than the first, then meter tickover is assumed to have occurred (that is, the meter has reached its limit and reset itself).

What makes these statements more complex? Clearly they are longer, but they are longer because they are trying to say more. They seem to be making more general statements about classes rather than individuals; and in being more general, they are also more stable, that is, they tend to remain true for a longer period. If this had not been the case, then programming would have been quite a different discipline.

Let us call these more complex statements **knowledge**. Taken in conjunction with the specific facts given previously, we can say, for example, that any claim for overtime made by Bill Smith will be rejected, and that the Jones family will be charged $155 for their electricity. How many statements of knowledge might be made regarding the organization – tens? thousands? tens of thousands? The answer is that there are probably millions. A great many, but still several orders of magnitude fewer than the simpler facts that accompany them.

Where do we store this knowledge? Do we have a knowledge base for complex facts, one that mirrors the use of a database for simple facts? In practice, we usually bundle together a number of them and encode them using the currently favored programming language. So the organization's computer programs constitute its knowledge base.

Do we have a knowledge base management system (KBMS) to manipulate and modify this knowledge? Most certainly not! Well ... we don't have a computerized KBMS, but one of the major roles of the Computing Department in any organization is to act as a knowledge base management system. One of that department's most important jobs is the maintenance and enhancement of the organization's knowledge base. This is done through the tasks of program maintenance and new systems development.

The knowledge base represents a kind of theory of that company. It represents the way that the company believes that it works and how it interacts with its environment. However, it is a theory that is being constantly revised and refined, as the organization adjusts to that environment.

1.3 Inside a Bank

For the remainder of this chapter, we will look at an example that tries to illustrate these ideas. The situation to be described is one with which most of us are familiar. We are inside a small suburban bank. A picture is presented in Figure 1.2.

Specific Facts about the Bank

The specific facts that are relevant to the situation are these.

- Teller T1 is open.
  Teller T3 is open.
  Teller T4 is open.

- Teller T3 is serving Sue.

- First in the queue is Ann.
  Second in the queue is Kim.
  Third in the queue is Dan.

- Liz is among the other customers.
  Jim is among the other customers.
  Bob is among the other customers.

Introduction 5

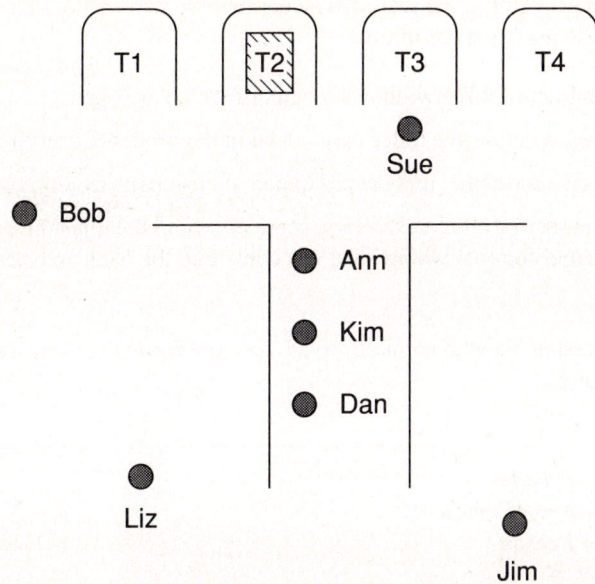

Figure 1.2 In the bank

The facts have been separated into four different groups. Each group corresponds to a certain type of fact. Every fact in a group has a fixed constant part and a variable part. For example, the first group has the form:

Teller __ is open.

Each hole is to be filled by the name or identity of a teller. The sentences themselves are not stored in the database. Rather, we store data that may be plugged into the holes of fact templates such as the one above. For example, the **Open** table contains three rows and each of these may be used to generate a true statement. Each group may give rise to one table or relation in a relational database. The bank database will contain four tables.

Open	Busy		Queue		Others
Teller	Teller	CustId	Place	CustId	CustId
T1	T3	Sue	1	Ann	Liz
T3			2	Kim	Jim
T4			3	Dan	Bob

Generally, there is *not* a one-to-one relationship between the fact types and the database tables. Usually, a number of fact types are compressed into a single table. Database design is, essentially, a process of deciding where to place the different types of fact that are to be stored.

6   Chapter 1

General Statements about the Bank

There are a number of more general statements that we can make. They are rules that describe the bank at any moment of time.

- There are a number of teller windows, not all of which are open.
- Even at an open window, the teller may not be in the process of serving a customer.
- There is a single first-come, first-served queue of customers awaiting attention.
- There are a number of other customers, some of whom have just been served and are about to leave and some of whom have just come into the bank and have not yet joined the queue.

Now we will restate these general observations more formally, using a **state schema** to describe this situation.

$$
\begin{array}{|l}
\hline
\text{Bank} \\
\hline
open : Set\ of\ Teller \\
busy : Teller \nrightarrow Person \\
queue : seq\ Person \\
others : Set\ of\ Person \\
\hline
dom\ busy \subseteq open \\
ran\ busy \cap ran\ queue = \{\} \\
ran\ queue \cap others = \{\} \\
ran\ busy \cap others = \{\} \\
\#(dom\ queue) = \#(ran\ queue) \\
\hline
\end{array}
$$

This state schema is intended to describe a *state of affairs* such as the one found in the bank. The schema and its contents are part of the Z specification language or **Z notation**. This is the language we will use to specify the situations and events that we intend representing in some subsequent information system.

The schema has two parts consisting of a **declaration** and a **predicate** separated by a short horizontal line. The declaration in the above schema introduces the four components of the state. The name of each component has been chosen to match the correspondingly named table in the database. You should note that a table such as **Open** reflects one aspect of the bank at a certain moment of time. Whereas a component of the bank schema such as *open* is meant to represent some permanent aspect of the bank.

The *Bank* Declaration

1. *open : Set of Teller*

   This is the set of tellers whose windows are currently open.

2. *busy : Teller $\nrightarrow$ Person*

   This is a relationship between tellers and people. It consists of a set of pairs with each pair being of the form (teller, person), for example **(T3,Sue)**.

The **domain** of this relationship, written *dom busy*, is the set of tellers actually serving someone. The *dom* operator is just one of a number of useful general purpose operators that may be employed in a specification written in Z. The operation may be applied to any set of pairs and it returns us (or more precisely, allows us to talk about) the set of left-hand components of each pair. If the set of pairs is regarded as a table such as **Busy**, then the domain is the left-hand column.

The **range** of this relationship, written *ran busy*, is the set of people in the process of being served. The *ran* operator complements the *dom* operator. It can also be applied to any set of pairs and if that set is thought of as a two-column table then the range is the right-hand column.

So although only four components were named directly in the declaration, we can access or describe other features of the bank that concern us.

3. *queue* : *seq Person*

    This is a sequence of people intended to represent the customers who are currently queuing. It is a set of pairs of the form (number, person), for example **(2, Kim)**. Each pair indicates a place in the queue and the person at that place.

    Because a sequence is a set of pairs, although of a special kind, we may talk about its domain and its range. The range of the queue, written *ran queue*, is the set of customers who are in the queue.

    We can specify the customer at any given place in the queue by **applying** *queue* to the place in question. For example the customer in second place can be denoted by the expression *queue*(2).

4. *others* : *Set of Person*

    This is a simple set of people intended to represent those customers in the bank but who are not queuing and who are not being served.

We have said what the components are intended to represent but we have not yet written the conditions that will make them such.

We should have a clear idea of the relationships between the components of the bank and now we must specify these. This is done in the predicate part of the schema. Here we **relate** the state components to one another. We provide a number of conditions that must hold within the bank at all times. For this reason the conditions that make the predicate are known as the state **invariant**. This invariant characterizes the bank for us.

The *Bank* Predicate

1. *dom busy* $\subseteq$ *open*

    The set of busy tellers (*dom busy*) must be contained ($\subseteq$) in the set of open tellers. In other words, only open tellers are allowed to serve customers.

2. *ran busy* $\cap$ *ran queue* = {}

    The set of customers being served (*ran busy*) has no elements in common with the set of customers queuing (*ran queue*). In other words, no customer is both being served and in the queue.

3. *ran queue* ∩ *others* = {}
   ran busy ∩ *others* = {}

   Similarly, no person is both queuing *and* among those other customers. And neither is anybody being served.

   These last three statements ensure that the three sets of customers are disjoint, that is, they have nobody in common.

4. #(*dom queue*) = #(*ran queue*)

   This is a more complex statement, yet merely states the almost self-evident fact that no customer will be found more than once in the queue. The queue was declared to be a sequence, but the sequence construct allows repetition. For example, the word "irresistible" is a sequence of characters in which certain of the letters repeat. So a sequence of objects of type *Person* will permit the same person to appear more than once in the queue. This can be prevented with the help of the set cardinality or set size operator #, which may be applied to any set. It allows us to talk about the number of elements in that set. We could write #*busy* to refer to the number of customers being served, or we could write #*open* − #*busy* to refer to the number of open tellers not actually serving at any moment.

   The set *dom queue* is the set of places in the queue; and #(*dom queue*) is the size of that set, that is, the number of places in the queue. The set *ran queue* is the set of customers in the queue; and #(*ranqueue*) is the size of that set, that is, the number of different customers in the queue.

We declared the bank as constituting four primary components. As may be seen in the predicate, however, we are able to use powerful operators such as *dom* and *ran* to "access" other parts of the bank that interest us. We can also use other operators, such as set intersection ∩ to combine two parts or set inclusion ⊆ to compare two parts of the bank.

It should be remembered, at this stage, that Z is not a programming language. When we write an expression such as *dom busy* we are not instructing a computer to return us the left-hand column of the **Busy** table. Rather, the term *dom busy* is a convenient means of naming that set of tellers. It is simply two words used together. We judge a specification language by its expressive power. We look for *economy of expression* and it is operators such as *dom* and *ran* that help us economize. However, you may still feel that the formal description of the bank did not add to your understanding and that the effort involved in learning the language is not justified. We will discuss this point shortly.

Suppose we now re-examine the database.

Open	Busy		Queue		Others
Teller	Teller	CustId	Place	CustId	CustId
T1	T3	Sue	1	Ann	Liz
T3			2	Kim	Jim
T4			3	Dan	Bob

This database is consistent with the rules stated in the *Bank* schema.

- Every teller in **Busy** is also in **Open**.
- No person appears in both **Busy** and **Queue**.
- No person appears in both **Queue** and **Others**.
- No person appears in both **Busy** and **Others**.
- No person appears more than once in **Queue**.

1.4 Next Please!

However, the database merely satisifes the rules. It does not contain them. Nor are the rules incorporated in the programs that are allowed to manipulate the database. But these programs must be aware of the rules, or at least written with an awareness in mind. Every one of them must be written so as to maintain the integrity of the *Bank* state. Whenever some event occurs that will change the situation within the bank, the program written to capture that event should guarantee that, if given a valid bank state, it also returns one. Consider what happens when a teller looks up at the queue and says "Next please!" How can we describe that event in general terms?

We can conveniently divide the description into two sets of conditions.

1. The pre-conditions

    These are the conditions that must apply before the change can proceed.

    - The teller must be open for business.
    - The teller must not be busy with a customer.
    - There must be someone in the queue.

    These are the conditions that we recognize as necessary for the event to be valid. If any *one* is not true then we know something is wrong.

2. The post-conditions

    These describe how the bank changes as a result of the customer moving from the queue to the teller. They relate the state of the bank before the event to its state after. For this event, the conditions are:

    - The teller is now serving the customer who was previously at the front of the queue.
    - The queue is now formed from the tail of the previous queue.
    - Nothing else has changed.

These conditions can now be combined and formalized in an **operation** schema.

10   Chapter 1

NextPlease

$\Delta Bank$
$t? : Teller$

$t? \in open$
$t? \notin dom\ busy$
$\#queue > 0$
$busy' = busy \cup \{(t?, head\ queue)\}$
$queue' = tail\ queue$
$open' = open$
$others' = others$

Before we look at this specification, you should note three conventions used.

1. The use of the delta symbol in $\Delta Bank$ indicates that this schema is describing a *change* to the bank.

2. The use of the question mark in the variable $t?$ indicates that the teller is identified as an *input* to the operation. It is information that will be supplied.

3. The four components of the *Bank* state are *open*, *busy*, *queue* and *others*. The primed variables $open'$, $busy'$, $queue'$ and $others'$ are used to indicate the value of the corresponding component of the bank *after* the event.

The schema can be interpreted in the following way:

The *NextPlease* Declaration

1. $\Delta Bank$

   This line indicates that the *NextPlease* operation is one that changes the *Bank* state in some way.

2. $t? : Teller$

   The variable $t?$ represents the teller who is looking to serve the next customer. The use of a question mark indicates that the teller is an input to the operation. In programming terms, the identity of the teller is a value to be supplied at run-time.

The *NextPlease* Predicate

The predicate part of the specification re-states, in formal terms, the pre- and post-conditions that were discussed informally.

1. $t? \in open$

   The teller is a member of the *open* set. In other words, the teller is open for business. The $\in$ symbol may be read as "is an element of" or "is a member of".

2. $t? \notin dom\ busy$

   The set $dom\ busy$ is the set of tellers actively serving a customer at this moment. The teller must not be a member of that set.

3. $\#queue > 0$

The $\#$ operator applied to *queue* gives the size of the queue. So this condition merely says that there must be somebody waiting to be served.

This takes us to the end of the pre-conditions. If they are all satisfied then we can proceed to describe how the bank changes as a result of this operation.

4. $busy' = busy \cup \{(t?, head\ queue)\}$

The teller $t?$ is paired with the head of the queue and, using set union $\cup$, that pair is "added" to the other pairings of tellers with customers.

The *head* operator may be applied to any non-empty sequence and it specifies the first object in the sequence. We know that *queue* is not empty because of the third pre-condition.

5. $queue' = tail\ queue$

The new queue is formed from the tail, that is, all but the head of the original queue. The *tail* operator is another special one that may be applied to any sequence.

Applying *tail* to *queue* has the effect we desire. It removes the head and shuffles everybody else forward one place.

6. $open' = open$

The set of open tellers is unchanged. No teller opened or closed as a result of this operation, which is as we would expect.

7. $others' = others$

The other customers in the bank are also unaffected by this operation.

You might again argue that this formal specification does not tell you anything that was not already clear from the original informal one.

There is another reason for preferring the formal version. We can use the formal specification. We can use it to *prove* that the operation will maintain the integrity of the bank, that is, the rules specified in the *Bank* schema. We cannot do that with the informal version; we can only hazard a guess.

For example, one of the conditions placed upon the bank is that all busy tellers are open. This was expressed formally as:

$dom\ busy \subseteq open$

After the *NextPlease* operation this condition must be held by the *after* versions of the bank state components; in other words:

$dom\ busy' \subseteq open'$

After the *NextPlease* change, the set of busy tellers, *dom busy'*, is contained in the set of open tellers, *open'*. Can we demonstrate that this latter condition does hold?

$dom\ busy'$

[We can start with the left-hand side of the equation, that is, the set of busy tellers, and try to prove that it is a subset of the open tellers.]

$= dom\,(busy \cup \{(t?, head\,queue)\})$

[In this line we have substituted for $busy'$ according to the line in *NextPlease* that states how the set is formed: $busy' = busy \cup \{(t?, head\,queue)\}$.]

$= dom\,busy \cup dom\,\{(t?, head\,queue)\}$

[Here we have "distributed" the use of the dom operation into two separate applications. This is similar to the way in which the multiplication in the expression $3 \times (2+4)$ can be distributed into two products as $3 \times 2 + 3 \times 4$.]

$= dom\,busy \cup \{t?\}$

[The expression $dom\,\{(t?, head\,queue)\}$ can be simplified to $\{t?\}$.]

$\subseteq open \cup \{t?\}$

[The previous expression must be a subset of the new one because of the line in the *Bank* schema that says: $dom\,busy \subseteq open$. We can assume that, before the *NextPlease* operation started, the bank was in a valid state.]

$= open$

[This can be simplified to $open$ because of the line in *NextPlease* requiring that: $t? \in open$.]

$= open'$

[The *NextPlease* operation leaves the set of open tellers unchanged as can be seen by the line: $open' = open$.]

Hence $dom\,busy' \subseteq open'$ which is what we were required to show.

We have now demonstrated that one of the bank conditions holds through the *NextPlease* operation. We have achieved this by a series of transformations based upon a valid *Bank* state and the *NextPlease* operation.

1.5 The *NextPlease* Program

Now we will look at a program that will update the database according to the specification laid down in the *NextPlease* schema. The program is written in the language SQL which we will use to **implement** our specifications. SQL is a straightforward language that allows us to inspect and manipulate a set of tables as if they were in front of our eyes rather on electronic storage.

Open	Busy		Queue		Others
Teller	Teller	CustId	Place	CustId	CustId
T1	T3	Sue	1	Ann	Liz
T3			2	Kim	Jim
T4			3	Dan	Bob

Suppose we want to find out who is at the front of the queue. We would probably do it this way:

1. We would start by determining which table contained information about queues. The table **Queue** is the one required. It is *from* that table that the answer will be extracted:

    `From Queue`

2. But that table contains information about the entire queue; so we need to narrow our search to the row *where* the place indicates that the customer is at the head.

    `Where Place = 1`

3. Having found the row we need, we can *select* from it the name of the customer involved.

    `Select CustId`

We can link these three clauses to form the SQL statement required.

```
Select CustId
From   Queue
Where  Place = 1
```

The entire program is presented as a sequence of steps to be obeyed by the computer. Each step consists of a simple instruction written in SQL. Each instruction will require the computer to either read the database or to amend it in some way. Steps that involve looking up the database will have an extra condition that determines whether the computer is to move to the next step or to abort the program. This condition will depend upon the results obtained from the retrieval.

The program is written in general terms, making reference to a teller **t?**. We will then examine what happens when t? = T1.

1. Is the teller open for business?

    ```
    Select Teller
    From   Open
    Where  Teller = 't?'
    ```

    If no rows are returned by the query, then the teller is not open. With t? = T1, there will be a row found.

2. Is the teller busy?

    ```
    Select *
    From   Busy
    Where  Teller = 't?'
    ```

    If a row satisfying the condition is found, then the teller *is* busy and so the program should be abandoned. With t? = T1, no row will be found and so the program can continue.

3. Is there someone in the queue?

    ```
    Select *
    From   Queue
    ```

14   Chapter 1

If any rows at all are returned, then the condition is satisfied. There are currently three rows in the **Queue** table and so the program may continue.

This is the last of the pre-conditions. The rest of the program is involved with making the necessary amendments to the database.

4. Move the customer at the front of the queue into the **Busy** table.

    ```
    Insert
    Into    Busy
    Select  't?', CustId
    From    Queue
    Where   Place = 1
    ```

    A row containing the name of the teller and the name of the customer first in the queue is created. This row is inserted into the **Busy** table. With t? = T1, the row (T1,Ann) is inserted into **Busy** and the table will now look like this:

    ```
    Busy
    ----------------
    Teller   CustId
    ----------------
      T3       Sue
      T1       Ann
    ----------------
    ```

    The database is now inconsistent. Ann is now at two places in the bank, breaking the rule that no customer may be queuing and being served at the same time.

5. Remove the customer from the front of the queue.

    ```
    Delete
    From    Queue
    Where   Place = 1
    ```

    The row with **Place** = 1 will be deleted from the **Queue** table which will now look like this:

    ```
    Queue
    ----------------
    Place    CustId
    ----------------
       2       Kim
       3       Dan
    ----------------
    ```

    Well, now Ann is in only one place, but the database is still inconsistent, this time because the queue is a sequence of people and our **Queue** table is not a proper representation of a sequence.

6. Shuffle up the remainder of the queue.

```
Update Queue
    Set Place = Place-1
```

This SQL statement will change each row in **Queue** subtracting one from the value stored in the **Place** column. The effect is to move everybody forward one place.

```
Queue
---------------

Place    CustId
---------------
  1      Kim
  2      Dan
---------------
```

Now the database looks like this:

```
Open             Busy                      Queue                   Others
------           -----------------         ---------------         ------
Teller           Teller    CustId          Place    CustId         CustId
------           -----------------         ---------------         ------
  T1               T3      Sue               1      Kim              Liz
  T3               T1      Ann               2      Dan              Jim
  T4             -----------------         ---------------           Bob
------                                                              ------
```

After these changes, the bank is still in the state defined for it:

- All busy tellers are open.
- Every customer is either:
    - in the queue, or
    - being served, or
    - elsewhere in the bank,

    but only in one of these sets.
- No customer appears at more than one place in the queue.

The sequence of SQL statements has maintained the bank in its proper state. Yet it would be impossible to tell. SQL is not amenable to formal methods. We can only rely on our intuition and on trial and error. We *believe* that the SQL is adequate and it seems to work on the test data supplied.

1.6 Summary

This book will cover the following topics.

- Chapters 2, 3 and 4 introduce simple facts and their specification.

    In the bank situation, the simple facts correspond to the bank components *open*, *busy*, *queue* and *others*. These chapters look at their structure. In particular, we will look at sets, functions and relations.

- Chapters 5, 6 and 7 introduce SQL, in particular its use as a database retrieval language.

  In the bank we used SQL retrieval statements to check that the pre-conditions were satisfied – that the given teller was open, and so on.

- Chapters 8, 9, 10 and 11 look at how we design a database.

  In the bank situation we used a rather simple-minded design. In these chapters we will treat the subject more seriously. Two alternative approaches to **data modeling** are presented. First we examine the **fact-based approach** which is founded on the belief that databases contain lots of simple facts and that from these we should develop our database structure. Then we look at the **entity-relationship approach** which takes a more pragmatic line, based on the assumption that we surely know the kinds of things that are going to form the basis for tables, and these are the basis for our database structure.

- Chapters 12, 13 and 14 look at general statements and their specification; these statements are ones that will eventually be implemented as programs.

  The predicate sections of the *Bank* and *NextPlease* schemas contained examples of these.

- Chapters 15 and 16 look at database definition and manipulation in SQL. This is the language that we will use to implement the general statements that were specified in the three preceding chapters. Chapter 16 looks at how we integrate the necessary SQL into a program.

- Chapter 18 contains case studies that show the specification in Z and implementation in SQL of two different situations. Chapter 19 contains another case study, but this time we use the idea of *data refinement*, and its associated rules, to more rigorously ensure that our SQL programs are a true implementation of the original specification.

Exercises

▶ Q1.1 Using the bank situation presented in this chapter, describe the pre-conditions and post-conditions for each of the following events. Express these conditions in English. What do you think the SQL program might be?

    a. A person $c?$ comes into the bank and joins the others.
    b. A person $c?$ leaves the bank.
    c. A teller $t?$ opens up his or her window.
    d. A teller $t?$ closes down his or her window.
    e. A customer $c?$ joins the queue.
    f. A customer $c?$ finishes his or her transaction and prepares to leave the bank.
    g. A customer $c?$ leaves the queue and goes to fill out a withdrawal slip.
    h. A customer at the end of the queue leaves to fill out a form but only if he or she is not at the front.

▶ Q1.2 Extending the bank model

Suppose that the bank is being enlarged. Instead of just one queue, there are several. Each queue is served by a dedicated set of tellers. How would the bank be described now? We might start by introducing a new class of objects *Stand*, where each object of this type represents a place where a queue may form. Each teller serves just one of these places, and so we might represent this relationship as a function:

    serves : *Teller* $\rightarrow$ *Stand*

Instead of just one queue, there will be several:

    queues : *Stand* $\rightarrow$ *seq Person*

This function maps each stand to a (possibly empty) sequence of people.

In the original model, we could have people in one of three places: queueing, being served, or among the others. In this model, instead of just one queue, we have several.

BiggaBank ────────────────────────────────

open : *Set of Teller*
busy : *Teller* $\leftrightarrow$ *Person*
queues : *Stand* $\rightarrow$ *seq Person*
others : *Set of Person*
serves : *Teller* $\rightarrow$ *Stand*
──────
. . .

───

How would your description of each event be changed, if at all?

CHAPTER 2

Specific Facts

2.1 Introduction

Computers are *not* magical. They are *marvellous*, but they are not magical. They may be extremely fast, with computation speeds measured in millions of instructions per second. They may have huge amounts of memory, measured in billions of characters. But there is nothing happening inside them that we could not contemplate doing ourselves. We may take a lot longer; we may get bored and make mistakes, but we *must* believe that we could. We must think of the computer as doing things that we could do with pencil and paper or with a blackboard and some chalk. If we cannot do this, then we are resigned to thinking of the computer as something beyond our comprehension. As a consequence of this necessary act of faith, it is the things that *we* can express (in conversation with a friend or on a piece of paper, say) that are of importance. And, unless we are day-dreaming, these expressions have some meaning. They are attempting to say something about reality. The **sentence** is the unit of language that allows us to say things about the world in which we live. Sentences, however, come in all shapes and sizes; there are commands, questions, forecasts and opinions to name just a few. This book will focus on one particular category consisting of what are called declarative sentences or, more simply, **facts**. A declarative sentence is one that is capable of being true or false. Consider the following sentences:

>Stop, in the name of love!
>Big girls don't cry.
>Will you still love me tomorrow?

Only one of these three is some kind of statement about the world. Only one is a representation. Only one can be added to the end of:

I declare that:

\-

and make a grammatical sentence. Maybe big girls don't cry; maybe they do. But it *is* certain that only the second sentence may sensibly be inserted into the above framework. Only the second sentence is declarative. This chapter examines specific facts – declarative sentences that relate particular people, places and things.

The chapter will also examine how we can formalize our everyday speech; that is, how we can take an English sentence and rewrite it in a highly structured way. Having expressed our meaning formally, the formal sentence may be evaluated to decide whether it is true or false. This evaluation is independent of whoever performs it. In this way, the formal sentence has a precise meaning; one that is independent of any particular reader or listener.

2.2 The Plain Facts

Imagine a situation involving two people who have just met for the first time. One of them is attempting to describe his or her circle of friends, relations and acquaintances. We will call that person the narrator. The other person is simply listening. The narrator begins with the following description.

> SNAPSHOT #1
> Alan is 21 years old; he plays tennis and golf. Sue is 18 and she plays tennis. Kim is 23 and she too plays tennis. Bob is also 23 and his sports are golf and hockey.

There are four sentences in the narrative, one for each person mentioned. Each of these sentences can be replaced by a number of simpler ones which, collectively, provide the same information. For example, the first sentence can be re-expressed as:

```
Alan is 21 years old.
Alan is a male.
Alan plays tennis.
Alan plays golf.
```

A similar kind of analysis could be performed on the other three sentences. The result would be 14 different sentences; and within those 14, there are three kinds or types of sentence: one type giving people's age, one for their sex and one specifying which sports they play.

Let us look at this last sentence type in some more detail. It has the general form:

```
_____ plays _____
```

There are two places where a substitution may be made. The underlining indicates the places involved. In this form, we have a kind of template for a sentence. After substitutions have been made, the resulting sentence may be true or false. A sentence template, where, after suitable substitutions, we are left with a declarative sentence, is called a **predicate**. Predicates may be simple, as in this example, or they may be quite complex, as we shall see in the remainder of this chapter and in Chapters 3, 4 and 12.

For a simple predicate like this, the word **plays** is the **predicate symbol**, and we can refer to the predicate as the **plays** predicate.

Suppose our narrator divulges a little more about the circle.

> SNAPSHOT #2
> There's also Mark, a bit past it at 48, but he still manages an occasional round of golf and an even more occasional hit on the squash court. Oh! and not forgetting Ann who's 45.

We can use our `plays` sentence templates to analyze some of this new information.

```
Mark plays golf.
Mark plays squash.
```

With the aid of the template, we insert `Mark` into the first place and a sport he plays into the second.

What else might have been substituted? Here are some possible ways.

```
Mark plays guitar.              Harpo plays the clown.
Menhuin plays violin.           Branagh plays Hamlet.
Menhuin plays Beethoven.        Wilson plays fullback.
Gekko plays the stockmarket.    Nancy plays on Saturdays.
```

There are a lot of possible substitutions, every one of which may produce a true statement and all of which are irrelevant to our purpose. We are only interested in the kind of substitutions that consist of a person and a sport. We will see, shortly, how we can declare this interest.

2.3 Facts as Relationships

2.3.1 Relations

We can summarize all the (`Person`, `Sport`) pairs that can be validly substituted in the following table.

```
-----------------
Person   Sport
-----------------
Alan     tennis
Alan     golf
Sue      tennis
Kim      tennis
Bob      golf
Bob      hockey
Mark     golf
Mark     squash
-----------------
```

Specific Facts 21

Suppose that we now examine this table in conjunction with the `_____ plays _____` predicate. If we substitute `Alan` in the first place, we get:

`Alan plays _____`

Looking at the table, now, it can be seen that there are two substitutions that will turn the above into a true statement; these are `tennis` and `golf`. Alan plays two sports; and, in general, a person may play several sports.

Conversely, if we return to the original predicate:

`_____ plays _____`

and, this time, we insert `tennis` into the second place, we get:

`_____ plays tennis`

There are three valid substitutions available to us, `Alan`, `Sue` and `Kim`; in general, a sport may be played by several people.

A relationship between two types of thing, such as this one between people and sports, is called a **relation**.

We should now introduce the `plays` relationship properly, by *declaring* it.

`_plays_ : Person <-> Sport`

The declaration says that:

- We can use `plays` to construct sentences, and it will be the verb in that sentence.
- Any such sentence is required to involve a `Person` and a `Sport`, in that order.
- The underscore on either side, `_plays_`, says that, when a sentence is being formed, the person is to precede the word `plays` and the sport is to follow it.

A sentence formed according to these rules may be either true or false; the rules relate to sentence construction and not to sentence meaning. This is an example of a **type declaration**. This particular one states that `plays` is something that is made true by a relation <-> between `Person` and `Sport`. The predicate is called `plays` as was discussed before; however, it is also common to use the same name to refer to the complete set of pairs that makes the predicate true. So we can talk about the `plays` relation and call "`plays`" the relation name or symbol.

2.3.2 Defining Fact Types

From now on, in this chapter, we will show a relation name and its associated relation in the way shown in Figure 2.1. There we see revealed the *nature* of the fact, through a type declaration, and the *extent* of the fact, through an equation that defines the entire fact as a set of pairs. This way of introducing a fact type is useful in an introductory chapter such as this one. However, it is generally unsatisfactory for two reasons:

1. In practical computing situations, the fact may involve thousands of pairs. We will want to store these on disk, not on paper.
2. More importantly, as presented, the `plays` fact is fixed. Nobody can take up a new sport; neither can anyone drop a sport. This is clearly unrealistic, and consequently undesirable.

Chapter 2

plays : Person <-> Sport	The **plays** fact is declared.
plays = {(Alan, tennis), (Alan, golf), (Sue, tennis), (Kim, tennis), (Bob, golf), (Bob, hockey), (Mark, golf), (Mark, squash)}	It is then defined in terms of the set of (Person, Sport) pairs that, when substituted into the fact template, give rise to a **true** statement.

Figure 2.1 Defining a fact type

2.3.3 Domains and Ranges

Frequently we will want to refer to those objects that are involved in a particular relationship such as the `_plays_` relation. If we want to specify the people who play a sport (of any kind) then we can refer to the **domain** of the relation. The domain of this relation corresponds to the left-hand column of the relation when it is presented as a table, that is, to:

    {Alan, Sue, Kim, Bob, Mark}

Ann doesn't appear because she doesn't seem to play any sport. This domain set can be written more briefly as:

    dom plays

In general, the domain of any relation can be referred to by prefixing the relation name by the word `dom`.

There is a corresponding way of denoting the set of sports played by these people. This is known as the **range** of the relation. This is the set:

    {tennis, golf, hockey, squash}

This set corresponds to the right-hand column of the table. The range can be referred to as:

    ran plays

In general, the range of a relation may be specified by prefixing the relation name with the word `ran`.

2.3.4 Base Types

Before proceeding any further, we had better clarify exactly what is meant by the words **Person** and **Sport**. These terms are two of the basic **types** of thing about which the narrator wishes to make some statement or statements. They are basic because all subsequent declarations will be founded upon these types. For this reason it makes sense to preface any narrative or specification with a brief introduction to these types.

Type	Intended interpretation
[CarMake]	the makes of car that interest the narrator
[Language]	the set of foreign languages
[N]	the set of whole numbers or integers {0,1,2,3,...}
[Person]	the people who make up the circle that the narrator intends to describe
[Sport]	those sports that interest the narrator

In describing these fundamental object or entity types, the narrator has the opportunity of clarifying exactly what he or she means by a particular type name. So, for example, Person is the set of people *in the circle*. It is *not* necessarily the set of all people, and it is not some arbitrary set of people that the listener might interpret it to mean. Similarly, the type Sport is the set of sports that interest the narrator and nothing else.

When being introduced, all of the types were enclosed within square brackets. These brackets are *not* part of the type name; they are used to delimit it. We may, if we wish, introduce several new types at the same time. We do this by enclosing, within square brackets, a list of type names separated by commas. So the above types could also have been introduced as follows.

```
[CarMake, Language, N, Person, Sport]
```

However, in this book, the preferred style is to introduce each type individually, and to describe it briefly.

2.3.5 Formalizing Sentences

Anything that we may wish to write down or to say in conversation may be expressed in a variety of ways, depending upon individual style and fluency. We could write about Alan's age in any of the following, more or less acceptable, ways.

```
Alan's age is 21.
Alan is 21 years old.
Alan is 21.
Alan was born 21 years ago.
The age of Alan is 21.
```

For the moment, we will use the first of these styles. Gathering together all the statements about the people's ages gives:

```
Alan's age is 21          Bob's age is 23
Sue's age is 18           Mark's age is 48
Kim's age is 23           Ann's age is 45
```

These sentences would seem to suggest a sentence template like:

```
_____'s age is_____
```

Chapter 2

We could then declare the sentence type as follows.

    `_'s age is_: Person <-> N`

The name `N` is the one conventionally given to the set of integers `0,1,2,3,...` The declaration above would follow the pattern set for `_plays_`. However, among other things in this chapter, we are trying to introduce the idea of a formal language to be used in describing or specifying situations. This language will be a simplified version of the original English, one that sacrifices flexibility for precision.

The first sacrifice that we must make is to use a single word or symbol to identify the relation. We are not allowed to use `'s age is` which starts with a punctuation symbol and contains spaces. Instead we must use a word, that is, a contiguous sequence of characters, or we can use some special symbol. We can try something like:

    `_____hasage_____`

Now we can write the formal version of:

    `Alan's age is 21`

as:

    `Alan hasage 21`

The sentence type may be declared as:

    `_hasage_: Person <-> N`

The declaration says that sentences constructed using `_hasage_` are made true by pairs drawn from the sets `Person` and `N`. Collectively, these pairs form a relation like that shown in Figure 2.2.

```
_hasage_ : Person <-> N

hasage =
        {(Alan, 21),
         (Sue,  18),
         (Kim,  23),
         (Bob,  23),
         (Mark, 48),
         (Ann,  45)}
```

Figure 2.2 The `hasage` relation

2.4 One-to-many Relationships

2.4.1 Functions

In many ways, the `_hasage_` relation is much more interesting than the `_plays_` one. Suppose, first, that we rephrase each sentence in this way.

Specific Facts 25

    `The age of Alan is 21.`

The general form would be:

    `The age of _____ is _____`

If we start by inserting a number in the second place, such as 23,

    `The age of _____ is 23`

There are two valid insertions for the person slot, that is, insertions that will make the sentence true; these are `Kim` and `Bob`. In general, in any group of people, there may be several of the same age. The converse is *not* the case. Suppose we insert `Alan` into the first place.

    `The age of Alan is _____`

Once we have inserted someone's name, then we are constrained to just one valid insertion for the remaining place; that is the number **21**. In general, a person has *one and only one* age. There is a pivotal point at the word **is**.

    `The age of Alan is 21.`
                `==`

The phrase `The age of Alan` is somehow balanced by the number **21**. The partial sentence: `The age of Alan is _____` can only be made true by the insertion of one number, **21**. A person's age is a single-valued fact about that person, whereas the sports they play is a many-valued fact. To reflect the difference between these two sentence types, we declare **age** in the following way:

    `age: Person -> N`

The declaration states that **age** is a special kind of relation called a **function**. A function is a single-valued fact about something. The notation tries to indicate that when the **age** function is **applied** to some person then we will be led or pointed to one particular number. This is written as, for example:

    `age(Alan) = 21`

The function symbol **age** is written next to its **argument**, in this case, `Alan`. The equality symbol = corresponds to the word **is**. It is a formal statement equivalent to the English sentence:

    `The age of Alan is 21.`

So, we have *two* ways of representing the age relationship, as may be seen in Figure 2.3.

    The underlying data is exactly the same, so why should we choose one style of declaration rather than the other? The difference between the two declarations is one of intended usage. When this relationship between people and numbers is named as **hasage** and declared to be of type `Person <-> N` then we expect to construct sentences such as:

    `Alan hasage 21`
    `Ann hasage 45`

Chapter 2

```
┌─────────────────────────────────┬─────────────────────────────────┐
│  _hasage_ : Person <-> N        │  age : Person --> N             │
├─────────────────────────────────┼─────────────────────────────────┤
│  hasage =                       │  age =                          │
│      {(Alan,  21),              │      {(Alan,  21),              │
│       (Sue,   18),              │       (Sue,   18),              │
│       (Kim,   23),              │       (Kim,   23),              │
│       (Bob,   23),              │       (Bob,   23),              │
│       (Mark,  48),              │       (Mark,  48),              │
│       (Ann,   45)}              │       (Ann,   45)}              │
└─────────────────────────────────┴─────────────────────────────────┘
```

Figure 2.3 Relation or function?

However, when we name the relationship **age** and declare it to be of type **Person --> N** then we intend to use it as a function, applying it to an appropriate argument. So the two sentences above can be written using function application as:

```
age(Alan) = 21
age(Ann) = 45
```

However, we may choose to use it anywhere that a number may be used:

```
  age(Alan) < age(Ann)
= 21 < 45
= true
```

By applying the function separately on two different arguments, we can determine that the age of Alan is less than the age of Ann, or more simply, Alan is younger than Ann.

2.4.2 Partial Functions

Whenever we have the possibility of an incomplete functional relationship, we have a **partial** function. We might have a partial **height** function.

```
height: Person -+> N
```

Everybody has just one height, so it is a functional relationship, but if we do not **know** every person's height, or cannot guarantee that we will know, then the function is partial. The symbol for a partial function is -+> which is similar to the --> symbol used for **total** functions but with a vertical bar.

Before we can refer to someone's height we must ensure that the person is in the domain of the height function, in other words, we must ensure that we know that person's height.

There are also many examples of what might be called naturally occurring partial functions.

> **SNAPSHOT #3**
> Alan has a Mercedes and Sue a Ford. Ann and Mark drive a Toyota. Bob drives a Porsche. Kim doesn't drive.

So everybody but Kim drives a car. We can represent this **drives** relationship as a partial function. See Figure 2.4.

```
drives : Person +> CarMake

drives =
         {(Bob,   Porsche),
          (Mark,  Toyota),
          (Ann,   Toyota),
          (Sue,   Ford),
          (Alan,  Mercedes)}
```

Figure 2.4 The **drives** partial function

The domain of the **drives** function is the set of people who drive or own a car of some type, that is, the left-hand column of the **drives** table. This domain can be written more briefly as **dom drives**, and:

dom drives = { Bob, Mark, Ann, Sue, Alan }

We can take any person from that domain, for example, **Bob**, and refer to the kind of car that Bob drives as **drives(Bob)**. The term **drives(Kim)** has no meaning, however.

The **range** of this particular function is the set of cars driven by one or more of the people in whom we are interested. This can be written as **ran drives** and:

ran drives = { Porsche, Ford, Toyota, Mercedes }

In general, the range of a function is the set of values into which the domain of that function maps.

Partial functions are a nuisance because, before we apply such a function to any arguments, we must ensure that they fall within the domain of the function. The subtraction and division of positive integers are both partial functions. This probably explains our slight hesitation in using them. However, partial functions are common in information systems.

2.5 One-to-one Relationships

The narrator now decides to reveal how, last night, everybody was seated round the table having a meal. This time, the description is given visually:

28   Chapter 2

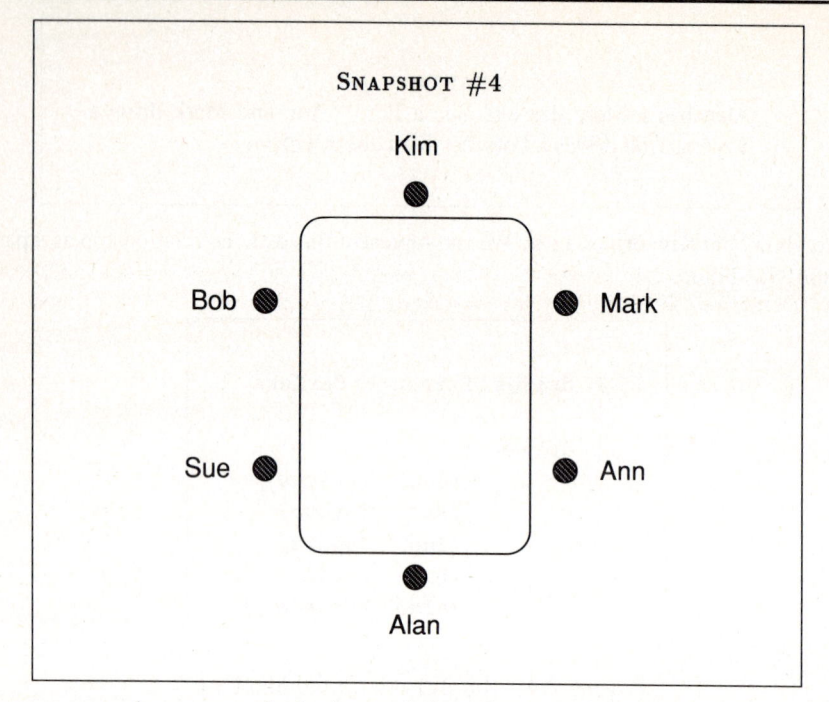

```
                    SNAPSHOT #4

                         Kim
                          ●
          ┌─────────────────────────┐
   Bob ●  │                         │  ● Mark
          │                         │
          │                         │
   Sue ●  │                         │  ● Ann
          │                         │
          └─────────────────────────┘
                          ●
                        Alan
```

Suppose we work our way clockwise, or leftwards, around the table. Everybody has someone to their immediate left; for example, Alan has Sue on his left. Moreover, everybody has *just one* person there. This indicates a total functional relationship; but it is more than that because everybody is *to the left* of just one person. There is a one-to-one relationship between each person and the person on their left. This relationship is defined in Figure 2.5.

```
┌─────────────────────────────────────┐
│ left : Person >─→ Person            │
│ ─────────────────                   │
│ left = {                            │
│         (Alan,  Sue),               │
│         (Sue,   Bob),               │
│         (Bob,   Kim),               │
│         (Kim,   Mark),              │
│         (Mark,  Ann),               │
│         (Ann,   Alan)}              │
└─────────────────────────────────────┘
```

Figure 2.5 The `left` total injection

The >─→ symbol indicates that `left` is an **injection** or one-to-one relationship. The injection symbol is an annotated version of the total function symbol →, indicating that `left` is a special kind of total function. It is total because everybody is seated at the table. There are also partial injections. Consider this insight into the circle.

Specific Facts

> SNAPSHOT #5
> Alan and Sue are married to one another, as are Ann and Mark. Bob isn't married which may help to explain how he drives a Porsche. Kim isn't married either.

Marriage is a well known one-to-one relationship, but it is not total. (Even if it is 'til death us do part.) Not everyone in the circle is married. The relationship is defined in Figure 2.6.

```
spouse : Person >+> Person

spouse =
        {(Ann,  Mark),
         (Mark, Ann),
         (Alan, Sue),
         (Sue,  Alan)}
```

Figure 2.6 The spouse partial injection

The >+> symbol indicates that **spouse** relationship is a partial injection. The domain of this injection is the set of people who are married and the range of that function is the set of people to whom they are married. Of course these two sets should be the same, and so:

`dom spouse = ran spouse`

This is an example of a general statement or rule about marriages.

2.6 The Construction of Simple Sentences

2.6.1 Function Application

Suppose that, again, we are presented with some additional information regarding the circle of people.

> SNAPSHOT #6
> Mark is Alan's father.

The relationship between a person and that person's father is a functional one – we can only have one father. This can be specified as:

`father : Person +> Person`

The **father** function is partial. We do not know everybody's father. In fact, we appear to know only Alan's.

```
father(Alan) = Mark
```

Function application is the name given to the symbolic expression formed by applying a function to its argument or arguments. The following terms are all examples of function application:

```
age(Bob)
father(Alan)
spouse(Mark)
```

These are symbolic expressions denoting objects we might more conveniently refer to as, respectively, the number **23**, the person **Mark** and the person **Ann**.

In computing terms, function application can be thought of as the process of reading down the left-hand column of the appropriate table until a match for the argument is found and then extracting the corresponding entry in the right-hand column.

Function application may be performed repeatedly. For example, since both the following statements are true:

```
Mark = father(Alan)
spouse(Mark) = Ann
```

we may combine them to give:

```
spouse(father(Alan)) = Ann
```

by using the equation for **Mark** provided by the first statement and substituting it in the second. The new sentence tells us that the spouse of the father of Alan is Ann (who is possibly, but not necessarily, the mother of Alan; we don't know).

Using this style of repeated function application, we can construct complex expressions that provide us with ways of identifying objects. So, this new sentence tells us that there are two ways, at least, of naming the person involved:

```
Ann
spouse(father(Alan))
```

We now know that the representation for a person need not be a simple name such as **Alan**. It can be of any form that allows us to identify an *individual* person. The importance of functional relationships (functions and injections) is that they provide us with an alternative way of identifying individual objects. The relationship called **left** provides us with another way of identifying people. Everybody at the table has just *one* person to their immediate left, for example, Alan is on Ann's left. We can construct a simple sentence to state this formally:

```
left(Ann) = Alan
```

This equation shows that there are (at least) two ways of representing the person in question, **left(Ann)** and **Alan**. The fact that Alan plays tennis, can also be said as:

Specific Facts

    `left(Ann) plays tennis`

In general, we will pair the symbol `left` with a person, as follows:

	Person
left	Representation

The symbolic expression that results is *yet another* `Person` representation. The declaration of `left`, which was:

    `left : Person >—> Person`

tells us that. The symbol `left` followed by a `Person` representation will map us (>—>) to another `Person` representation.

The representations used for a person may be as simple or as complex as we need or care to make them. We could refer to the person second on the left from Ann as:

    `left(left(Ann))`

Because of the nature of a functional relationship, for example, because each person has just *one* person to their immediate left, we use functions to identify individual objects. We expect to use `left` to identify somebody rather than using it to construct complete sentences in the way that `plays` was. It may seem that functions are being used in a lesser way than relations; but, in fact, they provide us with more flexibility of expression. The following table summarises the uses we may make of function application in describing the circle.

Function	Maps from	Type	Maps to	Comment
sex	Person	—>	Gender	Gives an alternative way of identifying the genders.
age	Person	—>	N	Gives an alternative way of identifying numbers.
drives	Person	—+>	CarMake	Gives an alternative way of identifying makes of car.
spouse	Person	>+>	Person	Gives an alternative way of referring to people.
left	Person	>—>	Person	...and another.
father	Person	—+>	Person	...and another.

The **Maps to** column shows various ways in which individual objects, of the type given, may be identified indirectly.

2.6.2 Terms

An equation such as:

    `Mark = father(Alan)`

tells us that `Mark` and `father(Alan)` stand for or **denote** the same thing. A symbolic expression that denotes some object or collection of objects is called a **term**. A term may be one of the following:

- the proper name of something, for example, `Mark`; these are sometimes referred to as constants;
- a noun phrase constructed using function application, for example, `father(Alan)`; or
- a pronoun in the form of a **variable**; examples of variables will be shown later.

A term is simply the kind of symbolic expression that may be used to complete a sentence. If we return to the `plays` predicate:

```
_____ plays _____
```

When we first completed this to form sentences, we substituted the names of people and the names of sports, as in, for example:

```
Mark plays squash
```

Yet, as we know, Mark is Alan's father, and so:

```
Mark = father(Alan)
```

It is reasonable to expect that anywhere that `Mark` is used, we could use the term `father(Alan)` instead; thus we could write:

```
father(Alan) plays squash
```

`Mark` and `father(Alan)`, and for that matter, `spouse(Ann)` are all terms denoting the same object.

The declaration of `plays` tells us that any simple sentence using this relation must be of the following form:

Person Term	plays	Sport Term

And any term representing a person may be placed before the word `plays` and any term representing a sport may appear after.

2.6.3 Variables

What do the following sentences have in common?

> Ask not for whom the bell tolls, it tolls for thee.
>
> Take that!
>
> You are my sunshine, my only sunshine.
>
> They also serve who only stand and wait.

In contrast to these sentences above, all our sentences have been of a rather prosaic nature, such as:

```
Alan plays golf.
Ann drives a Toyota.
Alan is 21 years old.
```

They have the advantage of being self-contained. In the context of the circle of people under discussion, each sentence is capable of standing on its own. There are other, quite grammatical, sentences that are not.

```
He plays golf.
She plays tennis.
Mark plays it.
```

Complete understanding of these sentences depends upon the context in which they are spoken. They all contain pointers or references to previously mentioned people or things. Does **he** refer to Alan or to Bob? They both play golf. Similarly, **she** might refer to either Sue or to Kim, and **it** could be either golf or squash. These special words are, of course, pronouns. A pronoun has a *variable* meaning whereas a word such as **Mark** or **45** or **golf** has a constant meaning, that is, one that does not vary from one usage to another, *in the context of the circle*.

In English we have a small number of pronouns. This can cause confusion.

```
Alan spoke to Bob who agreed to ask Sue. He also spoke to Ann.
```

Does **He** in the second sentence refer to Alan or to Bob? It should be Alan but we can't be certain. To overcome such ambiguity we will allow ourselves any number of pronouns or **variables** as they are called. And following the usual conventions of mathematics we will give these variables short names constructed from lower case letters, for example, **x**, **p**, **k** or **me**. We will also always declare the type of the variable, for example, **p: Person** indicates that the variable **p** will stand for a person and not a sport or a number. This "typing" is just what we do with a word such as **she** which can only ever stand for a feminine person or thing and a word such as **they** which can only ever refer to a set of things.

Finally, suppose that we have made the declaration **p: Person**. What can we say about its use in this sentence?

```
p plays golf.
```

From the **plays** table we see that only **Alan** and **Bob** can be successfully substituted for **p**. Thus the above sentence effectively defines a set of people, those who play golf. We will return to this particular use of variables in Chapter 3.

2.6.4 Infix and Prefix Form

In all the examples so far, predicate symbols have been written *between* the appropriate terms, for example, **Mark plays squash**. The terms **Mark** and **squash** are placed on either side of the predicate symbol **plays**. This predicate is said to be used in **infix** form. Such usage reflects the normal English manner of declarative sentence construction whereby a verb is placed between the subject and the object of the sentence. However, the notation we are developing also allows us to place the predicate symbol before any associated terms.

Finally, perhaps because the narrator is interested in overseas travel or the listener teaches modern languages, the narrator reveals one last glimpse of the circle.

> SNAPSHOT #7
> Both Alan and Sue speak French; Alan also speaks German and Sue Italian. Also, Kim can speak Japanese.

We might introduce a **speaks** predicate:

speaks: Person <—> Language

This form of declaration, without any underscores, indicates that any sentence using **speaks** will be such as the following:

speaks(Alan, French)

This is to be interpreted as meaning that Alan speaks French. This form of sentence construction uses the predicate symbol in **prefix** form.

We can analyze this snapshot into the following simple sentences.

speaks(Alan, French)
speaks(Alan,German)
speaks(Kim, Japanese)
speaks(Sue, French)
speaks(Sue, Italian)

Whether we use the predicate in infix or prefix form is indicated by the presence or absence of underscores in the corresponding declaration. This is the only indication we will get, or give.

Similar statements may be made regarding the usage of function symbols. So far, we have always declared functions for use in prefix form, for example:

age: Person —> N

The function symbol **age** prefixes any argument in any term formed through function application, for example **age(Mark)**. However we may also use functions in infix form. The arithmetic operators are typical of these. When we write a term such as **3 + 5**, the function symbol **+** is placed between its arguments **3** and **5**. Addition may be declared as follows:

_ + _ : N × N —> N

This declares that addition is a function that maps from a pair of numbers to a third one. Further, it states that any usage of the function to construct a term will require that the arguments appear on either side of the plus sign.

Again, terms may be constructed to whatever level of complexity is required. For example, if we want to discuss Ann's age in ten years' time, we can write the term:

age(Ann)+10

In this example, the addition function, **+**, is applied to its two arguments, one of which is a term constructed by applying the **age** function to **Ann** and the second of which is the constant term **10**.

2.7 The Circle Database

Let us summarize the narrative so far. There are seven relationships represented. Each of these relationships, in its own way, may be used to form simple sentences.

1. **_plays_ : Person <-> Sport**

   This relationship is called **play**. It is a relation (<->) between people and sports, that is, a person may play many sports and a sport may be played by many people. It may be used to construct such sentences as **Alan plays tennis**. It is used in *infix* form, that is, when used, it appears between a person and a sport. The form taken by sentences constructed with **plays** is dictated by the declaration. There we are told to use it this way by the appearance of underscores (_).

2. **speaks : Person <-> Language**

   This is also a relation. Some of the people speak more than one foreign language, and some of the languages are spoken by more than one member of the circle. It is used in *prefix* form to construct sentences such as: **speaks(Sue,Italian)**.

3. **sex : Person --> Gender**

   This is a total function, signified by the symbol -->, meaning that it is a special kind of relation, one that is special in two ways. *Everyone* has a gender and *nobody has more than one* gender. Functions are used, not to construct complete sentences, but, through function application, to describe objects such as **sex(Alan)**. These objects are then glued together to form sentences.

4. **age : Person --> N**

   This is another total function used to identify numbers such as **age(Kim)**. Everyone's age is known but nobody has more than one age.

5. **drives : Person -+> CarMake**

   This is a partial function, signified by the symbol -+>. A partial function is less restrictive than a total function in that not everyone need participate in the relationship. That is, not everyone need drive a car. It is used, like the two previous functions, to identify objects using such expressions as **drives(Ann)**.

6. **spouse : Person >+> Person**

   This is a partial injection, signified by the symbol >+>. Thus, it is a one-to-one relationship in which not everyone need participate. It should be treated as a particular kind of partial function, and it will be used like a function to identify objects such as **spouse(Alan)**.

7. **left : Person >--> Person**

   This is a total injection, signified by the symbol >-->. It is a one-to-one relationship in which everybody participates. Everyone has one person on their left, and everybody is immediately to the left of just one person.

A typical commercial database also consists of a number of different sentence types. However, that number is likely to be in the hundreds and thousands rather than just seven. But the difference is of degree, and of nothing else.

The five types of relationships that we are likely to encounter, their names and their synbols are shown in the following table.

Type of relationship	Name	Partial symbol	Total symbol
many-to-many	relation	<->	
one-to-many	function	-+>	->
one-to-one	injection	>+>	>->

2.8 Compound Sentences

2.8.1 Operations on Sentences

Given the above declarations and the associated data, we can take any arbitrary sentence and decide whether or not it is true. For example, `speaks(Alan,German)` is true because the pair `(Alan, German)` appears in the relation associated with `speaks`. Similarly, the sentence `Bob plays squash` is false because the pair `(Bob, squash)` does not appear in the table associated with `plays`.

What if we want to know if Alan plays both tennis and golf? We know, informally, that he does; but what if we attempt to formalize the question as:

`Alan plays tennis and golf`

The sentence is improperly formed because the second term must represent a single sport. We can rephrase the sentence as:

`Alan plays tennis and Alan plays golf`

The sentence is clearly one made of two simpler sentences, both of which are of the form `Person plays Sport`. Both constituent sentences are true and we would want the complete sentence to be true also.

Now what about Bob? Does he play tennis and golf? Again we can rephrase this as:

`Bob plays tennis and Bob plays golf`

This time only one of the constituent sentences is true and we know that the sentence, as a whole, is untrue.

The word **and** has been used to connect two sentences, both of which might be either true or false, in order to form a more complex sentence, which might itself be either true or false. In this section and the ones that follow, we will consider three ways in which complex sentences may be compounded from simpler ones.

The two values `true` and `false` are often referred to as Boolean (after the mathematician George Boole) values. Just as we have arithmetic operators that combine two numbers and return a third, we have Boolean operators that take Boolean values (that is, `true` and `false`) and return a Boolean answer. Those of particular interest at this stage are conjunction (**and**), disjunction (**or**) and negation (**not**). The purpose of these three operations is to enable us to take simple statements or sentences and to construct a more complex sentence, one whose truth or falseness depends solely upon the truth or falseness of the simpler sentences of which it is composed.

2.8.2 Negation

The **not** operator negates or reverses its argument.

Example 2.1 Ann is not 31 years old.

We can state that Ann *is* 31 as follows:

```
age(Ann) = 31
```

To claim that she is not 31, we prefix the above sentence with the word **not**.

```
  not age(Ann) = 31
= not 45 = 31
= not false
= true
```

It is **true** to say that Ann's age is not 31.

Example 2.2 Alan does not speak French.

```
  not speaks(Alan, French)
= not true
= false
```

It is **false** to say that Alan does not speak French.

The effect of this operator can be completely specified in what is called a **truth table**.

```
not
--------------
P        not P
--------------
true     false
false    true
--------------
```

In the table, P represents any Boolean expression or proposition, such as `age(Ann) = 21` or `6 > 2`.

The **not** truth table symbolizes our conviction that if some statement is **not true** then it is **false** and vice versa. Negation is a kind of prefix Boolean operator.

```
not: Boolean -> Boolean
```

We can apply the word **not** to a sentence that may be either true or false. This newly formed sentence has a truth value that is the reverse of the original.

2.8.3 Conjunction: When both sentences must be true

The **and** operator returns a value of **true** if both its arguments are **true**; otherwise it returns a value of **false**.

Example 2.3 Suppose we are looking for someone who speaks German and drives a Mercedes. Will Alan do?

```
speaks(Alan, German) and (drives(Alan) = Mercedes)
= true and (Mercedes = Mercedes)
= true and true
= true
```

Yes, Alan will do. He does both; he speaks German **and** drives a Mercedes.

Example 2.4 Suppose, next, that we are looking for someone aged between 18 and 35 (inclusive). Will Ann do?

```
age(Ann) > 17 and age(Ann) < 36
= 45 > 17 and 45 < 36
= true and false
= false
```

No, Ann is not in that age range. She is not both older than 17 **and** younger than 36.

A truth table can also be used to specify the **and** operator.

```
and
----------------------
P        Q        P and Q
----------------------
true     true     true
true     false    false
false    true     false
false    false    false
----------------------
```

This table summarizes and represents our experience that if, for example, police are on the lookout for a "middle-aged male" then they are looking for a suspect who is both male **and** middle-aged. Someone who meets one criterion but not the other will not do; and someone who meets neither criterion clearly will not do.

Conjunction is a kind of infix Boolean function.

and : Boolean × Boolean ⟶ Boolean

It takes two sentences, which may or may not be true, and joins them with the word **and** to form a new sentence which is true only if both of the participating sentences are also true.

2.8.4   Disjunction: When at least one of the sentences must be true

The **or** operator returns a value of `false` if neither its arguments is true, otherwise it returns a value of `true`.

Example 2.5 We are looking for someone who is either over 40 or who speaks Japanese; what about Kim?

```
age(Kim) > 40 or speaks(Kim, Japanese)
= 21 > 40 or true
= false or true
= true
```

Specific Facts

Yes, Kim satisfies at least one of the requirements.

The **or** operator also involves two arguments. It returns a value of **true** if either or both of its arguments are **true**.

Example 2.6 Now we are looking for someone who speaks French or Italian. Will Kim do this time as well?

```
speaks(Kim, French) or speaks(Kim, Italian)
= false or false
= false
```

No, Kim cannot help us; she speaks neither of these two languages.

The truth table for the **or** operator is as follows:

```
or
----------------------
P        Q        P or Q
----------------------
true     true     true
true     false    true
false    true     true
false    false    false
----------------------
```

Again, this table has been chosen to reflect our expectations and experience. If we were to ring a hotel and ask for a room with a view or a southerly aspect then we would expect a room that satisfies at least one and possibly both of these criteria.

Alternatively, suppose an employer advertises for someone who is a computing graduate or who has five years' experience. We might apply for the job if we satisfied either of the selection criteria. We would also expect to be considered if we satisfied both of them.

Disjunction is a kind of infix Boolean function.

_or_ : Boolean × Boolean → Boolean

It takes two sentences, which may or may not be true, and joins them with the word **or** to form a new sentence which is true if either of the participating sentences is also true.

2.8.5 Sentence Construction

We can create new sentences to whatever level of complexity is required. For example, the sentences that we might connect with an **and** may themselves have been constructed using **and**'s, **or**'s and **not**'s. We determine the truth of a complex sentence in a hierarchical manner. Simple sentences are evaluated first and their results slotted into the more complex ones which are themselves evaluated, and so on.

Example 2.7 Suppose we are looking for someone who does not drive a Ford and who speaks either French or Japanese. Will Sue do?

```
not drives(Sue)=Ford and (speaks(Sue,French) or speaks(Sue,Japanese))
= not true and (true or false)
```

```
= false and true
= false
```

While the sentence is not exactly what might be termed "user friendly", it has a major advantage; it has only one meaning. Provided that we correctly evaluate the sentence, there is only one possible answer. Two competent people, working independently, will get the same result; and so should a competently programmed computer.

The sentence becomes a useful means of communication as it has one and only one interpretation. It is a formal expression of our original requirement – a **formula**, in other words.

2.8.6 Evaluating Sentences

Suppose, now, that we are looking for someone who drives a Ford and who speaks French or German. Will Alan do? The equivalent formal sentence could be written as follows:

```
drives(Alan)=Ford and speaks(Alan,French) or speaks(Alan,German)
```

Unfortunately, depending upon how the sentence is evaluated, we can arrive at two different conclusions.

1. ```
   drives(Alan)=Ford and speaks(Alan,French) or speaks(Alan,German)
   = false and true or true
   = false or true
   = true
   ```
2. ```
   drives(Alan)=Ford and speaks(Alan,French) or speaks(Alan,German)
   = false and true or true
   = false and true
   = false
   ```

We have decided in the first evaluation that Alan will do and in the second that he won't. The conflict arises because of the order in which we evaluated the second line.

```
false and true or true
```

In one case the **and** operation was performed first and in the other case the **or** was.

The two distinct results directly contradict the claim that two competent people, working independently, *will* get the same answer.

So as to recover from this situation, we use round brackets ( ) to indicate the required order of evaluation. Thus we would probably write the sentence as:

```
drives(Alan)=Ford and (speaks(Alan,French) or speaks(Alan,German))
= false and (true or true)
= false and (true)
= false and true
= false
```

We retain the brackets until the enclosed sentence has been evaluated as `true` or `false` at which time we can dispense with them.

In general, any compound sentence using a mixture of **and**'s, **or**'s and **not**'s will require brackets to direct the order of evaluation.

2.8.7 Phrasing Sentences

Although it has been claimed that a validly constructed compound sentence will have just one correct evaluation, that does not mean that there is only one way of constructing a sentence to meet our requirements.

As a simple example, if we want to assert that Alan speaks French and German, we would hope that either of the following sentences:

```
speaks(Alan, French) and speaks(Alan, German)
speaks(Alan, German) and speaks(Alan, French)
```

would be an adequate expression of that claim. It does not matter which sentence precedes the word **and**, or which one follows it.

This interchangeability is one of a number of general rules or laws that indicate the equivalence of various alternative ways of phrasing sentences.

In the following discussion, two conventions are used: (1) **P**, **Q** and **R** are any arbitrary sentences; and (2) the symbol ≡ is to be read as "is equivalent to" or "can equally well be stated as".

1. Laws of commutation

    ```
    P and Q ≡ Q and P
    P or Q  ≡ Q or P
    ```

    These laws state that it does not matter in which order we insert the participating sentences when using conjunction (**and**) or disjunction (**or**).

2. Laws of association

    ```
    (P and Q) and R ≡ P and (Q and R)
    (P or Q) or R   ≡ P or (Q or R)
    ```

    When evaluating a sentence that only involves conjunction or only involves disjunction, then it does not matter in which order we perform the evaluation. This allows us safely to write the sentences as:

    ```
    P and Q and R
    P or Q or R
    ```

    Even without the brackets there is no danger of differing evaluations.

3. De Morgan's laws

    There are two laws under this heading.

    ```
    not (P and Q) ≡ (not P) or (not Q)
    ```

    This law states that, for example, if we say that Alan does not play both tennis and squash then we are saying, equivalently, that either he doesn't play tennis or he doesn't play squash.

    ```
    not (P or Q) ≡ (not P) and (not Q)
    ```

This law states that, for example, if we say that Alan cannot speak either Italian or Japanese, then this is equivalent to saying that Alan cannot speak Italian and he cannot speak Japanese.

2.9 Summary

In this chapter we have examined the use of the sentence as a means of representing reality.

- An informal narrative may be analyzed into a number of different sentence types or forms. Each sentence type, such as `_plays_` has, associated with it, a set of pairs. These are the pairs that make the sentence true. This set of pairs is called a relation. A relation is, in general, a many-to-many relationship between two sets of objects. A person may play many sports and a sport may be played by many people.

- There are particular sentence types where the corresponding relationship is one-to-many rather than many-to-many. For example, a person has only one mother, although that mother may have had several children. This kind of relationship is called a function. The idea of a function allows us to treat particular symbolic expressions as interchangeable. If Ann is Bob's mother, then `Ann` and `mother(Bob)` are equivalent terms. Any sentence that could be written using one of these terms can be rewritten using the other.

- There are particular kinds of functions where the relationship is one-to-one rather than one-to-many. These are **injections**. An injection is a special kind of function.

- More complex sentences may be constructed using negation (`not`), conjunction (`and`) and disjunction (`or`). Such a sentence may be evaluated in a mechanical or algebraic manner to decide whether it is true or false.

- There are a number of general rules or laws governing the equivalence of sentences. For example, the following two sentences mean the same.

```
Alan plays tennis and Bob plays squash
Bob plays squash and Alan plays tennis
```

Using these laws, two apparently different compound sentences may be shown to mean the same thing. Thus we have a variety of ways of expressing our meaning.

Exercises

▶ Q2.1   The CLUB Model

The following sets, functions and relations represent a (very) small computer club. There are four basic types in the model.

```
Member   = {Bill, Sue, Alan}
Language = {COBOL, FORTRAN, C, SQL, Pascal, Ada}
CarMake  = {BMW, Ford, GM, Honda, Mazda, Mercedes, Toyota}
N        = {0, 1, 2, 3, ...}
```

There are four relationships between the types. These are shown below in tabular form.

likes: Member <–> Member	_writes_: Member <–> Language
likes = {(Bill, Sue), (Bill, Alan), (Sue, Alan), (Alan, Bill)}	writes = {(Bill, FORTRAN), (Sue, C), (Sue, SQL), (Alan, FORTRAN), (Bill, SQL)}

age: Member –> N	drives: Member >+> CarMake
age = {(Bill, 19), (Sue, 19), (Alan, 16)}	drives = {(Sue, Honda), (Bill, Ford)}

a. Which of the above relationships are relations? Which are functions? Which are injections?

b. Not every member drives. Give two ways by which you can tell this.

c. Which of the four relationships are to be used in prefix form and which in infix form?

d. What is the range of `drives`? How do we express that formally?

e. What is the domain of `likes`? How do we express that formally?

▶ Q2.2   Which of the following sentences are true and which are false?

a. `Bill likes Sue`

b. `Sue writes Ada`

c. `age(Sue) = 19`

44 Chapter 2

    d.   `drives(Sue) = Honda`

    e.   `Alan writes C`

▶ Q2.3   If we wanted to say formally that Sue doted on Alan, the best we could do would be `Sue likes Alan`. Rewrite each of the following English sentences formally. State which are true and which are false and why.

    a.   Bill can write in SQL.

    b.   Bill is keen on Sue.

    c.   Sue drives a Ford.

    d.   Alan adores Sue.

    e.   Sue is nineteen years old.

▶ Q2.4   Complex sentences may be formed using conjunction (**and**), disjunction (**or**) and negation (**not**). Evaluate the following complex sentences.

    a.   `not (Bill likes Sue)`

    b.   `(Bill likes Sue) or (Sue likes Bill)`

    c.   `(Bill likes Sue) and (Sue likes Bill)`

    d.   `(age(Bill)=age(Sue)) and (age(Bill)>age(Alan))`

    e.   `not (drives(Sue)=BMW)`

    f.   `(Sue writes Ada) and (drives(Sue)=BMW)`

    g.   `not (not age(Sue)=19)`

    h.   `(not (Alan writes C)) and (not (Sue writes C))`

    i.   `not (Alan writes C or Sue writes C)`

    j.   `Sue likes Alan and Alan writes SQL`

▶ Q2.5   We can state that Bill doesn't like Sue as `not (Bill likes Sue)`. Formalize the following sentences. Determine whether each sentence is true or false.

    a.   Alan dislikes Bill.

    b.   Bill can't write in SQL.

    c.   Sue and Bill get on well together.

    d.   Bill is older than Sue.

    e.   Sue can write in both C and in Pascal.

    f.   Neither Alan nor Sue can write in FORTRAN.

    g.   Either Sue drives a Honda or Bill does.

    h.   Alan is five years older than Bill.

i. Sue and Bill both drive the same make of car.

j. Both Bill and Sue can write in SQL.

▶ Q2.6 We can tell that Alan doesn't drive a car because he is not in the domain of **drives**. Use the appropriate domain or range to say, in your own words, why each of the following statements is true.

a. Somebody likes Bill.

b. Nobody can write in COBOL.

c. Everybody can write in some language or another.

d. Everybody is liked by somebody.

e. All club members are in their teens.

▶ Q2.7 Given the variable declaration `m: Member`, decide which people satisfy each of the following sentences.

a. `m likes Alan`

b. `Alan likes m`

c. `age(m) > 16`

d. `drives(m) = Toyota`

e. `age(m) = age(Bill)`

f. `Bill likes m and m likes Bill`

g. `not(m writes SQL)`

h. `Bill likes m and m writes SQL`

i. `Bill likes m or m writes SQL`

Q2.8 Suppose that P is a sentence. The compound sentence: **P and true** can be reduced to P because the truth of **P and true** is entirely dependent on the truth of P. Simplify the following expressions in a similar way.

a. `P or true`

b. `not not P`

c. `P or P`

d. `P and P`

e. `P or (not P)`

f. `P and (not P)`

g. `P and false`

Chapter 2

▶ Q2.9 The GEOGRAPHY Model.

The following sets are used to record the states and major towns of Australia.

```
State = {QLD, NSW, VIC, WA, SA, TAS}
Town  = {Brisbane, Sydney, Cairns, Newcastle, ...}
```

Three particular relationships are involved.

1. cap : State >→ Town

    This injection returns the capital city of each state, for example, cap(NSW) would give Sydney.

2. loc : Town —→ State

    This returns the state in which a town is located, for example, loc(Cairns) would return QLD.

3. pop : Town —→ N

    This returns the population of each town, for example, pop(Brisbane) might return 950 000.

As well as these specific relationships, there will be the more general arithmetic functions and the numeric comparison operators.

Using function application, write terms to identify the following objects:

a. The capital of Queensland (QLD).
b. The population of Melbourne.
c. The population of the capital of Queensland.
d. The location of Cairns.
e. The difference between the population of Sydney and that of Melbourne.

▶ Q2.10 Using the functions of the previous question we can make assertions regarding the cities, states and populations. For example, if we wanted to say that Cairns and Sydney were in different states, we could write: not (loc(Cairns) = loc(Sydney))

Write formal assertions of the following English sentences.

a. The capital of New South Wales (NSW) is bigger, in terms of population, than the capital of Queensland.
b. There are more people in Sydney than in either Melbourne or Brisbane.
c. There are more people in Sydney than in Melbourne and Brisbane combined.
d. The capitals of South Australia (SA) and Tasmania (TAS) are, respectively, Adelaide and Hobart.
e. Newcastle is in either in New South Wales or in Western Australia (WA).

Q2.11 The PARLIAMENT Model

The following sets are used to model a parliament.

1. `Poli`

    This is the set of politicians, for example:
    `{ Wayne, Tom, Russell, Bob, Denzil, Molly, ... }`

2. `Party`

    This is the set of political parties, for example:
    `{ Labor, Farmers, Business, Green }`

3. `Dept`

    This is the set of government departments, for example:
    `{ Treasury, Transport, Health, Police, ... }`

The following functions and relations are also involved.

1. `belongs : Poli` $\rightarrow$ `Party`

    This maps each politician to his or her party, for example, `belongs(Wayne)` might give `Labor`.

2. `minister : Dept` $\rightarrow$ `Poli`

    This maps each department to the relevant minister, for example, `minister(Police)` might give `Terry`.

3. `leader : Party` $\rightarrowtail$ `Poli`

    This maps a party to its leader, for example, `leader(Business)` might map to `Denzil`.

4. `_talksto_ : Poli` $\leftrightarrow$ `Poli`

    This indicates whether one politician is prepared to talk to some other politician, for example, `Neville talksto Russell`.

Using either function application or a predicate, formally express the following:

a. The leader of the Farmers party.
b. The Justice Minister.
c. The party to which the Minister for Health belongs.
d. That David is the Minister for Transport.
e. That the Minister for Health is also the Minister for Police.
f. That Wayne talks to Russell.
g. That Wayne does not talk to the Justice Minister.
h. That Tom talks to Wayne but not vice versa.
i. That Molly talks to the leader of the Farmers Party.
j. That the leader of the Business Party actually belongs to that party.

CHAPTER 3

Sets

3.1 Introduction

Suppose someone writes down a list of people's names and hands that list to you. Then you are asked what these people have in common.

It is fairly safe to claim that one way or another you would find something to connect these people. Even if the names were as unlikely as John, Paul, George and Ringo. You would probably feel frustrated and disappointed with yourself if you were unable to discern some common feature.

A **set** is a collection of objects, with the objects usually sharing some property. The formation of a set allows us, mentally, to gather things that seem to belong together, and to provide them with a collective being. This process of **generalization** is a means of conquering complexity. Defining a set is a way of enforcing order upon our world and because of that order we can have reasonable expectations. We anticipate certain kinds of behavior and not others.

By isolating an object and stating that this thing is a "man", for example, we accomplish two things:

1. We provide a number of properties that can be ascribed to that object – beards, beer and baldness perhaps.

2. We group this person with other men – all the people who share these properties.

Having decided that a person is a man or a woman or a singer or a computer programmer we would expect a whole range of associated behavior patterns.

3.2 Sets and Everyday Language

There are two ways to specify a set: **set extension** and **set comprehension**. These two methods form an essential part of our everyday language.

Mum sets them straight

Imagine that a family is sitting at the dining table. They have just finished the evening meal; Mum has a meeting that night, and wants to get the evening chores over and done with. What kinds of things might she say?

- *"Kylie and Tim, go and do your homework."*
- *"The boys will tidy the table and wash the dishes."*
- *"Girls, you must tidy your room!"*
- *"Will Matthew, and anyone who didn't have a bath last night, have one tonight."*

She has used two basic styles of specifying the children that are involved. First, children have been named individually, using set extension.

- "Kylie and Tim"
- "Matthew"

Secondly, particular children are also identified through properties they hold, using set comprehension.

- "boys"
- "anyone who didn't have a bath last night"
- "girls"

Further, having identified the girls, she has then specified another set, the set of girls' rooms.

- "Girls, you must tidy your room!"

Finally, she has also used a set operation (union, in this case) to join two sets together to form another set.

- "Matthew and anyone who didn't have a bath last night"

In the following sections, we will look at how the ideas of set extension and set comprehension are formalized. This will be done by introducing a notation or language for specifying sets in each of these two ways.

3.3 Set Extension

In set **extension**, curly brackets {} are used to enclose the elements of the set. The set "Kylie and Tim" will be written as:

```
{Kylie, Tim}
```

Individual elements are separated by commas. The set "Matthew" contains just one element and will be written as:

{Matthew}

There are several rules or conventions regarding the definition of sets by extension. These we will consider next. Suppose we want a set of integers representing the number of days in each month, ignoring leap years. We can write it out as:

$\{31, 28, 30\}$

However, a set has no duplicates, so that writing down an element more than once does not change the nature of the set; for example, we could have specified the days by just running through each of the 12 months, from January to December, and writing down the number of days in each month.

$\{31, 28, 31, 30, 31, 30, 31, 31, 30, 31, 30, 31\}$
$= \{31, 28, 30\}$

Also, when writing out a set, the order in which we present its elements is of no significance. We could equally well have worked from December back to January, or we could have followed the old "Thirty days hath September ..." rhyme, so that:

$\{31, 28, 31, 30, 31, 30, 31, 31, 30, 31, 30, 31\}$
$= \{31, 30, 31, 30, 31, 31, 30, 31, 30, 31, 28, 31\}$
$= \{30, 31, 28\}$

This set of elements shown is just one particular **representation**. Consider another set of three integers:

$\{3, 7, 21\}$

The entire set has been written in a consistent fashion. Each of the elements has been expressed using one style – the arabic or decimal notation. An equally valid, if slightly old-fashioned representation of the same set would be:

{III, VII, XXI}

Other equally valid versions might be:

$\{3, 7, 3 * 7\}$
$\{2+1, 8-1, 2 * 10+1\}$
{three, seven, twenty one}
{trois, sept, vingt et un}

A slightly less acceptable version might be:

{3, VII, twenty one}

Here, three different but recognizable notations have been used in one set. Clearly, if the intention in writing down the set was to communicate its membership to other people, the notation should be both consistent and recognizable. It is important to understand the need for a suitable way of representing the members of a set. Why? Because the sets of records that make up a database are simply sets written, **in extension**, upon a computer's memory. When we design a database, we are faced with the situation where:

- several different ways of representing set elements may be available;
- some will be more appropriate than others; and
- it may be that none of them appeal; in which case, we might have to create an artificial representation.

As an example, suppose we had to write down a list of cities, for example the state capitals of Australia. A sensible representation would be:

{`Sydney`, `Perth`, `Brisbane`, `Adelaide`, `Melbourne`, `Hobart`}

The cities are represented by their everyday names. This would be the most sensible choice for normal communication. However, if these cities were to be named millions of times, as might be the case if we were maintaining a database of Australian city dwellers, then these representations would use relatively large amounts of disk space. Alternative methods of representation might be considered.

1. {2001, 6001, 4001, 5001, 3001, 7001}

   Here the GPO post code has been chosen. We would have to know that a set of cities was being represented.

2. {NSW, WA, Qld, SA, Vic, Tas}

   This is valid but potentially misleading. We would want to be quite sure that it was cities that were being discussed.

3. { S, P, B, A, M, H}

   This is rather cryptic, with the cities identified by their initial letter. However, at least there is no likelihood of a city being mistaken for a state.

4. { 2, 6, 4, 5, 3, 7}

   This is also cryptic, with the initial digit of the business district post code being used to identify each city.

In everyday conversation or in written communication, it is important that all parties are familiar and comfortable with the notation used. When two or more parties have access to a shared pool of sets (to a database, in other words) it is *essential* that all sets be encoded consistently.

3.4 A Sample Database

Before we look at set comprehension, we will set up a little database that records the family situation involving the children.

The basic sets include one for the children, one for sexes, one for (bed)rooms, one for sports and one for the ubiquitous integers.

```
Kids   = {Kylie, Tim, Matthew, Emma}
Sexes  = {F, M}
Rooms  = {sleepout, back, front}
Sports = {tennis, hockey, golf}
N      = {0, 1, 2, 3, ...}
```

An injection and two functions give access to each child's age, sex and bedroom.

```
age : Kids >—> N
sex : Kids —> Sexes
room : Kids —> Rooms
```

They can then be applied, for example, to determine the following:

```
age(Kylie) = 14
sex(Tim) = M
room(Emma) = sleepout
```

All of these relationships are *total*; in other words, we know everyone's age, everyone's sex and everyone's room.

Finally, there is also a relation that tells us which sports each child plays, if any.

```
_plays_ : Kids <—> Sports
```

This relation can be used in expressions such as:

```
Kylie plays tennis
Tim plays tennis
```

The specific facts concerning these children may be seen in Figure 3.1.

3.5 Set Comprehension

There is an alternative to physically writing out the contents of a set on a piece of paper or onto an electronic storage device. We can use set **comprehension** which enables us to specify the set by stating some property that every chosen element must satisfy. There are three forms that can be used.

3.5.1 Form 1: {Declaration | Predicate}

Suppose we want to specify the set "boys". This is simply those children of the male sex. If we were to pick out these children for ourselves then we would go through *all* of them checking whether or not each child was a male.

To specify the set of boys, we can write an expression of this form.

```
{k : Kids | sex(k) = M}
```

This expression can be thought of as giving rise to the following sequence:

age : Kids $\rightarrowtail$ N	sex : Kids $\rightarrow$ Sexes

age ={
   (Kylie,   14),
   (Tim,   12),
   (Matthew, 4),
   (Emma,   8)}
	sex ={
	   (Kylie, F),
	   (Tim, M),
	   (Matthew, M),
	   (Emma, F)}

room : Kids $\rightarrow$ Rooms	_plays_ : Kids $\leftrightarrow$ Sports

room ={
   (Kylie,   sleepout),
   (Tim,   back),
   (Matthew, front),
   (Emma,   sleepout)}
	plays ={
	   (Kylie, tennis),
	   (Kylie, hockey),
	   (Tim, golf),
	   (Tim, hockey),
	   (Emma, tennis)}

Figure 3.1 The KIDS Database

1. Let **k** be a variable that ranges over the set **Kids**.

    So **k**, in turn, takes on each of the values **Kylie**, **Tim**, **Matthew** and **Emma**.

2. As **k** takes on each value, evaluate the **predicate** or Boolean expression that follows the vertical bar |.

    The vertical bar can be read as **where** or **such that**.

3. If the predicate evaluates as **true**, then include this element in the new set that is being specified.

    In this example, if the expression **sex(k)** = **M** is true, then the corresponding child is a male.

4. Move to the next element in **Kids**, that is, move on to the next child.

The key word in the above description is *range*. We must picture the variable ranging over the set with which it is associated.

To see how the set of boys is formed, the following steps should be pictured.

We start the set by writing down { and then let **k** range over the set **Kids**, that is, over each of the four children.

1. The first child might be Kylie, so **k** = **Kylie**. The predicate is evaluated:

         sex(k) = M
    = **sex(Kylie) = M**
    = **F = M**
    = **false**

Applying the `sex` function to the argument `Kylie` returns a value `F`. This does not = `M` and so the predicate is false. `Kylie` is not a member of the set being formed.

2. The pointer `k` is moved to the next element of `Kids`, say `k` = `Tim`. Again the predicate is evaluated.

$$\begin{aligned}&\texttt{sex(k) = M}\\=\ &\texttt{sex(Tim) = M}\\=\ &\texttt{M = M}\\=\ &\texttt{true}\end{aligned}$$

The predicate is true so `Tim` is included in the set. We can now extend the set from `{` to `{ Tim`.

3. The pointer `k` is moved to `Matthew`. The predicate is evaluated as true, so the set is again extended, this time from `{ Tim` to `{ Tim, Matthew`.

4. The pointer `k` is moved on to `Emma`; the predicate is false, so `Emma` is not included.

There are no further elements in `Kids`, so the set is finished with a closing bracket `}` to become:

`{ Tim, Matthew }`

This process is summarized in Figure 3.2.

Example 3.1 Another example of this form of set comprehension would be an expression specifying the set of children over 10 years old.

$\{k : \text{Kids} \mid \text{age}(k) > 10\}$

Again, a variable `k` is allowed to range over all of `Kids`; but this time, the set is formed according to age not sex. The resulting set is:

$\{\text{Kylie}, \text{Tim}\}$

The variable used may be any validly named variable, `k` is used simply as a mnemonic. The above set could equally well have been specified as:

$\{t : \text{Kids} \mid \text{age}(t) > 10\}$

The declaration part of any piece of set comprehension allows us to state which set or type we will use as the basis for specifying the set that particularly interests us. In this case, `Kids` is the base set. The declaration also allows us to name a typical or representative element of that set.

The predicate part allows us to test that element in some way and to arrive at a `true` or `false` conclusion.

The braces `{ }` then indicate that we want to let `k` range over all elements of `Kids`, picking those aged over `10`.

Value of k	Evaluation of the predicate	Set constructed so far
-	-	{
Kylie	sex(k) = M = sex(Kylie) = M = F = M = false	{
Tim	sex(k) = M = sex(Tim) = M = M = M = true	{ Tim
Matthew	sex(k) = M = sex(Matthew) = M = M = M = true	{ Tim, Matthew
Emma	sex(k) = M = sex(Emma) = M = F = M = false	{ Tim, Matthew
-	-	{ Tim, Matthew }

Figure 3.2 Set Evaluation

3.5.2 Form 2: {Declaration | Predicate • Term}

There are occasions when we are interested not so much in the base set (the one named in the declaration) as in the elements of some related set. The base set is used as a kind of stepping-stone towards identifying the set that really interests us.

Suppose we want to specify the room(s) in which girls sleep. We can specify the girls in the same way as the boys were specified.

$$\{k : \text{Kids} \mid \text{sex}(k) = F\}$$

However, now we are interested in rooms rather than children. We can extend the above set comprehension as follows:

$$\{k : \text{Kids} \mid \text{sex}(k) = F \bullet \text{room}(k)\}$$

This statement says:

1. Run through the **Kids** set, picking out the females.
2. For each element chosen (that is, for each girl) select the associated room.
3. Form a set from all the rooms thus chosen.

The spot, •, is used to precede a term of some kind. In this example, the term is **room(k)** and it maps from a child (**k**) to that child's room (**room(k)**).

The spot can be read as **select** or **choose** or **pick**. The term that follows can be any valid statement that represents an object. Typically, it will involve the variable introduced in the preceding declaration.

This form of set comprehension can be considered as an extension of Form 1; however it is more useful to think of Form 1 as an abbreviation of Form 2.

The example given in Form 1 was:

$$(1)\ldots\{k : \text{Kids} \mid \text{sex}(k) = \text{M}\}$$

This can be written in Form 2 as:

$$(2)\ldots\{k : \text{Kids} \mid \text{sex}(k) = \text{M} \bullet k\}$$

What Form 1 allows us to say is that if the term part is omitted then it is assumed to consist of the variable named in the declaration. Thus **(1)** is a simpler version of **(2)**; and they both specify the same set.

3.5.3 Form 3: {Declaration • Term}

Just as we can omit the term part, we can also omit the predicate part, as in, for example:

$$\{k : \text{Kids} \bullet \text{room}(k)\}$$

This specifies the rooms of *all* children as there is no predicate to filter out any children.

What can be expressed in the term part? Any *thing* that makes sense, however simple or complex. For example, if we wanted to know what ages the children will be in two years' time, we could write:

$$\{k : \text{Kids} \bullet \text{age}(k) + 2\}$$

This would return the set { 14+2, 12+2, 4+2, 8+2 } or { 16, 14, 6, 10 }.

The term can involve some other piece of set comprehension. Suppose we want to know which children are of each sex.

$$\{s : \text{Sexes} \bullet (s, \{k : \text{Kids} \mid \text{sex}(k) = s\})\}$$

The outer set declares a variable **s** that ranges over the elements of the set **Sexes**. So **s** takes on, in turn, each of the values **F** and **M**. Each of these values is paired with the following term:

$$\{k : \text{Kids} \mid \text{sex}(k) = s\}$$

This gives the set of children whose sex is **s**. The set, in extension, looks like this:

{(F, {Kylie, Emma}), (M, {Tim, Matthew})}

Set comprehension is important because it is, in effect, what we do when we program a computer to retrieve and process information from a database. The above examples are small-scale versions of the kinds of information that can be obtained by means of a query language such as SQL. A retrieval statement in SQL defines a set by comprehension. The database management system searches the database and returns us *the same set in extension*.

3.6 Set Operations

What operations would we want to perform on sets? Suppose we have the following sets.

```
Men   = {Bob, Alan, Ivan, Mark}
Women = {Sue, Sam, Ann}
Rich  = {Bob, Alan, Ann}
Smart = {Sue, Alan}
```

The operations we will want to perform upon these sets are ones that will enable us to answer some simple everyday questions.

Set Membership: We will surely want to find out whether or not an element can be found in a set. This can be done using the **in** operator.

Example 3.2 Is Sam a man?

```
  Sam in Men
= Sam in {Bob, Alan, Ivan, Mark}
= false
```

No, Sam is not a man. The set membership operator is an infix relation that appears between an object of some type and a set of objects of the same type. The resulting expression is either true or false.

Set Union: We will want to amalgamate two sets to form a bigger set. This is called the **union** operator.

Example 3.3 Who is smart or rich (or both, we don't care)?

```
  Smart union Rich
= {Sue, Alan} union {Bob, Alan, Ann}
= {Sue, Alan, Bob, Ann}
```

The **union** operator creates a set with elements that are in either or both of the participating sets. It is an infix function that appears between two sets *of the same type*. The resulting expression is *yet another* set of that same type.

Set Subtraction: We might want to remove certain elements from a set. This is called set subtraction and is performed by the **minus** operator.

Example 3.4 Who are the not-so smart women?

```
    Women minus Smart
  = {Sue, Sam, Ann} minus {Sue, Alan}
  = {Sam, Ann}
```

A *new* set is formed. `Women minus Smart` is the set of people in `Women` who are *not* in `Smart`. Because `Sue` is the only member of both sets, she not in the resulting set.

Set Intersection: We will want to see which elements are common to both sets. This is called set intersection and is performed by the `intersect` operator.

Example 3.5 Who are the rich men?

```
    Men intersect Rich
  = {Bob, Alan, Ivan, Mark} intersect {Bob, Alan, Ann}
  = {Bob, Alan}
```

A new set is formed consisting of those people who are members of *both* sets. Only Bob and Alan belong to both, and so they must be the rich men.

Set Size: We will want to know how many members are in a set.

Example 3.6 How many smart people are there?

```
    count Smart
  = count {Sue, Alan}
  = 2
```

We can apply the `count` operator to any set and be returned the size of that set. It is a prefix function.

Example 3.7 How many poor (non-rich) people are there?

We answer this question by forming the set of all people, subtracting the rich from that set and counting the result.

```
    count ((Men union Women) minus Rich)
  = count ((({Bob, Alan, Ivan, Mark} union {Sue, Sam, Ann})
                              minus {Bob, Alan, Ann})
  = count ({Bob, Alan, Ivan, Mark, Sue, Sam, Ann}
                              minus {Bob, Alan, Ann})
  = count {Ivan, Mark, Sue, Sam}
  = 4
```

Example 3.8 Are there more poor men than rich women? This question concerns many men.

We find the set of poor men and the set of rich women; then we compare the sizes of these two sets.

```
    count (Men minus Rich) > count (Rich minus Men)
  = count ({Bob, Alan, Ivan, Mark} minus {Bob, Alan, Ann})
         > count ({Bob, Alan, Ann} minus {Bob, Alan, Ivan, Mark})
  = count ({Ivan, Mark}) > count ({Ann})
  = 2 > 1
  = true
```

3.7 Higher Order Sets

3.7.1 Power sets

Suppose we have two sets, say:

$A = \{1, 15, 25\}$
$B = \{1, 3, 5, 15, 25, 35\}$

All the elements of A are also elements of B. In such a case, A is said to be a **subset** of B. We can state this using the inclusion relation:

$A \subseteq B$

According to this definition, A is a subset of itself; every element of A is obviously an element of A. The empty set {} is also a subset of A; every element of {}, of which there are none, is an element of A. Every time we write an expression of the form { k:Kids | Predicate } we are specifying a subset of the set Kids. According to the predicate used, the set specified might be anything from the empty set to the complete set of all children, Kids.

	Predicate	Set specified
1.	$age(k) > 100$	{ }
2.	$age(k) = 8$	{Emma}
3.	$k = Matthew$	{Matthew}
4.	k plays golf	{Tim}
5.	$age(k) > age(Tim)$	{Kylie}
6.	$age(k) < 10$	{Matthew, Emma}
7.	$age(k) > 4$ and $age(k) < 14$	{Tim, Emma}
8.	$sex(k) = M$	{Tim, Matthew}
9.	$sex(k) = F$	{Kylie, Emma}
10.	$age(k) = 14$ or $k = Matthew$	{Kylie, Matthew}
11.	$age(k) > 10$	{Kylie, Tim}
12.	$k = Emma$ or $sex(k) = M$	{Tim, Matthew, Emma}
13.	$sleeps(k)$ in {sleepout, front}	{Kylie, Matthew, Emma}
14.	k plays tennis or k plays hockey	{Kylie, Tim, Emma}
15.	$age(k) = 14$ or $sex(k) = M$	{Kylie, Tim, Matthew}
16.	$age(k) < 100$	{Kylie, Tim, Matthew, Emma}

Regardless of how creatively we construct our predicate, we will inevitably specify one of the 16 sets shown. They represent the entire set of possibilities. What we achieve, by varying the predicate, is access to this higher level set or type. This is the set of all subsets of Kids. It is formally termed:

Set of Kids

and is known as the **power set** of Kids. The 16 entries in the **Set specified** column represent that set in extension.

Example 3.9 If we declare a variable:

    k : Kids

then k is an *individual* child drawn from the set Kids. If we declare a variable:

    p : Set of Kids

then p is a *set* of children, all of whom are drawn from the set Kids.

Power set construction

- The prefix Set of may be placed before any set T. The effect is to create a new set: Set of T, which is the set of all subsets of T, or, more simply, the power set of T.
- A power set may be used in a declaration wherever a set may appear.

Example 3.10 Consider the set of numbers X:

    X = $\{1, 3, 5\}$

The power set of X is:

    Set of X =
        $\{\ \{1, 3, 5\},$
        $\{1, 3\}, \{1, 5\}, \{3, 5\},$
        $\{1\}, \{3\}, \{5\},$
        $\{\ \}\ \}$

The set X has 3 elements and Set of X has $2^3 = 8$ elements. This relationship always holds; if X has n elements then Set of X will have 2^n elements, hence the name *power set*.

Example 3.11 A power set declaration may be used in set comprehension.

    $\{y : \text{Set of X} \mid \text{count } y = 2 \text{ and } 3 \text{ in } y\}$

This is the set of subsets of X that contain exactly 2 elements and where 3 is one of these elements. This is the set { {3,5}, {1,3} }.

3.7.2 Declarations

So far, all the declarations have involved just one variable, like the following:

    k : Kids

The variable k is of type Kids; this means that k represents or stands for an individual child. But we may introduce two variables in the same declaration, for example:

    j, k : Kids

Sets 61

We have introduced a *pair*, `j` and `k`, each of which represents individual children. They might even represent the same child; their identity has not yet been established.

To emphasize that we have coupled the children in some way, we may show the coupling in the form of a **tuple**.

   (j, k)

A tuple is a composite object formed from a number, two in this case, of component objects. The pairing process may involve two different kinds of object.

   k : Kids; s : Sports

This time two separate declarations have been connected by a semicolon. The pairing is now (k, s), for example, (Alan, tennis) or (Sue, golf).

We are not restricted to forming merely pairs. A tuple may involve any number of components of any type, for example:

   k : Kids; r : Rooms; s : Sports

This declaration introduces a triple (k, r, s) consisting of a child, a room and a sport, *in that order*.

The syntax of a declaration

Basic_Declaration:
   Symbol : *Set_Term*
 or *Symbol*, ..., *Symbol* : *Set_Term*

Declaration:
   Basic_Declaration
 or *Basic_Declaration*; ...; *Basic_Declaration*

The basic declaration style involves the introduction of one or more variables of the same type, for example:

   k : Kids
   i, j, k : Kids

The general form of a declaration allows us to introduce several variables of different types, using a semicolon as a separator:

   k : Kids; r : Rooms
   j, k : Kids; r, s, t : Rooms; p : Set of Sports

3.8 Product sets

We saw that varying the predicate part of a set comprehension gives rise to the power set. Now we will vary the declaration part. What happens if we use two variables?

$$\{j, k : Kids\}$$

The declaration pairs two children (j, k). When used within set comprehension, the effect is to specify the set of all possible *pairs* of children. There will be 16 elements in this set, as each of the four elements of Kids is paired with itself and the three others. So the set looks like this:

{(Kylie, Kylie),   (Kylie, Tim),   (Kylie, Matthew),   (Kylie, Emma),
 (Tim, Kylie),   (Tim, Tim),   (Tim, Matthew),   (Tim, Emma),
 (Matthew, Kylie), (Matthew, Tim), (Matthew, Matthew), (Matthew, Emma),
 (Emma, Kylie),   (Emma, Tim),   (Emma, Matthew),   (Emma, Emma)}

This could equally have been expressed as follows:

$$\{j, k : Kids \bullet (j, k)\}$$

When more than one variable is declared, then the default term is a tuple formed from these variables. The set of pairs may also be written:

Kids × Kids

This new set is called the **product** set and is formed by "multiplying" Kids by itself.

Product set construction

- The product operator × may be placed between any two sets S and T. The effect is to create a new set S × T which is the set of all pairs (s, t) where s is drawn from S and t from T.
- A product set may be used in a declaration wherever a set may appear.

Example 3.12 Suppose the set Sports is defined as follows:

Sports = {tennis, hockey, golf}

The product set Kids × Sports is the set of all (child, sport) pairs.

Kids × Sports =
    { (Kylie, tennis),   (Kylie, hockey),   (Kylie, golf),
      (Tim, tennis),   (Tim, hockey),   (Tim, golf),
      (Matthew, tennis), (Matthew, hockey), (Matthew, golf),
      (Emma, tennis),   (Emma, hockey),   (Emma, golf) }

Sets

The size of this set can be calculated as follows:

$$\text{count}(\text{Kids} \times \text{Sports}) = (\text{count Kids}) * (\text{count Sports}) = 4 * 3 = 12$$

Example 3.13 The set `Kids` × `Sports` is the set of all pairs `(k,s)` where `k` is a child and `s` a sport. This set can also be defined using set comprehension as follows.

$$\{k : \text{Kids}; s : \text{Sports}\}$$

Whenever more than one variable is declared, a product set is formed implicitly.

Example 3.14 We could add a condition requiring that the first child in each pair be older than the second.

$$\{j, k : \text{Kids} \mid \text{age}(j) > \text{age}(k)\}$$

This would give rise to this set:

```
{ (Kylie, Tim),     (Kylie, Matthew),   (Kylie, Emma),
  (Tim, Matthew),   (Tim, Emma),
  (Emma, Matthew), }
```

Kylie is older than the other three but not herself. Tim is older than Matthew and Emma. Only Matthew is younger than Emma.

Finally, rather than forming pairs of children, we could take the older one.

$$\{j, k : \text{Kids} \mid \text{age}(j) > \text{age}(k) \bullet j\}$$

This would give us the set of children who are older than some other child.

```
{ Kylie,
  Tim,
  Emma }
```

This is the set containing all but the youngest child (Matthew).

3.9 Sets, Relations and Functions

In the previous section, we looked at the power set and the product set. In this section, we combine these two ideas and see what arises.

3.9.1 Type Construction

Using the rules regarding power set and product set construction, we may define objects of any complexity. This allows us to describe the kinds of organizational views that appear in the shape of forms and reports. We could package all our knowledge regarding Kylie in the form of a record.

CHILD RECORD	
NAME:	Kylie
AGE:	14
SEX:	F
PLAYS:	tennis, hockey
ROOM:	sleepout

This record could be formally declared as follows:

    data : Kids × N × Gender × (Set of Sports) × Rooms

and our record of Kylie is a quintuple of data that could be defined as:

    data = (Kylie, 14, F, {tennis, hockey}, sleepout)

3.9.2 Relations and Functions

Suppose we were to form the product of Kids and Sports.

    Kids × Sports =
        { (Kylie, tennis),   (Kylie, hockey),   (Kylie, golf),
          (Tim, tennis),   (Tim, hockey),   (Tim, golf),
          (Matthew, tennis), (Matthew, hockey), (Matthew, golf),
          (Emma, tennis),   (Emma, hockey),   (Emma, golf) }

Another set has been constructed from the two more elementary sets. What if we were now to consider the power set of this new set? Suppose we declare a variable as follows.

    r : Set of (Kids × Sports)

This variable is constrained to be a set and the elements of that set are to be drawn from the product **Kids x Sports** shown above. Some possible values might be:

(1) ... { (Kylie, tennis), (Tim, tennis) }

(2) ... { (Matthew, golf) }

(3) ... { (Emma, hockey), (Emma, golf),
        (Emma, tennis) }

(4) ... { (Kylie, tennis), (Kylie, hockey),
        (Tim, golf), (Tim, hockey),
        (Emma, tennis) }

In particular, one of the above sets is just the same as the **plays** relation.

    plays : Kids <—> Sports

In general, all of the above are examples of relations. A **relation** is just an element of the power set of the product of two or more sets. Or, more simply, a relation between two sets is a subset of the product of these two sets. The following declarations mean the same.

    r : Set of (A × B)
    r : A <—> B

The latter is preferred because it helps to remind us that **r** is a *relation* between **A** and **B**.

Suppose now that we form the product of **Kids** and **Sexes**.

```
Kids × Sexes =
    { (Kylie, F),    (Kylie, M),
      (Tim, F),      (Tim, M),
      (Matthew, F),  (Matthew, M),
      (Emma, F),     (Emma, M) }
```

This is the set of all possible pairs of child and sex. One subset of this set is the following one.

```
{ (Kylie, F), (Tim, M), (Matthew, M), (Emma, F) }
```

This is the same as the **sex** function. So a function is a relation in that it is a subset of the product of two or more sets. However, a function is a special kind of relation. The function **sex** is declared as follows.

sex : **Kids** $\rightarrow$ **Sexes**

The notation $\rightarrow$ is used to indicate that through this function a child maps to one and only one sex. A function is a relation that carries this additional single-valued constraint. For each element of **Kids** there is only *one* element of **Sexes**.

3.9.3 Deriving New Relations

All the functions and relations that we have examined so far have been defined in extension, for example, **plays** and **sex**. This was done because these functions and relations were meant to form a database, which is that part of an information system where sets are written out on the secondary storage of some computer system.

In this section, we will look at deriving new relations based on ones previously defined.

Example 3.15 Suppose that we want to construct a new relation that allows us to test whether or not one child is the brother of another. The relationship is many-to-many as a child may have several brothers and, in turn, may be the brother of several children. We could declare it as follows:

isbrotherof : **Kids** $\leftrightarrow$ **Kids**

We can then use it in such sentences as **Tim isbrotherof Kylie** and so on. The corresponding relation can be pictured as:

```
isbrotherof =
    { (Tim,     Kylie),
      (Tim,     Matthew),
      (Tim,     Emma),
      (Matthew, Kylie),
      (Matthew, Tim),
      (Matthew, Emma) }
```

The relation is simply a set of pairs as shown above. We can use set comprehension to define this set.

> _isbrotherof_ : Kids <–> Kids
>
> ──────────
>
> isbrotherof = {j, k : Kids | sex(j) = M and not j = k}

The specified set consists of pairs of children (j,k) related in the following way.

1. sex(j) = M

   The first child in the pair, child j, is male. Only males can be the brother of anyone.

2. not j = k

   The second child in the pair, child k, is not the same as the first. A child, even a male one, cannot be his or her own brother.

This definition of a relation helps to emphasize that a relation is a mapping between sets; it is also a set of pairs; the pairs *are* the mapping.

3.9.4 Deriving New Functions

A function is just a special kind of relation, therefore we can also define functions using set comprehension.

Example 3.16 Suppose we want to be able to map from one child to the one immediately older. Let us call the function **next**. We would expect it to look like the following.

> next : Kids +-> Kids
>
> ──────────
>
> next =
>   { (Tim,   Kylie),
>   (Emma,   Tim),
>   (Matthew, Emma) }

The next child older than Tim is Kylie so **next(Tim) = Kylie**. Notice that Kylie does not appear in the domain of **next** (the left-hand column) because there is no child older than her. This means that **next** is a partial function, symbolized by +-> . The function may be fully specified in the following way.

> next : Kids +-> Kids
>
> ──────────
>
> next = {j, k : Kids | age(j) < age(k) and"
>   count {l : Kids | age(j) < age(l) and age(l) < age(k)} = 0}

The function **next** is a pairing of two children (j, k) where the first child j is younger than the child k *and* the number of children whose age lies between these two is zero.

In detail, the predicate appearing within the outer set comprehension requires that *both* of the following conditions be true:

1. $age(j) < age(k)$

   The first child in the pair, child j, must be younger than the second child, child k.

2. $count \{1 : Kids \mid age(j) < age(1)\ and\ age(1) < age(k)\} = 0$

   The inner item of set comprehension determines the set of children aged between child j and child k. We require that set to be empty before k can be **next** to j.

Example 3.17 A simpler example of a derived function is **older** which tells which children are older than some given child.

> older : Kids $\rightarrow$ Set of Kids
>
> ---
>
> older = $\{k : Kids \bullet (k, \{j : Kids \mid age(j) > age(k)\})\}$

This function is a pairing of each child with the set of children older than that particular child, for example, (Emma, {Tim, Kylie}). Note that this is a total function because although no child is older than Kylie, she can still be paired with the empty set. The complete function can be thought of in the following way:

```
older(Matthew) = { Emma, Tim, Kylie }
older(Emma)    = { Tim, Kylie }
older(Tim)     = { Kylie }
older(Kylie)   = { }
```

The complete function may be viewed in extension as follows:

```
older = { (Matthew, {Emma, Tim, Kylie}),
          (Emma, {Tim, Kylie}),
          (Tim, {Kylie}),
          (Kylie, {}) }
```

In this example, as in the previous one, there are two levels of set comprehension, one within the other. The outer level one has no predicate. This is because the function is total: all children participate. The term (k, {j:Kids | age(j) > age(k) }) is used to pair a child k with the set of children older than that particular child. A typical pairing would be (Emma, { Tim, Kylie }).

Example 3.18 Another related function, **youngest**, may be defined. This function maps from a set of children to the youngest child in that set.

> youngest : Set of Kids $\nrightarrow$ Kids
>
> ---
>
> youngest = $\{sk : Set\ of\ Kids; k : Kids \mid k\ in\ sk\ and$
> $age(k) = min\{j : sk \bullet age(j)\}\}$

This function pairs a set of children sk with one particular child k. It also requires that this child be a member of the set with which it is paired *and* that the age of this child be the least of all the ages of the various children within that group. The function is partial because it is not defined for an empty set, naturally. Some sample applications of this function are:

>   youngest{Kylie, Tim} = Tim
>   youngest{Emma} = Emma
>   youngest{Emma, Tim, Kylie} = Emma

This function may be applied in conjunction with the previous one in the following way:

>   youngest(older(Emma))
>   = youngest({Kylie, Tim})
>   = Tim

What this example says is that the youngest of those children older than Emma is Tim; but this is just the same as saying next(Emma) = Tim. We can define next using these two functions rather than defining it in terms of the base function age as we did originally.

>   next : Kids +> Kids
>   _____
>   next = {j, k : Kids | count older(j) > 0 and k = youngest(older(j))}

With this definition, next is a pairing of children (j, k). The predicate requires that both of the following conditions be true.

1. count older(j) > 0

    There are some children older than child j.

2. k = youngest(older(j))

    The second child k is the youngest of these children.

3.10 Set Terms

In Chapter 2 a term was defined as a symbol or symbolic expression that represents an object of some kind. We can also have a set term which is a symbolic expression that represents a *set* of objects.

1. A set may be represented simply by a symbol. Such a symbol may be a base type or a variable that has been declared to be set-valued.

2. A set may be defined in set extension.

3. A set may be defined by comprehension.

4. A set may result from a set expression that involves set operations such as union, minus and intersect.

5. A higher order set may be formed using the power set and product set type constructors.

6. A set may be defined as a fact type, which can be thought of as a set of pairs.

Sets 69

Set_Term:	Examples:
Symbol	Kids
or Set_Extension	or {Kylie, Tim}
or Set_Comprehension	or {k : Kids | age(k) < 10}
or Set_Operation	or Rich union Men
or Type_Construction	or Set of Kids
or Fact_Type	or Kids —> N

3.11 Summary

This chapter has examined ways of identifying or specifying **sets** of objects.

- There are two ways of identifying the elements of a set. There is **set extension** where the elements are named individually. Alternatively, we may use **set comprehension** where elements are specified through some shared property.

- When expressing a set in English, we may choose either of these two methods. The choice may depend on the relative ease with which we can use one form rather than the other. Sometimes it may be easier to simply list the set and sometimes it may be more convenient to specify the set through some shared attribute. We probably do a quick mental calculation to see whether it will take longer to express the set in extension or by comprehension.

- In a computer-based system, this choice is usually neither available nor appropriate. The sets involved are much, much larger than any we would consider expressing ourselves. There will be sets that are stored explicitly, that is, in extension. These sets form what is called the **database**. They are data because they are *given* to the information system which has no other way of determining that information. In addition to these sets there will be others that may be deduced or derived programmatically; these are sets defined by means of set comprehension.

- There are two **type constructors** that allow us to define higher level types and sets.

  1. There is the **power set** operator `Set of` which when applied to a type `T` gives us `Set of T` which is the set of all subsets of `T`. For example, an element of the `Set of Person` is itself a set whose elements are drawn from `Person`.

  2. The other constructor is the **product** operator × which operates on two types, say `S` and `T`, to form the type `S × T` which is the set of all pairs drawn from `S` and `T`. For example, `Person × Sport` is a new type consisting of a set of pairs of the form `(Bob, tennis)`.

- Finally, the combination of these two type constructors allows us to understand more clearly the nature of relations and functions which were introduced in the previous chapter. A relation is a set of pairs, and a function is a particular kind of relation in which no two pairs share the same first element.

Exercises

▶ Q3.1 The CLUB Model

Here are the four relationships used in the CLUB model that was introduced in the exercises at the end of Chapter 2.

likes : Member <–> Member	_writes_ : Member <–> Language
likes = {(Bill, Sue), (Bill, Alan), (Sue, Alan), (Alan, Bill)}	writes = {(Bill, FORTRAN), (Sue, C), (Sue, SQL), (Alan, FORTRAN), (Bill, SQL)}
age: Member –> N	drives: Member >+> CarMake
age = {(Bill, 19), (Sue, 19), (Alan, 16)}	drives = {(Sue, Honda), (Bill, Ford)}

The set: $\{m : \text{Member} \mid \text{age}(m) = 19\}$ is the set of members who are 19 years old. This set could have been written in extension as: $\{\text{Bill}, \text{Sue}\}$. Describe, in your own words, each of the sets specified below:

a. $\{m : \text{Member} \mid m \text{ likes Alan}\}$
b. $\{l : \text{Language} \mid \text{Sue writes } l\}$
c. $\{m : \text{Member} \mid m \text{ writes SQL} \bullet \text{age}(m)\}$
d. $\{m : \text{Member} \mid \text{age}(m) = \text{age}(\text{Bill})\}$
e. $\{m : \text{Member} \mid m \text{ likes Alan and Alan likes } m\}$

Re-state each set in extension.

▶ Q3.2 Express the following sets using set comprehension:

a. The people that Alan likes.
b. The ages of the people that Alan likes.
c. The people older than Alan.
d. The languages written by all the people of Sue's age.
e. The people of Sue's age that like her.

Sets 71

▶ Q3.3 The GEOGRAPHY Model

The following sets are used to record the states and major towns of Australia.

$$\text{State} = \{\text{QLD}, \text{NSW}, \text{VIC}, \text{WA}, \text{SA}, \text{TAS}\}$$
$$\text{Town} = \{\text{Brisbane}, \text{Sydney}, \text{Cairns}, \text{Newcastle}, \ldots\}$$

There are three relationships involved.

1. cap : State $\rightarrowtail$ Town

   This injection returns the capital city of each state, for example, cap(NSW) would give Sydney.

2. loc : Town $\rightarrow$ State

   This function returns the state in which a town is located, for example, loc(Rockhampton) would return QLD.

3. pop : Town $\rightarrow$ N

   This function returns the population of each town, for example, pop(Brisbane) might return 950,000.

Use set comprehension to specify the following sets.

   a. The cities located in New South Wales (NSW).
   b. The populations of the cities located in New South Wales.
   c. The state capitals.
   d. Towns that have a population greater than Newcastle's.
   e. The towns and the population of each town.

▶ Q3.4 Use set comprehension to specify the following sets.

   a. State capitals with a population of more than one million.
   b. The populations of the capital cities.
   c. Towns located in the same state as Cairns.
   d. Towns that are not capital cities.
   e. The states and the number of towns in each state.

▶ Q3.5 Suppose we have two sets of integers:

$$A = \{5, 3, 21, 16\}$$
$$B = \{10, 5, 4\}$$

Using set operations, we could obtain the union of A and B by requesting A union B and the resulting set would be $\{10, 5, 3, 4, 21, 16\}$.

What are the results of the following expressions?

72 Chapter 3

   a. A minus B
   b. {n:A | n > 11}
   c. count(A)
   d. count(B minus A)
   e. count(B minus B)
   f. A intersect {n:(B union A) | n < 16}
   g. A intersect (B union {n:A | n < 16})
   h. count ((A intersect B) union {n:A | n > 16})
   i. { n:B • n-1 }
   j. { n:B | n>5 • n*(n-1) }

▶ Q3.6 Using the sets A and B from the previous question, evaluate the following set expressions.

   a. { a:A; b:B | a=b }
   b. { a:A; b:B | a>b }
   c. { a:A; b:B | a<b }
   d. { a:A • (a, { b:B | a>b }) }
   e. { b:B • (b, { c:B | b>c }) }
   f. { a,b:A | a>b }
   g. { a,b:A | a>b • a }
   h. { as:Set of A | count as = 2 }
   i. { as:Set of A | 5 in as }
   j. { as:Set of A | count as = 3 • count as }

▶ Q3.7 Suppose that A is a set of some kind. What are the results of the following set expressions?

   a. A union {}
   b. A union A
   c. A minus {}
   d. {} minus A
   e. A minus A
   f. A intersect {}
   g. A intersect A

Q3.8 In the subject **Applied Psychology** there were both business and computing students. The marks achieved by these two sets of students are represented as two sets of integers **Bus, Comp : Set of N** and the results are:

Bus = {28, 33, 48, 55, 60, 62, 77, 95}
Comp = {19, 22, 58, 66, 75, 90}

Suppose also that we have two operations on sets:

min : Set of N +-> N
max : Set of N +-> N

These operations return, respectively, the minimum and the maximum element of a set of integers, for example **min Bus** = 28 and **max Comp** = 90.

We can write expressions to evaluate queries regarding the marks. For example, if we wanted to know the highest mark overall, we could write:

max (Bus union Comp)

Write expressions that will answer the following queries.

a. What was the lowest mark attained by a computing student?
b. Is the highest business mark higher than the highest computing mark?
c. Did any business student get a mark of 55?
d. Did any computing student get a mark over 80?
e. What was the second lowest business mark?

Q3.9 If **A** and **B** are both sets of integers, then the union of these sets **A union B** can be written, using set comprehension, as:

{k : N | k in A or k in B}

This can be read as "the set of integers that are in the set **A** or in the set **B**".

Rewrite the following expressions using set comprehension.

a. **A intersect B**
b. **A minus B**

▶ Q3.10 Here are two small sets:

Us = {Jim, Sue, Alan, Bob}
City = {Yeppoon, London, Paris}

Give one member and calculate the cardinality of each of the following sets.

a. **Us**

b. **Set of Us**
   c. **Us x City**
   d. **Set of (Us x City)**
   e. **(Set of Us) x City**
   f. **Set of (Set of Us)**
   g. **(Set of Us) x (Set of City)**

▶ Q3.11 Using the **Us** and **City** sets given in the previous question, to which set does each of the following elements belong?

   a. **Bob**
   b. **(Jim, Bob)**
   c. **{ Jim }**
   d. **{ Jim, Bob }**
   e. **{ (Jim, Yeppoon), (Sue, Paris) }**
   f. **(Jim, Bob, Alan)**
   g. **{ {Jim}, {Bob, Alan}, {} }**
   h. **{ (Jim, {Yeppoon, London}) }**

▶ Q3.12 Write out, in extension, the following sets. Test your answer by checking that it obeys the law regarding power set cardinality, which is: **count(Set of X)** = 2^{countX}.

   a. **Set of {spoon}**
   b. **Set of {fork, spoon}**
   c. **Set of (Set of {spoon})**
   d. **Set of {}**
   e. **Set of (Set of {})**

▶ Q3.13 Based on the GEOGRAPHY model, provide a type declaration and definition for each of the following.

   a. A prefix function **hascap** that maps a town to its capital city.
   b. A prefix function **alltowns** that maps a state to all the towns in that state.
   c. An infix relation **sameloc** that indicates whether or not two towns are located in the same state.
   d. A prefix function **samepop** that maps a town to all the other towns that have the same population.

e. A prefix function **exceed** that maps an integer to all the towns with a larger population.

Given these new operations, examine the set comprehension question associated with this model. How might the sets specified there be respecified using these operations?

Q3.14 In computing, it is common to use a double dot notation to represent a range of numbers, for example:

$$1..3 = \{1, 2, 3\}$$
$$7..12 = \{7, 8, 9, 10, 11, 12\}$$
$$99..99 = \{99\}$$
$$2..1 = \{\}$$

The operator is an infix function and may be declared as:

$$\_ .. \_ : N \times N \rightarrow \text{Set of } N$$

that is, it is a function that takes two integers as its arguments and returns a set of integers. Use set comprehension to define this function.

Q3.15 The PARLIAMENT Model

This model was introduced in the exercises at the end of the previous chapter. As a reminder, the following functions and relations are used.

1. **belongs: Poli → Party**

   This maps each politician to his or her party, for example, **belongs(Wayne)** might give **Labor**.

2. **minister: Dept → Poli**

   This maps each department to the relevant minister, for example, **minister(Police)** might give **Terry**.

3. **leader: Party ↣ Poli**

   This maps a party to its leader, for example, **leader(Business)** might map to **Denzil**.

4. **_talksto_: Poli ↔ Poli**

   This indicates whether one politician is prepared to talk to some other politician, for example, **Neville talksto Russell**.

Use set comprehension to specify the following sets.

a. The set of all ministers.
b. The set of Green politicians.
c. The party leaders.
d. Those politicians who are ministers of more than one department.

e. Those politicians who talk to the leader of their party.

Q3.16 We can pair each politician with his or her party leader through a function `takeme` which may be defined as follows:

> ```
> takeme: Poli —> Poli
> 
> takeme = { p: Poli • ( p, leader(belongs(p)) ) }
> ```

Using the above style, define sets of pairs to satisfy the following requirements. Make sure you declare the set as a function or as a relation.

a. Pair each party with the number of representatives that it has in parliament.
b. Pair each politician with the set of politicians to whom that politician talks.
c. Pair each politician with the set of politicians that talk to him or her.
d. Pair each party leader with the set of politicians that he or she leads.
e. Create pairs of party leaders such that the first one outranks the second in terms of the number of politicians in the respective parties.

CHAPTER 4

Relations

4.1 Introduction

In this chapter we take a step towards the implementation of our specific facts. In previous chapters, we attempted to represent situations in reasonably natural, if formal, way. We would usually consider a person's age and a person's father to be separate facts about that person; and so, in our specification, we would probably want to treat them separately. Don't forget that the specification is a description written for *our* benefit. An implementation, however, is a description written with automation in mind. While a specification may be written with a relatively free hand, an implementation is usually required to be efficient and effective, using a minimum amount of storage space and providing an acceptable response time.

This chapter provides a continuation of the formal notions of relations and sets that were introduced in the two previous chapters. It allows us to gather these ideas in a theoretical manner before discussing their implementation in a "real-live" computer language, namely SQL.

The chapter introduces the **relational model** of data. Using this approach, facts are combined to produce larger storage structures called relations. A relational database is a cohesive collection of relations. We use the relational model (1) because it allows us to access and to manipulate facts in a relatively easy manner, and (2) because there are many commercially available database management systems that support the relational model.

4.2 Merging Facts

The idea of a relation was introduced in Chapter 2 where it was described as a set of pairs. In that chapter, relations were frequently shown in the form of a two-column table. For that reason, we might call them **binary** relations to distinguish them from the more general relations that are the subject of this chapter. But, because each binary relation corresponds to a particular type of fact, we will also refer to binary relations as **fact types** to make their origin clear. Here are two examples of these fact types that were introduced in that chapter.

```
age : Person —> N                drives : Person -+> CarMake

age =                            drives =
   {(Alan,  21),                    {(Bob,   Porsche),
    (Sue,   18),                     (Mark,  Toyota),
    (Kim,   23),                     (Ann,   Toyota),
    (Bob,   23),                     (Sue,   Ford),
    (Mark,  48),                     (Alan,  Mercedes)}
    (Ann,   45)}
```

These two fact types, **age** and **drives**, are more specialized relations called functions. Viewed simply as tables, each table corresponds to a particular type of fact, and each row corresponds to one specific fact of that type. The relational model extends the notion of a two-column table to a table with any number of columns. Using the idea of an extended relation, we can merge facts into a space-efficient package. They may be merged safely, resulting in a table that has one row for each person: see Figure 4.1.

```
People
------------------------
Name     Age      Drives
------------------------
Alan     21       Mercedes
Sue      18       Ford
Kim      23       ?
Bob      23       Porsche
Mark     48       Toyota
Ann      45       Toyota
------------------------
```

Figure 4.1 An easy merger

As a result of the merge, a single three-column relation has replaced a pair of binary relations. Consequently, some space has been saved. One minor (is it?) problem has arisen because Kim does not drive. A question mark (**?**) has been inserted to indicate what is termed a **null** or missing **value**. However, the problem does seem minor compared with the savings that result, especially when this process is repeated for all the facts that are to be represented. We can save a lot of space by merging several smaller relations into one bigger one.

The merging process cannot be performed carelessly, however. Suppose we were to merge the **plays** fact with the **age** one. What happens?

```
     age : Person --> N                _plays_ : Person <--> Sport

     age =                             plays =
        {(Alan,  21),                     {(Alan,  tennis),
         (Sue,   18),                      (Alan,  golf),
         (Kim,   23),                      (Sue,   tennis),
         (Bob,   23),                      (Kim,   tennis),
         (Mark,  48),                      (Bob,   golf),
         (Ann,   45)}                      (Bob,   hockey),
                                           (Mark,  golf),
                                           (Mark,  squash)}
```

```
A Bad Merger                        A Good Merger
--------------------------          ----------------------------
Name     Age     Plays              Name    Age     Plays
--------------------------          ----------------------------
Alan     21      tennis             Alan    21      tennis, golf
Alan     ?       golf               Sue     18      tennis
Sue      18      tennis             Kim     23      tennis
Kim      23      tennis             Bob     23      golf, hockey
Bob      23      golf               Mark    48      golf, squash
Bob      ?       hockey             Ann     45      -
Mark     48      golf               ----------------------------
Mark     ?       squash
Ann      45      ?
--------------------------
```

Figure 4.2 Bad and good mergers

Problems arise if we use the **plays** fact to control the merge:

- What do we do with the ages of people who play more than sport, for example, Alan? Do we repeat the age for every sport he plays? Or, as has been done here, record his age for the first sport and make it null for all others?

- What do we do with people who don't play any sport, for example, Ann? Here we have recorded a null sport, but we would have to be careful should she decide to take one up.

From this one example, it is clear that the merging is not arbitrary. It is part of the database design process to determine which facts may be merged. Chapters 8 to 11 cover this.

There is an alternative way of merging these two fact types, one that avoids the need for null values. This merge requires that we have one row per person and associate each person with the *set* of sports that they play. In effect, we use the **age** fact as the basis for the merger. Alan plays the set of sports consisting of tennis and golf. Ann is associated with the empty set because she plays no sports. The empty set is a legitimate set value; it is not a null value. A null value would indicate that we do not *know* what sports she plays.

The relation so formed is quite valid. It is a way of representing facts that is well-established in computing. It makes its appearance in many file systems, where it would be termed a file with variable-length records. However, it is *not* allowed in the relational model as that term is normally understood. That model of data representation permits only table entries that have a simple or atomic value. So we have a conflict.

- There is the relational model that is theoretically possible. We will call this the **general** relational model. This may be used in a specification.
- There is the relational model that is in current use and that is available in many commercially available database management systems. We will call this the **standard** relational model. This must be used in an implementation.

We will look at the general relational model and then look at what compromises we must make to follow the standard model.

4.3 Relations

One of our less endearing features is a tendency to label things, that is, to put things into categories. Almost automatically, we try to see into how many slots we can place something.

Suppose, for example, that we were touring a second-hand car yard looking for a suitable car (we could equally well be browsing in a bookshop or a dress shop or a record shop). As soon as we see a car that we fancy, we make a mental note, such as:

Car Record	
Make:	Ford
Model:	Falcon
Color:	red
Year:	1985
Price:	7000

We have categorized the car in five different ways. We have noted five different aspects of the car. It is in the category of cars made by Ford; it is in the category of makes called Falcon; it is in the category of red cars; and so on.

If the car does not meet our requirements then we will pass on to the next one. We look at the car and notice its **attributes**. For each attribute, there is a set of allowable values, those that make the car acceptable. Then we decide which element, if any, of that set fits the car.

Attribute	Domain
Make	Ford, Toyota, Honda, BMW, Mitsubishi,...
Model	Falcon, Laser, Prelude, Accord, 723i, Magna, Golf,...
Color	red, purple, green, blue, white, pink,...
Year	1970, 1971, 1972,...
Price	50..100000

The set of values associated with the attribute is known as the **domain** of the attribute. While it would be nice to think that each attribute has its own independent set of allowable values, in practice the various domains may be highly *interdependent*. Suppose we are creating a new car record. Once we have filled the MAKE attribute with the value `Ford`, for example, our choice of values for the `Model` slot is immediately reduced to a certain subset of the original domain of that attribute; we cannot have a `Ford Accord`. There may be many other inter-domain constraints. We may be happy with a purple BMW but not with a purple Ford; we may be prepared to pay $2 000 for a 1970 BMW but not for a 1970 Toyota; and so on. The idea of a domain becomes so diluted that it ends up being some general set such as the set of integers or the set of character strings.

We might look at some other cars, perhaps writing down essential details as we go. A way of presenting this information is to write it **down** the page, with each car taking up a row and the result taking the form of a table.

```
Cars
-----------------------------------------
Make      Model     Color     Year   Price
-----------------------------------------
Ford      Falcon    red       1985    7000
BMW       723i      purple    ?       2500
Ford      Laser     blue      1978    1000
Toyota    Corona    brown     1972     100
Ford      Falcon    red       1981    1199
Toyota    Corolla   white     1971     199
-----------------------------------------
```

In computing, a table like the one above is often called a **relation**. A relation is a *dynamic* data object; that is, its contents are expected to change over time. So far we have seen six cars; when we started we had seen none; tomorrow – who knows how lucky we will be then? The `Cars` relation will vary accordingly. However, its structure will *not* change; it will always have exactly those five attributes that it had at the beginning and that it has now.

4.4 Tuples

4.4.1 Form Filling

When we start our car hunt, we may not be too fixed in our ideas about the kind of car that will suit us; but after seeing a few cars we will probably settle on those attributes that are important to us. Once we have decided on these particular attributes, then the search becomes rather like filling in a form, once for each potential purchase.

CAR RECORD	
MAKE:	....
MODEL:	....
COLOR:	....
YEAR:	....
PRICE:	....

The form is a kind of template for a suitable car, with a number of slots to be completed. Each slot or attribute has a corresponding set of allowable values. For example, the `Make` slot must be a `Ford` or a `Toyota` and so on. This composite collection of values is called a **tuple**. However, it is often simply referred to as a **record**. Suppose there is a classified advertisement for a car that might be suitable.

```
"BMW 723i, purple, low mileage; one careful owner; $2500."
```

This description presents several features or attributes of the car; some of these will be of interest; others we will ignore. We ignore the low mileage because it is not important to us, and discount the ownership claim as unconvincing. We then fill out our car record or tuple.

Car Record	
Make:	BMW
Model:	723i
Color:	purple
Year:	?
Price:	2500

The advertisement also omits one feature that we did consider to be important, the year of manufacture. What do we do about this attribute? That rather depends on how strongly we feel about that particular feature. If we are not prepared to even consider a car without knowing when it was made then we will be unable to complete the form and may have to miss out on this great bargain. In practice we would probably not wish to be quite so stringent. We should be able to discover, sooner or later, when the car was built. When we are prepared to leave a slot unfilled, then this is referred to as assigning a **null value**. The allowable values for this slot consist then of the attribute's domain plus the null value. There appear to be two distinct decisions to be made regarding each car attribute.

1. What exactly is the domain of the attribute, that is, what are the acceptable values?

2. Is it essential that we have a value for that attribute? Or are we prepared to consider cars, at least temporarily, where that attribute is unknown?

The three ideas of a tuple, its definition and the associated relation are closely connected.

A tuple definition specifies a particular kind or form of tuple; it states which attributes it has, the domain of each attribute, whether null values are to be permitted for that attribute and other constraints on what makes a valid tuple of that kind. The relation associated with a particular tuple definition is the set of tuples that satisfy the definition.

4.4.2 Tuple or Aggregate Objects

The process of gathering together relatively simple objects in order to create a more complex one is called **aggregation**. There are two different ways of declaring aggregate objects. We can use the Cartesian product operator, written $\times$, to introduce these objects.

$address : N \times Street \times Town \times PostCode$

Defined in this way, *address* is a four-part tuple. Constant tuple objects may be created by using round brackets to surround a collection of simple constants, for example:

$address = (1, Geo\ St, Brisbane, 4001)$

The tuple is an *ordered* list of values, so that:

$(9, 10, 1991) \neq (10, 9, 1991)$

Swapping the order creates another object, in this case, another date.

Almost as soon as we create an aggregate object, we will want to extract some component part. Look at the following tuples.

$date = (1, 10, 90)$

$address = (6, HuttonSt, Yeppoon, 4703)$

We may talk about the "second" part of *date* or the "fourth" part of *address*, but this is counter-intuitive. We really want to refer to the "month" part of *date* or the "postcode" part of *address*. There is a second style that we can use to define aggregate objects. This is the style we will use when we want to define an aggregate object and where the components of that object are to be identified by name rather than by position.

```
┌─ Date ──────────────────────────────────────
│  Day : N
│  Month : N
│  Year : N
└─────────────────────────────────────────────
```

This is an example of a **schema type** or **record type**. We can now use *Date* as a type in subsequent declarations.

$d : Date$

The variable *d* is a tuple with three components.

$d.Day$
$d.Month$
$d.Year$

The word "schema" means an outline, or a skeleton. A schema type outlines the valid tuples that may be inserted into a relation. The schema becomes, in effect, a relation schema as well. We could choose to introduce a record type for a car object.

```
┌─ CarRecord ─────────────────────────────────
│  Make : Make
│  Model : Model
│  Color : Color
│  Year : N|null
│  Price : Money
└─────────────────────────────────────────────
```

The *Make*, *Model* and *Color* attributes have been named after the parent type. This should not cause confusion. If it does, then other attribute names should be picked. The *Year* component may be unknown. The type associated with that attribute is a new one constructed from the disjoint union of the integers N and a special constant *null*. A car year may be an integer or it may be null.

4.4.3 A Definition

We are now able to define a relation.

Relations

Any object R that is declared, either directly or indirectly, in the following way:

$$R : Set\ of\ (A \times B \times \cdots \times P \times Q)$$

is a relation. The sets $A, B, \ldots, P, Q$ may themselves involve power sets and product sets. A **relation** is a set of composite objects called tuples. In its simplest form, a relation is a set of pairs.

The cars relation is merely a set of car records.

Cars : *Set of CarRecord*

If we substitute the definition of a *CarRecord*, we get:

Cars : *Set of* (*Make* × *Model* × *Color* × ($N|null$) × *Money*)

4.4.4 Identifying Individual Tuples

If the table is to serve its purpose as a set of suitable or adequate cars, then it must be possible to distinguish one car from another. How else can we drive away with the car of our choice?

```
Cars
-----------------------------------------
Make       Model      Color    Year    Price
-----------------------------------------
Ford       Falcon     red      1985    7000
BMW        723i       purple   ?       2500
Ford       Laser      blue     1978    1000
Toyota     Corona     brown    1972     100
Ford       Falcon     red      1981    1199
Toyota     Corolla    white    1971     199
-----------------------------------------
```

It may be that, depending upon what is available in the marketplace, we may see:

- only one Ford, but several Toyotas, so we cannot distinguish cars by means of their make alone;
- only one Ford Falcon, but several Ford Lasers, so we cannot distinguish cars by means of the combination of their make and their model;
- only one red Ford Falcon, but several blue ones, so the combination of make, model and color will not help us either;

– and so on.

We may decide that none of the attributes, either singly or in conjunction, is enough to uniquely identify each car. If this is so, we will have to add some other attributes such as the location of the car yard, or its phone number, or even the car's registration number. This is something that people do naturally. We can almost always go back in our minds and remember something about a car that made it different from the others. It may be a tear in the upholstery or a dent in the driverside door or even the shiny Studebaker that stood next to it.

When we are representing this kind of information within a computer system, we do not have this kind of recall. We must choose, in advance, the attributes that will enable us and the computer to uniquely identify each car. The attribute or attributes chosen for this purpose form what is called the **relation key**.

If none of the available attributes are of use, we will need to introduce an artificial attribute to help us. This is what we will do now. As we approve a car it will be assigned a unique number.

```
Cars
------------------------------------------------
Nr    Make      Model     Color    Year    Price
------------------------------------------------
1     Ford      Falcon    red      1985    7000
2     BMW       723i      purple   ?       2500
3     Ford      Laser     blue     1978    1000
4     Toyota    Corona    brown    1972     100
5     Ford      Falcon    red      1981    1199
6     Toyota    Corolla   white    1971     199
------------------------------------------------
```

4.5 Domains

There are three possible types of domain that may be defined for an attribute. These correspond to the three types that were introduced in Chapters 2 and 3.

1. There are **simple** domains where the set consists of atomic or single valued elements. The word atomic is used to indicate that no *useful* fragmentation of any value is likely to occur. The **Color** attribute has an atomic domain. There is no *separate* meaning or use in such fragments as `yel` or `lue`.

2. There are **compound** domains where the set consists of composite elements. When we fill in a form and one of the questions is broken into a number of subquestions then

the corresponding domain is compound. Typical examples of compound domains are dates and addresses. If we decide that we need to know on which day we saw a car, we could use a **DateSeen** attribute whose domain consisted of three subdomains; one for each of the day, month and year on which the car was seen. When the domain is defined as the product of two or more sets, for example, **Day** × **Month** × **Year**, then the underlying domain is compound.

3. There are **set valued** domains where each element of the domain is itself a set. When we fill in a form and one of the questions asks us to answer with a list of some kind, then the corresponding domain is set valued. As an example, suppose we wanted to record extra features that each car has, such as air-conditioning, power steering, automatic transmission, and so on. We could use an **Extras** attribute whose domain was set valued. When the domain is defined using the power set operator, for example, **Set of Extra**, then the underlying domain is set valued.

Any relation containing only attributes with simple domains is said to be in **first-normal form** or to be **normalized**. The conventional or standard relational model permits only simple domains. If we have relations that are not in first-normal form then they will have to be modified before being processed by any of the commonly used relational database management systems. However, there is no reason why our specification should not use non-first normal form (NF2) relations, as long as we map to normalized ones for our implementation.

Suppose that the car data entry form is now extended to include three new questions and three corresponding attributes.

1. There will now be a question that allows us to allocate an identifying number to the car.

2. There will be a question regarding the date on which the car was seen.

3. There will be a question asking which additional features or extras the car has, if any.

The record types will be:

```
┌─ Date ─────────────────────────────
│ Day : N
│ Mth : N
│ Yr : N
│
```

```
┌─ CarRecord ────────────────────────
│ Nr : N
│ DateSeen : Date
│ Make : Make
│ Model : Model
│ Color : Color
│ Year : N|null
│ Price : Money
│ Extras : Set of Extra
│
```

The car record has a composite *DateSeen* attribute and a set-valued *Extras* attribute.

The form now looks like this:

CAR RECORD	
NR:	1
DATESEEN:	12/10/92
MAKE:	Ford
MODEL:	Falcon
COLOR:	red
YEAR:	1985
PRICE:	7000
EXTRAS:	auto
	a/c
	radio
	....
	....

Cars

Nr	DateSeen Day Mth Yr	Make	Model	Color	Year	Price	Extras
1	12 10 92	Ford	Falcon	red	1985	7000	auto, a/c, radio
2	12 10 92	BMW	723i	purple	?	2500	radio
3	13 10 92	Ford	Laser	blue	1978	1000	-
4	13 10 92	Toyota	Corona	brown	1972	100	-
5	13 10 92	Ford	Falcon	red	1981	1199	radio, auto
6	15 10 92	Toyota	Corolla	white	1971	199	auto

4.6 Problems with the Automatic

Suppose now that we are planning to convert our manual or paper and pencil recording system into a computer-based one.

Instead of writing the information down on a sheet of paper, we will enter it through the keyboard of our laptop computer. The information entered will now form a database on the machine's disk. The questionnaire or form that we used to guide us in collecting the right information will now appear on the laptop's screen. (The more things change, the more they stay the same.) It would seem that all the program has to do is to capture the data and store it exactly as it is entered. The database will consist of a single relation that contains all the information we need. Unfortunately, there are a number of problems that must be overcome; the solutions to these will require that the database be split into a number of smaller relations.

1. Every time we see a Falcon that we like, we record that it is made by Ford, regardless of how many Falcons we see and like. A similar statement might be made regarding Ford Lasers, Toyota Corollas and so on. The practical consequence is that we are both wasting space in our database *and* irritating the user (ourselves in this case).

2. Most relational database management systems will not support, that is they will not permit, composite domains. This means that `DateSeen`, which has such a domain, must be modified in some way.

3. Most relational database management systems *in common use* will not support set valued domains such as required by the `Extras` attribute. The practical consequence is that we must avoid them somehow.

We will tackle each problem in turn.

4.6.1 Solving the Problem of Repetition

The solution to the first problem, where we repeated information, is to factor out the repetition and place it in a relation of its own. In this case, the split will result in the following relations.

```
Models
----------------
Make       Model
----------------
Ford       Falcon
BMW        723i
Ford       Laser
Toyota     Corona
Toyota     Corolla
----------------
```

Nr	DateSeen Day Mth Yr	Model	Color	Year	Price	Extras
1	12 10 92	Falcon	red	1985	7000	auto, a/c, radio
2	12 10 92	723i	purple	?	2500	radio
3	13 10 92	Laser	blue	1978	1000	-
4	13 10 92	Corona	brown	1972	100	-
5	13 10 92	Falcon	red	1981	1199	radio, auto
6	15 10 92	Corolla	white	1971	199	auto

The key of this new `Models` relation is the model name attribute `Model`. No two models have the same name and no manufacturer is ever likely to name one of their new models the same as some other manufacturer's. The `Make` attribute has been dropped entirely from the `cars` relation but the `Model` one has been retained. This is essential. If we removed both columns then we would have no way of knowing which make or model a particular car was. The `Model` attribute now appears in two relations. In one of these relations, `Models`, it is the relation key. Because of this, it is termed a **foreign key** within the other relation, `Cars`.

The sensible step now is to turn the `Models` relation into a table listing all acceptable models and their manufacturer. Whenever a value is to be entered into the `Model` attribute of the `Cars` relation, we refer to that attribute in `Models` to ensure that our entry is valid. This cross-checking to ensure accuracy helps to maintain the **referential integrity** of the database.

```
           CAR RECORD
NR:        1
DATESEEN:  12/10/92
MAKE:      Ford
MODEL:     Falcon
COLOR:     red
YEAR:      1985
PRICE:     7000
EXTRAS:    auto
           a/c
           radio
           ........
           ........
```

Now when entering car details from the keyboard, we will fill in the MODEL: slot and expect the computer system to look up the `Models` table, find the corresponding make and display that in the MAKE: slot as a form of confirmation.

4.6.2 Solving the Composite Domain Problem

The next problem occurs where we have attributes with composite domains. We must eliminate these, without losing any information.

```
----------
 DateSeen
Day Mth Yr
----------
12  10  92
```

There are two standard solutions to this problem.

1. The lower level attributes may be combined. The effect is to cram a collection of separate values into a single one.

```
   ----------          --------
    DateSeen           DateSeen
   Day Mth Yr
   ----------          --------
   12  10  92           121092
```

   This approach is commonly taken with dates and with addresses both of which are essentially composite.

2. The second solution is simply to drop the top level composite attribute and to raise its component attributes to this level.

```
    DateSeen              Day Mth Yr
    Day Mth Yr
    ----------            ----------
    12  10  92            12  10  92
```

The choice of solution depends on whether or not we want the machine to be able to access the components or whether we are prepared to do it ourselves. If we want to access all cars seen in October then we should keep the attributes separate, that is take the second approach. However, if all we would ever want is a date then the first approach would suffice.

4.6.3 Solving the Set Valued Domain Problem

The third problem to be solved is that of somehow getting rid of the set-valued **Extras** attribute, without losing any information. This is also done by splitting the **Cars** relation. Each car is uniquely identified by a number, say **1**, and each car has a set of extra features, say {**auto, a/c, radio**}. A new relation is formed and in this relation each feature will appear in a separate tuple, paired off with the appropriate car number.

```
Cars                                        CarExtras
-------------------------------             ----------
Nr     ...    Extras                        Nr    Extra
-------------------------------             ----------
1      ...    auto, a/c, radio              1     auto
                                            1     a/c
                                            1     radio
```

The result of the split leads us to the following division.

```
Cars                                                  CarExtras
------------------------------------------            ----------
Nr    Model     Color     Year    Price               Nr    Extra
------------------------------------------            ----------
1     Falcon    red       1985    7000                1     auto
2     723i      purple    ?       2500                1     a/c
3     Laser     blue      1978    1000                1     radio
4     Corona    brown     1972    100                 2     radio
5     Falcon    red       1981    1199                5     radio
6     Corolla   white     1971    199                 5     auto
------------------------------------------            6     auto
                                                      ----------
```

Again, although a split has occurred, we can still reconnect the relations because *both* relations have a car **Nr** attribute. Using this common attribute we can always find out which features a particular car has; or alternatively, we can find out which cars have a particular feature such as air-conditioning.

4.7 The Cars Database

Given the above analysis, we can now define a database for information regarding cars we have seen. There will be a record type for each of the three relations just discussed.

1. There will be a record type for models and their makers.

   ┌─ ModelRecord ───┐
   │ Make : Make   │
   │ Model : Model   │
   └───┘

2. There will be a record type for atomic attributes of each car.

   ┌─ CarRecord ───┐
   │ Nr : N   │
   │ Seen : Date   │
   │ Model : Model   │
   │ Color : Color   │
   │ Year : N | null   │
   │ Price : Money   │
   └───┘

3. There will be a record type for recording extra features that a car may have.

   ┌─ ExtraRecord ───┐
   │ Nr : N   │
   │ Extra : Feature   │
   └───┘

We can even use this formalism to define the Cars database.

   ┌─ CarsDatabase ──┐
   │ Models : Set of ModelRecord   │
   │ Cars : Set of CarRecord   │
   │ Extras : Set of ExtraRecord   │
   └───┘

Each component of the database is a relation. So we have an external user-view constructed by means of the **general** relational model; and we have an internal program-view, a relational database built by means of the **standard** relational model. It is the program's purpose to sustain a mapping between the two pictures, one that simulates the external picture by suitable manipulation of the internal picture.

- When the user sees a likely car, *one* new car record is added to his or her "database"; the data capture program will:

  1. Add a new record to the `Cars` relation.

2. Refer to the **Models** relation to supply the **Make**.

3. Add a new record to the **Extras** relation *for each* extra that this car features.

- When the user displays a car "record" on the screen, a reverse process will take place, with the "apparent" record being constructed by reference to the three database relations.

4.8 Anatomy of a Database

4.8.1 The Subject Database

Here is an example of a *relational* database. This database will be used throughout the rest of this chapter and extensively in the chapters on SQL that follow. It is worth taking some time to become familiar with the relation and attribute names and, to some extent, the database contents.

The database is used to keep track of student assessment for a subject at the Quilpie Institute of Theft. The subject is called an **Introduction to Crime**. There are three relations in the database, **Students**, **Assess** and **Results**.

Seven people enrolled in the subject and their personal details are recorded in the **Students** relation. Three items of assessment were set, two of these were to be done during the semester and the third was an end of semester examination. As the semester proceeded assignments were handed in and marked. The marks were then recorded in the **Results** relation along with the date of submission.

The contents of the database at the end of the semester were as follows.

Students

Id	First	Last
871	Hans	Zupp
862	Bill	Board
869	Rip	Orff
854	Ann	Dover
831	Hans	Orff
872	Betty	Kahn
868	Will	Gambol

Assess

Item	Description	Weight	Due
1	Petty Theft	10	0908
2	Tax Evasion	30	1021
3	Extortion	60	?

Results

Item	Id	Submitted	Mark
1	871	0908	80
1	862	0907	60
1	854	0908	70
1	872	0910	55
1	868	0906	90
1	869	0909	70
2	871	1021	70
2	869	1022	80
2	872	1021	65
2	862	1022	70
2	868	1021	75
3	869	?	95
3	872	?	45
3	862	?	40
3	868	?	50
3	871	?	60
3	854	?	65

The attributes `Due` and `Submitted` both hold dates in the form `MMDD`; so, for example, `1021` represents 21 October. This allows two dates to be compared numerically. A question mark is used to indicate a null value.

4.8.2 Keys

The relation keys are as follows:

Relation	Key attributes
Students	Id
Assess	Item
Results	Item and Id

Given the above keys, then it is guaranteed that:

- No two rows in the `Students` relation have the same `Id`.
- No two rows in the `Assess` relation have the same value in the `Item` column.
- No two rows in the `Results` relation have the same `Item` and `Id` in combination.

If we inspect the relations, two other keys might seem possible, since:

- No two students have the same `First` and `Last` name, in combination.
- No two items of assessment have the same `Description`.

The database designer, however, must choose a key that will provide uniqueness for *the lifetime* of the relation concerned. In this example, the designer thought that there might have been two or more `John Smith`'s in the class and that there might have been, for example, two `essay` assignments. In both cases an artificial key has been created specifically to overcome problems that would arise if such duplication did occur.

The best way to handle relations is to think of them as being in two parts.

- There is a set of objects represented by the key.
- Each non-key attribute is a simple fact concerning the elements of that set.

Using this as a guide, the `Students` relation divides in two.

```
                      ---               -----------------
                      Id                First     Last
                      ---               -----------------
                      871               Hans      Zupp
                      862               Bill      Board
                      869               Rip       Orff
         Students  =  854           +   Ann       Dover
                      831               Hans      Orff
                      872               Betty     Kahn
                      868               Will      Gambol
                      ---               -----------------
```

The relation decomposes into the following:

- a set of students represented by their Id's: $\{871, 862, 869, 854, 831, 872, 868\}$.
- two facts concerning each student, that is, his or her first and last name.

In the same way, the **Assess** relation can be decomposed into a set of assessments $\{1, 2, 3\}$ represented by their item number. Each assessment item has three facts recorded about it: a description, a weight and a due date.

The **Results** relation decomposes into a set of results $\{(1, 871), (1, 862), \ldots\}$ represented by (**Item**, **Id**) pairs, and for each item, there is information concerning the date of submission and the mark awarded.

Relation	Attribute	Domain
Students	Id	Integer
	First	CharString
	Last	CharString
Assess	Item	Integer
	Description	CharString
	Weight	Integer
	Due	Date
Results	Item	Integer
	Id	Integer
	Submitted	Date
	Mark	Integer

Figure 4.3 The database anatomy

There is more to anatomy than just structure. It is also concerned with the connections between structures. The links between relations are also important. These may be seen in the **Results** relation. Two of its attributes are the keys of other relations. When an attribute of one relation is the key in another then we have a link between the two relations. For example, the first row of the **Results** relation points to two other rows in two separate relations. See Figure 4.4.

The **Item** and **Id** attributes of the **Results** relation are **both** examples of foreign keys. Each is a **foreign key** because each is the key of some other relation. Any attribute or set of attributes within a relation may be a foreign key. It is by chance that **Item** and **Id** also form the key of the **Results** relation.

In summary, although a relational database may appear to consist of a number of quite disjoint relations, they are always connected by means of foreign keys which act as pointers from one relation to another. A relational database would be unusable without these connectors.

4.9 Relational Languages

A database is kept in a box on a computer system and that box is guarded by a piece of software known as a database management system or DBMS. The only access to the

```
Results
-----------------------------------
Item   Id      Submitted   Mark
-----------------------------------
  1   (871)      0908       80
```

Foreign keys provide the links that turn a collection of tables into a database.

```
Students
-----------------------------
Id        First       Last
-----------------------------
(871)     Hans        Zupp
```

```
Assess
-----------------------------------
Item  Description   Weight   Due
-----------------------------------
 (1)  Petty Theft     10     0908
```

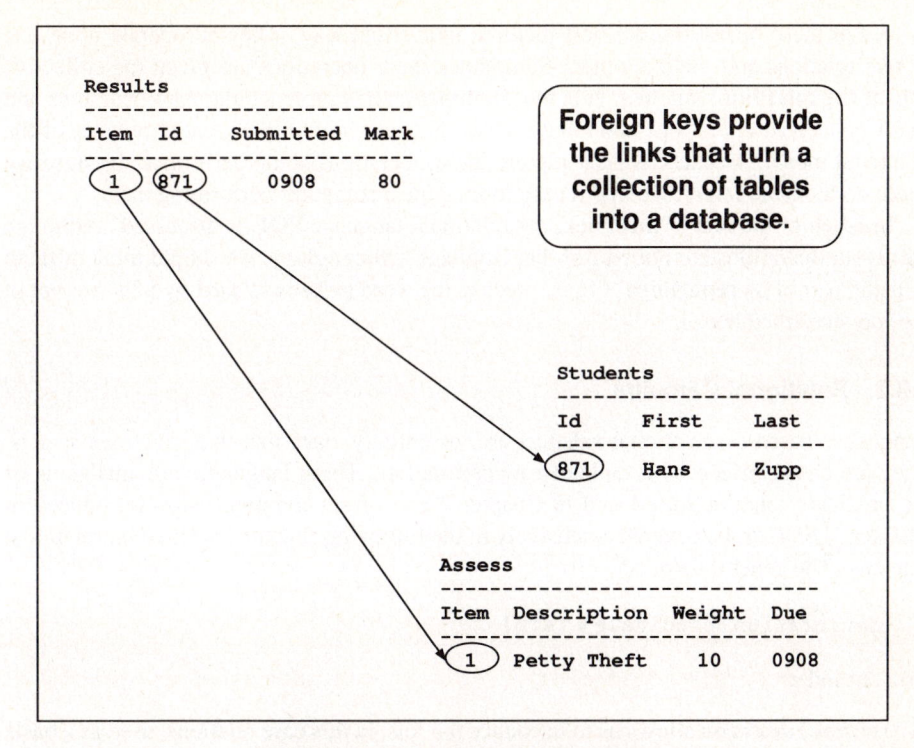

Figure 4.4 Links between tables

database is via the DBMS. *We* can only access the database indirectly, that is, by making a request to the software. This request must therefore be phrased in appropriate language. There are two kinds of language for manipulating relations: ones based on **relational algebra** and ones based on **relational calculus**. Although most of the discussion that follows will concern the calculus, there are important terms and concepts involved in the algebra.

4.9.1 Relational Algebra

Relational algebra attempts to treat relations as large units, capable of being manipulated as a whole. When parts of a relation are to be accessed then they are addressed by means of the appropriate attributes.

There are four operations that are particularly associated with relational algebra.

- The **select** operation allows tuples to be extracted from a relation. The extracted tuples then form a relation in their own right.
- The **project** allows attributes to be extracted from a relation to form another relation.
- The **product** operation creates a product relation from two relations.
- The **join** extends each tuple in one relation with an appropriate tuple from another relation. The effect is to make it look as if one relation is glued to the other.

All of these operations are best pictured in a visual way. They all operate upon one or two relations and yield another. Sometimes these operations are given the collective title of **the relational algebra**. It is the combination of simple tabular data structures and easily conceived operations upon these tables that accounts for the great popularity of the relational model. Because *we* can picture these operations being performed, because we could do them *ourselves*, we find it easy to imagine a computer performing them.

In much of the rest of this book, the relational language **SQL** is discussed. Although these four operations are not part of that language's **vocabulary**, we should think of them as being part of its **repertoire**. (To be precise, the word `select` is used by SQL but not in the way described here.)

4.9.2 Relational Calculus

Languages based on relational calculus are, essentially, ones that treat relations as sets. They are characterized by a tuple or row orientation. These languages are amalgams of the predicate calculus introduced in Chapter 2 and of set comprehension introduced in Chapter 3. SQL, to be covered extensively in the following chapters, is based on relational calculus. The general form is:

{declaration | predicate • term}

As a reminder:

- The `declaration` allows us to introduce the sets, in this case relations, used as a basis for the query.

- The optional `predicate` allows us to express conditions that elements of these sets must satisfy. In relational calculus, the elements are tuples of some kind. If no predicate is supplied then all tuples are selected.

- The optional `term` allows us to identify the exact nature of the new set that is to be formed. If no term is supplied then tuples from the base relations are to be used.

A very simple example is:

{s : Students}

This statement returns the entire **Students** relation. There is no predicate to filter out any students. The variable `s` is a **tuple variable**. It ranges over the entire relation taking in turn the value of each tuple.

What if we wanted details on certain students only? Perhaps we are interested in those whose first name is Hans. A tuple has a kind of segmented or composite value. There is one segment for each attribute in the relation. We use **tuple projection** to isolate one particular segment of a tuple. This is achieved by an expression such as:

s.First

A tuple variable name followed by a full stop followed by an attribute name represents the value of that attribute within the corresponding tuple. The expression `s.First` represents the first name attribute of any **Students** tuple represented by `s`.

4.9.3 The Select Operation

A typical request that might be made of a relational database would be to report on those tuples that satisfy some condition. This is called the **select** operation. The operation takes a relation and a condition; it returns the subset of that relation for which the condition holds.

Example 4.1 Find out about students called Orff.
To create a predicate requiring that the last name attribute be Orff, we can write:

$$s.Last = Orff$$

This predicate can then be incorporated into a set comprehension expression:

$$\{s : Students \mid s.Last = Orff\}$$

To execute this request, we must imagine the required rows or tuples being cut from the **Students** relation.

```
Students
---------------------------
Id      First       Last
---------------------------
871     Hans        Zupp
862     Bill        Board
869     Rip         Orff
854     Ann         Dover
831     Hans        Orff
872     Betty       Kahn
868     Will        Gambol
---------------------------
```

```
---------------------------
Id      First       Last
---------------------------
869     Rip         Orff
831     Hans        Orff
---------------------------
```

Figure 4.5 The select operation

The **Students** relation is *not* altered by this operation. We may imagine that a copy of it is taken, and that copy is chopped about in order to select the required tuples. The resulting relation is merely a subset formed from the original.

Example 4.2 Find out about failures in the final exam.
If we know that the final exam is assessment item **3**, and a failure is defined to be any mark less than 50%, then this query can be specified as follows:

$$\{r : Results \mid r.Item = 3 \text{ and } r.Mark < 50\}$$

Again, the resulting relation is a subset of the original.

```
-------------------------------
Item   Id    Submitted    Mark
-------------------------------
 3     872       ?         45
 3     862       ?         40
-------------------------------
```

Example 4.3 Which items of assessment have no due date scheduled yet?

$\{a : \textbf{Assess} \,|\, a.\text{Due} = \textbf{null}\}$

```
---------------------------------
Item   Description    Weight   Due
---------------------------------
 3     Extortion        60      ?
---------------------------------
```

We need a way of detecting null values. Since a null value is really the absence of a value, it is not truly a value and cannot be equal to anything. However, in practice, it is common to provide a special constant called **null**.

4.9.4 The Project Operation

This operation is an extension of the project operation defined on tuples. That particular operation allowed us to choose one attribute from a tuple. When used on a relation, the effect is as if an entire column is removed from that relation.

Example 4.4 What are the Id's of all students in the class?

To execute this request we must imagine the **Students** relation being split from top to bottom.

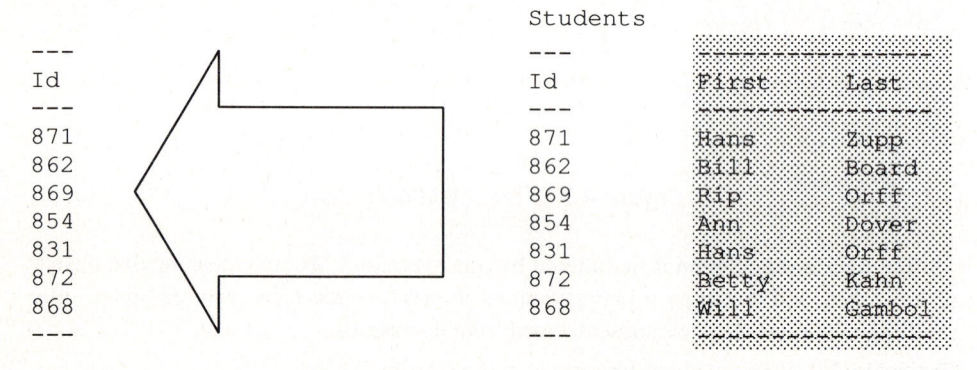

```
                                        Students
  ---                                      ---                 -------------------
  Id                                       Id              First         Last
  ---                                      ---                 -------------------
  871                                      871             Hans          Zupp
  862                                      862             Bill          Board
  869                                      869             Rip           Orff
  854                                      854             Ann           Dover
  831                                      831             Hans          Orff
  872                                      872             Betty         Kahn
  868                                      868             Will          Gambol
  ---                                      ---                 -------------------
```

Figure 4.6 The project operation

Again, the original relation is unchanged, and again, we may imagine that a copy is taken. From that copy, the **Id** attribute or column is retained and the others are discarded. The resulting column is a single attribute relation. In this case a relation acts like a simple set. This operation can be specified as:

$\{s : \textbf{Students} \bullet s.\text{Id}\}$

Example 4.5 What are the last names of all students?

$\{s : \textbf{Students} \bullet s.\text{Last}\}$

```
------
Last
------
Zupp
Board
Orff
Dover
Kahn
Gambol
------
```

The resulting relation is a set of names, and because it is a set, it should contain no duplicates. For this reason the second appearance of the name Orff has been suppressed.

Example 4.6 What are the first names of people whose last name is Orff?

$\{s : \text{Students} \mid s.\text{Last} = \text{Orff} \bullet s.\text{First}\}$

```
----
First
-----
Rip
Hans
-----
```

The project operation can be applied to relations that result from other operations. To answer this query, we **select** the correct tuples and then **project** the required attribute.

Example 4.7 What are the full names of all students?

So far, we have projected only one attribute. However, many queries require the projection of several attributes. In this version of project, the required attributes appear as a list between round brackets. To answer the query using this form of project we can write the expression:

$\{s : \text{Students} \bullet (s.\text{First}, s.\text{Last})\}$

```
--------------
First   Last
--------------
Hans    Zupp
Bill    Board
Rip     Orff
Ann     Dover
Hans    Orff
Betty   Kahn
Will    Gambol
--------------
```

4.9.5 The Product Operation

The Select and Project operations work on one relation. This means, for example, that we cannot, at least immediately, find out the **names** of students who got more than 80% in the final exam. To extract information from two or more relations we need an operation that enables us to combine them in some way. The **product** operation allows us to do that. The product of two relations is formed by connecting each tuple from one relation to each tuple from the other, in turn.

The product of two relations can be formed by introducing two variables into the declaration:

$$\{r : \text{Results}; \ a : \text{Assess}\}$$

The variable r ranges over the tuples of **Results**. For each tuple value taken on by r, the variable a is allowed to range over **Assess**. The product formed in this way is shown below.

Item	Id	Submitted	Mark	Item	Description	Weight	Due
1	871	0908	80	1	Petty Theft	10	0908
1	871	0908	80	2	Tax Evasion	30	1021
1	871	0908	80	3	Extortion	60	?
1	862	0907	60	1	Petty Theft	10	0908
:	:	:	:	:	:	:	:
:	:	:	:	:	:	:	:

The **Results** relation has 17 tuples and **Assess** has 3. Their product has **17 * 3 = 51** tuples, and each new tuple is formed by connecting two tuples, one from each of the relations involved.

Note that this product relation has two attributes with the same name. Two of the columns are headed **Item**. The resulting table is not a true relation.

As can be seen at a glance, many of these newly formed tuples are of little use, but some of them are. The first tuple in the product connects a tuple that contains specific information on a result achieved in the first assignment to a tuple containing some general information on that assignment. We could use such a tuple; for example, we can use it to find out whether or not the assignment was handed in on time. The second and third product tuples are not nearly so useful but we could use them (how?). The fourth one is, again, quite useful; and so on.

4.9.6 The Join Operation

The tuples that are most likely to be of use are those where the **Item** that originated from **Results** equals the **Item** that originated from **Assess**. To preserve these tuples and discard the others we can use a Select operation.

$$\{r : \text{Results}; \ a : \text{Assess} \mid r.\text{Item} = a.\text{Item}\}$$

The resulting relation looks like the following.

```
Results                          Assess
---------------------------------------------------------------
Item   Id    Submitted   Mark    Item   Description   Weight   Due
---------------------------------------------------------------
 1    871     0908        80      1    Petty Theft      10     0908
 1    862     0907        60      1    Petty Theft      10     0908
 1    854     0908        70      1    Petty Theft      10     0908
 1    872     0910        55      1    Petty Theft      10     0908
 1    868     0906        90      1    Petty Theft      10     0908
 1    869     0909        70      1    Petty Theft      10     0908
 2    871     1021        70      2    Tax Evasion      30     1021
 2    869     1022        80      2    Tax Evasion      30     1021
 2    872     1021        65      2    Tax Evasion      30     1021
 2    862     1022        70      2    Tax Evasion      30     1021
 2    868     1021        75      2    Tax Evasion      30     1021
 3    869      ?          95      3    Extortion        60      ?
 3    872      ?          45      3    Extortion        60      ?
 3    862      ?          40      3    Extortion        60      ?
 3    868      ?          50      3    Extortion        60      ?
 3    871      ?          60      3    Extortion        60      ?
 3    854      ?          65      3    Extortion        60      ?
---------------------------------------------------------------
```

The sequence of a Product followed by a particular Select is so commonly required that it is given its own name. It is called the **Join** operation.

4.9.7 Relational Expressions

In each of the four relational operations **select**, **project**, **product** and **join**, the result is yet another relation. This means that the result of one operation may be used by a second operation. This is just the same as when, in the expression `(7+3)/5`, the result of the addition is used by the division.

We can build up very complex relational expressions to answer correspondingly complex queries. Essentially, however, these relational expressions are to be thought of as no different from arithmetic expressions.

4.9.8 Relational Calculus Summary

This is, essentially, set comprehension based on the use of *tuple* variables. The general form is:

`{declaration | predicate • term}`

The restrictions placed upon each of the components are:

- The declaration uses *tuple* variables.
- The predicate does not allow the use of terms formed using function application. This rule is broken to allow simple arithmetic expressions.

- The term is a simple tuple, that is only *atomic* components are permitted.

Simple Formulae

A simple *formula* or predicate in the relational calculus has one of the following forms:

Simple Formula:	*Examples:*
t.A relop u.B	t.Age < u.Age
or t.A relop K	*or* p.Age > 25
or K relop t.A	*or* 18 < q.Age

where:

- **t** and **u** are tuple variables;
- **A** and **B** are attributes of **t** and **u** respectively;
- **K** is a constant;
- `relop` is a relational operator consistent with the attributes **A** and **B**.

Formulae in General

Suppose **F** and **G** are any arbitrary formulae, and **S** is a simple formula. Then, in general, a **well-formed formula** can take any of the following forms:

Well-Formed Formula:	*Examples:*
S	p.Age < 25
or not F	*or* not (p.Age < 25 and p.Sex = F)
or F and G	*or* p.Age < 25 and p.Age > 20
or F or G	*or* p.Sex = M or p.Name=Helen
or (F)	*or* (p.Age < 16)
or $\exists\, t : T \bullet F$	*or* $\exists\, p : People \bullet p.Age < 25$
or $\forall\, t : T \bullet F$	*or* $\forall\, p : People \bullet p.Age > 16$

The last two options, which use the quantifiers $\exists$ and $\forall$, have been included for completeness at this stage. Quantification will be introduced in Chapter 12.

4.10 The Circle Database

4.10.1 Circle Record Types

Chapter 2 introduced us to a circle of people and certain facts about them. All the facts were presented as sets of pairs. In this chapter we have seen another way of representing simple facts using aggregate data structures called records which are gathered into sets called relations. This section compares the two representations and the purpose of each.

Before we can do that we will introduce record types for the circle. The choice of record structure is determined by the results of a database design effort which will be discussed in later chapters. For the moment we will take on trust that the circle may be adequately represented using three record types.

1. There will be a record type based on the functions and injections involving people. Partial functions and injections need to allow for the possibility of a null value.

   ─── PersonRecord ───────────────────────────
   Id : Name
   Sex : Gender
   Age : N
   Drives : CarMake | null
   Left : Name
   Spouse : Name | null
   ──

2. There will be a structure to record information about the playing of a specific sport by a specific person.

   ─── PlayingRecord ──────────────────────────
   Player : Name
   PlaysAt : Sport
   ──

3. There will be another structure to record the speaking of a language.

   ─── SpeakingRecord ─────────────────────────
   Speaker : Name
   FluentIn : Language
   ──

The database can now be defined as follows.

─── CircleDatabase ─────────────────────────────
People : Set of PersonRecord
Plays : Set of PlayingRecord
Speaks : Set of SpeakingRecord

count $\{p : \text{People} \bullet p.\text{Id}\} = \text{count People}$
$\{p : \text{People} \bullet p.\text{Spouse}\} \subseteq \{p : \text{People} \bullet p.\text{Id}\}$
$\{p : \text{People} \bullet p.\text{Left}\} = \{p : \text{People} \bullet p.\text{Id}\}$
──

The **People** relation would look like the following table, using the data from Chapter 2.

```
People
-------------------------------------------------
Id      Sex    Age    Drives     Left    Spouse
-------------------------------------------------
Alan    M      21     Mercedes   Sue     Sue
Sue     F      18     Ford       Bob     Alan
Bob     M      23     Porsche    Kim     ?
Kim     F      23     ?          Mark    ?
Mark    M      48     Toyota     Ann     Ann
Ann     F      45     Toyota     Alan    Mark
-------------------------------------------------
```

The database definition has not only declared the relations used, but has also added two examples of constraints that would normally be placed upon these relations.

Relation Key Constraints

These are required to enforce the functional dependencies that existed before the aggregation. For example, there is nothing in the declaration part of the database definition requiring every `PersonRecord` to have a different name. To recover from this, a constraint is added requiring that the number of names (Id's) in the People relation be the same as the number of tuples in the relation.

$$\text{count } \{p : \text{People} \bullet p.\text{Id}\} = \text{count People}$$

Foreign Key Constraints

These are required to enforce the *referential integrity* of the database. For example, the person named as being somebody's spouse should also exist in the database. This condition may be expressed using set comprehension.

$$\{p : \text{People} \bullet p.\text{Spouse}\} \subseteq \{p : \text{People} \bullet p.\text{Id}\}$$

The set of people identified as being spouses should be a subset of the set of people in the circle.

Other Constraints

The database definition should also specify any other constraints that might apply to the particular database in question. The original `left` relationship, for example, was a total injection. We can convey this constraint in the following way:

$$\{p : \text{People} \bullet p.\text{Left}\} = \{p : \text{People} \bullet p.\text{Id}\}$$

4.10.2 Comparing the Two Views of the Circle

We have now seen two different ways of describing the circle of people that was introduced in Chapter 2. In this section, we will compare the expressiveness of the two methods of description on three queries.

Query 1: Who are the males?
Using set comprehension, as discussed in Chapter 3, we might specify the males as follows:

$\{p : \text{Person} \mid \text{sex}(p) = \text{M}\}$

The variable **p** ranges over each person in the circle, where people are represented by their names. If the gender of the person is **M** then he is added to the set being formed.

Using relational calculus, we might write an expression such as:

$\{p : \text{People} \mid p.\text{Sex} = \text{M} \bullet p.\text{Id}\}$

This time, the variable **p** ranges over the tuples of the **People** relation. For each tuple, the **Sex** attribute is examined, and if it is equal to **M** then the **Id** attribute is projected from the tuple and added to the set being formed.

Query 2: Who is on Sue's left?
This is a simple case of function application.

`left(Sue)`

The one-to-one function or injection `left` maps from Sue to the next person. But, using relational calculus, we have:

$\{p : \text{People} \mid p.\text{Id} = \text{Sue} \bullet p.\text{Left}\}$

Relational calculus is a special form of set comprehension and so every query will return a set of some kind. So we are obliged to form the set of people immediately to Sue's left. It is a set of one but a set nonetheless. The query seems long and awkward.

Query 3: What is the gender of the person on Sue's left?
Since `left(Sue)` is a person, we can apply the `sex` function to that person and be mapped to his or her gender.

`sex(left(Sue))`

Alternatively, we may write:

$\{p, q : \text{People} \mid p.\text{Id} = \text{Sue and } p.\text{Left} = q.\text{Id} \bullet q.\text{Sex}\}$

In Query 2, we were able to find out the person on Sue's left merely by looking at the **Left** attribute of Sue's tuple. To get the gender of that person, we need to look at that person's tuple. So we need two tuples from the **People** relation, (1) Sue's to find the name (**Id**) of that person, and (2) that person to find his or her gender.

p						q					
Id	Sex	Age	Drives	Left	Spouse	Id	Sex	Age	Drives	Left	Spouse
Sue	F	18	Ford	Bob	Alan	Bob	M	23	Porsche	Kim	?

Projection provides the equivalent of a single application of a function but any greater degree of application, such as is required in this case, requires a join.

4.11 Summary

- Relations are the data structures in which we embed the simple specific facts about some situation that we wish to represent. A relation is a set of aggregate structures known as **records** and it is from the richness of the record structure that relations inherit their own potential variety.
- The relational data structure, *in general*, is very flexible, and is capable of representing the wide variety of formats that we use to present organizational views – whether these are management reports or data entry forms.
- Unfortunately, there is a gap between these kinds of relations and the kind that are supported by most commercially available relational database management systems. These products can manipulate relations with only simple attributes. This is the **standard** relational model, as that term is normally used.
- The gap between the two is bridged programmatically, that is, we write programs to turn data retrieved from a relational database into the kinds of richer relations and records that people use to view their organizations.

The relational model of data can be more accurately described as the relational **view** of data. We only picture the data as being stored in relations or tables. Since most forms of electronic bulk storage consist of concentric tracks on a disk storage device, there is no way that the data can really be stored as a table. However, we, as the users of the data, are allowed to refer to the data and to manipulate it as if it were.

A table is commonly used as a way of presenting a collection of similar pieces of information. However, although *we* may suppose the information is in a table, the way that the information is stored within a computer system is another matter. But as long as we can operate under the impression that the information is in a table, then that is all that we require.

It is the role of the Data Base Management System to take our request for information, to decipher it, to determine the best access strategy, to execute that strategy, and to return us the results. All that is required of us is that we have a tabular mental picture of the relations and how they might be manipulated. We talk to the DBMS as if the relations **are** tables and we use the operations of relational algebra as if they are executed in the simple-minded manner shown in this chapter.

This relational carpentry is central to the attraction of relational databases. Such a database is pictured as a number of tables and these tables can be processed by a number of appealingly visual operations. The operations allow existing tables to be chopped, shaped and stuck together to form a new (result) table. In a way, this might be compared to writing a research report. There we take the results of laboratory experiments or of consumer surveys and, by cutting and pasting, we massage these results until they are in a form that enables us to communicate the essential details of our findings.

Exercises

▶ Q4.1 The ACADEMIC Database

The University of Wiseacres is divided into a number of schools and each school consists of a number of academic staff and a Head of School who is also an academic. The following relations are to be used to store information regarding the organizational structure at Wiseacres University. The database also records details of staff and their qualifications. There are three relations in the database and they have the following structure.

```
        Schools             Staff                Quals
        -------             -----                -----
    (*) School_Id       (*) Staff_Id         (*) Staff_Id
        School_Name         Staff_Name       (*) Degree
        Phone               School_Id            Place
    (?) Head_Id                                  Year
```

An asterisk (*) indicates that the attribute is (part of) the primary key of the relation. A question mark (?) indicates that null values are to be permitted for that attribute in the associated relation. The domains of some of the attributes are as follows.

- The School_Id is to be a two-character code uniquely identifying a particular school; for example, the accountancy school might be coded AC.
- The Staff_Id is to be an integer uniquely identifying a member of staff.
- The Head_Id attribute is simply the Staff_Id of the appropriate staff member. The Head of School is to be recorded as a member of the staff within that school.
- The Degree is the name of a qualification, such as BSc or PhD.
- The Place is the initial letters of the university or institute conferring the degree; for example, Wiseacres is encoded as UW.
- The Year is the year in which the degree was conferred.

The following data is taken from the 1996 University Handbook.

School of Computing Science
Head: Prof B.Tree BSc(UW, 1925), PhD(UQ, 1928)
Phone: 2299
Staff: I.Drone BSc(UQ, 1979), MSc(UNSW,1984)
        L.R.Parser BAppSc (QIT, 1987)

School of Accountancy
Head: Ms C.R.Double-Entry BBus(QIT, 1972), MBA(UWA, 1975)
Phone: 8756
Staff: D.Fraud BComm(UQ, 1995), MBA(UCLA, 1998)
        M.Bezzle BBus(UW, 1989)
        P.P.Lounge-Lizard BBus(QUT,1989), MBA(UQ, 1990)

```
            School of Chemistry
            Head:   Vacant
            Phone:  1869
            Staff:  C.A.Quick-Lime BSc(UNT, 1956), PhD(UW, 1958)
                    A.G.Silver BSc(UW, 1975), MSc(UW, 1977), PhD(UW, 1980)
                    H.H.Esso-Fore BSc(MU, 1970), PhD(UNT, 1974)
```

Take a sheet of paper and use the above data to create a database following the layout suggested below. Choose a suitable two-character `School_Id` for each school. Allocate each member of staff a number, starting at 1, so that the ten members of staff shown in the handbook will be numbered 1 to 10 consecutively.

```
Schools
-------------------------------------------
School_Id    School_Name    Phone    Head_Id
-------------------------------------------


Staff
---------------------------------------
Staff_Id    Staff_Name        School_Id
---------------------------------------


Quals
--------------------------------
Staff_Id    Degree   Place   Year
--------------------------------
```

▶ Q4.2   **For each** of the relations used in the previous exercise, answer the following:

   a.   How many attributes does the relation have?

   b.   How many tuples does it have?

   c.   What foreign key appears in this relation?

▶ Q4.3   The RESOURCES Database

Across town from Wiseacres is the Witsend Institute of Technology, where resource allocation is a bigger issue than staff qualifications. This is reflected in the structure of their database.

```
            Staff              Theaters              Allocation
            -----              --------              ----------
       (*) Teacher        (*) Theater           (*) Subject
           Room               Capacity              Enrolled
       (?) Phone                                    Theater
                                                    Teacher
```

The **Staff** and **Theaters** relations represent the Institute's resources and the **Allocation** relation shows, for each subject taught, the current enrollment as well as the lecture theater and teacher normally allocated to that subject. There may be more students enrolled for a subject than the allocated lecture theater can hold. Here is the current state of the database.

```
Staff                              Theaters
---------------------------        ------------------
Teacher    Room    Phone           Theater   Capacity
---------------------------        ------------------
Drone      21      2240            Tiny      15
Slack      16      ?               Chockers  20
Tripp      21      2240            Cramp     15
Hacker     18      2868            Cosy      30
---------------------------        ------------------

Allocation
------------------------------------------------
Subject        Enrolled   Theater    Teacher
------------------------------------------------
Music          10         Tiny       Drone
Ballet         25         Cosy       Tripp
TapDancing     35         Cosy       Tripp
Programming    10         Cramp      Hacker
Singing        25         Tiny       Drone
Surgery        15         Cramp      Hacker
Poetry         10         Cramp      Drone
------------------------------------------------
```

For each of the relations:

    a.   How many attributes does the relation have?

    b.   How many tuples does it have?

    c.   What foreign keys, if any, are there in the relation?

▶ Q4.4   Dr Slack has no phone number recorded. Does this mean he has no phone?

▶ Q4.5   How many tuples will there be in the product of **Allocation** and **Staff**? Write down a sample tuple from this product.

▶ Q4.6   Write out the join of **Allocation** and **Staff**. Is this the same as the join of **Staff** and **Allocation**?

▶ Q4.7   Evaluate the following expressions and show the results. Suggest a possible equivalent English expression.

a. $\{s : \text{Staff} \bullet s.\text{Teacher}\}$

b. $\{s : \text{Staff} \bullet s.\text{Teacher}\} \text{ minus } \{a : \text{Allocation} \bullet a.\text{Teacher}\}$

c. $\{t : \text{Theaters} \mid t.\text{Capacity} > 15\}$

d. $\{s : \text{Staff}; a : \text{Allocation} \mid s.\text{Teacher} = a.\text{Teacher} \bullet (a.\text{Subject}, s.\text{Phone})\}$

e. $\{a, b : \text{Allocation} \mid a.\text{Subject} = \text{Ballet and } b.\text{Enrolled} >= a.\text{Enrolled} \bullet (b.\text{Subject}, b.\text{Enrolled})\}$

▶ **Q4.8** For each of the following queries:

(i) Using the relational calculus, write an expression that specifies the required answer.

(ii) State the relational operations (selects, projects, products and joins) implied by your answer.

a. What is Ms Hacker's phone no?

b. What number is the Music teacher's room?

c. Which staff teach in the Cramp theater?

d. Which subjects are over-enrolled?

e. Which teachers share a room with Mr Drone?

f. Which theaters are not currently allocated?

g. Which theaters have a capacity of over 25?

h. Which theaters have a greater capacity than the Chockers theater?

i. The singing class is over-enrolled for the room allocated. Is there any other room that would be big enough?

j. What are the names and phone numbers of teachers involved with subjects that are over-enrolled?

CHAPTER 5

Introducing SQL

5.1 Introduction

In this chapter we introduce one of the most important computer languages so far developed, SQL. It represents a major departure from the languages we usually think of in connection with computer programming. These more conventional languages are primarily concerned with giving instructions to a computer. SQL is different.

SQL is, first and foremost, a **means of communication**, a means of expressing our requirements. These requirements are passed to a complex software product known as a database management system (DBMS). This software is designed to control access to and usage of the database. SQL is a means of telling the DBMS what we want done. Because the nature of the language allows us to concentrate on specifying the information to be retrieved from our database, there is a consequential load placed upon the DBMS. It must be able to determine a sufficiently rapid means of accessing the data, sufficiently rapid, that is, to satisfy our need for the data.

SQL is an acronym for **S**tructured **Q**uery **L**anguage, and the key word is **query**. This word is to be taken in a more general sense than simply "retrieval". The central idea in SQL is that of identifying the portion of the database that interests you. Having done that, you may apply some operation to that portion: you may display it, you may update it, or you may delete it.

This chapter is intended to provide a brief look at some of the language's major features. These features are divided into four groups concerned with:

- **database definition**, whereby the major components of the database may be defined, modified or discarded;
- **database retrieval**, whereby the portion of the database that meets certain conditions may be identified and examined;
- **database manipulation**, whereby some part of the database may be extended, updated or deleted;

- **database security**, whereby the right to access and modify the database is defined.

All the examples in this chapter are based upon the SUBJECT database introduced in Chapter 4.

5.2 SQL Databases

SQL is a language for dealing with a set of relations known as a relational database. It takes a very pictorial view of a relation. This means that the standard relational terminology of the previous chapter is replaced by SQL's own terms:

Standard term	SQL term
relation	table
attribute	column
tuple	row

The usual way of presenting a relation is in the form of a table, so in SQL a relation is called a **table**; a tuple of the relation is presented horizontally, so it is called a **row**. Each attribute of the relation appears vertically as a **column**.

```
a table
-------------------
Id    First   Last
-------------------
 .    Hans     .
 .    Bill     .
 .    Rip      .
854   Ann     Dover    <------- a row
 .    Hans     .
 .    Betty    .
 .    Will     .
-------------------
       ^
       |
      a column
```

An SQL database is a collection of tables but it is more than just some tables thrown together arbitrarily. It is a unified and interlocking set of tables; it is an organized body with an administrative component. The make-up of every SQL database reflects this organization.

- There are the **base** tables which contain the data for which the database was designed. For the Subject database, these are the `Students`, `Assess` and `Results` tables.
- There is a background component known as the **system catalog**. This consists of a number of **system** tables which contain additional knowledge regarding the contents of the database. This knowledge consists of information regarding which columns make up each base table, what type of data is stored in each column, and so on.

Introducing SQL   113

The division between the base tables and the system tables is reflected in the language itself. There is one style of statement for handling the base tables. There is another style for **defining** the database – handling the system tables, in other words.

So the SQL context or environment incorporates both a database consisting of the base tables and knowledge of that database contained in the system tables.

5.3 Database Definition

The first category of SQL statements to be examined contains those concerned with defining the database. These statements are used to create new structures within the database, to modify these structures and to dispose of them.

Example 5.1 Define the Students table of the Subject database.

```
Create table Students
(Id      integer    not null,
 First   char(10),
 Last    char(10)   not null)
```

The statement names the table (**Students**) and the three columns (**Id**, **First** and **Last**) that form the table. For each column you must also declare the type of data that can be stored in that column. Thus the **Id** column can hold only integers, and the **First** and **Last** columns can hold only character data up to a maximum of 10 characters. The final part of a column definition is optional; it allows you to specify whether or not null values (that is, empty column entries) are to be permitted. The definition indicates that only the **First** name column may contain nulls.

The statement creates an empty table called **Students**, which we can picture thus:

```
Students
-------------------------
Id       First      Last
-------------------------


-------------------------
```

As well as creating an empty **Students** table, the statement will cause entries to be inserted into the system catalog, in particular into two system relations, **Syscatalog** and **Syscolumns**.

If the Students table is the first to be defined in the database, then these two system relations might appear as follows:

```
Syscatalog              Syscolumns
----------              ---------------------------------------------
Tname                   Cname       Tname        Coltype      Length
----------              ---------------------------------------------
Students                Id          Students     integer      ?
----------              First       Students     char         10
                        Last        Students     char         10
                        ---------------------------------------------
```

Other database definition statements allow us to alter tables by adding a new column, or by dropping an entire table from the database. There are three kinds of database objects that can be defined and modified.

- The **table** is the most important kind of object in the database. Almost every single SQL statement requires a table to be named as part of the user's expression of requirements.

- The **view**, as the name suggests, provides one particular aspect or subset of the database. This aspect can cover just a portion of a single table, or it can be widened to spread across several tables. A view is always presented as a table and the `create view` statement is a way of naming that table. A view may be defined for either of two reasons.

    1. It can be used to restrict a user's access to the database. The user only sees that part of the database revealed through the view.

    2. It can be used to simplify retrieval statements with the view name being used in the statement as if it was just another table.

- The **index** may serve two distinct purposes (and causes confusion because of this dual function).

    1. It may be used to ensure that no two rows in a table are the same. If a table is to be a true set, then it must be indexed in this way.

    2. It may be used to improve database access times. In this regard, an index is used in the same way that a book index may be used to speed access to selected topics.

The table is the only object that may be modified. Views and indexes may only be created or deleted.

Example 5.2 Define an index on student Id's in the Students table.

```
Create unique index Student_Key
             on Students (Id)
```

The index `Student_Key` will be used for two purposes. It will be used to ensure that no two rows in the `Students` table will have the same Id. This is indicated by the appearance of the word `unique`. Secondly, the index will be used to provide rapid access to individual rows in the table. This rapid access will be based upon knowledge of the relevant Id. Indexing and view properties are covered in more detail in later chapters.

Example 5.3 It is the end of the semester and we are finished with the `Results` and `Assess` tables but we want to keep the `Students` table for next semester.

```
Drop table Results
Drop table Assess
```

These two tables are not just emptied, they are completely removed from the database; any space they use will be released and the corresponding entries in the system catalog are also removed.

5.4 Database Retrieval

The next category is concerned with database retrieval. The category contains only one statement, but that statement characterizes the whole of SQL. The `select` statement is used to retrieve or identify some portion of the database.

The best way to understand the `select` is to see it at work. The following examples all put forward queries that we ourselves could answer from the Subject database. Each query is followed by an example of how SQL could be used, instead, to generate an answer.

Example 5.4 What are the Id's and last names of all students?

```
Select    Id, Last
From      Students
---------------
Id        Last
---------------
871       Zupp
862       Board
869       Orff
854       Dover
831       Orff
872       Kahn
868       Gambol
---------------
```

The retrieval statement is very brief; indeed it is hard to imagine how we could express our requirements more briefly. We merely say which columns we want and where they are to be found.

Example 5.5 Give details of all students called Orff.

```
Select    *
From      Students
Where     Last = 'Orff'

---------------------
Id        First    Last
---------------------
869       Rip      Orff
831       Hans     Orff
---------------------
```

The asterisk (*) indicates that all columns in the table are to be shown in the query answer. The clause `Where Last = 'Orff'` is used to specify a condition that all displayed rows must satisfy.

Example 5.6 What are the last names of all students?
There are two ways of answering this query:

```
(1)                          (2)
Select    Last               Select    distinct Last
From      Students           From      Students
```

116   Chapter 5

```
------              -----
Last                Last
------              -----
Zupp                Board
Board               Dover
Orff                Gambol
Dover               Kahn
Orff                Orff
Kahn                Zupp
Gambol              -----
------
```

The second method uses the keyword **distinct** to tell SQL to remove duplicates. So the second Orff does not appear; but not only that, SQL has chosen, in this instance, to remove duplicates by sorting the result table prior to output. When scanning this sorted table duplicates can easily be detected and skipped. The manner in which duplicates are removed is left to SQL. Sorting is just one way that might be used.

Example 5.7 List, in name order, the details of all students.

```
Select    *
From      Students
Order by Last, First
```

```
------------------------
Id      First   Last
------------------------
862     Bill    Board
854     Ann     Dover
868     Will    Gambol
872     Betty   Kahn
831     Hans    Orff
869     Rip     Orff
871     Hans    Zupp
------------------------
```

The result can be forced into some order by using the **order** clause. In this example, the resulting rows are displayed in alphabetic order of last name. If two or more students have the same last name, the names will be displayed in order of first name, so Hans Orff appears before Rip Orff.

Example 5.8 List Assignment One performance in order of merit.
For this query, we want to be able to direct SQL to produce the highest mark first.

```
Select    Id, Mark
From      Results
Where     Item = 1
Order by Mark desc
```

The keyword **desc** (short for descending) may be used to reverse the default sequence.

```
------------
Id      Mark
------------
868     90
871     80
854     70
869     70
862     60
872     55
------------
```

Example 5.9 How many students are enrolled?

```
Select   count(*)
From     Students
```

```
--------
count(*)
--------
    7
--------
```

The special **count** function is used to count the number of rows determined by the rest of the query, in this case the whole of the Students table. The effect of the asterisk(*) makes this query the equivalent of asking "how many rows are there in this table?" **Count** is a **summary** function, and there are a number of similar summary functions in SQL.

Example 5.10 What was the average mark in the final exam?

```
Select   avg(Mark)
From     Results
Where    Item = 3
```

```
---------
avg(Mark)
---------
   59.2
---------
```

The **avg** function averages the **Mark** column values for each row containing 3 in the Item column.

5.5 Database Modification

The third group of SQL statements to be examined in this chapter involves those used to make changes to the database. The types of change allowed by these statements are fine-grained ones aimed at adding, changing and deleting rows in just **one** table. More specifically, these statements are:

- the `Insert` which allows new rows to be added to the table concerned;
- the `Update` which allows one or more rows to be amended; and
- the `Delete` which allows one or more rows to be deleted.

These database-modifying commands, and their correct use, are covered in more detail in later chapters. Some examples only are given in this section.

Example 5.11 The lecturer in the subject has discovered student 831's mark for the first assignment. Add this result.

```
Insert
Into     Results
Values   (1,831,0908,55)
```

The values that make up this new row of the `Results` table are separated by commas; they are allocated to the columns of that table in the order specified for the table in the System Catalog. Obviously the values must match in both number and type.

Example 5.12 Student 862 has been given an extra 5% for the second assignment. Make the appropriate change.

```
Update  Results
Set     Mark = Mark + 5
Where   Id = 862
  and   Item = 2
```

The row containing the result is located and the mark modified.

Example 5.13 Student 872 has been granted permission to withdraw from the subject. Remove all details of her enrollment.

```
Delete
From     Results
Where    Id = 872


Delete
From     Students
Where    Id = 872
```

Two separate statements are required, one for each table involved.

Example 5.14 It is the end of the semester. Clear out the `Results` and `Assess` tables.

```
Delete
From     Results


Delete
From     Assess
```

After these deletes, the tables still continue to exist. They are just empty. The system catalog still contains details of their structure. Thus the effect differs from similar `Drop table` statements of Example 5.3.

5.6 Database Security

The fourth and final part of SQL deals with database security. A database is a **shared** organizational model; it is a kind of gigantic company noticeboard.

Consider a typical database. It consists of hundreds of tables containing a range of information from the managing director's silent phone number to the retail price of a can of baked beans. Its users are a mixture of the corporate life form, both high and low. They will be clerks, managers, assembly-line workers, engineers, programmers, and so on. These people have correspondingly mixed needs and responsibilities with regard to the database.

Yet, through SQL, they are able to delete entire tables with a single statement, for example, `Delete From Employees`; or they might give everyone a payrise. Clearly it is undesirable to allow all users to have totally unconstrained access to the entire database. People should have exactly those rights that they need to do their job, and no more.

To prevent potential disasters, SQL recognizes database users and is prepared to grant access rights to these users.

Example 5.15 Suppose there are two kinds of user accessing the `Subject` database, *student* and *lecturer*. Give student users the right to read the `Assess` table and lecturers the right to read and generally modify it.

```
Grant  Select
   on  Assess
   to  Student

Grant  Select, Insert, Update, Delete
   on  Assess
   to  Lecturer
```

SQL makes appropriate entries in the system catalog. Whenever a user attempts to access the database in some way, SQL first checks the catalog to see if the user has the appropriate rights before going ahead. There is a corresponding `revoke` statement to remove access rights from a user.

The view feature, which was discussed in an earlier section, can also be used to protect the database. Not only does a view present the user with a restricted portion of the database, but the `grant` and `revoke` statements may be used to further control the user's actions against that portion.

5.7 Using SQL

How do we issue SQL requests? So far, the exact context in which SQL statements may be issued has been ignored. We have suggested that the statements are issued directly. This is only one of three ways in which SQL is likely to operate.

- We can use SQL **interactively** by issuing requests from a keyboard and having the response appear on a screen. The results may be further manipulated by having the general layout altered, by formating columns, and even by dropping columns entirely. The eventual results may be printed or stored on a file for future use.

- A second way of using SQL is to have one or more statements **embedded** in a program written in some other language, typically COBOL. This second language is said to be the **host** language. When used in this way, the results of an SQL query will be stored in the program's own variables. The program can be written to use these results in whatever way the designer chooses.

- Most versions of SQL are accompanied by an application development tool or **application generator**. Such software tools enable new information systems to be generated with relative speed and ease, at least when compared with COBOL. These tools provide many features to help the software developer, features that are not part of SQL.

    1. They assist with screen and dialog management.
    2. They enforce data capture rules, using SQL where necessary.
    3. They automatically update the database when appropriate.
    4. They will translate end-user query requirements, written in some other way, into SQL retrieval statements.
    5. They will format these results automatically, according to predefined specifications.

A terminal user should not be able to distinguish between the second and third of these methods of employing SQL. They need neither know nor care whether SQL is being used. By contrast, an interactive terminal user needs to be familiar with the language, with its power and with the dangers of using that power thoughtlessly.

5.8 Summary

In this chapter, we have seen how SQL provides four groups of statements to use and manage a database made up of tables. There are statements which define relations, statements to retrieve relation contents, statements to alter the database's information content and statements to control access to the database.

From this brief introduction, it can be seen that the actual vocabulary of SQL is not large. Most of the power of SQL is in its role as a retrieval language. Examples in the following chapter show how SQL can be used to solve complex information requests, which would require much more complicated programs if implemented in a conventional procedural language such as COBOL or C.

Exercises

▶ Q5.1 The following table represents the results of games played by the Shinhackers Rugby Club this season so far.

```
Games
-------------------------------------------
Day     Month   Team            Ours    Theirs
-------------------------------------------
 7       3      Toecrushers       6       25
14       3      Headbutters       0       10
21       3      Necktwisters     21       10
28       3      Ankletappers     18       16
 4       4      Armlockers        0        6
11       4      Kneeknockers      0        9
18       4      Bellyfloppers     9        3
25       4      Headbutters      14        6
 2       5      Toecrushers       6       16
-------------------------------------------
```

So the table tells us, for example, that on 7 March we lost to the Toecrushers team by 25 points to 6. The table can be accessed by means of an SQL statement such as:

```
Select  Team
From    Games
Where   Ours = 0
```

This would tell us the names of any teams that we (Shinhackers) failed to score against.

State, in everyday English, the information that you think each of the following SQL statements is intended to provide.

a. ```
    Select *
    From   Games
    Where   Month = 4
    ```

b.  ```
    Select  Team
    From    Games
    Where   Ours > Theirs
    ```

c. ```
    Select *
    From   Games
    ```

d.  ```
    Select  Day, Month, Team
    From    Games
    Where   Ours = Theirs
      and   Month = 5
    ```

Chapter 5

```
        e.  Select   Ours, Theirs
            From     Games
            Where    Team = 'Bellyfloppers'
               or    Team = 'Kneeknockers'
        f.  Select   count(*)
            From     Games
            Where    Ours > Theirs
        g.  Select   max(Ours - Theirs)
            From     Games
        h.  Select   *
            From     Games
            Order by Month, Day
```

▶ Q5.2 Using the **Games** table, write SQL to answer the following queries.

    a. How many games have we played so far, and what are the total points scored by us and against us?

    b. What teams have beaten us by 10 points or more?

    c. List details of all matches, in order of points scored by us, with our highest score first.

    d. What were the results in the second half of April?

    e. Name all the teams we have played so far.

▶ Q5.3 Suggest a suitable **create** statement for the **Games** table.

▶ Q5.4 Write database modification statements to record the following events.

    a. On 9 May we beat the Knuckledusters by 6 points to 3.

    b. A mistake was made when entering the result of 14 March. Our opponents scored 5 more points than was originally recorded.

    c. The Toecrushers have been ejected from the competition for over-gentlemanly play. Cancel any results that involve them.

▶ Q5.5 Define an index that ensures that only one result is recorded for any given date.

Q5.6 Write **grant** or **revoke** statements in response to the following club decisions.

    a. The club **secretary** is to be allowed to see the **Games** table and to insert match results into it.

    b. The club **members** are to be allowed to see the table.

    c. The club **president** is to be allowed to modify and even to delete rows from the table.

Q5.7 A computer dating company keeps track of its members in a table such as:

```
People
---------------------------------------------------------
Name     Age   Sex   Earns    Likes      Dislikes
---------------------------------------------------------
Bill     55    m     18000    golf       politics
Sue      28    f     15000    music      beer
Ivan     19    m     25500    football   dancing
Dave     21    m     18000    music      sport
Judy     33    f     28000    walking    men
Karen    41    f     48000    dancing    SQL
Alan     40    m     45000    golf       golf
Mark     32    m     17500    football   alcohol
Mario    18    m     17500    dancing    water
Paul     25    m     62500    music      students
Jim      32    m     38500    squash     alcohol
Kathy    19    f     14500    dancing    politics
---------------------------------------------------------
```

Write SQL to satisfy the requirements below.

a. List everybody's name and age, with the youngest first.

b. List details of everybody, males then females and, within each of these categories, by earning power.

c. List the names of all people in their teens who like dancing.

d. How many people are recorded in the table?

e. What is the biggest income?

Q5.8 Suggest a suitable `create` statement for the `People` table.

Q5.9 Write a suitable database modification statement to suit each of the following situations.

a. Paul lied about his income. He really earns $92 500.

b. The women have decided that the men are wimps. Get rid of them all.

c. Inflation has been bad. Give everybody a 10% payrise.

d. Another year has passed. Age everybody by 1 year.

e. A new member has joined (thank goodness). His name is Harry; he's 25, likes sport, hates politics and earns $28 000.

f. What if Harry did not want to reveal his age – how would we insert a row for him then?

CHAPTER 6

SQL Retrieval

6.1 Introduction

This chapter contains a series of examples of database retrieval using SQL. The examples attempt to show the basic retrieval capabilities of the language.

There are three basic ways in which information may be extracted or derived from a table. These relate to the ways that we ourselves might extract information presented to us in tabular form.

Sometimes we are interested in detailed information. We scan down particular columns looking for values that interest us, stopping when we find such a value. Then we will examine the rest of the row upon which we found the value. This is how people look up telephone numbers or exam results or sports results or a timetable. The search operation will be repeated until we have, for example, noted our own exam results and those of our friends.

There is another kind of retrieval. This kind is performed when, essentially, we are looking for one particular value. The value may be one that can be extracted from the table, or it may be a derived value. The situations when we scan a table in this way are, for example, when looking for the lowest mark in an exam or the total number of people who passed or the time of the last train or bus.

The third kind of retrieval is the kind performed when we want to compare one group of figures with another. Did chemistry students perform better than computing students? Are there more trains to town than buses?

These are the basic means of retrieval offered by SQL. There is nothing performed by SQL that we could not contemplate doing ourselves. SQL is a language, after all; it is a means of expressing our wishes.

All examples are based on the SUBJECT database introduced in Chapter 4. This database contains three tables:

- **Students**, which contains the names of students enrolled in the single subject offered;
- **Assess**, which contains details of assessment involved in the subject; and

- **Results**, which records marks achieved by the students in the various items of assessment.

6.2 Simple Queries

Queries that extract some portion of a single table are the simplest form of query. The portion may be a subset of the columns of the table, of its rows, or of both.

Example 6.1 Describe all items of assessment, showing the weight attached to each.

```
Select   Description, Weight
From     Assess
```

```
----------------------
Description    Weight
----------------------
Petty Theft      10
Tax Evasion      30
Extortion        60
----------------------
```

The query is answered quite simply by naming the columns required, and by naming the table in which the data will be found.

Example 6.2 Which students failed the final exam?

```
Select   *
From     Results
Where    Item = 3
and      Mark < 50
```

The asterisk (*) in the **select** clause signifies that, for rows meeting the two conditions specified, all columns are to be displayed:

```
----------------------------------------
Item    Id      Submitted       Mark
----------------------------------------
 3      872        ?             45
 3      862        ?             40
----------------------------------------
```

The order in which the columns appear will be determined by the order in which they appeared in the **create** statement used to define the table.

Example 6.3 Which students got marks in the range 70 to 90 in the first assignment? What were their marks?

```
Select   Id, Mark
From     Results
Where    Mark between 70 and 90
and      Item = 1
```

```
----------
Id     Mark
----------
871    80
854    70
868    90
869    70
----------
```

The **between** clause may be used to specify a range of values. The end-points of the range are included as can be seen from the resulting table. The **where** clause above is equivalent to the following:

```
Where  Mark >= 70
and    Mark <= 90
```

Example 6.4 Which item or items of assessment have no due date assigned to them?

```
Select   *
From     Assess
Where    Due is null
```

```
---------------------------------
Item   Description   Weight   Due
---------------------------------
3      Extortion     60       ?
---------------------------------
```

This is the only way that we can check whether or not a column has a missing (i.e. null) value. We are not allowed to say **Where Due = null** because **null** is not a value and so cannot be compared with anything. A question mark is sometimes used to indicate the presence of a null value, that is, the absence of a value.

6.3 Join Queries

A well-designed relational database is devoid of any redundant data. For example, a student's name is recorded only once. The effect of this design is to produce some rather cryptic or code-like tables. The Results table is an example; this table refers to students by means of their Id, and to items of assessment by means of their item number. To recover from this state of affairs we must be able to bring the tables together in such a way as to, for example, find the **names** of students who did well in the second assignment. This very important process is called a **join**.

Suppose we were interested in how well students have done in the subject; we might try the following SQL.

```
Select   *
From     Results
```

SQL Retrieval

This would tell us how each student performed, but it would tell us in a rather unhelpful style. We would have to be able to match the Id to a particular student. This is likely to be of limited use in practical situations.

The table from which the data is drawn is specified in the **from** clause. If we wanted to link a result to a student, we can try:

```
Select    *
From      Students, Results
```

The **from** clause is used to list the tables from which the displayed data can be produced.

What does this query achieve? SQL responds as follows:

Students			Results			
Id	First	Last	Item	Id	Submitted	Mark
871	Hans	Zupp	1	871	0908	80
871	Hans	Zupp	1	862	0907	60
871	Hans	Zupp	1	854	0908	70
871	Hans	Zupp	1	872	0910	55
871	Hans	Zupp	1	868	0906	90
871	Hans	Zupp	1	869	0909	70
871	Hans	Zupp	2	871	1021	70
871	Hans	Zupp	2	869	1022	80

(111 more rows will be generated in the output table.)

What has happened? SQL has taken the two tables named in the **from** clause and "multiplied" them. It does this by creating a new table in which each row in Students is paired with each row in Results. The table names are placed at the top here simply to help identify the parentage of each part of the row. For example, the first row:

Students			Results			
Id	First	Last	Item	Id	Submitted	Mark
871	Hans	Zupp	1	871	0908	80

is formed from the first rows of Students and Results. As there are 7 student rows and 17 result rows, the relation resulting from the **select** statement has $7 * 17 = 119$ rows. This new table is the relational **product** of **Students** and **Results**.

The resulting table is much bigger than the original database. Obviously, this feature of SQL will have to be used with some caution. Despite this, the relational product achieved in this way is the only means by which we can **directly** compare the rows of one table with those of another. It is also a means by which we can compare a row in a table with other rows in the **same** table.

128   Chapter 6

A relational product will almost always be followed by some condition that reduces the size of the product. The most common form of restriction is the **join** condition. This occurs when two tables each have a column that draws its values from a common set of values. For example, both the `Students` and `Results` tables have a column called `Id`. Not only are the names the same, but the values that might appear in each are essentially the same. The join condition states that the values in these shared columns must be equal; thus:

```
Select    *
From      Students, Results
Where     Students.Id = Results.Id
```

There are two `Id` columns in the product, and they are distinguished by prefixing them with the name of the parent relation followed by a full stop.

The resulting table is:

Id	First	Last	Item	Id	Submitted	Mark
871	Hans	Zupp	1	871	0908	80
871	Hans	Zupp	2	871	1021	70
871	Hans	Zupp	3	871	?	60
862	Bill	Board	1	862	0907	60
862	Bill	Board	2	862	1022	70
862	Bill	Board	3	862	?	40
869	Rip	Orff	1	869	0909	70
869	Rip	Orff	2	869	1022	80
869	Rip	Orff	3	869	?	95
854	Ann	Dover	1	854	0908	70
854	Ann	Dover	3	854	?	65
872	Betty	Kahn	1	872	0910	55
872	Betty	Kahn	2	872	1021	65
872	Betty	Kahn	3	872	?	45
868	Will	Gambol	1	868	0906	90
868	Will	Gambol	2	868	1021	75
868	Will	Gambol	3	868	?	50

Further conditions may be added to the join condition. If we wanted the results for the final exam (item number 3) then we would add the appropriate condition:

```
Select    *
From      Students, Results
Where     Students.Id = Results.Id
and       Results.Item = 3
```

The new condition `Results.Item = 3` causes all but item 3 results to be discarded from the join to produce the following table.

```
---------------------------------------------------------------
Id      First   Last    Item    Id      Submitted       Mark
---------------------------------------------------------------
871     Hans    Zupp    3       871     ?               60
862     Bill    Board   3       862     ?               40
869     Rip     Orff    3       869     ?               95
854     Ann     Dover   3       854     ?               65
872     Betty   Kahn    3       872     ?               45
868     Will    Gambol  3       868     ?               50
---------------------------------------------------------------
```

It is only necessary to prefix a column name when it is defined in more than one of the tables being joined **and** when that column is used in the query.

Example 6.5 What are the names and the marks of those people who failed the final exam?

```
Select    First, Last, Mark              ...... 5.
From      Students, Results              ...... 1.
Where     Students.Id = Results.Id       ...... 2.
  and     Item = 3                       ...... 3.
  and     Mark < 50                      ...... 4.
```

The events that take place in order to answer this query can be thought of as taking the following sequence. However, the data management software can use whatever method it chooses.

1. The product of **Students** and **Results** is formed.
2. The product is reduced to a join by equating the two **Id** columns. The join is shown above.
3. All but final exam marks are removed. The resulting table is also shown above.
4. All but failures are removed.

   The table defined by steps 1 to 4 now looks like this:

```
---------------------------------------------------------------
Id      First   Last    Item    Id      Submitted       Mark
---------------------------------------------------------------
872     Betty   Kahn    3       872     ?               45
862     Bill    Board   3       862     ?               40
---------------------------------------------------------------
```

5. Finally, **Select First, Last, Mark** causes the desired columns to be projected.

```
-----------------------------
First     Last      Mark
-----------------------------
Betty     Kahn      45
Bill      Board     40
-----------------------------
```

130   Chapter 6

Example 6.6 How much did the final exam contribute to each student's overall total? This is another query requiring a join of two tables, Results and Assess. The reason for this is that the Results table contains a mark out of 100, but each item of assessment has its own particular weighting. For example, student 868 got 50% in the final exam, where the latter is worth 60% of the overall subject assessment. So the final exam contributes 50*60/100 = 30 marks to student 868's overall total for the subject.

```
Select    Id, Mark, Weight, Mark*Weight/100
From      Results, Assess
Where     Results.Item = Assess.Item
and       Results.Item = 3
```

Id	Mark	Weight	Mark*Weight/100
869	95	60	57
872	45	60	27
862	40	60	24
868	50	60	30
871	60	60	36
854	65	60	39

Again, the result table can be **thought** of as being produced by the following sequence.

1. First, the relational product of **Results** and **Assess** is formed. This is accomplished by the clause From Results,Assess.

2. From that product, the join of Results and Assess is created. This is accomplished by the clause Where Results.Item = Assess.Item. (The resulting join is shown in Section 4.9.6.)

3. From that join, results for item 3 are retained and the rest discarded.

4. Finally, the result table shown above is produced.

Example 6.7 What are the names of students who were late in submitting their first assignment?

This example requires information from all three tables:

- **Students** is needed to provide the names;
- **Results** because it contains the date of submission; and
- **Assess** because it contains the due date.

Straight away, we can write the from clause.

```
From    Students, Results, Assess
```

This clause will cause the creation (in our minds) of a product table that combines all the rows from all three tables. This will contain 7 * 17 * 3 = 357 rows. The first row and two other typical rows will look like the following:

```
Students            Results                   Assess
----------------------------------------------------------------------
Id   First Last   Item  Id   Submitted  Mark  Item  Description  Weight  Due
----------------------------------------------------------------------
871  Hans  Zupp    1    871    0908      80    1    Petty Theft    10   0908
      :     :                   :                    :
862  Bill  Board   2    868    1021      75    3    Extortion      60    ?
      :     :                   :                    :
869  Rip   Orff    1    869    0909      70    1    Petty Theft    10   0908
      :     :                   :                    :
----------------------------------------------------------------------
```

The second row compares student **Bill Board** against a mark achieved in assessment item **2** by some other student against details of assessment item **3**. Rows like this one one must be discarded. These rows are removed by supplying the appropriate join condition, one that joins three tables.

> Where   Students.Id = Results.Id
> and   Results.Item = Assess.Item

These two conditions leave us in a position where all remaining rows relate a student to a mark attained by that student to details of that item of assessment. Now we can apply the other conditions that will give us specific answers to our query.

> and   Results.Item = 1
> and   Submitted > Due

For the first of these two conditions, we could also have said **and Assess.Item = 1** since the two Item columns must have the same value, as required by the join condition. Whichever column we choose, however, we must use a prefix. The second condition requires that the date of submission must come **after** (>) the due date. No prefixes are required, although it might be better to be consistent, so that once prefixes are required, we use them for all columns, whether they are needed or not. This is a matter of personal style and convenience.

We are now in a position to write the **select** clause.

> Select   Id, First, Last, Submitted, Due

The **select** clause must appear first in any SQL query; however, as a strategy for forming queries, it is often better to leave selection until last. Determining the tables required and supplying conditions to be met are decisions that are easier done first.

The complete **select** statement is as follows.

> Select   Id, First, Last, Submitted, Due
> From   Students, Results, Assess
> Where   Students.Id = Results.Id
> and   Results.Item = Assess.Item
> and   Results.Item = 1
> and   Submitted > Due

```
Id    First   Last    Submitted    Due

872   Betty   Kahn    0910         0908
869   Rip     Orff    0909         0908
```

6.4 Statistical Queries

There are five **built-in** functions that enable us to ask SQL to provide summary rather than detailed information.

1. `count` which counts rows for us;
2. `max` which gives us the maximum of a set of values;
3. `min` which gives us the minimum of a set;
4. `avg` which averages a set of values; and
5. `sum` which adds up a set of values to provide a total.

As may be seen, this summary information is of a rather simple statistical nature.

Example 6.8 How many items of assessment are there?

```
Select    count(*)
From      Assess


--------
count(*)
--------
   3
--------
```

The `count` function may be used to count the number of rows determined by the conditions in the rest of the query.

Example 6.9 What were the highest, lowest and average marks in the final exam?

```
Select    max(Mark), min(Mark), avg(Mark)
From      Results
Where     Item = 3


-----------------------------------------
max(Mark)      min(Mark)      avg(Mark)
-----------------------------------------
    95            40             59
-----------------------------------------
```

Example 6.10 As a check on our arithmetic, what is the total weighting for all items of assessment?

```
Select    sum(Weight)
From      Assess
```

```
-----------
sum(Weight)
-----------
    100
-----------
```

The **sum** function adds up the values in the column specified as the function's argument, in this case the `Weight` column.

Example 6.11 What was student 871's overall total for the subject?

```
Select    sum(Mark*Weight/100)
From      Results, Assess
Where     Results.Item = Assess.Item
and       Id = 871
```

```
--------------------
sum(Mark*Weight/100)
--------------------
         65
--------------------
```

To see how this works, it is best to picture the intermediate table defined by the **from** and **where** clauses above:

Item	Id	Submitted	Mark	Item	Description	Weight	Due
1	871	0908	80	1	Petty Theft	10	0908
2	871	1021	70	2	Tax evasion	30	1021
3	871	?	60	3	Extortion	60	?

The **sum** function performs the calculation for each row in the above table, thus:

```
sum(Mark*Weight/100) = 80*10/100 + 70*30/100 + 60*60/100
                     = 8         + 21        + 36
                     = 65
```

6.5 "Group by" Queries

So far, we have seen examples of SQL that either provide detailed answers to queries, or a single summary figure such as a count or a total. The **group by** clause allows a kind

134   Chapter 6

of half-way house between the two. It allows a table to be partitioned into groups. Each group can then be summarized.

Example 6.12 What was the average performance in each item of assessment?

```
Select    Item, avg(Mark)
From      Results
Group by Item
Order by Item
```

We can picture the Results table being divided into groups according to the value in the Item column. This means that there are three groups, one for each item of assessment. This is specified in the clause `Group by Item`.

Item	Id	Submitted	Mark
1	871	0908	80
1	862	0907	60
1	854	0908	70
1	872	0910	55
1	868	0906	90
1	869	0909	70
2	871	1021	70
2	869	1022	80
2	872	1021	65
2	862	1022	70
2	868	1021	75
3	869	?	95
3	872	?	45
3	862	?	40
3	868	?	50
3	871	?	60
3	854	?	65

The appearance of a **group by** clause signals SQL to produce one line of output **per group**, so the actual output shows one line for each item of assessment. Each line produced by the `select` clause will contain an item number and the average mark for that item.

Item	avg(Mark)
1	71
2	72
3	59

SQL Retrieval   135

Because SQL will only produce one line per group, whatever items we select must be **single-valued** for each group. Once we have used a **group by** clause, the items that we we may select for output are restricted to one of the following:

- the column **group**ed by (**Item**, in this case);
- a statistical function applied to some column within the group (**avg(Mark)** in this case).

Finally, the **order by** clause is used to ensure that the results appear in item number order. However, the likelihood is that, as part of the grouping process, SQL has already performed a sort.

Example 6.13 Which students have done all three items of assessment?

```
                          Item   Id     Submitted   Mark
                          ---------------------------------
                          1      854    0908        70
                          3      854    ?           65

Select    Id              1      862    0907        60
From      Results         2      862    1022        70
Group by  Id              3      862    ?           40
Having    count(*) = 3
                          1      868    0906        90
---                       2      868    1021        75
Id                        3      868    ?           50
---
862                       1      869    0909        70
868                       2      869    1022        80
869                       3      869    ?           95
871
872                       1      871    0908        80
---                       2      871    1021        70
                          3      871    ?           60

                          1      872    0910        55
                          2      872    1021        65
                          3      872    ?           45
                          ---------------------------------
```

The **group by** clause used here will partition the Results table into six groups, one for each of the six students who submitted some work for assessment (student 831 never submitted anything at all!). The effect of the grouping is shown in the table on the right-hand side above. Of the six groups obtained, five will contain three rows and the other will contain two rows (student 854 failed to submit item number 2). SQL will probably sort the table as the best way of grouping; so that the table **may** be in student Id order.

The **having** clause, which follows the **group by**, may be used to eliminate entire groups from the output. In this example, any group that does **not** contain exactly three rows will be removed. Because the **having** clause is used to eliminate groups, the condition it enforces should be one applying to the whole group.

Example 6.14 Which students failed at least one item of assessment?

```
Select    Id
From      Results
Group by  Id
Having    min(Mark) < 50
```

```
---
Id
---
862
872
---
```

Again, the Results table is divided into groups, one for each Id. Only groups where the minimum mark is less than 50 are reported in the output. For Id to appear, then the student must have failed at least one item.

6.6 Multi-table "Group by" Queries

The **group by** clause, used on a single table, partitions that table into a number of groups according to the column used as the basis for the grouping. The clause can also be used on two or more tables that have been linked together for some reason. The same restrictions apply to the kind of expressions that may be used in the **select** clause. Once a **group by** clause has been used, the items that may be selected are restricted to either (1) the column(s) used in the **group by** clause or (2) a statistical function applied to the group as a whole. SQL is only prepared to display one row per group, regardless of the number of rows in each group. These two restrictions have the effect of guaranteeing that whatever is chosen must be single-valued for the group.

Example 6.15 For each item of assessment, describe that item and give the average mark attained.

```
Select    R.Item, max(A.Description), avg(R.Mark)
From      Results R, Assess A
Where     R.Item = A.Item
Group by  R.Item
```

```
------------------------------------------
R.Item   max(A.Description)    avg(R.Mark)
------------------------------------------
  1      Petty Theft               71
  2      Tax Evasion               72
  3      Extortion                 59
------------------------------------------
```

SQL Retrieval 137

The use of the `max` function on the `Description` column is a most dreadful fudge. SQL will not allow us to simply say:

```
Select    ... , A.Description, ...
```

The `Description` column was not used in the `group by` clause and so cannot appear on its own in the `select` clause, even though we know that within any group the `Description` column will only ever have one value, because an item of assessment only ever has one description. So we are obliged to resort to trickery in order to fool SQL. The `max` function, when applied to a character string column, returns the highest alphabetic value. For example:

```
Select  max(Last)
From    Students
```

```
---------
max(Last)
---------
  Zupp
---------
```

Example 6.16 List, in order of merit, the final totals for each student.

```
Select     S.Id, max(S.First), max(S.Last),
           sum(R.Mark*A.Weight/100)
From       Students S, Results R, Assess A
Where      S.Id = R.Id
and        R.Item = A.Item
Group by S.Id
Order by 4 desc
```

Id	max(S.First)	max(S.Last)	sum(R.Mark*A.Weight/100)
869	Rip	Orff	88
871	Hans	Zupp	65
868	Will	Gambol	62
872	Betty	Kahn	52
862	Bill	Board	51
854	Ann	Dover	46

Once again, to get SQL to display first and last names, we use a built-in function to overcome SQL's rules. Note also that student 831 makes no appearance in this final table. This is because there is no mark for that student in the `Results` table.

The results were to be displayed in order of merit, that is, in descending order of total mark. The total mark column is the fourth column displayed. It is a **derived** column, not one existing in the database itself, but specially formed just to answer the query. Where such a column is to be used in the sorting process, then it must be identified by its position in the `select` clause. In this case, the final total is the fourth column and can only be referred to in this numerical way.

6.7 Product Queries

In Section 6.3 we discussed what were called join queries. The first step towards joining two tables requires that the relational product of the tables be formed. It was, perhaps, implied that the only reason for multiplying two tables was as a step towards the join. This is not the case. There are occasions when the product is of use in its own right. This is especially true when we want to compare the rows of a table against other rows in the same table. To do this we need to multiply a table by itself.

Example 6.17 Which students did better in assignment 1 than in assignment 2?

```
Select    R1.Id, R1.Mark, R2.Mark
From      Results R1, Results R2
Where     R1.Id = R2.Id
  and     R1.Item = 1
  and     R2.Item = 2
  and     R1.Mark > R2.Mark
```

```
-------------------------------
R1.Id     R1.Mark    R2.Mark
-------------------------------
871       80         70
868       90         75
-------------------------------
```

The aliases `R1` and `R2` must be used in this example. The `from` clause, in the above SQL, will cause the `Results` table to be multiplied by itself, squared so to speak! The product will contain 17 x 17 = 289 rows, pairing every row in the table against every other row. The table below shows one typical row and one row of the kind we want.

```
        Results (R1)                          Results (R2)
----------------------------------------------------------------------
Item   Id    Submitted   Mark      Item   Id    Submitted   Mark
----------------------------------------------------------------------
  :                                  :
  3    869        ?        95        1    862       0907     60
  :                                  :
  1    871      0908       80        2    871      1021      70
  :                                  :
----------------------------------------------------------------------
```

Each row is in two parts, but both originate from the same table. We cannot use the table name to distinguish each part. This is why the aliases are required. However, aliases may be used in any query. Often they are used simply to reduce the amount of typing necessary.

6.8 Pattern Matching

SQL allows a limited form of pattern matching. This can be of use when we cannot remember or do not know the exact value of some data item. It can also be useful when we want to specify a complex range of possible values.

Example 6.18 Which students have a first name starting with the letter **B**?

```
Select   First, Last
From     Students
Where    First like 'B%'
```

```
-------------
First   Last
-------------
Bill    Board
Betty   Kahn
-------------
```

The percent character **%** is used to indicate a place where zero or more characters may appear.

Example 6.19 Which students have the letter **o** in their last name?

```
Select   First, Last
From     Students
Where    Last like 'O%'
or       Last like '%o%'
```

```
-------------
First   Last
-------------
Bill    Board
Rip     Orff
Ann     Dover
Hans    Orff
Will    Gambol
-------------
```

We have to use two separate pattern strings because the `like` operator is case sensitive, that is, it distinguishes between upper case **O** and lower case **o**.

The second pattern string cannot be simply '%o' because that would imply that we were looking for people whose last name **ended** in the letter **o**.

Example 6.20 Which students have the letter **i** as the second letter of their first name?

```
Select   First, Last
From     Students
Where    First like '_i%'
```

The string _i% requires *exactly one* character before the letter **i** and any number after.

```
-------------
First    Last
-------------
Bill     Board
Rip      Orff
Will     Gambol
-------------
```

The underscore character _ is used to indicate a place where any **one** character may be substituted. This ensures that the second character must be an **i**. After the **i** there may be any number of other characters as indicated by the ensuing % symbol.

Example 6.21 Which students have a four-letter surname?

```
Select    First, Last
From      Students
Where     Last like '____'
```

```
-------------
First    Last
-------------
Hans     Zupp
Rip      Orff
Hans     Orff
Betty    Kahn
-------------
```

The pattern string '____' indicates that the last name must contain **exactly** four characters.

6.9 Summary

In this chapter, you have seen examples of the basic SQL retrieval statements. These basic capabilities reduce to three major categories.

- There are queries that involve examination of a table and the suppression of unwanted rows and columns. The rows we want to see are retained by means of the `where` clause. The columns we want are specified in the `select` clause. The table from which these rows and columns are drawn may be one of the base tables of the database. However, the table may equally be one formed by multiplying together all the tables mentioned in the `from` clause. Regardless of how the table is formed, the same basic means of retrieval apply.

- There are queries that work by subdividing a table into a number of groups according to some value shared by all rows in the group and by no others. Some of these groups may be eliminated by applying a condition that each group must satisfy. After that, we are allowed to select just one line of output per group. As in the first category, the table that is partitioned in this way may be one of the base tables or it may be the product of several tables.

- There are queries that allow us to summarize a table by reporting some statistics concerning that table such as the number of rows in the table. Again, the table reported in this way may be a base table or the product of several tables.

SQL can provide much more complicated queries than these, but only by extending the use of the features in this chapter. For example, queries can be nested. These more advanced features are described in the following chapter.

Exercises

▶ Q6.1 The ACADEMIC Database

Here is the University of Wiseacres database that was used in the exercises at the end of Chapter 4.

```
    Schools                Staff                Quals
    ---------              -------              -------
(*) School_Id          (*) Staff_Id         (*) Staff_Id
    School_Name            Staff_Name       (*) Degree
    Phone                  School_Id            Place
(?) Head_Id                                     Year
```

An asterisk (*) indicates that the attribute is (part of) the primary key of the relation. A question mark (?) indicates that null values are to be permitted for that attribute in the associated relation. Write SQL to satisfy the following requirements.

a. List the names and phone numbers of all the schools.
b. List the entire contents of the **Staff** table.
c. Name any schools where the Head of School position is vacant.
d. Name each member of staff along with the name of his or her school. Produce the list in alphabetic order of staff name.
e. Provide the name of each school and the name of the head of that school.
f. Name members of staff along with their degrees. You will need a separate line for each degree. Produce the list in alphabetic order of staff name and, within that, by year of conferral.
g. How many staff are there altogether?
h. When was the earliest degree conferred on any staff member?
i. For each staff member, provide the staff Id and the number of degrees held.
j. Give each school's Id, its name and the number of staff in the school (including the Head of School).
k. Give the staff Id of everyone who has more than one degree.
l. For any member of staff who has more than one degree, provide their staff Id and the time between receiving their first and their last degree.
m. Name each member of staff and give the year in which they received their most recent qualification.
n. Give the staff Id of anyone who received degrees in both 1975 and 1985.
o. Give the staff Id of all those who received a bachelor degree before 1950.
p. Give the name of all staff who received their bachelor's degree from an Institute of Technology (IT).

► Q6.2 An auction of ex-police cars had the following results. The `Kilo` column represents how many thousand kilometers the car has on its odometer.

```
Cars
------------------------------------
Lot     Color      Aircon   Kilo     Sale
------------------------------------
1       gray       y        48       9650
2       white      n        41       9200
3       white      n        50       8500
4       white      y        41       9200
4a      beige      n        46       9550
4b      green      n        50       9600
5       white      y        50       9700
6       vanilla    y        53       10100
6a      white      n        46       9300
7       white      y        95       8650
------------------------------------
```

State the outcome of each of the following SQL statements.

a. ```
    Select   count(*)
    From   Cars
    ```

b.  ```
    Select   avg(Kilo)
    From     Cars
    ```

c. ```
    Select   avg(Kilo)
    From   Cars
    Where   kilo < 70
    ```

d.  ```
    Select   min(Sale)
    From     Cars
    Where    Aircon = 'y'
    and      Color <> 'white'
    ```

e. ```
    Select   Aircon, max(Sale)
    From   Cars
    Group by Aircon
    Order by 2 desc
    ```

f.  ```
    Select   Kilo, count(*)
    From     Cars
    Group by Kilo
    Having   count(*) > 1
    Order by 2 desc
    ```

g. ```
    Select   Aircon, Color, count(*)
    From   Cars
    Group by Aircon, Color
    Order by Aircon, Color, 3 desc
    ```
    ```

Q6.3 Here is the `People` table again, with the addition of one new member, `Harry`.

```
People
-----------------------------------------------------
Name    Age    Sex    Earns    Likes      Dislikes
-----------------------------------------------------
Bill    55     m      18000    golf       politics
Sue     28     f      15000    music      beer
Ivan    19     m      25500    football   poms
Dave    21     m      18000    music      sport
Judy    33     f      28000    walking    men
Karen   41     f      48000    dancing    SQL
Alan    40     m      45000    golf       golf
Mark    32     m      17500    football   alcohol
Mario   18     m      17500    dancing    water
Paul    25     m      62500    music      students
Jim     32     m      38500    squash     alcohol
Kathy   19     f      14500    dancing    politics
Harry   ?      m      28000    sport      politics
-----------------------------------------------------
```

Using the `People` table, write SQL to satisfy the requirements below.

a. List each like, and the number of people who have that like.
b. List each shared like and the number of people sharing, in order of popularity.
c. Do females or males earn more, on average?
d. How many men and how many women are there?
e. List each like shared by members of the opposite sex. (Multiply the table by itself.)
f. Do women who like music earn more, on average, than women who like dancing?
g. Do women who like dancing earn more, on average, than men who like football?
h. Give the names of all people in their twenties.
i. Give the names of all people with an `a` as the second letter of their name.
j. Give the names of all people whose name ends in a `y`.
k. Whose age is not recorded?

▶ Q6.4 The ROCKY CONCRETE Database

The Rocky Concrete Company makes a range of concrete products from laundry tubs to park benches to garden gnomes. Rocky's regular customers include hardware shops, local councils, nurseries, farmers and other small businesses. These customers are considered to be the company's "bread and butter" and Rocky likes to satisfy their orders as quickly as possible. To this end the company tries to keep an adequate level of stock for each product made. Whenever the stock in hand falls below some predetermined level then another batch is made.

There are four relations used to keep track of products, orders and customers:

```
    customers           products            orders              order_details
    ---------           --------            ------              -------------
(*) cust_no         (*) prod_code       (*) order_no        (*) order_no
    cust_name           description         order_date      (*) prod_code
    street              prod_group          cust_no             order_qty
    town                list_price                              order_price
    post_code           qty_on_hand
    cr_limit            remake_level
    curr_bal            remake_qty
```

Relation key columns are marked with an asterisk (*). Some columns, such as `cust_name`, are self-explanatory; however, others need some explanation:

`cr_limit`   The maximum that a customer is allowed to owe Rocky Concrete; this may be exceeded at the manager's discretion.

`curr_bal`   The amount currently owed by the customer.

`list_price`   The advertised price for a single unit of a particular product; the price charged to a customer might vary from this.

`order_date`   The date on which the order was made; for these exercises you may assume that the date is held in `YYMMDD` form.

`order_price`   The unit price charged on this order for this product.

`prod_group`   A code that indicates whether a product is grouped as agricultural (A), or council (C), or garden (G) or household (H) in nature.

`remake_level`   The level at which the quantity on hand is compared; if stocks fall below this level then Rocky will usually make another batch to avoid stockout.

`remake_qty`   The amount usually involved in any new production.

The questions that follow have been divided into a number of categories according to the kind of SQL that you are to use in answering them. In practice, however, a query may be phrased in a variety of ways.

Simple Queries (SQ)

These are straightforward queries requiring access to only one of the four tables.

SQ1. List the names of all customers.

SQ2. List the description and list price of all products.

SQ3. List all details of all customers.

SQ4. List all details of those products with a list price of more than $100.

SQ5. List the names and balances of all customers who owe more than $250.

SQ6. List all products in the agricultural product group.

SQ7. List all details of products where stock on hand is worth (at list price) more than $1000.

SQ8. List the customer number, credit limit and current balance of all customers whose current balance exceeds their credit limit.

SQ9. List all details of all customers living in Queensland (post code in the range 4000 to 4999).

SQ10. Which product lines require replenishing and how much should be made?

Join Queries (JQ)

These are relatively simple queries requiring access (as the title suggests) to more than one table.

JQ1. List the product code, description, order price and quantity ordered for each line on order number 1234.

JQ2. List, in date order, the customer name and address and the order date of all orders taken in June 1991.

JQ3. List the order number, order price, product code and list price of those orders where the order price differed from the list price.

JQ4. List the customer name, the order date and the value of each order line worth more than $500. Produce the output in date order and, within date, in ascending order of value.

JQ5. List the product descriptions and customer names for all orders made by Brisbane customers.

JQ6. List the customer name, current balance, credit limit, order date and order line value for all customers whose current balance has been allowed to exceed their credit limit.

JQ7. List the names of all customers who ordered garden gnomes in April 1991. (`prod_code = 'GNOME'`)

JQ8. List the product code, description, order date and order quantity of all orders for gardening products.

JQ9. List the product code, order number and order date where the order quantity is more than the remake quantity.

JQ10. List the customer name, order quantity, list price and order price for all orders for agricultural products taken from Queensland customers.

Statistical Queries (ST)

These queries are to be answered using one or more of the five special functions: `max`, `min`, `avg`, `count` and `sum`.

ST1. What is the total value of order 1234?

ST2. What are the largest and smallest credit limits held by any customers?

ST3. What is the largest amount of credit available to any customer?

ST4. What is the maximum amount by which any customer is over their credit limit?

ST5. When was the first order ever taken?

ST6. When was the latest order taken?

ST7. What is the value of the best order for a large cattle trough? (`prod_code` = `'LOO'`)

ST8. What is the least remake cost for any product line where the quantity on hand is less than the remake level?

ST9. What is the most number of medium cattle troughs ever sold in a single order? (`prod_code` = `'MOO'`)

ST10. How many orders have been made by customer 2255?

Simple Group-by Queries

These (relatively) simple queries are to be answered by means of a `group by` clause. Only one table will be involved.

SG1. List the number of customers in each town, in town order.

SG2. List the number of orders made by each customer, in descending order of frequency.

SG3. For each product group, list the value of stock held. Value at list price.

SG4. For each town, provide a list of the number of customers whose current balance is at least 90% of their credit limit.

SG5. For each product, list the product code and total value of orders taken, in descending value. Ignore products that have never been ordered.

SG6. For each order, list the order number and the total value of that order in descending value. List only those orders worth more than $1000.

SG7. List those towns where the average credit limit is more than $1000.

SG8. For each product, list the product's lowest and highest ever order price.

SG9. Consider June 1991. For each day on which an order was made, list the day and the number of orders taken on that day. Produce the list in date order.

SG10. For each product, list the product code and the total value of orders taken, where the average order line value was more than $1000.

Multi-table Group-by Queries (MG)

These queries are to be answered using a `group by` clause. More than one table may be involved.

MG1. For each product ordered in May 1992, list the product code and the total value of orders for that product.

MG2. For each product group, list the total value of orders taken and the total number of units sold.

MG3. On what days in June 1991 did the sum of the value of all orders taken on that day exceed $1000?

MG4. For each order taken in May 1991, list the order number, the date and the value of the order. Produce the list in date order.

MG5. For each customer who ordered in May 1991, list the customer's number, name and the number of orders made. Produce the list by customer number.

MG6. For each product group, list the group code, the total value of all orders at list price and at order price. Produce the list in product group order.

MG7. From orders taken in 1991, produce a list showing each customer number, name and the total value of orders taken from that customer. Produce the list in descending order of value.

MG8. For each product, list the product code, its description, the number of orders involving this product in June 1991 and the total value of these orders.

MG9. For each product ordered in June 1991, list the product code and the number of customers who ordered the product.

MG10. For each customer receiving a discount in May 1991, list the customer number, name and the amount of discount. Produce the list in descending order of total discount.

Product Queries (PQ)

These queries are to be answered by multiplying one table against another or against itself. This is in contrast to Join queries.

PQ1. Customer 2345 is in financial trouble. Are there any other customers, in the same town, with a larger current balance?

PQ2. Name any customers who have ordered twice in the same day.

PQ3. Customer 6789 is just below the credit limit and wants to buy a large cattle trough. How much below the list price will we have to drop the price to prevent them from going over their limit – as an amount and as a % of the list price?

CHAPTER 7

SQL Modularization

7.1 Introduction

In computing, a **module** is the name we give to an item of work. A program module is a discrete component of that program. It performs a particular task, such as finding the minimum of a set of numbers. All the various modules of a large program are put together in such a way as to achieve the program's overall goal.

This process of conquering complexity is sometimes called **modularization**. Using this technique a complex task may be reduced to a number of relatively simpler tasks. Suitable program modules are then built to accomplish each of these tasks.

This chapter is concerned with how the fundamental query building methods of Chapter 6 may be combined in different ways. In creating these more complex queries we can answer more complex questions.

Three mechanisms are discussed. They are:

- query **nesting** whereby the results of one query are fed into another;
- the **union** operator which allows the results of two or more queries to be merged to produce a single result table; and
- the **view** which allows the results of a query to be given a name and subsequently treated as just another database table.

7.2 Query Nesting

The first kind of query modularization considered in this chapter is query nesting. This involves passing results from one query directly into another. Thus two queries may be executed, one after the other, with no "manual" intervention required.

Example 7.1 What is the Id of the student who got the lowest mark in the first assignment? We could issue the following command:

```
Select    min(Mark)
From      Results
Where     Item = 1
```

```
---------
min(Mark)
---------
   55
---------
```

But this doesn't entirely answer the question. We could then take the query result (55) and, by using it in a second query, get what is wanted:

```
Select    Id from Results
Where     Item = 1
  and     Mark = 55
```

```
---
Id
---
872
---
```

The two queries can be merged into a single **nested** query.

```
Select    Id
From      Results
Where     Item = 1
  and     Mark = (Select min(Mark)
                  From    Results
                  Where   Item = 1)
```

The SQL inside the brackets (`Select min(Mark)...`) is called a **subquery**. This inner subquery is executed first and the answer, 55, is fed back into the outer query to provide the right answer.

There are two ways of looking at the kinds of query nesting that can occur.

1. The first way is according to the **manner** in which the inner and outer queries interact.

    - There is once-only nesting where the inner query is executed once and the outer query then uses that result. So the inner query is executed and then the outer one. Example 7.1 is of this kind.
    - There is query correlation where the outer query executes a little and then the inner query executes a little; and this is repeated until the outer query is complete. This is rather like a module being executed within a program loop.

2. The other way of analyzing query nesting is by the **matter** of the interaction between the inner and the outer query, in other words, by the kind of information that is returned by the subquery.

SQL Modularization

- There are subqueries that return conventional data, such as names, addresses and phone numbers; that is, they return the kind of information stored in the database.
- There are subqueries that simply return a `true` or `false` answer.

7.3 Simple Nesting

There are situations where the query cannot properly be answered without first answering some preliminary query.

Example 7.2 What is the name of the student who got the lowest mark in the first assignment?

This question has already been partially answered in Example 7.1 where we found the Id of the student who got the lowest mark. To get the name of that student, we can turn the query that gave us the Id into a subquery.

```
Select    *
From      Students
Where     Id = (Select   Id
               From      Results
               Where     Item = 1
               and       Mark = (Select min(Mark)
                                 From    Results
                                 Where   Item = 1))
```

```
------------------
Id     First    Last
------------------
872    Betty    Kahn
------------------
```

Here we have a three-level hierarchy of queries. At the bottom level there is one to extract the lowest mark; at the next there is one to get the Id of the student who got that mark; at the top there is one to get us the name of that student.

Example 7.3 Which students were late handing in assignment one? When did they submit?

```
Select    S.*, R.Submitted
From      Students S, Results R
Where     S.Id = R.Id
and       R.Item = 1
and       R.Submitted > (Select   Due
                         From     Assess
                         Where    Item = 1)
```

The inner query returns the due date for the first assignment. The outer query joins the Students and Results tables (because we want student names) and then checks to see whether the student handed in late *that same assignment*.

```
----------------------------------
Id    First    Last     Submitted
----------------------------------
872   Betty    Kahn     0910
869   Rip      Orff     0909
----------------------------------
```

The subquery obtains the due date of the first assignment, which is 0908 or 8 September. The outer query joins the Students and Results tables, so as to be able to provide the names of students who submitted the first assignment after that date.

An alternative solution to the one above is to join all three tables.

```
Select    S.*, R.Submitted
From      Students S, Results R, Assess A
Where     S.Id = R.Id
and       R.Item = A.Item
and       R.Item = 1
and       R.Submitted > A.Due
```

Neither solution is better than the other. It is a matter of personal preference. The reason for showing this alternative is that it provides some clues as to when we can use a subquery and when we need to perform a join. Although we need the assignment due date to answer the question, it is not required as part of the result table and so can be accessed using a subquery. If the due date was to be displayed then we would need to join all three tables as was done in the alternative solution. This three-way join enables us to select and display any column from the three tables.

7.4 "In" Queries

There are occasions when we might expect the inner query to result in a set of values, rather than a single value. When this is the case, we can use the **in** clause to see if an item of data is a member of this set.

Example 7.4 Which students failed at least one item of assessment?

```
Select    *
From      Students
Where     Id in (Select Id
                From   Results
                Where  Mark < 50)
```

```
----------------------
Id    First    Last
----------------------
872   Betty    Kahn
862   Bill     Board
----------------------
```

The inner query returns two **Id**'s, 872 and 862. The outer query then works its way through this set, matching the **Id**'s with student details from the **Students** table.

Example 7.5 Which students did either of the first two items of assessment?

```
Select    Id
From      Results
Where     Item is in (1,2)
```

As can be seen from this example, the **in** clause need not necessarily be used with a subquery. The clause above is equivalent to `Where Item = 1 or Item = 2`. This form of the **in** clause is convenient when we have a long list of alternative values.

7.5 "All–Any" Queries

In Section 7.4 we used the **in** clause to check for set membership. The clause returns a true or false answer because an item is either a member of a set or it is not. Any kind of subquery that returns a true or false answer can be incorporated directly into the condition of a **where** clause.

In Section 7.3 we saw examples of simple subqueries. These all returned a single value such as a mark. This value can then be used in a comparison operator such as = or >. The result of the comparison is either true or false and this answer can be incorporated into the **where** clause.

In this section we will look at situations where the subquery is expected to return a set of values **and** we want to perform more than just a membership test. We want to compare, in a more general way, some item against the set returned.

Example 7.6 What is the Id of the student who got the lowest mark in assignment 1? This is the same as Example 7.1, and there the solution was:

```
Select    Id
From      Results
Where     Item = 1
and       Mark = (Select   min(Mark)
                 From      Results
                 Where     Item = 1)
```

This is an example of a subquery that is expected to provide a single answer, otherwise we could not put the = sign in front of it.

An alternative solution is to use the **all** keyword, as follows:

```
Select    Id
From      Results
Where     Item = 1
and       Mark <= all (Select   Mark
                       From     Results
                       Where    Item = 1)
```

Two changes have been made.

- The = has been changed to `<= all`.
- The subquery now selects `Mark` instead of `min(Mark)`.

The inner query now returns the set of values (80, 60, 70, 55, 90). The second 70 has been removed. The `where` clause of the outer query now becomes:

```
Where    Item = 1
and      Mark <= all (80, 60, 70, 55, 90)
```

Any item 1 mark that is less than or equal to **all** of these marks will satisfy the condition. Clearly 55 is the only mark that is less than or equal to all of these and so is the minimum mark. If we had specified `Mark >= all (...)` then we would have got the maximum mark.

SQL allows either of the two keywords **all** or **any** to be placed between a comparison operator and a subquery. This is known as operator modification. The effect of each of these keywords is as follows.

all The item must bear the specified comparison against **all** members of the set returned by the subquery. For example, `Mark <= all (80, 60, 70, 55, 90)` requires that `Mark` be `<=` all the elements of the set, which means that it must be less than or equal to 55.

any The item must bear the specified comparison against **at least one** member of the set. For example, `Mark > any (80, 60, 70, 55, 90)` requires that the mark be greater than one of the set, which means that it must be greater than 55.

Example 7.7 Which item of assessment was best done, as measured by the average mark?

We could try this.

```
Select    Item, avg(Mark)
From      Results
Group by Item
Order by 2 desc
```

```
-----------------
Item    avg(Mark)
-----------------
 2         75
 1         71
 3         59
-----------------
```

If we pick the first row in the result then we have answered the question. However, computing people are lazy, we always want to get the computer to tell us the answer, no matter how hard that might be.

We want to say something like `Select max(avg(Mark))` ... but this offends SQL and will be rejected. Built-in functions may only be applied to simple columns such as `Mark` or to expressions involving these columns such as `Mark*Weight/100`. They may **not** be used on other built-in functions, for example.

An alternative solution is as follows.

```
Select      Item, avg(Mark)
From        Results
Group by    Item
Having      avg(Mark) >= all (Select   avg(Mark)
                              From     Results
                              Group by Item)
```

The **having** clause is used to restrict groups reported to those where the average mark is greater than or equal to all three of the averages obtained. This is equivalent to the maximum average.

Any of the six standard comparison operators (<, <=, =, ^=, >=, >) may be used in this way. Thus to get the lowest average we could amend the **having** clause to:

```
Having      avg(Mark) <= all (Select avg(Mark) ... )
```

Example 7.8 Which students handed in assignment 1 after students 871 **and** 869?

```
Select      Id, Submitted
From        Results
Where       Item = 1
and         Submitted > all (Select   Submitted
                             From     Results
                             Where    Item = 1
                             and      Id in (869, 871))


----------------
Id      Submitted
----------------
872     0910
----------------
```

The subquery returns the dates on which 869 and 871 handed in their assignments (**0909**, **0908**). Only student 872 submitted after **all** of these dates.

7.6 Correlated Subqueries

Rather than having an inner query finish before the outer query is attempted, there are times when the inner and the outer query work as a team, iteratively executing the inner and the outer query in tandem.

Example 7.9 Which students did better in the first assignment than in the second?

```
Select      Id
From        Results One
Where       Item = 1
and         Mark > (Select Mark
                    From   Results
                    Where  Id = One.Id
                    and    Item = 2)
```

```
---
Id
---
871
868
---
```

The above query is an example of a correlated subquery. In simple subqueries it is best to think of SQL as performing the subquery first and then passing the result to the outer query which then executes. With correlated subqueries it is better to think of the outer query as doing a certain amount of work and then asking the subquery to do some. The outer query then does some more work and then the inner does some more, and so on until the outer query is finished. Thus the outer and inner queries are correlated.

The reference **One** is called a **pseudonym** or **alias**. Aliases are often an easy way to refer several times to a table with a very long name – we simply give it a short alias when it first appears, in the **from** clause. However, in this correlated subquery, **Results** has to have an alias, because the query passes an Id value into the subquery for comparison every time the inner query is executed: if the inner query referred to **Results.Id** rather than **One.Id**, it would be comparing the same Id value to itself.

Example 7.10 Who was the **second** best student in the final exam?

```
Select    Id, Mark
From      Results R1
Where     R1.Item = 3
and       2 = (Select   count(*)
               From     Results
               Where    Item = 3
               and      Mark >= R1.Mark)


----------
Id    Mark
----------
854   65
----------
```

The outer query steps through the results for the final exam and for every one, asks the inner query to count the number of marks that were better than or equal to it. If that count is 2 then we have the second best student.

This query works only if just one student had the second best mark. How would it need to be modified to handle situations where several students share a mark?

7.7 "Exists" Queries

There are occasions when we might want to know of the existence of certain rows in a table and act accordingly. This can be achieved by use of an **exists** clause within the **where** clause. An **exists** clause evaluates the subquery; if the subquery returns an empty table then the **exists** clause returns a value of false; otherwise it returns a value of true.

SQL Modularization   157

Example 7.11 Name any student who got more than 90% in any item of assessment.

```
Select     *
From       Students S
Where      exists (Select *
                   From    Results
                   Where   Id = S.Id
                   and     Mark > 90)
```

```
--------------------
Id     First    Last
--------------------
869    Rip      Orff
--------------------
```

SQL picks a row from the Students table. It then passes control to the inner query. If the student has achieved a mark higher than 90% then the inner query is successful and the student row is displayed. If no such mark exists then SQL passes straight on to the next row in the Students table. This process is repeated until all rows have been examined.

Example 7.12 Which students failed to submit any work for assessment?

```
Select     *
From       Students S
Where      not exists (Select *
                       From    Results
                       Where   Id = S.id)
```

```
--------------------
Id     First    Last
--------------------
831    Hans     Orff
--------------------
```

In this example, each student row is examined and, if there are no results for that student, the student row is displayed.

Example 7.13 Which students submitted assignment 1 but **not** assignment 2?

```
Select     *
From       Students S
Where      exists      (Select  *
                        From    Results
                        Where   Item = 1
                        and     Id = S.Id)
           and not exists (Select  *
                           From    Results
                           Where   Item = 2
                           and     Id = S.Id)
```

```
--------------------
Id    First   Last
--------------------
854   Ann     Dover
--------------------
```

In this example, the **Students** table is examined and for each row two subqueries are evaluated, one for each assignment. If the subquery returns a row then the student did the assignment, otherwise they did not. In this way the conditions required to satisfy the question may be evaluated.

7.8 Subquery Usage

The ability to issue subqueries is an important and powerful feature of SQL. Subqueries are not restricted to the **select** statement, but may be used within **update** and **delete** statements.

A subquery may use any number of tables; it may involve a **group by** clause and a **having** clause. A subquery may invoke other lower level subqueries.

When writing a subquery, the following constraints are placed upon the the phrasing of the subquery.

- The **order** clause must not be used.
- The **select** clause must contain only one column name or expression; for example, **(select p from ...)** but not **(select p, q from ...)**. An exception is the **exists** clause where any number of columns may be selected.

The outer query may use several subqueries at the same level; see Example 7.13 which has two. However, there are limitations placed upon the way in which a subquery may be invoked by the query in which it is embedded.

- Subqueries must always appear within round brackets.
- Subqueries can only appear **after**, that is, to the right of an operator. So we can have, for example, 8 = **(subquery)** but not **(subquery)** = 8.
- Subqueries cannot be used as part of **between** or **like** clauses.
- A subquery should return only **one** value unless the subquery is preceded by one of the keywords **in**, **exists**, **all** or **any**.

7.9 The Union Operator

Use of the **union** operator offers the second kind of query modularization discussed in this chapter.

The results of two or more queries may be merged to form a single result table. SQL treats the result of each query as a set. It then creates the set union of each participating query.

The keyword **union** is inserted between the **select** statements whose results are to be merged. The rows produced by each individual query are amalgamated with duplicate rows being removed.

Example 7.14 Which student got less than 70 in either assignment 1 or 2?

```
Select    Id
From      Results
Where     Item = 1
and       Mark < 70

Union
Select    Id
From      Results
Where     Item = 2
and       Mark < 70
```

The two query results are merged as shown below:

```
---                 ---            ---
Id        Union     Id      =      Id
---                 ---            ---
862                 872            862
872                 ---            872
---                                ---
```

This query could have been answered more conventionally:

```
Select    Id
From      Results
Where     (Item = 1 or Item = 2)
and       Mark < 70
```

The use of the **or** in this answer should not surprise us. The union of two sets, A and B, is the set whose elements are in A **or** B (or both).

Example 7.15 List the results for assignment 1, and give zero to any student who did not submit any work at all.

```
Select    Id, Mark
From      Results
Where     Item = 1

Union
Select    Id, 0
From      Students S
Where     not exists (Select  *
                      From    Results
                      Where   Item = 1
                      and     Id = S.Id)
```

In the previous example, it was possible for the two sets of students involved to overlap. A student might get less than 70 in both items of assessment. In this example, however, the two sets should be disjoint. The two queries would give rise to the following amalgamation.

```
          Id    Mark    union    Id    0      =    Id    Mark?
          ---------             ---------            ---------
          871   80               831   0             831   0
          862   60               ---------           854   70
          854   70                                   862   60
          872   55                                   868   90
          868   90                                   869   70
          869   70                                   871   80
          ---------                                  872   55
                                                    ---------
```

The first query gets item 1 results and the second supplements these with a zero mark for any student who did not do this assignment.

The result has been shown in Id order. SQL **may** decide that the easiest way of performing a union is first to sort the sets involved and then to merge them.

Example 7.16 List the results for assignment 1. Give a zero to any student who did not do this assignment. Take 5 marks off any student who submitted it after the due date. Produce the list in order of merit.

```
Select    R.Id, R.Mark
From      Results R, Assess A
Where     R.Item = A.Item
  and     R.Item = 1
  and     R.Submitted <= A.Due

Union
Select    R.Id, R.Mark - 5
From      Results R, Assess A
Where     R.Item = A.Item
  and     R.Item = 1
  and     R.Submitted > A.Due

Union
Select    Id, 0
From      Students S
Where     not exists (Select   *
                      From     Results
                      Where    Item = 1
                        and    Id = S.Id)

Order by 2 desc
```

Three separate queries are used. The first identifies those who submitted on or before the due date. The second takes 5 marks off anyone who submitted *after* that date. The third "awards" a zero to anybody who failed to submit at all. They will give rise to the following union:

```
       -----------                 -----------                 -----------
       Id    Mark     union        Id    Mark?    union        Id    Mark?
       -----------                 -----------                 -----------
       871   80                    872   50                    831   0
       862   60                    869   65                    -----------
       854   70                    -----------
       868   90
       -----------
```

The **order** clause requires that the results of the union be displayed in descending order of the second column. So the final table is:

```
       -----------
       Id    Mark?
       -----------
       868   90
       871   80
       854   70
       869   65
       862   60
       872   50
       831   0
       -----------
```

In the final table, the second column is headed **Mark?**. The question mark is there to indicate that while *we* know that the column represents marks, SQL has no such knowledge. As far as SQL is concerned, the values in this column have three sources.

- Four values are taken directly from the database.
- Two are the results of calculations.
- One is generated by a **select** clause.

The three **select** statements in the above union correspond to three organizational rules regarding the submission of work.

1. IF   a submission is made on time
   THEN no penalty is occurred.
2. IF   a submission is late
   THEN a 5 point penalty is applied.
3. IF   no submission is made at all
   THEN a mark of zero is awarded.

7.10 Union Usage

The union operator can be used to merge essentially similar items of information obtained from two or more separate queries. The information may come from quite different parts of the database. It may even be constructed by one of the participating queries.

There are, unfortunately, a number of restrictions on the use of the union.

- The corresponding items in each `select` clause must have matching data types. So we cannot merge an `integer` column with anything but another `integer` column. We cannot even merge `char(4)` with `char(5)` as the lengths must also match.
- The items to be merged must have matching **nullity**. We cannot merge a column that might contain nulls with one that cannot.
- The **order** clause appears once only at the end, if at all. The columns used in the sort must be identified by **number**.
- In some versions of SQL, the union cannot be used within a subquery.
- In some versions of SQL, the union cannot be used in the definition of a view. See the following section.

The first three restrictions are ones we can live with. In versions where the latter two apply, they limit the power of SQL considerably.

The union does give us the ability to perform `IF...THEN...ELSE...` queries. Some problems are best thought of in the following terms:

```
IF      condition
THEN    extract certain information
ELSE    extract some alternative information
```

This kind of query can be converted to a union query using the following template:

```
Select   certain information
From     ...
Where    condition

Union
Select   alternative information
From     ...
Where    inverse-condition
```

7.11 Views

In Chapter 3, where sets were introduced, it was stated that there are two ways of specifying a set: in extension and by comprehension. The base tables are sets in extension. A view is a name given to a set defined by comprehension. The view mechanism is the third kind of query modularization to be considered in this chapter. The result of an SQL query is always shown as a table. A **view** is simply a name that we give to a result table.

Example 7.17 Define a view containing the results of the first assignment.

```
Create View Ass_1
     as Select Id, Submitted, Mark
        From    Results
        Where   Item = 1
```

SQL Modularization 163

```
Ass_1
----------------------
Id     Submitted   Mark
----------------------
871    0908        80
862    0907        60
854    0908        70
872    0910        55
868    0906        90
869    0909        70
----------------------
```

We can now, with certain restrictions, use this view as if it is a database table.

```
Select   Id, Mark
From     Ass_1
Where    Mark > 70


----------
Id    Mark
----------
868   90
871   80
----------
```

We can join the view to other tables, for example, to display the names of the two students above.

```
Select   S.Id, First, Last, Mark
From     Students S, Ass_1 A
Where    S.Id = A.Id
  and    Mark > 70


-------------------------
Id    First   Last    Mark
-------------------------
868   Will    Gambol   90
871   Hans    Zupp     80
-------------------------
```

However, a view has no real existence as a separate table; it merely exists as a definition in the system catalog.

In this example, we have given the name `Ass_1` to a particular subset of the `Results` table. From now on, any usage of that name is a reference to that set. The set of values defined is **dynamic**. It is not necessarily the set of values that apply when the view is defined. It is the set applying whenever the view is used in a query. The membership of this set may vary from time to time because the underlying table may be updated from time to time.

Example 7.18 Create a view of the overall results for each student.

```
Create View Overall(Id, Total)
       as Select   R.Id, sum(R.Mark*A.Weight/100)
          From     Results R, Assess A
          Where    R.Item = A.Item
          Group by R.Id
```

With this view, it is as if we now had a table called **Overall** in the database. The names of the columns in this new table are given in brackets after the view name. If no names are given in this way then SQL takes them from the **select** clause. In this example, column names must be provided because one of the columns involves a calculation.

Unfortunately, we cannot join this table with the Students table to name the students. Naturally, we would like to be able to do something like the following.

```
Select    S.Id, First, Last, Total
From      Students S, Overall O
Where     S.Id = O.Id
Order by Total desc
```

When a view has been constructed with the aid of a **group by** clause, it cannot be joined to another table or view.

Another restriction results from the use of a built-in function in the view definition. The **Total** column is based on a **sum** function. For any view column derived in this way, SQL prevents us from using the column in the condition of a **where** clause. For example, we might like to list those who passed the subject, **Select * From Overall Where Total >= 50**. This is not allowed.

Nor can we use such a column in a built-in function, for example, to find the top mark, **Select max(Total) From Overall**. This is forbidden also.

7.12 View Usage

In its view facility, SQL shows us a glimpse of a marvellous chance to be able to:

- **exclude unwanted information** from the view user by making the view incorporate only the information wanted by the view user;
- **hide information** that is not the business of the user by making the view contain only what the user needs to know; and by granting the user access to that view alone; and
- **perform complex calculations** for the user and present a result table that can be treated like any other table.

Unfortunately, SQL then neuters the facility with a whole series of limitations on how the view can be used, saying, in effect "you can treat a view as if it is just another database table except when ... and when ... and when ...".

7.13 Summary

In this chapter, we have extended the retrieval capabilities of SQL that were introduced in Chapter 6. That chapter showed three simple forms of SQL query whereby information may be extracted from a table.

- We can **extract** from some table the rows and columns that we want.
- We can **partition** a table into groups and summarize each group.
- We can **summarize** an entire table in a single line.

This chapter showed three ways in which simple queries may be combined to form more complex ones.

- We can **nest** queries so that the results of one query are passed directly to another.
- We can use the union operator to **amalgamate** the results of two or more queries to form a single result table.
- We can use the view facility to **name** a query and then refer to the results of that query in subsequent retrievals.

These extensions of the basic retrieval mechanisms allow us to respond to a complex request for information. We construct an answer from more simple queries and combine these to form a single result table. This process is similar to the way in which complex programs may be constructed from simpler program modules. Hence we have put query nesting, the union operator and the view mechanism under the joint title of **SQL modularization**.

Exercises

▶ Q7.1 The MATCHING Database

People

Name	Age	Sex	Earns	Likes	Dislikes
Bill	55	m	18000	golf	politics
Sue	28	f	15000	music	beer
Ivan	19	m	25500	football	dancing
Dave	21	m	18000	music	sport
Judy	33	f	28000	walking	men
Karen	41	f	48000	dancing	SQL
Alan	40	m	45000	golf	golf
Mark	32	m	17500	football	alcohol
Mario	18	m	17500	dancing	water
Paul	25	m	62500	music	students
Jim	32	m	38500	squash	alcohol
Kathy	19	f	14500	dancing	politics

Required:

Write nested queries to satisfy the requirements below.

a. Who earns the most?
b. Which men earn less than the average male earnings?
c. Who likes the same thing as Mario?
d. Who dislikes students, politics or SQL? [Use a simple **in**]
e. Which men earn more than all women? [Use **all**]
f. Which women earn more than at least one man? [Use **any**]
g. Which men like things liked by females? [Use **in**]
h. Which women are older than Kathy?

▶ Q7.2 Use the union operator to satisfy the following requirements.

a. Find out how many men and women there are in the table. Produce a table like this:

```
------------
Men      8
Women    4
------------
```

b. People under 30 are classified as young; those between 30 and 49 are middle-aged and those 50 or over are elderly. Produce a table showing how many men there are in each age range.

```
               ----------------
               young           4
               middle-aged     3
               elderly         1
               ----------------
```

    c.   It is time to send out the annual accounts. The fees charged depend upon how much a member earns.

Earns	Fee
under 15 000	0.5%
15 000 – 29 999	0.75%
30 000 and above	1.25%

Display all members, their incomes and the fees payable.

▶ Q7.3   Define views to satisfy the following requirements.

    a.   Create a view `Men` that contains details of all men in the `People` table.

    b.   Create a view `Rich (Name, Sex, Income)` which contains information on people who earn $40 000 or more.

    c.   Use the views `Men` and `Rich` to create a view `Rich_Men (Name, Age, Worth)`.

▶ Q7.4   ROCKY CONCRETE

All of the following exercises are base upon the Rocky Concrete database described in the exercises at the end of the preceding chapter.

Simple Nested Queries (SN)

These are queries to be answered by simple nested queries. Use of more than one table might be required; also, queries might be nested to more than one level.

SN1.   What is the name of the customer with the largest credit limit?

SN2.   What is the name and number of the customer most over his or her credit limit?

SN3.   What is the name of the customer who made the latest order? (nested 2 deep)

SN4.   Describe the product that is normally the most expensive.

SN5.   What product costs the most to remake?

SN6.   Which customers have a larger credit limit than customer 2255?

SN7.   Name the customer(s) that paid the most for a small septic tank. (`prod_code = 'STANK'`)

SN8.   On what date did we get our most valuable order ever?

SN9.   What is the name of the customer that ordered our first garden gnome? (least order no. involving prod_code `GNOME`).

SN10. For each customer that has not yet ordered this year, say 1991, give their number, name and the date on which they last ordered.

In Queries (IQ)

These queries are to be answered using `in` or `not in` expressions.

IQ1. Give the names and addresses of all customers who made orders on 12 August 1991.

IQ2. List the names of all customers who ordered garden gnomes in April 1991 (same as JQ7).

IQ3. List the product code and description of those products that were involved in order no. 1234.

IQ4. List the names of all customers who have made orders worth more than $1000 in total.

IQ5. List the number of orders made in April 1991 by customers from Bundaberg.

IQ6. For each product that requires remaking, list the product code and the total value of orders taken in April 1991.

IQ7. List the product codes of those products sold to Gympie customers in July 1991 (double `in`).

IQ8. On what days in April 1991 were individual orders for more than one garden gnome taken?

IQ9. List the names of customers who did not order in 1991.

IQ10. What are the product codes of products not ordered in July 1991?

Complex Group-by Queries (CG)

These queries are to be answered using a `group by` clause. They may require `any` or `all` clauses, subqueries and more than one table.

CG1. Which product has led to the biggest volume of sales, in terms of units sold?

CG2. Which product has been the most valuable, in terms of value of orders taken?

CG3. Which order(s) contained the greatest number of lines? Give the order no. only.

CG4. Which customers are based in the town with the largest average current balance?

CG5. Give details of customers based in the town with the lowest maximum credit limit.

CG6. In which towns are there customers with more than twice the average available credit for that town? Give the number of such customers in each town.

CG7. What was our most successful day in terms of value of orders taken?

CG8. List the order no. and order date of all those 1991 orders that involved the most popular product of that year (popularity measured in terms of units sold).

CG9. Which product group represents the biggest proportion of the total value of stock on hand?

CG10. List customers based in Bundaberg that made less than 10 orders in 1991.

Correlated Subqueries (CR)

These queries are to be answered using correlated subqueries.

CR1. List the product code and description of those products that have, at some time, been sold below list price.

CR2. For each town, list the customers based in that town that have less than the average current balance for that town.

CR3. For each product group, list the product code, description and list price of the most expensive product in that group.

CR4. For the product with the code **GNOME**, list the addresses of all customers that ordered that product between 1 April and 16 May 1991.

Exists Queries (EQ)

These queries are to be answered using **exists** or **not exists** expressions.

EQ1. List any orders for which there is no corresponding customer.

EQ2. List order details for which there is no corresponding order.

EQ3. List order details for which there is no corresponding product.

EQ4. List orders for which there is no order detail.

EQ5. List any customers that have never ordered.

EQ6. List any products that have never been ordered.

Union Queries (UQ)

These queries are to be answered using the **union** operator to merge the results of two or more separate select statements.

UQ1. List the name and address of customers based in the towns of Bundaberg or Toowoomba.

UQ2. List the product code and description of all those products that have either been ordered in April 1991 or that were ordered at least twice in May 1991.

UQ3. For all products, list the product code, the total value of orders taken and the description (some products may never have been ordered).

UQ4. For all customers, list the customer no., the name and the total value of orders made. Produce the list in descending value of orders (some customers may never have made an order).

CHAPTER 8

Facts and Relations

8.1 Introduction

A **fact** is a declarative sentence; that is, it is a statement which may be either true or false. It describes a particular relationship between two or more things or **entities**; for example:

```
Billy Connolly was born in Scotland.
```

We use computers when we have lots of similar facts to remember.

```
Bill Cosby was born in the USA.
John Cleese was born in England.
Barry Humphries was born in Australia.
  :        :       :   :    :
```

When we recognize that certain facts are similar, we can generalize them into a **fact type** which is a relationship between two types of entity rather than between individual entities. In this case the relationship is between people and countries. Or is it? Perhaps it's between comedians and countries, or between men and countries? To be more certain we need to investigate the *universe of discourse* or UoD which is simply the situation that we intend representing in our information system. In attempting to design the most appropriate database structure for a given situation, we need to know the kinds of things that are involved and the kinds of facts that relate them.

Fact types are not stored individually; rather, they are embedded within **relations** with each relation dedicated to representing a fixed number of fact types. This chapter looks at some of the problems we face when deciding where to place a fact type when designing a database. We will find that each fact type may be merged or grouped only with certain others. Some we will be unable to merge; they must remain on their own. We will use **conceptual schema diagrams** to help achieve this grouping. These diagrams are used to depict the knowledge we need to design a database.

8.2 Facts

Consider this statement:

```
Harry lives in New York.
```

This is an example of a fact. Is it a fact more about Harry than New York? It seems to be more about Harry. Why is this so?

If we wanted to represent many facts of this particular type, we could tabulate them.

```
LivesIn
-----------------
Person   City
-----------------
Harry    New York
Bruce    Sydney
John     New York
Sue      Perth
Angus    Aberdeen
-----------------
```

This table or relation has five rows, one for each person. In contrast, one of the cities, New York, appears in two of the rows. Perhaps this was what made us think that `"Harry lives in New York."` is a fact about Harry rather than New York. In general, the `"lives in"` fact type is a fact about people rather than cities. As a rule, a person lives in just one city, but a city will have many residents.

The relation is called a **binary** relation because it has two attributes. This binary table has two important features that might easily go unnoticed.

1. People's first names have been used to represent or **symbolize** the people concerned. A one-for-one substitution has been made. This will probably not be satisfactory if the set of people is large. Also, city names have been used to represent the cities. This does not seem quite so likely to lead to problems. This symbolism may be disclosed if we rewrite one of the facts rather pedantically as:

   ```
   The PERSON with the first name 'Harry'
   lives in
   the CITY with the name 'New York'.
   ```

2. The `lives in` relationship between each person and a city has been made **identical** and can hence be used as a heading. This is an example of **abstraction** at work, the suppression of what is considered to be irrelevant detail. Harry might be happy in New York and Bruce bored in Sydney. We can't tell from this table; all that we can say is that Harry lives in New York and Bruce in Sydney. This is the price we pay for the simplicity of a tabular representation.

This method of fact expression is called the "telephone heuristic". We imagine that we are trying to communicate the fact down a rather bad line to a rather dim-witted friend. It also helps to remind us that `'Harry'` and `'New York'` are merely symbols or **labels** that we stick on these two objects and that *naming* is the particular form of labeling that we used for both.

Finally, the particular method of writing the fact:

```
Harry lives in New York.
```

is just one way of stating the information; we could equally have written it as:

```
New York is the residence of Harry.
```

The two sentences have the same meaning. This second form is rather awkward. Perhaps that is why we prefer to think of it as a fact about Harry.

What the two forms help to show is the **role** that each entity plays in the relationship. Harry plays a `lives in` role with regard to New York; and New York plays a `residence of` role with respect to Harry. We can now display the entire fact type *schematically*; that is, we can show the basic structure of the fact in terms of:

- the kinds of things that participate in the fact; and
- the roles taken by each kind of thing involved.

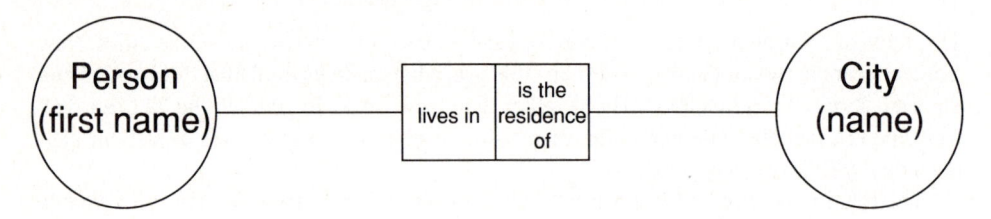

1. The fact is one between people and cities; or between a `Person` type and a `City` type. These are the **entity types** involved.

2. Each individual person is represented or **symbolized** by his or her name. Each city is represented by its name. The manner of representation is shown in brackets below the entity type.

3. The **roles** that each entity plays in the relationship have been shown alongside the corresponding role box.

We need to be able to generalize from specific facts relating specific objects to the corresponding fact type. When designing a database, we are very much concerned with and, of necessity, restricted to the *type* of information to be stored. We have no way of knowing the information that will *actually* be stored in the relations we design.

What about this fact?

Suppose we have more facts to record. Here is one of them.

```
New York is in the USA.
```

Is this a fact about New York or about the USA? More about New York, it would seem.

Again, if we had many facts of this kind, we could tabulate them.

Facts and Relations

```
LocatedIn
--------------------
City        Country
--------------------
New York    USA
Sydney      Australia
Perth       Australia
Aberdeen    Scotland
--------------------
```

Each fact relates a city to a country. The first row of the table can be expressed as:

> The CITY with the name 'New York'
> is located in
> the COUNTRY with the name 'USA'

The alternative phrasing, putting the country as the subject of the sentence might be:

> The COUNTRY with the name 'USA'
> is the location of
> the CITY with the name 'New York'.

So the City entity type plays the role `is located in` in the fact type and the Country entity type plays the role `is the location of`. We can now represent this fact type diagrammatically.

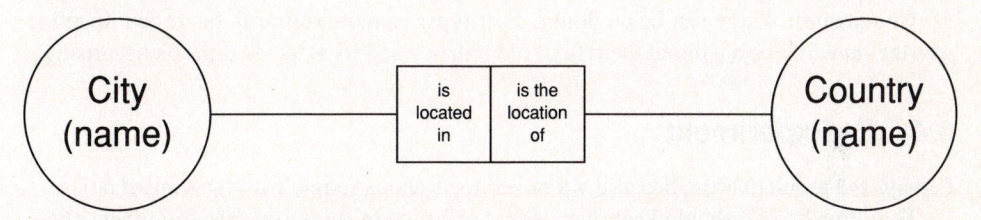

[Diagram: City (name) —[is located in | is the location of]— Country (name)]

As before, the diagram emphasizes the two types of entity that participate in the fact and the role that each entity plays. However, rather than representing each new fact type as a separate diagram, we will extend the diagram to include additional fact types.

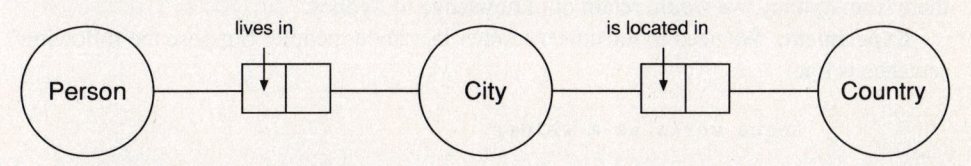

[Diagram: Person —[lives in]— City —[is located in]— Country]

In this way we get a composite picture of the relationship between people, cities and countries. The two fact types involving cities are seen as stemming from the one City entity type.

8.3 A Simple Design

Suppose these two fact types were all that we wished to record. We might, quite innocently, decide to incorporate them in a single relation.

```
LivesIn              LocatedIn              MergeTable
----------------     ---------------------  ---------------------------
Person  City       + City       Country   = Person  City       Country
----------------     ---------------------  ---------------------------
Harry   New York    New York    USA         Harry   New York   USA
Bruce   Sydney      Sydney      Australia   Bruce   Sydney     Australia
John    New York    Perth       Australia   John    New York   USA
Sue     Perth       Aberdeen    Scotland    Sue     Perth      Australia
Angus   Aberdeen    ---------------------   Angus   Aberdeen   Scotland
----------------                            ---------------------------
```

Figure 8.1 Merging fact types

Is anything amiss here? We have had to incorporate a little bit of redundancy in the table. The fact that **New York is in the USA** has been recorded twice, once for each person who lives there. If there were 100 people recorded as living in New York then the location of New York would also be recorded 100 times. Worse, if New York was likely to move from one country to another then we would have to remember to make changes to every one of the rows involving that city. Otherwise we risk recording New York as being located in more than one country. Fortunately, this is not the case! What is perhaps even worse is that should Bruce decide to leave Sydney and live in New York, we would lose our knowledge of Sydney's location entirely.

Conclusion: There can be no doubt. Fact types cannot arbitrarily be thrown together into the same relation without the risk of redundancy and its associated problems arising.

8.4 An Experiment

Perhaps the problem arose because we mixed facts about people with facts about cities.

Hypothesis: We should keep facts about one type of thing separate from facts about some other kind of thing. So, in the above examples we should have one relation for facts about people and another for facts about cities. Now we would record the location of New York only once no matter how many people we know there; and also, should Bruce move there from Sydney, we would retain our knowledge of Sydney.

Experiment: We need to introduce another fact about people. Suppose the following sentence is true:

> **Angus works as a welder.**

This seems to be a fact about Angus rather than about welding. Suppose we know the following facts about people and their jobs:

> **Harry works as a stockbroker.**
> **Bruce works as an actor.**
> **John works as a waiter.**
> **Sue works as a welder.**
> **Angus works as a welder.**

Facts and Relations 175

We can construct a corresponding `WorksAs` table and compare it against the `LivesIn` table. The result is shown in Figure 8.2. The `LivesIn` and `WorksAs` tables can be merged without redundancy arising. This is possible because there is **one** row per person in **both** tables.

```
                   LivesIn                       WorksAs
                   -----------------             --------------------
                   Person   City                 Person    Job
                   -----------------             --------------------
                   Harry    New York             Harry     stockbroker
        People  =  Bruce    Sydney         +     Bruce     actor
                   John     New York             John      waiter
                   Sue      Perth                Sue       welder
                   Angus    Aberdeen             Angus     welder
                   -----------------             --------------------


                   --------------------------------
                   Person   City        Job
                   --------------------------------
                   Harry    New York    stockbroker
                =  Bruce    Sydney      actor
                   John     New York    waiter
                   Sue      Perth       welder
                   Angus    Aberdeen    welder
                   --------------------------------
```

Figure 8.2 Merging single-valued facts

The merging is straightforward. The resulting table has been called `People` because it contains facts about people. We can add this new fact directly to the previous diagram.

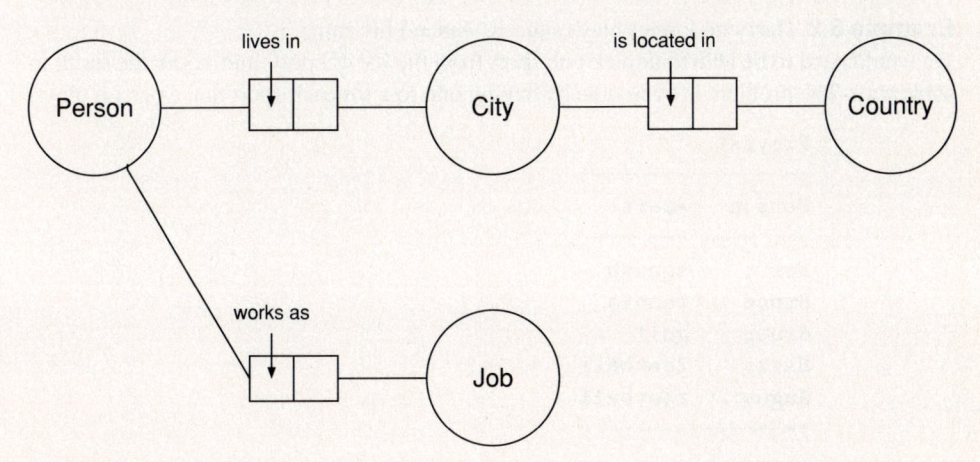

8.5 Another Experiment

Just to be safe we had better try some more sample data. Consider this fact:

```
Harry plays squash.
```

This looks like another fact about Harry. Let us gather all facts of this kind. Harry plays squash; Bruce plays tennis and golf; and both Harry and Angus play football.

This data could be presented as a table in the following way.

```
PlaysAt
-------------------------
Person    Sports
-------------------------
Harry     squash, football
Bruce     tennis, golf
Angus     football
-------------------------
```

This seems a very natural way of tabulating the data, but SQL is not very adept at handling multi-valued or set-valued columns, such as the `Sports` column above.

Example 8.1 Who plays football?

```
Select    Person
From      PlaysAt
Where     Sports like '%football%'

------
Person
------
Harry
Angus
------
```

We would need to use the `like` operator to search for an occurrence of the word `football` somewhere within the `Sports` attribute.

Example 8.2 Harry no longer plays squash. Amend his entry.

We would need to be able to unpick one sport from the list of sports and rejoin the result in some way. The problem is overcome by having one row for each sport that a person plays.

```
PlaysAt
------------------
Person    Sport
------------------
Harry     squash
Bruce     tennis
Bruce     golf
Harry     football
Angus     football
------------------
```

Now if Harry's doctor tells him to quit squash, we can easily amend the table.

```
Delete
From    PlaysAt
Where   Person = 'Harry'
and     Sport  = 'squash'
```

With this way of presenting the sports data, writing SQL is easier, but we are left with other difficulties. What if we merge `LivesIn` and `PlaysAt`? If we combine the tables, we get:

```
People
------------------------------------
Person   City       Sport
------------------------------------
Harry    New York   squash
Harry    New York   football
Bruce    Sydney     tennis
Bruce    Sydney     golf
John     New York   ?
Sue      Perth      ?
Angus    Aberdeen   football
------------------------------------
```

John and Sue play no sport and null values have had to be introduced for this reason. However, this is not a problem. What is a nuisance is that, despite both being facts about people, redundancy has arisen in the combined table. This is a direct result of the two people who play more than one sport.

Conclusion: We can merge fact types about the same kind of thing, but only under certain circumstances.

What are these circumstances? If we summarize the fact types involving people, we have:

Fact type	Related entity type	Number that one person may relate to
lives in	City	one
works as	Job	one
plays at	Sport	many

1. The first line in the table states that a person lives in only **one** city. A person's city of residence is a **single-valued** fact about that person.

2. The second line says that a person's job is also a **single-valued** fact about a person. In our universe of discourse, a person has only one job.

3. On the other hand, the third line states that a person may play **many** sports. The sport a person plays is a **many-valued** fact about a person.

The circumstances under which we can merge two fact types occur when:

- both fact types are directly concerned about the same kind of thing, that is, one of the sets participates in both fact types; and

- these facts are both single-valued facts about that kind of thing.

We need some way of differentiating single-valued facts from many-valued facts. What we need, in effect, is to decide how the things **participate** in the relation. Does a person live in one city or many? Does a person play one sport or many?

We can add this new fact to our conceptual schema diagram. At the same time we can annotate the diagram to show these **uniqueness constraints**: see Figure 8.3.

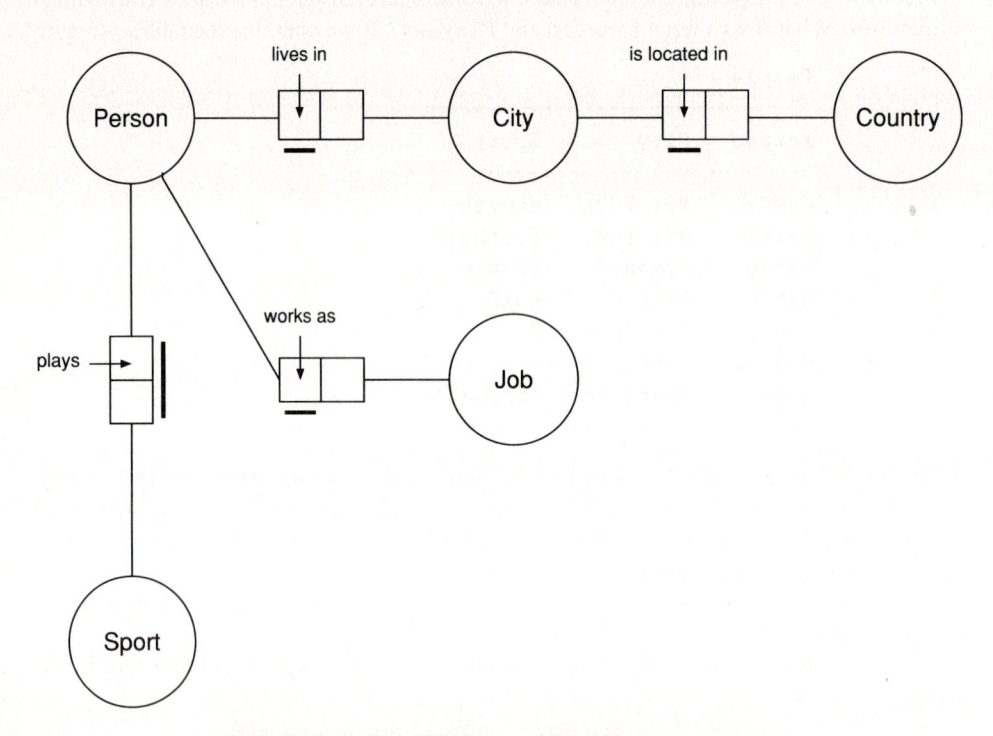

Figure 8.3 Introducing uniqueness constraints

A bar is put alongside the appropriate role box to indicate the following knowledge:

- Each person lives in *one* city.
- Each person works at *one* job.
- Each city is located in just *one* country.

But for the fact about sports, the bar goes alongside both role boxes which indicates that:

- A person may play *many* sports and a sport may be played by *many* people.

So the diagram tells at a glance what facts about people may be merged. A bar alongside a role box to which an entity type is attached indicates a single-valued, and hence mergeable, fact about that entity. Once we have the bars marked, it is relatively easy to decide what may be merged. But first we must learn how to place these bars. We will do that in the following section.

8.6 Uniqueness Constraints

Let us return to the first fact type, one example of which was that Harry lives in New York. This fact type is represented schematically:

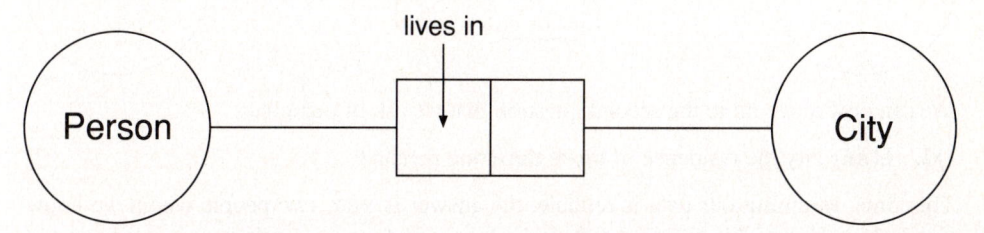

```
                    lives in
                       │
                       ▼
   ╭─────╮    ┌─────┬─────┐    ╭─────╮
  │Person │───┤     │     ├───│ City  │
   ╰─────╯    └─────┴─────┘    ╰─────╯
```

To find out whether this is a single-valued fact about a person, or a city, or both, we ask ourselves two simple questions.

Q1. Does **any** person live in **more than one** city?

We can't answer that question without being sure about the set of people we are modeling. And we are not merely interested in the people that we know now. The relations in our database are dynamic data objects; their contents can be expected to vary over time.

The tabulated form of the facts was as follows:

```
LivesIn
-----------------
Person   City
-----------------
Harry    New York
Bruce    Sydney
John     New York
Sue      Perth
Angus    Aberdeen
-----------------
```

Let us suppose that this table contains a *significant* set of facts of this type; that is, it may not be the entire set, either currently or in the future, but it is extensive enough to enable us to generalize about the nature of the relationship.

Suppose we *again* ask the question.

Q1. Does **any** person live in **more than one** city?

Using our sample data, the answer is NO. Each person appears only once. There is no repetition in the **Person** column. This restriction is called a **uniqueness constraint**. We signify this constraint by placing a bar over, under or alongside the role box to which the Person entity type is connected, that is, to the **lives in** role box.

```
     lives in
 ┌──────┐    ┌──┬──┐    ┌──────┐
 │Person│────┤▼ │  ├────│ City │
 └──────┘    └──┴──┘    └──────┘
```

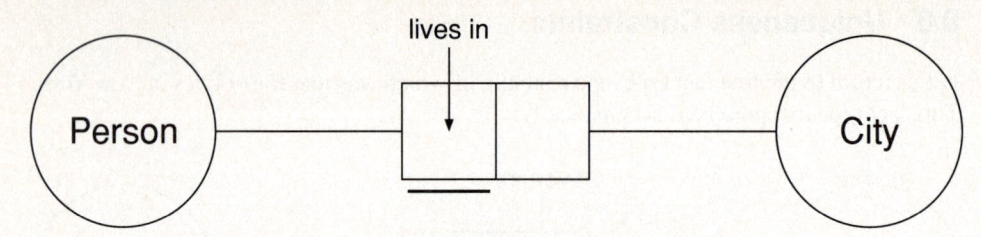

We can now move on to the second question that we ask of ourselves.

Q2. Is **any** city the residence of **more than one** person?

This time, assuming our data is reliable, the answer is YES; two people whom we know live in New York. This means that the `is the residence of` role is unconstrained and so we leave the corresponding role box unmarked.

In summary, to find out whether there are any uniqueness constraints in a fact type, we take the entity types and each role and form these into an "Is **any** _____ _____ **more than one** _____ ?" sentence framework. If the answer to any question posed this way is NO then there is a uniqueness constraint on the role.

Let us now try this technique with the fact type relating people and jobs. The sample data was as follows, and it too is assumed to be significant.

```
WorksAs
--------------------
Person    Job
--------------------
Harry     stockbroker
Bruce     actor
John      waiter
Sue       welder
Angus     welder
--------------------
```

The two questions and their answers are:

Q1. Does any person work at more than one job?

The answer is NO; so there is a uniqueness constraint on the `work at` role.

Q2. Is any job (type) worked at by more than one person?

The answer is YES; there are two welders.

So the fact type has a uniqueness constraint placed over the `works as` role box.

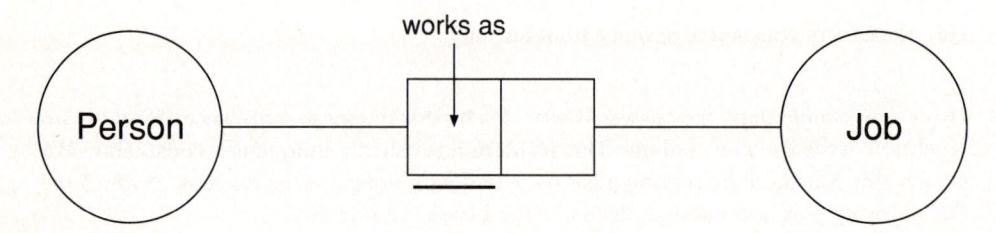

```
      works as
 ┌──────┐    ┌──┬──┐    ┌──────┐
 │Person│────┤▼ │  ├────│ Job  │
 └──────┘    └──┴──┘    └──────┘
```

Next we can examine the facts we have about people and sports.

```
PlaysAt
-----------------
Person   Sport
-----------------
Harry    squash
Bruce    tennis
Bruce    golf
Harry    football
Angus    football
-----------------
```

The two questions are as follows:

Q1. Does any person play at more than one sport?

>The answer is YES. Harry plays football and squash.

Q2. Is any sport played by more than one person?

>YES, both Harry and Angus play football.

The answer was YES to both questions and so there no uniqueness constraint associated with any individual role in this fact type. The pairing of a person with a sport is unrestricted. But *the combination* will be unique; we do not expect to see the same *row* twice and so we can say that there is a uniqueness constraint across the roles in conjunction. So we place a bar alongside *both* role boxes.

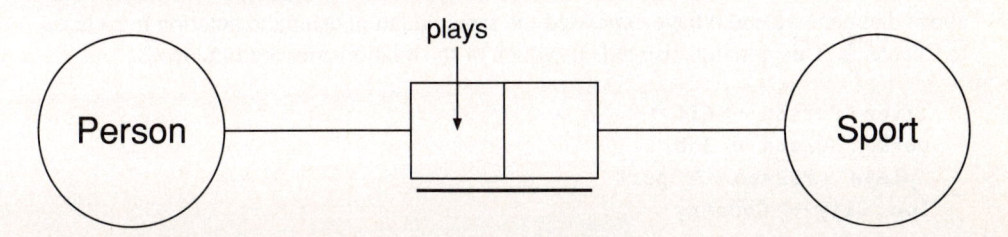

8.7 Single and Many-valued Fact Types

We saw, in Section 8.5, that we cannot mix single-valued facts about people, such as the city they live in, with many-valued facts about people, such as the sports they play. If we do mix them then redundancy can arise. How do we quickly decide whether a fact type is single or many-valued? If we examine the conceptual schema so far, the answer should become evident: see Figure 8.4.

We can tell at a glance that:

>a person lives in *one* city;

>a person works at *one* job;

>but a person may play *many* sports.

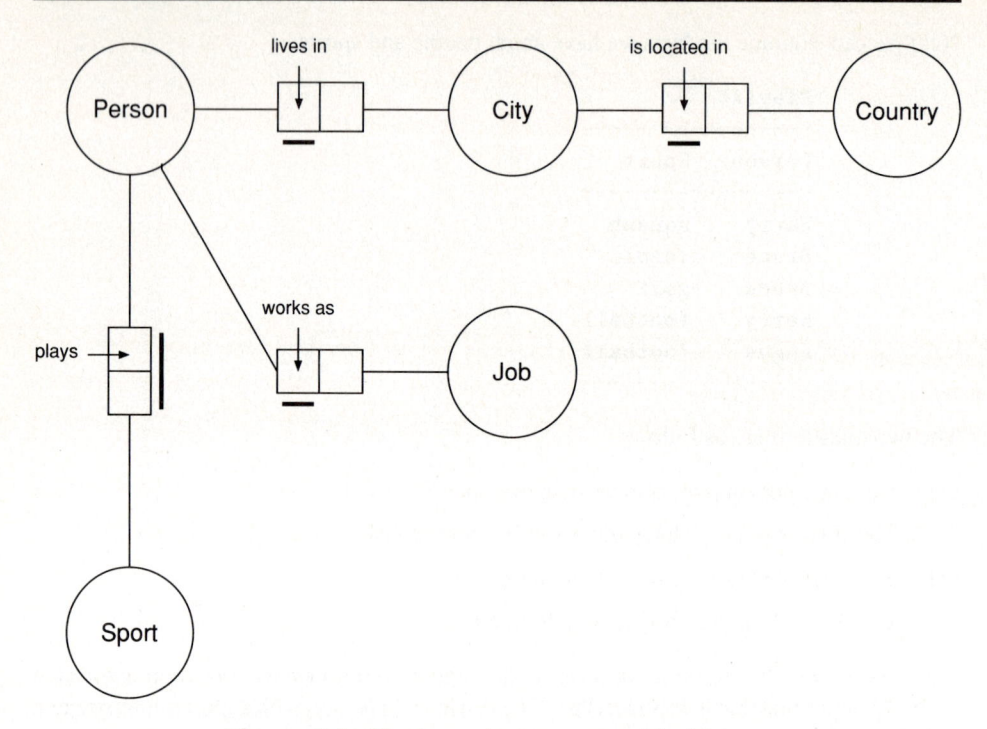

Figure 8.4 Single and many-valued fact types

The diagram allows us to easily decide which fact types may be **aggregated**. Instead of the above diagram, we could have expressed the same situation using the notation introduced in Chapter 2. This notation also tells us which of the relationships are functions.

```
lives : Person +> City
works : Person +> Job
_plays_ : Person <-> Sport
loc : City +> Country
```

We can tell from these declarations that `lives` and `works` may be merged. They are both functions, that is, they are both single-valued facts about the `Person` entity type. If we already have a notation for describing these ideas, why do we need another? The difference is between a verbal notation and a visual one. With the verbal notation, we must scan the relationships and decide for ourselves what facts may be merged. The conceptual schema diagram, in contrast, helps to show that three of the facts apply to one entity type *because three arcs lead off the Person entity*. What the graphical notation allows us to do is to show the *connectivity* of the situation being modeled. If we try to write a single verbal description of Harry, that is, if we write one sentence about him, we might write something like this:

> Harry plays squash and football; he works as a stockbroker and lives in New York which is in the USA.

Because the sentence is a one-dimensional stream we are obliged to use pronouns to point back to previously introduced objects. The "he" refers to Harry and the "which" to New York. In a graphical representation, pointers are not required; we can directly connect the objects.

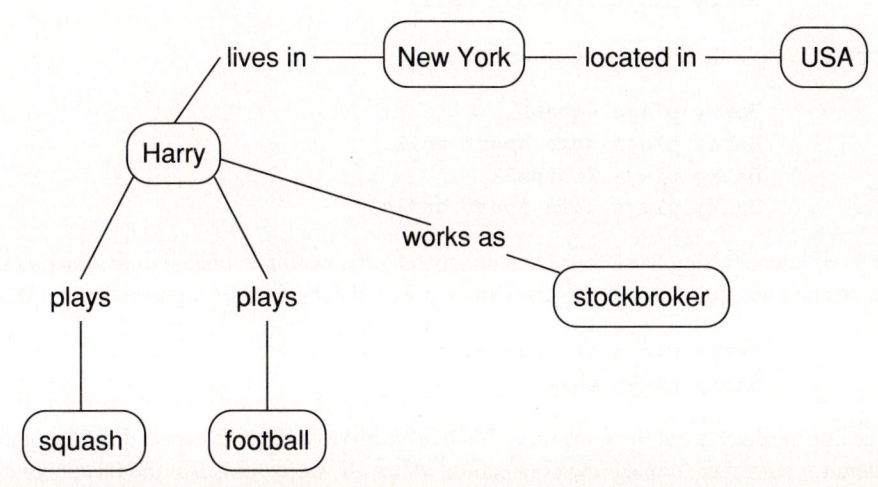

```
                  lives in ─── New York ─── located in ─── USA
                 ╱
            Harry
           ╱    ╲   ╲
          ╱      ╲    works as
         ╱        ╲         ╲
      plays      plays       stockbroker
        │          │
      squash    football
```

A conceptual schema diagram merely tries to generalize these connections to express something about the entire UoD rather than about a few individuals. It helps establish the universe of discourse by allowing us to state the kinds of things that are to be found there, whether they are connected and the nature of these connections. And it is the nature of these connections that provides us with a design for our database. The diagram is a very useful aid to database design. After that task has been done, we will no longer need the diagram. It will have served its purpose.

8.8 Irreducible Facts

So far, all the facts we have discussed have been *binary*. They involved just two entity types. It is quite common to have fact types that involve three, four, five or more entity types. Suppose that some knowledge of the sporting ability of these people is revealed to us. We are told this in sentences like the following.

        Harry plays squash well.

We can present all the information provided in tabular form.

```
    ------------------------------
    Person    Sport      Skill
    ------------------------------
    Harry     squash     well
    Harry     football   badly
    Bruce     tennis     well
    Bruce     golf       well
    Angus     football   badly
    ------------------------------
```

These facts are **irreducible**, which means that we cannot reduce them to simpler facts without some loss of information. For example, take the two facts involving Harry:

```
Harry plays squash well.
Harry plays football badly.
```

Suppose we split these facts as follows:

```
Harry plays squash.
Harry plays some sport well.
Harry plays football.
Harry plays some sport badly.
```

Someone encountering these four facts, independently, would be unable to reconstruct the two original sentences; and that is the situation with databases. Yet suppose the two facts:

```
Harry plays at squash.
Harry plays well.
```

come into the database at the same time. It would seem reasonable to expect the information system to remember to make the connection. After all, we would. But the facts may end up in separate rows of a table or even in separate tables; and there will be other similar facts about Harry.

The only way that we can make the information system remember to make the connection is for it to retain the connection. And that means simply keeping the fact as one sentence:

```
Harry plays squash well.
```

We can represent this three-part fact type diagrammatically: see Figure 8.5. Rather than attempting to provide three different roles, it is simpler merely to show the outline of the fact.

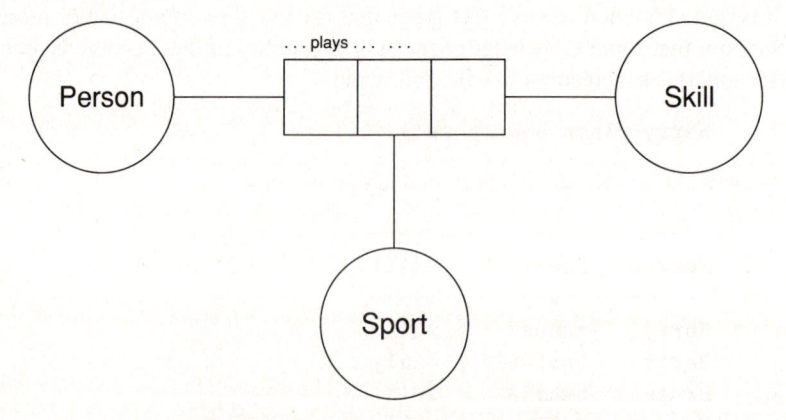

Figure 8.5 An irreducible fact type

8.9 Nested Fact Types

The new fact type just introduced may not be merged with any of the other fact types discussed so far. Can it ever be merged? To answer that question, we must first find out whether there are any uniqueness constraints to be applied. There is such a constraint because, at least judging from the sample data provided, each person plays a particular sport with *just one* skill level: see Figure 8.6.

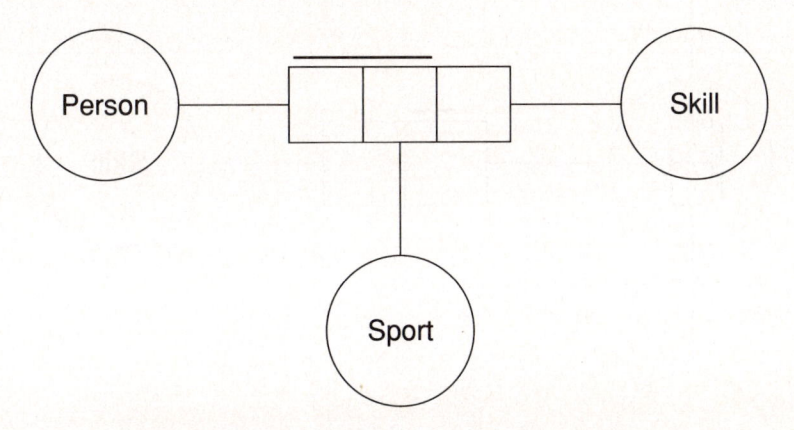

Figure 8.6 A uniqueness constraint on two roles

The uniqueness constraint bar is drawn across the role boxes attached to both the **Person** and the **Sport** entity types. This is consistent with the table where no two rows have the same `Person + Sport` combination.

Another interpretation of this uniqueness constraint is to think of the fact as a single-valued fact about a person's sporting abilities with regard to his or her playing of some given sport. It is not surprising that the skill levels are expressed in terms of adverbs ("well", "badly") because the sentence is about the ability with which an individual **plays** a particular sport. It is a fact about a fact. To emphasize this, we can redraw the three-part fact type as a **nested** fact: see Figure 8.7. This nested form helps to emphasize that the skill level is a fact about the playing of a sport. The relationship is said to be **objectified**; a fact has been turned into an object. The fact type has been turned into a composite entity type, with an entity circle (or ellipse) enclosing the role boxes that symbolize the relationship.

We can extend the diagram (see Figure 8.8) to incorporate any other single-valued facts about the playing of sports. These could include the following.

- We may wish to record the club at which a person currently plays some given sport. The word "currently" is a common way of making a fact single-valued.
- We may also wish to record the year in which they took up a sport. To discuss when someone *first* (or *last*) did something is another common way of making a fact single-valued.

Now we have three single-valued facts about a composite entity type. However, the aggregation rule still applies. These three facts may be combined into the one table without fear of redundancy. The table might look like this:

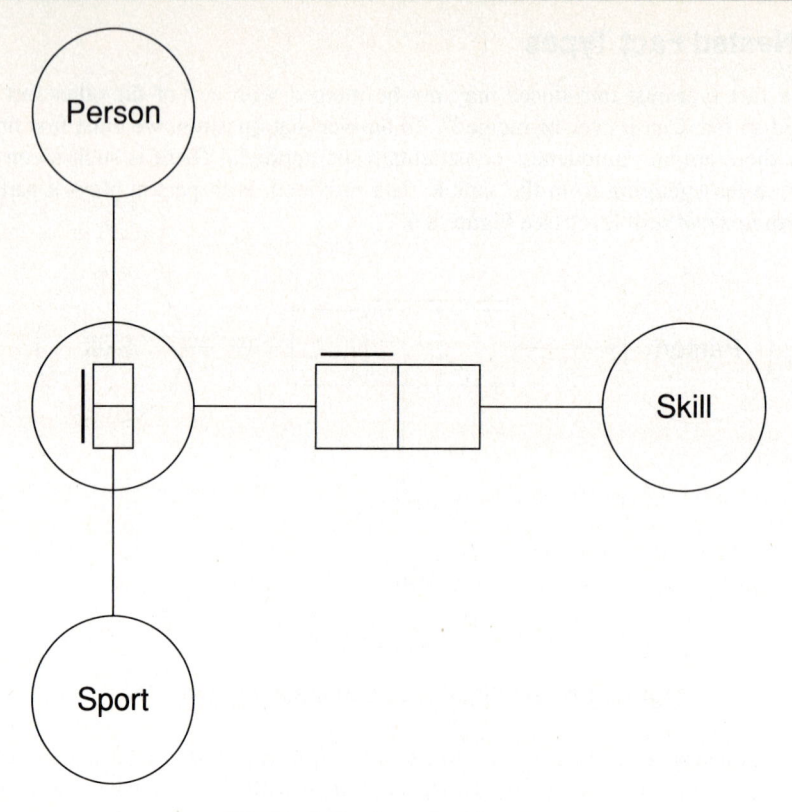

Figure 8.7 A nested fact type

```
Plays
------------------------------------------------
PersonName   Sport      Skill   Club     TakeUpYear
------------------------------------------------
Harry        squash     well    Hibs     1991
Harry        football   badly   Hibs     1991
Bruce        tennis     well    Squibs   1985
Bruce        golf       well    Hibs     1991
Angus        football   badly   Squibs   1995
------------------------------------------------
```

Note that the table incorporates the original fact concerning people and the sports they play.

8.10 Aggregation

Before discussing the process of turning a conceptual schema into a relational database schema, we will introduce one final fact type. Suppose we want to record which languages these people speak.

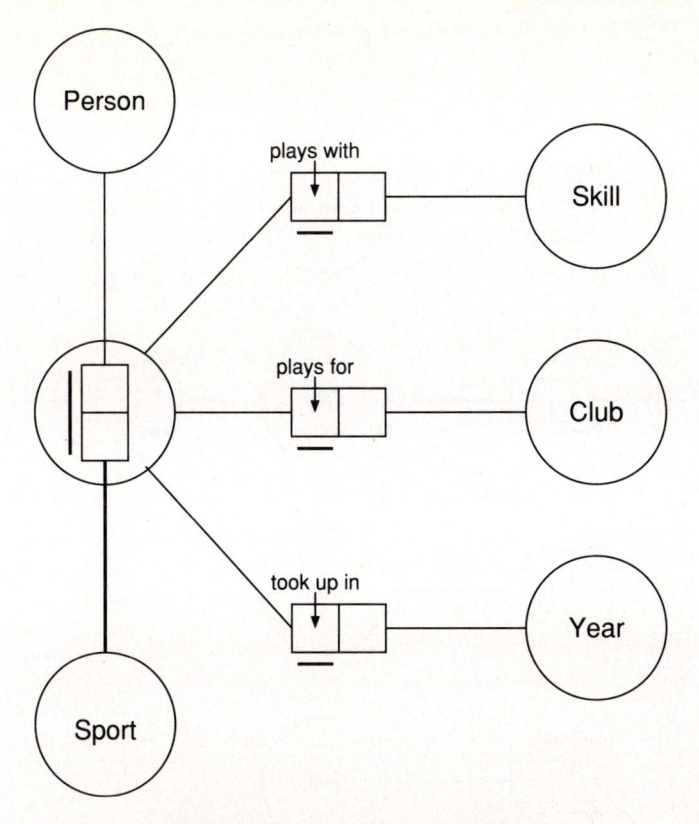

Figure 8.8 Multiple nested facts

```
Speaks
------------------
Person   Language
------------------
Harry    Spanish
Harry    Japanese
Harry    German
John     Spanish
Sue      German
Angus    English
Angus    Gaelic
------------------
```

A person may speak many languages and a language may be spoken by many people; thus it is a many-to-many relationship and is incorporated into the final conceptual schema diagram which is shown in Figure 8.9.

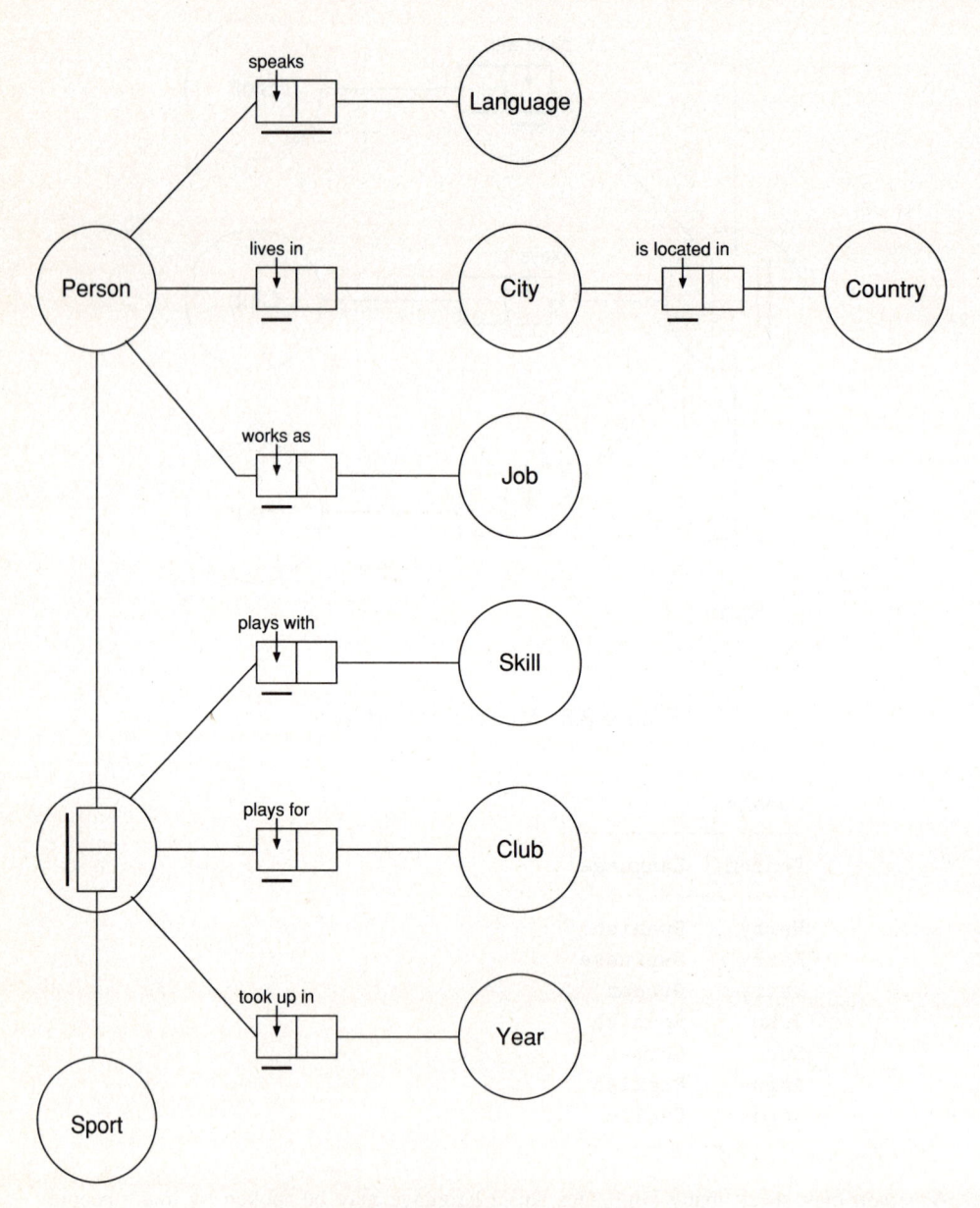

Figure 8.9 The final conceptual schema

8.10.1 Determinants

The conceptual schema indicates the following.

- We can safely merge "`lives in`" and "`works as`" because they are both single-valued facts about the same entity type.
- We can safely merge the "`plays with`", "`plays for`" and "`took up in`" fact types because they are all single-valued facts about the same complex entity type.
- We must leave the "`speaks`" relationship in a table of its own; it is many-to-many and these may never be merged.
- We must also leave the "`is located in`" fact in a table of its own; but only because there is no other single-valued fact about cities with which it may be merged.

Determinants

Wherever an entity type appears in a conceptual schema diagram *and* it is connected to a role box against which there is a uniqueness constraint, then the associated relationship is a single-valued fact about that entity type. The entity type is said to be a **determinant**.

A single conceptual schema diagram is to be replaced by a collection of relations. Each relation corresponds to a particular fragment of the diagram. Yet, whereas the original diagram represents a *universe* of discourse, the fragments are not self-contained. They are interrelated, and it is the determinants that are connected. We must make sure that the database *symbolically* represents the connections that are shown *graphically* in the diagram. The process of merging is called **aggregation** which means a "flocking" or coming together. The conceptual schema diagram will be divided into a number of disjoint segments. An aggregate data object or record type will be defined for each of these segments. The following table shows how the conceptual schema is divided.

Nr	Determinant	Entity type(s)	Fact type(s)
1.	Person	Person	lives in works as
2.	City	City	is located in
3.	Plays	Person + Sport	plays with plays for took up in
4.	Speaks	Person + Language	-

Where the determinant involves only one entity type, it is named after that entity type. Where more than one is involved then the determinant is named after the relationship. Strictly speaking, the `Speaks` determinant is not really a determinant at all; it determines nothing. But as far as the process of deriving record types is concerned, it may be treated as one. So there are four record types to be extracted from this particular conceptual schema.

8.10.2 Record Types

We will use a **record type table** to show the development of a record type and its relationship to other record types and other restrictions to be placed upon records of any given type. This is shown by example for the `Person` record type:

	Person Record Type		
Fact	Key?	Attribute	References?
	(*)	PersonName	
lives in		CityName	City Record
works as		WorksAs	

The four columns are used in the following ways:

- The **Fact** column allows us to identify the associated fact in some way.
- The **Key?** column allows us to express two things:

  (*) signifies that the corresponding attribute is (part of) the relation key of relations built upon this record type.

  (?) indicates that, in any instance of this type, the attribute may be null.

  For the `PersonRecord` type we can see that the key is the `PersonName` attribute, and that the `CityName` and `WorksAs` attributes may be null.

- The **Attributes** column merely lists all the attributes of the record type.
- The **References?** column allows to say whether there should be referential integrity between this attribute and the key of some other record type. We can see that the `CityName` attribute depends on the existence of some parent record type which contains information specifically regarding cities.

8.10.3 Attribute Naming

Here are three rules for naming attributes. The naming is done from the viewpoint of one particular record type. The process is repeated for the others.

N1 Key attributes arise from the determinant that is the basis for this record type.

   1.1 Each such attribute may be named by taking the name of the associated entity type and appending the manner of its representation. So for the key of the `Person` record type, we have an attribute:

   `PersonName` which has the form:

   `Entity RepresentationManner`

   1.2 Alternatively, we may simply want to suggest that this attribute somehow identifies a particular entity type and append the letters "**Id**" to the entity name to form, for example:

          `PersonId`

   1.3 Or, we may simply use the entity type name, for example:

          `Person`

N2 Non-key attributes may be divided into two categories:

   2.1 There are those that provide a link to some other determinant. It is desirable that all determinants (or their components) are named in a consistent way, wherever they appear in the database. It makes joining tables less error-prone. Thus the attribute that corresponds to the "`lives in`" fact should be named according to rule **N1**, for example: `CityName`.

   2.2 Other non-key attributes may be named using any one of the following rules.

       2.2.1 Use the role that most naturally characterises the information provided. Thus the job that the person does may be named the `WorksAs` attribute.

       2.2.2 If the corresponding fact is the only one that links this record's determinant to the other entity involved, then we might use the entity name itself. As `works as` is the only fact that links a person to a job, we might name the attribute `Job`.

       2.2.3 As a variation on the previous rule, we might prefix the entity by the determinant name. Thus, for `works as` we might name the attribute `PersonJob`.

       2.2.4 There may be some well-established name that it would be silly to ignore, such as `Father` or `Mother`.

N3 Once you have established your own naming conventions then *try* to stick with them. However, if application of any rule leads to an ungainly, ugly or misleading name, then construct one of your own.

8.10.4 Looking for Nulls

Every instance of a `PersonRecord` consists of three components or attributes. But can every slot be filled? In using a record structure for people we are effectively forcing everyone into the same mold. We anticipate keeping the same two facts about everybody – everybody's city of residence and everybody's job. But what if somebody doesn't have a job, or we don't know where he or she lives?

    The problem is overcome by permitting a special **null** value for the `WorksAs` attribute for that person. What other attributes should be allowed to be null? To help answer that question, we can immediately divide the record's attributes into two disjoint (non-overlapping) sets.

1. There are the key attributes; those that correspond to the entity type or types around which the aggregation occurred. In the case of the `PersonRecord` there is only one key attribute – `PersonName`. These attributes form the key of the relation that will be founded upon this record type. The **entity integrity** rule states that *none* of these particular attributes may ever be null because otherwise we would be unable to identify properly the entity involved.

2. There are the non-key attributes, each of which is a fact about the entity identified by the key attributes. For the `PersonRecord` type the non-key attributes are `CityName` and `WorksAs`. For each of these attributes we must perform some additional analysis. This we will do next.

To determine whether or not a given attribute may ever be null, we must return to the fact type that was its basis. For the `CityName` attribute, we return to the `lives in` fact type and ask two questions: see Figure 8.10.

```
Will EVERY person live          ── no ──▶   Nulls ARE
in SOME city?                                allowed.
         │
        yes
         ▼
Will we ALWAYS KNOW in          ── no ──▶   Nulls ARE
which city a person lives?                   allowed.
         │
        yes
         ▼
Nulls are NOT
allowed.
```

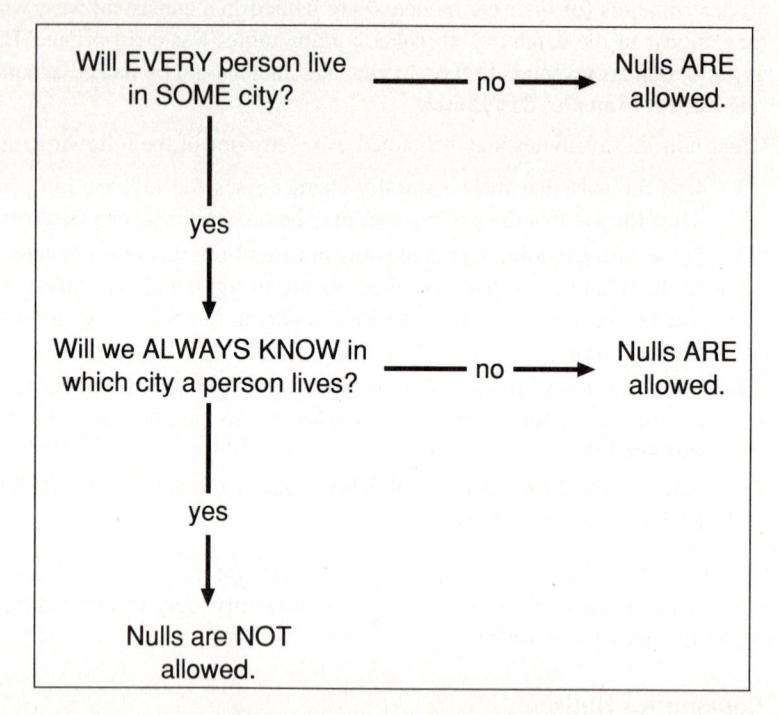

Figure 8.10 Looking for nulls

The questions are intended to be asked with a "for the duration of the database" time frame in mind, not just for the specific facts at hand.

Two questions are involved in the decision because there are two distinct reasons why a null may be required.

1. *Not applicable*

   It may be that the fact is simply not applicable to the entity involved. If a person is out of work then we have no job to record. Or, if a person is unmarried we can't record his or her spouse.

   The first question: "Will **every** person live in **some** city?" is designed to handle this kind of null.

2. *Don't know*

   It may be that the information is not known. And yet we may wish to retain knowledge of the entity and of other facts relating to that entity. A shopper does not ignore a potentially interesting purchase just because he or she does not yet know how much it will cost.

The second question: "Must we **always know** in which city a person lives?" is designed to handle this kind of null.

Suppose that we wished to continue recording people even if we have lost track of their whereabouts or if they are out of a job. Then nulls should be allowed for the corresponding attributes. Our final record type will be as follows:

Person Record Type

Fact	Key?	Attribute	References?
lives in works as	(*) (?) (?)	PersonName CityName WorksAs	City Record

We perform this analysis of null values for all record types that result from the aggregation of *one or more* single-valued facts. This means that we must also look at the record type created from the `is located in` fact type. It seems reasonable to suggest that:

YES, every city is located in some country; and

YES, we will always know that country.

In other words nulls are not to be allowed. So the record type can be introduced as follows.

City Record Type

Fact	Key?	Attribute	References?
is located in	(*)	CityName Location	

The third record type is the `Plays` record type.

Plays Record Type

Fact	Key?	Attribute	References?
plays with plays for took up in	(*) (*)	PersonName SportName SkillLevel Club TakeUpYear	Person Record

194   Chapter 8

The analysis for the allowability of null values proceeds as before.

```
Key        PersonName, SportName
Non-key    SkillLevel, Club, TakeUpYear
```

The key attributes represent the (complex) entity type about which each non-key attribute is a single-valued fact. The key attributes should not be null. Looking at the first of the non-key attributes, we apply the same two questions as before; see Figure 8.11.

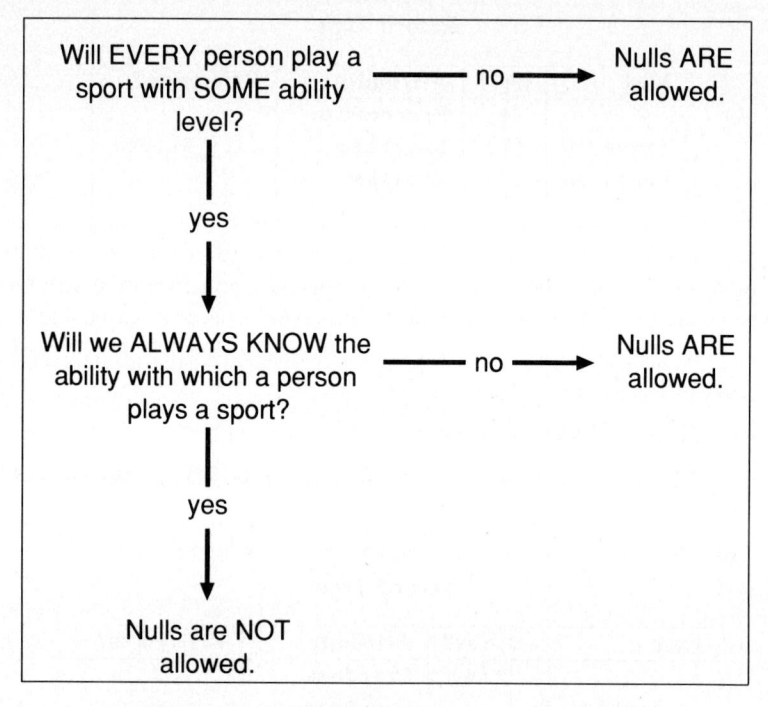

Figure 8.11   Looking at a nested facts for nulls

Everybody who plays a sport must play at some level or another, but we might not know that level. So we should answer YES to the first question and NO to the second. Therefore nulls *should* be allowed.

We might analyze the other two fact types in the following way:

YES, we will always know for which club a person plays.

NO, we will sometimes not know in which year a person took up a sport.

Thus, we will have a record with the following structure.

Facts and Relations   195

		Plays Record Type	
Fact	Key?	Attribute	References?
	(*)	PersonName	Person Record
	(*)	SportName	
plays with	(?)	SkillLevel	
plays for		Club	
took up in	(?)	TakeUpYear	

Any other record types are ones that do not result from the aggregation of fact types. For these records, nulls are never allowed for any attribute. The fourth and final record type in case under consideration is in this category. It is based upon the **speaks** fact type, which is a many-to-many relationship. It causes the construction of a record type based upon *all* of the entity types involved (in this case two).

		Speaks Record Type	
Fact	Key?	Attribute	References?
	(*)	PersonName	Person Record
	(*)	Language	

The decision not to allow *any* null values may seem rather arbitrary, but it more useful to think of **speaks** not as a many-to-many fact type but as a more complex entity type. And this new entity type corresponds to the speaking of a language by a person. It is a complex entity about which we have *no* single-valued facts, and so there are no non-key attributes and consequently there are no nulls to be considered.

8.11 Establishing the Database

We have now established four different types of records and we may now introduce them formally.

```
┌─ PersonRecord ─────────────────────────────────
│  PersonName : Person
│  CityName : City
│  WorksAs : Job | null
└────────────────────────────────────────────────


┌─ CityRecord ───────────────────────────────────
│  CityName : City
│  Location : Country
└────────────────────────────────────────────────
```

```
┌─ PlaysRecord ─────────────────────────────────────────┐
│ PersonName : Person                                    │
│ SportName : Sport                                      │
│ SkillLevel : Skill | null                              │
│ Club : Club                                            │
│ TakeUpYear : Year | null                               │
└────────────────────────────────────────────────────────┘

┌─ SpeaksRecord ────────────────────────────────────────┐
│ PersonName : Person                                    │
│ Language : Language                                    │
└────────────────────────────────────────────────────────┘
```

If these were all that were required, we could now define a relational database based upon them.

```
┌─ Database ────────────────────────────────────────────┐
│ People : Set of PersonRecord                           │
│ Cities : Set of CityRecord                             │
│ Plays : Set of PlaysRecord                             │
│ Speaks : Set of SpeaksRecord                           │
└────────────────────────────────────────────────────────┘
```

Each relation would be a set based upon one of the record types. However, this definition is not enough; it does not mention some of the important constraints that must be enforced in order to make the database more accurately reflect the situation being represented. There are, in patricular, two very important restrictions on the kind of data that may be inserted into the database as a whole. These are as follows:

1. **Relation key constraints**

    There is nothing in the definition of, for example, the `People` relation to prevent there being two people with the same name. Yet it was decided earlier that people were to be identified by their names. We can specify this constraint by requiring that the number of records in the `People` relation be the same as the number of people (when identified by name).

    $$\texttt{count People} = \texttt{count } \{\texttt{p : People} \bullet \texttt{p.PersonName}\}$$

    Similar constraints must be placed on the keys of the other two relations.

2. **Referential Integrity**

    It is reasonable to expect that anybody mentioned in a `PlaysRecord` should also appear in a `PersonRecord`. On accessing a `PlaysRecord`, we should be able to *refer* to the appropriate record in the `People` relation for more information. This will be true of everybody named in the `Plays` relation. We can express this constraint as follows:

    $$\{\texttt{p : Plays} \bullet \texttt{p.PersonName}\} \subseteq \{\texttt{p : People} \bullet \texttt{p.PersonName}\}$$

The people in `Plays` are a subset of those in `People`. This is sometimes called an **inclusion dependency**. There will be a similar relationship between the cities in `People` and those in `Cities`.

We may now extend our defintion of the database:

Database

People : Set of PersonRecord
Cities : Set of CityRecord
Plays : Set of PlaysRecord
Speaks : Set of SpeaksRecord

---

count People = count $\{p : \text{People} \bullet p.\text{PersonName}\}$
count Cities = count $\{c : \text{Cities} \bullet c.\text{CityName}\}$
count Plays = count $\{p : \text{Plays} \bullet (p.\text{PersonName}, s.\text{SportName})\}$
$\{p : \text{Plays} \bullet p.\text{PersonName}\} \subseteq \{p : \text{People} \bullet p.\text{PersonName}\}$
$\{p : \text{People} \bullet p.\text{CityName}\} \subseteq \{c : \text{Cities} \bullet c.\text{CityName}\}$
$\{s : \text{Speaks} \bullet s.\text{PersonName}\} \subseteq \{p : \text{People} \bullet p.\text{PersonName}\}$

8.12 Summary

This chapter has been an introduction to fact-based analysis which is an approach to designing a database. The fact-based approach sees the database as a repository of simple irreducible facts regarding some situation. However, these facts are not stored haphazardly.

- All the facts of a similar nature are stored together, forming what is termed a **fact type**.
- A fact type, as a rule, is not stored separately; rather, it will be grouped or merged with other fact types into data structures called **relations**.

Certain problems arise.

- What is the basis for the merging? Exactly what fact types may be merged? The early sections of the chapter demonstrated that we should not arbitrarily group facts into relations. Certain rules exist regarding what may be merged. Conceptual schema diagrams were introduced to help us follow these rules.
- Having decided to merge individual facts into record structures, we will inevitably be faced with the problem of missing or null values. A record is a group of values and the circumstances surrounding its creation may be such that we cannot supply all the data required.
- And there is also the problem of deciding what exactly *is* an irreducible fact? How do we know when a fact may be split without loss of information? Certainly, when the fact is binary, that is, when it relates just two specific objects, then it is not splittable. But there may be more complex facts, that is, ones involving three or more objects; and it may be that these should not be split either. We must rely on our analytical skills.

Exercises

▶ Q8.1   The Pig Intelligence Experiment

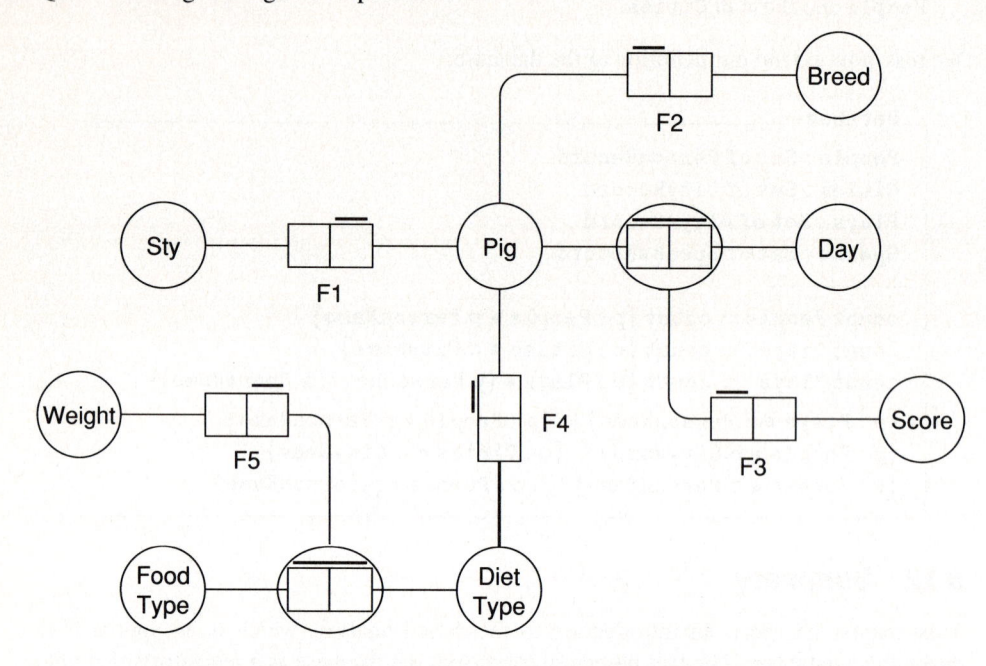

A veterinary institute is carrying out some investigations into the effect of diet on pigs, with the work being funded by a research grunt, of course. The results are to be recorded in a database, and a conceptual schema has been designed. Examples of the facts recorded on this schema are:

> F1: The pig "Black Beauty" is in sty number 8.
>
> F2: Black Beauty is of the Saddleback breed.
>
> F3: On March 21, 1995, Black Beauty scored 118.
>
> F4: Black Beauty is on a Multi-grain diet.
>
> F5: In a Multi-grain diet, the daily allowance of caraway seeds is 50 gms.

From inspection of the conceptual schema, decide which of the following statements are true and which are not. Explain your answer.

a. A pig is on only one kind of diet.

b. Every pig is in a different sty.

c. A pig may have its score recorded several times a day.

d. A given type of food may be in only one type of diet.

e. A given pig may, for example, receive 50 gms of caraway seeds one day and 100gms the next.

Facts and Relations 199

▶ Q8.2 From the conceptual schema given in the previous question:

  a. Decide which facts may be aggregated, and develop a complete set of record types.

  b. Based on these record types, what questions need to be asked regarding null values?

  c. Formally define each record type, and based upon these, formally define the database.

▶ Q8.3 The CLUB Model

The following entity types are involved in a computer club.

Type	Current Instances of the Type
[Member]	{ Bill, Sue, Alan }
[Language]	{ COBOL, Pascal, C, Ada, SQL, Modula, FORTRAN }
[Carmake]	{ BMW, Ford, GM, Honda, Mazda, Mercedes, Toyota }
[N]	{ 0, 1, 2, 3, ... }

There are also four relationships between these types:

1. **likes** which indicates whether one member likes another;
2. **writes** which indicates which languages each member can write;
3. **age** which says how old each member is;
4. **drives** which indicates the make of car driven by those members who do.

The current states of each of these relationships are tabulated below.

```
likes                writes              age              drives
---------------      ----------------    ----------       ----------------
Member  Member       Member  Language    Member   N       Member   CarMake
---------------      ----------------    ----------       ----------------
Bill    Sue          Bill    FORTRAN     Bill     19      Sue      Honda
Bill    Alan         Sue     C           Sue      19      Bill     Ford
Sue     Alan         Sue     SQL         Alan     16      ----------------
Alan    Bill         Alan    FORTRAN     ----------
---------------      Bill    SQL
                     ----------------
```

For **each** of the four relationships:

  a. Write one sample fact of the type represented by the relationship. Rewrite the fact in the reverse order. In this way, the roles played by each entity type should be seen.

  b. Draw a conceptual schema diagram representing just this fact type. Show each role.

Chapter 8

c. Assuming the data in the associated table *is* significant, add any uniqueness constraints that apply.

▶ Q8.4 Use the conceptual schema diagrams that you developed in answering the previous question to respond to the following.

a. Connect the diagrams into a single conceptual schema.
b. Which fact types may be merged?
c. Using the data supplied, show the contents of the table or tables that result from the merging.

▶ Q8.5 The KIDS Model

The following entity types are involved in modeling the children in a family.

Type	Current Instances of the Type
[Kid]	{ Kylie, Tim, Matthew, Emma }
[Gender]	{ f, m }
[Room]	{ sleepout, back, front }
[Sport]	{ tennis, hockey, golf }
[N]	{ 0, 1, 2, 3, ... }

There are also four relationships between these types:

1. **age** which says how old each child is;
2. **sex** which indicates which gender a child is;
3. **bedroom** which indicates the room in which a child sleeps;
4. **plays** which indicates which sports each child plays.

The current states of each of these relationships are tabulated below.

```
age                 sex                  bedroom              plays
-----------         ---------------      ---------------      ---------------
Kid         N       Kid       Gender     Kid       Room       Kid       Sport
-----------         ---------------      ---------------      ---------------
Kylie       14      Kylie       f        Tim       back       Kylie     tennis
Tim         12      Emma        f        Matthew   front      Kylie     hockey
Matthew     4       Matthew     m        ---------------      Tim       golf
Emma        8       ---------------                           Tim       hockey
-----------                                                   Emma      tennis
                                                              ---------------
```

For **each** of the four relationships:

a. Write one sample fact of the type represented by the relationship. Rewrite the fact in the reverse order to show the role played by the other entity type.

b. Draw a conceptual schema diagram representing the fact type. Show each role.

c. Assuming the data in the associated table *is* significant, add any uniqueness constraints that apply.

▶ Q8.6 Use the conceptual schema diagrams that were developed in the previous question to respond to the following.

a. Connect the diagrams into a single conceptual schema.

b. Which fact types may be merged?

c. Using the data supplied, show the contents of the table or tables that result from the merging.

d. For each table, and assuming the data supplied is significant, say which attributes of that table may be null.

▶ Q8.7 The PARLIAMENT Model

The following entity types are involved in modeling a state parliament.

Type   **Meaning**

[Poli]   All state representatives.
[Party]   Political parties, e.g. { Labor, Business, Green, ... }
[Dept]   Government bureaucracies, e.g. { Transport, Justice, ... }

There are four basic relationships between these types:

1. `belongs: Poli` —▷ `Party` which maps a politician to his or her party;

2. `minister: Dept` —▷ `Poli` which maps a government department to its minister;

3. `leader: Party` ▷—▷ `Poli` which indicates the politicans who are party leaders;

4. `_talksto_ Poli` ◁—▷ `Poli` which indicates which politicians talk and to whom.

Draw a conceptual schema for this model and construct record types based on your diagram.

Q8.8 The GEOGRAPHY Model

The following entity types are involved in modeling Australia.

[State, Town, River, PeopleCount]

The basic relationships between these types are as follows:

1. `loc: Town` —▷ `State` maps each town to the state in which it is located;

2. `pop: Town -> PeopleCount` indicates the population of each town;
3. `cap: State >-> Town` relates each state with its capital;
4. `_flowsthru_: River <-> State` shows which rivers flow through which states;
5. `source: River -> State` says in which state each river has its source;
6. `sink: River -> State` says in which state each river terminates.

Draw a conceptual schema for this model.

CHAPTER 9

Uncovering Facts

9.1 Introduction

Suppose we are required to design a database to support a new information system. In the preceding chapter some rules were formulated regarding which facts may and which may not be merged into relations. Once we have, in front of us, the kinds of facts that are to be stored in the database then it is a relatively mechanical process to follow these rules and to arrive at a design for the database.

Unfortunately, this information is rarely presented to us in a neatly packaged and labeled way. In other words, the basic facts types do not usually show themselves clearly and obviously. We, the designers, must identify them.

The people who are going to use this new system will want the computer to extract information from the database, to sort it, to merge it with other information, to summarize it, and so on. They are most unlikely to be interested in receiving long lists of quite trivial facts. They have sophisticated ideas of how the organization works and may want these ideas reflected in complex reports.

A report is simply a view of the organization. This chapter introduces a language that may be used to describe the structure of such views. From these descriptions, the underlying simple facts may be uncovered.

9.2 Defining Syntax

The **syntax** of a language is a set of rules that govern exactly what may be said in that language. This definition applies as much to programming languages as it does to any other kind.

The language to be presented in this chapter is a special language used to describe the syntax of programming languages. It is the language in which we write the rules of syntax. The syntax of SQL, for example, tells us that "`Select * From Students`" is legal SQL whereas "`From Students Select *`" is not. Syntax is concerned with the superficial order of words and symbols within a language rather than with what any statement in the language means. The syntax of SQL requires that the `select` clause appears before the `from` clause within a `select statement`. It will also say that both these clauses must appear and that the others (the `where`, the `group`, the `having` and the `order` clauses) are optional.

This syntax definition language is called **Extended Backus-Naur Form**. The original Backus-Naur Form was developed in order to describe the language **Algol 60**. It is named after two of the people involved in the original report of that language, John Backus and Peter Naur. The extensions were proposed by Nicklaus Wirth, the inventor of the Pascal programming language.

9.3 Analyzing a View

The view to be examined is one we all know. It is a telephone directory.

```
Smith J., 21 Bell St .................... 223 2240
Smith T.J., 8 Mutual Rd ................. 875 6827
Smith W., 59 Palmerston St .............. 388 9756
Speedie Deliveries, Hutton St ........... 339 1123
Spendthrift Savings Bank, High St ....... 987 1000
Stamp T., 35 Cliff St ................... 339 1234
Stamper R., 23 Bell St .................. 223 1119
StoneGround Flour Co., Mill Rd .......... 777 2121
Stonehouse A.P., 11 Hutton St ........... 339 5549
```

How can we describe the structure of this directory? Spend some time examining it.

All the entries are similar in some respects; and some are more similar than others. We can start by recognizing that there is a recurring number of entries, and define the directory as follows:

```
Directory ::= { Entry }
```

The curly brackets are used to indicate that any enclosed item or items repeat a number of times. The `::=` symbol is to be read as "is composed of". So the definition can be read as saying the following:

- "A directory is composed of a number of entries."

The use of curly brackets is borrowed from set notation. Another way of reading the definition would be to say that:

- "A directory is a set of entries."

Defined in this way, we have provided a description of the overall structure of the directory; the problem of defining the structure of the entries has been postponed. In this way, we solve one problem at a time in what is known as a **top-down** fashion. We have concentrated on the similarities in the directory rather than on the differences. Now it is time to look at the differences.

There seem to be, in general, two major kinds of entry. There are entries for private subscribers and there are ones for businesses. Now we can define an entry as follows:

```
Entry ::= [ Private | Business ]
```

This definition states that an entry is composed of either a private or a business entry. The square brackets `[ ]` are used to enclose a number of alternatives. The vertical bar `|` is used to separate these alternatives. We may specify as many alternatives as is required.

Now we continue the analysis by providing definitions of **Private** and **Business**. The latter is slightly simpler, so in good top-down style, we will tackle it first. Each business entry involves a business name, a street and a phone number. This may be defined in the following way:

```
Business ::= BusinessName + StreetName + PhoneNo
```

The plus sign is used to concatenate two components of the structure being defined. It should be read as "followed by". So the above definition says that a business entry is composed of a business name followed by a street name followed by a phone number.

The next stage is to examine each of the components **BusinessName**, **StreetName** and **PhoneNo**. If any of them has an internal structure that interests us then that component will require its own definition as a structure. If there can be no useful subdivision then the component is called a data element. All three of these components are of this elementary kind.

When we reach a data element then this is as far as the analysis need proceed *on this path*. Now we retrace our steps until we arrive back at a structure that has not yet been defined. In this example, we return to the **Private** component and examine it.

Each private subscriber is given a name, an address and a phone number, so it can be defined as follows.

```
Private ::= Name + Address + PhoneNo
```

The **PhoneNo** is a data element as we have already discussed. What about the **Name**? Are we interested in parts of the name? We probably are. If we are looking for Jim Smith then the initial letters will help us locate him. Are we interested in individual initial letters? Again the answer is that we probably are. If we can't find Jim under **Smith J.** then we might try **Smith A.J.** and so on.

So the definition of name could be:

```
Name ::= Surname + { Initial }
```

A name consists of a surname followed by a set of initial letters.

Finally, what about the address? Are we interested in components of the address? We probably *do* want to know the street number, so the definition could be:

```
Address ::= StreetNo + StreetName
```

These two components are unlikely to need further dissection. So now we have completely analyzed the directory. The final set of definitions is as follows:

```
Directory ::= { Entry }
Entry     ::= [ Private | Business ]
Business  ::= BusinessName + StreetName + PhoneNo
Private   ::= Name + Address + PhoneNo
Name      ::= Surname + { Initial }
Address   ::= StreetNo + StreetName
```

Everything we have named is either a data structure or a data element and every structure has its definition.

9.4 Another Analysis

There will be many ways of correctly describing the structure of the directory. There is not just one valid analysis. It is a matter of individual judgement and style. We will briefly examine the directory in another way.

It is possible to look at the directory and decide that "yes, it does consist of a number of entries", just as we did before.

```
Directory ::= { Entry }
```

But this time, rather than having two main styles of entry, we may feel that there is a single style; one that varies slightly at the beginning.

```
Entry ::= [ BusinessName | PrivateName ] + Address + PhoneNo
```

We have decided that the variation in each entry is determined by whether it starts with a business name or with an individual's name. After that, each entry is essentially the same, consisting of an address and a phone number.

The business name is elementary. The individual name might be analyzed as before:

```
PrivateName ::= Surname + { Initial }
```

This time we define the address as:

```
Address ::= ( StreetNo ) + StreetName
```

The round brackets ( ) are used to enclose an optional component. This definition states that an address consists of a street name optionally preceded by a street number. Perhaps we didn't notice that only private subscribers have a street number. Perhaps we thought that it was unimportant. Maybe we wanted to retain flexibility.

We end up with a quite different analysis.

```
Directory   ::= { Entry }
Entry       ::= [ BusinessName | PrivateName ] + Address + PhoneNo
PrivateName ::= Surname + { Initial }
Address     ::= ( StreetNo ) + StreetName
```

9.5 A Summary of the Notation

Here is a table showing the extent of the notation:

Symbol	Description
`::=`	Use like an assignment symbol. It allows a name to be assigned to a structure.
`...+...`	Use a plus sign to link one component of the structure to the one that follows it.
`{...}`	Curly brackets are used to enclose a component of the structure that may occur zero or more times.
`[...]`	Square brackets are used to enclose alternative components.
`...|...`	A vertical bar is used to separate alternatives. It is used within square brackets.
`(...)`	Round brackets are used to enclose an optional component.
`"..."`	Quotation signs may be used to enclose a constant value of some kind, for example, `"male"`.

9.6 Some More Examples

Here are three views to be analyzed. Each is a particular picture of our friends and acquaintances. Of course, we don't use computers to keep track of people this way; however, the reports *are* like the ones produced by information systems.

1. The Green-Eyed Monster Report

    We are puzzled as to how all our friends can go on holiday to exotic locations while we have to stay at home.

    ```
    The Green-Eyed Monster Report
    -------------------------------------------------
    Name    Job        Earns      Holiday
                                  Year    Place

    Sue     lecturer   peanuts    1986    Bali
                                  1984    Monte Carlo
                                  1985    Acapulco

    Bill    plumber    heaps      1985    Cairns
                                  1982    Rio

    Doug    doctor     heaps      1988    China
                                  1987    France
    -------------------------------------------------
    ```

A definition of the structure of this report might be the following.

$$\texttt{GreenEyedMonster ::= \{ Name + Job + Earnings + \{ Year + Place \} \}}$$

The view contains an entry for each friend; and for each one we give their name, job, the earning capacity of that job. Finally, for each friend, we detail their recent holidays, in particular, when and where they went.

2. The Hot Gossip Report

We have a juicy piece of gossip and want to spread it around. We will ring people who live locally, but are too mean to ring long distance, so we need the address of anyone who lives at a distance.

```
The Hot Gossip Report
---------------------------------
Name    Contact

Ann     22 Strand Bvd, Copenhagen
Bill    391 1615
Sue     223 2555
Doug    3 Via Appia, Rome
---------------------------------
```

This view also has an entry for each friend (except those whom the gossip concerns, of course). Each entry consists of the friend's name followed by either their address or their phone number.

$$\texttt{HotGossip ::= \{ Name + [Address | Phone] \}}$$

It can be assumed from this definition that we are not interested in any further breakdown of the address; that is, it can be treated as if it is a data element.

3. The Match-making Report

We want to interfere in their private lives. What else are friends for?

```
The Match-making Report
---------------------------------------------
Name    Sex    Age    Interests

Bill    m      29     sport, travel
Sue     f      31     travel
Ian     m             music, art, photography
Ann     f      32     Ian
---------------------------------------------
```

This view lists each friend's name followed by their sex, which we know, followed by their age if we know it; and finally any spare time interests they might have.

$$\texttt{MatchMaking ::= \{ Name + Sex + (Age) + \{ Interest \} \}}$$

9.7 View Analysis

We have used the syntax definition language to specify the structure of each view. This is the first stage of a three-stage process that should help us to understand the user's world and to uncover the elementary types of fact that are used to build pictures of this world.

The process involves the following three stages.

1. Derive view structures

   Analyze all the various pictures or views of the user's world that we can obtain. Develop **view structures** for each of these views. Using our friends and acquaintances as our world, we derived three view structures.

   ```
   GreenEyedMonster ::= { Name + Job + Earnings
                          + { Year + Place } }
   HotGossip ::= { Name + [ Address | Phone ] }
   MatchMaking ::= { Name + Sex + (Age) + { Interest } }
   ```

2. Derive view relations

   In the next stage, each view structure is examined in turn. Any structure that contains repeating components is "flattened" out into a number of **view relations**. Any structure that contains alternative components is split into a number of separate view relations.

3. Extract elementary fact types

   In the third and final stage, each view relation that results from the previous stage is examined. Each view relation has a corresponding sentence. Sample sentences of that type are formed. This sentence may be reduced to two or more simpler sentences, without loss of information. Alternatively, it may be irreducible. Either way we are reducing our more complex sentences into a number of elementary sentences.

The outcome of this entire process is a set of elementary sentence or fact types. These are the basic sentences that are to be stored in the database. The next step is to use participation rates to determine which fact types may be merged and where.

9.8 Deriving View Relations

As discussed above, this second stage of the view analysis is a two-part process in which the possibly complex view structures are decomposed into a number of relatively simple view relations.

9.8.1 Flattening Structures

The first part of the process of simplifying view structures is to remove any repeating components. Two of the structures contain repetition.

```
GreenEyedMonster ::= { Name + Job + Earnings + { Year + Place } }
MatchMaking ::= { Name + Sex + (Age) + { Interest } }
```

The first structure repeats the year and place at which people went on holiday. The second one repeats any spare time interest the friend might have. The flattening can be done in two steps. We will perform these steps on the `GreenEyedMonster` structure first.

1. Identify the key component of the outermost level. The outermost level incorporates all the components not involved in the repetition. In this case, it involves the three components `Name`, `Job` and `Earnings`. Which of these three items of data can we use to distinguish one friend from another? Let us assume that the name alone is enough.

2. Split the structure into two separate ones by removing the repeating component entirely and forming a new structure consisting of the key in conjunction with this repeating component. The repeating component, in this case, is `{ Year + Place }`. The result of the split is as follows:

```
VR1 ::= { Name + Job + Earnings }
VR2 ::= { Name + Year + Place }
```

Each flat structure is called a view relation (VR) and as we define one, we can assign it a number for future reference.

Because a structure may contain repeating components that themselves contain repetition, these two steps may have to be performed a number of times until the original structure has been completely flattened.

The other view that contains repetition is the Match-making Report.

```
MatchMaking ::= { Name + Sex + (Age) + { Interest } }
```

Again the key component is the name. Splitting this structure gives these two view relations:

```
VR3 ::= { Name + Sex + (Age) }
VR4 ::= { Name + Interest }
```

9.8.2 Separating Alternatives

The second part of the process of simplifying view structures is to split any view that contains alternative components and to create a view relation for each alternative. There is only one example of this kind here:

```
HotGossip ::= { Name + [ Address | Phone ] }
```

This view is separated out to become:

```
VR5 ::= { Name + Address }
VR6 ::= { Name + Phone }
```

The outer level of the view, that is `Name`, is paired off with each of the alternative components of the view, `Address` and `Phone`.

9.8.3 Gather Them Together

Now we have a number of simple view relations derived from the original view structures.

```
VR1 ::= { Name + Job + Earnings }
VR2 ::= { Name + Year + Place }
```

```
VR3 ::= { Name + Sex + (Age) }
VR4 ::= { Name + Interest }
VR5 ::= { Name + Address }
VR6 ::= { Name + Phone }
```

9.9 Extracting Elementary Fact Types

Each view relation corresponds to a type of sentence. Many of these are capable of being reduced to simpler, more fundamental, sentence types. The final process involves examining each view relation to see if any further reduction can be performed.

There are two steps to this process.

1. Carefully construct a sample sentence based on the view relation. Use some of the data that was employed in forming the original view structure.
2. Examine that sentence to see if it can equally well be written as two or more simpler sentences.

Each sentence will either be decomposable, in which case we form the appropriate number of elementary fact types; or, alternatively, it will not be decomposable, in which case the view relation itself becomes one of the basic fact types.

We will now examine each view relation in turn.

```
VR1 ::= { Name + Job + Earnings }
```

A sample sentence is:

```
Sue is a lecturer; she earns peanuts.
```

We must examine this sentence and make sure that it says *exactly* what we mean it to say. In this case, which of the following sentences more accurately expresses its meaning?

```
(1) Sue is a lecturer, and as everybody knows, lecturers earn
peanuts.
(2) Sue is a lecturer who also happens to earn peanuts.
```

In other words, is Sue's earning capacity determined by her job or is it simply a fact about Sue? We will take the first of these alternatives as our choice. Therefore two separate fact types are embedded in the sentence:

```
Sue works as a lecturer.
Lecturers earn peanuts.
```

Now we can generalize these into two fact *types*. We decide what types of thing participate in the fact and we give a name to the relationship. For the first sentence, the entity types would be something like `Friend` and `Job`; the relationship might be called `works as a`. So this first sentence, in general, says that:

```
F1. Friend works as a Job.
```

The second sentence seems to involves jobs and the earning power of these jobs. It might be generalized into a fact type like this:

    `F2. Job earn EarningPower.`

`VR2 ::= { Name + Year + Place }`

A sentence of this type might be:

    `In 1986, Sue went on holiday to Bali.`

Examination of the original report in Section 9.6 suggests that people have only one holiday a year, at most. If this is the case, then this sentence is an irreducible fact type. So the complete view relation is one of the elementary fact types we are looking for. It becomes our next fact type:

    `F3. In Year, Friend went on holiday to Place.`

`VR3 ::= { Name + Sex + (Age) }`

A sample sentence of this type would be:

    `Bill, a male, is 29 years old.`

Obviously there are two basic sentences. A person's sex has no bearing on his or her age. Even if we did not pick this, a significant clue is given by the optionality of the age component. This is a clear signal that sex and age are separable.

    `F4. Friend is a Sex.`
    `F5. Friend is N years old.`

We will use the standard name `N` for the entity type consisting of the set of integers, as was done in Chapter 2.

`VR4 ::= { Name + Interest }`

This is a binary relation and consequently must be an elementary fact type. Here is an example:

    `Sue likes travel.`

In general, the fact type would be something like this:

    `F6. Friend likes Interest.`

`VR5 ::= { Name + Address }`

This is another binary relation, so no decomposition is possible. A sample fact could be:

    `Sue lives at 22 Strand Bvd, Copenhagen`

The corresponding fact type would be:

    `F7. Friend lives at Address.`

```
VR6 ::= { Name + Phone }
```
This is another binary relation. A sample fact could be:

```
Bill's phone number is 391 1615.
```

The fact type would be something like the following:

```
F8. Friend can be telephoned on N.
```

Summary: All the fact types can be written down together as follows:

```
F1. Friend works as a Job.
F2. Job earn EarningPower.
F3. In Year, Friend went on holiday to Place.
F4. Friend is a Sex.
F5. Friend is N years old.
F6. Friend likes Interest.
F7. Friend lives at Address.
F8. Friend can be telephoned on N.
```

All the views have now been converted into a number of elementary fact types. The next step is to find out how and where these facts can be merged. To do this, we need to look at the participation rates involved in each fact type. However, as we have no intention of ever keeping a database on our friends, we will stop this exercise now.

9.10 Further Abstraction

The Extended Backus-Naur Form (EBNF) language has been used to describe the *appearance* of views or reports. It has links, however, with other notations used in this book. In particular, it may be compared with the higher-order sets introduced in Chapter 3.

- The repetition construct {...} of EBNF corresponds to the power set operator. A view of the form:

    ```
    R ::= {A}
    ```

    can be "translated" into a declaration:

    R : Set of A

    For example, a series of people: `Kim, Ann, Bob, ...` is nothing more than a *set* of people.

- The concatenation construct ...+... of EBNF corresponds to the product set operator. A view of the form:

    ```
    R ::= A + B
    ```

    can be translated into a declaration:

    R : A × B

    For example, the sequence `Bob tennis` is nothing more than a *tuple* that pairs a person with a sport.

We may use this method of conversion to turn our description of views into declarations in our formal specification language.

Example 9.1 The Green-Eyed Monster Report
The definition of the structure of this report was:

```
GEM ::= { Name + Job + Earnings + { Year + Place } }
```

This may be turned into a formal declaration:

GEM : Set of (Person × Job × EarningPower × Set of (Year × Place))

```
The Green-Eyed Monster Report
-----------------------------------------------
Name    Job         Earns       Holiday
                                Year    Place

Sue     lecturer    peanuts     1986    Bali
                                1984    Monte Carlo
                                1985    Acapulco

Bill    plumber     heaps       1985    Cairns
                                1982    Rio

Doug    doctor      heaps       1988    China
                                1987    France
-----------------------------------------------
```

However, the **Person** (name) is the key of this (generalized) relation, and so there is a functional relationship between the key and the rest of the tuple. We may choose to define it as:

GEM : Person ⇸ Job × EarningPower × Set of (Year × Place))

The view may be regarded as a (rather large) function that maps each person to the kind of information on which we choose to base our prejudices about each person. The description is still clumsy, and we may prefer to declare it in the following way. First we declare two record types.

Holiday
Year : N
Destination : Place

GemInfo
WorksAs : Job
Earns : EarningPower
Holidays : Set of Holiday

The underlying nature of the **GEM** function may now be clearly revealed:

```
GEM : Person +-> GemInfo
```

Example 9.2 The Match-making Report
This view lists each friend's name followed by their sex, which we know, followed by their age if we know it; and finally any spare time interests they might have.

```
MM ::= { Name + Sex + (Age) + { Interest } }
```

If we look at the sample report, we can see that it is also a function.

```
The Match-making Report
-----------------------------------------
Name    Sex    Age    Interests

Bill    m      29     sport, travel
Sue     f      31     travel
Ian     m             music, art, photography
Ann     f      32     Ian
-----------------------------------------
```

We may declare it directly as:

```
MM : Person +-> Sex × (N|null) × Set of Interest)
```

Example 9.3 The Hot Gossip Report
This report provides two alternative pieces of information about each friend.

```
The Hot Gossip Report
---------------------------------
Name    Contact

Ann     22 Strand Bvd, Copenhagen
Bill    391 1615
Sue     223 2555
Doug    3 Via Appia, Rome
---------------------------------
```

It has the following structure:

```
HotGossip ::= { Name + [ Address | Phone ] }
```

This report is better seen as an amalgamation of two separate reports:

```
HG1 ::= { Name + Address }
HG2 ::= { Name + Phone }
```

Both of these are functions, and we may declare them as:

```
HG1 : Friend +-> Address
HG2 : Friend +-> Phone
```

9.11 Summary

Designing a relational database involves the following steps.

1. First of all, we must discover the basic kinds of information that are to be stored in the database.
2. Then we need to examine each type of fact to see what kind of relationship is involved. Is it a functional one? We can use the idea of uniqueness constraints.
3. Having determined the participation rates we can then merge certain of these fact types according to rules formulated in Chapter 8.

The second and third steps are relatively straightforward. The problems we encounter are usually met in the first of these steps.

The people for whom the database is being designed will not expect to and will probably be unable to tell us the basic kinds of facts that are to be stored in their database. They will present us with a number of complex overlapping pictures of their world. These pictures are the facts that *they* wish to store. *We*, the designers, need to break up these views into a much larger number of elementary pictures or fact types. From these we can develop a good design.

This chapter has looked at how we can perform this first step of user view analysis.

- We have looked at a language that we can use to place some order on each view. The language allows us to define the structure of the view.
- We have looked at how we can decompose these view structure definitions into simpler structures called view relations. From these flat relations we can extract the elementary fact types that are built into them.

Exercises

▶ Q9.1 The following advertisement is an extract from the latest issue of the computing magazine PC PLOD.

THE SOFTWARE SOFTIES

Here is a list of the cheapest software prices on the market!

Spreadsheet		**Integrated**	
Lotus 1–2–3	$500	PFS	$675
Multiplan	795	Framework	999
Quattro	250	Symphony	795

Languages		**Word Processing**	
Microsoft C	$100	Wordstar	$500
Turbo Pascal	125	Word Perfect	550
Turbo Prolog	125		

		Games	
		War	$70
		Chess	15
		Gato	45

Purchasers are entitled to free after-sales service from our acknowledged experts. For spreadsheet, word processing and integrated packages, ring **BILL BOARD** on 228 1165; for languages and games, ring **FRED HARDLY-EVERIN** on 223 5162.

!!! STOP PRESS !!!

We are offering discounts for a short while only, 10% off all spreadsheet and word processing software, 25% off all games.

There are three distinct views here; one giving prices, a second the support available and a third discounts.

a. Derive the structure of each view.

b. Derive view relations from these structures.

c. Extract the elementary fact types.

▶ Q9.2 A small library wants to keep track of books that are out on loan and to whom they are on loan. The librarian envisages needing two reports.

```
On Loan Report
-----------------------------------------------------
Patron     Patron            Item(s)       Due Date
Nr         Name              On Loan
-----------------------------------------------------
899        Bill Thompson     12099         13/08/91

151        John Smith        13678         21/08/91
                             54911         21/08/91
                             99887         23/08/91

755        Anne Davidson     22989         12/08/91
                             33244         27/08/89

234        John Smith        43559         9/08/89
-----------------------------------------------------


Loan Type Report
--------------------------------------------------------------------------
Title              Author(s)             Copy Nr    Item Nr    Loan Type
--------------------------------------------------------------------------
Autumn Leaves      Smith, Jones, Hale       1        45689      2 week
                                            2        76119      4 week

Spring Rolls       Edmond                   1        87112      4 week

Summer Sales       Walsh, Lee               1        26853      2 week

Winter Freeze      Frost, Hale, Snow        1        98789      4 week
                                            2        65456      4 week
                                            3        11223      1 week
--------------------------------------------------------------------------
```

    a. Derive the structure of these reports.

    b. Derive view relations from these structures. Assume that author names and book titles are unique but patron names are not.

    c. Extract the elementary fact types.

Q9.3 The Antarctic Computer Society publishes an occasional magazine called *Cold Comfort*. Here is the contents page of their latest issue.

```
            C O L D         C O M F O R T

                    Vol. 21    1995

                    List of Contents

        Page    Title                       Author(s)

          3     Use of neural nets to       Smith J., Ross C.
                solve the Tower of
                Hanoi problem

         10     UNIX: How Secure?           George I., Smith J.
                                            and Dos P.C.

         12     An A to Z of formal         Berg I.C.
                specification

                    Editor:   K.G. Lyon
```

a. Derive the structure of the this title page and all the previous ones.
b. Derive view relations from this structure. You may assume that, for all issues of the magazine, people are uniquely represented by their names and that the titles of articles will never repeat.
c. Extract the elementary fact types.

Q9.4 The following information was extracted from a list of the complete results of the 1995 World Soccer League.

Date	Stadium	Team	Score	Scorer(s)
21/3/95	Wembley	Liverpool	5	O'Reilly(2), Smith(2), Jones
		Real Madrid	3	Charles, Humble, Santana
	Hampden Park	Rangers	1	Souness
		Milan	2	Galileo, Michael
28/3/95	Lang Park	Brisbane	1	Lewis
		Liverpool	0	
	MCG	Melbourne	0	
		Milan	4	Angel o(3), Galileo

a. Derive the structure of the list.
b. Derive view relations from this structure.
c. Extract the elementary fact types.

CHAPTER 10

Fact-based Analysis

10.1 Introduction

This chapter is presented as a worked example in a technique which we will call **fact-based analysis**. This is a way of designing a relational database. In particular, it is concerned with developing a design that guarantees that in any resulting database each fact is stored *just once*. Here are the stages that we follow.

1. Uncover the relevant entity types and the fact types that join them.

    In this step, we apply the techniques of Chapter 9 to find the relevant elementary fact types.

2. Look for any uniqueness constraints involved in each fact type.

    In this step, we apply the question and answer technique of Section 8.6 to decide whether a fact type is a many-to-many, a many-to-one or a one-to-one relationship.

3. Construct record types by merging fact types, where appropriate.

    In this step, we merge fact type according to the rule that permits the merging of single-valued facts about the same kind of thing.

4. Decide which attributes may be null.

    In this step we process each record type in turn, examining each non-key attribute of that record. Those that may contain null values are flagged.

5. Define the database.

    In this step, we provide an outline of the database.

6. Review the design.

    Finally, we should check that the database design is satisfactory. Has any computable or derivable information slipped through into our design? Using SQL, can the major views be reproduced with this design?

Fact-based Analysis 221

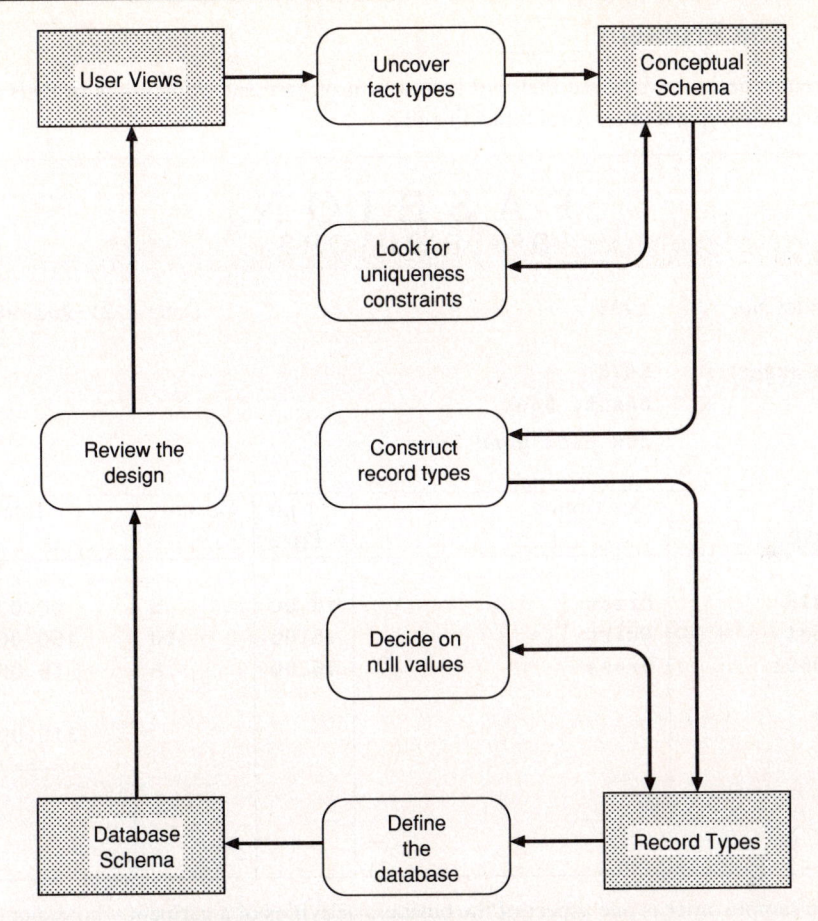

Figure 10.1 An outline of fact-based analysis

Figure 10.1 shows the processes and their outcomes.

- **User Views**

  These are "pictures" of the users and their environment.

- **Conceptual Schema**

  This consists of entity types and the fact types that join them, typically shown in graphical form.

- **Record Types**

  These are the various aggregate data structures that form the basis of our relational database.

- **Database Schema**

  This is both a formal definition *and* and a number of **Create Table** statements to define the database.

10.2 The Problem

We need to design a database that will help a firm of garment wholesalers in their order processing. A typical order form looks like this:

F A S H I O N
DISTRIBUTORS

Order No: 1234   Date: 21-Jul-95

Customer: 5678
              Beauty Nook
              369 Left Hand Lane

Style Code	Description	Unit Price	Quantity	Total
6216	Dress	18.00	5	90.00
Y53A	Skirt	15.00	10	150.00
S9501	Dress	15.00	5	75.00

				315.00
				======

The sample order is one aspect of the business activities of a garment wholesaler such as Fashion Distributors. A valid analysis is not possible without an understanding of the events leading to its receipt. Further, we need some general knowledge of the business environment in which the company operates.

Fashion Distributors (FD for short) sell women's clothes to boutiques, pharmacies, souvenir shops and small department stores. None of their customers run more than one shop. Sales representatives travel with samples of FD's current styles. They have a fairly stable customer base and a reputation for quality and reliability. Once a customer has made an order, this is sent to FD's head office for credit approval. If approved, the order is passed onto the warehouse. There a warehouse attendant attempts to fill the order, but sometimes there might not be sufficient stock on hand. Details of the shipment are sent to the accounts department where an order is prepared and sent out to the customer.

10.3 Step 1: Uncover the fact types

This step requires that we write down all the entity types that we see on the order, that is, the **kinds** of things that will appear on order forms. The step also says that we should write down any significant facts that connect these entity types. Although these two requirements might be done separately, they are better accomplished concurrently.

The process involves the following three stages as was discussed in Section 9.7.

1. Derive view structures

   Analyze all the various pictures or views of the user's world that we can obtain. Develop **view structures** for each of these views.

2. Derive view relations

   In the next stage, each view structure is examined in turn. Any structure that contains repeating components is "flattened" out into a number of **view relations**. Any structure that contains alternative components is split into a number of separate view relations.

3. Extract elementary fact types

   In the third and final stage, each view relation that results from the previous stage is examined. Each view relation has a corresponding sentence. Sample sentences of that type are formed. This sentence may be reduced to two or more simpler sentences, without loss of information. Alternatively, it may be irreducible. Either way we are reducing our more complex sentences into a number of elementary sentences.

The outcome of this entire process is a set of elementary sentence or fact types. These are the basic sentences that are to be stored in the database.

10.3.1 Derive View Structures

We have been presented with only one picture of the user's world, the order form. Each completed form represents just one order but we are interested in the set of all orders, so an appropriate view definition could be the following.

- `Orders ::= { OrderForm }`

  The orders view consists, quite simply, of a set of order forms.

- `OrderForm :: = Heading + { IndividualOrder } + OverallTotal`

  Each order form, such as the one shown, contains a heading, a number of individual orders for specific styles followed by an overall figure giving the total value of the entire order.

- `Heading ::= OrderNr + OrderDate + CustomerNr + CustName + Street`

  This is what will appear in the top part of each order form.

- `IndividualOrder ::= StyleCode + StyleType + UnitPrice + Quantity + StyleTotal`

  This is the information shown on each detail line of the order.

Amalgamating these into a single definition gives us:

```
Orders ::=
   { OrderNr + OrderDate + CustomerNr + CustName + Street
 + { StyleCode + StyleType + UnitPrice + Quantity + StyleTotal }
 + OverallTotal }
```

There are two data elements that can be derived from others, the individual style total, `StyleTotal` and the overall total, `OverallTotal`. For the purpose of designing a database, these may be discarded. As a result, we now have the view that we will analyze:

```
Orders ::=
   { OrderNr + OrderDate + CustomerNr + CustName + Street
 + { StyleCode + StyleType + UnitPrice + Quantity } }
```

10.3.2 Derive View Relations

The `Orders` structure contains a repeating component, and so we must flatten it into two, simpler, view relations.

First we need to identify a key component of the structure. The view consists, essentially, of a set of orders. The key will be whatever information we can use to distinguish one order from another. The `OrderNr` was clearly designed for this purpose.

The structure is flattened by removing the repeating component entirely from `Orders` and placing it in a new relation consisting of this component and the key, `OrderNr`. The resulting view relations are:

```
VR1 ::= { OrderNr + OrderDate + CustomerNr + CustName + Street }
VR2 ::= { OrderNr + StyleCode + StyleType + UnitPrice + Quantity }
```

10.3.3 Extract Elementary Fact Types

The final part of this first step in fact-based analysis is to take the above view relations and extract whatever irreducible fact types they contain.

`VR1 ::= OrderNr + OrderDate + CustomerNr +CustName + Street`

This view corresponds to the heading on an order form, so we should now construct a sample sentence using the data on the form provided.

- Order number `1234`, which was taken on `21-Jul-95`, was made by customer number `5678`; this customer trades as `Beauty Nook` at `369 Left Hand Lane`.

This is a long-winded and awkwardly phrased sentence; a sure sign that it can, and should, be decomposed. The sentence breaks most obviously at the semi-colon, so we can rewrite it as:

- Order number `1234`, which was taken on `21-Jul-95`, was made by customer number `5678`.

- Customer number `5678` trades as `Beauty Nook` at `369 Left Hand Lane`.

In the first of these sentences, it should be clear that the date on which the order was taken is independent of the customer who made the order. Looking at the second, it should be seen that the customer's trade name and address are separate facts about the customer. So the two sentences can be further reduced.

- Order number **1234** was taken on **21-Jul-95**.
- Order number **1234** was made by customer number **5678**.
- Customer number **5678** trades as **Beauty Nook**.
- Customer number **5678** is located at **369 Left Hand Lane**.

These are all binary facts and so are irreducible. Generalizing them gives rise to four fact types:

    F1. **Order was taken on Day**.
    F2. **Order was made by Customer**.
    F3. **Customer trades as Name**.
    F4. **Customer is located at Address**.

VR2 ::= OrderNr + StyleCode + StyleType + UnitPrice + Quantity

This view corresponds to a line on the order, so we can use data from one of these lines to construct a sample sentence from this relation.

- On order number **1234** there was a request for **5** units of style **6216** which is a dress and sells for **$18.00**.

The phrase "which is a dress and sells for $18.00" contains two asides which are aimed solely at the style code 6216. The sentence can be restated as follows.

- Style **6216** is a **dress**.
- Style **6216** sells for **$18.00**.
- On order number **1234** there was a request for **5** units of style **6216**.

The first two of these sentences are irreducible but what about the third? If we were to re-express it as three simple sentences we would get:

- On order number **1234** there was a request for **5** units (of some style or another).
- On order number **1234** there was a request for style **6216** (but we don't know how many).
- There has been an order (but we don't know which) for **5** units of style **6216**.

These three facts are *not* enough to permit us to reconstruct the original sentence; this sentence is also irreducible. This leaves us with three fact types to be extracted from this view relation:

    F5. **Style is a StyleType**.
    F6. **Style sells for Money**.
    F7. **On Order, Quantity units of Style were requested**.

The Results of Step 1

This step requires that we decide on the relevant entity types and the fact types that join them. We have now accomplished this task. The fact types and the entity types they connect are as follows:

F1. Order was taken on Day.
F2. Order was made by Customer.
F3. Customer trades as Name.
F4. Customer is located at Address.
F5. Style is a StyleType.
F6. Style sells for Money.
F7. On Order, Quantity units of Style were requested.

The conceptual schema diagram for these seven facts is shown in Figure 10.2.

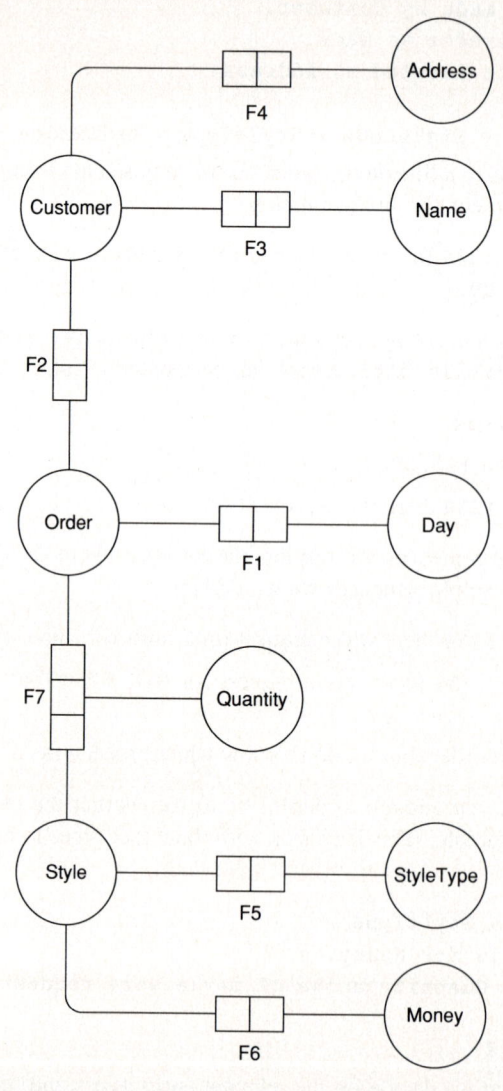

Figure 10.2 The first-draft conceptual schema diagram

10.4 Step 2: Look for uniqueness constraints

Now we will examine each of the fact types uncovered in step 1 and try to establish the nature of the relationship between the entity types that participate in the fact. We will be looking for uniqueness constraints and will mark the conceptual schema diagram according to our findings.

F1. **Order was taken on Day.**

In diagrammatic form this fact type looks like:

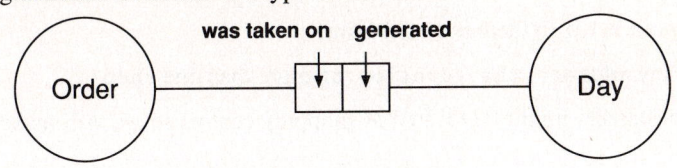

```
     was taken on   generated
  ( Order )─────[ │ │ ]─────( Day )
```

The questions that we must answer are as follows.

Q1. Was any **order taken on** more than one **day**?

The answer is NO so there is a uniqueness constraint.

The other question is phrased using the opposite form of the relationship, namely **generated**.

Q2. Did any **day generate** more than one **order**?

The answer, we hope, is YES and so there is no uniqueness constraint.

The role boxes can now be marked to show the constraint involved in this fact type.

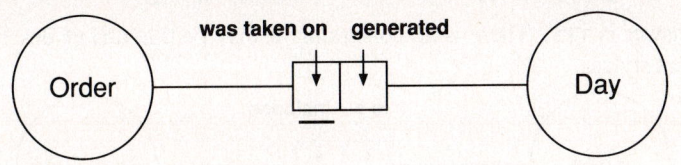

```
     was taken on   generated
  ( Order )─────[ │ │ ]─────( Day )
                   ───
```

F2. **Order was made by Customer.**

Q1. Was any **order made by** more than one **customer**?

The answer is NO so there is a constraint.

Q2. Has any **customer made** more than one **order**?

The answer is surely YES so there is no constraint on this role.

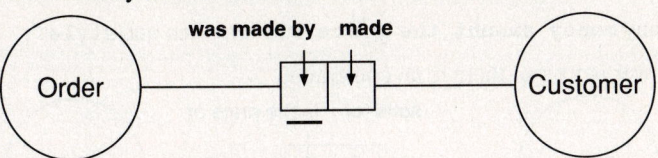

```
     was made by    made
  ( Order )─────[ │ │ ]─────( Customer )
                   ───
```

F3. **Customer trades as Name.**

Q1. Does any **customer trade as** more than one **name**?

We will make it NO but the answer is one we might have to discuss with our client.

Q2. Is any **name traded under by** more than one **customer**?

The answer is NO (a legal requirement), so there is a constraint here.

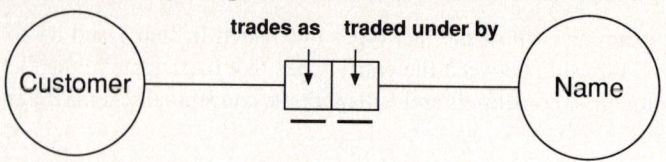

```
              trades as   traded under by
   ╱‾‾‾╲         ┌──┬──┐         ╱‾‾‾╲
  │Customer│────│▼ │▼ │────│ Name │
   ╲___╱         └──┴──┘         ╲___╱
```

F4. `Customer is located at Address.`

Q1. Is any customer located at more than one **address**?

The answer is NO so there is a constraint.

Q2. Is any **address the location of** more than one **shop**?

Some customers might be located at shopping centres so we will make the answer YES.

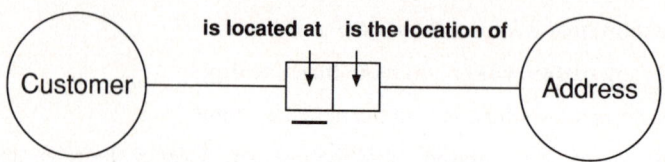

```
              is located at   is the location of
   ╱‾‾‾╲         ┌──┬──┐         ╱‾‾‾╲
  │Customer│────│▼ │▼ │────│Address│
   ╲___╱         └──┴──┘         ╲___╱
```

F5. `Style is a StyleType.`

Q1. Does any style have more than one **style type**?

The answer is NO so this is a constraint.

Q2. Does any **style type include** more than one **style**?

The answer is YES. There is no constraint. It may be that **shirt** describes several different styles.

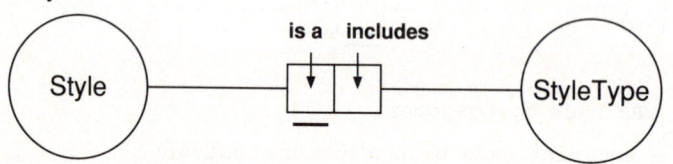

```
                 is a    includes
   ╱‾‾‾╲         ┌──┬──┐         ╱‾‾‾‾‾╲
  │ Style │────│▼ │▼ │────│StyleType│
   ╲___╱         └──┴──┘         ╲____╱
```

F6. `Style sells for Money.`

Q1. Does any style sell for more than one **amount (of money)**?

The answer is NO so there is a constraint.

Q2. Is any **money amount the price of** more than one **style**?

The answer is YES so there is no constraint.

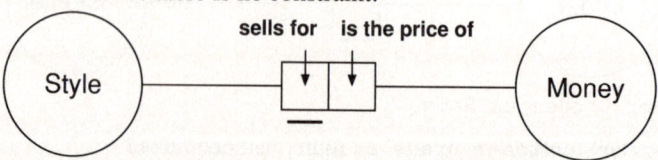

```
               sells for   is the price of
   ╱‾‾‾╲         ┌──┬──┐         ╱‾‾‾╲
  │ Style │────│▼ │▼ │────│ Money │
   ╲___╱         └──┴──┘         ╲___╱
```

F7. `On Order, Quantity units of Style were requested.`

This fact type involves three entity types, **Order**, **Style** and **Quantity**.

Fact-based Analysis

The question-answer technique can be modified to deal with three-part fact types. This done by pairing two of the entity types and relating them to the third. Because there are three participants, there are three ways of performing this permutation. These are (1) **Order** and **Style** against **Quantity**; (2) **Order** and **Quantity** against **Style**; and (3) **Style** and **Quantity** against **Order**.

Q1. Does any **style on an order have** more than one **quantity**?

The answer is NO and so there is a constraint.

Q2. Is any **quantity on an order** that of more than one **style**?

The answer is YES and so there is no constraint on the **quantity + order** combination.

Q3. Does any **quantity of a style** appear on more than one **order**?

The answer is YES, because more than one customer may order 10 units of some given style. So there is no constraint on the **quantity + style** combination. See Figure 10.3.

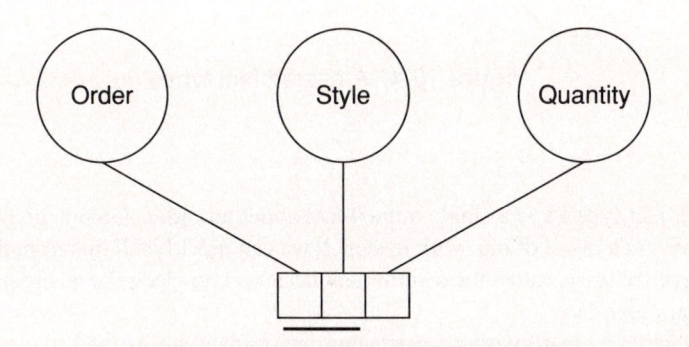

Figure 10.3 An irreducible fact type

We should now redraw this fact type as a nested one, as shown in Figure 10.4.

The revised conceptual schema diagram, now incorporating the uniqueness constraints and the nested fact type, is shown in Figure 10.5.

10.5 Step 3: Construct record types

In this step we merge the fact types into record types. The basis for merging is the determinant.

> Wherever an entity type appears in a conceptual schema diagram *and* it is connected to a role box against which there is a uniqueness constraint, then the associated relationship is a single-valued fact about that entity type. The entity type is said to be a **determinant**.

Chapter 10

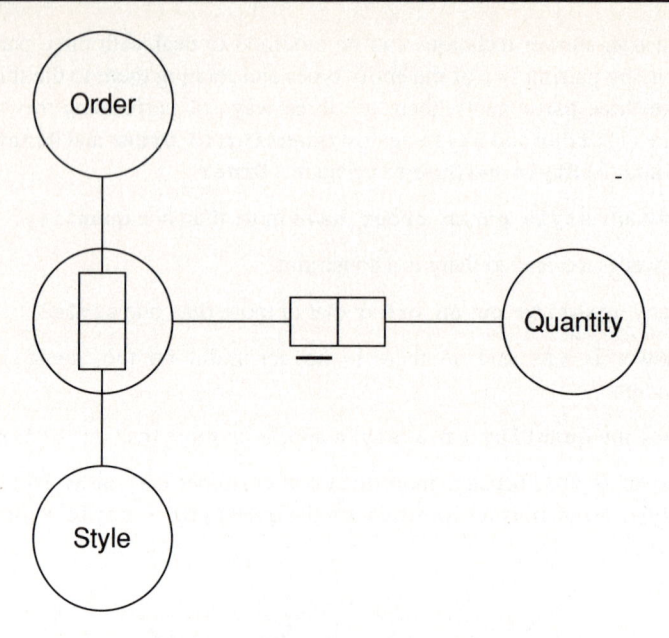

Figure 10.4 A nested fact type

For example, fact type **F1** is a single-valued fact about an order. Orders are taken on *one* particular day. As a result of our work in step 2, we can quickly tell this from the diagram. The entity type **Order** is called the determinant because knowledge of an order *determines* one particular order date.

All the fact types that involve a particular determinant are merged to create a record type. The determinants, with their associated entity and fact types, are summarized below.

Determinant	Entities	Fact types involved
Order	Order	F1, F2
Customer	Customer	F3, F4
Name	Name	F3
Style	Style	F5, F6
StyleOrder	Order + Style	F7

Fact type **F3** is a one-to-one fact involving customers and their names. As a consequence, it appears twice, once with Customer as the determinant and once with Name. We choose to aggregate **F3** with other facts relating to Customers. The record types that result from the merging process are:

Fact-based Analysis 231

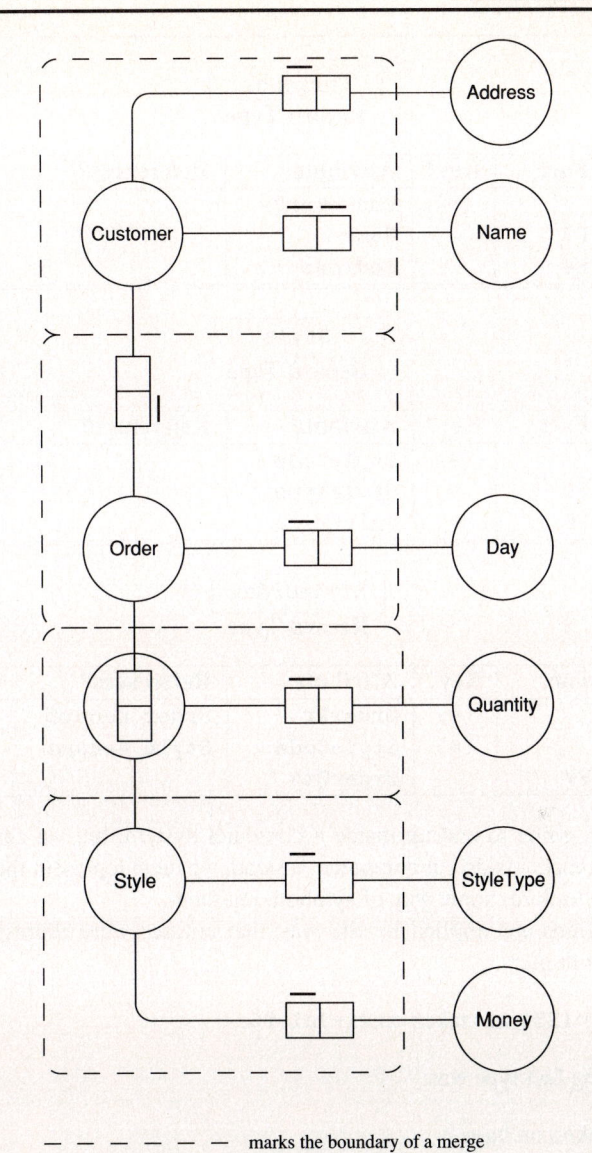

– – – – – marks the boundary of a merge

Figure 10.5 The final schema

		Order Record Type	
Fact	Key?	Attribute	References?
F1 F2	(*)	OrderNr OrderDate CustomerNr	Customer Record

232   Chapter 10

		Customer **Record Type**	
Fact	Key?	Attribute	References?
	(*)	CustomerNr	
F3		Name	
F4		Address	

		Style **Record Type**	
Fact	Key?	Attribute	References?
	(*)	StyleCode	
F5		StyleType	
F6		UnitPrice	

		StyleOrder **Record Type**	
Fact	Key?	Attribute	References?
	(*)	OrderNr	Order Record
	(*)	StyleCode	Style Record
F7		OrderQty	

Our model is going to end up inside a computer system, but we can't put shops or garments or customers inside our computer. Instead, we must represent them in some way. What we do is to look for some way of symbolizing them.

The substitutions are implied by the way that entities were represented in sample sentences. For example:

- Order number **1234** was taken on **21-Jul-95**.

The corresponding fact type was:

- **Order** was taken on **Day**.

The generalization from the sample sentence to the fact type involved a recognition that (1) an order number represented the entity type **Order**; and (2) a date represented the entity type **Day**. What we are doing in this step is returning to the symbolic level. A complete list of the substitutions used is as follows:

Entity type	Representation
Order	Order Number
Day	Date
Style	Style Code
Customer	Customer Number

10.6 Step 4: Decide which attributes may be null

We must now decide which attributes of each relation will permit null values. This requires that we return to the relevant fact type and find out the *least* participation rates *for the determinant only.*

F1. **Order was taken on Day.**

To determine whether or not null values are to be allowed in the **Day** attribute, we must answer the following questions.

Q1. Will every **order** be taken on some **day**?

YES, it could hardly be done outside of space and time, so we must go on and ask the supplementary question.

Q2. Must we always know on which **day** an **order** was taken?

The answer cannot be answered from the sample order form we have been using so far; we should really ask the users. If there is any doubt then the answer should be NO. That is the one we will use now.

The consequence of a negative answer is that nulls *should be permitted* for the **Day** attribute in the **Order** proto-relation.

F2. **Order was made by Customer.**

Q1. Is every order made by some customer?

The answer is YES.

Q2. Must we always know which customer made an order?

The answer must surely be YES. Nulls should not be allowed in the **Customer** attribute of the **Order** proto-relation.

F3. **Customer trades as Name.**

Q1. Does every customer trade under some name?

The answer is YES.

Q2. Must we always know under which name a customer trades?

Again, the answer must surely be YES. Nulls are not to be permitted for the **Name** attribute of the **Customer** proto-relation.

F4. **Customer is located at Address.**

Q1. Is every customer located at some address?

The answer is YES.

Q2. Must we always know at which address a customer is located?

Again, the answer must be YES.

F5. **Style is a StyleType.**

Q1. Is every style of some type?

The answer is YES.

Q2. Must we always know which type the style is?

We cannot be sure, so the answer must be NO.

F6. Style sells for Money.

Q1. Does every style sell for some amount of money?

The answer is YES.

Q2. Must we always know how much a style sells for?

The answer must surely be YES.

F7. On Order, Quantity units of Style were requested.

Q1. Will there always be some quantity specified for every style appearing on an order?

It would seem appropriate.

Q2. Must we always know how many units of a style were requested on an order?

The answer must be YES.

Two record types should now be revised to include the results of these questions. A question mark (?) is placed alongside any attribute that can contain nulls.

Order Record Type

Fact	Key?	Attribute	References?
	(*)	OrderNr	
F1	(?)	OrderDate	
F2		CustomerNr	Customer Record

Style Record Type

Fact	Key?	Attribute	References?
	(*)	StyleCode	
F5	(?)	StyleType	
F6		UnitPrice	

10.7 Step 5: Define the database

We begin the formal definition of the database by defining schema record types for each record type.

OrderRecord

OrderNr : Order
OrderDate : Date
CustomerNr : Customer

┌─ *CustomerRecord* ────────────────────────────────
│ *CustomerNr* : *Customer*
│ *Name* : *Name*
│ *Address* : *Address*
└──

┌─ *StyleRecord* ───────────────────────────────────
│ *StyleCode* : *Style*
│ *StyleType* : *StyleType*
│ *UnitPrice* : *Money*
└──

┌─ *StyleTypeRecord* ───────────────────────────────
│ *OrderNr* : *Order*
│ *StyleCode* : *Style*
│ *OrderQty* : $\mathbb{N}$
└──

Now we can define the database schema itself.

┌─ *Database* ──────────────────────────────────────
│ *Orders* : Set of *OrderRecord*
│ *Customers* : Set of *CustomerRecord*
│ *Styles* : Set of *StyleRecord*
│ *StyleOrders* : Set of *StyleOrderRecord*
│ ───
│ count *Orders* = count $\{o : Orders \bullet o.OrderNr\}$
│ count *Customers* = count $\{c : Customers \bullet c.CustomerNr\}$
│ count *Styles* = count $\{s : Styles \bullet s.StyleCode\}$
│ count *StyleOrders* = count $\{s : StyleOrders \bullet (s.StyleCode, s.OrderNr)\}$
│ count $\{c : Customers \bullet c.CustomerNr\}$ = count $\{c : Customers \bullet c.Name\}$
│ $\{o : Orders \bullet o.CustomerNr\} \subseteq \{c : Customers \bullet c.CustomerNr\}$
│ $\{s : StyleOrders \bullet s.OrderNr\} \subseteq \{o : Orders \bullet o.OrderNr\}$
│ $\{s : StyleOrders \bullet s.StyleCode\} \subseteq \{s : Styles \bullet s.StyleCode\}$
└──

The relation key constraints are given first. Then the one-to-one relationship between customers and their names is specified. Finally, we define the referential integrity or inclusion constraints between foreign keys and their parent tables.

The SQL **create table** statements may now also be defined. Each record type gives rise to a separate **create** statement, with the attributes of the table being taken from those of the record type, as is the nullity of each. The **primary key** clause is based on the **Key?** column of the record type table. The **foreign key** clauses are based on the **References?** column.

```
Create Table Orders
        (OrderNr    number(4,0) not null,
        OrderDate   date,
        CustomerNr  number(4,0) not null,

        Primary key (OrderNr),
        Foreign key (CustomerNr) references Customers(CustomerNr))

Create Table Customers
        (CustomerNr  number(4,0) not null,
        Name         char(30)    not null,
        Address      char(30)    not null,

        Primary key (CustomerNr))

Create Table Styles
        (StyleCode   char(8)      not null,
        StyleType    char(20),
        UnitPrice    number(7,2) not null,

        Primary key (StyleCode))

Create Table StyleOrders
        (OrderNr    number(4,0) not null,
        StyleCode   char(8)      not null,
        OrderQty    number(4,0) not null,

        Primary key (OrderNr, Stylecode)
        Foreign key (OrderNr)    references Orders(OrderNr),
        Foreign key (StyleCode) references Styles(StyleCode))
```

10.8 Step 6: Review the design

During a typical exercise in fact-based analysis, we examine user views in order to extract fact types. The order form shown at the beginning of this particular exercise is an example of a view. The narrative that accompanies the order provides another. This final step in fact-based analysis is not really part of the design process, nor does it truly validate the design. Rather, it provides some kind of check on whether major flaws exist in the relations we have defined. One way of validating the design is to see whether a view can be We begin with the heading:

```
Select   OrderNr, Date, CustomerNr, Name, Address
From     Orders, Customers
Where    Orders.CustomerNr = Customers.CustomerNr
 and     OrderNr = 1234
```

```
----------------------------------------------------------------
OrderNr   Date      CustomerNr   Name            Address
----------------------------------------------------------------
1234      950421    5678         Beauty Nook     369 Left Hand Lane
----------------------------------------------------------------
```

The following SQL will give us the body of the order:

```
Select    Styles.StyleCode, Styles.StyleType, Styles.UnitPrice,
          OrderQty, OrderQty * Styles.UnitPrice
From      Styles, StyleOrders
Where     Styles.StyleCode = StyleOrders.StyleCode
  and     StyleOrders.OrderNr = 1234
```

```
----------------------------------------------------------------
StyleCode   Type      UnitPrice      OrderQty          Cost
----------------------------------------------------------------
6216        Dress     18.00          5                 90.00
Y53A        Skirt     15.00          10                150.00
S8701       Blouse    15.00          5                 75.00
----------------------------------------------------------------
```

The following SQL will provide us with the overall order total:

```
Select    sum(OrderQty * Styles.UnitPrice)
From      Styles, StyleOrders
Where     Styles.StyleCode = StyleOrders.StyleCode
  and     StyleOrders.OrderNr = 1234

--------
Overall
Total
--------
315.00
--------
```

10.9 Summary

This chapter has presented a worked example of relational database design. It has attempted to integrate the tools and techniques introduced in Chapters 8 and 9.

Designing a database, like most other activities requiring skill, is something at which we improve with practice. The fact-based analysis (FBA) method has been shown as a rather large number of small steps. This has been done so as to make the steps manageable for newcomers. The danger is that a multitude of steps will daunt. It is, therefore, worth comparing this situation to that of learning to drive. When we start, driving seems to require the almost simultaneous use of many new skills. Once we have driven for some time, all these skills are applied with ease. We steer, change gear, put on indicators and scan the road ahead without a hitch.

The same kind of comment applies to relational database design. An experienced designer will apply all the steps of fact-based analysis almost without realizing it.

Exercises

Q10.1 MEGA CONSTRUCTORS

Mega Constructors is an international company that specialises in large-scale construction. They build such things as bridges, dams, office blocks, hotels and factories.

The company is divided into a number of departments. Each department specializes in one form of construction; for example, department 654 deals exclusively with the erection of bridges, regardless of their geographical location.

Head Office, however, is interested in the activities of the various geographical areas in which the company operates. This is for political and financial reasons.

Each individual construction activity is termed a project. Each project is given a code, which is used to uniquely identify the project in any reports.

Prior to the commencement of construction, the project is analyzed into a number of tasks. This is done by the project leader and his or her assistants. Each task is given a code, unique *to that project*. For each task, a time estimate is made. A monthly budget is developed for the expected lifetime of the project. As each project progresses, actual expenditure is monitored.

There are three reports to be analyzed.

1. The Departmental Summary

This report appears monthly. Each department's projects are listed. For each project run by that department, the actual and budgeted expenditure for the previous month are compared. The month and year are therefore significant.

```
------------------------------------------------------------------

                       Departmental Summary

                         Department: 654

          Activity: Bridge Construction    Manager: Sam Small

                                     August 1998 Figures
   Project          Description       Budget         Actual
   -------          -----------       ------         ------

   NOOSA            Noosa Bridge          950 000        821 006
   DIEGO            San Diego Overpass  1 011 965      1 201 943
   SAUCE            Spaghetti Junction     21 854         30 446
   TAY              Perth Swan Bridge     124 300        110 477

------------------------------------------------------------------
```

2. The Project Status Report

This report appears on demand. Each task within a project is listed along with the original time estimates, the effort so far, revised estimates and the project leader's feeling about the state of the task.

Project Status Report

Project: NOOSA

Leader: Harry Hasting   Department: 654

Task	Description	Original Estimate	Days So Far	Days Now Expected
DIG	Dig Foundations	6	3	7
POUR	Pour Cement	16	10	12
ERECT	Erect Scaffolding	2	2	2
BOX	Lay Girders	25	0	25

---

3. The Area Summary

This appears on demand. It simply lists current projects in each area of the world. The original contract value of the project also appears.

Area Summary

Area: 21   Australia   Controller: Bill O'Reilly

Department	Project	Description	Contract ($M)
654	NOOSA	Noosa Bridge	56.82
826	HEAP	Hay Point Ship Loader	101.00
112	SWEETY	Bondoola Sugar Mill	35.25
189	DTS	Bondi Brewery	15.50

Required:

Perform a fact-based analysis of the situation described above. You may assume that people are identifiable by their name.

► Q10.2 Marge Butter and the Cholesterols have recently released a compilation of their greatest hits on an album entitled *Best Spread*. This work consists of a number of tracks taken from previously released albums. The sleeve notes provide information on those involved with each track. Here is a typical note.

> Track 3: *Case Tool Cool* (4:30)
> Music: Hans Zupp/ Rip Cord/ Norman D. Butter
> First released on *Seek Well* in 1985
> Producer: Norman D. Butter
> Vocals: Marge Butter
> Drums: Hans Zupp/Bill Board
> Bass: Kerry Gould
> Guitar: Marge Butter/Rip Orff/Norman D. Butter
> Clarinet/Sax: Split Reed
>
> Split Reed appears courtesy of
> ILL WIND Records, Rip Orff courtesy
> CANNY LAD Records.

Perform a fact-based analysis of the album. You can assume the following.

- Most of the people are involved on several of the tracks.
- Margie and friends have occasionally released more than one album in the same year.
- There is only ever one producer per track.
- "Vocals" is just another kind of instrument.

CHAPTER 11

Entity-relationship Modeling

11.1 Introduction

Entity-relationship modeling is a very popular method for designing databases. ER modeling, as it is often called, may be described as a **top-down** approach in that it encourages to look at the "big picture" first. We begin by describing the world in terms of **entity** types that are **related** to one another in various ways. We may then refine that picture to show the **attributes** of each entity type. Thus we start by looking for the major kinds of things that populate the situation to be modeled. These entity types will give rise, eventually, to the major relations in our database. In a hospital situation, for example, the entity types might be:

- patients
- wards
- beds
- surgeons
- nurses

We then establish any relationships that exist between these entity types, such as:

- Patients are operated on by surgeons.
- Patients are located in beds.
- Beds are placed in wards.
- Nurses are allocated to wards.

The relationships enliven the otherwise static picture of the hospital that is provided by the entity types on their own. In database terms, some of these relationships might also be represented by relations. For example, if details of the time and place of operations are required, we might need an Operations relation. Other relationships might be adequately represented by foreign key linkages between relations. Finally, we flesh out the entity types by attaching properties to them. For example, we might want to know each surgeon's specialty, qualifications and home telephone number. Similarly, we can attach attributes to relationships, adding the operating theatre as an attribute of the **operation** relationship. Thus we look for important features before examining them in detail. The technique is *not* as clear-cut as this. We may need to cycle through the process a number of times until we are satisfied with our model.

11.2 An Example

Moreton Bay University is a large institution with several campuses scattered across the city of Moreton. Academically, the University is also divided, consisting of a number of faculties, such as the Arts Faculty, the Science Faculty, and so on. Some of the faculties operate on a number of campuses. Faculties, in turn, are divided into schools; for example, the Science Faculty has a School of Physics and a School of Chemistry. It is University policy, however, not to split schools.

11.2.1 Entities

Suppose we try to model what has been described so far. Using the narrative as a guide, the first step would be to recognize that campuses are an important feature of the University. In Entity-relationship modeling, we can do this by enclosing the name of that feature in a rectangle, as is shown in Figure 11.1.

Campus

Figure 11.1 The campus entity type

Why did we not start with the University itself? It is obviously an important entity. Why did we choose to ignore it? There are two reasons. To begin with, it is the University *itself* that we are modeling; so we are not ignoring it at all. However, there is another reason. We are not so much interested in specific entities as in *types* of entities. Note that the type name is singular. Thus the box represents both a typical campus and the set of *all* campuses. The second entity type is clearly the faculty. This new type is added to the diagram we are constructing. See Figure 11.2.

The first two entity types show how diverse the concept of an entity can be. The Campus entity type divides the University in a physical sense. The Faculty divides it intellectually, so to speak.

Entity-relationship Modeling 243

```
┌─────────┐                    ┌─────────┐
│ Campus  │                    │ Faculty │
└─────────┘                    └─────────┘
```

Figure 11.2 And now we have two!

11.2.2 Relationships

The third entity type is the School, and by the time that we have drawn a box for schools, we will be feeling like showing how these three kinds of thing are related. The connection between faculties and schools is clear. A faculty is divided into a number of different schools, as can be seen in Figure 11.3. We show this relationship as a diamond-shaped symbol that connects the types of entity involved.

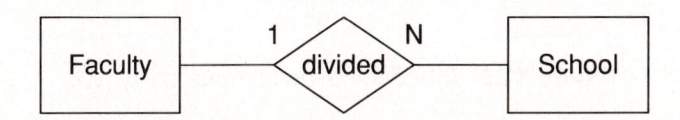

```
┌─────────┐      1  ◇  N   ┌─────────┐
│ Faculty │─────<divided>──│ School  │
└─────────┘      ◇         └─────────┘
```

Figure 11.3 Faculties are divided into schools

The **cardinality** of the relationship is also noted. This particular relationship is one-to-many (1 to N). The N (for many) is written at the School side of the diamond to indicate that a faculty may be divided into a number of schools. Conversely, however, a school is part of just 1 faculty. The representation of any relationship may be interpreted at both the individual and at the general level. At the individual level, an instance of the relationship might be that the Biology School is one of four schools into which the Science faculty is divided. See Figure 11.4.

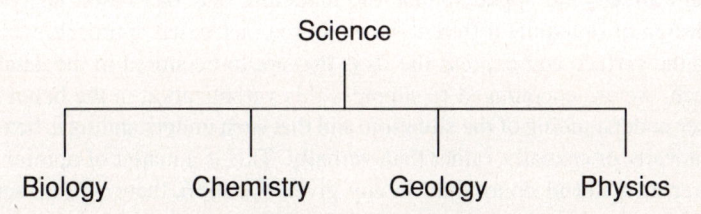

```
                    Science
                       │
        ┌──────┬───────┼───────┬──────┐
        │      │               │      │
     Biology Chemistry      Geology Physics
```

Figure 11.4 The Science Faculty is divided

The division of the Science Faculty is represented as four separate individual relationships between that faculty and its constituent schools. At the general level, the relationship cardinality indicates that no school is part of more than one faculty. As presented in the diagram, the relationship has been named from the faculty point of view. Obviously, it is the faculty that is divided, not the school. Given that we have only one chance at naming the relationship, it is better to name it so that we can read the diagram from left to right as we normally do. However, it remains that we are seeing just one side of the relationship. We can extend the diagram to include the relationship between schools and campuses.

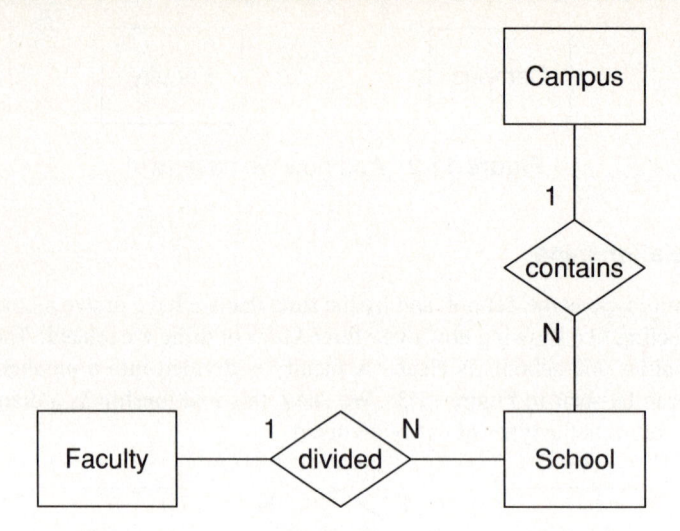

Figure 11.5 Introducing the campus entity type

This is another one-to-many relationship. A school is located on just one campus, although a campus may be the location of many schools. This time, the relationship has been named from the campus point of view, because the Campus entity box is above that of the School, and we tend to read from top to bottom.

The narrative actually discussed how faculties are spread across campuses. It might be argued that we should have described this location as a relationship between faculties and campuses rather than between schools and campuses. However, because a school is part of just one faculty as well as being located on just one campus, we can determine over what campuses any particular faculty is spread.

It should already be apparent that ER modeling and fact-based analysis approach database design in two quite different ways. In the fact-based approach, we are required to bring to the surface and express the facts that are to be stored in the database. In the ER approach, we are encouraged to suppress this verbalization in the belief that there is some deeper understanding of the situation, and that such understanding is better expressed diagrammatically or spatially, rather than verbally. This is a matter of opinion.

However, it is not in doubt that, in any given situation, there will be some kinds of things that are more important than others. The ER approach encourages us to start with these, to establish the relationships between them, and to refine from there. If we look at ER modeling as a graphical approach to database design, it says that there will be relations for campuses, faculties, schools and so on. It then becomes a matter of deciding what kind of information, that is what columns, these relations will have. Before we do that, we will introduce some more important facts.

There are students, obviously, and each student is enrolled in a single course of study which involves a fixed core of subjects specific to that course as well as a number of electives taken from other courses. Each course is offered by one particular school. The schools also employ lecturing staff to teach the students taking these subjects. A student is awarded a grade in any subject taken; the nature of the grade may mean that the student has to take the subject again! Finally, each campus has its club, where the cares of the day are eased, in one way or another. The diagram in Figure 11.6. shows how these things are connected.

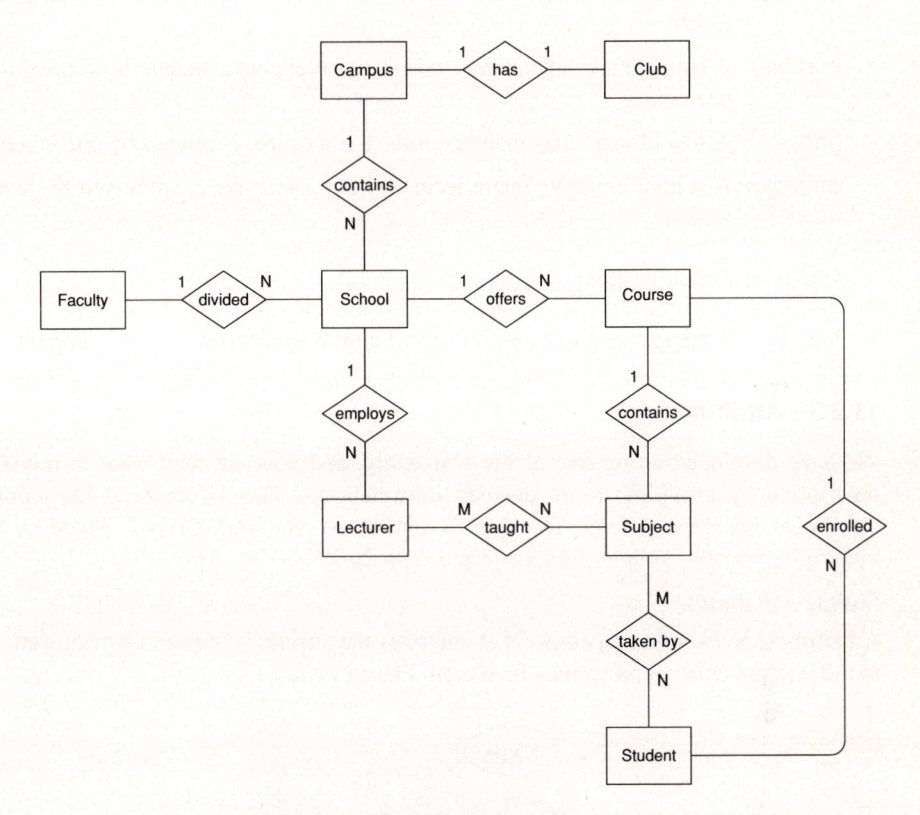

Figure 11.6 The story so far

There are now course, subject, lecturer and student entity types, in addition to those already introduced. These entity types are related in the way shown. There are three possible kinds of relationship:

1. Many-to-many relationships:

   taught   A lecturer may have taught many different subjects and even the same subject on many different occasions. A subject may also have been taught by many different lecturers.

   taken by   A subject may be taken by many students and a student may take many subjects.

2. One-to-many relationships:

contains   A campus may contain *many* schools, but a school is located on just *one* campus.

contains   A course contains many subjects, but a subject is in just one course.

divided   A faculty is divided into many schools, but a school is part of just one faculty.

enrolled   A course may have many students enrolled, but a student is enrolled in just one course.

offers   A school may offer many courses, but a course is offered by one school.

employs   A school employs many lecturers, but a lecturer is employed by just one school.

3. One-to-one relationships:

has   A campus has just one club and a club is located on just one campus.

11.2.3 Attributes

We have developed an outline of the University, and now we may want to refine that description by providing more detailed information. This is achieved by supplying **attributes** that show different facets of the entity and relationship types. There are three kinds of attributes – simple, composite and set-valued.

Simple Attributes

An attribute is shown as an ellipse that encircles the attribute name and which is attached to the relevant entity type, as may be seen in Figure 11.7.

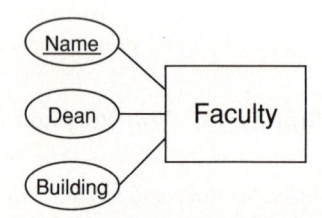

Figure 11.7 Faculty attributes

Identifying attributes, that is attributes that distinguish one entity from another of the same type, are underlined. So, according to the diagram, each faculty has a different name.

Simple attributes may be regarded as functions mapping from the entity type to the set of values associated with the attribute.

Dean : *Faculty* ↦ *Person*
Building : *Faculty* ↦ *Buildings*

Each faculty is symbolized by its identifying attribute, that is, by its name. The domain of each function is the entity type itself. The range of each function is the **value set** of the

Entity-relationship Modeling   247

attribute. The range of the Dean function is the set of people who are deans. The range of the Building function is the set of University buildings in which faculties are housed.

Relationships may also have attributes. We might choose to represent the year that a school moved to its current location as an attribute of the relationship rather than of the school itself. We will avoid this and make it an attribute of the school itself.

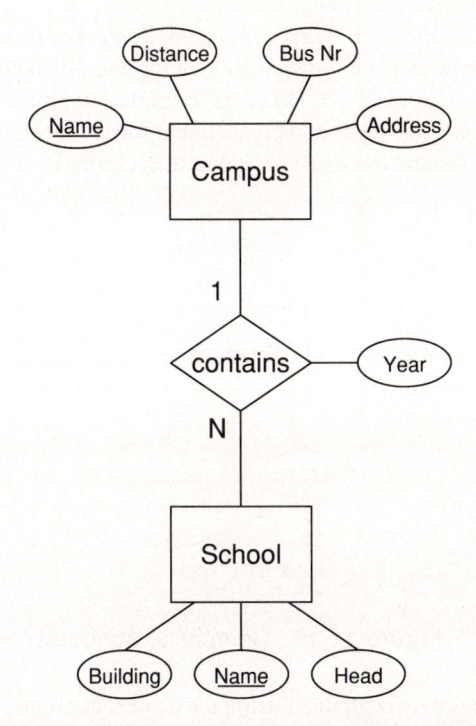

Figure 11.8 Relationships may also have attributes

There are relationships, however, for which we may need to record attributes. These are the many-to-many relationships.

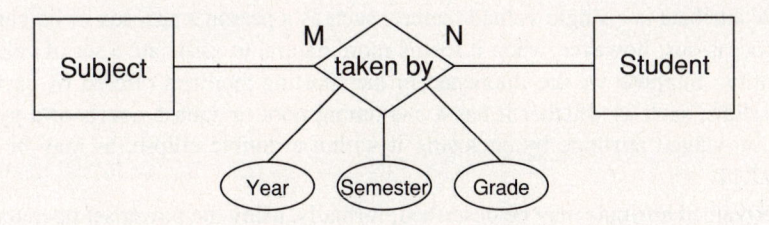

Figure 11.9 Attributes of a many-to-many relationship

A subject may be taken by many students and a student may take many subjects. If we assume that a student takes a particular subject just once then we can represent the year, semester and grade as simple attributes of that relationship. This is shown in Figure 11.9.

An attribute of a relationship may be also be considered as a function. The **Grade** attribute may be represented as follows:

$Grade : Subject \times Student \twoheadrightarrow N$

Composite Attributes

Certain attributes may be shown as being composite. Typical of these are names, addresses and dates. We can show this subdivision by making the attribute have attributes of its own, as may be seen in Figure 11.10. However, even this subdivision much simplifies the situation. Addresses may take a great many different forms. It might be better to omit this detail as it is likely to obscure the situation rather than clarify it.

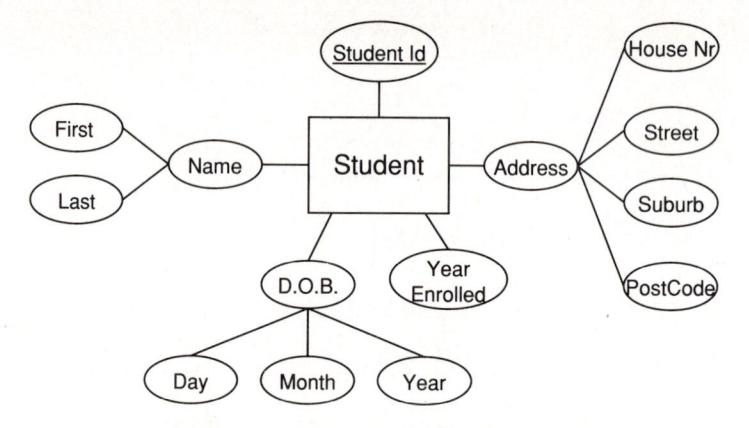

Figure 11.10 Composite attributes

Composite attributes may be defined using the Cartesian product operator or by means of a schema type:

$DOB : Student \twoheadrightarrow Day \times Month \times Year$

Set-valued Attributes

A typical attribute is a single-valued feature, such as a person's age, sex or height. There may be occasions, however, when it seems more natural to associate a set of values with some entity. Suppose we are interested in the sporting facilities offered by each of the campus clubs, such as whether it has a swimming pool or squash courts or a gym. We show a set-valued attribute by enclosing it within a double ellipse, as may be seen in Figure 11.11.

A set-valued attribute may be described, formally, using the power set operator.

$Facilities : Club \twoheadrightarrow Set\ of\ Sport$

11.2.4 Dependent or Weak Entity Types

So far, all the entities within a given type have been distinguishable from one another. Each campus has its own name, as does each school and each faculty. There may be occasions

Entity-relationship Modeling   249

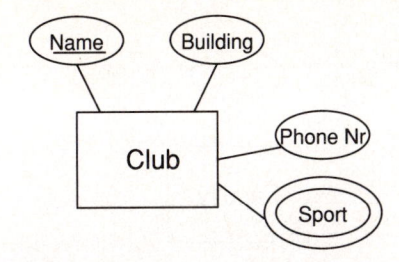

Figure 11.11 A set-valued attribute

when it is not possible to provide such unique identification. Take the case of committees. Every university operates by committee and Moreton Bay University is no exception. By University policy, each faculty has to have a set number of committees, the Faculty Executive, the Post-Graduate Studies Committee, the Health and Sanity Committee, and so on. These committees meet at regular intervals, such as weekly or monthly. The frequency is determined by the faculty involved. Because each faculty has committees with the same titles, the title is not enough to identify a particular committee, University-wide. We need to add the faculty name to fully establish its identity. Having done so, we can talk quite specifically about the Faculty of Science Executive Committee or the Faculty of Arts Post-Graduate Studies Committee.

The committee is said to be a **weak** or **dependent** entity type. We will use the latter term. A dependent entity type is enclosed within a double rectangle as shown in Figure 11.12. Each committee entity may be fully identified by adding in the faculty name. This identifying relationship is enclosed within a double diamond shape. A dependent entity type may be involved in other relationships besides the identifying one. A committee's membership is taken from the lecturers. A lecturer may be a member of several committees, however, and so this is *not* an identifying relationship. The member relationship will be represented within the single diamond shape.

The non-dependent entity types, such as Faculty and School, are said to be **regular** entity types to distinguish them from the dependent ones.

11.2.5 Recursive Relationships

So far, all the relationships discussed are ones between different entity types. It is quite common, however, to have relationships between entities of the same type. For example, at Moreton Bay, it may be necessary for any student taking a particular subject to have taken, and passed, one or more prerequisite subjects. In turn, this subject may be a prerequisite for a number of other subjects. So we have a **recursive** relationship. This may be represented as shown in Figure 11.13. This particular relationship is many-to-many.

A one-to-many recursive relationship may be used to represent a hierarchical situation. Suppose that there is a pecking order amongst the lecturers. A lecturer may be in charge of several lecturers, each of whom may be in charge of several other lecturers, and so on. A lecturer, however, reports to just one superior. This hierarchy and its manner of representation are shown in Figure 11.14.

The complete model for Moreton Bay University is presented in Figure 11.15.

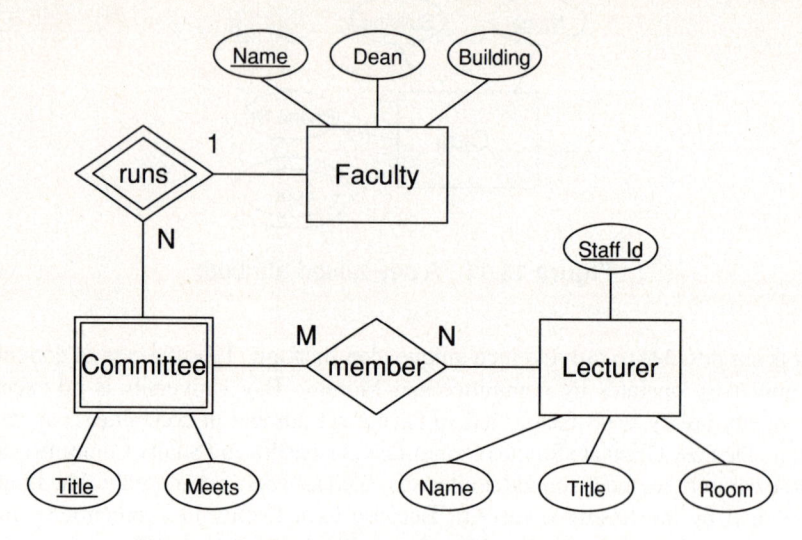

Figure 11.12 Weak or dependent entity types

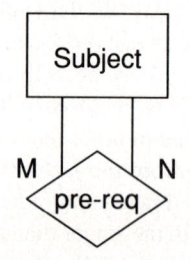

Figure 11.13 A recursive relationship

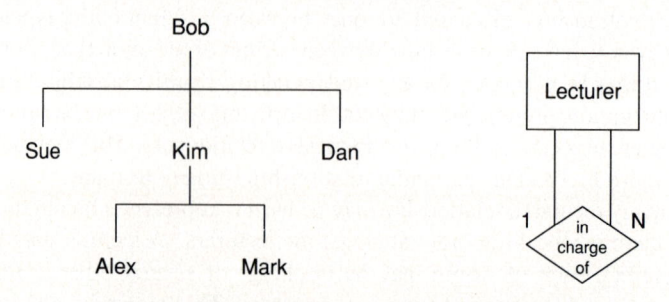

Figure 11.14 A hierarchical relationship

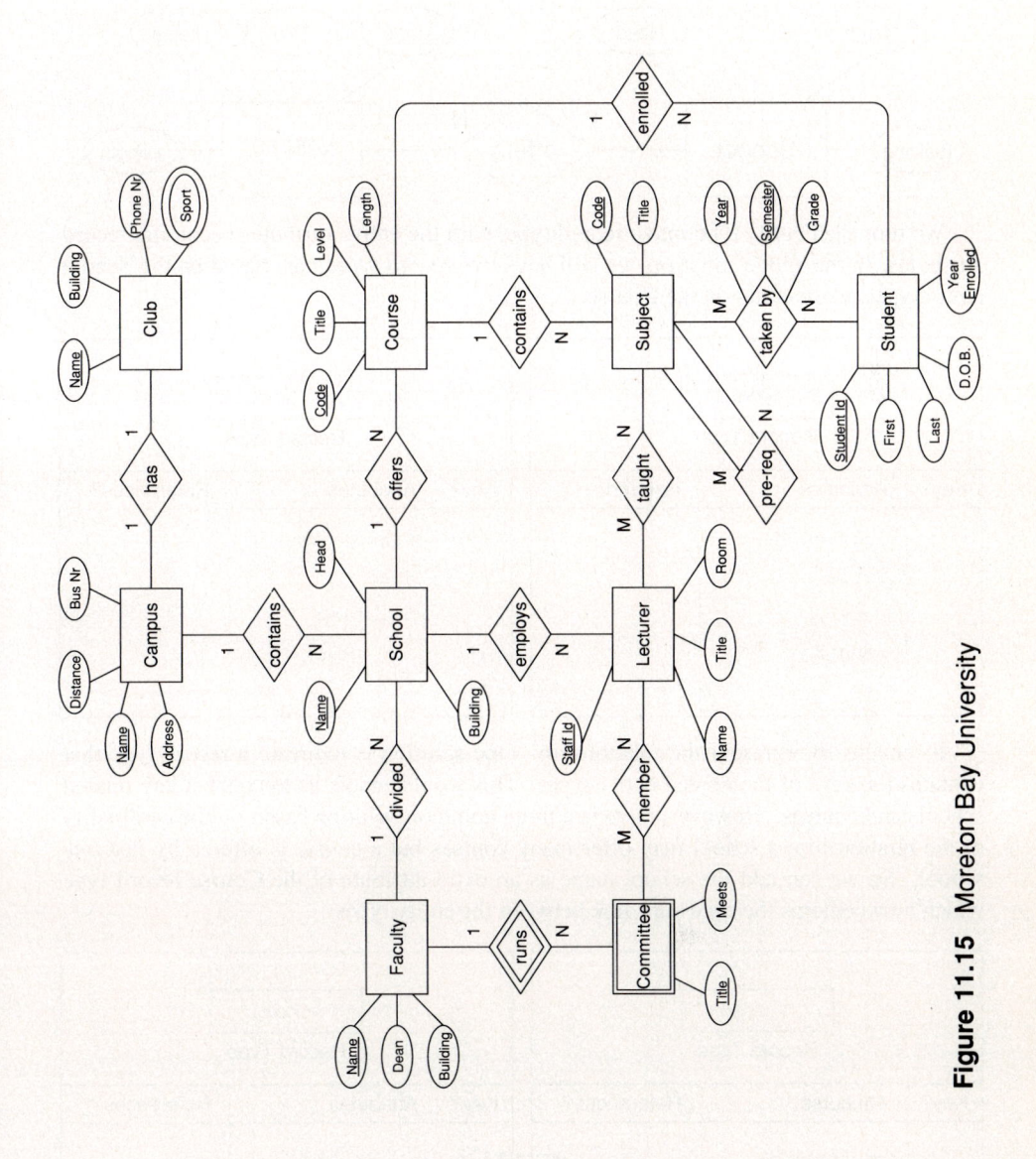

Entity-relationship Modeling 251

Figure 11.15 Moreton Bay University

11.3 Database Design

We will begin with a simple example that shows the more important elements.

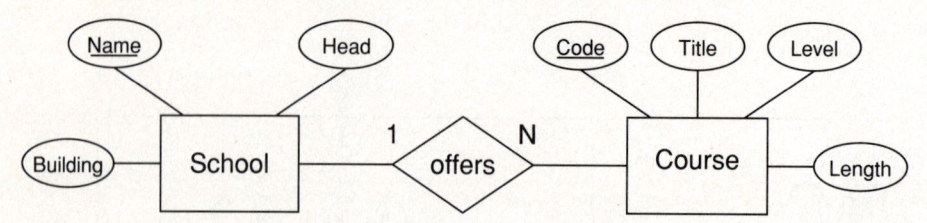

```
    (Name)        (Head)              (Code) (Title)  (Level)
       \           /                     \    |       /
        \         /        1        N     \   |      /
(Building)— School  —————<offers>————————  Course  —(Length)
```

We turn each entity type into a record type, with the entity attributes becoming record attributes. In the above situation, we will have two record types, one based on the School entity type and the other on the Course.

	Course Record Type			School Record Type	
Key?	Attributes	References?	Key?	Attributes	References?
(*)	CourseCode		(*)	SchoolName	
	Title			Head	
	Level			Building	
	Length				

It remains to represent the relationship. One solution is to create a record type that contains the keys of the related entity types. This would enable us to connect any related schools and courses. However, there is a more common solution based on the cardinality of the relationship; a school may offer many courses but a course is offered by just *one* school. So we can add the school name as an extra attribute of the Course record type which now contains the necessary link between the entity types.

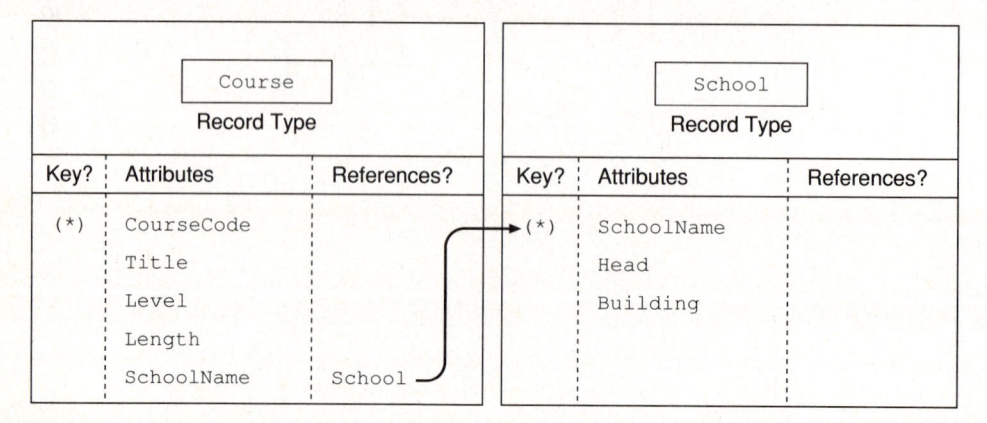

	Course Record Type			School Record Type	
Key?	Attributes	References?	Key?	Attributes	References?
(*)	CourseCode		►(*)	SchoolName	
	Title			Head	
	Level			Building	
	Length				
	SchoolName	School ┘			

11.4 The Conversion Process

Step 1: Entity types

Introduce a record type for each regular entity type. The key of this record type will be the key attribute(s) of the entity type. All *simple* attributes are incorporated directly. Composite attributes are replaced by their (simple) components. Set-valued attributes are ignored at this stage.

Those attributes forming the key should be marked as such. The Moreton Bay model contains eight of these entity types. The resulting record types are shown in Figures 11.16 and 11.17.

Step 2: Dependent entity types

Introduce a record type for each dependent entity type in the same way as was done for regular entity types. To each record, add the key of the owning entity type(s). The key of this new record type is the combination of the key of the owning entity type in conjunction with the partial key of the dependent entity type.

There is one such entity type in our model, the Committee. This record type will be as shown in Figure 11.18. In adding the owning entity reference, we have dealt with the relationship between these types.

Step 3: Many-to-many relationships

Introduce a new record type consisting of any attributes of that relationship. Add the keys of the record types associated with the entity types that participate in the relationship. In our model, there are four of these relationships:

Relationship	Entity Types
took	Student, Subject
taught	Lecturer, Subject
member	Lecturer, Committee
prereq	Subject, Subject

The resulting record types are shown in Figure 11.19.

Step 4: One-to-many relationships

Next we handle one-to-many (or many-to-one) relationships. These are distinguished from the many-to-many relationships just discussed. Consider the **divided** relationship. A faculty may be divided into several schools but a school is part of just one faculty. We have two options.

1. We can add the faculty name as an attribute of the school record type. We may do this because a school can only ever be part of one particular faculty.

2. Alternatively, we can introduce a record type specifically to represent the relationship, as was done with the many-to-many relationships.

The first option is the one more likely to be taken, because it will help reduce the total number of relations in the eventual database. However, if it is possible for schools to exist without being part of any faculty, then we must allow nulls in the faculty name attribute

Course Record Type

Key?	Attributes	References?
(*)	CourseCode	
	Title	
	Level	
	Length	

School Record Type

Key?	Attributes	References?
(*)	SchoolName	
	Head	
	Building	

Campus Record Type

Key?	Attributes	References?
(*)	CampusName	
	Address	
	Distance	
	BusNumber	

Club Record Type

Key?	Attributes	References?
(*)	ClubName	
	Building	
	PhoneNr	

Faculty Record Type

Key?	Attributes	References?
(*)	FacultyName	
	Dean	
	Building	

Lecturer Record Type

Key?	Attributes	References?
(*)	StaffId	
	Name	
	Title	
	Room	

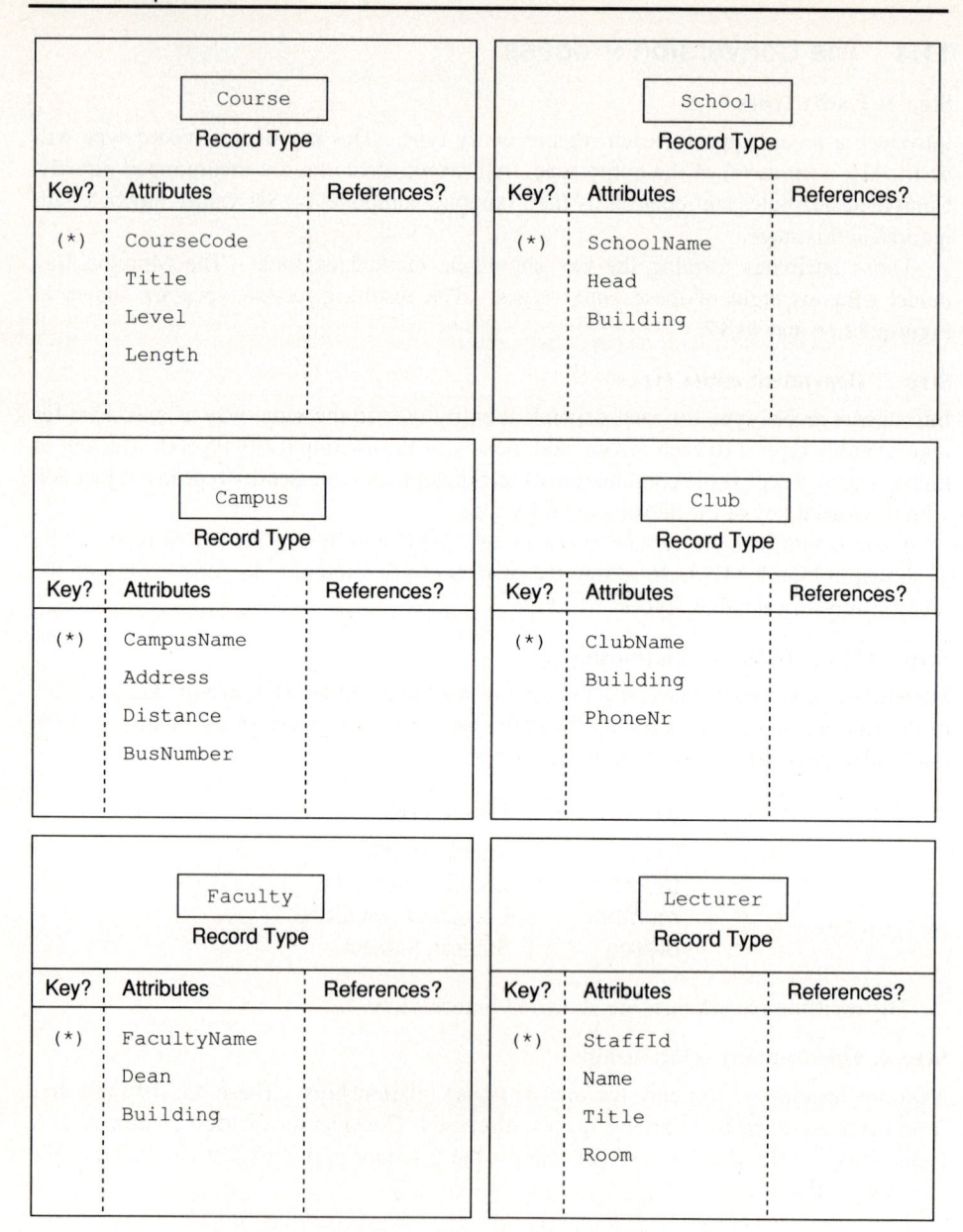

Figure 11.16 Record types based on entity types (part 1)

of the school record. If most of the schools are like this then we might choose the second option, creating a relation for those few schools that are linked to a faculty.

To handle these relationships it is helpful to list them in the following tabular form:

Entity-relationship Modeling 255

```
               Subject
              Record Type
```

Key?	Attributes	References?
(*)	SubjectCode	
	Title	

```
               Student
              Record Type
```

Key?	Attributes	References?
(*)	StudentId	
	FirstName	
	LastName	
	DateOfBirth	
	YearEnrolled	

Figure 11.17 Record types based on entity types (part 2)

```
              Committee
              Record Type
```

Key?	Attributes	References?
(*)	Title	
	Meets	
(*)	FacultyName	Faculty

Figure 11.18 A dependent entity

Relationship	N-Side	1-Side
contains	School	Campus
divided	School	Faculty
offers	Course	School
employs	Lecturer	School
contains	Subject	Course
enrolled	Student	Course

The table shows the relationship name and the entity type names. The runs relationship is omitted. It has already been processed in dealing with the dependent committee entity type. The column headed **N-Side** contains the record types that are to be extended by another attribute. The attribute to be added will be the key of the record type in the corresponding entry under the column marked **1-Side**. So, for example, with the contains relationship, the School record type will be extended to include the key of the Campus record type. This new attribute should be annotated to show which record type is being

Member Record Type

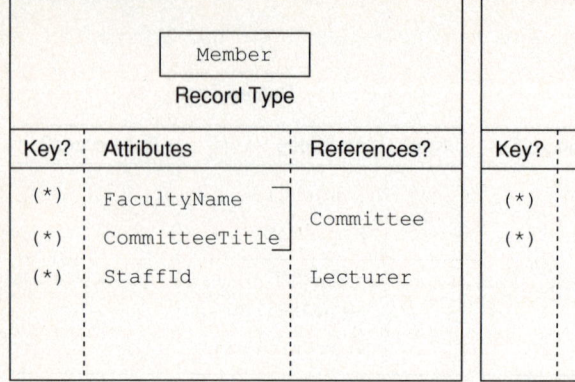

Key?	Attributes	References?
(*)	FacultyName	Committee
(*)	CommitteeTitle	
(*)	StaffId	Lecturer

Taught Record Type

Key?	Attributes	References?
(*)	StaffId	Lecturer
(*)	SubjectCode	Subject

Took Record Type

Key?	Attributes	References?
	Year	
	Semester	
	Grade	
(*)	StudentId	Student
(*)	SubjectCode	Subject

PreReq Record Type

Key?	Attributes	References?
(*)	SubjectCode	Subject
(*)	PreReqCode	Subject

Figure 11.19 The many-to-many relationships

referenced. In extending these record types we are adding a foreign key. The extended record types are shown in Figure 11.20.

Step 5: One-to-one relationships

These are a special case of the one-to-many situation, allowing us yet more options. There is just one example in the University, the has relationship between campuses and clubs.

1. We can represent the relationship as a separate relation, as we can with the other two kinds.

2. We can add the relationship to *either* of the record types associated with the participating entity types, rather than just one of them. We could have a Club record with a CampusName attribute or a Campus record with a ClubName attribute.

3. Finally, we can even merge the two record types together, in this case, forming a single Campus/Club record.

Perhaps we decide that the campus and the club *are* separate entities and should be represented separately. There is a final problem, however. Suppose we decide to add the CampusName to the Club record. The likelihood is that the ClubName is the same as that

Entity-relationship Modeling   257

School Record Type		
Key?	Attributes	References?
(*)	SchoolName	
	Head	
	Building	
	CampusName	Campus
	FacultyName	Faculty

Course Record Type		
Key?	Attributes	References?
(*)	CourseCode	
	Title	
	Level	
	Length	
	SchoolName	School

Lecturer Record Type		
Key?	Attributes	References?
(*)	StaffId	
	Name	
	Title	
	Room	
	SchoolName	School

Subject Record Type		
Key?	Attributes	References?
(*)	SubjectCode	
	Title	
	CourseCode	Course

Student Record Type		
Key?	Attributes	References?
(*)	StudentId	
	FirstName	
	LastName	
	DateOfBirth	
	YearEnrolled	
	CourseCode	Course

Figure 11.20 The One-to-many Relationships

of the campus on which it is located. So, after all this discussion, we decide to leave these two record types with the same attributes that they had after we had handled the entity types in Step 1; see Figure 11.16.

Step 6: Set-valued attributes

At this stage, we are left with one part of the model that has not been discussed. This consists of entity types with set-valued attributes. These were ignored in Steps 1 and 2. We could not incorporate them in the record types formed at that time because relations can only have simple or atomic-valued attributes.

The usual solution is to introduce a new record type that consists of two parts: (1) the key of the record type associated with the owning entity type, and (2) a single-valued version of the set-valued attribute. The key of this record consists of *all* the attributes of the record.

```
              ClubSport
             Record Type

   Key?  │  Attributes      │  References?

   (*)   │  ClubName        │  Club
   (*)   │  Sport           │
```

Figure 11.21 Resolving set-valued attributes

There is only one such attribute in the model, the **Sport** attribute of the Campus entity. The rule requires that we form a record type, say ClubSport, that consists of two attributes, ClubName and Sport. See Figure 11.21. The effect is to create a relation that allows us to add new sports that a club may offer and to remove ones that are no longer offered. This relation certainly provides us with flexibility, but it may be a flexibility that perhaps is not required. It may be that the information stored in this relation is quite static. Or it may be that, typically, there are only one or maybe two sports for a club, or that the set of entities is very small.

11.5 Issues in ER Modeling

In this section, we will discuss some issues that arise when we attempt to represent a situation using entities, attributes and relationships as our modeling tools.

11.5.1 Entity or Attribute?

There is unlikely to be just one correct ER diagram for a given situation. Sometimes what one person might see as an entity in its own right, another person will see as an attribute of some other entity. For example, the building in which a school is located is modeled as an attribute of that school. It might be argued that, more truly, there is a **location** relationship between schools and a new entity type **Building**. This view is supported by there being **Building** attributes for the faculty and club entity types as well, suggesting that buildings are important. But there are no facts specifically about buildings. It is the need to record information about the buildings themselves that makes buildings into an entity type. Should we need to know the age or height of a building, or whether or not it is air-conditioned, *then* we would introduce a **Building** entity type. In general, it is the need to collect information about things that makes them entities.

We can find three different kinds of attributes:

1. There are identifying attributes, which usually are labels, such as numerals or names, that we use to symbolize the entity.
2. There are the more conventional attributes which give us some measure of an entity. Examples are age, height, gender, and so on.
3. There are lesser relationships, involving things that failed the "entity of interest" test, such as the location relationship between schools and buildings. A building was not considered important enough to warrant an entity type of its own and so was made an attribute instead.

11.5.2 Entity or Relationship?

The distinction between entities and relationships may also be unclear.

In the Moreton Bay model, the taking of a subject by a student was represented as a relationship **takenby**. Each instance of this relationship corresponds to an attempt by a specific student on a specific subject in a specific semester and year. We might see the attempt as an entity and model it as shown in Figure 11.22.

The **Attempt** entity type is dependent on both the student and subject types, so it has an identifying relationship with the combination. This new relationship is one-to-many, whereas the original **takenby** relationship was many-to-many.

In terms of its effect on any eventual database design, the choice of whether to model the situation as an entity or as a relationship makes no difference, in this case. Instead of generating a record type in Step 3 of the conversion process, an identical record will arise in Step 2 instead.

11.5.3 Naming

Given that we might have trouble distinguishing between entities, attributes and relationships, it is important that we name carefully each component of our ER diagram.

Entity Types: These should be given singular names that correspond to individual instances of the type. Use **Campus** rather than **Campuses**. This follows the convention used in Chapter 2 regarding the introduction of basic types. Naturally, every type should have a unique name.

Relationships: Each entity that participates in a relationship will play a particular role in that relationship. A student **takes** a subject; a subject is **taken by** a student. The student plays the **takes** role, and the subject the **taken** one.

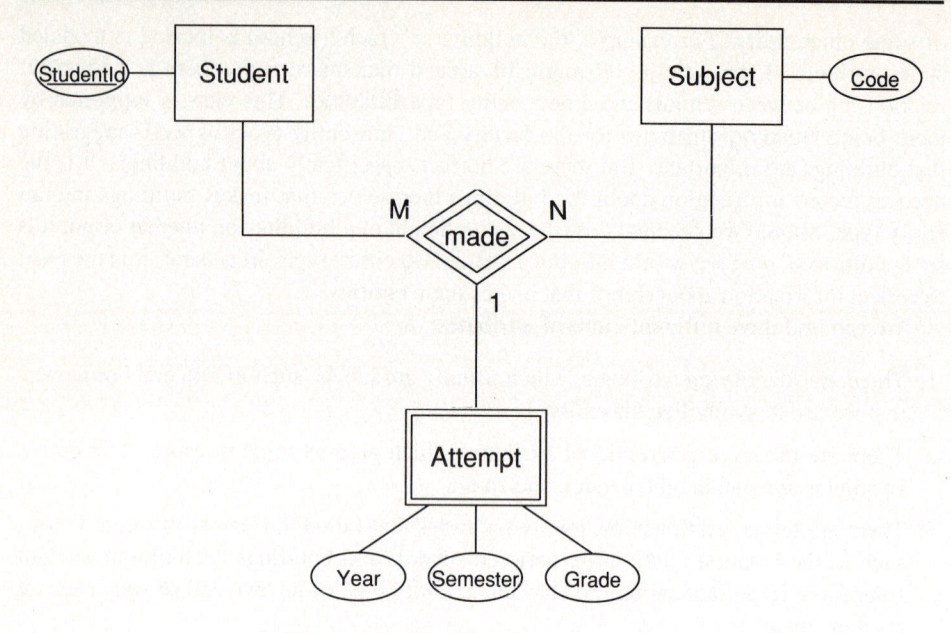

Figure 11.22 The Attempt entity

There are a number of options for naming the relationship, given that we have a small diamond-shaped symbol into which we must squeeze the meaning of the relationship.

1. We may decide that one of the roles is more important than the other or others, and use *that* role to identify the relationship.
2. We may choose, as has been done in this chapter, to use the role of the entity type that is either above or to the left of the relationship symbol. This allows us to read the diagram from top to bottom and from left to right in the usual way.
3. We may derive a noun that amalgamates the roles, such as **membership** between committees and lecturers or **offering** between schools and courses.

Note that relationship names need not be unique. It is enough that the name be unique to all the relationships between the particular entity types involved.

Attributes: In Section 11.5.1 it was suggested that there are three kinds of attributes. There are three correspondings options regarding their names.

1. Identifying attributes are symbols or labels by which the owning entities are recognized. These will be names, titles, codes, numerals and other forms of identification.
2. Measuring attributes are ones such as height, width, distance, value, counts and so on. There is little point in attaching an attribute **Number** or **Money** to an entity type. It is sensible to use the name of the corresponding property such as **Distance** or **CostPrice**.
3. There are attributes, such as the **Building** attribute of the school entity type, which correspond to lesser or failed relationships. There are two choices. We can use the name of the failed entity type, as in the case of the building attribute. Alternatively,

we can name the role played by that lesser entity type, as was done in the case of the Head attribute of the school.

Attribute names need only be unique for a particular entity type, although when developing records for the database, we will need to be careful.

11.5.4 Optional and Mandatory Roles

It is reasonable to suggest the following.

- Not every lecturer is a member of any committee.
- Not every student need have taken a subject yet (because he or she has just enrolled at the University).
- Not every campus need necessarily have a club.

If a lecturer need not be a member of a committee, then we say that the role is **optional** for the lecturer entity type. Not every instance of the current lecturing population need participate in the relationship; it is inappropriate or irrelevant for some.

Conversely, it is reasonable to suggest that every lecturer is employed by some school or another. That role is said to be **mandatory** for lecturers. The compulsory nature of this role is indicated by a double line connecting the lecturer entity type to the employs relationship, as shown in Figure 11.23.

Figure 11.23 Every lecturer belongs to a school

This analysis suggests that, when we construct a record type for lecturers and add the SchoolName as a foreign key, we should not allow the SchoolName attribute to be null. If every lecturer belongs to a school then there should never be a null value there. However, the issue is more complex. It may be that we need to record details of lecturers even if we are unaware which school employs them. Thus the semantics of the situation become confused with the restrictions imposed upon our recording of that situation. It may be better, therefore, to postpone analysis of optionality until we have developed *record* structures, that is, until the basic record types have evolved from the conversion process.

A similar situation arises with attributes. Every campus is a certain distance from the city center; it cannot be otherwise. Yet, it may be that we do not know that distance, or have not bothered to measure it, and so cannot record it. So we may have to permit a null value in the Distance attribute of the Campus record type.

11.6 Summary

In this chapter we have looked at the entity relationship approach (ERA) as an alternative to the fact-based approach (FBA) to database design that was introduced in Chapter 8 and used in Chapter 10.

- ERA says:

    Look for the *objects* that populate the situation to be modeled.

    FBA says:

    Write down the *facts* about the situation that are of interest to us.

- ERA says:

    Let's be practical. In any situation, it will very quickly become clear which objects are important. Inevitably, we will have relations based on these objects.

    FBA says:

    Let's not be hasty. A database is a repository of facts. We should look at these first, analyze them, and let the rules about merging facts determine which relations we will have.

- ERA says:

    But your approach makes all objects of equal importance, whereas ERA allows us to say that some objects are important, we call them entities; others are of lesser importance, we call them attributes. This hierarchy allows us more flexibility.

    FBA says:

    Yes, but to decide whether something is an entity or an attribute, for example, requires some kind of analysis of the facts in which the thing is involved. In other words, you are performing fact-based analysis but you won't admit it!

- ERA says:

    Lots more people use ER modeling than fact-based analysis.

    FBA says:

    Lots of people used to think the world was flat, but we have progressed since then.

- ERA says:

    Graphical representations are an essential part of data modeling.

    FBA says:

    Yes, graphical representations are an essential part of data modeling.

Exercises

▶ Q11.1 The ROCKY CONCRETE Model

An entity-relationship diagram has been developed for the Rocky Concrete Company.

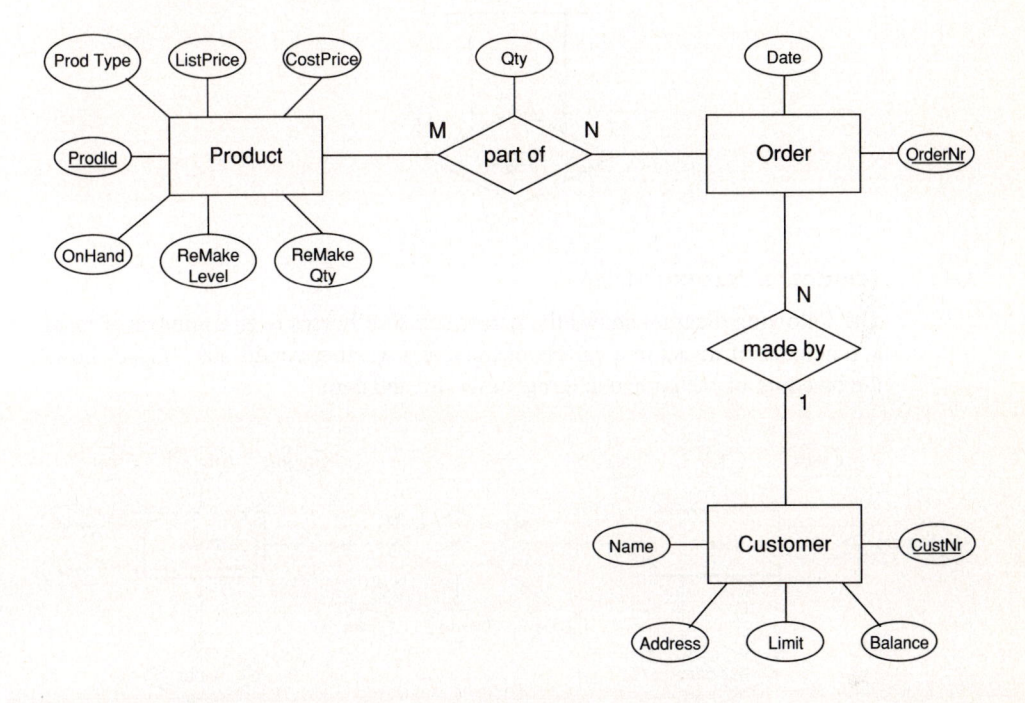

```
(Prod Type)  (ListPrice) (CostPrice)         (Qty)                    (Date)
         \        |     /                     |                         |
   (ProdId)--[ Product ]----M---<part of>---N----[ Order ]----(OrderNr)
         /       |    \
   (OnHand) (ReMake  (ReMake
             Level)   Qty)
                                                    |
                                                    N
                                                 <made by>
                                                    1
                                                    |
                                    (Name)--[ Customer ]--(CustNr)
                                           /     |     \
                                    (Address) (Limit) (Balance)
```

a. List the entity types in this model and for each entity type, list the identifying attribute(s).

b. List the relationships and the cardinality of each.

c. Develop a database design from this model.

Q11.2 The CARE Model

A community action group, known as CARE, has been established. It plans to maintain database on its members in which it will record their names, addresses and phone numbers as well as any specific help they feel able to offer. The group occasionally needs to quickly pass information to its members regarding meetings and other actions. This is to be done by means of a "telephone tree" whereby the person at the top of the tree rings a few people, each of whom in turn ring a few people, and so on. Develop a database design from this model.

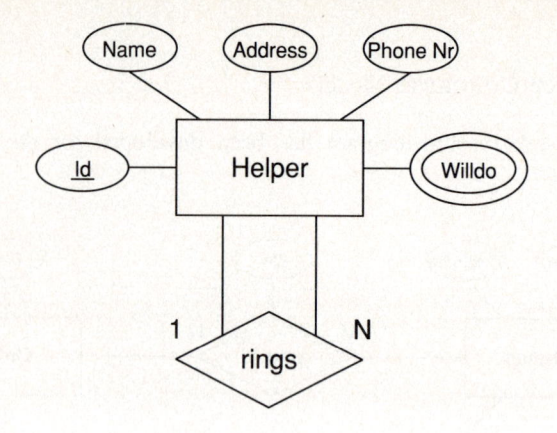

Q11.3 The HORSE RACING Model

The following diagram shows the performance of horses over a number of races at a number of tracks in a variety of track and weather conditions. It also shows the breeding of each horse in terms of its sire and dam.

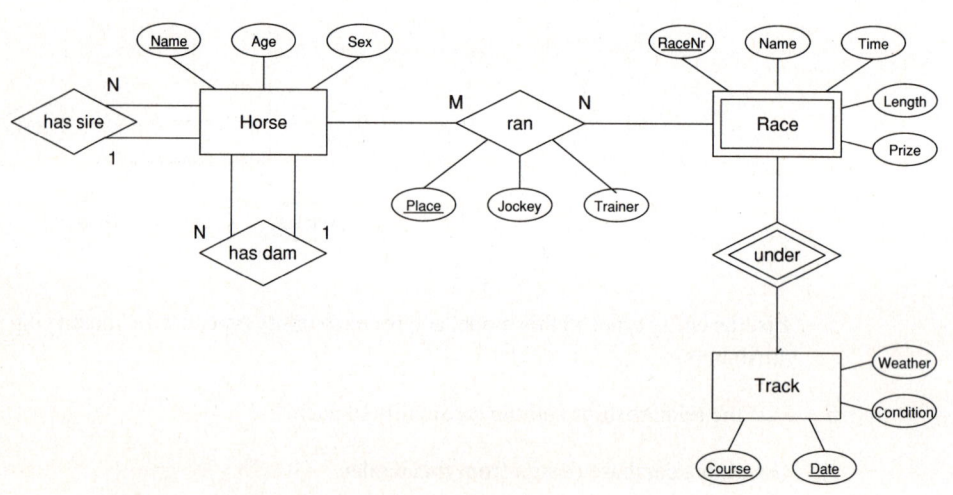

Develop a database design from this model.

Q11.4 The BEST SPREAD Model

Here is an entity-relationship diagram for Marge Butter and the Cholesterols. See the corresponding question in the exercises at the end of Chapter 10.

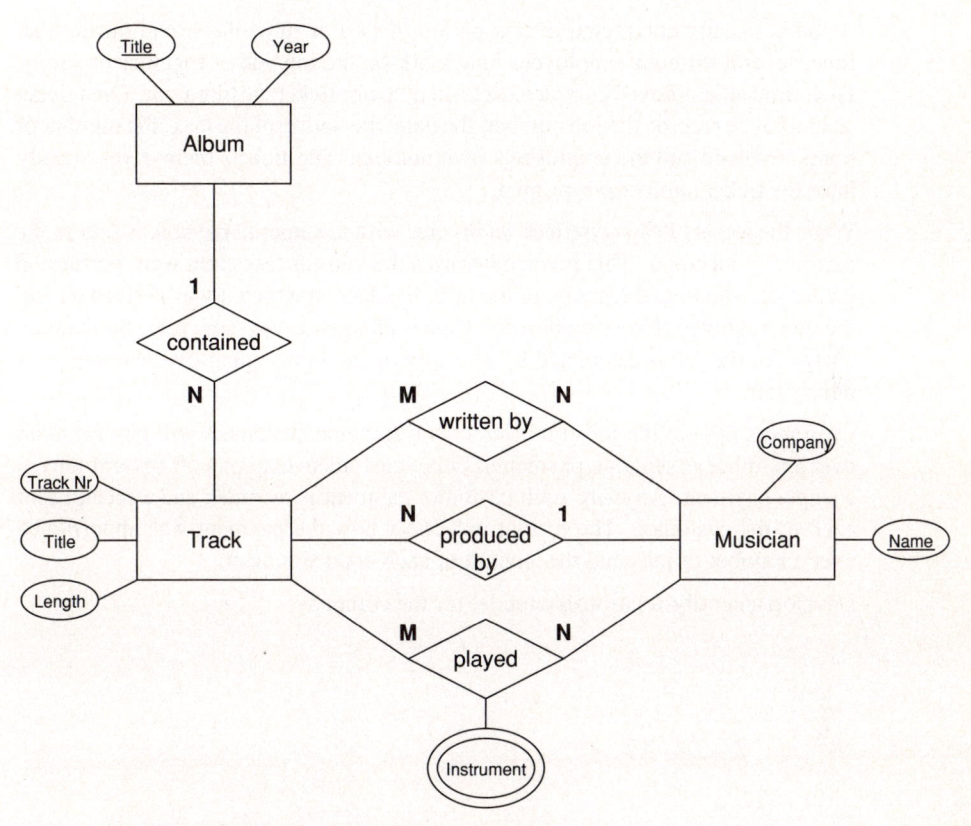

[Entity-relationship diagram: Album entity (with attributes Title, Year) is linked via a 1:N "contained" relationship to Track entity (with attributes Track Nr, Title, Length). Track is linked to Musician entity (with attributes Company, Name) via an M:N "written by" relationship and an N:1 "produced by" relationship. Track is also linked to Musician via an M:N "played" relationship, which has a multi-valued attribute Instrument.]

Develop a database design from this model.

Q11.5 The ODD JOB Company

The Odd Job Co. was started by some out-of-work computing graduates from the Moreton Bay University. They were unfortunate enough to graduate in the middle of a recession. The company claims to be able to accomplish any task, simple or challenging, clean or dirty, as befits the company motto:

Tedium ad Nauseam

which roughly translates as:

Anything is better than writing COBOL!

How ironic, then, that the company is made up of four divisions.

The company will take on any job, no matter how unqualified it might be and no matter how many other jobs it is already tackling or is committed to tackling. It guarantees to finish the job on time. (Actually the fine print of the company's contract states that it guarantees to get a job 95% complete.)

A job is usually completed over a period of two or three days, and during that time, several different employees may work on the job, either together or singly. Each time an employee completes a task, a "work ticket" is filled out. On a ticket an employee records the job number, the date, the nature of the task, the number of hours involved and the employee's own number. The tickets themselves already have the ticket number pre-printed.

When the job is (95%) complete, an invoice with the amount payable is sent to the customer concerned. This invoice itemizes the various tasks that were performed on the job, showing the nature of the task, the date on which it was performed and the time involved. Every employee's time is charged at the same rate. So the total charge for the job is calculated by multiplying the hours spent by the company's hourly rate.

Customers pay for the jobs in different ways. Some customers will pay for a job over a number of separate payments. Other customers may pay off several jobs in a single payment. Anyway, each customer payment is recorded and a receipt sent back to the customer. The receipt will show how the payment was apportioned over a number of jobs and the amount of each apportionment.

Develop an entity-relationship model for the company.

CHAPTER 12

Knowledge

12.1 Introduction

This chapter is an introduction to the **Z Notation** which is a language that allows us to express our understanding of any given situation in a concise and precise way. In Chapter 1, it was suggested that if we write down all that we know about something, then our statements may be divided into (1) simple specific statements that were termed **facts** and (2) more general statements that were termed **knowledge**. This chapter is concerned with the more general statements, that is, it is about knowledge representation. Z is the language we will use to express that knowledge.

The generality of knowledge is achieved by the statements involved saying something about whole classes or sets of objects. Such knowledge will eventually be encoded as computer programs, so Z will be used to **specify** these programs. The resulting specification will then be **implemented** using a programming language. It is important, however, to realize that the implementation is yet another description of the *same* situation that was portrayed in the original specification. The implementation is a kind of re-specification of that situation, this time written in a specification language that the computer can follow and obey or execute. This implementation is, in effect, an **executable** specification; that is, it will be written using a programming language such as C or COBOL or SQL or some combination of these.

The Z Notation is a particular style of writing two mathematical languages, **set theory** and **predicate calculus**. Z is an amalgam of these. Most of the ideas relating to set construction and manipulation were discussed in Chapter 3. In this chapter, we will see how to write set expressions in Z. Mostly, this involves using a special symbol rather than a word. For example, Z uses the symbol ∪ for set union whereas in Chapter 3 and in the coverage of SQL that followed, we would have used the word `union` instead.

The second element of Z is predicate calculus, and many of the ideas behind this theory have also been discussed previously. This was done in Chapter 2 where we discussed basic simple facts and their construction. In Z, basic facts are also constructed in the same way, so Chapter 2 was also an introduction to the language. In that chapter, we also saw how compound sentences may be formed from simpler ones using negation, conjunction and disjunction. Z also allows us to compound sentences except that again, special symbols, rather than words, are used. For example, the symbol ¬ is used for negation rather than the word **not**.

There is a part of predicate calculus that has not yet been discussed. This chapter examines **quantification** which is the fundamental method by which we may make a statement about a class or set of objects.

12.2 The Predicate Calculus

This is the name given to a system for constructing and manipulating statements about the world, or, at least, our perceptions of selected aspects of some situation. The statements are referred to as predicates, and the rules relating to their manipulation are the calculus – hence the name **predicate calculus**.

The system contains two kinds of rules.

1. There are rules about how we construct predicates. These rules determine the way in which we represent our knowledge of some world.

2. There are also rules and methods to help us manipulate existing predicates to derive or **prove** hitherto unstated knowledge of that world.

We can summarize the system in the following "equation":

PREDICATE CALCULUS = KNOWLEDGE REPRESENTATION + PROOF METHODS

This chapter is concerned with the representational aspects, and discusses how to construct predicates of increasing complexity and generality.

12.2.1 Simple Sentences

We will return to the database of facts concerning the circle of friends, relations and acquaintances that was introduced in Chapter 2. There are six basic types:

$$[Person, Sport, N, Gender, Language, CarMake]$$

There are also seven basic relationships represented. Each of these relationships, in its own way, may be used to form simple sentences.

1. $\_plays\_ : Person \leftrightarrow Sport$

   This relationship is called *plays*. It is a relation ($\leftrightarrow$) between people and sports, that is, a person may play many sports and a sport may be played by many people. It may be used to construct such sentences as *Alan plays tennis*. It is used in *infix* form, that is, when used, it appears between a person and a sport. The form that sentences constructed with *plays* take is dictated by the declaration. There we are told to use it this way by the appearance of underscores (_).

2. $speaks : Person \leftrightarrow Language$

This is also a relation. Some of the people speak more than one foreign language, and some of the languages are spoken by more than one member of the circle. It is used in prefix form to construct sentences such as: *speaks(Sue, Italian)*.

3. *sex* : *Person* → *Gender*

    This is a total function, signified by the symbol → , meaning that it is a special kind of relation, one that is special in two ways. Everyone has a gender *and* no-one has more than one gender. Functions are used, not to construct complete sentences, but, through function application, to describe objects such as *sex(Alan)*. These objects are then glued together to form sentences.

4. *age* : *Person* → *N*

    This is another total function used to identify numbers such as *age(Kim)*. Everyone's age is known but nobody has more than one age.

5. *drives* : *Person* ↦ *CarMake*

    This is a partial function, signified by the symbol ↦ . A partial function is less restrictive than a total function in that not everyone need participate in the relationship. That is, not everyone need drive a car. It is used, like the two previous functions, to identify objects using such expressions as *drives(Ann)*.

6. *spouse* : *Person* ⤖ *Person*

    This is a partial injection, signified by the symbol ⤖ . Thus it is a one-to-one relationship in which not everyone need participate. It should be treated as a particular kind of partial function, and it will be used like a function to identify objects such as *spouse(Alan)*.

7. *left* : *Person* ↣ *Person*

    This is a total injection, signified by the symbol ↣ . It is a one-to-one relationship in which everybody participates. Everybody round the table has one person on their left, and everybody is immediately to the left of just one person.

12.2.2 Terms

Given the declaration of *plays*, we know that any simple sentence using this relation must be of the following form:

Person		*Sport*
Representation	*plays*	Representation

The representation for a person need not be a simple name such as *Alan*. It can be of any form that allows us to identify an *individual* person. The relationship called *left* provides us with another way using **function application**. Everybody at the table has just *one* person to their immediate left, for example, Alan is on Ann's left. We can construct a simple sentence to state this formally:

$$left(Ann) = Alan$$

This equation shows that there are (at least) two ways of representing the person in question, *left(Ann)* and *Alan*. The fact that Alan plays tennis, can also be said as:

$$left(Ann) \; plays \; tennis$$

Because of the nature of a functional relationship, for example, because each person has just *one* person to their immediate left, we use functions to identify individual objects. We expect to use *left* to identify somebody rather than using it to construct complete sentences in the way that *plays* was. It may seem that functions are being used in a more limited way than relations; but, in fact, they provide us with more flexibility of expression.

In general, we will pair the symbol *left* with a person, as follows:

	Person
left	Representation

And again, the representation used for a person may be as simple or as complex as we need or care to make it. We could refer to the person second on the left from Ann as:

$$left(left(Ann))$$

We give the name **term** to any symbol or symbolic expression that represents an object, so we can follow the symbol *left* with any term that represents a person. More generally, a term may be any of the following:

- a **constant** such as *Ann* or *tennis* or 41; or
- a **variable** such as x or p; or
- an expression constructed using function application, as discussed above, for example, $left(Alan)$ or $sex(spouse(p))$.

12.2.3 Compound Sentences

We can construct more complex sentences from simpler ones using **sentential operators**. There are five of these. Three of them, negation, conjunction and disjunction, were introduced in Chapter 2 and were used extensively in the chapters that followed.

1. Negation (*not*)

    Previously, to say that Alan doesn't speak Chinese, we would have written:

    $not \; speaks(Alan, \; Chinese)$

    In Z, we use the symbol $\neg$ instead of the word *not* and write the sentence as:

    $\neg \; speaks(Alan, \; Chinese)$

    Apart from that difference, its usage is the same as discussed in Section 2.8.2.

2. Conjunction (*and*)

    For this operation, we use the symbol $\wedge$ instead of the word *and*. To say that Bob and Kim are both 23, we can write:

    $age(Kim) = 23 \wedge age(Bob) = 23$

3. Disjunction (*or*)

   For this operation, we use the symbol ∨ instead of the word *or*. To say that Alan plays tennis or golf (or possibly both), we write:

   Alan plays tennis ∨ *Alan plays golf*

The other two operators, implication and equivalence, are new and have a role in the construction of the more general statements that are the concern of this chapter. These operations are discussed in more detail later.

12.3 Quantification

12.3.1 Existential Quantification

We can use the *plays* relation to verify such statements as:

   Alan plays tennis

This statement is true because the *plays* relation contains the pair (*Alan, tennis*) as one of its elements. What if we wanted to make a slightly weaker but more general statement? Perhaps we want to say something such as:

   Somebody plays tennis

This, we are sure, is true; but we cannot claim that it is true in the same way as we claim that Alan plays tennis. There is no pair (*Somebody, tennis*) in the relation involved. We could fudge the situation by inserting such a pair; but that would introduce many more problems than it would solve. What if we wanted to say that:

   Somebody speaks Spanish

We could insert a pair (*Somebody, Spanish*) into the *speaks* relation. But would that somebody be the same person who plays tennis?

Another, somewhat more acceptable, solution is to use set comprehension to define the set of people who play tennis and then to count the result.

   $\#\{p : Person \mid p \text{ plays tennis}\} > 0$

This statement says that the number of people who play tennis is greater than zero. It has the meaning we intend, but it is hardly a natural way of expression; it does not match the English equivalent.

The statement may be rephrased more naturally using **existential quantification**:

   $\exists p : Person \bullet p \text{ plays tennis}$

The predicate *p plays tennis* has been taken from within the set expression and prefixed by the quantifier $\exists p : Person$. The spot • is used to separate them. The overall expression corresponds very closely to the English expression:

   There exists a person who plays tennis.

The role of the pronoun *who* has been taken by the variable p. Note, however, that the expression is more accurately translated as:

There is *at least one* person who plays tennis.

There may be more than one person, there may not. There is a special form of existential quantification used when we want to make a statement about *one* person or thing:

$\exists! \, p : Person \bullet p \; plays \; tennis$

This is to be read as:

There is *exactly one* person who plays tennis.

Existential Quantification:

$\exists \, Declaration \bullet Predicate$

Unique Quantification:

$\exists! \, Declaration \bullet Predicate$

Example 12.1 Somebody drives a Mercedes.

$\exists \, p : Person \bullet drives(p) = Mercedes$

This can be interpreted as saying that at least one person drives a Mercedes, whereas:

$\exists! \, p : Person \bullet drives(p) = Mercedes$

means that only one person drives a Mercedes. This latter form is really just a short way of saying that:

There is somebody who drives a Mercedes *and* there is no other person who does.

Put formally, this can be stated as:

$\exists \, p : Person \bullet (drives(p) = Mercedes \, \wedge$
$\neg \, \exists \, q : Person \bullet (drives(q) = Mercedes \wedge q \neq p))$

In other words:

There is a person p who drives a Mercedes and there is no person q ($\neg \, \exists \, q : Person$) who drives a Mercedes and who is not p.

The existential quantifier ($\exists$) is often written using a predicate that involves the conjunction ("and"-ing) of two simpler predicates. Fortunately, they are not all as complex as the last one. If we want to say that:

There are people over 40 who play squash.

Knowledge 273

we can write this as:

$\exists\, p : Person \bullet age(p) > 40 \wedge p\ plays\ squash$

This can be read as saying that there exists at least one person who is aged over 40 and who plays squash.

When an existentially quantified predicate involves conjunction, then we are effectively strengthening our statement about the situation. We are not merely saying that somebody plays squash, but that somebody *over 40* plays squash. By making a weak statement about a subset (those over 40) as distinct from the entire set (everybody in the circle), we are making a stronger statement. A general pattern to follow is given in Figure 12.1.

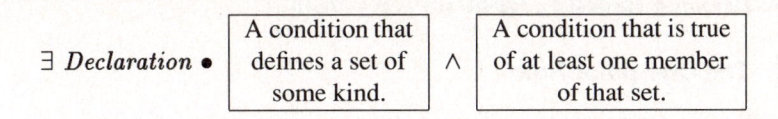

$\exists\, Declaration \bullet$ | A condition that defines a set of some kind. | $\wedge$ | A condition that is true of at least one member of that set.

Figure 12.1 Existential quantification with conjunction

Example 12.2 Some women speak Japanese.
The first condition defines the set of women and the second that some of them speak Japanese.

$\exists\, p : Person \bullet sex(p) = F \wedge speaks(p, Japanese)$

Sets and Existential Quantification

Set specification is exactly the same in Z as it was described in Chapter 3. For example, if we want to specify the set of men in the circle, we can write it in extension as:

$\{Alan, Bob, Mark\}$

or, we can define it by comprehension as:

$\{p : Person \mid sex(p) = M\}$

However, the set membership operator, in Z, is the symbol $\in$ rather than the word *in*. For example, to say that Bob is in the set of males, we would write:

$Bob \in \{p : Person \mid sex(p) = M\}$

The above predicate can be read variously as:

Bob is an element of ...
Bob is a member of ...
Bob is in ...
Bob belongs to ...

We can interchange expressions such as the one above with similar statements written using existential quantification. For example, to say that Kim speaks Japanese, we would probably write:

$speaks(Kim, Japanese)$

However, we could say that "Kim is one of those people who speak Japanese" and write this in terms of set membership as follows.

$Kim \in \{p : Person \mid speaks(p, Japanese)\}$

We could also express the same fact as "somebody called Kim speaks Japanese". This form seems to map to existential quantification.

$\exists p : Person \bullet speaks(p, Japanese) \land p = Kim$

12.3.2 The One-point Rule

This is an equivalence rule that allows us to move from a set theoretical expression to a predicate calculus expression and vice versa. The rule is as follows:

The One-point Rule:

$\exists x : S \bullet x = t \land P \equiv t \in S \land P[t/x]$

S is some set
P is a predicate of some kind
t is a term
$P[t/x]$ is the predicate P with all free occurrences of x replaced by the term t, and is read as "P with t for x"

To say that:

"There is an object x of type S that satisfies P, and t is another name for x."

is the same as saying that:

"t is a member of the set S and P is true of t."

and vice-versa. For example:

$\exists p : Person \bullet p = Alan \land p \text{ plays tennis}$

has the form of the left-hand side of the equivalence, with:

x replaced by p
S by $Person$
t by $Alan$
P by p plays tennis

The form: $P[t/x]$ becomes $(p \text{ plays tennis})[Alan/p]$ which is: $Alan \text{ plays tennis}$, and the right-hand side becomes:

$Alan \in Person \land Alan \text{ plays tennis}$

12.3.3 Universal Quantification

Suppose we want to say that:

> Everybody plays golf

We could claim that this is false because (*Everybody*, *golf*) does not appear in the *plays* relation; the problem is solved.

What if we want to say that:

> Everybody is under 80 years old.

Again, we could fudge this by inserting the pair (*Everybody*, 79) into the relation; and, again, this would introduce more problems than it would solve. It would allow us to say, for example, that Mark is younger than everybody; which, of course, is untrue.

This problem can also be overcome by using set notation:

$$\#\{p : Person \mid age(p) < 80\} = \#Person$$

The number of people aged under 80 is the same as the total number of all people.

There is a neater way of making our claim using **universal quantification**:

$$\forall p : Person \bullet age(p) < 80$$

The predicate $age(p) < 80$ has been extracted from the set expression and prefixed by the quantifier $\forall p : Person$. The new expression corresponds to the English:

> All people are aged under 80.

The general form of universal quantification is:

Universal Quantification:

$\forall$ *Declaration* $\bullet$ *Predicate*

12.3.4 Implication

Frequently we will want to make statements that narrow the extent of the quantification. Thus we may want to write something such as:

> All men are over 20.

This is a sentence that would suggest the use of universal quantification. However, we do not have a type *Man* and so *cannot* say:

$$\forall m : Man \bullet age(m) > 20$$

We could look at the original sentence another way and say that:

> Everybody is either not male or is over 20.

Now we can use quantification:

$$\forall p : Person \bullet (\neg sex(p) = M) \vee age(p) > 20$$

There are two conditions in the predicate (1) $\neg sex(p) = M$ and (2) $age(p) > 20$. These are "or"-ed together; that is, the entire predicate is true if *either* of these two conditions is true.

The entire predicate $(\neg sex(p) = M) \vee age(p) > 20$ is true for all women, regardless of their age, because $\neg sex(p) = M$ must always be true for these people.

For men, for the predicate to be true, it requires that the second condition $age(p) > 20$ be true because the first, $\neg sex(p) = M$, will *always* be false for men. The effect is that the entire quantification is true only if all *men* are aged over 20.

This argument is considerably simplified if a new Boolean operator or sentence connective is introduced. This new operator is called **implication** and is written as $\Rightarrow$. The statement $P \Rightarrow Q$ is read as:

P implies *Q*; or

if *P* then *Q*.

It is defined as:

$$P \Rightarrow Q \equiv \neg P \vee Q$$

The original statement on men's ages can now be written as:

$$\forall p : Person \bullet sex(p) = M \Rightarrow age(p) > 20$$

which can be interpreted as saying:

For all people, *p*, if *p* is a male then *p* is aged over 20.

For all people, *p*, *p* being male implies *p* is over 20.

Implication is frequently used with universal quantification to narrow down the class of objects about whom or which the predicate is universally true. Implication is a way of weakening a universal general statement. The pattern for its usage is shown in Figure 12.2.

$\forall$ Declaration $\bullet$ | A condition that defines a set of some kind. | $\Rightarrow$ | A condition that is true of *all* members of that set.

Figure 12.2 Universal quantification with implication

Example 12.3 All women are over 25 years old.

$$\forall p : Person \bullet sex(p) = F \Rightarrow age(p) > 25$$

The first condition specifies the set of women; the second states what is true of all members of that set.

A summary of the implication operator is given in Figure 12.3.

Operation:	Implication
Z Symbol:	$\Rightarrow$
Usage:	$P \Rightarrow Q$
Pronounced:	if P then Q P implies Q
Sometimes:	$\rightarrow$ or $\supset$
Example:	If Mark is over 45 then he plays tennis. $age(Mark) > 45 \Rightarrow Mark\ plays\ tennis$
Truth Table:	$\begin{array}{ccc} P & Q & P \Rightarrow Q \\ \hline true & true & true \\ true & false & false \\ false & true & true \\ false & false & true \end{array}$
Notes:	A sentence of the form $P \Rightarrow Q$ is true if either $\neg P$ or Q, or both, are true and false otherwise. This suggests that we can define the implication operator in terms of negation and disjunction. $$P \Rightarrow Q \equiv \neg P \vee Q$$ The truth table is better interpreted by going in from the left and right columns to the middle one. In particular, the first line of the table says that, given the truth of P and of $P \Rightarrow Q$, we can deduce that Q is true. This is the rule of inference known as **modus ponens**. Implication is further discussed in Section 12.3.4.

Figure 12.3 Implication

12.3.5 A Summary of Quantification

The various forms of quantification provide ways of making general statements of various degrees of strength. There are four major forms involved and they are presented in

Figure 12.4 as a spectrum from the strongest to the weakest.

Strong .... Weak

1.	2.	3.	4.
Everybody plays tennis.	Everybody over 50 plays tennis.	Somebody over 50 plays tennis.	Somebody plays tennis.
$\forall\, p : Person \bullet$ $p\ plays\ tennis$	$\forall\, p : Person \bullet$ $age(p) > 50 \Rightarrow$ $p\ plays\ tennis$	$\exists\, p : Person \bullet$ $age(p) > 50 \wedge$ $p\ plays\ tennis$	$\exists\, p : Person \bullet$ $p\ plays\ tennis$

Figure 12.4 General statements

12.3.6 Quantifier Equivalences

Although universal and existential quantification may seem to be quite different in the kinds of statements that we would wish to make using them, any statement written using universal quantification may, in fact, be rewritten using existential quantification, and vice versa.

1. We would probably feel that the following two statements are equivalent:

    Everybody plays badminton.

    There isn't anybody who doesn't play badminton.

    These may be written, respectively, as:

    $\forall\, p : Person \bullet p\ plays\ badminton$

    $\neg \exists\, p : Person \bullet \neg(p\ plays\ badminton)$

    These examples reflect the following general equivalence:

    > First Equivalence:
    >
    > $\forall\, Declaration \bullet Predicate \equiv \neg \exists\, Declaration \bullet \neg Predicate$

    In the above example, the declaration is $p : Person$ and the predicate is $p\ plays\ badminton$.

2. We would probably also feel that the following statements are equivalent:

    Not everybody plays squash.

Some people don't play squash.

These may be expressed, respectively, as:

$\neg \forall p : Person \bullet p\ plays\ squash$
$\exists p : Person \bullet \neg (p\ plays\ squash)$

These examples reflect a second general equivalence:

Second Equivalence:

$\neg \forall\ Declaration \bullet Predicate \equiv \exists\ Declaration \bullet \neg Predicate$

In the above example, the declaration is $p : Person$ and the predicate is $p\ plays\ squash$.
When writing an expression that involves some kind of quantification, we may use either $\exists$ or $\forall$ depending on our personal style.

It was previously stated that, in existential quantification, the predicate part often involves the conjunction or and'ing of two conditions.

This is not accidental; the above two statements reflect two different styles of saying the same thing. Suppose that T is some type of thing that interests us and that P and Q are two conditions involving some element t of type T.

$\forall t : T \bullet P \Rightarrow Q$
$\equiv \forall t : T \bullet \neg P \vee Q$
(from the definition of $\Rightarrow$)
$\equiv \neg \exists t : T \bullet \neg(\neg P \vee Q)$
(quantifier equivalence)
$\equiv \neg \exists t : T \bullet \neg\neg P \wedge \neg Q$
(De Morgan's laws)
$\equiv \neg \exists t : T \bullet P \wedge \neg Q$
(simplification)

Using the following substitutions:

T becomes $Person$
P becomes $sex(p) = M$
Q becomes $age(p) > 20$

and the first and last lines of the above equations, we get:

$\forall p : Person \bullet sex(p) = M \Rightarrow age(p) > 20$
$\neg \exists p : Person \bullet sex(p) = M \wedge \neg age(p) > 20$

Or, in English, the two equivalent sentences:

All men are over 20.

There isn't a man who is not over 20.

12.4 Defining New Symbols

The development of a new computer system presents us with what seem, at first, to be almost insuperable problems. The task threatens to overwhelm us. The problems we face range from user interface design to performance requirements, and from operational and development costing to functional requirements. Suppose we look at the last of these, at the functional requirements, that is, at what the system is basically meant to do. Even there, the task is huge. The usual approach to this kind of situation is to divide the task into a number of smaller tasks, and then attempt to handle and overcome each of these in turn. We continue this process of decomposition until the tasks become ones that the computer can perform itself, without any further direction.

As we do so, we will inevitably find that certain basic tasks are required in a number of different parts of the system. Suppose the system is a loans system for a library. We might discover that, in handling the return of overdue books, there is a need to calculate the difference in days between the date the book was due back and the date on which it was returned. In some other part, when calculating the average length of loans, we might need to calculate the difference between the day on which the book was borrowed and the day it was returned.

We make use of this commonality by creating a single program module (subroutine, procedure, section, subprogram or whatever). That module is used whenever and wherever required. Those programs needing the calculation merely refer to the module *by name*. The corresponding instructions are accessed and executed.

An analogous situation occurs when specifying a system. In discussing or describing a situation, we will repeatedly need to refer to certain relationships and objects. The solution to this problem is to *name* that situation or object, that is, to introduce a single name that stands for the set of conditions that make up the situation. To see how we might introduce new symbols, suppose we try to formalize the following fact about the circle.

> Sue is married to Alan.

We could look at this two ways, depending, perhaps, on whether we take Sue's part or Alan's.

> Either: $spouse(Sue) = Alan$ Or: $spouse(Alan) = Sue$

We know that both these versions are correct because of a general law concerning marriages.

$$\forall\, p, q : dom\ spouse \bullet$$
$$spouse(p) = q \Leftrightarrow spouse(q) = p$$

We can interpret this as follows.

> Suppose we take any two people p and q from the set of all married people, then if q is the spouse of p then p is the spouse of q and vice versa.

Because we took *any* two people from the set, the equivalence is universally true for all pairs from that set. We can use this combination of an equivalence with some kind of universal application to help introduce new symbols.

The phrase "If P then Q and vice-versa" means "If P then Q and if Q then P" which may be written formally as:

$$P \Rightarrow Q \land Q \Rightarrow P$$

This pattern is used frequently enough to justify the introduction of a new sentence connective called **equivalence**. Using this new connective, the above predicate is written as:

$$P \Leftrightarrow Q$$

Equivalence is summarized in Figure 12.5.

Example 12.4 Suppose, in talking about the circle, we often want to say that one person is *older* than another. This can be represented as a relation. In Chapter 3, where we looked at sets, we would have defined the relation in the following way:

$$\_older\_ : Person \leftrightarrow Person$$
$$older = \{p, q : Person \mid age(p) > age(q)\}$$

By this means, *older* is said to be a set of pairs of people, with the first person always being older than the second. Using set comprehension as the means of construction helps remind us that a relation is a set of pairs.

There is an alternative means of defining this relation, one that uses universal quantification and the equivalence operator.

$$\_older\_ : Person \leftrightarrow Person$$
$$\forall p, q : Person \bullet$$
$$p \; older \; q \Leftrightarrow age(p) > age(q)$$

The advantage of this second style is that it highlights the interchangeability of the expressions involved. Suppose we know that the following statement is true:

(1) ...   *Mark older Alan*

We can then argue that:

(2) ... $age(Mark) > age(Alan)$

We can also argue the reverse. We can do this because of the equivalence used in the definition of *older* and because the equivalence is true *for all* people.

We are not so much defining a new relation as giving a name to an existing and hitherto anonymous one. The *older* relation between people existed before we named it. This naming or symbolizing allows us to simplify what might otherwise have been awkward, long-winded or unnatural expressions. For example, consider the equivalent expressions (1) and (2) shown above. Both have the same meaning, but one has three symbols and the other has five. Since economy of expression is one of the ways in which we will judge

Operation:	equivalence
Z Symbol	$\Leftrightarrow$
Usage:	$P \Leftrightarrow Q$
Pronounced:	`P if and only if Q` `P exactly when Q`
Sometimes:	$\leftrightarrow$
Example:	Alan is the spouse of Sue if and only if Sue is the spouse of Alan. $Alan = spouse(Sue) \Leftrightarrow$ $Sue = spouse(Alan)$
Truth Table:	$\begin{array}{ccc} P & Q & P \Leftrightarrow Q \\ \hline true & true & true \\ true & false & false \\ false & true & false \\ false & false & true \end{array}$
Notes:	A sentence of the form $P \Leftrightarrow Q$ is true if (i) both P and Q are true or (ii) both P and Q are false. We can define equivalence in terms of other operators. $$P \Leftrightarrow Q \equiv (P \Rightarrow Q) \land (Q \Rightarrow P)$$ Given $P \Leftrightarrow Q$, we can interchange P for Q in any sentence involving Q without affecting the truth or falseness of the sentence. We can also interchange Q for P.

Figure 12.5 Equivalence

a specification, this reduction is important. However, there will always be some kind of trade-off. We will need to remember the new symbol and its exact meaning. Will it be worth learning? That will depend on how often we might expect to use it.

Knowledge

Example 12.5 Maybe we frequently need to discuss who is sitting next to whom, rather than restricting ourselves to whether one person is to the left of another. We might want to say that Alan is sitting next to Sue, not caring whether he is to her left or she to his.

$Alan\ nextto\ Sue$ if and only if $left(Alan) = Sue$ or $left(Sue) = Alan$

We can generalize this relationship to one between any two people.

$$\_nextto\_ : Person \leftrightarrow Person$$

$$\forall p, q : Person \bullet$$
$$p\ nextto\ q \Leftrightarrow left(p) = q \lor left(q) = p$$

Two people p and q are sitting next to one another if q is to the left of p or p is to the left of q.

The general pattern for defining new relation symbols is given in Figure 12.6.

The general form for defining new relations is as follows.

$$\_R\_ : X \leftrightarrow Y$$

$$\forall x : X;\ y : Y \bullet$$
$$x\ R\ y \Leftrightarrow \text{some predicate relating } x \text{ and } y.$$

A relation R between two types X and Y is defined by introducing a variable of each type, say $x : X$ and $y : Y$. The pair (x, y) is in the relation R if x and y are related in the way specified.

Figure 12.6 Defining new relations

12.4.1 Introducing New Total Functions

A function may be considered as merely a special kind of relation and so a new function symbol may be introduced in a very similar manner.

Example 12.6 Suppose we frequently need to refer to the number of sports that a person plays.

$$playcount : Person \rightarrow N$$

$$\forall p : Person;\ n : N \bullet$$
$$playcount(p) = n \Leftrightarrow n = \#\{s : Sport \mid p\ plays\ s\}$$

A person p plays a total of n sports if (and only if) the size of the set of sports he or she plays is n.

In this particular example, the intermediate number n may be avoided if the function is defined in the following equivalent manner.

$$playcount : Person \rightarrow N$$

$$\forall p : Person \bullet$$
$$playcount(p) = \#\{s : Sport \mid p \; plays \; s\}$$

The number of sports that a person p plays *is* the size of the set of sports played.

Example 12.7 Now that the symbol *playcount* has been formally introduced, further new symbols may be defined in terms of it. Suppose we need to know whether one person is more athletic or sportier than another. This would require the introduction of a new relation symbol.

$$\_sportier\_ : Person \leftrightarrow Person$$

$$\forall p, q : Person \bullet$$
$$p \; sportier \; q \Leftrightarrow playcount(p) > playcount(q)$$

Person p is sportier than person q if p plays more sports than q.

Example 12.8 Suppose that Alan is rather choosy about where he sits at the table. He only sits next to men, and even then, only if he is sportier than them. We can use our newly introduced symbols.

$$\forall p : Person \bullet$$
$$Alan \; nextto \; p \Rightarrow sex(p) = M \wedge Alan \; sportier \; p$$

The general pattern for defining new total functions is shown in Figure 12.7.

Example 12.9 The "up to" function, defining a contiguous set of numbers, is commonly used in computing. For example:

$$5..8 = \{5, 6, 7, 8\}$$

Thus, $5..8$ is the set of all numbers between 5 and 8 inclusive. If we take this second definition and express it formally, we would have:

$$5..8 = \{n : N \mid n \geq 5 \wedge n \leq 8\}$$

It is an infix function that, when applied to a pair of numbers, represents the set of numbers in between. We can take the set comprehension version of $5..8$ and use it as the basis of a general definition.

$$\_..\_ : N \times N \rightarrow Set \; of \; N$$

$$\forall i, j : N \bullet$$
$$i..j = \{n : N \mid n \geq i \wedge n \leq j\}$$

The term $i..j$ is the set of numbers greater than or equal to i and less than or equal to j.

Knowledge 285

There are two forms for defining total functions.

1. When a term can be constructed directly.

   $f : X \to Y$
   ___
   $\forall x : X \bullet$
   $\qquad f(x) =$ some term of type Y

2. When the term cannot be expressed directly.

   $f : X \to Y$
   ___
   $\forall x : X; y : Y \bullet$
   $\qquad f(x) = y \Leftrightarrow$ some predicate defining y

---

Figure 12.7 Defining new total functions

12.4.2 Introducing New Partial Functions

With partial functions, we must establish the domain of the function.

Example 12.10 We need to be able to refer to a man's wife, where appropriate to do so, in other words, when we have established that the man is married.

$wife : Person \nrightarrow Person$
___
$dom\ wife = \{p : dom\ spouse \mid sex(p) = M\}$
$\forall p : dom\ wife \bullet$
$\qquad wife(p) = spouse(p)$

The *wife* function is partial. Not every person has a wife. Its domain is the set of married men. The first condition of the definition establishes that. The second condition then says that for each such person, that person's wife is the same as his spouse.

The two forms for defining new partial functions are more general forms of those used for total functions and are shown in Figure 12.8.

Example 12.11 The *min* function takes a set of numbers and returns the smallest member of that set. It is partial because it cannot operate on the empty set. Here are three examples of its use: are they true or false?

$min\{5, 3, 9\} = 11$
$min\{5, 3, 9\} = 5$
$min\{5, 3, 9\} = 3$

We know that the first line is untrue because the number 11 is not even *in* the set $\{5, 3, 9\}$. The second line is untrue because, although the number 5 is in the set, it is not less than

Like total functions, there are two general forms for introducing new partial function symbols.

1. When the term can be expressed.

   $$\begin{array}{|l} f : X \nrightarrow Y \\ \hline dom\ f = \text{some set expression that defines the domain of } f \\ \forall x : dom\ f \bullet \\ \quad f(x) = \text{some expression of type } Y \end{array}$$

   Note that the quantification is restricted to the domain of the function being defined. We are saying nothing about what happens when the function is applied to some element outside the domain.

2. When the term cannot be expressed directly.

   $$\begin{array}{|l} f : X \nrightarrow Y \\ \hline dom\ f = \text{some set expression that defines the domain of } f \\ \forall x : dom\ f;\ y : Y \bullet \\ \quad f(x) = y \Leftrightarrow \text{some predicate defining } y \end{array}$$

Figure 12.8 Defining new partial functions

or equal to *all* the members of the set and so cannot be the minimum. The third line satisfies both these conditions and these two conditions seem to be enough to determine the minimum element. We can summarize this as:

$$min\{5, 3, 9\} = 3 \text{ because } 3 \in \{5, 3, 9\} \text{ and } \forall n : \{5, 3, 9\} \bullet 3 \leq n$$

And we can generalize this to any non-empty set of numbers.

$$\begin{array}{|l} min : Set\ of\ N \nrightarrow N \\ \hline dom\ min = Set\ of\ N - \{\} \\ \forall nset : dom\ min;\ m : N \bullet \\ \quad m = min\ nset \Leftrightarrow m \in nset \land \forall n : nset \bullet m \leq n \end{array}$$

Its definition takes the second, more complex, form of function definition.

12.5 Generic Functions and Relations

In the previous section we looked at defining functions and relations that operated on specific types such as *Person* and N; for example, the *min* function may be applied to a set of integers and nothing else.

There are, fortunately, many general-purpose operations that may be applied to *any* type. The *dom* and *ran* operators are examples. They may be applied to any set of pairs. There are also some even better known operators such as the union ($\cup$), intersection ($\cap$) operators and the subset ($\subseteq$) relation of set theory.

We will examine the *dom* operator first. This function may be applied to any set of pairs and it returns the set consisting of all the first or left-half elements of each pair. In other words, we may apply it to any relation since a relation is defined to be a set of pairs. Here is an example.

$$\_plays\_ : Person \leftrightarrow Sport$$

$$plays = \{ \\
(Alan, tennis), \\
(Alan, golf), \\
(Sue, tennis), \\
(Kim, tennis), \\
(Bob, golf), \\
(Bob, hockey), \\
(Mark, golf), \\
(Mark, squash)\}$$

The domain of *plays* is the left-hand column, so:

$$dom\ plays = \{Alan, Sue, Kim, Bob, Mark\}$$

Just by looking at the relation we can see that a person is in the domain of *plays* if and only if there is some sport played by that person, that is, if and only if:

$$\exists s : Sport \bullet p\ plays\ s$$

where p is the person in question. Looking at *plays* as a set of pairs, we could say this as:

$$\exists s : Sport \bullet (p, s) \in plays$$

The domain of *plays* is the set of people who satisfy that condition. Put more formally, we have:

$$dom\ plays = \{p : Person\ |\ \exists s : Sport \bullet (p, s) \in plays\}$$

If we were only interested in a *dom* function that worked on sets of (*person*, *sport*) pairs such as *plays*, we could introduce it in the usual way.

$$dom : (Person \leftrightarrow Sport) \rightarrow Set\ of\ Person$$

$$\forall R : Person \leftrightarrow Sport \bullet \\
dom\ R = \{p : Person\ |\ \exists s : Sport \bullet (p, s) \in R\}$$

For all relations R between *Person* and *Sport*, the domain of that relation is the set of people p for whom there is some sport with which they are connected through the relation.

Now we can apply the *dom* operator, as defined, to any such relation; for example, given:

$$\_loathes\_ : Person \leftrightarrow Sport$$
$$\_watches\_ : Person \leftrightarrow Sport$$
$$\_usedto\_ : Person \leftrightarrow Sport$$

We can refer to:

dom loathes – the set of people who loathe some sport;
dom watches – the set of people who watch some sport;
dom usedto – the set of people who used to play some sport.

Of course, we have no intention of restricting ourselves to using this operator only upon to relations between people and sports. It has widespread applicability. We can extend its definition so that it may be used on any set of pairs.

$$[X, Y]$$
$$dom : (X \leftrightarrow Y) \rightarrow Set\ of\ X$$

$$\forall R : X \leftrightarrow Y \bullet$$
$$\quad dom\ R = \{x : X \mid \exists y : Y \bullet (x, y) \in R\}$$

We have generalized the definition from one involving sets of (*person, sport*) pairs to one that applies to arbitrary sets of pairs of the form (x, y). The definition has been *parameterized* on two types X and Y. If we were to replace X by *Person* and Y by *Sport* then we would be back to our initial definition of *dom*.

Example 12.12 The union operator is also a function. It takes two sets *of the same type* and returns another set, of that same type. In Z, the symbol for union is $\cup$.

The union of two sets of people A and B is the set of people who are in either A or B or both. We can extend this to the union of two sets of any type.

$$[X]$$
$$\_\cup\_ : Set\ of\ X \times Set\ of\ X \rightarrow Set\ of\ X$$

$$\forall A; B : Set\ of\ X \bullet$$
$$\quad A \cup B = \{x : X \mid x \in A \vee x \in B\}$$

The definition of $\cup$ is *parameterized* on the type X. In other words, we may substitute any type of our choosing, which is what we have been doing, off and on, throughout this book.

Example 12.13 Set subtraction is another function involving sets. Like set union, it also takes two sets *of the same type* and returns another set, of that same type. The symbol for subtraction is $-$.

Subtracting the set of people B from the set of people A gives us the set of people who are in A but not in B. The difference between any two sets may be defined as follows:

$$
\begin{array}{|l}
\hline [X] \\
\hline \_-\_ : \text{Set of } X \times \text{Set of } X \rightarrow \text{Set of } X \\
\hline
\forall A; B : \text{Set of } X \bullet \\
\qquad A - B = \{x : X \mid x \in A \wedge \neg x \in B\} \\
\hline
\end{array}
$$

Generic Relations

Generic relations may be defined in a similar way; for example, the containment of one set within another is a generic relation. A set may be a subset of many sets and, equally, a set may have many subsets. This means that the subset operator, wriiten $\subseteq$ in Z, is a relation. A set may have many different subsets. The set of people in Queensland has, as subsets, the set of people in Brisbane, the set of people in Rockhampton, and so on. In turn, the same set may be a subset of many other sets. The set of people in Queensland is a subset of the people in Australia; it is also a subset of the people who live in the Southern Hemisphere, and so on. This generic relation may be defined as follows:

$$
\begin{array}{|l}
\hline [X] \\
\hline \_\subseteq\_ : (\text{Set of } X) \leftrightarrow (\text{Set of } X) \\
\hline
\forall A, B : \text{Set of } X \bullet \\
\qquad A \subseteq B \Leftrightarrow \forall x : X \bullet x \in A \Rightarrow x \in B \\
\hline
\end{array}
$$

A set A is a subset of set B if and only if x being an element of A implies that x is also an element of B.

Example 12.14 Suppose we now return to the suburban bank that was introduced in Chapter 1. The situation at the tellers is shown in Figure 12.9.

There are two components in this situation that are relevant here.

1. *open* : *Set of Teller*
   The component *open* is the set of tellers who are ready to do business. At this moment tellers T1, T3 and T4 are open, so:

   $open = \{T1, T3, T4\}$

2. *busy* : *Teller* $\nrightarrow$ *Person*
   The other component *busy* describes which tellers are in the process of serving by pairing each busy teller with the customer involved, so:

   $busy = \{(T1, Bob), (T3, Sue)\}$

As part of the general conditions that characterize the bank at any and every moment of time, we had:

$dom\ busy \subseteq open$

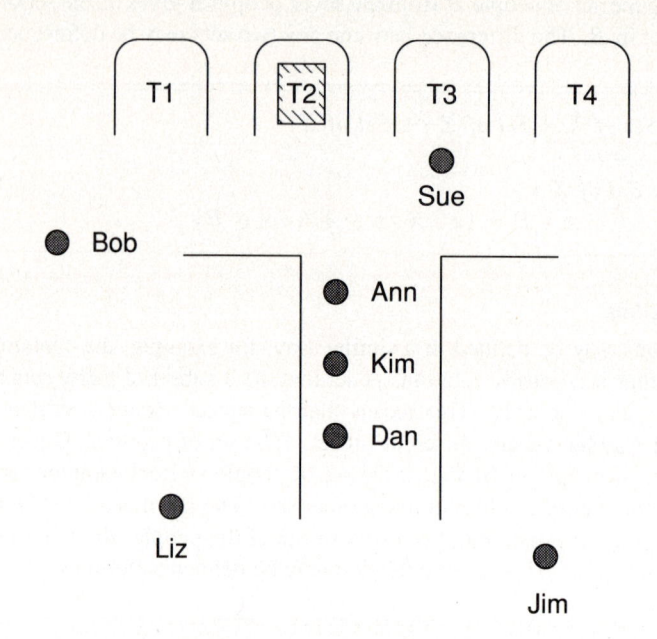

Figure 12.9 In the bank

The domain of *busy* is the set of tellers actually serving a customer. The condition requires that set to be a subset of the open tellers. In other words, every serving teller must also be open. This is a general statement about the bank and yet seems to make no use of quantification. Does this mean that not all general statements involve quantification? No, the quantification has been hidden through the use of the *dom* operator and the $\subseteq$ relation. We can reveal the relative complexity of this statement by removing the *dom* and $\subseteq$ symbols. Suppose we first replace the subset symbol by its definition. The relevant line from its generic definition is:

$$A \subseteq B \Leftrightarrow \forall x : X \bullet x \in A \Rightarrow x \in B$$

The predicate *dom busy* $\subseteq$ *open* requires the substitution of:

   X by *Teller* as the base set involved
   A by *dom busy*
   B by *open*

$$\forall t : Teller \bullet t \in dom\ busy \Rightarrow t \in open$$

The predicate now states that : "For every teller t, if that teller is in the domain of *busy* then the teller is also in *open*."

Knowledge

We can now replace *dom busy* using the generic definition of the *dom* operator; its generic definition was:

$$dom\ R = \{x : X \mid \exists y : Y \bullet (x, y) \in R\}$$

We need to make the following replacements.

X by *Teller*
Y by *Person*
R by *busy*

We get:

$$dom\ busy = \{x : Teller \mid \exists y : Person \bullet (x, y) \in busy\}$$

This gives a complete replacement of *dom busy* ⊆ *open* by:

$\forall t : Teller \bullet$
$t \in \{x : Teller \mid \exists y : Person \bullet (x, y) \in busy\} \Rightarrow t \in open$

The predicate now states that : "For every teller *t*, if that teller is in the set of tellers for whom there is a person being served by that customer, then the teller is also in *open*." Compare the complexity of this statement with the relative simplicity of the original version.

12.6 Describing Change

In this section we will examine some new general-purpose functions. These are all used to describe how a situation changes in response to some given event. What kinds of events might happen, ones that change the circle? Here are three typical ones.

1. Bob takes up rugby.

    There will be changes that cause the *addition* of new facts to the database of facts relating to the circle. This is an example. The *plays* relationship must be extended to include a pairing of Bob and rugby.

2. Alan drops tennis.

    There will be changes that require the *removal* of facts that are no longer relevant. The pairing of Alan and tennis must be removed.

3. Bob celebrates his birthday.

    There will be changes that *modify* facts. The *age* relationship must be altered so as to pair Bob with his new age rather than his previous one.

12.6.1 Adding New Facts

Extending our database can be described in terms of set union. We form a new version of the appropriate relationship by adding new facts to the existing ones.

Example 12.15 Bob takes up rugby.

$$plays' = plays \cup \{(Bob, rugby)\}$$

In all the examples in this section we will use a primed version of a relationship (*plays'* in this example) to represent the *after* version of the relationship that is changing. This primed version *must* have the same type in its declaration. So, in this example, we require that *plays'* be introduced as follows:

$$\_plays'\_ : Person \leftrightarrow Sport$$

Example 12.16 Sue learns Spanish.

$$speaks' = speaks \cup \{(Sue, Spanish)\}$$

This time the relationship to be extended is the *speaks* one. The revised version of that relationship, *speaks'* must be declared to be of the same type as the "before" version.

$$\_speaks'\_ : Person \leftrightarrow Sport$$

Example 12.17 Kim comes into a small inheritance and buys her first car, a Ford.

$$drives' = drives \cup \{(Kim, Ford)\}$$

This time the change involves a function. The new version will be declared in the same way as *drives* was, that is:

$$drives' : Person \nrightarrow CarMake$$

We must ensure that, in describing the change, we construct an equation that is consistent with the type of the relationship involved. In this case, we must ensure that whatever extension we make, *drives'* truly is a function. That means that before making the change we need to check that *Kim* is not in the domain of *drives*, in other words, Kim must not currently be driving a car.

Example 12.18 Kim and Bob get married (or, at least, enter into a spouse-like relationship).

$$spouse' = spouse \cup \{(Kim, Bob), (Bob, Kim)\}$$

Like the previous example, we would need to check that neither *Kim* nor *Bob* are currently involved with other people. As this example shows, we are not restricted to adding just one new fact or pairing.

Example 12.19 In a touching display of marital support, Kim decides to take up all the sports that Bob plays.

$$plays' = plays \cup \{(Kim, golf), (Kim, hockey)\}$$

This assumes knowledge of the sports that Bob plays. If we didn't then we could write the change as:

$$plays' = plays \cup \{s : Sport \mid Bob\ plays\ s \bullet (Kim, s)\}$$

This description pairs Kim with each of the sports that Bob plays.

12.6.2 Removing Facts

There are three different ways in which we can describe a change that involves forgetting something. The basic method is set subtraction, but there are two other methods that make the descriptions more compact. These are domain subtraction and range subtraction.

Example 12.20 Alan drops tennis.

$$plays' = plays - \{(Alan, tennis)\}$$

We can always remove a fact by creating a set containing just that fact and subtracting it from the corresponding relationship as represented by a set of pairs.

Example 12.21 Bob loses heavily in the 1997 stockmarket crash and has to sell his car.

$$drives' = drives - \{(Bob, Porsche)\}$$

If we didn't remember exactly what kind of car Bob drove, we could identify it through function application.

$$drives' = drives - \{(Bob, drives(Bob))\}$$

The pair identifies Bob and whatever make of car he previously drove.

This kind of change is so commonly required that a special operation called **domain subtraction** has been defined to allow us to describe the change in the minimum number of symbols.

$$drives' = \{Bob\} \vartriangleleft drives$$

The domain subtraction operator $\vartriangleleft$ says to look for any pair in *drives* that involves Bob and form a new set of pairs *drives'* that contains no pair involving Bob on the *domain* side, that is, involving Bob as the first half of any pair. Note how this third description of the change uses the least number of symbols that could have been used. Compare this with the first and second versions. Its generic definition is as follows:

$$
\begin{array}{l}
\underline{\quad [X, Y] \quad}\\
\_ \vartriangleleft \_ : (\text{Set of } X) \times (X \leftrightarrow Y) \to (X \leftrightarrow Y)\\
\hline
\forall A : \text{Set of } X; R : X \leftrightarrow Y \bullet\\
\quad A \vartriangleleft R = \{x : X; y : Y \mid x \notin A \land (x, y) \in R\}
\end{array}
$$

$A \vartriangleleft R$ is the set of pairs (x, y) that are in R except those where x is not in A.

Example 12.22 Mark's doctor strongly insists that he gives up all forms of sport. If we know that he plays just golf and squash, we can write:

$$plays' = plays - \{(Mark, golf), (Mark, squash)\}$$

If we cannot remember exactly (in extension) what he plays, then we can use set comprehension to do the job:

$$plays' = plays - \{s : Sport \mid Mark \text{ plays } s \bullet (Mark, s)\}$$

The set expression forms a set of pairs consisting of Mark and each of the sports he plays. Again, this kind of change may be expressed using domain subtraction:

$$plays' = \{Mark\} \vartriangleleft plays$$

This means exactly the same, as we shall see when the operation is defined. Again, note the economy of this expression compared with the previous ones.

Example 12.23 Sue and Alan separate. As before, this change might be described in several ways.

$$spouse' = spouse - \{(Sue, Alan), (Alan, Sue)\}$$
$$spouse' = spouse - \{(Sue, spouse(Sue)), (spouse(Sue), Sue)\}$$
$$spouse' = \{Sue, Alan\} \vartriangleleft spouse$$

There is a complementary operation, **range subtraction**, that targets the range side of a set of pairs.

Example 12.24 Suppose the golf club has increased its fees enormously and everyone has decided to stop playing golf. We can create a suitably modified version of the *plays* relation through the expression:

$$plays \vartriangleright \{golf\}$$

The result is a relation that contains all the (*person, sport*) pairs from *plays* except those where the sport is golf.

The generic definition is as follows:

$$[X, Y]$$
$$\_ \vartriangleright \_ : (X \leftrightarrow Y) \times (Set\ of\ Y) \rightarrow (X \leftrightarrow Y)$$

$$\forall R : X \leftrightarrow Y;\ B : Set\ of\ Y \bullet$$
$$R \vartriangleright B = \{x : X;\ y : Y \mid y \notin B \wedge (x, y) \in R\}$$

The set $R \vartriangleright B$ is the set of pairs (x, y) that are in R except those where y is not in B.

12.6.3 Modifying Facts

When a fact type or relationship involves a function, we often find ourselves in the position of adding and dropping facts at the same time.

Example 12.25 Kim turns 23. This new information requires that we drop the fact that she is 22 and add a new one stating that she is 23. We can express this as:

$$age' = (age - \{(Kim, 22)\}) \cup \{(Kim, 23)\}$$

We can express this change using **function override**, an operator especially devised for describing changes to relationships that are functions.

$$age' = age \oplus \{(Kim, 23)\}$$

Knowledge 295

The pair after the operator symbol, ⊕, overrides any pair in *age* to the extent that whatever Kim's age was before, she is *now* 23. No-one else's age is changed. Function override allows us to superimpose one function upon another. The function that *follows* the override symbol ⊕ has precedence over the function that appears before the symbol. The expression {(Kim, 23)} is a small function that overrides, that is, it has precedence over *age*.

Example 12.26 It is Kim's birthday.
Suppose we did not know how old Kim now is, merely that it's her birthday. We can still access her previous age.

$$age' = age \oplus \{(Kim, age(Kim) + 1)\}$$

We find out her previous age, add one to that and override her current age with that number. It is no-one else's birthday.

A guide for using function override is shown in the following diagram.

| The relationship to be modified. | ⊕ | A set of pairs describing just those modifications required. |

It shows that we place the relationship (function name, typically) *before* the override symbol ⊕ and a precise description of the changes to be made *after*.

Example 12.27 Suppose that Sue has sold her Ford and bought a Mazda instead. We need to amend the *drives* function to reflect this change.

$$drives \oplus \{(Sue, Mazda)\}$$

Whatever Sue drove before, she *now* drives a Mazda.
Its generic definition is as follows:

$$\begin{array}{l} [X, Y] \\ \_\oplus\_ : (X \nrightarrow Y) \times (X \nrightarrow Y) \rightarrow (X \nrightarrow Y) \\ \forall f, g : X \nrightarrow Y \bullet \\ \quad f \oplus g = (dom\ g \vartriangleleft f) \cup g \end{array}$$

Summary: The subtraction operators ◁ and ▷ are useful for knocking pairs off a relation and giving us *whatever is left over*.

Function override ⊕ is useful for allowing us to speak of amendments to the information in a database, when that information is in the form of a function.

12.7 Abbreviations

In Section 12.4, we were introduced to a method for defining new symbols. That method allows us, primarily, to simplify the writing of predicates. This was highlighted in the case of the bank. A complex condition, that all busy tellers are open, would otherwise have involved both universal and existential quantification. With the introduction of the *dom* operator and the ⊆ relation, the predicate was reduced to the compact *dom busy* ⊆ *open*.

Chapter 12

In this section, we will see a technique that simplifies the writing of predicates by introducing symbols that are used within declarations. We have already made frequent use of one such symbol, the function symbol $\rightarrow$. Consider the declaration of the *age* function.

$age : Person \rightarrow N$

It says that *age* is a set of pairs, each pair mapping a person to a number. It also makes two restrictions or constraints on that set.

1. No person has more than one age, that is, no person is linked through the *age* relationship to more than one number. The relationship is a *function*.

2. Every person is involved in this relationship, that is, every person is mapped to a number. The function is said to be *total*.

We do not need to specify these two constraints in any predicate using *age*. Its declaration as a total function does that for us. The knowledge has been encoded in the definition of the total function symbol $\rightarrow$. The way in which this symbol is defined is part of a more general technique, within Z, for simplifying statements by introducing new symbols that are to be used within a declaration of some kind.

The total function symbol has a fairly complex definition, so we will look at some simpler examples first.

Example 12.28 Perhaps we might need to establish that a person is a woman before making some further statement about such people (treading carefully). We could define the set of women as:

$Women == \{Ann, Sue, Kim\}$

The double equal sign is read as "is defined to be". So the set *Women* is defined to be the set consisting of Ann, Sue and Kim. If we were unsure of their proper names, we could play safe and define it as:

$Women == \{p : Person \mid sex(p) = F\}$

Either way, we can use this set to make some claim such as that all the women are over 30 years old.

$\forall w : Women \bullet age(p) > 30$

Example 12.29 We can use this newly introduced symbol *Women* as the basis for defining another. If we want to name the set of married women, we could introduce it as follows.

$Wives == Women \cap dom\ spouse$

The set *Wives* is the set of married women.

The left-hand side of an abbreviation definition may include symbols that have already been introduced. A **relation** is a set of pairs drawn from the set of all pairs, that is the product of two sets, *Person* and *Sport* say.

$$Person \leftrightarrow Sport == Set\ of\ (Person \times Sport)$$

As a reminder:

- *Person* × *Sport* is the product set consisting of *all* (*Person*, *Sport*) pairings.
- *Set of* (*Person* × *Sport*) is the power set consisting of all subsets of that product set.

So the declaration $\_plays\_ : Person \leftrightarrow Sport$ is an abbreviated way of declaring that *plays* is an element of that power set, that is, *plays* is a set of (*Person*, *Sport*) pairs. In particular, it is one in which not all people need necessarily participate.

More generally, the relation symbol may be defined as relating two arbitrary sets X and Y in the following way:

$$X \leftrightarrow Y == Set\ of\ (X \times Y)$$

A **partial function** is a special kind of relation, one with a uniqueness constraint on the domain side of the relation. For example:

$$drives : Person \rightarrowtail CarMake$$

Not everyone need drive a car, but no-one drives more than one. We can describe this constraint formally:

$$\forall p : dom\ drives \bullet (\exists!\ c : CarMake \bullet (p, c) \in drives)$$

For all those people who do drive a car, there is exactly one car that they drive. It is this constraint that enables us to use function application.

We can define the partial function symbol in terms of the relation symbol with that one constraint:

$$X \rightarrowtail Y == \{R : X \leftrightarrow Y \mid \forall x : dom\ R \bullet \exists!y : Y \bullet (x, y) \in R\}$$

A **total function** is a partial function with yet another constraint, that every element from the domain side takes part. We know everybody's age, so it was declared as:

$$age : Person \rightarrow N$$

Its totality can be expressed as $dom\ age = Person$. Total functions between people and numbers may be defined as follows:

$$Person \rightarrow N == \{f : Person \rightarrowtail N \mid dom\ f = Person\}$$

They are the set of partial functions f from *Person* to N such that the domain of f is the same as *Person*. This definition may be generalized to any two types X and Y.

$$X \rightarrow Y == \{f : X \rightarrowtail Y \mid dom\ f = X\}$$

A **partial injection** is a one-to-one partial function. The *spouse* relationship between certain members of the circle is an example.

$$spouse : Person \rightarrowtail Person$$

If two people, p and q, have the same spouse, then p and q must be the same people. We can express this formally as:

$$\forall p, q : dom\ spouse \bullet spouse(p) = spouse(q) \Rightarrow p = q$$

And we can generalize this to arbitrary types X and Y:

$$X \rightarrowtail Y == \{f : X \nrightarrow Y \mid \forall p, q : dom\ f \bullet f(p) = f(q) \Rightarrow p = q$$

A **total injection** is a one-to-one function that is also a total function. An example is the *left* relationship. Each person is on the left of just one person and everybody has just one person on their left.

$$left : Person \rightarrowtail person$$

We can define the set of all total injections between people as follows:

$$Person \rightarrowtail Person == (Person \rightarrowtail Person) \cap (Person \rightarrow Person)$$

Then we can generalize this definition to one involving arbitrary types X and Y.

$$X \rightarrowtail Y == (X \rightarrowtail Y) \cap (X \rightarrow Y)$$

12.8 Sequences

There are many occasions, in practice and in theory, when we would wish to talk about one element of a set coming before or after some other element. The **order** clause of SQL is a recognition of this need. Suppose we make another return to the bank. See Figure 12.9.

Now we want to talk about the people queuing for service. If we use a set to describe some objects, there is no concept of order or sequence; so, for example:

$$\{Ann, Kim, Dan\} = \{Kim, Dan, Ann\} = \{Dan, Ann, Kim\}$$

All three expressions describe the same set of people. Nothing tells us that there is a certain order to the queue. Yet we know that we cannot move Ann, Kim and Dan around and claim that the queue is still the same. Declaring the queue to be a simple set of people is not enough.

We could model the queue as an "is in front of" relation.

$$\_infrontof\_ : Person \leftrightarrow Person$$

$$infrontof = \{$$
$$\qquad (Ann, Kim),$$
$$\qquad (Ann, Dan),$$
$$\qquad (Dan, Kim)\}$$

This relation allows us to determine whether one person is in front of another, for example *Ann infrontof Kim*; however, it does not enable us, *with ease*, to decide who is first in the queue, who is second and so on. We could use quantification:

1. The first person in the queue, say $p1$, is the one who has nobody in front of him or her:
   $\neg \exists q : Person \bullet q \; infrontof \; p1$
2. The second in the queue, $p2$, is the person with only one other person in front.
   $\exists q : Person \bullet q \; infrontof \; p2 \land \neg \exists r : Person \bullet r \; infrontof \; p2 \land r \neq q$

This use of quantifiers, while it accurately expresses the concepts involved, does seem rather lengthy. There is a nicer way, and that is to declare *queue* as a **sequence**.

$queue : seq \; Person$

This is almost equivalent to the declaration:

$queue : N \twoheadrightarrow Person$

This latter form says that *queue* is a partial function mapping from the integers, N, to the set *Person*. The function can be thought of in tabular form as follows:

$queue : seq \; Person$

$queue = \{$
  $(1, Ann),$
  $(2, Kim),$
  $(3, Dan)\}$

We can now use *queue* as a function and apply it to an integer, for example $queue(1)$ would determine who is first in the queue, $queue(2)$ would give the person in second place.

The function is a partial function because the domain is not the entire set of integers but simply the set $\{1, 2, 3\}$ because there are three people in the queue. In general, the domain of a sequence function will be a contiguous set of numbers $1..n$ where n is the number of entries in the sequence.

So the queue is a partial function with a domain consisting of a contiguous set of numbers ranging from 1 up to n where n is the size of the sequence. For every sequence s:

$\exists n : N \bullet n = \#s \land dom \; s = 1..n$

Or, by eliminating the need for the intermediate n:

$dom \; s = 1..\#s$

We can use this constraint to define the set of all sequences of people:

$seq \; Person == \{s : N \twoheadrightarrow Person \mid dom \; s = 1..\#s\}$

And this definition, in turn, may be generalized into the set of sequences of some arbitrary type X:

$seq \; X == \{s : N \twoheadrightarrow X \mid dom \; s = 1..\#s\}$

We could model the history of car driving within the circle as:

$hasdriven : Person \rightarrow seq \; CarMake$

While *queue* is a valid use of the sequence, it does not quite provide the complete picture as in a sequence of people one particular person may occur several times.

Suppose we want to model the results of a race and we are not interested in the names of individual athletes but only in the names of the countries represented. There may be several athletes from each country competing. The race may written out in full as:

> *race* : *seq Country*
>
> *race* = {
> (1, *USA*),
> (2, *Australia*),
> (3, *Australia*),
> (4, *GB*),
> (5, *USA*)}

Because there may be several athletes from each country, that country appears several times, once for each athlete.

12.8.1 Sequence Construction

There is a sequence equivalent to set extension. This notation allows us to write out, in full, the contents of a sequence; for example, the *race* sequence may be written as:

[*USA, Australia, Australia, GB, USA*]

The square brackets signify that the enclosed data forms a sequence. For that reason, the order in which the countries are named *is significant*. This sequence is equivalent to the set of pairs:

{(1, *USA*), (2, *Australia*), (3, *Australia*), (4, *GB*), (5, *USA*)}

Written as a set, the order is not important because the sequencing information is encoded within each pair.

We can have a sequence containing just one entry, for example [*NZ*], which is equivalent to the set {(1, *NZ*)}. We can have an empty sequence [ ] which is the same as the empty set { }.

One of the most natural operations to be performed on sequences is to **concatenate** or string together two or more sequences. If we want to concatenate two sequences of characters [*T, O, O*] and [*F, A, R*] we can write:

[*T, O, O*]⌢[*F, A, R*] = [*T, O, O, F, A, R*]

Any number of sequences may be concatenated:

[*S, U, N, D, A, Y*]⌢[*T, O, O*]⌢[*F, A, R*]⌢[*A, W, A, Y*]

No brackets are required because it does not matter which sequences are joined first; the result will always be the same.

12.8.2 Sequence Decomposition

As well as constructing new sequences we will want to pull them apart so as to isolate some component or another. There are two operations for accomplishing this, *head* and *tail*.

The *head* operation extracts the first entry in a sequence and returns the associated element.

$$\begin{aligned}&head\ race\\ =\ &head\,[USA,\ Australia,\ Australia,\ GB,\ USA]\\ =\ &USA\end{aligned}$$

This is simply another way of saying *race*(1) which returns the first element in the *race* sequence. Thus we cannot apply *head* to the empty sequence.

The *tail* operation removes the head of a sequence and returns a sequence consisting of whatever is left over.

$$\begin{aligned}&tail\ race\\ =\ &tail\,[USA,\ Australia,\ Australia,\ GB,\ USA]\\ =\ &[Australia,\ Australia,\ GB,\ USA]\end{aligned}$$

The tail of a sequence starts immediately after the head. So we are talking about a snake's tail and not a dog's.

If there is only one entry, then applying *tail* to that sequence returns the empty sequence.

$$\begin{aligned}&tail[A]\\ =\ &[\,]\end{aligned}$$

We cannot apply *tail* to the empty sequence.

12.8.3 Operations on Sequences

There is a kind of hierarchy involved in the operations that may be performed upon a sequence or in conjunction with sequences.

1. Sequence operations

   We can use the constructor operation [ ] and the concatenation operator ⌢ to build new sequences; we can also use *head* and *tail* to access components of a sequence.

2. Function operations

   Because a sequence is a special kind of function, we can use function application to identify entries in the sequence; for example *race*(2) returns the country that came second.

3. Relation operations

   Because a function is a special kind of relation, we can use relation operators such as *dom* and *ran* to determine the domain or range of a sequence considered as a relation.

For example the expression *ran race* will return the set of countries represented in the race.

4. Set operations

   Because a relation is a special kind of set, we can use all the set operations on sequences; for example, we can use the set size operator in #*race* to find out how many runners there were in the race.

We should be prepared to use whatever level of operation most naturally and appropriately expresses our requirements.

12.9 Summary

In this chapter we have looked at several important aspects of information modeling.

- We have looked at the use of universal and existential **quantification** as means of making statements about classes of people or things. This should be seen as an extension of the ideas of Chapter 2 where we looked at ways of making statements about specific things.

- We have looked at how new symbols may be introduced into a specification in order to reduce the complexity of our predicates. In particular, the set operators, set union (∪), set intersection (∩), and set subtraction can all be introduced in this way.

- We also looked at three operators – domain subtraction, range subtraction and function override. These operators are of particular use when we want to describe how a situation is to change as a result of changed circumstances.

- We have seen how abbreviation definitions may be introduced in order to save us from repeatedly stating commonly used relationships.

- Finally, we have looked at a commonly used abbreviation, the **sequence**, a modeling tool or notion that allows us to talk about ordered sets such as queues. As part of the idea of a sequence we have special operators that enable us to construct sequences and to pull them apart.

Exercises

▶ Q12.1   The CLUB Model

The following sets, functions and relations represent a (very) small computer club. There are five basic types in the model.

$$[Member, Language, CarMake, N, Gender]$$

We can think of these types in the following terms.

1. Member = { Bill, Sue, Alan }
2. Language = { COBOL, FORTRAN, C, SQL, Pascal, Ada, RPG, Modula-2 }
3. CarMake = { BMW, Ford, GM, Honda, Mazda, Mercedes, Toyota }
4. N = { 0, 1, 2, 3, ... }
5. Gender = { F, M }

There are five relationships between the types. These are shown below in tabular form.

$\_likes\_ : Member \leftrightarrow Member$

likes =
  {(Bill, Sue),
  (Bill, Alan),
  (Sue, Alan),
  (Alan, Bill)}

$\_writes\_ : Member \leftrightarrow Language$

writes =
  {(Bill, FORTRAN),
  (Sue, C),
  (Sue, SQL),
  (Alan, FORTRAN),
  (Bill, SQL)}

$age : Member \rightarrow N$

age =
  {(Bill, 19),
  (Sue, 19),
  (Alan, 16)}

$drives : Member \rightarrowtail CarMake$

drives =
  {(Sue, Honda),
  (Bill, Ford)}

$sex : Member \rightarrow Gender$

sex =
  {(Bill, M),
  (Sue, F),
  (Alan, M)}

In Z, the statement that Alan dislikes Bill would be written as: $\neg(Alan\ likes\ Bill)$. Rewrite each of the following English sentences using Z.

   a.   Bill can't write in SQL.

b. Sue and Bill get on well together.
c. Sue can write in both C and in Pascal.
d. Neither Alan nor Sue can write in FORTRAN.
e. Either Sue drives a Honda or Bill does.
f. Both Bill and Sue can write in SQL.

▶ Q12.2 Rewrite the following English expressions formally, using quantifiers.

a. Everybody likes Alan.
b. Somebody likes Alan.
c. Nobody likes Alan.
d. No one is older than Bill.
e. No one is younger than Sue.

▶ Q12.3 Use quantifiers to express the following statements.

a. Only women drive Hondas.
b. Women only drive Hondas.
c. Only those who can write in SQL drive a BMW.
d. Only BMW drivers can write in C.
e. Alan only likes people who drive a BMW.
f. Alan only likes females.
g. Alan can write in every language that Sue can.
h. Sue likes everybody that Bill likes.
i. All the men can write COBOL.
j. Some men can write SQL.

▶ Q12.4 Use quantifiers to express the following statements.

a. Everybody is liked by somebody.
b. Only one person can write in FORTRAN.
c. Alan is the second youngest person.
d. There is no man who is not liked by some woman.
e. Every woman drives a car.

▶ Q12.5 Write out, in extension, the set that results from each of the following domain subtraction operations.

a. $\{Bill\} \triangleleft likes$

b. $\{Bill\} \triangleleft age$
c. $\{Bill, Sue\} \triangleleft likes$
d. $\{Bill, Sue\} \triangleleft age$
e. $(dom\ drives) \triangleleft likes$
f. $dom(\{Bill\} \triangleleft likes)$
g. $dom(\{Bill, Sue\} \triangleleft likes)$
h. $ran(\{Bill\} \triangleleft likes)$

▶ Q12.6 Write out, in extension, the set that results from each of the following range subtraction operations.

a. $likes \triangleright \{Bill\}$
b. $age \triangleright \{16\}$
c. $age \triangleright 18..20$
d. $drives \triangleright \{Ford, Toyota\}$
e. $writes \triangleright \{FORTRAN\}$
f. $writes \triangleright \{l : Language \mid Sue\ writes\ l\}$
g. $sex \triangleright \{F\}$
h. $dom(sex \triangleright \{F\})$

▶ Q12.7 Write out, in extension, the set that results from each of the following function overrides.

a. $age \oplus \{(Bill, 20)\}$
b. $age \oplus \{(Sue, age(Bill))\}$
c. $drives \oplus \{(Sue, Toyota)\}$
d. $drives \oplus \{(Sue, Toyota), (Alan, Ford)\}$
e. $\{(Bill, 20)\} \oplus age$

Q12.8 The PARLIAMENT Model

This model was introduced in the exercises at the end of Chapters 2 and 3. Two basic types were used:

[Poli, Party]

The following functions and relations are used to represent the facts that we want to represent here.

1. $belongs : Poli \rightarrow Party$

   This maps each politician to his or her party, for example, *belongs(Wayne)* might give *Labor*.

2. *minister* : *Dept* → *Poli*

   This maps each department to its minister, for example, *minister*(*Police*) might give *Terry*.

3. *leader* : *Party* ⇸ *Poli*

   This maps a party to its leader, for example, *leader*(*Business*) might map to *Denzil*.

4. *_talksto_* : *Poli* ↔ *Poli*

   This indicates whether one politician is prepared to talk to some other politician, for example, *Neville talksto Russell*.

We can map each politician to his or her party leader through a total function *takeme* which may be defined as follows.

$$takeme : Poli \to Poli$$

$$\forall p : Poli \bullet$$
$$takeme(p) = leader(belongs(p))$$

Using the above style, define functions or relations to satisfy the following requirements.

a. Pair each party with the number of representatives that it has in parliament.
b. Pair each politician with the set of politicians to whom that politician talks.
c. Pair each politician with the set of politicians that talk to him or her.
d. Pair each party leader with the set of politicians that he or she leads.
e. Create pairs of party leaders such that the first one outranks the second in terms of the number of politicians in the respective parties.

Q12.9 The results of the men's 100 m final in the 1996 Olympics were as follows.

Places	Runners	Countries	Times
1	Bill	USA	9.78
2	Frank	GB	9.85
3	Ahmed	Kenya	9.93
4	Stefan	Jamaica	10.01
5	Bruce	Australia	10.03
6	Bevan	USA	10.18
7	Barry	Australia	10.25
8	Jean	France	10.35

The race results are modeled using the types [*N*, *Runner*, *Country*, *Time*] and the following functions between the types.

1. $place : Runner \rightarrow N$

   This enables us to determine which place a runner achieved, for example $place(Frank) = 2$.

2. $rep : Runner \rightarrow Country$

   This tells us which country an athlete represented, for example $rep(Bevan) = USA$.

3. $time : Place \rightarrow Time$

   This tells us the time taken by whoever took a particular place, for example $time(8) = 10.35$.

Rewrite the following English sentences using quantification.

a. Every one came in under 11 seconds.
b. No one bettered 9.5 seconds.
c. There were no Australians in the top three.
d. Every Australian did better than 8th.
e. No Australian beat a Kenyan.
f. Only one person took less than 9.80 seconds.
g. No country got more than one medal.

Q12.10 Using only the set of integers, N, rewrite the following statements by means of quantification.

a. There is a number greater than 1.
b. There is no number that is half of 25.
c. Every number greater than 1 is less than its square.
d. There is a number less than 25 that is the sum of 6 and 12.
e. Every number less than 10 has a square less than 100.

Restate your answer using the quantifier equivalents.

Q12.11 Which of the following statements are true and which are false?

a. $\exists n : N \bullet 3^n + 4^n = 5^n$
b. $\exists n : N \bullet n * n = 625$
c. $\forall m, n : N \bullet m + n = 2n \Rightarrow m = n$
d. $\forall n : N \bullet (\exists m : N \bullet m = n + 1)$
e. $\forall n : N \bullet n < 1000 \Rightarrow n > 5$

Q12.12 Write out, in extension, the following expressions.

a. { 2 } ◁ { (1,5), (2,10), (3,1) }
b. { 1,3 } ◁ { (1,5), (2,10), (3,1) }
c. { (1,3) } ⊕ { (1,5), (2,10), (3,1) }
d. { (1,5), (2,10), (3,1) } ⊕ { (1,3) }
e. { (1,5), (2,10), (3,1) } ⊕ { (2,5), (8,6) }
f. { (1,5), (1,8), (3,1) } ▷ { 1 }
g. { (1,5), (2,10), (3,1) } ▷ { 1,8 }

▶ Q12.13 Write the following sequences in set extension form.

a. [B,A,T]
b. [T,A] ⌢ [B]
c. [T,A] ⌢ [T,A]
d. [A]
e. [A] ⌢ [B] ⌢ [C]
f. [ ]
g. [ ] ⌢ [A]
h. [A] ⌢ [ ]

▶ Q12.14 Rewrite the following sets as sequences.

a. { (1,Q), (2,U), (3,T) }
b. { (2,Q), (1,U) }
c. { (1,U) } ∪ { (2,N), (3,I) }
d. { (4,E), ,(1,B) } ∪ { (3,A), (2,C) }
e. { (1,N), (2,O) } - { (2,O), (1,N) }

▶ Q12.15 Given the following sequences of characters:

k = [K,I,N,G]
q = [Q,U,E,E,N]
b = [B,I,S,H,O,P]

simplify the expressions below.

a. head k
b. tail q
c. tail tail b
d. [head k] ⌢ (tail tail q)
e. 4..6 ◁ b

CHAPTER 13

The Knowledge Base

13.1 Introduction

Documentation is one of the most disliked features of computing. This is rather unfortunate since program documentation is where we store our knowledge in its most (human) readable form. As an example, consider a simple rule stating that a customer's current balance must not be allowed to exceed his or her credit limit. A rule like this is typically specified using a program design technique such as pseudocode or a decision table. The rule might then be encoded within a COBOL program. Thus the program becomes the rule enforcer. The rule is specified in pseudocode and implemented in COBOL.

What happens next? If we are honest with ourselves we know that from now on all attention turns to the program code; the specification takes on a secondary role of documentation. Changes to the rule occur, such as amendments, extensions, special cases and so on. These are implemented directly in the program and the documentation becomes increasingly obsolete, simply confirming the programmer's prejudice against documentation. The result is that the database is encapsulated by a collection of programs, with each program implementing any number of undocumented rules. The database starts to suffer from hardening of its arteries. Organizational knowledge becomes buried in programs. When the system is to be replaced, all this knowledge must be rediscovered by the next generation of systems developers.

One answer to this problem is to keep the documentation up to date and to make the programs subordinate to this documentation. In doing so, we would move towards a more evolutionary style of systems development. Maybe the term *specification* should be discarded. In the minds of many programmers, any specification is a disposable means to an end; the end being an executable program. A better approach is to consider that the programs constitute a knowledge-base of some kind; and that knowledge needs to be expressed in at least two forms: (1) in a way that humans can understand; and (2) in a way that machines can execute. Both forms are necessary; the first for us, and the second for the machines. A knowledge base of the kind being proposed is simply continuously updated documentation that is being used to drive the implementation rather than being treated as an afterthought.

13.2 Information Systems Development

Historically, in the development of organizational information systems, three distinct styles have arisen:

1. There is a process-oriented style characterized by an emphasis on the physical basis of any new system, that is, on the kinds of storage devices used to store data and on the instructions to be given to the computer. Development tools include system and program flowcharts. This kind of development peaked with the structured analysis and design schools. The processing is central and the data peripheral.
2. There is a data-oriented style in which the roles are reversed so that the database is central and programs peripheral. Programs are seen as merely the means by which the database is queried and updated. Entity-relationship modelling, conceptual schema design and SQL are part of this school.
3. There is a knowledge-based style which can be thought of as an amalgamation of the process and data styles. Programs and data are *both* seen to model or represent the organization, each in their own way. Programs contain general knowledge, rules, equations or formulae. Databases contain specific knowledge or facts. Expert systems are part of this school. CASE (Computer-Assisted Software Engineering) tools, especially those based on repositories, are also a move to this style.

Although there is a historical trend, the process-oriented and data-oriented style are still in active use.

13.3 Knowledge

An organizational information system models some aspect of the organization. If we take the knowledge-based approach, then an information system comes in two parts. One part implements organizational rules and the other contains specific facts about the organization, but both model the organization in their different ways.

One of the prime reasons for data (or conceptual) modeling is that the end product, such as a conceptual schema or an ER diagram, is a stable community view of an organization. The resulting model provides a secure platform from which information systems may be developed. The usefulness of this platform stems primarily from its stability. From the model a relatively static data base structure may be derived. So, for example, a fact like:

```
Dave works in Dispatch.
```

may be replaced, in the database, by one like:

```
Dave works in Maintenance.
```

but the more general fact that:

```
People work in Departments.
```

remains unchanged. So the database changes but the knowledge base does not. The term knowledge is used in this book to describe information that is true for a relatively long period of time, that is, knowledge is more stable. It consists of *generalized* facts, that is, facts not just about specific objects but about whole classes of objects. A knowledge base contains the essence of organizational wisdom and experience, or at least, such of that essence as may be formally represented.

A data model, such as a conceptual schema or an ER diagram, is a kind of knowledge base, although a rather rudimentary one. It allows us to nominate enduring relationships and to specify a little of the nature of these relationships (that is, whether they are one-to-one, one-to-many or many-to-many). A data model, however, limits itself to basic types and basic relationships because its purpose is to help us design the database. A more useful knowledge base would be one that allows us to specify any type of object and any relationships. Some examples of the kind of things that we would like to specify are as follows:

1. We should be able to specify general constraints regarding things, for example, that a customer's current balance should always be less than their credit limit.

2. We should be able to specify that, after a bank teller says "Next please!", and the person at the front of the queue has moved forward to be served, the queue is now formed strictly from the tail of the queue beforehand.

3. We should be able to derive and specify new relationships based upon existing relationships, for example, the total on an invoice is the sum of the totals for each line of the invoice.

These usually form part of the program specification because they are implemented programmatically, rather than becoming part of a database.

13.4 Representing Organizational Knowledge

How do we represent or specify the knowledge to be kept in our knowledge base? In other words, how do we best specify our information systems? What alternatives are there? Current forms of program specification include:

- pseudocode
- decision tables or trees
- program flowcharts
- data flow diagrams
- structure charts
- Nassi-Shneiderman diagrams
- and, frequently, the programs themselves

There are two contrasting problems with these techniques and their usage.

1. On the one hand, some of them are too oriented towards the computer and it is difficult to distinguish the rule from its implementation.

2. On the other hand, some of them allow rules to be expressed too vaguely; the user is happy with one interpretation and the programmer with another.

However, the number of alternatives and their variety of approaches do show that it is possible to represent knowledge in many different ways. In this book we choose to express the human-readable form of our knowledge using a language called **Z**. It can be thought of as a language that integrates data and program design.

Z is a *specification* language. It is *not* a programming language, in the sense that a statement in Z may not be directly executable or automatically translated into executable instructions. It is a means of expressing our ideas and of organizing them in some way.

So our knowledge base will consist of two quite distinct descriptions of the organization:

- The first description will be called the **specification**. This will be for us.
- The second description will be called the **implementation**. This will be a machine-executable version of the first.

It must be possible to say how these two versions are related or linked, and to demonstrate their equivalence. Chapter 19 provides an example of what we need to prove in order to be satisfied that they are equivalent. There are several comments that may be made as a result.

1. The link between the specification and any implementation should be maintained *at all times* as one of the normal functions of the data processing department within the organization.
2. This link, itself an information system, should be used as a means of gaining access to the implementation. It forms a *bridge* between the non-executable and the executable versions of the knowledge base.
3. Access to the implementation should be permitted *only by means of* this link.
4. Changes to any part of the implementation should *only be permitted if they are consistent* with the specification; and such consistency will be provided by means of this linking software.

In practice things are *not* done this way. Instead:

1. The link is only ever in the mind of the programmers involved, disappearing as they disappear to create even bigger and better information systems.
2. Instead of using the specification to guide them, the maintenance programmer jumps into the implementation with boots on.
3. The specification no longer matches the implementation; so it withers.

13.5 A look at Z

The chapter introduces some of the features of **Z**. In particular, we will look at the **schema** which is the unit of specification within the language. Schemas are used to modularize a specification written using Z, and a complete Z specification will consist of a number of interdependent schemas. In essence, a schema allows us to state some truth regarding the things that we are specifying. Each schema consists of two parts, a signature and a predicate. The signature is where variables are declared and associated with some set or type. The predicate is where constraints are placed upon these variables.

Example 13.1 Here is an example of a schema called *Employee* that might contain the information that we want to keep regarding each employee.

Employee

$name : seq\ Character$
$age : N$
$jobhistory : Set\ of\ Promotion$

$17 \leq age < 65$

The schema signature states that we are interested in three things about an employee:

- a *name* which is a sequence of characters;
- an *age* which is a number;
- a *job history* which is a set of promotions.

The schema predicate states that an employee is required to be at least 17 and younger than 65.

Example 13.2 Another schema might be used to define what we mean by a promotion.

Promotion

$date : day$
$job : seq\ Character$
$rate : Money$
$dept : seq\ Character$

$job \in \{\texttt{plumber}, \texttt{joiner}, \texttt{nurse}, \texttt{manager}\}$
$rate > 10$
$dept \in \{\texttt{Finance}, \texttt{Computing}, \texttt{Marketing}, \texttt{Production}\}$

According to its signature, every promotion consists of:

- the date upon which the promotion occurred;
- the new job taken that day;
- the rate of pay attached to this job;
- the department.

The predicate part requires every promotion to satisfy three conditions:

- the job can only be one of **plumber**, **joiner**, ...;
- the rate of pay must exceed $10.00 per hour;

- the department involved must be one of `Finance`,...

In summary a schema looks like this:

―― *A Z Schema* ――――――――――――――――――――――
| *THE SIGNATURE*
| *a collection of type declarations*
| *that name variables and associate*
| *each variable with a particular*
| *set or type.*
|――――
| *THE PREDICATE*
| *a collection of rules or constraints*
| *governing the values held by the*
| *variables named in the signature.*
――――――――――――――――――――――――――――――――――

Just like a COBOL program with its data division and its procedure division! Let us pursue that analogy a little further.

13.6 Signatures

A signature is like the data division of a COBOL program. It consists of a series of type declarations whereby each variable is associated with a type or set. A signature is written in a data or type sublanguage that enables us to declare the kinds of things that interest us and about which we want to make statements. However, there are differences. In a COBOL data division we are **reserving storage inside a computer** in order to perform calculations or to make comparisons. In a Z signature we are not restricted to the kinds of data that some compiler is prepared to recognize. We can introduce any kind of object that interests us.

Example 13.3 This can be seen in the following schema which has no predicate, consisting only of a signature.

―― *FirstSampleSignature* ――――――――――――――――
| $b : Bore$
| $x, y : Property$
| $p : Person$
| $c, d : Client$
――――――――――――――――――――――――――――――――――

We can introduce variables that stand for things that no self-respecting COBOL compiler would be prepared to let pass.

Example 13.4 The type associated with a variable may be given as a simple name such as in the examples above. However, it may be a more complex expression.

$\boxed{\begin{array}{l} \textit{SecondSampleSignature} \\ \textit{location} : N \times N \\ \textit{team} : \textit{Set of Player} \\ \textit{sqrt} : N \rightarrow N \\ \textit{min} : N \times N \rightarrow N \\ \textit{queue} : \textit{seq Customer} \end{array}}$

Briefly, the types associated with each of these variables are as follows:

- A *location* is a pair of integers (N is the name usually given to the set of integers 0, 1, 2, ...).
- A *team* is a set of players, not *the* set of players, but a subset of that set.
- *sqrt* is a function that maps from one integer to another, say from 4 to 2 or from 144 to 12; we can place this function in front of the first of the pair and expect it to equal the second, for example, $sqrt(4) = 2$.
- *min* is a function that maps a pair of integers to another integer, say from (4,9) to 4; again we can apply the function so that $min(4, 9) = 4$.
- *queue* is a sequence of customers, that is, it is an ordered list of some kind, one that allows us to talk of one customer being in front of another.

13.6.1 Declaration

A signature consists of a series of *type declarations* and each declaration has one of these formats:

$\boxed{\begin{array}{l} \textit{Declaration}: \\ \quad \textit{Basic\_Declaration} \\ \quad \textit{or } \textit{Basic\_Declaration}; \ldots; \textit{Basic\_Declaration} \\ \textit{Basic\_Declaration}: \\ \quad \textit{Symbol} : \textit{Set\_Term} \\ \quad \textit{or } \textit{Symbol}, \ldots, \textit{Symbol} : \textit{Set\_Term} \end{array}}$

Essentially, a declaration introduces a symbol which will be used to represent an object of the kind indicated.

Example 13.5 We might use the symbol p to represent a person, as follows.

$p : \textit{Person}$

A symbol may be any mark that we (collectively) can construct, recognise and reproduce. We are not restricted merely to letters and words, although the keyboard is a convenient way of making new symbols (in the form of words). We may borrow symbols from other alphabets, for example Σ, or build new ones, for example $\oplus$.

Example 13.6 The basic declaration style also allows us to introduce several new objects of the same type at the same time.

$p, q, r : Person$

We must take care, however. Just because the symbols are different does not mean that the objects they represent are different. They may be, they may not; it depends on any subsequent constraints we choose to place upon these objects.

Example 13.7 Several basic declarations may be connected by semi-colons.

$p, q : Person;\ s : Sport;\ d, e, f : Date$

Example 13.8 Although the semicolon has been shown as the separator, a new line may also be used.

$p, q : Person$
$s : Sport$
$d, e, f : Date$

Although all the examples so far have declared objects to be of a certain type, we may use any symbolic expression (*Set Term*) that represents a set. A *Set Term* may be a primitive or basic type, that is, one whose existence is to be accepted without question, for examples, people or cars or rivers. Alternatively it may be of a derived nature. We will discuss these two alternatives next.

13.6.2 Type Introductions

The world according to Z is divided into a number of disjoint sets called types. Every object has or belongs to just one type. No object can belong to more than one. When we discuss an object, we must always declare its type, and we must have introduced its type beforehand.

Type_Introduction
  [*Symbol*]
  or [*Symbol*, ..., *Symbol*]

Example 13.9 We may introduce several new types together.

[*Person, Sport, Skill*]

Example 13.10 However, it is better to introduce them one at a time and provide some explanatory comment.

Type	Interpretation
[*Person*]	The set of people who may belong to the circle.
[*Sport*]	The set of sports that they might take up.
[*Skill*]	The different levels of skill with which people may play a sport.

A type should be thought of as a fixed immutable background set. It must be capable of incorporating *all* candidate members by being defined broadly enough to cover all likely changes to the situation being described.

We do not need to introduce all required types at the same time, but may choose to spread their introduction throughout the specification, subject to the restriction that no type is used before being introduced.

13.6.3 Sets

The second kind of set that may be used in a declaration is one defined by means of any one of a number of ways in which sets may be constructed. These are as follows:

Set_Term:
  Symbol
  or *Set_Extension*
  or *Set_Comprehension*

  or *Type_Construction*
  or *Set_Operation*
  or *Special_Set_Operation*
  or *Fact_Type*
  or *Sequence_Operation*

  or (*Set_Term*)
  or *Symbol Set_Term*
  or *Set_Term Symbol Set_Term*

13.6.4 Set Extension

The set may be defined by listing out its elements in full.

Set_Extension:
  {*Term*}
  or {*Term, Term, ..., Term*}

Example 13.11 To introduce an object and identify it as being either Bob or his father:

$p : \{Bob, father(Bob)\}$

Example 13.12 To introduce an odd number less than ten:

$n : \{1, 3, 5, 7, 9\}$

13.6.5 Set Comprehension

The set to which an object belongs may be defined through some property shared by all its members. This is done by set comprehension, which takes all the forms discussed in Chapter 3.

$Set\_Comprehension$:

    $\{Declaration\}$
or $\{Declaration \mid Predicate\}$
or $\{Declaration \mid Predicate \bullet Term\}$
or $\{Declaration \bullet Term\}$

Example 13.13 To declare an object as being one of the sports that Alan plays:

$s : \{t : Sport \mid Alan\ plays\ t\}$

13.6.6 Type Construction

All objects in the knowledge base are of one of three kinds:

$Type\_Construction$:

or $Set\ of\ Set\_Term$
or $Set\_Term \times Set\_Term$

There are simple or **atomic** objects of some previously defined base type. There are also two ways of constructing more complex types:

1. The **power set** operator, $Set\ of$. Any object of a type built using this constructor is a set in its own right.

2. The Cartesian **product set** operator, $\times$. Any object of a type built using this constructor is a composite object.

Example 13.14 We may declare an object P to be a set of people.

$P : Set\ of\ Person$

Example 13.15 We may declare an object to be a pair of numbers.

$loc : N \times N$

Example 13.16 We can combine the constructors to declare an object to be a set of pairs of numbers.

$k : Set\ of\ (N \times N)$

Example 13.17 We can declare an object to be a pair of sets of numbers.

$k : (Set\ of\ N) \times (Set\ of\ N)$

13.6.7 Set Operations

The commonly used set operations, set union, set intersection and set difference give rise themselves to sets.

> $Set\_Operation$:
> $\quad\quad Set\_Term \cup Set\_Term$
> $or \quad Set\_Term \cap Set\_Term$
> $or \quad Set\_Term - Set\_Term$

Example 13.18 We could declare an object to be a sport that is played by Bob or Alan.

$s : (\{t : Sport\ |\ Bob\ plays\ t\} \cup \{t : Sport\ |\ Alan\ plays\ t\})$

Example 13.19 We could declare a person to be one of the people that Sue does not like.

$p : (Person - \{q : Person\ |\ Sue\ likes\ q\})$

13.6.8 Special Set Operations

There are also a number of other, less well known but just as useful, set operations. They were discussed in Chapter 12.

> $Special\_Set\_Operation$:
> $\quad\quad Set\_Term \triangleleft Set\_Term$
> $or \quad Set\_Term \triangleright Set\_Term$
> $or \quad Set\_Term \oplus Set\_Term$
> $or \quad dom\ Set\_Term$
> $or \quad ran\ Set\_Term$

All of these operations result in sets, and so may be used in a declaration.

- the domain subtraction operator $\vartriangleleft$
- the range subtraction operator $\vartriangleright$
- function override $\oplus$
- the domain operator dom
- the range operator ran

Example 13.20 We can declare an object to be any pair in the *plays* relation not involving Alan.

$g : (\{Alan\} \vartriangleleft plays)$

Example 13.21 We can declare an object to be a married person.

$p : dom\ spouse$

13.6.9 Fact Types

In Chapter 2, a fact involving two objects was seen as a pairing of these objects. The fact that Alan plays tennis was seen as a pairing (*Alan*, *tennis*). All facts of this kind can be gathered into a set of pairs.

$Fact\_Type$:
$\quad Set\_Term \leftrightarrow Set\_term$
or $Set\_Term \nrightarrow Set\_Term$
or $Set\_Term \rightarrow Set\_Term$
or $Set\_Term \rightarrowtail\kern-0.5em\rightarrow Set\_Term$
or $Set\_Term \rightarrowtail Set\_Term$

There are five kinds of fact types. See Chapter 2 for further discussion.

- The set $A \leftrightarrow B$ is the set of *all* relations (many-to-many relationships) between A and B.
- The set $A \nrightarrow B$ is the set of *all* partial functions (one-to-many relationships) from A to B.
- The set $A \rightarrow B$ is the set of *all* total functions from A to B.
- The set $A \rightarrowtail\kern-0.5em\rightarrow B$ is the set of *all* partial injections (one-to-one relationships) from A to B.
- The set $A \rightarrowtail B$ is the set of *all* total injections from A to B.

Example 13.22 To declare that *plays* is a relation between people and sports:

$\_plays\_ : Person \longleftrightarrow Sport$

Example 13.23 To declare two quite different relationships between people and numbers:

$age, height : Person \rightarrow N$

Both *age* and *height* have the same type. They are not, of course, the same thing.

13.6.10 Sequences and Sequence Operations

A sequence is a special kind of set, and so may be used in a declaration.

```
Sequence_Operation:
        seq Term
    or  Term ⌢ Term
    or  tail Term
```

Example 13.24 Declare a queue as a sequence of people.

$queue : seq\ Person$

The set *seq A* is the set of sequences of type *A*. Any individual element of *seq A* is itself a set.

Example 13.25 Declare an object to be one of the people in the above queue.

$queuer : ran\ queue$

The queue is a set of pairs. Its range is the people themselves.

Example 13.26 Declare an object to be one of the people in the queue, but not the person at the front.

$p : ran\ (tail\ queue)$

13.7 Predicates

A predicate is a condition that is to hold or is held by one or more variables, typically those variables declared in the preceding signature.

Example 13.27 Suppose we have the schema:

```
─ FirstSamplePredicate ─────────────────
  cost : Product → Money
  ─────────────────────────────────────
  ∀ p : Product • cost(p) < 100
  ∃ p : Product • cost(p) > 95
────────────────────────────────────────
```

The signature declares a function *cost* that enables us to map from a product to the cost of that product. The predicate contains two statements:

- the first uses the universal quantifier (∀) and it says that for all products, the cost is less than $100, or more simply, every product costs less than $100;
- the second statement uses the existential quantifier (∃) and it says that there exists a product that costs more than $95, or more simply, some products cost more than $95.

Example 13.28 The emphasis so far has been on the use of predicates to constrain or limit the values taken by variables. However, the use of predicates can be extended to defining computations or calculations.

Suppose that a company has a policy of allowing a discount of 15% on any order of 100 units or more. The charge for an order might be specified as in the following schema:

―― *ChargeFormula* ――――――――――――――――――――――――
$cost : Product \to Money$
$charge : Product \times N \to Money$
―――――――――――
$\forall p : Product;\ n : N \bullet$
$\quad n < 100 \Rightarrow charge(p, n) = n * cost(p)\ \wedge$
$\quad n \geq 100 \Rightarrow charge(p, n) = n * cost(p) * (1 - (15/100))$
――――――――――――――――――――――――――――――――

In this kind of predicate, the charge for a particular quantity of some product is defined in terms of other things, the quantity ordered and the discount allowed.

13.7.1 The Structure of a Predicate

The predicate of a schema was likened to the procedure division of a COBOL program. In this section we have seen predicates that relate to the kinds of things done in a procedure division, checking constraints and performing calculations. However, predicates are not necessarily restricted to the kinds of things that we expect to see in a procedure division.

> *Predicate*:
>
>   *Simple_Predicate*
>   or *Compound_Predicate*
>   or *Quantified_Predicate*

A predicate may be a simple sentence, or one involving connectives such as ∧, or one using quantifiers.

13.7.2 Simple Predicates

The kinds of sentences that come under this heading are shown below:

> *Simple_Predicate*:
>
> > *Symbol Term*
> > or *Term Symbol Term*
> > or *Term* ∈ *Set_Term*
> > or *Term* = *Term*

Example 13.29 To say that person p speaks Japanese:

speaks(p, *Japanese*)

Example 13.30 To say that Alan plays tennis:

Alan plays tennis

Example 13.31 To say that Bob is married:

Bob ∈ *dom spouse*

Example 13.32 To say that Mark is Alan's father:

Mark = *father*(*Alan*)

13.7.3 Compound Predicates

These are statements formed using sentential connectives. See Chapters 2 and 12.

> *Compound_Predicate*:
>
> > ¬*Predicate*
> > or *Predicate* ∧ *Predicate*
> > or *Predicate* ∨ *Predicate*
> > or *Predicate* ⇒ *Predicate*
> > or *Predicate* ⇔ *Predicate*

Example 13.33 To say that Bob is not Alan's father:

¬(*Bob* = *father*(*Alan*))

Example 13.34 To say that Alan is aged somewhere between Sue and Ann:

age(*Alan*) > *age*(*Sue*) ∧ *age*(*Alan*) < *age*(*Ann*)

Example 13.35 To say that Sue is married to Alan or Bob:

$$spouse(Sue) = Alan \lor spouse(Sue) = Bob$$

Unfortunately, this allows Sue to be married to both these men.

Example 13.36 To say that Sue is married to either Alan or Bob, but not both:

$$(spouse(Sue) = Alan \lor spouse(Sue) = Bob) \\ \land (\neg (spouse(Sue) = Alan \land spouse(Sue) = Bob))$$

This last example shows that the predicates used to build a compound predicate may themselves be compound.

13.7.4 Quantified Predicates

These allow us to make statements about classes of objects, rather than about individual objects.

> *Quantified_Predicate*:
>
> $\quad \forall$ *Declaration* • *Predicate*
> or $\exists$ *Declaration* • *Predicate*
> or $\exists!$*Declaration* • *Predicate*

Example 13.37 To say that everybody plays tennis:

$\forall p : Person$ • $p\ plays\ tennis$

Example 13.38 To say that at least one person is over 45 years old:

$\exists p : Person$ • $age(p) > 45$

Example 13.39 To say that exactly one person drives a Porsche:

$\exists! p : Person$ • $drives(p) = Porsche$

13.8 Kinds of Schema

The schema structure is very simple and yet enables us to make a number of different kinds of statements.

13.8.1 Process Descriptions

These allow us to describe a process or what we think of as a dynamic situation.

Example 13.40 Here is a schema that describes the process of taking two numbers and returning their sum.

```
┌─ Add ─────────────────────────
│ first?, second? : N
│ sum! : N
├───────────────────────────────
│ sum! = first? + second?
└───────────────────────────────
```

A process is something that takes some input and returns some output. The *Add* process takes two numbers, *first?* and *second?*. It returns or produces a third number *sum!* To help us interpret process schemas, two conventions are followed:

1. Input variables are **decorated** with or end in a question mark: so, without any additional comment, we can tell that *first?* and *second?* are inputs to the *Add* process.
2. Output variables are decorated with an exclamation mark: so *sum!* is the output of this process.

Example 13.41 Here is a schema *Square* that takes a number *n?* and returns its square *sn!*

```
┌─ Square ──────────────────────
│ n?, sn! : N
├───────────────────────────────
│ sn! = n? * n?
└───────────────────────────────
```

There is only one input and one output. We can declare them on the same line or on separate lines as was done in the *Add* schema. It would seem better to separate the declaration of input and output variables to help clarify the schema.

Example 13.42 Here is a schema *SquareRoot* that takes a number *n?* and outputs its square root *sr!*

```
┌─ SquareRoot ──────────────────
│ n? : N
│ sr! : N
├───────────────────────────────
│ sr! * sr! = n?
└───────────────────────────────
```

You think: what a cheat! The schema makes no attempt to describe how to derive the root. It leaves that up to the programmer. The schema simply relates the input to the output. But how would we test the program? We would square its output and compare that with the input provided. If they are the same then the program would seem to meet its specification. So that even if the specifier were to present the programmer with an algorithm for calculating the square root, there would still be a "hidden agenda" that would come out during testing.

Example 13.43 Here is a schema *Upto* that takes a number *n?* and returns *all!*, the set of numbers in the range 0 to *n?*

```
┌─ Upto ─────────────────────────────────
│  n? : N
│  all! : Set of N
├────────────────────────────────────────
│  all! = {k : N | k ≤ n?}
└────────────────────────────────────────
```

The output is a set of numbers and so is declared as such. Set comprehension is used to define the output.

13.8.2 State Descriptions

The schema structure can equally well be used to describe a situation in a *static* way. We use the schema to provide a snapshot of some **state** of affairs that interests us.

Example 13.44 We can represent a college or university in terms of its students and their names.

```
┌─ WiseacresUni ─────────────────────────
│  students : Set of People
│  called : People ⇸ Name
├────────────────────────────────────────
│  dom called = students
└────────────────────────────────────────
```

As far as we are concerned, Wiseacres consists of a set of people called *students* and a partial function *called* that maps from people to their name. The variables *students* and *called* are called the **components** of the state. The predicate says that we are interested in the names of just these people who are students. The domain of *called* is the set of people for whom we know a last name. The predicate part of a state description is called the state **invariant**. It characterizes the state. Regardless of what specific changes the University undergoes, we will *always* want the invariant to be true.

Example 13.45 Here is a schema that makes a simple statement about a parliament.

```
┌─ Parliament ───────────────────────────
│  poli : Set of People
├────────────────────────────────────────
│  #poli = 89
└────────────────────────────────────────
```

Parliament, as defined in this schema, consists of a set of people. The set is called *poli* and consists of exactly 89 members.

13.8.3 Type Descriptions

This kind of schema is useful when we want to define a new **type** of object.

Example 13.46 Suppose we wish to define the structure of a rugby union team.

The Knowledge Base

```
┌─ Team ─────────────────────────────────
│ players : Set of People
│ forwards, backs : Set of People
├────────────────────────────────────────
│ players = forwards ∪ backs
│ forwards ∩ backs = {}
│ #forwards = 8
│ #backs = 7
└────────────────────────────────────────
```

The team consists of three sets of people – *players*, *forwards* and *backs*. However these sets are not disjoint. The predicate contains the following conditions.

1. The *players* set is made up of the forwards and the backs.
2. No person is both a forward *and* a back.
3. There are 8 forwards.
4. There are 7 backs.

A rugby team is often called a rugby XV or fifteen. We can demonstrate that a team must have 15 players.

$\quad \#players$

$= \#(forwards \cup backs)$
[from line 1 of the predicate part of the schema]

$= \#forwards + \#backs - \#(forwards \cap backs)$
[a law of set cardinality: $\#(A \cup B) = \#A + \#B - \#(A \cap B)$]

$= 8 + 7 - \#\{\}$
[lines 2,3 and 4]

$= 15 - 0$

$= 15$

Now that we have established that a team has 15 players, we can use the *Team* schema with increased confidence. One way of using the schema is to declare a variable to be of type *Team*, for example:

$\quad t : Team$

The variable t is now a composite variable with three components and these may be accessed using **projection** as $t.players$, $t.forwards$ and $t.backs$. These components of t are related in the way described in the predicate of *Team*.

Example 13.47 We can describe a school as follows. A school consists of the staff, the head of school and a secretary. The head is a member of staff; the secretary is not.

┌─ *School* ──────────────────────────────────┐
│ *head* : *People*   │
│ *secretary* : *People*   │
│ *staff* : Set of *People*   │
├───┤
│ *head* ∈ *staff*   │
│ *secretary* ∉ *staff*   │
└───┘

13.9 Summary

It is one of the ironies of computing that software writers are relatively unprovided for in terms of computing support. When was a programmer ever asked what kind of information system he or she would like? But what kinds of information systems *do* organizational computing people need? They need software aids to help with the **long-term management** of information systems. This computer support must help computing people to take a more evolutionary approach to their work. If we take the view that programs contain encoded organizational knowledge, then the true job of data processing professionals is that of knowledge base management. They must revise their thoughts and habits accordingly.

To differentiate between data and programs is to make a distinction that is partly technological and partly historical. Both data *and* programs contain information.

Programmers need to alter their mental image of what their job principally entails – from a notion of construction to one of evolution. They need to see themselves less as hackers and more as technical writers of programming and other languages. They need to see themselves as knowledge maintainers.

1. They must start to see the provision of information systems in evolutionary rather than revolutionary terms. User needs are continually changing. A computer system is just a temporary implementation of user requirements, one using the current technology.

2. They must see that specification is not simply a means to an end, not merely a way of reaching the desired goal of a new information system. The specification contains organizational knowledge in its most concentrated form; it is a valuable organizational asset. One of the DP department's major responsibilities is the management of this asset.

3. They must change their attitude towards documentation. They must see themselves as producers of high quality documentation using CASE tools.

Organizational computing will continue without direction for as long as computing professionals are obliged to play a purely support role. Computing people are quite without the kind of computing support that other staff take for granted.

Of course, computing professionals (everywhere) must take some of the blame for this state of affairs. We (from the computing viewpoint) encourage an "us and them" attitude between computing people and so-called end-users. Unfortunately, the effect of this is that:

1. we are placed in a service, and consequently reactive, role with regard to users; and

2. we never see ourselves as possible end-users in our own right.

Another barrier to our seeing ourselves as users is that we have no feel for what kinds of information systems we should have ourselves. Other people can go out and touch the things that *their* information systems record. Engineers can swim in their rivers, jump in their dams or canoe down their canals. Managers can talk to their staff, pat them on the back, kick them out the office and so on. In contrast, computing people deal with intangible things.

In this chapter we have seen the use of the **schema** which is the basic structure upon which we will hang the mathematical statements that form the essence of our knowledge base. The schema has a simple structure and allows us to make a variety of statements.

- It can be used to describe processes in an active or dynamic way.
- It can equally be used to present a snapshot or static description.
- It can also be used to introduce and describe a new type of object which can then be incorporated in other schemas.

Essentially, the schema allows us to express knowledge in the same way that we do in proverbs such as:

"He who hesitates is lost."

The warning is issued to the variable (He) in the sentence; but it applies to us all!

Exercises

▶ Q13.1 Write process description schemas to satisfy each of the following requirements. Make sure that input and output variables are decorated according to convention.

   a. A schema *Successor* which takes an integer and returns the next integer in sequence.

   b. A schema *Max* which takes two integers and returns the larger of the two.

   c. A schema *Largest* which takes a set of integers and returns the largest integer in the set. The set must therefore contain at least one element.

   d. A schema *Between* which takes two integers and returns any integer in the range defined by the smaller and the larger of these two numbers.

▶ Q13.2 Write a schema that describes a family according to the following requirements.

A family consists of two (tired) people *mum* and *dad* as well as a set of people *children*.

   1. Mum is female; Dad is male.
   2. All the children are appropriately related to Mum and Dad.
   3. All the children are at least 16 years younger than both Mum and Dad.
   4. No family has more than 15 children.

You may use the following functions which should be self-explanatory.

$sex : People \rightarrow Sexes$
$mother : People \rightarrow People$
$father : People \rightarrow People$
$age : People \rightarrow N$

CHAPTER 14

From Specification to Implementation

14.1 Introduction

In this chapter we will look at how the various schemas that form a Z specification might be put together. The situation to be modeled is that of a class of students who are studying a particular subject. The specification covers such typical activities as students being enrolled, being awarded marks, having marks amended and, hard to believe, students dropping the subject. We will begin by introducing a **state schema** which provides a static picture of the classroom. Based on that picture we specify a number of **operation schemas** which describe the ways in which the classroom may change. Then we return to the state schema and discuss how it might be developed. Finally, we discuss the relationship between this **specification**, which consists of a state schema and a number of operation schemas, and the **implementation**, which consists of a database and a number of programs.

14.2 The State Schema

Suppose we describe the classroom in the following way.

$$
\begin{array}{|l}
\hline
\textit{Class} \\
\hline
students : Set\ of\ Person \\
last : Person \nrightarrow Name \\
mark : Person \nrightarrow 0..100 \\
\\
dom\ last = students \\
dom\ mark \subseteq students \\
\hline
\end{array}
$$

This is called a **state** schema and is intended to capture or represent a particular state of affairs that interests us. The *Class* schema is a *single, global and static* picture of the classroom. It introduces the students, their names and any marks they might have been awarded for the subject under study. There are three basic sets or types used:

[*Person*]   The set of all possible students.
[*N*]   The set of integers 0, 1, 2, ...
[*Name*]   The set of names.

The schema above can be interpreted in the following way.

The *Class* Declaration

1. *students* : *Set of Person*

    The variable *students* represents the set of people enrolled at any particular time.

2. *last* : *Person* $\nrightarrow$ *Name*

    This is a function that maps people to their last name.

3. *mark* : *Person* $\nrightarrow$ *N*

    This is a function that maps people to any mark that they may have been awarded.

The *Class* Predicate

1. *dom last* = *students*

    This says that we will know or require to know the last name of just those students enrolled in the class.

2. *dom mark* $\subseteq$ *students*

    This says that we may not necessarily have a mark for every student enrolled.

14.3 Schema Inclusion

One of the things we can do with a named schema is to **include** it within other schemas. Suppose we wanted to define a small class, something like our original class but where the class size was to be restricted to no more than 10 students. We can define this as follows:

```
─ SmallClass ──────────────────────────────
  Class
  ─────────────────────
  #students ≤ 10
───────────────────────────────────────────
```

The schema *Class* is named in the declaration of *SmallClass* and the effect is to introduce all the variables of *Class* and to conjoin (logically "and") the predicate of *Class* to that of *SmallClass*. So, *SmallClass*, when fully expanded, looks like this:

―― *SmallClass* ―――――――――――――――――――――――――――――――
students : *Set of Person*
last : *Person* ⇸ *Name*
mark : *Person* ⇸ 0..100
―――――――――――――――――
#*students* ≤ 10
dom last = *students*
dom mark ⊆ *students*
―――――――――――――――――――――――――――――――

Using schema inclusion, we are able to emphasize that a small class is the same as any other class with the additional constraint that there be no more than 10 students enrolled.

14.4 Schema Decoration

There is a convention that if we use a schema and **decorate** its name in some way, typically with a prime ', then the effect is to consistently decorate or rename all the variables within the schema, both within the declaration and within the predicate.

―― *TrialDecoration* ―――――――――――――――――――――――――――
Class'
―――――――――――――――――――――――――――――――

This expands to the following:

―― *TrialDecoration* ―――――――――――――――――――――――――――
students' : *Set of Person*
last' : *Person* ⇸ *Name*
mark' : *Person* ⇸ 0..100
―――――――――――――――――
dom last' = *students'*
dom mark' ⊆ *students'*
―――――――――――――――――――――――――――――――

Note that only the variables are decorated, not their types.

14.5 State Transition

Another use of the schema is to allow us to capture the essentials of any change that may happen to a particular state of affairs. Suppose we want to be able to talk about changes that might occur to our class. These changes could include such events as:

- enrolling a new student;
- awarding a mark to a student;
- adjusting a student's mark;
- allowing a student to drop out.

We will need to be able to talk about the set of students before and after a change, and about their names and marks as well. We might define a new schema:

$$
\begin{array}{|l}
\hline \Delta\,Class \\
\hline
students, students' : Set\ of\ Person \\
last, last' : Person \nrightarrow Name \\
mark, mark' : Person \nrightarrow \mathbb{N} \\
\hline
dom\ last = students \\
dom\ mark \subseteq students \\
dom\ last' = students' \\
dom\ mark' \subseteq students' \\
\hline
\end{array}
$$

These are the kinds of variables that we might want to use, and these are the conditions to be attached to them. But this can be achieved much more neatly using schema inclusion and decoration.

$$
\begin{array}{|l}
\hline \Delta\,Class \\
\hline
Class \\
Class' \\
\hline
\end{array}
$$

We have built a **frame** schema, in this case $\Delta\,Class$, that describes the features that are common to all possible changes to some state, in this case the $Class$ state.

14.6 Operation Schemas

A schema that is intended to specify how something such as an event is expected to affect a particular state of affairs is called an **operation** schema. The variables used in an operation are ones that allow us to specify the allowable change of state and any inputs and outputs involved in the change.

1. Variables are required to represent the state *before* the change. These variables are defined in the corresponding state schema. The $Class$ schema is an example.

2. Variables are required to represent the state *after* the change. These variables can be obtained from a version of the state schema decorated with a prime or apostrophe. The schema $Class'$ is an example.

3. Variables are possibly required to represent any *input* to the operation. These variables are conventionally decorated with a question mark to indicate their role in the operation.

4. Variables may also be required to represent any *output* from the operation. These are conventionally decorated with an exclamation mark.

Using the above conventions we will look at some operation schemas.

14.6.1 Enrolling a New Student

In this operation we will add a new student to the class. There are two inputs, the person $p?$ enrolling and his or her *name?*.

Enrol

$\Delta Class$
$p? : Person$
$name? : Name$

$p? \notin students$
$students' = students \cup \{p?\}$
$last' = last \cup \{(p?, name?)\}$
$mark' = mark$

In this and each of the specifications that follow, we will provide an accompanying explanation of both the declaration and the predicate parts of the schema.

The *Enrol* Declaration

1. $\Delta Class$

   This signals a change to the *Class* state.

2. $p? : Person$

   This is the number or identifier of the student.

3. $name? : Name$

   This is the new student's name.

The *Enrol* Predicate

1. $p? \notin students$

   The student must not already be in the class.

2. $students' = students \cup \{p?\}$

   The student is added to those already enrolled.

3. $last' = last \cup \{(p?, name?)\}$

   An entry mapping this student to his or her name is added to the list of last names.

4. $mark' = mark$

   No change is made to any marks awarded to the students.

All the conditions in the predicate part of an operation schema must be made true by any program implementing that specification. There is an implied conjunction of *all* the conditions in the predicate. It does not supposedly matter in which order they appear. In practice, however, the program will validate any input it receives *before* making any changes to the database that are required. It is useful, therefore, to write the operation schema conditions in a certain sequence.

1. The pre-conditions are presented before the post-conditions. That is why the condition:

    $p? \notin students$

   appears first.

2. The post-conditions appear next, but they too appear in a certain order. Those conditions describing changes appear first. Thus the lines:

    $students' = students \cup \{p?\}$
    $last' = last \cup \{(p?, name?)\}$

   come next because the *students* and *last* components are changed by this operation. The condition:

    $mark' = mark$

   appears last because the *mark* component is unchanged.

These are merely guidelines. It may be more convenient, in certain circumstances, to vary or even ignore these suggestions.

14.6.2 Award a Mark

A mark is to be awarded to a student. There are also two inputs to this operation, the person $p?$ being awarded a mark and $m?$, the mark itself.

Award

$\Delta Class$
$p? : Person$
$m? : 0..100$

$p? \in students$
$p? \notin dom\ mark$
$mark' = mark \cup \{(p?, m?)\}$
$students' = students$
$last' = last$

The *Award* Declaration

1. $\Delta Class$

    This signals a change to the *Class* state.

2. $p? : Person$

    This is the number or identifier of the student.

3. $m? : 0..100$

    This is the mark that the student is to receive. It must be an integer in the range 0 to 100.

The *Award* Predicate

1. $p? \in students$

   The student must be in the class.

2. $p? \notin dom\ mark$

   The student must not already have a mark.

3. $mark' = mark \cup \{(p?, m?)\}$

   An entry mapping this student to his or her mark is added to the list of marks.

4. $students' = students$

   No change is made to any students enrolled.

5. $last' = last$

   No change is made to the list of last names.

14.6.3 Amend a Mark

This operation allows an existing mark to be amended.

AmendMark

$\Delta Class$
$p? : Person$
$m? : 0..100$

$p? \in students$
$p? \in dom\ mark$
$mark' = mark \oplus \{(p?, m?)\}$
$students' = students$
$last' = last$

The *AmendMark* Declaration

1. $\Delta Class$

   This signals a change to the *Class* state.

2. $p? : Person$

   This is the number or identifier of the student.

3. $m? : 0..100$

   This is the new mark that the student is to receive.

The *AmendMark* Predicate

1. $p? \in students$

   The student must be in the class.

2. $p? \in \text{dom } mark$

   The student must already have been awarded a mark.

3. $mark' = mark \oplus \{(p?, m?)\}$

   The entry mapping this student to his or her mark is amended or overridden with the new mark.

4. $students' = students$

   No change is made to any students enrolled.

5. $last' = last$

   No change is made to the list of last names.

14.6.4 A Student Drops Out

This operation records the person $p?$ dropping the class.

```
┌─ DropOut ──────────────────────────
│ Δ Class
│ p? : Person
├────────────────────────────────────
│ p? ∈ students
│ students' = students − {p?}
│ last' = {p?} ⩤ last
│ mark' = {p?} ⩤ mark
└────────────────────────────────────
```

The *DropOut* Declaration

1. $\Delta \, Class$

   This signals a change to the *Class* state.

2. $p? : Person$

   This is the number or identifier of the student dropping out.

The *DropOut* Predicate

1. $p? \in students$

   The student must be in the class.

2. $students' = students - \{p?\}$

   The student is removed from the list of those enrolled.

3. $last' = \{p?\} ⩤ last$

   The student's name is also removed.

4. $mark' = \{p?\} ⩤ mark$

   Any mark awarded to the student is removed.

14.7 Read-only Transactions

There are occasions when we simply wish to inspect some component of the state, rather than changing the state. The first step is to define a special version of the Δ schema, $\Delta\,Class$.

$$
\begin{array}{|l}
\Xi\,Class \\
\hline
\Delta\,Class \\
\hline
students' = students \\
last' = last \\
mark' = mark
\end{array}
$$

The Ξ is to be read as "no change", so $\Xi\,Class$, when used within a operation schema, signals that the transaction does not change any part of the state.

As an example of the use of this convention, here is a read-only transaction that simply tells us the number of students enrolled in the class.

$$
\begin{array}{|l}
HowMany \\
\hline
\Xi\,Class \\
count! : \mathbb{N} \\
\hline
count! = \#students
\end{array}
$$

The *HowMany* Declaration

- $\Xi\,Class$

    This signals an inspection of the *Class* state.

- $count! : \mathbb{N}$

    This output variable will contain the number of students.

The *HowMany* Predicate

- $count! = \#students$

    The number of students in the class is simply the size of the *students* set.

14.8 Maintaining the State Invariant

The classroom situation was formally described by a state schema *Class*.

┌─ *Class* ─────────────────────────────────────┐
│ *students* : *Set of Person*   │
│ *last* : *Person* $\nrightarrow$ *Name*   │
│ *mark* : *Person* $\nrightarrow$ 0..100   │
├───┤
│ *dom last* = *students*   │
│ *dom mark* ⊆ *students*   │
└───┘

The *Class* state consists of three parts.

1. There is a set of people; let us call that set *students*.
2. There is a mapping from some people to their name; let us call this mapping *last*.
3. There is a mapping from some people to an integer; let us call this mapping *mark*.

Nothing *specific* is said about these things. The purpose of the state schema is to describe the class *in general terms*. We don't know which people are going to enrol, what their names will be or what marks they will be awarded. But we do know that:

1. Every student's name will be known.
2. Marks will only be awarded to students and to nobody else, although not every student need have been awarded a mark.

These are *permanent* features of the class, and they are expressed in the predicate part of the schema. They form the *state invariant*. No matter what changes the class undergoes, it will retain these characteristics.

But how can we be sure of this? How can we be certain, for example, that the *Enrol* operation will not corrupt the class in some way? If we are given:

- a valid class, and
- an operation of some kind,

can we prove that:

- we get a valid state afterwards?

A valid class *after* an operation is one that satisfies the state invariant when that invariant is expressed in terms of *after* variables; that is, it satisfies the conditions:

dom last' = *students'*
dom mark' ⊆ *students'*

When writing an operation schema, we should be ensuring that these two conditions are satisfied. Let us try to establish the first of them. We are allowed to assume (1) that we had a valid state before the operation, and (2) that the operation went ahead as specified.

dom last'
(We start with the left-hand side of our equation)

$= dom\,(last \cup \{(p?, name?)\})$
(substituting the post condition in the *Enrol* schema)

$= dom\,last \cup dom\,\{(p?, name?)\}$
(using a general law of the form: $dom(A \cup B) = dom\,A \cup dom\,B$)

$= dom\,last \cup \{p?\}$
(using an obvious law that $dom\{(x, y)\} = \{x\}$)

$= students \cup \{p?\}$
(using the first condition of the state invariant equating *dom last* and *students*)

$= students'$
(using the relevant post-condition from the *Enrol* operation)

Thus we have demonstrated that, given a valid *Class* state, the *Enrol* operation maintains, in general terms, the rule that every student's last name must be known.

Suppose an operation will, when given one valid instance of a state, create another valid instance. It remains to ensure that, at the very beginning of its existence, the *Class* is valid. We can do this by specifying the initial state. This can be done conveniently, as follows.

```
┌─ ClassInitially ─────────────────────────────────
│ Class
│ ────────
│ students = {}
└──────────────────────────────────────────────────
```

This single condition, in conjunction with the state invariant, requires that *last* and *mark* both be empty.

14.9 Developing a State Schema

Where did the *Class* schema come from? How was it developed? Perhaps it was like this:

- Imagine that the user (the lecturer) saw the students, to begin with, as just a set of numbers.
- After a while, as he got to know them better, he was able to put a name to them.
- At the end, he started to award marks for the subject.

The situation may be as shown in Figure 14.1.

So we have three views of a situation, but they are not completely distinct; they overlap each other to some extent. We could say that the class situation is merely an amalgamation of these views – it is a global all-encompassing view. We can use the extended Backus-Naur Form (EBNF) language of Chapter 9 to describe these views.

```
studentsView ::= {Person}
lastView     ::= {Person + Name}
markView     ::= {Person + Number}
```

```
   AtFirst            LaterOn              LaterStill
   -------          -------------          ----------
     Nr              Nr     Last            Nr    Mark
   -------          -------------          ----------
     871             871    Zupp            871    75
     862             862    Board           869    60
     869             869    Orff            872    60
     854             854    Dover           868    80
     831             831    Orff           ----------
     872             872    Kahn
     868             868    Gambol
   -------          -------------
```

Figure 14.1 Three views of the classroom

Next we can further abstract them. The repetition construct $\{\ldots\}$ is replaced by the power set operator *Set of* and the concatenation construct $\ldots+\ldots$ is replaced by the product set operator $\times$. This gives us three declarations:

students : *Set of Person*

last : *Set of* (*Person* $\times$ *Name*)

mark : *Set of* (*Person* $\times$ *N*)

But *last* and *mark* are more than just sets of pairs or relations; they are also functions. And further, the *mark* function maps a student not to any number, but to a particular subset – the numbers from 0 to 100.

students : *Set of Person*

last : *Person* $\nrightarrow$ *Name*

mark : *Person* $\nrightarrow$ 0..100

Now we can gather these formalised view declarations into a single global declaration that covers the class:

Class

students : *Set of Person*
last : *Person* $\nrightarrow$ *Name*
mark : *Person* $\nrightarrow$ 0..100

There is still some work to be done. We must show all the constraints that apply to these views collectively; that is, we must show how they relate to one another. This we do in the predicate.

$$
\begin{array}{|l}
\hline
\textit{Class} \\
\hline
students : Set\ of\ Person \\
last : Person \nrightarrow Name \\
mark : Person \nrightarrow 0..100 \\
\hline
dom\ last = students \\
dom\ mark \subseteq students \\
\hline
\end{array}
$$

What lessons does this particular development have for us? Turning what we have done into what we should do, we:

- Gather as many views as we need to adequately cover the situation.
- Use the EBNF language to show the structure of each view.
- Turn each view structure into the corresponding Z declaration.
- Refine each view declaration by incorporating any constraints that are specific to that view.
- Gather the individually defined and constrained views into the declaration part of the state schema.
- Form the predicate part of the state schema by writing the constraints that apply to the views collectively.

We can expect the schema to look like this:

$$
\begin{array}{|l}
\hline
\textit{The State Schema} \\
\hline
\quad \text{THE SIGNATURE} \\
\qquad \textit{A number of type declarations,} \\
\qquad \textit{each of which introduces a view} \\
\qquad \textit{and possibly constrains that view} \\
\qquad \textit{in some way.} \\
\\
\quad \text{THE PREDICATE} \\
\qquad \textit{A collection of rules or constraints} \\
\qquad \textit{that specify how these views relate to} \\
\qquad \textit{and overlap one another.} \\
\hline
\end{array}
$$

14.10 Implementation

In the rest of this chapter, we will examine how the *Class* situation might be implemented. By implementation, we mean the rewriting of the specification in some programming language. In this book, the language used is SQL. The programming of a specification will involve two major steps.

1. The state schema, *Class* in this case, will be turned into a relational database. In particular, we use the declaration part of that schema. The declaration introduces each

component of the state and the basic structure of that component. It says whether it is, for example, a function or a relation or whether it is a simple object or a set of simple objects.

2. Each operation schema will be turned into a program of instructions that will examine and manipulate the database.

- The pre-conditions will become SQL `select` statements which, by retrieving information from that database, allow the "before" state to be checked.
- The post-conditions will become `insert`, `update` or `delete` statements (or a mixture) depending upon the exact nature of the conditions involved.

14.11 Developing the Database

Two approaches to database design have been presented in this book. We will consider each in turn.

A Conceptual Schema

According to Figure 14.1, there are two types of facts in the class and they both involve people. We need to know people's names and their marks, if any. We can analyze each fact type and find any uniqueness constraints that apply (Figure 14.2).

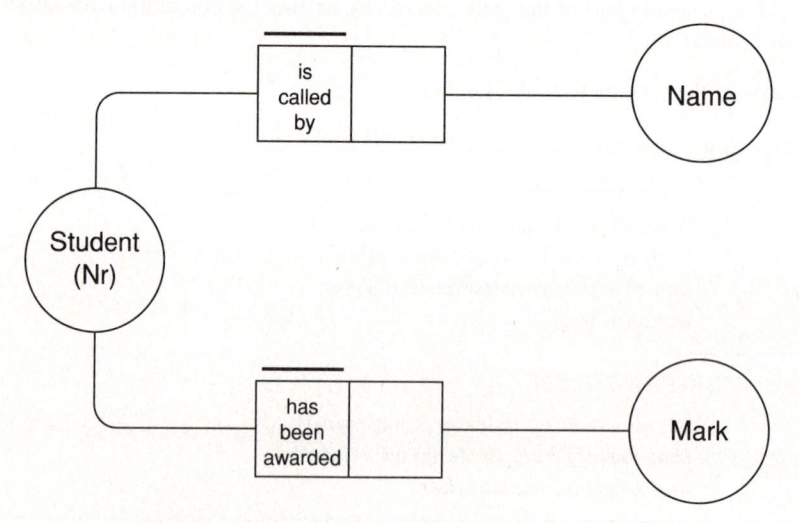

Figure 14.2 Conceptual schema diagram

Each person has just *one* last name, but two people share the same one. Similar remarks may be made regarding people's marks. Two or more facts may be merged, without risk of redundancy, if they all provide single-valued information about the same entity type. The rules about aggregation suggest, therefore, that we should develop a `Student` record type by merging the "`is called`" and "`awarded`" fact types.

An Entity-relationship Model

Alternatively, if we use the ER approach, we might develop a diagram such as the one shown in Figure 14.3.

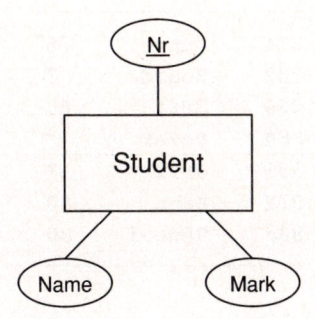

Figure 14.3 Entity-relationship diagram

According to that model, there will be a single entity type **Student** with an identifying attribute **Nr** and two other attributes **Name** and **Mark**. From this model, we will extract a **Student** record type.

The Class Database

Whatever data modeling approach we take, our database will consist of one record type:

	Student Record Type	
Key?	Attribute	References?
(*)	Nr	
	Last	
(?)	Mark	

The formal definition of this record type is:

```
┌─ StudentRecord ─────────────────────────────
│ Nr : Person
│ Last : Name
│ Mark : 0..100
└─────────────────────────────────────────────
```

The database will consist of a single relation:

```
┌─ Database ──────────────────────────────────
│ Students : Set of StudentRecord
│ ────────────────────────────────────────
│ count Students = count {s : Students • s.Nr}
└─────────────────────────────────────────────
```

In SQL terms, we will have a **Students** table and we might have the following data in that table. This is a specific instance of the *Database* state.

```
Students
--------------------
Nr      Last      Mark
--------------------
871     Zupp      75
862     Board     ?
869     Orff      60
854     Dover     ?
831     Orff      ?
872     Kahn      60
868     Gambol    80
--------------------
```

Figure 14.4 The Class Database

14.12 The State Schema and the Database

The development of the state schema and that of the database had the same starting point – user views. This is not a coincidence. The state schema and the database are simply two different pictures of the same situation. Figure 14.1 shows the classroom at the *Class* state level, and Figure 14.4 shows it as a database. The state schema is written for our benefit. It uses (or may use) the full range and richness of the Z specification language. The database picture is written solely in terms of relations because that is the only structure that a relational database management system will allow, and we have chosen to use this as our implementation "vehicle". See Figure 14.5.

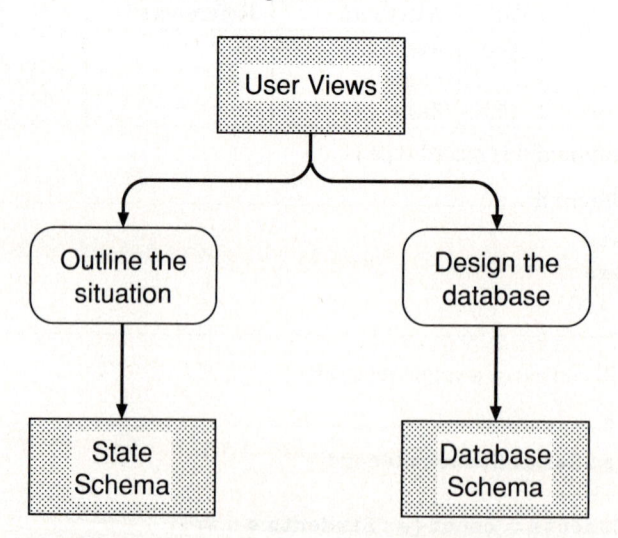

Figure 14.5 Abstract and concrete states

The database is a machine-oriented realization of the state schema. We can show this relationship between the database and the state schema by means of a **mapping** schema.

Mapping
Class
Database

$students = \{s : \text{Students} \bullet s.\text{Nr}\}$
$last = \{s : \text{Students} \bullet (s.\text{Nr}, s.\text{Last})\}$
$mark = \{s : \text{Students} \mid s.\text{Mark} \neq \text{null} \bullet (s.\text{Nr}, s.\text{Mark})\}$

This schema defines the components of *Class* in terms of Database components. The following table shows how each component of the state schema is represented in terms of the database.

Component	How represented	In SQL terms
students	The Nr attribute of the Students relation: $\{s : \text{Students} \bullet s.\text{Nr}\}$	The Nr column of the Students table: Select Nr From Students
last	The Nr and Last attributes: $\{s : \text{Students} \bullet (s.\text{Nr}, s.\text{Last})\}$	The Nr and Last columns: Select Nr, Last From Students
mark	The Nr and Mark attributes where the latter is not null: $\{s : \text{Students} \mid s.\text{Mark} \neq \text{null} \bullet (s.\text{Nr}, s.\text{mark})\}$	The Nr and Mark columns where the latter is not null: Select Nr, Mark From Students Where Mark is not null

We can take this mapping process further and see how some of the secondary components are represented.

dom last Given the representation of *last* above, this must be the Nr column on its own.

```
Select Nr
From    Students
```

This is the same as the *students* component above, so we can see that the *Class* invariant:

$$\text{dom } last = students$$

is satisfied at the concrete level.

dom mark Similarly, given the representation of *mark* above, the domain of *mark* must be:

```
Select  Nr
From    Students
Where   Mark is not null
```

14.13 Implementing an Operation

We have seen how the state schema is implemented as a database, but we still have to implement the operation schemas as programs. In this section, we will look at how the *Award* operation may be programmed.

1. The Pre-Conditions

    We can take each of the pre-conditions of the *Award* operation schema; use the mappings above and convert the condition to SQL syntax.

Condition	In SQL terms
$p? \in students$	`p? in (Select Nr From Students)`
$p? \notin dom\ mark$	`p? not in (Select Nr From Students Where Mark is not null)`

2. The Post-Conditions

    The post-conditions will specify changes to the database, whether in the form of **Insert**s, **Update**s or of **Delete**s. What changes are required here?

    Suppose student number 862 is to be awarded a mark of 80. The Students table needs to be amended as follows:

    ```
    Students                          Students'
    --------------------              --------------------
    Nr      Last    Mark              Nr      Last    Mark
    --------------------              --------------------
    871     Zupp    75                871     Zupp    75
    862     Board   ?  *              862     Board   80 *
    869     Orff    60                869     Orff    60
    854     Dover   ?        =>       854     Dover   ?
    831     Orff    ?                 831     Orff    ?
    872     Kahn    60                872     Kahn    60
    868     Gambol  80                868     Gambol  80
    --------------------              --------------------
    ```

    We do not need to add any new rows nor do we need to delete any. The only change required is that the `Mark` column for student 862 be set to 80. For that, we use an **Update** statement.

    ```
    Update Students
        Set Mark = m?
        Where Nr = p?
    ```

This single SQL statement satisfies all three of the post-conditions.

(a) $mark' = mark \cup \{(p?, m?)\}$

The before version, $mark = \{(871, 75), (869, 60), (872, 60), (868, 60)\}$.

The after version, $mark' = \{(871, 75), (862, 80), (869, 60), (872, 60), 868, 60)\}$

(b) $students' = students$

The **set** clause of the **update** statement does not involve the **Nr** column, so this column, which is the concrete version of the *Class* component *students*, is unchanged.

(c) $last' = last$

Similarly, the **set** clause does not affect either the **Nr** or the **Last** columns which together form the concrete version of the *Class* component *last*. This is therefore unchanged.

14.14 From Operation to Program

We discussed the relationship between the state schema and the database and how we can (and must be able to) map from one to the other. Can we map between an operation and the corresponding program?

We certainly cannot easily map between the *Award* schema, for example, and an SQL program that implements it. The two languages have quite different syntaxes. We can, however, write an operation schema that awards a mark to a student, but that changes the database rather than the *Class* state.

───── *AwardProgram* ──────────────────────────────────
$\Delta Database$
$p? : Person$
$m? : 0..100$
─────────────────────────────────────
$\exists S : Students \bullet$
$\qquad S.Nr = p?$
$\qquad S.Mark = null$
$\qquad \exists S' : StudentRecord \bullet$
$\qquad\qquad S'.Nr = S.Nr$
$\qquad\qquad S'.Last = S.Last$
$\qquad\qquad S'.Mark = m?$
$\qquad\qquad Students' = Students - \{S\} \cup \{S'\}$
─────────────────────────────────────

We can interpret the predicate as requiring that:

1. There exists, in the *Students* relation, a record S with the same number as the one supplied, and where the mark is null.

2. Afterwards, the new *Students* relation is the same as before, except that the record S is replaced by a record S' that has the same *Nr* and *Last* attributes, but with a *Mark* attribute set to the mark supplied.

We will need to ensure that the language used is restricted to the relational calculus. That language is as close as we can get, in Z, to SQL. So now we have two versions of the operation:

- An *Award* operation that modifies the situation as represented by the abstract *Class* state.
- An *AwardProgram* that modifies the situation as represented by the concrete *Database* state.

The question still stands. How do we know that the award program, as described by *AwardProgram*, is correctly implemented? This important issue is discussed in Chapter 19.

14.15 Summary

In this chapter we have seen how the schema may be used in a number of quite different ways to **specify** different aspects of a situation.

- We have used the schema to describe or present a general view of some state of affair, one that avoids, of necessity, any specific details. Rather, it tries to characterize the siuation by providing some general rules or conditions known as the **state invariant**. In particular we created the *Class* state schema which described a class of students.

- Then we used schema decoration and schema inclusion to build a **frame** schema, in this case $\Delta Class$, that describes the features that are common to all possible changes to some state, in this case the *Class* state.

- Next we used the frame schema in conjunction with process description schemas to create **operation** schemas that allow changes of state to be described. Each operation schema will describe the necessary pre-conditions for some event and the post-conditions that describe how the state is changed as a result of the pre-conditions being met.

- Then we looked at how we might satisfy ourselves that an operation schema maintains the state invariant.

Then we looked at how we might **implement** the specification collectively provided by these schemas.

- First we translated the state schema into a relational database.
- Then we translated an operation schema into a program that applies the rules of that schema in making changes to the database.

Figure 14.6 shows the interaction of the processes involved in specifying and implementing an information system.

And finally, we are able to use the programs in conjunction with the database to maintain and reproduce the user views. So we are back to our starting point.

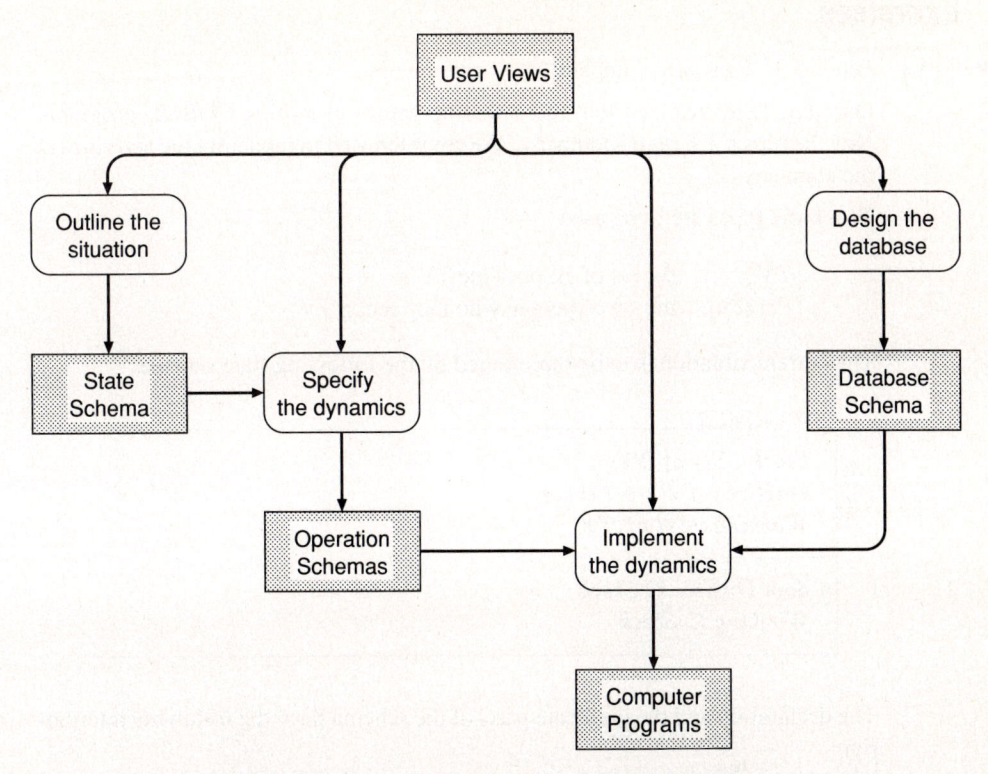

Figure 14.6 From specification to implementation

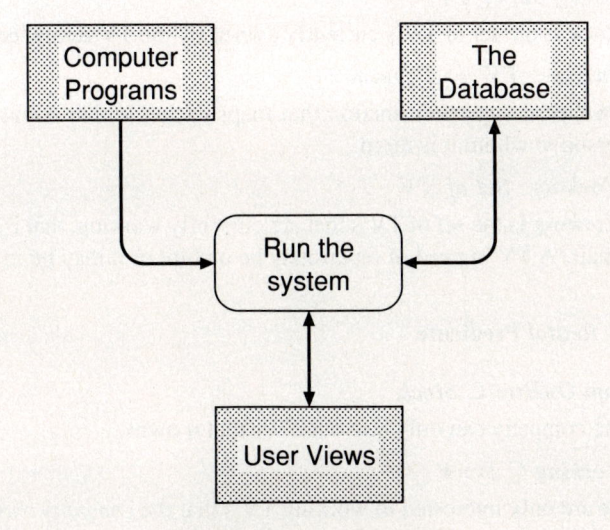

Figure 14.7 Full circle

Exercises

▶ Q14.1 Pete's TV RENTAL Company

One day, Peter realized that there was no future in writing COBOL programs. Now he runs a TV rental company. We are interested in modeling the activities of the company.

Two basic types are to be used.

> $[TV]$ the set of all possible TV's.
> $[Person]$ the set of people who may rent a TV.

The current situation is to be represented by the following state schema.

```
┌─ TVRental ─────────────────────────────────
│ Stock : Set of TV
│ OnHire : TV +→ Person
│ Working : Set of TV
│
│ dom OnHire ⊆ Stock
│ Working ⊆ Stock
└────────────────────────────────────────────
```

The declaration and the predicate parts of the schema have the following interpretation.

The *TVRental* Declaration

1. *Stock : Set of TV*

   Stock is the set of TV's currently owned by the TV Rental company.

2. *OnHire : TV +→ Person*

   OnHire is a partial function that maps each TV that is out on hire to the person to whom it is hired.

3. *Working : Set of TV*

   Working is the set of TV's that are currently working, that is, not in need of repair. A TV in need of repair may be on hire or it may be in the shop.

The *TVRental* Predicate

1. *dom OnHire ⊆ Stock*

   The company can only hire out TV's that it owns.

2. *Working ⊆ Stock*

   We are only interested in working TV's that the *company* owns.

Here is an operation schema that describes a TV being rented out to a customer.

```
┌─ RentTV ─────────────────────────────
│ Δ TVRental
│ t? : TV
│ p? : Person
├──────────────────────────────────────
│ t? ∈ Stock
│ t? ∈ Working
│ t? ∉ dom OnHire
│ OnHire' = OnHire ∪ {(t?, p?)}
│ Stock' = Stock
│ Working' = Working
└──────────────────────────────────────
```

Explain the significance of each line of the schema, both its declaration and its predicate. Use the style of the introduction to this question.

▶ Q14.2 Using the *TVRental* state schema given in the previous question, write operation schemas for the following events.

a. *NormalReturn* – a TV $t?$, currently out on hire, is returned at the end of its period of contract.

b. *BreakDown* – a TV $t?$, currently out on hire, has broken down.

c. *BigDeal* – a customer $p?$ rents a number of TV's $tvset?$, all of which are in working order of course.

d. *Target* – a list *whingers*! of those customers with a faulty TV is to be produced.

e. *FixIt* – a faulty TV $t?$ is repaired at the customer's home or premises.

f. *SwitchTV* – a working TV $ok?$, one that is not on hire, is provided in place of a faulty TV $rs?$ that *is* currently on hire.

▶ Q14.3 At the corner shop

In this question, we will attempt to model or represent the situation and happenings in a self-service corner shop. There is only one person behind the counter. Typically, people come into the shop, locate the goods they want, pay for them and leave.

There is to be one basic type, [*Person*], representing the set of all people who may, at some time, be customers. The state of the shop is to be modeled by the following schema.

354   Chapter 14

$\underline{\quad Shop \quad\quad\quad\quad\quad\quad\quad\quad\quad\quad\quad\quad\quad\quad\quad\quad\quad\quad\quad\quad\quad\quad\quad\quad\quad}$
$shopping : Set\ of\ Person$
$queue : seq\ Person$

$ran\ queue \cap shopping = \{\}$
$\forall i,j : dom\ queue \bullet i \neq j \Rightarrow queue(i) \neq queue(j)$

The first state component, *shopping*, represents the set of customers who are still shopping, that is, still looking for items to purchase. The second state component, *queue*, contains those customers who have found what they want and are waiting to pay.

Using the conventions regarding state transition schemas and operation variable naming, specify the following operations and queries.

a. How long is the queue?
b. How many people are there in the shop altogether?
c. Someone, $c?$, enters the shop.
d. Someone, $c?$, joins the queue.
e. The person at the front of the queue pays and leaves the shop.
f. Someone, $c?$, waiting in the queue leaves the queue but not the shop.
g. Which customers are still "just looking"?

Q14.4   At the supermarket

The situation to be considered in the supermarket is one involving customers, checkouts and and the queue at each checkout. Each customer may either still be shopping or have joined a queue.

The basic types are:

[*Person*]   the set of all possible customers
[*Checkout*] the set of checkouts

The state of the supermarket is to be modeled by a state schema with the following declaration.

$\underline{\quad Supermarket \quad\quad\quad\quad\quad\quad\quad\quad\quad\quad\quad\quad\quad\quad\quad\quad\quad\quad\quad\quad\quad}$
$shopping : Set\ of\ Person$
$queues : Checkout \rightarrow seq\ Person$

We will assume that every checkout is in operation at all times. The components of the schema have the following interpretations.

shopping – the set of customers still shopping
queues   – the queue (possibly empty) of customers waiting at each checkout

Assume that the first customer, if any, of a queue is being checked out.

Required:
Specify conditions to match each of the following requirements.

    a.   Nobody shopping in the aisles is also queueing at a checkout.

    b.   Nobody appears twice in the same queue.

    c.   Nobody appears in two different queues.

Q14.5   Specify schemas for the following operations or queries.

    a.   Which checkouts are free?

    b.   Someone comes into the supermarket and joins those in the aisles.

    c.   Someone shopping, $p?$, joins the queue at checkout $c?$

    d.   Someone, $p?$, moves from one queue to the end of the queue at checkout $c?$ That person will not be at the front of whatever queue he or she leaves.

    e.   The person $p?$, at the front of the queue at some checkout, pays and leaves.

    f.   Someone, $p?$, leaves a queue and returns to the aisles.

▶ Q14.6   In the bank

Inside the bank there are, at any time, a number of tellers operating. Each teller has his or her own window. However, not all windows need be open at any time. And even if a teller's window is open, there need not be a customer being served at that window. There may also be a single queue of customers waiting to be served; and there may also be a number of other customers who either have not yet joined the queue or who have completed their transactions and have not yet left the bank.

The basic types are *Person*, the set of all possible customers, and *Teller*, the set of all tellers. The state of the bank is to be modeled using the following state schema.

    ┌─ *Bank* ───────────────────────────────
    │ *open* : Set of *Teller*
    │ *busy* : *Teller* ↛ *Person*
    │ *queue* : seq *Person*
    │ *others* : Set of *Person*
    └──

This schema is to be interpreted as follows:

356　Chapter 14

open	– the set of tellers whose window is currently open
busy	– a function that maps from tellers whose window is open to any customer that they might be serving
queue	– a sequence that indicates those who are waiting and their place in the queue
others	– the set of people who have either been served or who have not yet joined the queue

Specify operation schemas to handle the following situations or requirements. Use the standard sequence operations, where appropriate.

a. Someone comes into the bank.
b. Someone leaves the bank.
c. Someone completes a transaction and leaves the teller's window.
d. Someone goes from the front of the queue to a teller.
e. A teller opens his or her window.
f. A teller closes down, but only if he or she is not handling a customer and only if there is at least one other teller still open.
g. Someone joins the queue.
h. Someone leaves the queue without commencing a transaction.

▶ **Q14.7 Files on floppy**

We are interested in modeling the contents of a floppy disk and the operations that may be performed upon it. Three basic types are to be used:

Name	– the possible names of files
Byte	– the data (of whatever form) that may be stored in files
N	– the set of integers $0, 1, 2, 3, \ldots$

The contents of the floppy at any given moment are to be represented by the following state schema.

─── *Floppy* ───────────────────────────
$FileData : Name \nrightarrow seq\ Byte$
$Used, Left : N$
─────────────────────────
$Used + Left = 360\,000$
$Used = \Sigma f : dom\ FileData \bullet \#FileData(f)$
─────────────────────────

The declaration and the predicate parts of the schema have the following interpretation.

The *Floppy* Declaration

1. $FileData : Name \nrightarrow seq\ Byte$

   FileData is a partial function that maps the name of any files on the disk to the data contained in the file.

2. $Used, Left : \mathbb{N}$

   Used and *Left* are numbers representing, respectively, the number of bytes used and the number of bytes left on the disk.

The *Floppy* Predicate

1. $Used + Left = 360\,000$

   The number of bytes used and the number of bytes left unused must add up to 360 000.

2. $Used = \Sigma f : dom\ FileData \bullet \#FileData(f)$

   The total space used is the sum of the sizes of all the individual files stored on the disk.

Here is an operation schema that specifies the effect of deleting a file from the disk.

$$
\begin{array}{|l}
\hline
\textit{DeleteFile} \\
\hline
\Delta Floppy \\
f? : Name \\
\hline
f? \in dom\ FileData \\
FileData' = \{f?\} \vartriangleleft FileData \\
Used' = Used - \#FileData(f?) \\
Left' = Left + \#FileData(f?) \\
\hline
\end{array}
$$

Explain the significance of each line of the schema, both its declaration and its predicate. Use the style of the introduction to this question.

▶ Q14.8 Using the *Floppy* state schema given in the previous question, write operation schemas for each of the following. For each schema briefly explain the significance of each line of its predicate.

  a. A new file called $f?$ containing data $d?$ is to be created on the disk.
  b. The contents of a file called *from?* are to be copied to a new file to be called *to?*.
  c. The file currently called *old?* is to be renamed as file *new?*.
  d. A list *all!* of all the files on the disk and their sizes is to be output along with the number of files *count!* and the amount of space available *free!*.
  e. The contents of the file called $f?$ are to be replaced with new data $nd?$.

CHAPTER 15

Database Definition in SQL

15.1 Introduction

This chapter describes how to define the major objects that may appear in an SQL database.

- There are **tables** without which the database would be empty. These are sometimes referred to as **base** tables.
- There are **views** which define **virtual** tables.
- There are **indexes** which enable the DBMS to respond to queries within an acceptable period of time.

The word definition is used in the general sense of describing or delimiting the properties of these objects. So, this chapter will discuss the creation, alteration and, in the extreme case, removal of these properties.

Information about the properties of database objects is stored in the **system catalog** or dictionary. The catalog itself takes the form of a set of tables which we may examine ourselves using SQL. It forms a relational database that resides alongside our own.

15.2 Tables

15.2.1 Table Creation

A new table is introduced into the database by means of the `create table` statement which, in its simplest form, only requires that we name the table and then name and provide a datatype for each column in the table.

```
table_creation:
    CREATE TABLE table_name
    (list_of_column_definitions)
column_definition:
    column_name data_type [NULL|NOT NULL]
```

There are a number of conventions used in presenting syntax for the statements discussed in this chapter. They are discussed in more detail in Appendix A. Briefly:

- Upper case words in typewriter font, such as `CREATE TABLE`, must appear verbatim.
- Lower case words in typewriter font, such as `table_name`, represent places where we must substitute something of our own choosing, for example, `Students`.
- The *list_of_* X*s* structure, for example, *list_of_*`column_definition`*s*, means that we should substitute one or more column definitions separated by commas.
- Square brackets are used to enclose options, vertical bars to separate them.

For example, to define the `Students` table:

```
Create Table Students
    (Id     integer,
     First  char(10),
     Last   char(10))
```

Every row of the `Students` table, as defined above, is guaranteed to have three attributes labelled `Id`, `First` and `Last`. And further, each `Id` attribute will be associated with an integer value, and the `First` and `Last` attributes will both be associated with strings of up to ten characters. This is the lowest level of integrity support offered by SQL. It guarantees the tabular appearance that we expect of a relation and the consistent type of data appearing in each column of the table. However, apart from these constraints, the definition allows a lot of freedom in what we might choose to store in the table. So, at some stage, the table might contain any of the following data.

1.
Students

Id	First	Last
?	John	Smith
223	?	Smith
235	John	?
?	?	Smith
?	John	?
247	?	?
?	?	?

2.
Students

Id	First	Last
299	John	Smith
299	John	Smith
299	John	Smith
299	John	Smith
299	John	Smith
299	John	Smith
299	John	Smith

3.
Students

Id	First	Last
299	John	Smith
299	Jack	Daw
299	Billy	Kahn
299	Anna	Purna
299	Eva	Rest
299	Ben	Nevis
299	Cosy	O'Scu

Look at each sample in turn.

1. How many students do we really have here? There are at least three and maybe as many as seven. When creating a table, the default is for columns to be allowed to contain null values unless otherwise specified. It is part of the database design process to decide which attributes may be null and which must never be.

2. In the second sample, we can see that, unless otherwise constrained, a table may hold any number of identical rows. While the data in the table might be quite valid, it is potentially misleading. We might count the rows believing that the result would indicate the number of students in the subject.

3. As a consequence of the possibilities implied by the third sample, we must ensure that if no two students can have the same Id, then the database reflects this constraint. In other words, if the key of the relation is the student Id then there will only be *one* row in the table with a particular Id.

In designing the database we took the view that each relation represented a set of entities and zero or more single-valued facts concerning these entities. This caused each relation to be divided into two disjoint sets of attributes.

1. There are the **key** attributes, of which there must be at least one. This attribute or this combination of attributes uniquely identify each entity. For example, the key of the `Students` table is the `Id` attribute.

    - Key attributes are *never* null. This rule prevents us from keeping information about some as yet unidentified entity and is known as the **entity integrity** rule.

    - We will normally define a unique index on the primary key. This requirement will be further discussed in Section 15.6.1. This index will ensure that no two rows in the table have the same key value. For the `Students` table, no two rows will have the same `Id` value.

2. There are the **non-key** attributes. In some relations, there may not be any. Each of these attributes supplies one single-valued fact about the entity identified by the key. For `Students`, the non-key attributes are `First` and `Last`. Each provides a separate fact about a student.

    - Non-key attributes may or may not be null depending on the analysis performed during database design. In this example we will assume that the first name may not be known but the last name always will be.

This division of a relation and the rules that apply to each part leads to a revised definition:

```
Create Table  Students
        (Id     integer   not null,
         First  char(10),
         Last   char(10)  not null)
```

15.2.2 Table Alteration

From our database design effort, two outcomes may arise.

1. We got the design right first time and, more than that, we foresaw *all* the possible changes that might occur *and* our design was flexible enough to cope with these changes.
2. Alternatively, as a result of using their information system, users have developed a much better feel for the nature and extent of the information they *really need* to record in the database.

The second scenario is much more likely and consequently, in order to respond to organizational changes, there is a need to be able to alter the characteristics of a table. This includes (1) adding entirely new columns, (2) modifying the nature of existing columns such as the nullity, and (3) removing unnecessary columns.

The general syntax is:

```
table_alteration:
    ALTER TABLE table_name
    [ADD|MODIFY] (list_of_column_definitions)
```

Example 15.1 Suppose we now need to record the initial letter of each student's middle name.

```
Alter Table Students
    Add(Middle char(1))
```

We have now added an entirely null column called **Middle** to the **Students** table.

There may be restrictions upon the nature of any new or modified columns. For example, a column added to a table must permit nulls, for the simple reason that we are, in effect, adding an all null column.

- If we are modifying a column to the extent of disabling nulls then the column must not currently contain any null values.
- The datatype or width of a column may only be changed if the contents of that column are entirely null at the time of alteration.
- A column declared as `not null` may only be added to an empty table.

Example 15.2 The descriptions associated with items of assessment are becoming increasingly verbose. We need to widen the **Description** column:

```
Alter Table Assess
    Modify(Description char(30) not null)
```

This statement will succeed only if the **Assess** table is empty.

15.2.3 Table Removal

There will be occasions when we want to create a temporary table for some special purpose. Afterwards we may discard it with a **drop table** statement.

```
table_removal:
     DROP TABLE table_name
```

Example 15.3 Suppose we only wish or need to know a student's last name. We need to be able to remove the **First** name column.

We cannot delete a column with an **alter table** statement. We can, however, make a copy of the parts of the table we wish to retain.

```
Create Table New_Students
       (Id    integer,
        Last char(10))

Insert
Into   New_Students
Select Id,Last
From   Students

Drop Table Students
```

If we want to retain the name **Students**, then we will either copy the data back from **New_Students** to a reconstructed version of **Students**. Alternatively, we may rename the table if permitted.

15.3 SQL Datatypes

15.3.1 Datatypes

Most versions of SQL will offer a range of datatypes that match those available in more conventional programming languages. These will include integers, floating point and fixed point numbers as well as character strings.

Every item of data, large or small, that is stored in a database will be of a certain **type**. A relation is a **set** of rows and a row is of type **tuple**. Each row is made up of a number of elementary items of data. These are the attributes of the row. In the **Students** relation each row has three attributes. An attribute is the smallest unit of storage that SQL is prepared to handle. Each attribute has an associated **datatype**.

There is more to a datatype than merely data storage.

- There are rules specifying how constants or **literals** may be written or displayed in order to represent individual instances or values of the type. For example, **1945** is a legitimate representation of an integer literal but **1,945** is not. Note that these rules relate to the *external* representation of instances of a datatype.

- There is the *internal* representation used by the database management system in conjunction with the particular computer system upon which the database resides. This representation will, of necessity, be quite unlike the external one. This internal representation may be of concern to us because it may significantly determine the size of the column and hence the size of the table and the database.
- There are the operations that accompany the type. With numbers, for example, the operations will include functions such as addition (+) and subtraction (−) as well as relations such as <, = and >. The operations may involve only one type or may relate two types.

In the following sections we will discuss the datatypes are available from the ORACLE relational database management system. However, these datatypes are typical of SQL systems.

15.3.2 Numbers

Numbers come in all shapes and sizes. Here are some well-known ones. (No pun intended!)

```
1066
2.18718
1.618033988
-273
1.38 * 10^71
```

There are several questions to be considered when writing down a number.

- Is it a whole number or is there some fractional component? If a fraction is involved then how many places are required after the decimal point? The number of digits to the right of the decimal point is referred to as the **scale** of the number.
- How many digits of **precision** are required?
- Is there a sign involved?

The **number** datatype may be declared in any of three formats.

```
Number(p,s)
Number(p)
Number
```

where:
   p   is the precision, the total number of digits available;
   s   The scale, that is the number of digits to the right of the decimal point.

A datatype declaration of **number(5,2)** would allow us, for example, to represent numbers in the range **−999.99** to **+999.99** such as might be used for supermarket prices. When entering a value into a numeric column, two checks are made on the value.

1. Does it exceed the precision specified for the column? If so, the value is *rejected*. For example, entering a value **12.25** into a column of type **number(3,2)** will cause the value to be rejected because it has four digits but the column is restricted to no more than three.

2. Does it exceed the scale specified for the column? If so, the number is *rounded*. For example, entering a value of **123.45** into a column of type **number(6,1)** will cause the number to be rounded to one decimal place and the value **123.5** will be stored.

ORACLE SQL has just *one* internal representation for *all* types of numbers. However, we can use the precision and scale factors to ensure that only acceptable numbers are allowed through to the database. Certain of these precision and scale combinations have been given names of their own.

Datatype	Equivalent to ...
Integer	Number(38,0)
Decimal	Number(38,0)

As stated already, each datatype will have a package of operations that process and relate elements or instances of that type. The most familiar of these are the arithmetic functions +, −, * and /, and the relational operations (<, <=, >=, >, <>). There are also a number of more specialized functions and relations.

Abs(n)   This is a prefix function that returns the absolute value of the given number n.

         abs(21) = 21
         abs(-13) = 13

Ceil(n)   This is a prefix function that returns the smallest integer that is larger than or equal to n.

         ceil(8.1) = 9
         ceil(8.5) = 9
         ceil(8) = 8

Floor(n)   This is a prefix function that returns the largest integer that is less than or equal to n.

         floor(8.1) = 8
         floor(8.5) = 8
         floor(8) = 8

Mod(m,n)   This is a prefix function that returns the remainder of m divided by n.

         mod(8,5) = 3
         mod(8,4) = 0
         mod(8,0) = 8

Power(x,n)   This is a prefix function that returns x to the power n (x^n). The exponent (n) must be an integer.

         power(3,2) = 9
         power(1.2,2) = 1.44

Round(m,n)   This is a prefix function that returns m rounded to n decimal places.

> round(8.35,1) = 8.4
> round(8.355,2) = 8.36

If n is omitted then 0 is assumed.

> round(8.35) = 8
> round(8.5) = 9

Sqrt(n)   This is a prefix function that returns the positive square root of n.

> sqrt(9) = 3
> sqrt(2) = 1.41421356

The square root is just another number and may be rounded.

> round(sqrt(2),3) = 1.414

Trunc(m,n)   This is a prefix function that returns m truncated to n decimal places.

> trunc(8.35,1) = 8.3
> trunc(8.355,2) = 8.35

If n is omitted then 0 is assumed.

> trunc(8.35) = 8
> trunc(8.5) = 8

15.3.3 Character Strings

The character string datatype has one basic form:

`Char(n)`

Where n is the maximum number of characters allowed in the associated column.
String literals are formed by enclosing the required characters between apostrophes.

```
'Bill'
'Niagara Falls'
'Hobart, Tasmania'
'Boosey & Hawkes'
```

There is a minor problem when the apostrophe character itself is to form part of the string. In this case, two apostrophes in succession are used to indicate that a single apostrophe is to be included in the string. Here are some examples.

Required string	Literal value
O'Reilly	'O''Reilly'
rock'n'roll	'rock''n''roll'
plumber's mate	'plumber''s mate'

The operations associated with character strings are as follows.

`str1 || str2`   This is an infix function that concatenates (strings together) two strings to form another.

> `'Jack'||'Smith' = 'JackSmith'`
> `'Desperate'||' '||'Dan' = 'Desperate Dan'`

`Initcap(str)`   This is a prefix function that capitalizes the first letter of all words in the string.

> `initcap('BILLY') = 'Billy'`
> `initcap('billy jones') = 'Billy Jones'`
> `initcap('RADio 4DK') = 'Radio 4dk'`

`Instr(str1,str2)`   This is a prefix function that attempts to locate string `str2` within string `str1`.

> `instr('Mt. Everest','t') = 2`
> `instr('Jim','e') = 0`

`Length(str)`   This is a prefix function that returns the number of characters in a given string.

> `Length('String')=6`

`str1 like str2`   This is an infix relational operator used for pattern matching: see page 139 for examples.

> `%` matches zero or more characters.
> `_` matches exactly one character.

All other characters match themselves, `Name like 'Mac%'` would match any name starting with Mac, for example, MacTavish or MacDonald. However, `Name like 'Mac_'` would match any name containing four characters and starting with Mac, for example, Mace or Mack.

`Lower(s)`   This is a prefix function that turns all *letters* in the string `s` into lower case.

> `lower('BOOM!') = 'boom!'`
> `lower('case') = 'case'`

`Lpad(str1,n,str2)`   This is a prefix function that pads string `str` on the left to length `n` with the string `str2`.

```
lpad('28.45',8,'0') = '00028.45'
lpad('here',8,'->') = '->->here'
```

Ltrim(str1,str2)   This is a prefix function that trims string **str1** from the left until the first occurrence of a character not in the string **str2**.

```
ltrim('Mr. Smith','Mr. ') = 'Smith'
ltrim('001345','0') = '1345'
```

Replace(s1,s2,s3)   This is a prefix function that replaces each occurrence of string **s2** found in string **s1** with the string **s3**.

```
replace('raspberry','r','l') = 'laspbelly'
replace('21st January 1995','January','Jan')
    = '21st Jan 1995'
replace('21 May 1989',' ','-') = '21-May-1989'
```

Rpad(str1,n,str2)   This is a prefix function that pads out string **str1** on the right to length **n** with string **str2**.

```
rpad('Help',7,'!') = 'Help!!!'
rpad('Exit',8,'->') = 'Exit->->'
```

Rtrim(str1,str2)   This is a prefix function that trims string **str1** from the right until a character not in **str2** is encountered.

```
rtrim('Seth Jones Snr',' Snr') = 'Seth Jones'
rtrim('B. Anderson',' Snr') = 'B. Anderso'
```

Soundex(str)   This is a prefix function that returns the **soundex** value of a character string. It is used to compare names on a phonetic basis rather than on spelling.

```
Select  *
From    Employees
Where   soundex(name) = soundex('Magee')
```

Substr(str,m,n)   This is a prefix function that returns a selected substring from some other string.

substr('Sally',2,3) returns the 3 characters from **'Sally'** starting at position 2.

substr('Sally',2,3)='all'

`Upper(str)`   This is a prefix function that turns all lower case letters into upper case.

```
upper('Congo') = 'CONGO'
upper('Gum Tree') = 'GUM TREE'
```

15.3.4 The Date Datatype

This is a datatype that programming languages do not provide as standard. This is really rather odd as the great majority of organizational information systems are simple historical models. They record the occurrence of events relevant to the organization. These are everyday events such as receiving an order from a customer, ordering from a supplier or paying an employee. Normally, the time of occurrence is also noted, and the unit of time most commonly used is the date.

Many versions of SQL provide an inbuilt `date` datatype because of the need not only to record dates but also to perform calculations and comparisons involving dates. ORACLE SQL provides a single `date` datatype that handles units of time from seconds to centuries.

The standard form for date literals is `'DD-MON-YY'`, for example, `'21-AUG-93'`. When (ORACLE) SQL encounters a character string literal where a date might be expected then it will assume that it is in the above format. To register a date in one of the many other forms in which dates (and times) may appear, we must state the format explicitly and use a conversion function.

`To_Date(DateString, FormatString)`

For example:

```
To_Date('12-MAY-1801', 'DD-MON-YYYY')
To_Date('23-NOV-93 11:15 AM', 'DD-MON-YY HH:MI AM')
```

A `FormatString` is a character string consisting of one or more format "models". Each model represents some unit of time, such as `MON` for a month name in three character form. The format string is used to state how a date value is to be displayed or how it is being entered. Some of the more common format models are shown below.

Model	Example	Comment
YYYY	1745	4 digit year
YY	67	2 digit year
MM	09	2 digit month
MONTH	SEPTEMBER	full name of month (padded to 9 characters)
WW	03	2 digit week of the year
DDD	35	3 digit day of the year
DD	28	2 digit day of the month
D	3	1 digit day of the week

The operations that may be used with dates are as follows.

`Add_Months(d,m)`   This is a prefix function that adds `m` months on to the date `d`.

Database Definition in SQL 369

```
             Add_Months('1-JAN-93',6) = '01-JUL-93'
             Add_Months('18-NOV-95',2) = '18-JAN-96'
```

Last_Day(d)   This is a prefix function that determines the date of the last day of the month in which date **d** falls.

```
             Last_Day('18-NOV-95') = '30-NOV-95'
```

Months_Between(d,e) This is a prefix function that returns a number representing the months between dates **e** and **d**.

```
             Months_Between('15-MAR-95','1-FEB-95')
             = 1.4516129
```

We would probably want to round the result.

```
             round(Months_Between('15-MAR-95',
                                  '1-FEB-95'),1)
             = 1.5
```

Next_Day(d,day)   This is a prefix function that returns the date of the next **day** of the week after date **d**.

```
             Next_Day('25-MAR-91','WEDNESDAY')
             = '27-MAR-91'
```

The next Wednesday after 25 March 1991 was dated 27 March 1991.

Round(d,fmt)   This is a prefix function that "rounds" the date **d** depending on the format string **fmt**.

```
             Round(To_Date('25-MAR-95'),'MONTH')
             = '01-APR-95'
             Round(To_Date('25-MAR-95'),'YEAR')
             = '01-JAN-95'
```

Sysdate   This is a variable that contains the current date and time.

Trunc(d,fmt)   This is a prefix function that "truncates" the date **d** depending on the format string **fmt**.

```
             Trunc(To_Date('25-MAR-95'),'MONTH')
             = '01-MAR-95'
             Trunc(To_Date('25-MAR-95'),'YEAR')
             = '01-JAN-95'
```

15.3.5 Conversion Between Datatypes

There will be, of necessity, a number of conversion operations that enable us to convert from, for example, character strings to dates.

15.4 Referential Integrity and Other Constraints

The original version of SQL, SQL/DS, was released in 1983. It made no provision for the definition of keys. However, newer products, such as Version 6 of ORACLE, allow us to define the primary key of a table and the consequent foreign key connections. It does this through the extensions to the `create table` statement. See Figure 15.1.

```
table_creation:
    CREATE TABLE table_name
    (list_of_[column_definition| table_constraint]s)
column_definition:
    column_name data_type [column_constraint]
column_constraint:
    NULL|NOT NULL
  or CHECK (condition)
table_constraint:
    PRIMARY KEY(list_of_column_names)
  or UNIQUE(list_of_column_names)
  or FOREIGN KEY(list_of_column_names)
    REFERENCES table_name [(list_of_column_names)]
  or CHECK (condition)
```

Figure 15.1 Revised `create table` syntax

Column constraints are attached to the definition of a column and apply specifically to that column. There are two kinds to consider.

- NULL|NOT NULL

    This is the same as before, either allowing or disallowing null values in the column.

- CHECK (condition)

    This kind of constraint will ensure that any value placed in this column will satisfy the condition specified.

```
Mark integer check(Mark between 0 and 100)
```

The condition may only refer to the column concerned and to constants. The check will be made prior to the execution of relevant `insert` and `update` statements. If the condition is not satisfied then the statement will be rejected.

Table constraints are more generalized restrictions applying to the table as a whole and relating different rows and possibly several columns of the table. There are four kinds.

- **PRIMARY KEY**(*list_of_column_names*)

  This constraint allows us to nominate the column or columns that make the primary key of the table.

  ```
  Primary Key (Id)         for the Students table.
  Primary Key (Item, Id)   for the Assess table.
  ```

  With the above constraint on **Students**, we are guaranteed that no two rows in that table will have the same **Id**. There may only be one such constraint per table. The column or columns involved must not allow nulls, that is, they must be declared `not null`.

- **UNIQUE**(*list_of_column_names*)

  This constraint allows us to nominate other columns where uniqueness is required. With it we can enforce one-to-one relationships between the columns and the primary key.

  ```
  Unique (Due) in the Assess table.
  ```

  The column or columns should *not* have been declared as a primary key. Nor should they allow nulls.

- **FOREIGN KEY**(*list_of_column_names*)
  REFERENCES `table_name` [(*list_of_column_names*)]

  This constraint allows us to enforce referential integrity between two tables.

  ```
  Foreign key(Item) references Assess(Item)
  ```

  The above example will ensure that for every row inserted into the **Results** table, there is a row in **Assess** with a matching **Item** number. The effect of this kind of table constraint on the data manipulation statements is discussed more fully in Section 16.6.

- **CHECK (condition)**

  This is an extension of the column `check` constraint. At the table level, the condition may refer to several columns in the table, but not to columns in other tables.

For the SUBJECT database:

```
Create Table Students
        (Id          number(3.0) not null,
        First        char(10),
        Last         char(10)    not null,

        Primary key (Id))
Create Table Assess
        (Item        number(1,0) not null,
        Description  char(30),
        Weight       number(3,0) check(Weight between 0 and 100),
        Due          date,

        Primary key (Item))
Create Table Results
        (Item        number(1,0) not null,
        Id           number(3,0) not null,
        Submitted    date,
        Mark         number(3,0) check(Mark between 0 and 100),

        Primary key (Item,Id),

        Foreign key (Id)   references Students(Id),
        Foreign key (Item) references Assess(Item))
```

At this stage (Version 6 of ORACLE), the column and table constraints serve as a comment. The uniqueness of the key must still be maintained through the application or through a unique index (see Section 15.6.1).

15.5 Views

Views play a variety of roles in a database system.

- They can be used to provide a convenient name for a commonly used subset of the database.
- As a consequence of this, they may be used to secure the database by restricting users to just that data they need to know.
- They can be used to make inferences and to perform calculations based on values in the database.

Example 15.4 Suppose we frequently have to deal with students who have failed any item of assessment.

```
Create View Fails(Item, Id, Mark)
    as Select Item, Id, Mark
       From    Results
       Where   Mark < 50
```

Database Definition in SQL

This names as `Fails` all the rows in `Results` where the mark is less than 50.

> Fails = Results where Mark < 50

The `Fails` table is a virtual table. It has no *physical* presence in the database, existing merely through its definition. However, it may be treated as if it were a real table. For example, to find out who failed the second assignment, we need only refer to the `Fails` view.

```
Select *
From   Fails
Where  Item = 2
```

This query is taken and expanded, with the word `Fails` being replaced by its definition.

```
Select Item, Id, Mark
From   Results
Where  Mark < 50
and    Item = 2
```

This expanded version of the query refers only to base tables and may now be executed.

Example 15.5 Views are not merely subsets of the database. They can provide information derived by calculations, such as the average mark for each assessment item:

```
Create View Assess_Average(Item, Mean)
    as Select   Item, avg(mark)
       From     Results
       Group by Item
```

This provides a table that contains the results of calculations.

Example 15.6 We can take views further and use them to derive "new" information. The following view counts the number of assignments that each student has submitted.

```
Create View Ass_Count(Id, Did)
    as Select Id, count(*)
       From Results
       Group by Id
       union
       Select   Id, 0
       From     Students
       Where    Id not in (Select Id
                           From   Results)
```

The view combines the results of two separate queries. The first `select` statement counts the number of submissions made where the student actually made a submission. The second deduces that any student without a result must have submitted a total of zero assignments.

In general the view mechanism allows us to make inferences stemming from data stored in the database.

View Definition

A **base** table is simply a set specified in extension, that is, one written out in full. A view or **virtual** table is a set specified by comprehension, that is, its elements or rows are defined through some property common to all rows in the view.

The `select` statement is SQL's version of set comprehension. Through its `select` clause we may form rows that, by means of the `where` clause, have some shared property. The syntax for view definition reflects this.

```
view_definition:
    CREATE VIEW view_name [(list_of_column_names)]
    AS select_statement
```

- The view name is optionally followed by a list of column names. If these are omitted then the names of the view columns are "inherited" from the column names that appear in the `select` clause.
- If the `select` clause contains a calculation then this *must* be named.
- If the view needs to be changed or we no longer need it then it can be dropped.

```
view_removal:
    DROP VIEW view_name
```

15.6 Indexes

15.6.1 Unique or Primary Indexes

In Section 15.2.1 it was pointed out that, unless advised otherwise, SQL will allow duplicate rows in a table. This is clearly undesirable. We need to ensure that, for example, no two students have the same Id. When inserting a new row into **Students**, we should first check that there is not already some student (row) with the new student's Id. In general terms, when inserting a new row into a table, we should check that no row already exists with the same key value. To help speed up this process, it is recommended that there be a unique index on the key. There will be one such index for each table in the database. The key of the **Students** relation is the student **Id** and a corresponding index would be defined. It may be that this is done automatically, as is the case with IBM's SQL/DS product.

```
Create Unique Index Student_Key
    on Students (Id)
```

This is our way of telling SQL that we need to be able to rapidly access individual student rows based on the **Id** value *and* that only one row in the **Students** table may have a given **Id** value. The index can be thought of as providing access to the **Students** table in the following way.

```
Student_Key              Students
-------------            --------------------
Id      Pointer          Id      First   Last
-------------            --------------------
831     5            1.  871     Hans    Zupp
854     4            2.  862     Bill    Board
862     2            3.  869     Rip     Orff
868     7            4.  854     Ann     Dover
869     3            5.  831     Hans    Orff
871     1            6.  872     Betty   Kahn
872     6            7.  868     Will    Gambol
-------------            --------------------
```

The index is based on the primary key of the relation. There is one entry in the index for each row in the relation. Each entry is presented as consisting of a value and a pointer to the row that has that value for its key. For example, the first entry contains the value 831 and the number, 5, of the row for student 831.

There are two features of the index that should be noted in comparing it with the associated table.

1. First and foremost it is an *ordered* structure. The student Id's are held in numeric order. As a result, the index may be searched in a binary way. For example, if we take the mid-point of the index as being Id 868 then we are assured that all Id's less than 868 will be *before* that entry in the index. All those Id's greater than 868 will appear after. This is the way we search a telephone directory. We don't need to search anything like the entire directory to find an entry.

2. Secondly, the index is physically smaller than the table. There is not much difference in this example, but in general there will be.

It should be defined at the same time as the table is defined and maintained over the lifetime of the associated table.

This type of index is used for two purposes.

1. It is used to preserve the integrity of the database by guaranteeing the uniqueness of the primary key. For example, if we tried to insert a new row in **Students** with an Id of 871 then the insertion would be rejected because there already exists such a row. This is the significance of the word **Unique** in the index definition.

2. The index is also used to speed access to individual rows of the table. Because the index is, typically, a much smaller structure than the corresponding table and because it is ordered, the index can be searched in a much shorter time than it would take to search the table. Once the correct entry in the index is found, the pointer or address can be used to **directly** locate the corresponding row.

Based on this rather simplified view of the structure of an index, what improvement in access time might we expect? Suppose that there are 100 rows in the **Students** table. What if we were to scan the table itself for a particular student's row? We might find the row at the very beginning of the table but we might equally have to search all the way to the end, and even then, not find it. On the average, we would expect to find the required row halfway through the table; that is, after reading 50 rows. In general, when there are S student rows we can expect to search through $S/2$ records.

Using the index, with its ordered structure, we search by dividing the index in two, checking whether the key is in the first or the second half by examining the mid-point value. Then we repeat this process on the reduced search area, stopping when we can divide no longer. The search space will be reduced from 100 entries to 50 then 25, 13, 7, 4, 2 and 1, taking us 7 **binary chops**. With S student rows we can expect to search $log_2 S$ entries.

The difference in search time can be seen in the following table:

S	$S/2$	$log_2 S$
4	2	2
8	4	3
128	64	7
1024	512	10

The syntax for defining indexes requires that we name the index and specify the table and attributes upon which it is based. Note that, although we have to provide the index with a name, that name is *never* mentioned in any query that involves the associated table. We must trust that SQL knows when and how to use the relevant indexes. We can create an index on an empty table or on one with rows already in it.

```
index_definition:
    CREATE [UNIQUE] INDEX index_name
    ON table_name (list_of_index_components)
index_component:
    column_name [ASC|DESC]
```

Where the Relation has a Composite Key

The `Results` table has a composite key made up of the `Item` and `Id` attributes. When this kind of situation arises, there will be several different ways of defining the unique index required. In this particular case, we can create an index that will put the `Item` first or one that puts the `Id` first.

```
Create Unique Index              Create Unique Index
       Results_Key_One                   Results_Key_Two
    on Results (Item, Id)             on Results (Id, Item)
```

15.6.2 Secondary Indexes

Suppose that we wanted to gain access to all the items submitted for assessment and the marks obtained by individual students. A student may be expected to have several results.

Database Definition in SQL 377

If we build an index to help us access one particular student's results then each entry in this index will consist of a key value and several pointers, one for each result record for that student.

Student_Results			Results			
Key	Pointers		Item	Id	Submitted	Mark
854	3, 17	1.	1	871	0908	80
862	2, 10, 4	2.	1	862	0907	60
868	5, 11, 15	3.	1	854	0908	70
869	6, 8, 12	4.	1	872	0910	55
871	1, 7, 16	5.	1	868	0906	90
872	4, 9, 13	6.	1	869	0909	70
		7.	2	871	1021	70
		8.	2	869	1022	80
		9.	2	872	1021	65
		10.	2	862	1022	70
		11.	2	868	1021	75
		12.	3	869	?	95
		13.	3	872	?	45
		14.	3	862	?	40
		15.	3	868	?	50
		16.	3	871	?	60
		17.	3	854	?	65

This is an example of a **secondary** index. Now if we want to find student 854's marks we can use the considerably smaller index which tells us that the results are located at rows 3 and 17. We can access these rows directly. Without the index we would have needed to read through the entire table to find the marks. The index can be created as follows:

```
Create Index Student_Results
    on Results (Id)
```

Secondary indexes have only one function and that is to speed access to one or more rows, that is why they are designed to allow for several pointers per entry. There will be as many of these indexes as it takes to make the database useable.

15.6.3 The Role of Indexes in a Join Operation

Suppose we want a list showing how each student went in the items of assessment he or she submitted.

```
Select    First, Last, Item, Mark
From      Students, Results
Where     Students.Id = Results.Id
```

378   Chapter 15

Option 1: The Nested Loop Approach

One rational method of answering this query, without the benefit of any indexes, is called the **nested loop** method. It involves reading through the `Results` table then scanning `Students` for the corresponding student row. This can be presented as an algorithm:

For each row in the Results table, do:

    For each row in the Students table, do:

        • If the Id in the Students = the Id in the Results row, then:

            • Print the `First`, `Last`, `Item` and `Mark` columns

How long will this query take to execute? Using the above steps, we will be required to make a scan of the entire `Results` table. For each row, we will have to scan the `Students` table. Since the student row could be anywhere in that table, we can expect to scan half the table on the average. So the cost is:

$$\begin{aligned} & R * (S/2) \\ = & 17 * (7/2) \\ = & 59.5 \end{aligned}$$

Option 2: Using Indexes

As stated before, in a relational database, there should be a primary or unique index on each relation key and a secondary index for each foreign key.

```
Student_Key              Student_Results
-------------            -----------------
Id     Pointer           Id       Pointers
-------------            -----------------
831    5                 854      3, 17
854    4                 862      2, 10, 4
862    2                 868      5, 11, 15
868    7                 869      6, 8, 12
869    3                 871      1, 7, 16
871    1                 872      4, 9, 13
872    6                 -----------------
-------------
```

Because both indexes are in Id order, we can work through both indexes concurrently. If we have an entry in the left-hand index but none in the right- hand one, then that student has no results to report. This is the case for student **831**. We can skip this student and move down to the next entry on the left. Now we have entries for student **854** on the left and the right. We can follow the pointer on the left to access the student's first and last name; and we can follow the pointers in the right-hand entry to access the two results for that student. We can print as we go. In this way, we can join the tables speedily.

How can we cost this method? Suppose we make the following assumptions.

- We need two reads to access a student row, one to read the entry in the index and another to follow the pointer and read the record itself.

- For results, we need one read to access the entry and one read for each individual result record. This will vary from student to student, but it is not unreasonable to average this at no more than three because there are three items of assessment and most students will do all three. That makes four reads altogether.

The cost is therefore $6S$ where there are S students enrolled.

$$\begin{aligned} & 6*S \\ =\ & 6*7 \\ =\ & 42 \end{aligned}$$

The relatively small sizes of the two tables used in the discussion gives a false impression of the worth of the indexes. Let us move to a more realistic situation. Suppose there are 1000 students enrolled. That means, proportionately, that we might expect $1000*(17/7) = 17\,000/7 = 2429$ result rows. Let $R = 2429$.

The Nested Loop Approach

The cost is:
$$\begin{aligned} & R*(S/2) \\ =\ & 2429*(1000/2) \\ =\ & 2429*500 \\ =\ & 1214500 \end{aligned}$$

Using the Indexes

The cost is:
$$\begin{aligned} & 6*S \\ =\ & 6*1000 \\ =\ & 6000 \end{aligned}$$

Now the benefits of indexing are clearly highlighted. With more typical table sizes, the nested loop method is many times slower than the second option. This difference will continue to grow as the table sizes increase.

15.6.4 Advantages and Disadvantages of Indexes

If indexes provide such benefits, why don't we define indexes on every attribute on every table? Then we would be guaranteed speedy access almost regardless of the kind of queries we make. One drawback attached to each index is the maintenance required. Every time a change is made to a table and that change involves an indexed column, then all associated indexes must also be updated. Everybody involved in applying a change will need to wait while this is done. The cost may prove too much because these overheads slow down a crucial transaction to an unacceptable extent. What we are doing with indexes is spreading the cost of a query across all the changes that are made. A second drawback is the additional space required to store each index. Typically, the disk space overhead is 20% of the base table size *per index*.

The expected advantages gained from indexes are as follows:

1. With a unique index, that is, one based upon the key of the table, rapid access is enabled to *the* row with a given key value.
2. With a secondary index, rapid access to groups of records is enabled.

There are also *unexpected* advantages to be gained from an index.

1. Sometimes a query may be answered by reference to the index alone. For example, if we wanted to know which students had submitted all three items of assessment, then the index can answer that by counting the number of pointers attached to each Id.

2. Sorted output can be achieved at a reduced cost. For example, if we wanted to list student details in Id order then this can be done via the `Student_Key` index which is in Id sequence.

An index may be dropped at any time:

```
index_removal:
    DROP INDEX index_name
```

15.7 Summary

In this chapter we have discussed three of the major features of a relational database.

- There is the base **table**. This feature corresponds to the notion of a set defined in extension. The elements or rows of such sets are written out in full on the bulk memory of a computer system.

- There is the **view** or virtual table. This corresponds to the notion of set comprehension in which a set is defined by means of some property common to all its members.

- There is the **index** of which there are two kinds. We use unique or primary indexes to ensure the uniqueness of the primary key of a table and to speed access to individual rows in the table. We use secondary indexes to improve the speed at which a query is executed.

Exercises

▶ Q15.1 **The ACADEMIC Database**

In the exercises at the end of Chapter 4 we were introduced to the University of Wiseacres. They have a database with the following structure.

```
        Schools              Staff                Quals
        -------              -----                -----
    (*) School_Id        (*) Staff_Id         (*) Staff_Id
        School_Name          Staff_Name       (*) Degree
        Phone                School_Id            Place
    (?) Head_Id                                   Year
```

An asterisk (*) indicates that the attribute is (part of) the primary key of the relation. A question mark (?) indicates that null values are to be permitted for that attribute in the associated relation.

a. Write `create table` statements for this database. As a guide, use the sample data provided in the corresponding question at the end of Chapter 4.

b. Create unique indexes appropriate to the database.

c. Create secondary indexes appropriate to the database.

▶ Q15.2 Write `create table` statements for the ACADEMIC database that ensure the following constraints.

a. The primary keys of each table are unique.

b. There is referential integrity between the tables.

c. No two schools will have the same name.

This time, use the extended `create table` syntax discussed in Section 15.4.

Q15.3 **The RESOURCES Database**

As before, across town from Wiseacres is the Witsend Institute of Technology where resource allocation is still a bigger issue than staff qualifications. The structure of their database is as follows.

```
        Staff                Theaters             Allocation
        -----                --------             ----------
    (*) Teacher          (*) Theater          (*) Subject
        Room                 Capacity             Enrolled
    (?) Phone                                     Theater
                                                  Teacher
```

The `Staff` and `Theaters` relations represent the Institute's resources and the `Allocation` relation shows, for each subject taught, the current enrolment as well as the lecture theatre and teacher normally allocated to that subject.

a. Write **create table** statements for this database. As a guide, use the sample data provided in the corresponding question at the end of Chapter 4.
b. Create unique indexes appropriate to the database.
c. Create secondary indexes appropriate to the database.

Q15.4 Write **create table** statements for the RESOURCES database to ensure that:

a. The primary keys of each table are unique.
b. There is referential integrity between the tables.

Use the extended **create table** syntax discussed in Section 15.4.

▶ Q15.5 Assume you have access to a table **Mins** that contains all the integers from 0 to 1439. The table is shown below on the left.

```
    Mins              Time_24
    ------            -------
    Minute            HH   MM
    ------            -------
       0               0    0
       1               0    1
       :               :    :
      59               0   59
      60               1    0
       :               :    :
    1439              23   59
    ------            -------
```

Develop a view **Time_24**, like the one shown on the right above, that represents each minute in 24-hour form.

Q15.6 Using the **Mins** table of the previous question, create another view **TimeString** that represents each minute of the day in 24-hour form using a five-character string.

```
       TimeString
       --------------
       Minute   Time
       --------------
          0     00:00
          1     00:01
          :       :
         59     00:59
         60     01:00
          :       :
       1439     23:59
       --------------
```

Database Definition in SQL 383

Q15.7 Using the `TimeString` view of the previous question, create a view `MinsDiff` that indicates the difference, in minutes, between two times.

```
MinsDiff
--------------------
TimeA   TimeB   Diff
--------------------
00:00   00:00      0
00:00   00:01      1
  :       :        :
00:00   23:59   1439
00:01   00:00     -1
00:01   00:01      0
  :       :        :
09:00   09:44     44
  :       :        :
--------------------
```

How many rows will there be in the entire view?

▶ Q15.8 GRUMBLERS

The famous old gentlemen's club GRUMBLERS recently elected a new management committee. One of this committee's first decisions was to move the membership accounting system onto computer. Because of the historical importance of the club it was decided to record all members, past and present. A table has been created showing membership information exactly as it was recorded in the original books.

```
Grumblers
---------------------------------------------------
Id    Grumbler              Day  Mth  Year
---------------------------------------------------
 1    Sir Roger Planter      30  Feb  1776
 2    Lord Overall           32  Jul  1901
 3    Lord Dungarees         31  Jun  1965
 4    Mr Hank van Plump      25  Mar  1821
 5    Mr Sam Sepia           29  Feb  1695
 6    Sir Uther Twitt        29  Feb  1900
 7    Prof I.T.E. Rolls      30  Jul  1875
---------------------------------------------------
```

As may be seen, the data is not as accurate as it should be.

The rules regarding valid dates are as follows:

1. Thirty days hath September, April, June and November.

2. All the rest have 31 except February alone

3.1 In a year not divisible by 4, February has 28 days.

3.2 In a year divisible by 4 and, if divisible by 100 then also divisible by 400, February has 29 days.

3.3 Otherwise February has 28 days.

Create a view `Fixit(Id, Day, Mth, Year, RuleBroken)` that will flag each invalid row in `Grumblers` and indicate the code of the rule broken.

(Hint: Write a separate `select` statement for each rule and then combine them using the `union` operator.)

▶ Q15.9 The HORSE RACING Database

Suppose we are a group of professional punters and we keep a database of horse racing results. There are four basic tables.

```
    Horses              Races                   Results                Conditions
    ------              -----                   -------                ----------
(*) Horse_Name      (*) Race_No             (*) Course             (*) Course
    Age                 Race_Name           (*) Race_Date          (*) Race_Date
    Sex                 Time                (*) Race_No                Weather
(?) Sire                Length                  Gate_No                Track
(?) Dam             (*) Course                  Handicap
                    (*) Race_Date           (?) Odds
                        Prize_Money             Horse_Name
                                                Jockey_Name
                                                Trainer_Name
                                        (*) Place
                                            Distance
```

General comments:

1. Columns that form (part of) the key are marked with an asterisk (*).

2. Columns that may be null are marked with a question mark (?).

3. The handicap is kept in kilograms.

4. Odds are expressed as a single number, for example:

Odds	Stored As
2-1 on	0.5
evens	1.0
2-1	2.0
11-2	5.5

5. The `Distance` column represents how far the horse was behind the horse in front of it when the winner passed the post.

6. Prize money is awarded for first place only.

7. A horse's sire is its father.

8. A horse's dam is its mother.

Required:

a. For each table, identify any foreign keys it contains.
b. Write `create table` statements for this database.
c. Define primary indexes.
d. Define secondary indexes for the foreign keys.

Q15.10 Write SQL statements in response to each of the following.

a. How much money has the horse Lucky Streak won in total?
b. Define a view `Winner` that enables us to identify race winners quickly.

```
Winner
-----------------------------------------------------
Course  Race_Date  Race_No  Horse_Name  Prize_Money
-----------------------------------------------------
```

Use this view to determine Lucky Streak's prize winnings.

c. Define a view `First_Place` that summarizes a horse's race wins.

```
First_Place
--------------------------
Horse_Name  Wins  Winnings
--------------------------
```

Be sure to allow for horses that have *never* won a race.

d. From the base tables alone, list horses with more than 25 wins, in order of merit. Repeat this query using the view `First_Place`.

e. Assuming the existence of two views:

`Second_Place(Horse_Name,Seconds)`, and
`Third_Place(Horse_Name,Thirds)`

that provide the number of second and third places that a horse has had, write a view `First_Place`, like the following, that provides a summary of a horse's performance:

Horse	Winnings	Wins	Seconds	Thirds
Two Bit	25531	13	18	11
Flea Bitten	8328	6	5	0
Cat Food	0	0	0	1

CHAPTER 16

Database Manipulation in SQL

16.1 Introduction

In this chapter we look at the three data manipulation commands of SQL.

- The `insert` statement enables one or more new rows to be added to a table.
- The `update` statement allows one or more existing rows to be modified in some way.
- The `delete` statement allows one or more existing rows to be removed from a table.

These statements allow the user's model (or information system) to be *manipulated* so as to reflect changes that have occurred in the user's environment.

16.2 Adding New Rows

The `insert` statement allows one or more rows to be inserted into a table.
There are two forms of the statement, one that allows us to insert a single row, and one that allows the insertion of a set of rows.

16.2.1 Single Row Insert

This form allows one new row to be placed in the table specified.

Example 16.1 We want to add a new student number 999, with the name Meg Murphy. To do this we construct the row with a `values` clause and then insert that into the `Students` table.

```
Insert
Into Students
Values(999, 'Meg','Murphy')
```

Database Manipulation in SQL

The three values supplied are attached to attributes according to the order of their appearance in the `create` statement used to set up the `Students` table.

If we didn't know Ms Murphy's first name, then we must leave a gap. We can do this in either of two ways:

```
Values(999,,'Murphy')
Values(999, null, 'Murphy')
```

It is better style to state explicitly where any null values are to be used; that is, of the above two examples, the second form is preferable.

It is even better style to state explicitly the attributes to which values are to be associated. This can be done by specifying the columns into which the values are to be placed:

```
Insert
Into Students(Id, Last)
Values (999, 'Murphy')
```

Not only does this document the `insert`, it also allows us to write the values in any order; so we could have written:

```
Insert
Into Students(Last, Id)
Values('Murphy', 999)
```

The general syntax of this form of insert is as follows:

---
single_row_insert:
    INSERT
    INTO table_name [(*list_of_column_names*)]
    VALUES (*list_of_values*)

The value may be a constant such as `999` or `'Murphy'`, or a program variable. It may also be an expression of the type appropriate to the associated column, it cannot involve a `select` statement.

16.2.2 Multi-row Insert

The second form allows any number of rows to be inserted into a table. This can be useful if we want to make a copy of the table or to extract a significant amount of data from elsewhere in the database. However, since the database will have been designed to avoid any redundancy, we might ask if it is wise to duplicate information already in existence. This will be discussed shortly.

We could create a table `ShortStudents` that contains only the last name and Id attributes:

```
Create Table ShortStudents
        (Id      integer,
         Last    char(10))
```

Now we can fill this table with a "mass" insert:

```
Insert
Into    ShortStudents
Select  Id, Last
From    Students
```

Why would we want to do this when we can create a view that offers the same information?

```
Create View ShortStudents
as
Select  Id, Last
From    Students
```

The view will save space, existing only as a definition in the catalog. It will also automatically include any new students added to the underlying base table **Students**.

This form of the **insert** does offer a way of dropping a column from a table. With **ShortStudents** we have, in effect, dropped the **First** column from the **Students** table. The mass insert also enables us take a snapshot of the database. If we want to examine the state of some portion of the database at a certain moment, then we can do so with this form of **insert**. The syntax is as follows:

---

multi_row_insert:
  INSERT
  INTO table_name [(*list_of_column_names*)]
  select_statement

Example 16.2 Suppose we want to add a new student and automatically allocate a new **Id** to that student.

```
Insert
Into    Students(Id, First, Last)
Select  max(Id)+1, 'Doug', 'Deep'
From    Students
```

16.3 Modifying Existing Rows

The **update** statement allows us to make changes to rows that already exist in the database. All the rows will be from the same table, that is, only one table at a time can be updated.

Database Manipulation in SQL 389

```
update_statement:
    UPDATE table_name
    SET list_of_assignments
    [WHERE condition]
assignment:
    column_name = value
```

Example 16.3 The update may target one row if the **where** clause refers to the key. Suppose we discover that student 871 is called Stan Zupp, not Hans Zupp.

```
Update Students
Set    First = 'Stan'
Where  Id = 871
```

The **set** clause allows us to assign a new value to a column. The value assigned may be one of:

- a constant
- a program variable
- an expression constructed using either or both of the above in conjunction with any built-in function
- a subquery that returns a single value
- **null**

Obviously the value must be of the same type as the column to which it is being assigned.

Example 16.4 We can change a number of columns in the set clause, separating each new assignment with a comma. Suppose we find that student 854 is not Betty Kahn after all, but Liz Kant.

```
Update Student
Set    First = 'Liz',
       Last  = 'Kant'
Where  Id = 854
```

Example 16.5 We can change a number of rows with a single statement. Suppose we want to increase everybody's marks in assignment 1 by 5%.

```
Update Results
Set    Mark = Mark + 5
Where  Item = 1
```

Example 16.6 The **where** clause may involve a subquery. Suppose we want to take 5 marks away from anybody who submitted the second assignment after the due date.

```
Update Results
Set Mark = Mark - 5
Where Item = 2
  and  Submitted > (Select Due
                    From    Assess
                    Where   Item = 2)
```

This would cause two results to be changed, those marked with an asterisk below:

```
----------------------------------
Item    Id     Submitted   Mark
----------------------------------
 2      871     1021        70
 2      869     1022        80     *
 2      872     1021        65
 2      862     1022        70     *
 2      868     1021        75
----------------------------------
```

The assignment was due on 1021 that is the twenty-first of October. Two students handed in their assignments after that date, **869** and **862**; they will have 5 marks deducted.

```
----------------------------------
Item    Id     Submitted   Mark
----------------------------------
 2      871     1021        70
 2      869     1022        75     *
 2      872     1021        65
 2      862     1022        65     *
 2      868     1021        75
----------------------------------
```

Example 16.7 Having penalized some of the students we can now be kind to them all by scaling the marks upwards. We do this here by taking the best mark, which was 75 and set this to 100 and then adjust all the others accordingly.

```
75   -->   75*100/75 = 100

70   -->   70*100/75 = 93
65   -->   65*100/75 = 87
```

It would seem straightforward to turn this calculation into an **update** statement.

```
Update Results
Set Mark = (Mark*100)/(Select max(Mark)
                       From    Results
                       Where   Item = 2)
Where Item = 2
```

Unfortunately this form of assignment is not allowed. If the `set` clause uses a subquery then the assignment must be of the form:

```
set column_name = (subquery)
```

whereas the statement above uses a `set` clause of the form:

```
set column_name = mark*100/(subquery)
```

We can overcome this problem by incorporating the `mark*100` factor into the subquery and using a `min` function instead of a `max`:

```
Update Results R
Set     R.Mark = (Select min(R.Mark*100/Mark)
                 From   Results
                 Where  Item = 2)
Where  R.Item = 2
```

The revised table now contains the scaled marks.

Item	Id	Submitted	Mark	
2	871	1021	93	(was 70)
2	869	1022	100	(was 75, the top mark)
2	872	1021	87	(was 65)
2	862	1022	87	(was 65)
2	868	1021	100	(was 75)

Note that the new version uses a correlated subquery and may be expected to be slower to execute because the `min` function is calculated for every row updated.

16.4 Removing Rows

We can remove unwanted or outdated rows from the database by using the `delete` statement. Like the `insert` and `update` statements, the `delete` targets just one table.

Example 16.8 We can rid ourselves of a troublesome student.

```
Delete
From  Students
Where Id = 831
```

Example 16.9 We can even rid ourselves of all students.

```
Delete
From Students
```

The table is now empty. It remains defined in the catalog. To get rid of the table entirely we would need to `drop` it.

```
delete_statement:
    DELETE
    FROM table_name
    [WHERE condition]
```

Example 16.10 The condition in the `where` clause may involve a subquery. Suppose we want to remove any student who has failed to submit any item for assessment.

```
Delete
From Students
Where Id not in (Select Id
                 from    Results)
```

The subquery `(Select Id From Results)` identifies students who have a result of some kind. The `delete` statement removes those who are not in this list.

16.5 Transactions

Each of the data manipulation statements operates on just one table at a time. Yet there will be events that, to be adequately captured, require changes to several tables. For example, in the SUBJECT database, if a student drops out, then not only should his or her student row be removed, but any result rows associated with that student should also be removed. These two deletions cannot be achieved through a single delete statement. Two are required. Consequently, after the first delete, the database is no longer in a consistent state. There are two possible ways of dropping the student.

1. If we perform the update as:

    ```
    Delete
    From   Students
    Where Id = 872
    ```

    At this stage the database has results for a non-existing student.

    ```
    Delete
    From   Results
    Where Id = 872
    ```

    Now the results are gone as well and once again the database is consistent.

2. Alternatively we might change the database in the reverse order.

    ```
    Delete
    From   Results
    Where Id = 872
    ```

Now we have a student 872 without any results, and should the transaction stop here then it might appear as though the student had not obtained any results, which is not the case.

```
Delete
From   Students
Where Id = 872
```

The database is again consistent.

At the halfway stage of this transaction, and regardless of which table we tackle first, the database will be in an inconsistent state. Now there are two ways to recover consistency; we can either go forward and complete the second delete; or we can attempt to undo the first `delete`, which might be rather difficult.

Why would we want to undo the work done so far?

1. We might be sitting at a terminal typing in the commands interactively when suddenly we realize that it was student 862 who dropped out, not 872.

2. More likely, we are operating on the database through a program, and that program is issuing the SQL statements on our behalf. We merely identify the student as 872 (or was it 862?) and the program fires off both `delete` statements for us. Our one action gives rise to two database actions. Should there be a hardware or software error in the middle of this transaction then the database is potentially in error.

Regardless of exactly how we are modifying the database, there is a need to be able to unpick our current activities and get back to where we started. But where did we start? Perhaps we have just successively dropped two students with the error occurring while processing the second. Clearly we must wipe out the current transaction. Do we want to wipe the first one as well? Probably not but how can SQL tell how far to rollback? As far as it is concerned it is merely receiving a stream of commands and executing them one at a time. How can SQL tell that certain comments are packaged together as a transaction? While processing a transaction we have two ways of signaling completion.

1. The `COMMIT` Statement

   This command indicates to SQL that we are satisfied with the current transaction and are prepared to have its effects irrevocably fixed in the database. Once issued there is no return.

2. The `ROLLBACK` Statement

   This command undoes any changes that have been made since the most recent `commit`.

We will return to transaction management in Chapter 17 where we consider it from the user's point of view.

16.6   Referential Integrity

If the tables in the database have been defined with `Foreign key` references, there are two such linkages in the SUBJECT database, both are from the `Results` table. This was shown in Section 15.4. For the SUBJECT database:

```
Create Table Students
    (Id          number(3.0) not null,
     First       char(10),
     Last        char(10)    not null,

     Primary key (Id))

Create Table Assess
    (Item        number(1,0) not null,
     Description char(30),
     Weight      number(3,0) check(Weight between 0 and 100),
     Due         date,

     Primary key (Item))

Create Table Results
    (Item        number(1,0) not null,
     Id          number(3,0) not null,
     Submitted   date,
     Mark        number(3,0) check(Mark between 0 and 100),

     Primary key (Item,Id),

     Foreign key (Id)   references Students(Id),
     Foreign key (Item) references Assess(Item))
```

As we build up the database, SQL will maintain this referential integrity.

1. **Insert**

    If we attempt to insert a row into the **Results** table, then the value in the **Id** attribute must match the **Id** attribute of some existing row in the **Students** table. For example, if we try to add a result for student Id **999**, then student **999** must exist in the **Students** table.

    Similar comments apply to the **Item** attribute of any result being inserted. There must exist a corresponding item in the **Assess** table.

2. **Update**

    Once a result row is successfully inserted, we may change it with an update statement. However, the same conditions apply. The new value to which the Id is set must still match an existing student row,

3. **Delete**

    For the delete statement, we must switch our attention to the parent tables, **Students** and **Assess**. We cannot delete a row from the **Students** table, for example, if that student is recorded as having any results. Nor can we delete an assessment item from **Assess** if results have been awarded for that item.

16.7 View Update

In all the discussion in the chapter so far, it has been assumed that the table being manipulated is a *base* table. What might happen if we were to try, for example, to insert a row into a view rather than an ordinary base table? Later we will consider why we might wish to insert through a view.

Suppose we define two views of the Students table, one that gives each student's first name and one that gives the student's last name.

```
Create View First_View         Create View Last_View
as                             as
Select Id,First                Select Id,Last
From Students                  From Students

Select *                       Select *
From   First_View              From   Last_View
```

```
First_View                     Last_View
-----------                    ------------
Id     First                   Id     Last
-----------                    ------------
871    Hans                    871    Zupp
862    Bill                    862    Board
869    Rip                     869    Orff
 :      :                       :      :
868    Will                    868    Gambol
-----------                    ------------
```

The `First_View` can never be used to update the database. It omits a column that was defined as `not null` in the `create table` statement. SQL can work out into which base table a row should be inserted, but cannot construct an adequate `values` clause because an essential base table column is missing from the view. However, if we want to add a student whose first name is unknown then we could use the `Last_View`

```
Insert
Into Last_View
Values(999, 'Murphy')
```

SQL can, through the view definition, turn this into an insert into the base table.

```
Insert
Into Students(Id, Last)
Values(999, 'Murphy')
```

This is a valid insert statement for the Students table.

Suppose we now define a view which selects certain rows rather than certain columns.

```
Create Views Scots
as
Select Id, First, Last
```

```
            From Students
            Where Last Like 'Mc%'
               or Last Like 'Mac%'
```

Anybody whose last name starts with Mc or Mac will appear on the view. Nobody does at the moment. Clearly we can insert into Students through this view because all three columns are involved.

```
            Insert
            Into Scots(Id, First, Last)
            Values (314, 'Angus','Mackay')
```

This translates directly into a straightforward insert into the base table. If we try using the view in a query we will expect to see Angus.

```
            Select *
            From    Scots

            Scots
            --------------------
            Id    First   Last
            --------------------
            314   Angus   Mackay
            --------------------
```

What if we try another insert?

```
            Insert
            Into Scots
            Values (999,'Bob','Smith')
```

This can be translated into an insert into **Students**. But if we look at the view now, we still get only Angus because his row is the only one that satisfies the view condition. Bob's clearly does not. This is rather unfortunate. After a seemingly successful insert into the **Scots** view the row has disappeared. This is particularly undesirable because the user may be completely unaware that he or she is working with a view and not a table.

To overcome this problem we can require that all inserts into a view can be seen through the view. This is done by using the optional **check** clause:

---

view_definition:

   CREATE VIEW view_name [(*list_of_column_names*)]
   AS select_statement
   [WITH CHECK OPTION]

Suppose we now try to insert Bob. SQL will now check that this new row satisfies the view condition. If it does not, then the insert will be rejected.

The check is also made on any update statements applied to the view. If we change Angus' name to Hamish:

```
Update Scots
Set First = 'Hamish'
Where Id = 314
```

the record will satisfy the view condition so the update is allowed to proceed. However, if we try to change the last name:

```
Update Scots
Set Last = 'Jones'
Where Id = 314
```

this update will be rejected because afterwards the row involved will not appear through the view, so the update will have operated like a delete. To make this kind of change we will have to revert to the base table.

16.8 Controlling Database Access

In almost all of the discussion of SQL that has taken place so far, it has been assumed that either there was only one user or that the users formed a single homogeneous group of people. This is *not* normally true. Typically, the database is a composite picture of the organization or of some part of it. It is, in fact, constructed from a number of individual views, some of which overlap and some of which have nothing in common. Yet, when integrated, the result is a kind of communal organizational noticeboard containing information ranging from the managing director's expense sheet to the date of acquisition and purchase price of somebody's personal computer. We must be able to control access to the database so that sensitive information is available only to those who need it. We also need to ensure that those entrusted with updating the database have the right kind of access. Controlling access to the database is achieved through the **grant** and **revoke** statements. We will consider each of these in turn.

16.8.1 Granting Access

The **grant** statement has the following syntax.

```
grant_statement:
    GRANT [list_of_privileges | ALL]
    ON table_name
    TO list_of_user_names
    [WITH GRANT OPTION]
privilege:
    [SELECT | INSERT | DELETE | ALTER | INDEX]
    or UPDATE list_of_column_names
```

Suppose we have the following users.

User	Role
`lecturer`	supervises the whole affair
`student`	suffers throughout the whole affair
`admin`	adds new students to the class, corrects any mistakes in the spelling of student names, and drops students when they fail to pay their fees
`receiver`	receives items of assessment submitted by students
`marker`	awards marks to students

Example 16.11 The `admin` user not only needs to add new rows to the student table but also needs to read the table to ensure that the student is not already enrolled. He or she also may need to change names, and to drop students.

```
Grant Select,
      Insert,
      Update First, Last,
      Delete
   On Students
   To admin
```

Example 16.12 The marker needs to add rows to the results table.

```
Grant Select, Insert
   on Results
   to marker

Grant Select
   on Students
   to marker

Grant Select
   on Assess
   to marker
```

Example 16.13 The lecturer might be granted complete access to all privileges on all tables.

```
Grant All
   on Students
   to lecturer
```

16.8.2 Revoking Privileges

There is a complementary command for removing privileges.

```
revoke_statement:
    REVOKE [list_of_privileges|ALL]
    ON table_name
    FROM list_of_user_names
```

Either individual, and possibly all, access rights may be removed from users; and either just one user and possibly several different users may be involved.

Example 16.14 Once the semester has finished and results have been finalized, we may want to prevent any subsequent changes to the database.

```
Revoke All
    on Students
    from admin, student, marker
```

16.9 Summary

In this chapter we have examined the three data manipulation commands of SQL.

- The `insert` statement enables one or more new rows to be added to a table.
- The `update` statement allows one or more existing rows to be modified in some way.
- The `delete` statement allows one or more existing rows to be removed from a table.

We have also looked at how these statements operate (1) when applied in a situation where the database management system supports referential integrity, and (2) when the statements are applied to a view rather than to a base table.

Finally, we have looked at how access rights may be granted and/or revoked.

Exercises

▶ Q16.1 The ACADEMIC Database

```
    Schools              Staff                Quals
    -------              -----                -----
(*) School_Id        (*) Staff_Id         (*) Staff_Id
    School_Name          Staff_Name       (*) Degree
    Phone                School_Id            Place
(?) Head_Id                                   Year
```

Change the database to reflect each of the following events.

a. A new staff member has been hired by the School of Accountancy [School_Id = 'AC']. The person involved has been allocated the Staff_Id = 25 and his name is J. Muir, BA, MBA. John was awarded his arts degree by the University of Florida at Orlando (UFO) in 1985 and his MBA by the University of Bute (UBute) in 1992.

b. Mr M. Bezzle [Staff_Id = 6] has resigned.

c. Prof. B. Tree [Staff_Id = 1] has, at last, been persuaded to retire.

d. L. R. Parser has finally (1995) been awarded his PhD by the University of Central Casting (UCC).

e. The School of Chemistry has closed due to lack of interest.

▶ Q16.2 The RESOURCES Database

```
    Staff                Theaters             Allocation
    -----                --------             ----------
(*) Teacher          (*) Theater          (*) Subject
    Room                 Capacity             Enrolled
(?) Phone                                     Theater
                                              Teacher
```

Change the database to reflect each of the following events.

a. The Cosy Theater has been partitioned into two smaller ones, Tiddly and Winks, with capacities of 5 and 25 respectively.

b. The Tiny and Cramp Theaters have been knocked together resulting in a new larger Cramp Theater. The overall capacity is unchanged.

c. Any class allocated to too small a room is to be cancelled.

d. Yet another student has enrolled for a course in Tap Dancing.

e. All Ms Tripp's classes are to be taken by Mr Hacker instead.

Q16.3 PARLIAMENT

```
Members             Parties             TalksTo
-------             -------             -------
(*) Member          (*) Party           (*) Talker
    Party           (?) Leader          (*) Listener
    Seat
```

Change the database to reflect each of the following events.

a. Mike has been elected as the Labor member for the seat of West Wyalong.

b. Duane has resigned as the leader of his party. An election for a new leader has yet to take place.

c. Denzil is the new leader of the Business Party.

d. Duane no longer talks to Denzil.

e. Nobody talks to Duane any more.

f. Marge has resigned from parliament.

Q16.4 The following tables are being used to represent the situation in a supermarket:

```
Queues              Checkouts           Shopping
------              ---------           --------
CustId              CheckId             CustId
CheckId
Place
```

Change the database to reflect each of the following events.

a. Alan comes into the supermarket and joins those people still shopping.

b. Sue joins the end of the queue at checkout C3.

c. The customer at the front of checkout C2 pays and leaves.

d. Bob, queueing somewhere, returns to the aisles.

e. Jackie goes from the end of the queue at checkout C5 to checkout C6 which may have no customers.

Q16.5 A takeover

Wiseacres has taken over the tiny University of Hard Knox (UHK) and is in the process of merging some academic departments (as UHK calls them) and closing down others. Some information about Hard Knocks has already been copied from their database into Wiseacres own ACADEMIC database. The relevant tables are as follows:

```
            Depts                   Employees
            -----                   ---------
       (*) Dept_No             (*) Empl_No
           Dept_Name               Empl_Name
                                   Bachelor
                               (?) Masters
                                   Doctorate
                                   Dept_No
```

Some of the contents of these two tables should indicate the kind of information they contain in general.

```
Depts
--------------------
Dept_No   Dept_Name
--------------------
   1      Arts
   2      Business
   3      Computing
   4      Dentistry
   :      :
--------------------
```

```
Employees
----------------------------------------------------------------
Empl_No   Name      Bachelors   Masters   Doctorate   Dept_No
----------------------------------------------------------------
   1      D.Smith   BSc         MPhil     No          10
   2      B.Bop     BA          ?         No          1
   3      A.Lulu    BDSc        ?         Yes         4
   :      :         :           :         :           :
----------------------------------------------------------------
```

Change the ACADEMIC database to reflect the following decisions taken by the "Joint Amalgamation Committee" (stacked, of course, to ensure that the *correct* decisions are made).

a. The Department of Business [Dept_no = 2] is to be merged into Wiseacres' School of Accountancy [School_Id = 'AC']. Every member of that department is to be offered a place.

b. Wiseacres' School of Chemistry will only be required to take in UHK chemists who have a PhD.

Q16.6 The CARE Database

A community action group known as Citizens Against Ruining the Environment (CARE) has been set up to protest against a proposed freeway. CARE has set up

Database Manipulation in SQL

a database containing information on helpers and the help they are able to offer. This has required the creation of three tables.

```
    Helpers              Help                 Tree
    -------              ----                 ----
(*) Id               (*) Id               (*) Id
    First            (*) Willdo               Is_Rung_By
    Last
    Street
    Phone
```

The key of the Helper table is the Id column, that of the Tree table is also the Id column. The key of the Help table is both the Id and the Willdo columns.

Helpers

Id	First	Last	Street	Phone
21	Jim	White	28 Lizzie St	260 3145
36	Ann	Binks	Hill Road	?
:	:	:	:	:

Help

Id	Willdo
21	Drafting
28	Typing
35	Leafleting
21	Typing
:	:

Tree

Id	Is_Rung_By
21	38
22	38
38	15
15	?
:	:

The **Tree** table is used to quickly disseminate information, for example, to notify people of an urgent public meeting or for a demonstration. The method used is known as a telephone tree. The person at the top rings several people and they, in turn, ring several other people. So person 15 must be at the top of the tree because nobody rings him or her.

Write SQL to answer the following queries.

    a.   What is the phone number of Bill Smith?

    b.   How many helpers live on Hill St (not to be confused with Hill Rd)?

    c.   Give the name and phone numbers of all helpers who can type.

    d.   We need some leafleting done quickly. How may people can we get to help?

    e.   Bill Smith claims that he has never been contacted through the telephone tree. What is the name of the person who should be ringing him?

f. What is the name of the person at the top of the telephone tree?

g. How many helpers do we have who cannot be contacted through the telephone tree?

h. Who are at the bottom of the tree? Who rings each of these people? Give names.

i. Who rings the most people?

j. Which is the largest group at the bottom of the tree and who rings that group?

k. Are there any people on the tree who do not have a phone?

Q16.7 Write SQL that amends the CARE database to reflect the following events.

a. One of the helpers, Mary Wood, has been shy about herself. It turns out that she is an experienced political lobbyist. Update the **Help** table to reflect this new knowledge. [**Willdo='Lobbying'**]

b. A new helper has volunteered:

Angus Mackay
53 Essex St
633 9912

Angus can type and is prepared to do leafleting. Add him to the database, giving him the next available Id number.

c. One of the helpers, Doug Deep [**Id=55**], is disgusted with the political infighting. He wants to leave CARE.

1. Remove him from the **Helpers** and **Help** tables.
2. Pick someone from the largest group at the bottom of the telephone tree and make that person take Doug's place on the tree. You may assume that Doug is somewhere in the middle of the tree.

CHAPTER 17

Application Programming

17.1 Introduction

This chapter is concerned with how we program our information systems or **application**. The system will, typically, consist of a database and a set of programs. This split reflects that division first discussed in Chapter 1.

- The database contains simple specific facts concerning the organisation.
- The programs contain more general statements or knowledge.

The programs themselves can be divided into two groups according to the kind of knowledge they encode. Some of them are **report** programs. They inspect the database, make calculations using the data retrieved, and report on the results of their calculations. The other group of programs **process transactions**, that is, they allow events and changes in the real world to be represented in the database. Each of these latter programs will be dedicated to handling one particular kind of event.

A large part of the work involved in operating an organisational information system is concerned with this latter group of programs. The information system *must* be able to record changes in the organisation's environment and circumstances.

This chapter is mainly concerned with such transaction processing. It examines how the operation schemas that are used to *specify* the transactions are *implemented* as SQL programs.

Each operation schema could be divided into two separate sets of conditions.

- There are the pre-conditions which, collectively, state what conditions must apply before some event may truly be said to have occurred.

- There are the post-conditions which, on the basis of the pre-conditions being satisfied, say how the situation changes as a result of this event.

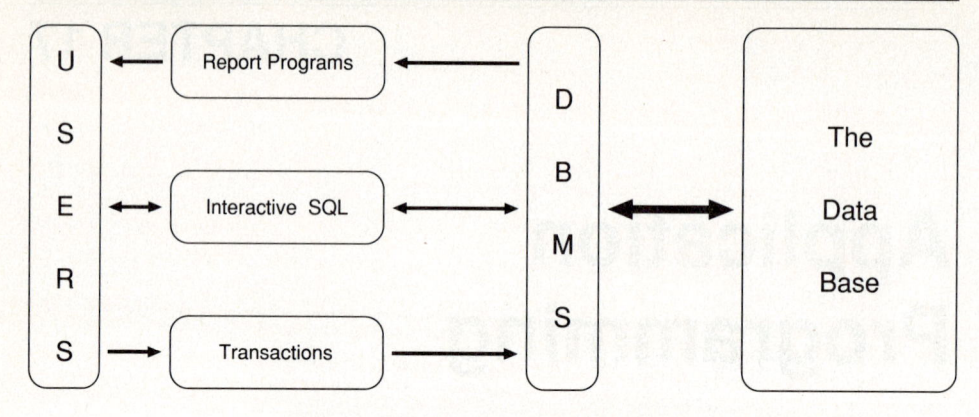

```
┌─────┐     ┌──────────────────┐
│  U  │ ←── │ Report Programs  │ ←──┐
│     │     └──────────────────┘    │   ┌─────┐                ┌──────────┐
│  S  │                              │   │  D  │                │          │
│     │                              │   │  B  │                │   The    │
│  E  │     ┌──────────────────┐     │   │  M  │ ←────────────→ │   Data   │
│     │ ←── │  Interactive SQL │ ←───┼──→│  S  │                │   Base   │
│  R  │     └──────────────────┘     │   │     │                │          │
│     │                              │   └─────┘                └──────────┘
│  S  │ ──→ │  Transactions    │ ────┘
└─────┘     └──────────────────┘
```

Figure 17.1 Modes of SQL Usage

In this chapter we will look at how these operation schemas may be turned into computer programs that use SQL retrieval statements to check the pre-conditions and SQL data manipulation statements to implement the post-conditions.

17.2 Using SQL

In all the discussion relating to SQL, it has been tacitly assumed that the user was entering queries directly by means of a keyboard, and the results were being displayed on the screen. There are three major ways in which the language may be used, as is shown in Figure 17.1.

1. There are users who *receive* reports from the system, perhaps on a daily, weekly or other regular basis, or perhaps on demand. These people might rarely use the system directly. Let us call such people managers.

2. There are people who use SQL *directly* to inspect the database by means of queries specific to their needs at the time. They may also use SQL *interactively* with the results of one query being used to trigger other queries.

3. There are people whose usage of the system is closely bound with the work they do. These people might be order entry clerks, airline reservation clerks, nurses or air traffic controllers. These people mainly *supply* information to the system.

These three groups may overlap in some systems and be quite separate in others. However, the major difference is between the direct users and the other two groups combined. Direct users need to know SQL and they need to know about the tables that make the database and the columns that make each table. They have, or are obliged to have, a simple relational view of the world represented by the information system.

Other users will have views determined by the programs with which they interact; and these views are unlikely to be simple relational ones. Hopefully, if the users have been properly consulted during the requirements analysis stage and participate in it properly, these programs will present pictures of the world as the users see it. This chapter looks at how we might construct these **non-first normal form** interfaces that provide richer views than the one provided by the database alone. In doing so, we will also implement the operation schemas that specify the programs concerned.

This chapter examines the two ways in which we can do this:

1. We can use SQL in conjunction with a conventional **third generation** procedural programming language such as COBOL or C.

2. We can use a **fourth generation** product that allows us to develop forms for each transaction and to attach **triggers** or relatively short sequences of SQL to appropriate points on a form.

17.3 Host Language Interface

17.3.1 Introduction

Third generation or procedural languages, such as COBOL and C, are flexible and multi-purpose programming tools. Millions of information systems meeting many different needs and satisfying many different kinds of users have been written in such languages. Yet they do not provide the brevity and simplicity of database access that SQL provides. Their file-handling capabilities are very limited. To overcome this problem it is common to **embed** SQL statements in programs written in languages like COBOL. In this way, we achieve a blend of the fine control provided by procedural languages with the powerful database access facilities of a query language. The SQL is said to be embedded in the **host** procedural language. The rules governing the way in which the embedding occurs is the **host language interface**. The description of the interface that follows is written in terms of a COBOL interface. Besides being a "venerable language of the '50's", COBOL is *the* most commonly used application development language *and* it is readable to people with some knowledge of programming. However, the general style of the interface is common to any of the languages, such as C, Pascal, FORTRAN and Ada, for which interfaces have been developed. The differences between them stem from the variations in the ways in which, for example, statements are separated.

In this section we will discuss the major components of the interface. These are as follows.

1. The Declare Section

   This is a part of the program set aside specifically for us to introduce any **host language variables** that are required. These variables are any program variables that are involved in an SQL statement of any kind.

2. The SQL Communications Area

   This is a record structure (group, in COBOL terms) in which the DBMS will return information regarding any SQL statement that the program attempted to execute. It will tell us whether the SQL was successful or not, and if not, then why not. An unsuccessful call to SQL will fail, typically, because no rows were found to match the condition specified.

3. Exception Handling

   Rather than having to write program code that checks for errors and other exception conditions after every call to SQL, it is possible to direct the interface to handle them.

4. Cursors

An SQL `select` statement is designed to return a set of rows in one "go", so to speak. A typical procedural language handles a set by means of a `do while` or other loop structure. The **cursor** is the way in which the host language interface handles this mismatch. It is a mechanism for releasing the results of a query to the program, one row at a time.

5. Null Values

In the datatypes used in programming languages, there is no concept of a null value. A variable declared as an integer will *always* have some integer value associated with it. Yet a row retrieved from the database, may contain null values. How are these signalled to the receiving program? The problem is overcome by introducing **indicator variables**. These are used to indicate whether or not some related variable would have received a null value, had that been possible.

17.3.2 Pre-processing

Any program that results from embedding SQL within a COBOL program is not itself a COBOL program. It cannot be compiled. Before it can, it is converted into a conventional COBOL program by a special converter program known as a **pre-processor** or **pre-compiler**. The program produced by this process contains all the COBOL code contained in the original one plus new COBOL code generated and inserted at appropriate places. After preprocessing, the normal sequence of compilation and linking is followed in producing an executable program. See Figure 17.2.

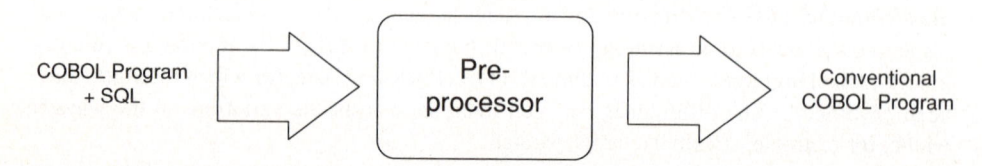

Figure 17.2 Pre-processing

The host language interface is designed to mark clearly those sections of the program that contain either embedded SQL or information relevant to the embedding. Mostly, this is achieved by having each relevant section commence with `Exec SQL` and finish with `End-exec`. The pre-processor can then concentrate solely on sections of code marked in this way, expanding them into conventional COBOL and merely transcribing the rest of the program.

17.3.3 The `Enrol` Program

This program will be used to show how the following interface features are used:

- the declare section
- the communications area
- exception handling

Application Programming 409

It is an implementation of the *Enrol* operation that was originally specified in Chapter 14. The complete program is shown at the end of this subsection. The program allows students to be enrolled in a class of study. There is only one table in the database:

```
         Students
         -----
    (*)  Id
         Last
    (?)  Mark
```

When first enrolled, a student will not yet have been awarded a mark. That is the role of some other program. A typical dialog will look like this:

```
    Enter Student Id: 831
            Last Name: Zupp

    ... enrolled
```

The program asks for the student's Id and last name. It then signals that the student has been (successfully) enrolled. Were someone now to enrol a student with the Id 831, then the dialog would look like this:

```
    Enter Student Id: 831
    The student Zupp is already enrolled.
```

If an error is encountered, for example, if someone has dropped the **Students** table, then the dialog will look like this:

```
    Enter Student Id: 831
    Too bad -- no such table or view
```

The program will then close down.

```
*  ---------------------------------------------------------------
*
*                   Enrol Transaction
*
*  This program logs on to the CLASS database, prompts the user
*  for a student Id and last name. A new row is then added to
*  the Students table.
*
*  ---------------------------------------------------------------

   Environment Division.

   Data Division.

   Working-Storage Section.

       Exec SQL Begin Declare Section End-Exec.
```

Chapter 17

```
        01  Database-Name      Pic X(12) Varying.
        01  Password           Pic X(12) Varying.

        01  Student.
            05  Id             Pic XXX.
            05  Last-Name      Pic X(10).

        Exec SQL End Declare Section End-Exec.

        Exec SQL Include SQLCA End-Exec.

Procedure Division.

Enrol-Main.

    Exec SQL whenever SQLerror Goto SQL-Error End-Exec.

Connect-to-Database.

    Move "CLASSDB" to Database-Name-Arr.
    Move 7 to Database-Name-Len.
    Move "OCHAYE" TO Password-Arr.
    Move 6 TO Password-Len.
    Exec SQL Connect :Database-Name identified by :Password End-Exec.


Get-Student-Id.

    Display "".
    Display "Enter Student Id: " with no advancing.
    Accept Id.
    Exec SQL Select Last
             Into    :Last-Name
             From    Students
             Where   Id = :Id
    End-Exec.
    If SQLcode = 0
      Then
        Display "The student ", Last-Name, " is already enrolled."
        Exec SQL rollback release End-Exec
        Stop run.


    Display "      Last Name: " with no advancing.
    Accept Last-Name.



Insert-New-Row.

    Exec SQL Insert
```

```
                Into Students(Id,Last)
                Values(:Id,:Last-Name)
    End-Exec.


    Exec SQL commit release End-Exec.
    Display "".
    Display "...enrolled.".
    Stop run.


SQL-Error.

    Display "".
    Display "Too bad -- ", SQLerrmc.
    Exec SQL whenever SQLerror continue End-Exec.
    Exec SQL rollback release End-Exec.
    Stop run.
```

17.3.4 The Declare Section

As stated previously, this is a section of the program where we introduce any host language variables that are required. These are program variables that are involved in an SQL statement of any kind. All such variables must be declared in this section. The variables required in the **Enrol** program are shown below:

```
    Exec SQL Begin Declare Section End-Exec.

    01   Database-Name     Pic X(12) Varying.
    01   Password          Pic X(12) Varying.

    01   Student.
         05   Id            Pic XXX.
         05   Last-Name     Pic X(10).

    Exec SQL End Declare Section End-Exec.
```

The **Database-Name** and **Password** variables will allow us to identify the database we want to access and the password required. The **Student** record contains two fields that allow us to supply the identity and last name of the enrolling student.

17.3.5 The SQL Communications Area

This is a record with a standard structure. It is used by the DBMS to return information regarding any SQL statement that the program attempted to execute. We can request many different services of the DBMS and the communications area must be able to deliver a corresponding variety of responses. These include error messages, warnings and information on the number of rows processed during execution of a request. The record is shown below:

```
01  SQLCA.
    05  SQLCAid         Pic X(8).
    05  SQLABC          Pic s9(9) comp.
    05  SQLcode         Pic s9(9) comp.
    05  SQLerrm.
        10  SQLerrml    Pic s9(9) comp.
        10  SQLerrmc    Pic X(70).
    05  SQLerrp         Pic X(8).
    05  SQLerrd         occurs 6 times
                        Pic s9(9) comp.
    05  SQLwarn.
        10  SQLwarn0    Pic X.
        10  SQLwarn1    Pic X.
        10  SQLwarn2    Pic X.
        10  SQLwarn3    Pic X.
        10  SQLwarn4    Pic X.
        10  SQLwarn5    Pic X.
        10  SQLwarn6    Pic X.
        10  SQLwarn7    Pic X.
    05 SQLext           Pic X(8).
```

Some of the fields are reserved for future use and others are beyond the scope of this text, and so only certain fields will be discussed here.

- **SQLcode**

    This field will tell us whether some particular use of SQL was successful or not. An unsuccessful call to SQL will fail, typically, because no rows were found to match the condition specified.

- **SQLerrmc**

    If a call does fail, then this 70-byte character string will contain the text of any relevant error message.

- **SQLwarn**

    This is a group of eight warning flags only some of which are ever used. They warn us of possibly non-fatal occurrences such as the truncation of data retrieved from the database.

17.3.6 Exception Handling

We can write program code to check for possible errors or exceptions after every call to SQL. However, we may also direct the interface to handle them automatically. Suppose that, in the event of an error, we mostly want to close down the program and exit. We can include a directive, like the following, at the start of the program's procedure division:

```
Exec SQL whenever SQLerror Goto SQL-Error End-Exec.
```

Such a directive causes the pre-processor to generate code that tests the **SQLcode** field and if it is negative then program control is transferred to the paragraph labeled **SQL-Error**.

This code is generated after every SQL call that follows the directive, and the pre-processor continues to generate it until it encounters another directive, such as the one in the `SQL-Error` paragraph itself.

```
SQL-Error.

    Display "".
    Display "Too bad -- ", SQLerrmc.
    Exec SQL whenever SQLerror continue End-Exec.
    Exec SQL rollback release End-Exec.
    Stop Run.
```

Errors are handled merely by displaying the error message returned in the field `SQLerrmc`, rolling back any changes that might have been made, releasing the database and stopping the program. However, before we rollback and release, a different error-handling directive is issued:

```
Exec SQL whenever SQLerror continue End-Exec.
```

The program will now `continue` in the event of an error. This prevents the program from getting into a loop should there be a failure in attempting to rollback and release.

```
whenever_declaration:
    WHENEVER exception action
exception:
    [SQLerror | SQLwarning | NOT FOUND]
action:
    [GOTO label | CONTINUE | STOP]
```

The interface recognizes three different exception conditions.

- **SQLerror**

    This occurs when an error (usually fatal) is detected. They are fatal because the program will not be able, sensibly, to continue. They include such events as:

    - the program being denied access to the database;
    - the table involved in a `select` statement not existing; or
    - a column involved in a `select` statement not being defined for any of the tables involved.

- **SQLwarning**

    This occurs when a non-fatal error, such as truncation, occurs.

- **NOT FOUND**

    This occurs when no rows were found (retrieved) when processing a `select` statement.

Three possible actions may be specified.

- `GOTO label`

    Program control is transferred according to the label supplied.

- `CONTINUE`

    Any errors or warnings are to be ignored. This is the action taken in programs without a `whenever` declaration.

- `STOP`

    The program is to stop without delay. This is not normally an acceptable course of action.

17.3.7 Assignment

One of the most characteristic statements in any programming language is the assignment statement, in which new values are inserted into program variables. The host language interface allows us to extract data from the database, to be inserted into one or more host variables. This is made possible by the introduction of another clause into the `select` statement. The `into` clause comes immediately after the `select` clause. The following excerpt from the `Enrol` program shows an example.

```
Get-Student-Id.

    Display "".
    Display "Enter Student Id: " with no advancing.
    Accept Id.
    Exec SQL Select Last
            Into   :Last-Name
            From   Students
            Where  Id = :Id
    End-Exec.
```

The code prompts for the Id of the enrolling student. It checks whether or not there already is someone with that Id. If there is, then that student's last name will be stored in the host variable `:Last-Name`. Note how the host language variable `Id` is distinguished from the column name `Id` by being prefixed with a colon. Outside the `Exec SQL...End-Exec` delimiters, there is no need to prefix.

---

assignment:

    SELECT *list_of_expressions*
    INTO *list_of_*:variable_name[:indicator]*s*
    FROM *list_of_table_names*
    [WHERE condition]
    [GROUP BY *list_of_expressions*
    [HAVING condition]]

17.3.8 The `SQLcode` Variable

This variable is a field in the SQL communications area. The DBMS will use it to return some indication of the success or otherwise of a request made to it. There are three values of interest.

- `SQLcode = 0`

  If a value of zero is returned then the call to SQL was successful. In the case of the above request to `select`, this means that a student with the given Id *was* found. For the `Enrol` program, this is an error, and an error message is displayed.

  ```
  If SQLcode = 0
    Then
    Display "The student ", Last-Name, " is already enrolled."
    Exec SQL rollback release End-Exec
    Stop run.
  ```

  The program then stops! Of course, it should ask if the user wants to enter another Id.

- `SQLcode = 100`

  A value of `100` is the standard indication that no rows were returned, that is, no data was found to match the `where` clause or the table was empty.

- `SQLcode < 0`

  A negative value indicates an error of some kind. These could arise because of a number of problems. The programmer does not need to check for a negative value because of the directive discussed earlier which will cause the pre-processor to generate a check for errors after every ensuing SQL statement.

17.3.9 The `ClassList` Program

The second program in this section is designed to show the following two interface features:

- how a set of rows may be retrieved and then processed under program control; and
- how null values are handled.

The program is shown at the end of this subsection. It displays, in alphabetical order, a list of all the students in the class. Apart from this, it does little more than display the letters `n/a` for students who have not been awarded a mark. Suppose the table contains the following data:

```
Students
------------------
Id    Last    Mark
------------------
831   Zupp    74
256   Bight   ?
128   Power   86
------------------
```

Chapter 17

The program will display the following class list:

```
256    Bight    n/a
128    Power    86
831    Zupp     74

End of Class List
```

```cobol
Identification Division.

Program-Id. ClassList.


* ---------------------------------------------------------------
*
*                    The CLASS Database
*
*                    Class List Report
*
* This program lists all the students in the Students table.
*
* ---------------------------------------------------------------

Environment Division.

Data Division.

Working-Storage Section.

    Exec SQL Begin Declare Section End-Exec.

    01  Database-Name     Pic X(12) varying.
    01  Password          Pic X(12) varying.

    01  Mark-Info.
        05  Mark          Pic 999.
        05  MarkInd       Pic S9(4) comp.

    01  Student-Line.
        05  Id            Pic XXX.
        05  Filler        Pic XXX     value spaces.
        05  Last-Name     Pic X(20).
        05  Filler        Pic XXX     value spaces.
        05  Show-Mark     Pic ZZ9.
        05  SM redefines Show-Mark.
            10  No-Mark   Pic XXX.

    Exec SQL End Declare Section End-Exec.

    Exec SQL Include SQLCA End-Exec.
```

```
Procedure Division.

ClassList-Main.

    Exec SQL whenever SQLerror Goto SQL-Error End-Exec.

Connect-to-Database.

    Move "CLASSDB" to Database-Name-Arr.
    Move 7 to Database-Name-Len.
    Move "OCHAYE" TO Password-Arr.
    Move 6 TO Password-Len.
    Exec SQL Connect :Database-Name identified by :Password End-Exec.

    Exec SQL Declare cursor S for
            Select   Id, Last, Mark
            From     Students
            Order by Last
    End-Exec.

    Exec SQL Open S
    End-Exec.

    Exec SQL Fetch S into :Id, :Last-Name, :Mark:MarkInd
    End-Exec.

    Perform until SQLcode = 100

      If MarkInd is not = -1
         then
         Move Mark to Show-Mark
         else
         Move "n/a" to No-Mark
      End-If

      Display Student-Line
      Exec SQL Fetch S into :Id,:Last-Name, :Mark:MarkInd
      End-Exec

    End-Perform.

    Close S.
    Exec SQL commit release End-Exec.
    Display "".
    Display "End of Class List".
    Stop run.

SQL-Error.
```

```
Display "".
Display Too bad -- ", SQLerrmc.
Exec SQL whenever SQLerror continue End-Exec.
Exec SQL rollback release End-Exec.
Stop run.
```

17.3.10 Cursors

An SQL `select` statement will return a *set* of rows. In contrast, a procedural language handles a set by looping under the control of a `do while` or other loop structure. In COBOL, the loop structure is the `Perform End-Perform`. The `cursor` is the mechanism by which the host language interface handles this mismatch. It releases the results of a query to the program, one row at a time.

The `ClassList` program is intended to produce, in alphabetical order, a list of all the students in the class and any mark they may have been awarded. A cursor is associated with the appropriate `select` statement.

```
Exec SQL Declare cursor S for
         Select   Id, Last, Mark
         From     Students
         Order by Last
End-Exec.
```

A cursor, `S`, is declared and linked to a query. However, the query is not executed until the cursor is **opened**. Once the cursor is open, the result rows are made available to the program, one at a time, by means of a `fetch` statement. This new command is only available as part of the host language interface. The cycle of fetch and display is shown below:

```
Exec SQL Open S
End-Exec.

Exec SQL Fetch S into :Id, :Last-Name, :Mark:MarkInd
End-Exec.

Perform until SQLcode = 100

  If MarkInd is not = -1
     then
     Move Mark to Show-Mark
     else
     Move "n/a" to No-Mark
  End-If

  Display Student-Line
  Exec SQL Fetch S into :Id,:Last-Name, :Mark:MarkInd
  End-Exec
```

```
                End-Perform.

            Close S.
```

The first row is fetched outside the loop, which is then repeatedly performed until the **SQLcode** variable contains **100** which indicates that the most recent **fetch** statement was unable to be satisfied. The cursor is then closed. It may be opened again later in the program, if required.

```
        fetch_statement:
                FETCH cursor_name
                INTO  list_of_:variable_name[:indicator]s
```

When the cursor is declared, it is associated with a particular **select** statement. The order in which host variables are listed in a **fetch** should match the **select** clause of that **select** statement.

```
        cursor_declaration:
                DECLARE CURSOR cursor_name FOR
                select_statement
```

17.3.11 Indicator Variables

In the **Students** table, the **Mark** attribute may be null, as some students may not yet have received one. The program must deal with these students slightly differently. They require that **n/a**, for "not applicable", appear instead of a number. The **fetch** statement must be instructed to indicate when a null value is returned. It can do this because it is supplied with an **indicator** variable. This special variable is piggy-backed onto the **Mark** host variable in the form **:Mark:MarkInd**.

```
                Exec SQL Fetch S into :Id,:Last-Name, :Mark:MarkInd
                End-Exec
```

This instructs the **fetch** statement to set the **MarkInd** according to the value found in the **Mark** attribute. The settings are as follows.

- **MarkInd = -1**

    This indicates that a null value was found in the **Mark** column for that student.

- **MarkInd = 0**

    This indicates that a normal mark was found.

- `MarkInd > 0`

   A positive value indicates that some kind of truncation was performed. This would be the case if the host language variable `Mark` was not large enough to hold the student's mark.

The code within the loop then checks to see whether a null mark was fetched and displays the student information accordingly.

```
If MarkInd is not = -1
   then
   Move Mark to Show-Mark
   else
   Move "n/a" to No-Mark
End-If
```

We can attach an indicator variable to all or any of the host variables used in a `fetch` statement. Indicator variables should be declared as two-byte integer fields.

17.4 Form-based Application Development

17.4.1 Transaction Processing

In the development of any new information system, a large amount of effort is spent in specifying and writing **transaction processing** programs. These are programs that update the information system, in particular, the database, to reflect changes in the situation modeled by the information system. They have developed a well-defined style, being screen-based and interactive. The user is presented with a fixed layout or form on which the details of the transaction will be displayed. The transaction follows a common pattern.

1. There is a set-up stage during which the user specifies the input. The program will validate user input and warn of any errors detected.

2. Once the user is satisfied with the set-up, then he or she signals that the transaction should go ahead. If the input values are valid, then the database will be updated accordingly.

3. However, it may be that either the user is unable to satisfy the program or, possibly, the user decides to abandon the transaction.

Here is an example of how an event, such as enrolling a student in a class, may be entered into the database. The user will enrol the student by filling out a form like the one shown below.

```
          The Class Information System

              Enrollment Operation

           Id:    ┌──────────────┐
                  │ 871          │
                  └──────────────┘
           Last:  ┌──────────────┐
                  │ Zupp         │
                  └──────────────┘
```

The user will normally follow the layout of the form and enter data into the two fields in a top-to-bottom flow.

1. The **Id** field

   When the user enters the Id of an enrolling student, the program will look up the database to establish whether or not a student with this Id is already enrolled. If someone is, then an error message is displayed and the user will have to correct the Id or abort the entire transaction.

2. The **Last** field

   Once an acceptable Id has been entered, the program will take the user on to the last name field, for which no particular checks are likely to be made.

The user may then be satisfied with the data entered and signal that the transaction should be accepted, in which case, a new row will be inserted into the **Class** table. Alternatively, upon checking the data, the user may realize that mistakes have been made, for example, the last name may have been misspelt. If so the user may move back, change the mistake or mistakes and then signal that the transaction is complete.

The need for programs that operate in this way is so great that a class of development tools called **application generators** has arisen. These tools allow form-based programs to be generated rapidly.

17.4.2 Using Forms

Before looking at how we might build a form program, we should have a clear picture of how the form is presented to its user and how the user **fills** it in, because these programs are a continuation and an extension of the paper forms that we are all obliged to complete at most stages in our lives.

There is a certain appearance common to most forms.

- There will be a number of questions to be answered.
- These questions will be presented in the sequence that seems the most natural for the information to be entered.
- Each question will be numbered and there will be a small "prompt" indicating the kind of information to be entered with an appropriate amount of space for the answer.

- There will be notes to help us with individual questions and with the form as a whole.

Doing the Deed

Having established that we can fill it out or that we will die in the attempt, we answer the questions as best we can, perhaps returning to earlier questions to amend our original answer, perhaps skipping forwards because we are unable to work out what the question means.

Now we (should) scan the form to check it as a whole and then submit it. Alternatively, we screw it up into a ball and throw it away, perhaps starting a new form, perhaps not.

Office Use Only

There will, inevitably, be a part of the form marked "Office Use Only". We view this section with a mixture of relief and suspicion. We are pleased that this is something that we don't have to answer; yet we are concerned as to the meaning of the various cryptic codes that appear there, such as `OMDB` or `NOYL`.

This part is used by the bureaucrats in two ways.

1. It is used to check that the form has been filled in correctly, that all claims have been verified.

2. It is used to note that the appropriate changes have been recorded and dealt with, or to record how far through the bureaucratic process the form has reached.

In other words, it is used to check the pre-conditions and implement the post-conditions, or to monitor their implementation.

17.4.3 Using Automated Forms

Filling out an electronic form involves *essentially* the same actions as completing a paper one. See Figure 17.3.

1. The monitor or screen takes the place of the paper.

2. The keyboard (or mouse, etc.) takes the place of the pen or pencil.

3. There will be a **cursor** on the screen to indicate the current position of the "tip" of the pencil, that is, where the next item of input will appear.

4. There will be a number of form navigation and control keys.

5. We will be presented with a series of questions. Each question will involve, typically, a small label or prompt and a data entry area.

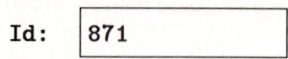

    Id: 871

    The data entry area will be called a **field**. The label will be used to identify the field.

6. Some of the fields will be mandatory and some will be optional.

7. Some of the fields will be used for display purposes only. These allow the user access to information that will assist them in the transaction but which should not be changed.

8. The data to be entered in a field will be of a certain type or **format** such as a date or a name or a money amount.

9. A default value may be placed in a field by the program. This will be the most commonly used value for that field, thus reducing the keystrokes required by the user who may skip over the field.
10. There will be an area for the program to send messages to the user. These messages may describe errors in input or information about the kind of data that should be placed in the current field, or help on using the form.

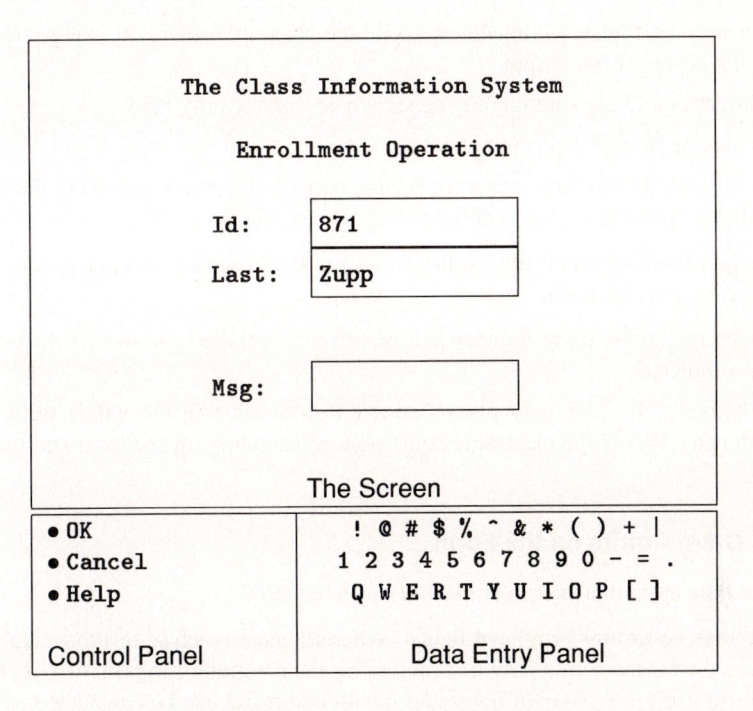

```
             The Class Information System

                 Enrollment Operation

             Id:    [ 871 ]

             Last:  [ Zupp ]


             Msg:   [      ]

                       The Screen
```

• OK	! @ # $ % ^ & * ( ) + |
• Cancel	1 2 3 4 5 6 7 8 9 0 - = .
• Help	Q W E R T Y U I O P [ ]
Control Panel	Data Entry Panel

Figure 17.3 An electronic form

There is a section of the keyboard that can be likened to the control panel of any machine, such as a car. On some computer systems this control panel may take the form of a "soft" panel located on the screen and activated by a mouse.

For electronic forms we use this control panel for activities such as the following.

- **Rubout** to erase or undo the most recently pressed data key.
- **Blank** to start a field over again.
- **Next** and **Previous Field** to allow users to navigate the form.
- **Next** and **Previous Page** to move between the pages of a multi-page form.
- **Help** as a token gesture to the user interface.
- **OK** to indicate that the form has been completed to our satisfaction.
- **Cancel** to abandon the transaction entirely.

These control keys may not be marked as such, appearing as the function keys **F1**, **F2**, and so on, or as `Ctrl`, `Alt` or `Shift` in conjunction with some other key, for example, `Ctrl-U`.

Office Use Only

The major difference between a hand-filled paper form and an electronic form is here. A paper form is completed *off-line*, that is, away from the bureaucracy that will process it. The electronic form is *on-line*, that is, its completion is being supervised by a computer program. The consequences are as follows.

1. Errors may be detected immediately, with the program refusing to budge from a field until it receives correct input.
2. Confirmation of data entered may be shown on display only fields.
3. Help may be brought up automatically.
4. Lists of currently correct values for a field may be shown on request in the form of a **pick list** with the user able to choose a value from the list.

Once the user has entered all the required data and the program has approved it, then two distinct actions may be taken.

1. The user may press `OK` to indicate that he or she is satisfied and wishes the transaction to be completed.
2. Alternatively, the user may press `Cancel` to indicate that the whole thing is to be abandoned. This is the electronic equivalent of screwing up the form and throwing it away.

17.4.4 Other Points on the Form

A form will be more than a string of individual data fields.

- There may be groups of related fields. When the user reaches, or more likely leaves, a group then some action may be required by the computer program driving the form. The form itself is a group of fields and the `OK` command can be considered as a signal, from the user, that he or she has finished that group.
- There may be sets of fields or sets of groups, upon which reaching or leaving, some action may be required by the program.

The structure of the form and the data fields it contains may best be described by means of the BNF language introduced in Chapter 9. The **Enrollment** screen may be summarized by the following definition:

```
Enrollment ::= Id + Last
```

According to this definition, there are two data fields involved in enrolling a student. The fields and their manner of use may be summarized in a **Field Usage** table.

\multicolumn{4}{c}{Enrollment Field Usage}
Field	Usage	Format	Default
Id	Entry, mandatory	integer	
Last	Entry, mandatory	name	

The kind of information about a field that may appear in the columns is summarized below.

Usage

This indicates whether the field is to be used for data entry (by the user) and, if so, whether the user must enter some data (mandatory) or whether the field may be skipped (optional). There are three kinds of usage.

Usage	Purpose
Entry	for the entry of data
Display	for fields to be used, *by the program*, to display information to the user
Hidden	for fields that will contain data relevant to the workings of the transaction, but which need not, or perhaps should not, concern the user

Format

This column indicates the kind of data that may be entered, or displayed, in the field. Typical formats are:

Format	Allowable Keystrokes
Integer	a sequence of digits
Money	a sequence of digits followed by a period (full stop) followed by two more digits
Date	a valid date, perhaps with a further restriction of the kind of date, for example, `YYMMDD` or `DD-MON-YY`
Time	a valid time, also perhaps with a variety of options
Name	for moderately sized character strings such as might be required to represent someone's name
Text	for arbitrarily sized blocks of text, perhaps giving access to word-processing facilities

A format is similar to, but not quite the same as, a datatype. It indicates a kind of syntactic filter that permits certain keystrokes and disallows others. These format filters are provided by the application generator and relieve the programmer of considerable effort. The programmer merely has to specify the kind of format required.

Default

This is a preset value automatically inserted into the field by the program. It is useful when there is one particularly common value for the field, for example, the city center postcode for a postcode field.

17.4.5 Triggered Actions

So far, we have only specified some superficial checks that the form program must make. For the **Enrollment** form, for example, we have only required that the Id be an integer and that the last name be a name. Now we need to connect the form to the database, both to do some integrity checking and to add the new student to the class. We specify this extra activity by associating actions with appropriate points on the form. For example, we might require that the program, on receiving an Id from the user, checks that no enrolled student has that particular Id. These actions are triggered whenever the user passes through that point and are often called **triggers** for that reason.

The actions that are required may be summarized in a **Form Action** table.

<table>
<tr><td colspan="3" align="center">Enrollment
Form Action Table</td></tr>
<tr><td>**Position**</td><td>**Structure**</td><td>**Action**</td></tr>
<tr><td>Start of Form</td><td></td><td></td></tr>
<tr><td></td><td>Id
+ Last</td><td>CheckId</td></tr>
<tr><td>End of Form</td><td></td><td>AddStudent</td></tr>
</table>

There are two actions. One is triggered when the Id is entered; the other when the user signals that the transaction is `OK`. The details of these actions are shown below.

- The `CheckId` Action

  The `Class` table is checked to ensure that no student with the given Id is currently enrolled.

  1. Check the table retrieving the student's last name if possible.

     ```
     Select Last
     Into   :Last
     From   Class
     Where  Id = :Id
     ```

     If no row was returned then the user's input is valid and the user may proceed to the next field. If data was retrieved, then a student with the same Id as the one entered (`:Id`) is already enrolled. That student's last name is now displayed in the `Last` field. An error message should be displayed and the user can either enter the correct Id or abandon the transaction.

- The `AddStudent` Action

  This action is taken when the user signals that he or she is satisfied that the data on the screen is valid *and* complete.

  1. Add a new row to the `Class` table.

     ```
     Insert
     Into   Class(Id, Last)
     Values(:Id,:Last)
     ```

17.4.6 Awarding a Mark

This form allows a mark to be awarded to a student and is an implementation of the *AwardMark* operation of Chapter 14.

```
┌─────────────────────────────────────────────┐
│         The Class Information System        │
│                                             │
│              Award Operation                │
│                                             │
│          Id:     ┌──────────┐               │
│                  │   871    │               │
│                  └──────────┘               │
│          Last:   ┌──────────┐               │
│                  │   Zupp   │               │
│                  └──────────┘               │
│                                             │
│          Mark:   ┌──────────┐               │
│                  │    55    │               │
│                  └──────────┘               │
│                                             │
└─────────────────────────────────────────────┘
```

In a typical successful transaction, the user will enter the student's Id; the program will respond with the student's last name as confirmation; and the user will then enter that student's mark.

The structure of the form is as follows.

```
AwardForm ::= Id + Last + Mark
```

Award Field Usage

Field	Usage	Format	Default
Id	Entry, mandatory	integer	
Last	Display	name	
Mark	Entry, mandatory	integer	

Award Form Action Table

Position	Structure	Action
Start of Form		
	Id	GetStudent
	+ Last	
	+ Mark	CheckMark
End of Form		AwardMark

- The `GetStudent` Action

    1. Retrieve the student's record and move his or her name and any mark awarded onto the screen.

        ```
        Select Last, Mark
        Into   :Last,:Mark
        From   Class
        Where  Id = :Id
        ```

    2. Check that the student has not already been awarded a mark.

        ```
        :Mark is null
        ```

- The `CheckMark` Action

    1. Check that the mark is in the range 0 to 100. This will take place *after* the user has keyed something into this field.

        `:Mark between 0 and 100`

- The `AwardMark` Action

    1. Update the student's record.

        ```
        Update Class
           Set Mark = :Mark
           Where Id = :Id
        ```

17.5 Summary

When a transaction is specified by an operation schema, no constraints are placed upon how we might implement that specification. Nor is any guidance given. In this chapter we have seen two quite contrasting ways by which a program may be built to meet a given specification.

- We may embed the necessary SQL within the framework of a conventional third generation programming language such as COBOL.
- We may employ an application development package which allows us to create a form-based program saving us from much of the work involved in the user interface and where the SQL is attached to appropriate places on the form.

Exercises

Q17.1   Amend a mark

The following form allows an existing mark to be amended. It is an implementation of the *AmendMark* operation.

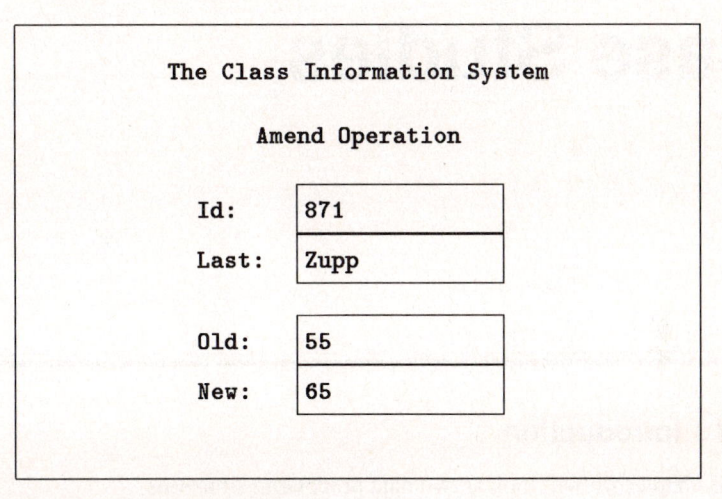

```
              The Class Information System

                    Amend Operation

           Id:    871

           Last:  Zupp


           Old:   55

           New:   65
```

  a.   Define the structure of the form.
  b.   Specify a Field Usage Table for the form.
  c.   Specify a Form Action Table for the form.

Q17.2   A student drops out

This form removes a student from the class. It is an implementation of the *DropOut* operation.

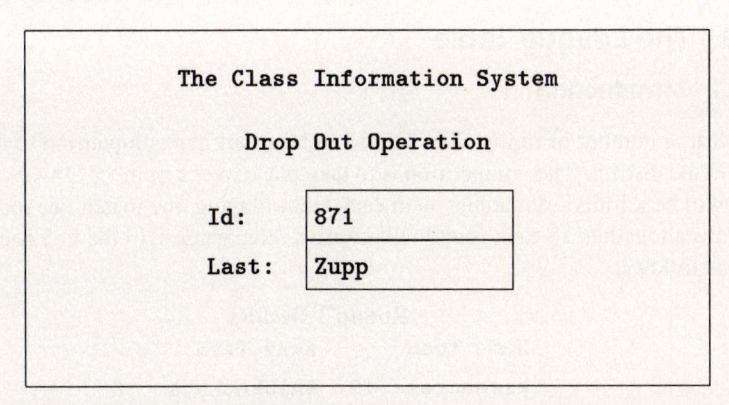

```
              The Class Information System

                    Drop Out Operation

           Id:    871

           Last:  Zupp
```

  a.   Define the structure of the form.
  b.   Specify a Field Usage Table for the form.
  c.   Specify a Form Action Table for the form.

CHAPTER 18

Case Studies

18.1 Introduction

In this chapter we will look at two data processing situations.

- The first situation involves deriving a compact yet complex report or view from some simple data.
- The second situation involves monitoring the handling of orders made on a small manufacturer.

For both situations, we will (1) present an informal introduction, (2) describe it formally, and (3) look at an implementation in SQL.

18.2 The League Table

18.2.1 Introduction

Last year, a number of rugby clubs agreed to take part in a competition to decide the best team in the district. The competition is to take place over a number of weeks. Every week there will be a round of matches with each team playing one match per round. There are six clubs altogether, so each round will involve three games. In the first round, the results were as follows:

```
              Round 1 Results
       Home Team        Away Team
       Wiseacres   12   Shinhackers    8
       Rosewell     8   Witsend       20
       Rovers       5   Jeeps          5
```

The convention about presenting results is that the home team and its score are given first and the away team and its score second. Each team will play all the others twice, once at home and once away. This helps eliminate any bias resulting from the home team's ground advantage.

After each round, the results are added to the results recorded previously and a summary table is produced. This table shows the relative standing of each team. After round 1, the table looked like this:

Team	Wins	Losses	Draws	For	Against	Points
Witsend	1	0	0	20	8	2
Wiseacres	1	0	0	12	8	2
Jeeps	0	0	1	5	5	1
Rovers	0	0	1	5	5	1
Shinhackers	0	1	0	8	12	0
Rosewell	0	1	0	8	20	0

Each column in the table provides a specific piece of summary information regarding a team's performance for the competition so far. The meaning of each column is as follows.

`Wins`   The total number of matches that the corresponding team has won in the competition so far. For example, after round 1, both Witsend and Wiseacres have had a total of 1 win so far. They were the only victorious teams in the first round, so all the other have had 0 wins.

`Losses`   The total number of matches that the team has lost so far in the competition. Only Shinhackers and Rosewell have lost at all, so they have lost a total of 1 match; all the others have lost 0 matches.

`Draws`   A draw occurs when each team scores the same number of points in a game. This column indicates the total number of drawn matches involving the team in question. Jeeps and Rovers drew their first match, so they have a total of 1 draw so far.

`For`   This column shows the total number of points scored by the team in all its matches so far. It is the total points counting **for** the team. For example, Witsend scored 20 points in its first round game and so has scored a total of 20 points in all its (one) matches.

`Against`   This column shows the total number of points scored by other teams **against** this particular team. For example, Witsend had 8 points scored against it in its round 1 match, so its total against is also 8.

`Points`   This column shows the total number of **merit** points awarded to each team as a result of its performance in the competition so far. It is these merit points that primarily determine the ranking of each team in the competition and the eventual winner. The merit points are awarded according to the following rules:

      2 merit points are given for each game *won* by a team;

      1 point is awarded for each *drawn* game;

      no points are awarded for a *lost* game.

Both Witsend and Wiseacres have won once and drawn no times; so they both have a total of 2 merit points. Jeeps and Rovers drew their first match, and so have 1 merit point each.

Conventionally, the summary table is presented in order of merit. The team with the most merit points is shown first, the second best team next, and so on. Where two or more teams have the same number of merit points, these teams are ranked according to the *difference* between the team's `For` and `Against` columns. For example, after round 1, both Witsend and Wiseacres have 2 merit points; but, for Witsend, `For` - `Against` = 20 - 8 = 12 and for Wiseacres, `For` - `Against` = 12 - 8 = 4 and so Witsend is placed ahead of Wiseacres in the summary table.

```
                  Round 2 Results
        Home Team          Away Team
        Witsend      25    Shinhackers   6
        Jeeps        10    Wiseacres     0
        Rosewell      6    Rovers        6
```

The status of each team after two rounds can be seen in the updated summary table:

```
        Team           Wins    Losses   Draws    For    Against   Points

        Witsend         2        0        0       45      14        4
        Jeeps           1        0        1       15       5        3
        Rovers          0        0        2       11      11        2
        Wiseacres       1        1        0       12      18        2
        Rosewell        0        1        1       14      26        1
        Shinhackers     0        2        0       14      37        0
```

Witsend has won both its matches and is the only team to have done so. It now tops the "ladder" with 4 merit points. Witsend won its latest match by 25 points to 6 and so has $20 + 25 = 45$ points in total for and $8 + 6 = 14$ against. Jeeps has won one match and drawn the other; so it now has 3 merit points. Wiseacres and Rovers have 2 merit points each, but Rovers is placed ahead because its `For` - `Against` difference is $11 - 11 = 0$ whereas it is $12 - 18 = -6$ for Wiseacres.

18.2.2 Defining the League

The league simply consists of a set of teams and the results of matches played between these teams. We will use the following basic types.

Type   **Interpretation**

[*Team*]   The set of teams that *may* participate in the tournament.

[*N*]   The set of integers 0,1,2,3,...

We will also use a schema type to represent the result of a game.

```
┌─ Result ────────────────────────────────────────
│ round : N
│ home, away : Team
│ hscore, ascore : N
├─────────────────────────────────────────────────
│ home ≠ away
└─────────────────────────────────────────────────
```

A result consists of the home and away teams, their scores, and the round in which the game was played. The only constraint is that a team cannot play against itself.

Now we can present a schema that outlines the state of the competition at any moment.

```
┌─ League ────────────────────────────────────────
│ Teams : Set of Team
│ Results : Set of Result
├─────────────────────────────────────────────────
│ ∀ r : Results • r.home ∈ Teams
│ ∀ r : Results • r.away ∈ Teams
│ ∀ r, s : Results • (r.round = s.round ∧ r.home = s.home) ⇒ r = s
│ ∀ r, s : Results • (r.round = s.round ∧ r.away = s.away) ⇒ r = s
│ ∀ rnd : {r : Results • r.round}
│            {r : Results | r.round = rnd • r.home} ∩
│            {r : Results | r.round = rnd • r.away} = {}
└─────────────────────────────────────────────────
```

The *League* Declaration

1. *Teams : Set of Team*
   There is a particular set of teams involved in the competition;
2. *Results : Set of Result*
   and there is a set of results.

The rules relating these teams and these results are given in the predicate.

The *League* Predicate

1. ∀ r : Results • r.home ∈ Teams
   ∀ r : Results • r.away ∈ Teams
   All the home teams must be rugby teams participating in the tournament; and so must all the away teams.
2. ∀ r, s : Results • (r.round = s.round ∧ r.home = s.home) ⇒ r = s
   No two results in the same round have the same home team.
3. ∀ r, s : Results • (r.round = s.round ∧ r.away = s.away) ⇒ r = s
   No two results in the same round have the same away team.
4. ∀ rnd : {r : Results • r.round}

434   Chapter 18

In any given round, say *rnd*, no team played both home and away. For that round, the set of teams that played at home does not overlap with the set of teams that played away.

18.2.3 Adding New Results

We should specify the operation of adding new results to the set of results posted so far.

AddResult

Δ *League*
$r?$: *Result*

$r?.home \in Teams$
$r?.away \in Teams$
$\neg \exists r : Results \bullet r.round = r?.round \land$
$\qquad (r.home = r?.home \lor r.away = r?.home)$
$\neg \exists r : Results \bullet r.round = r?.round \land$
$\qquad (r.home = r?.away \land r.away = r?.away$
$Results' = Results \cup \{r?\}$
$Teams' = Teams$

The interpretation of this schema is as follows.

The *AddResult* Declaration

1. Δ *League*
   This operation changes the league state.
2. $r?$: *Result*
   The result being added is input as a result record $r?$. This means that there will be variables $r?.round$ for the round, $r?.home$ for the home team, and so on. Note that the definition of *Result* requires that $r?.home \neq r?.away$.

The *AddResult* Predicate

1. $r?.home \in Teams$
   $r?.away \in Teams$
   Both teams must be registered with the league.
2. $\neg \exists r : Results \bullet r.round = r?.round \land$
   $(r.home = r?.home \lor r.away = r?.home)$
   There is no other result for the home team in this round.
3. $\neg \exists r : Results \bullet r.round = r?.round \land$
   $(r.home = r?.away \lor r.away = r?.away)$
   There is no other result for the away team in this round.
4. $Results' = Results \cup \{r?\}$
   The new result is added to the results recorded so far.

5. $Teams' = Teams$
   No teams enters or leaves the competition.

18.2.4 Producing a Summary Table

Now we can specify how each team's position on the ladder is to be calculated. To do this, we can introduce a record type that summarizes a team's performance in the competition so far.

―― *Summary* ――――――――――――――――――――――――――
$team : Team$
$wins, draws, losses,$
$for, against, pts : \mathbb{N}$
――――――――――――――――――――――――――――――

This record matches a line on the summary table.

The following schema specifies how the summary table, which is a set of *Summary* records, is to be formed.

―― *ShowTable* ――――――――――――――――――――――――――
$\Xi League$
$ladder! : Set\ of\ Summary$
――――――――――――――――――――――――――――――
$\{t : ladder! \bullet t.team\} = Teams$
$\forall t : ladder! \bullet$
$\quad t.wins = \#\{r : Results \mid (t.team = r.home \land r.hscore > r.ascore) \lor$
$\qquad (t.team = r.away \land r.ascore > r.hscore)\}$
$\quad t.draws = \#\{r : Results \mid r.hscore = r.ascore \land$
$\qquad (r.home = t.team \lor r.away = t.team)\}$
$\quad t.losses = \#\{r : Results \mid (t.team = r.home \land r.hscore < r.ascore) \lor$
$\qquad (t.team = r.away \land r.ascore < r.hscore)\}$
$\quad t.for = \Sigma(r : Results \mid t.team = r.home \bullet r.hscore)$
$\qquad +\Sigma(r : Results \mid t.team = r.away \bullet r.ascore)$
$\quad t.against = \Sigma(r : Results \mid t.team = r.away \bullet r.hscore)$
$\qquad +\Sigma(r : Results \mid t.team = r.home \bullet r.ascore)$
$\quad t.pts = 2 * t.wins + t.draws$
――――――――――――――――――――――――――――――

The interpretation of this schema is as follows.

The *ShowTable* Declaration

1. $\Xi League$
   Producing the ladder involves an examination of the current state of the league. No changes are involved.

2. $ladder! : Set\ of\ Summary$
   This operation produces the summary table or ladder which shows the status of each team in the competition.

The *ShowTable* Predicate

1. $\{t : ladder! \bullet t.team\} = Teams$
   Just those teams in the league have an entry in the ladder.

2. $\forall t : ladder! \bullet$
   All status records in the ladder are to be defined in the following way:

3. $t.wins = \#\{r : Results \mid (t.team = r.home \land r.hscore > r.ascore) \lor (t.team = r.away \land r.ascore > r.hscore)\}$
   The number of times that a team has won can be determined by counting the number of results in which either the team played at home and the home team won ($t.team = r.home \land r.hscore > r.ascore$) *or* the team played away and the away team won ($t.team = r.away \land r.ascore > r.hscore$).

4. $t.draws = \#\{r : Results \mid r.hscore = r.ascore \land (r.home = t.team \lor r.away = t.team)\}$
   The number of drawn games in which a team has been involved can be found by counting the number of results in which the both teams had the same score ($r.hscore = r.ascore$) *and* the team in question ($t.team$) was one of the participating teams ($r.home = t.team \lor r.away = t.team$).

5. $t.losses = \#\{r : Results \mid (t.team = r.home \land r.hscore < r.ascore) \lor (t.team = r.away \land r.ascore < r.hscore)\}$
   The number of losses is the number of results in which the team has played at home and the home team has lost *or* the team has played away and the away team has lost.

6. $t.for = \Sigma(r : Results \mid t.team = r.home \bullet r.hscore)$
   $+ \Sigma(r : Results \mid t.team = r.away \bullet r.ascore)$
   The total number of points scored by a team is the sum of all the points scored by the team at home plus the sum of all the points scored in away games.

7. $t.against = \Sigma(r : Results \mid t.team = r.away \bullet r.hscore)$
   $+ \Sigma(r : Results \mid t.team = r.home \bullet r.ascore)$
   The total number of points scored against a team is obtained by calculating the total number of points scored against that team while playing at home ($\Sigma(r : Results \mid t.team = r.away \bullet r.hscore)$) and adding to that the total number of points scored against that team when playing away.

8. $t.pts = 2 * t.wins + t.draws$
   The total number of merit points may be calculated from the total number of wins and draws.

18.2.5 The League Database

We will create two tables, one for the teams participating in the competition and another to keep a record of all the results so far.

```
Create Table Teams
         (TeamId   Char(12) not null)
```

This table provides us with a list of the teams participating in the competition.

```
Teams
-----------
TeamId
-----------
Jeeps
Rosewell
Rovers
Shinhackers
Wiseacres
Witsend
-----------
```

The second table will contain a row for each result.

```
Create Table Results
        (Round   Integer     not null,
         Home    Char(12)    not null,
         Hscore  Integer     not null,
         Away    Char(12)    not null,
         Ascore  Integer     not null)
```

The `Results` table seems a natural way of representing the raw data that will eventuate from each game played. After two rounds the table will look like the following.

```
Results
-----------------------------------------------------
Round   Home            Hscore    Away           Ascore
-----------------------------------------------------
  1     Wiseacres         12      Shinhackers      8
  1     Rosewell           8      Witsend         20
  1     Rovers             5      Jeeps            5
  2     Witsend           25      Shinhackers      6
  2     Jeeps             10      Wiseacres        0
  2     Rosewell           6      Rovers           6
-----------------------------------------------------
```

However, there are difficulties with the table. Suppose we try to process the results for an individual team. That team, it is likely, will have played some games at home and some away. To find out how many games `Witsend` have won we can try the following SQL.

```
Select  count(*)
From    Results
Where   (Home = 'Witsend'
         and
         Hscore > Ascore)
or      (Away = 'Witsend'
         and
         Ascore > Hscore)
```

```
--------
count(*)
--------
   2
--------
```

In general, a team may, like `Witsend`, have won games both at home and away.

To find out the total `For` is more difficult. Witsend have scored 45 points but this is calculated by adding the 20 points from their round 1 away match to the 25 points from their round 2 home game. Suppose we try this:

```
Select    sum(Hscore) + sum(Ascore)
From      Results
Where     Home = 'Witsend'
   or     Away = 'Witsend'
```

The query will perform the following calculations:

```
sum(Hscore) =  8 + 25 = 33
sum(Ascore) = 20 +  6 = 26
                        --
                        59
```

This is clearly incorrect. What we have calculated is the total points scored in all the matches in which Witsend have been involved. This total includes points scored by both Witsend *and* their opponents. What we need is a view that places a team in one slot, so to speak. The following table shows what is meant.

```
ForAgin
-----------------------------------------------
Round   TeamId         ForScore    AginScore
-----------------------------------------------
  1     Wiseacres          12           8
  1     Shinhackers         8          12
  1     Rosewell            8          20
  1     Witsend            20           8
  1     Rovers              5           5
  1     Jeeps               5           5
  2     Witsend            25           6
  2     Shinhackers         6          25
  2     Jeeps              10           0
  2     Wiseacres           0          10
  2     Rosewell            6           6
  2     Rovers              6           6
-----------------------------------------------
```

Each match result, that is, each row in the `Results` table, will give rise to two rows in this view showing the scores for and against each team. Each row in the view provides information on just *one* team. The view can be defined as follows:

```
Create View ForAgin(Round, Team, ForScore, AginScore)
as
Select  Round, Home, Hscore, Ascore
From    Results
Union
Select  Round, Away, Ascore, Hscore
From    Results
```

The required doubling up is achieved by processing the entire `Results` table twice and merging the resulting rows with a union operation. The view may be usefully manipulated with a **group by** clause. Suppose we were to group by the `TeamId`. The view will be partitioned as follows:

```
ForAgin
-------------------------------------------------
Round   TeamId          ForScore    AginScore
-------------------------------------------------
1       Jeeps               5           5
2       Jeeps              10           0

1       Shinhackers         8          12
2       Shinhackers         6          25

1       Rosewell            8          20
2       Rosewell            6           6

1       Rovers              5           5
2       Rovers              6           6

1       Wiseacres          12           8
2       Wiseacres           0          10

1       Witsend            20           8
2       Witsend            25           6
-------------------------------------------------
```

We can use the view to give us two of the columns of the summary table.

```
Select   TeamId, sum(ForScore), sum(AginScore)
From     ForAgin
Group by TeamId

-------------------------------------------------
TeamId       sum(ForScore)    sum(AginScore)
-------------------------------------------------
Jeeps             15                 5
Shinhackers       14                37
Rosewell          14                26
Rovers            11                11
Wiseacres         12                18
Witsend           45                14
-------------------------------------------------
```

This satisfies the specification regarding the calculation of the **For** and **Against** columns of the summary table. Although each of these columns was defined as the addition of two separate summations, we have reduced that to one. We might expect to be able to use this view to calculate the other columns of the summary table. To find the number of wins by Witsend, we could write:

```
Select    count(*)
From      ForAgin
Where     TeamId = 'Witsend'
and       ForScore > AginScore
```

```
--------
count(*)
--------
   2
--------
```

This gives us the correct answer, but not for all teams:

```
Select    TeamId, count(*)
From      ForAgin
Where     ForScore > AginScore
Group by  TeamId
```

```
----------------------
TeamId         count(*)
----------------------
Jeeps             1
Wiseacres         1
Witsend           2
----------------------
```

The other three teams make no appearance. Their rows in **ForAgin** were excluded by the **where** clause. We can overcome this problem by simply "adding" in these three teams by means of a union operation.

```
          union
          Select    TeamId, 0
          From      Teams
          Where     TeamId not in (Select TeamId
                                   From    ForAgin
                                   Where   ForScore > AginScore)
```

The subquery returns the teams that have won at least one match. The outer query goes through the list of all teams and returns each team that is not in the list of winners.

```
        --------------------
        Rosewell          0
        Rovers            0
        Shinhackers       0
        --------------------
```

Now we can create a view that counts the number of wins achieved by each team.

```
Create View WinSum(TeamId, Wins)
as
Select    TeamId, count(*)
From      ForAgin
Where     ForScore > AginScore
Group by TeamId
union
Select    TeamId, 0
From      Teams
Where     TeamId not in (Select TeamId
                         From   ForAgin
                         Where  ForScore > AginScore)
```

This view has now provided us with another column for the summary table.

```
Select    TeamId, Wins
From      WinSum
Order by Wins desc
```

```
-----------------------
TeamId           Wins
-----------------------
Witsend           2
Jeeps             1
Wiseacres         1
Rosewell          0
Rovers            0
Shinhackers       0
-----------------------
```

The losses and draws columns can be delivered by two views similar to `WinSum`.

```
Create View LoseSum(TeamId, Losses)
as
Select    TeamId, count(*)
From      ForAgin
Where     ForScore < AginScore
Group by TeamId
union
Select    TeamId, 0
From      Teams
Where     TeamId not in (Select TeamId
                         From   ForAgin
                         Where  ForScore < AginScore)

Create View DrawSum(TeamId, Draws)
as
```

```
Select    TeamId, count(*)
From      ForAgin
Where     ForScore = AginScore
Group by  TeamId
union
Select    TeamId, 0
From      Teams
Where     TeamId not in (Select TeamId
                        From   ForAgin
                        Where  ForScore = AginScore)
```

The final column in the summary table is for merit points and this can be calculated. We can now define the summary table as yet another view.

```
Create View Summary(Team, Wins, Losses, Draws,
                    For, Against, Pts)
as
Select    TeamId,
          Wins,
          Losses,
          Draws,
          For,
          Against,
          2*Wins + Draws
From      WinSum W
          LoseSum L,
          DrawSum D,
          ForAgin FA,
Where     W.TeamId = L.TeamId
and       L.TeamId = D.TeamId
and       D.TeamId = FA.TeamId
```

We can now print the summary table in order of merit.

```
Select    *
From      Summary
Order by  Pts desc, For-Against desc
```

18.3 The Rocky Concrete Company

We have been commissioned by that well-known manufacturer of highly regarded concrete products. The company wants us to develop an information system. The system is to help it answer questions such as:

- What kinds of products does Rocky sell? How much does it have in stock? Should it make another batch of product X or not?

- Who are its customers? How are they distributed across the country? How much do they owe?

- What orders have been taken and when? Who made them? What products and how many of each product were involved in an order?

A. Rocky's Product Line-Up

Perhaps the best introduction to the company is to have a look at part of its catalog. See Figure 18.1.

```
              Rocky Concrete Products

              Agricultural Products

    Product   Description                List Price

    MOO       Medium Cattle Trough          150
    LOO       Large Cattle Trough           250


              Domestic Products

    STANK     Small Septic Tank             300
    LTANK     Large Septic Tank             450
    LTUB     Laundry Tub                    100
    GNOME     Garden Gnome                   10


              Local Council Products

    STAND     Bicycle Stand                  50
    WALLY     Statue of Rugby Player        500
```

Figure 18.1 Catalog of products and prices

The catalog is for customer use. Rocky is just as much interested in other aspects of its stock. An inventory is shown in Figure 18.2.

List of Stock

Product	Type	Cost Price	On Hand	ReMake Level	ReMake Qty
MOO	A	70	6	3	5
LOO	A	100	1	1	3
STANK	D	200	10	5	15
LTANK	D	300	1	2	2
LTUB	D	60	20	15	20
GNOME	D	2	100	150	200
STAND	C	20	50	35	20
WALLY	C	100	10	15	40

Figure 18.2 List of Stock Report

When the quantity on hand of a particular product falls below a given level then a new batch of that product will be made. The batch size is determined by the product. For example, the number of garden gnomes in stock has fallen dangerously low. It is down to only 100 units. This is below the re-make level of 150 units. (Rocky must have had a busy Sunday.) Therefore a batch of 200 units, the re-make quantity for this product, will need to be made. However, before a request is made, a list is made, showing all products that need replenishing and the cost involved. An example is shown in Figure 18.3.

Production Request

Product	On Hand	Remake Qty	Unit Cost	Total Cost
LTANK	1	2	300	600
GNOME	100	200	2	400
WALLY	10	40	100	4000

Figure 18.3 Production Request

B. Rocky's Customer Base

Next we will look at the kinds of customers that Rocky serves. Figure 18.4 shows an excerpt from its customer ledger.

Each customer is granted a credit limit, beyond which they are never allowed to stray; that is, the total amount that a customer currently owes Rocky, the current balance, is never allowed to exceed the particular limit of credit imposed on that customer.

List of Customers

Customer	Name	Address	Credit Limit	Current Balance
1066	Nev's Nursery	White Hart Lane, Bundaberg, 4670	500	450
1314	Alfred Shire Council	Meadow Bank, Alfieton, 4555	3000	1000
1776	Di Hunter	Thornton Farm, Rosevale, 4765	500	500
2001	Glad's Gladdies	Turkey Beach, Gladstone, 4750	500	0

Figure 18.4 List of Customers

C. Customer Orders

These are the company's lifeblood! Every customer order is recorded on an order form. Figure 18.5 shows a typical example of one. The order is allowable, from Rocky's point of view, because it satisfies the following conditions:

1. The quantity of each product ordered is less than or equal to the quantity on hand for that product. In other words, Rocky had enough in stock.

2. The total value of the order, $1400, when added to the customer's current balance, which is $1000, is less than or equal to the customer's credit limit of $3000.

Note that the unit price charged for two of the products is less than the list price. This is the benefit of being a valued customer. The effect that this order will have on Rocky's records can be seen in the excerpts shown in Figure 18.6.

For each of the products ordered, the OnHand quantity is reduced by the amount ordered. The current balance of the customer making the order is increased by the total value of the order.

18.3.1 Developing a Specification

We start by introducing some base types that we will clearly need.

```
         ┌─────────────────────────────────────────────────────────────┐
         │                                                             │
         │          ROCKY CONCRETE PRODUCTS                            │
         │              212 Bell St. Rocklea                           │
         │                                                             │
         │  Order:        1601                        Date:  16-Mar-95 │
         │                                                             │
         │  Customer:     1314                                         │
         │                Alfred Shire Council                         │
         │                Meadow Bank, Alfieton,                       │
         │                4555                                         │
         │                                                             │
         ├──────────┬──────────────────────┬─────┬───────┬─────────────┤
         │ Product  │ Description          │ Qty │ Unit  │    Total    │
         │ Code     │                      │     │ Price │             │
         │          │                      │     │       │             │
         │ STAND    │ Bicycle Stand        │ 10  │   40  │     400     │
         │ GNOME    │ Garden Gnome         │ 10  │   10  │     100     │
         │ WALLY    │ Statue of Rugby Player│  2 │  450  │     900     │
         │          │                      │     │       │     ----    │
         │          │                      │     │       │    1400     │
         │          │                      │     │       │    ====     │
         │          │                      │     │       │             │
         │          │                      │     │       │             │
         └──────────┴──────────────────────┴─────┴───────┴─────────────┘
```

Figure 18.5 Order Form

Type	Interpretation
[*Product*]	All the products that Rocky might ever make
[*ProdType*]	The product types, e.g. domestic, agricultural, and so on
[*Customer*]	All the company's possible customers
[*Order*]	All possible orders
[*Text*]	For names and addresses
[*N*]	The integers 0, 1, 2, ...
[*Date*]	For order dates and whatever other dates might be required

We need a money type, but will treat it as a synonym for integers.

Money == *N*

Next we will create some schema or record types that gather together relevant information on some of the major entity types just introduced.

The Product Record Type

This record gathers together all the simple data that Rocky keeps about product, *except* for the identity of the product itself.

Stock Changes

Product	Description	On Hand BEFORE	Order Qty	On Hand AFTER
GNOME	Garden Gnome	100	10	90
STAND	Bicycle Stand	50	10	40
WALLY	Statue of Rugby Player	10	2	8

Customer Changes

Customer	Name	BEFORE Balance	Order Total	AFTER Balance
1314	Alfred Shire Council	1000	1400	2400

Figure 18.6 Before and after

ProdRec

Desc : *Text*
Type : *ProdType*
List, *Cost* : *Money*
Onhand : N
ReMake_Level, *ReMake_Qty* : N

This record may be thought of as an individual product view. It is an amalgamation of the information provided about a product on the `List of Stock` report (see Figure 18.2) and the catalog (see Figure 18.1).

The Customer Record Type

This schema type gathers some important facts about a customer. It is an individual customer's view of its relationship with Rocky.

CustRec

Name,
Address : *Text*
Limit,
Balance : *Money*

Balance $\leq$ *Limit*

It corresponds to the information about a customer found on a row of the `List of Customers` report (see Figure 18.4).

Every customer is required to have a current balance that is less than or equal to their credit limit.

The Order Record Types

Two record types will be defined to help specify orders. The first corresponds to a physical line on an order form.

―― $OrderLine$ ―――――――――――――――――――――――――――
$ProdCode : Product$
$Qty : N$
$SoldAt : Money$
―――――――――
$Qty > 0$
―――――――――――――――――――――――――――――――

Every order line must involve an order quantity greater than zero.

The second record type captures the essential details of a complete order. It corresponds, approximately, to an individual order form including heading and body. See Figure 18.5.

―― $OrderRec$ ―――――――――――――――――――――――――――
$OrderDate : Date$
$CustId : Customer$
$Lines : Set\ of\ OrderLine$
―――――――――
$\#Lines = \#\{l : Lines \bullet l.ProdCode\}$
―――――――――――――――――――――――――――――――

The predicate requires that every line on the order involve a different product, that is, the number of lines on the order must equal the number of different kinds of product ordered.

18.3.2 The Rocky State

We can now bring these types together in a schema that attempts to summarize the analysis that appeared in the introduction. The components or observations introduced in the schema correspond to the three major reports, the List of Stock, the List of Customers and the Order Form.

―― $Rocky$ ――――――――――――――――――――――――――――
$Products : Product \nrightarrow ProdRec$
$Customers : Customer \nrightarrow CustRec$
$Orders : Order \nrightarrow OrderRec$
―――――――――
$\forall ord : dom\ Orders \bullet$
$\qquad Orders(ord).CustId \in dom\ Customers$
$\qquad \forall line : Orders(ord).Lines \bullet line.ProdCode \in dom\ Products$
―――――――――――――――――――――――――――――――

The schema is to be interpreted as follows.

The *Rocky* Declaration

1. *Products* : *Product* $\nrightarrow$ *ProdRec*
   Information relating to all the products currently manufactured by Rocky is represented as a partial function that maps each product to all the information relevant to that product. The domain of the function, *dom Products*, represents the products themselves. An application of the function, say *Products*(p), provides us with a *ProdRec* tuple of information about product p.

2. *Customers* : *Customer* $\nrightarrow$ *CustRec*
   The customer base is also represented as a partial function, one that maps each existing customer to information about that customer. The domain of the function, *dom Customers* is the set of existing customers. An application of the function, say *Customers*(c), provides a record of the customer c.

3. *Orders* : *Order* $\nrightarrow$ *OrderRec*
   In a similar fashion to products and customers, each order is mapped to information about that order.

The *Rocky* Predicate

1. $\forall$ *ord* : *dom Orders* •
   In every order ...

2. *Orders*(*ord*).*CustId* $\in$ *dom Customers*
   the customer identified is one of Rocky's and ...

3. $\forall$ *line* : *Orders*(*ord*).*Lines* • *line*.*ProdCode* $\in$ *dom Products*
   every product identified on the order is from Rocky's stock.

18.3.3 Adding a New Customer

The following schema describes how a new customer may be added to Rocky's customer base and the conditions that apply.

```
┌─ AddCustomer ─────────────────────────────────
│ Δ Rocky
│ newrec? : CustRec
├───────────────────────────────────────────────
│ newrec?.Balance = 0
│ ∃ nextid : Customer • nextid ∉ dom Customers
│            Customers' = Customers ∪ {(nextid, newrec?)}
│ Products' = Products
│ Orders' = Orders
└───────────────────────────────────────────────
```

The schema is to be interpreted as follows.

The *AddCustomer* Declaration

1. $\Delta Rocky$
   This signals that the operation causes a change to the *Rocky* state.

2. $newrec? : CustRec$
   All the necessary information, apart from the customer's Id, is supplied in this input customer record.

The *AddCustomer* Predicate

1. $newrec?.Balance = 0$
   The customer will start with a zero current balance.

2. $\exists\, nextid : Customer \bullet nextid \notin dom\ Customers$
   This condition establishes that there is a customer (Id) *nextid* for this new customer and that the Id is not already allocated to some existing customer.

3. $Customers' = Customers \cup \{(nextid, newrec?)\}$
   The customer base is extended to include a mapping from the customer to the customer's record.

18.3.4 Taking a New Order

In this section, we will discuss the operation of taking an order and how that operation affects the *Rocky* state. We will start by seeing what inputs the operation will require and what output it will produce.

1. $custid? : Customer$

   We will need to know the customer making the order to ensure both that they have enough credit and that their current balance is updated.

2. $d? : Date$

   We need to know on what date the order was made.

3. $lines? : Set\ of\ OrderLine$

   The most important input will be a set of *OrderLine* records that show what products were ordered, how many of each were ordered and what price they were sold at.

4. $total! : Money$

   The total value of the order is to be calculated.

The operation affects all three of the components of the state schema and before we introduce the *TakeOrder* schema, we will describe how these state components are altered. These descriptions also take the form of schemas and, eventually, they will be incorporated into the complete description of the ordering process.

1. The *Products* Component

   The effect of an order on the *Products* component is to reduce the quantity on hand of each of the products involved by the amount ordered. We do not need to worry whether there are enough in stock. This will be handled in the operation schema itself.

Case Studies

EffectOfTakeOrderOnProducts

$Products, Products' : Product \twoheadrightarrow ProdRec$
$lines? : Set\ of\ OrderLine$

$Products' = Products \oplus$
$\qquad \{l : lines?, p, p' : ProdRec$
$\qquad\qquad |$
$\qquad\qquad p = Products(l.ProdCode) \wedge$
$\qquad\qquad p'.OnHand = p.OnHand - l.Qty \wedge$
$\qquad\qquad p'.Desc = p.Desc \wedge$
$\qquad\qquad p'.Type = p.type \wedge$
$\qquad\qquad p'.List = p.List \wedge$
$\qquad\qquad p'.Cost = p.Cost \wedge$
$\qquad\qquad p'.ReMake\_Level = p.Remake\_Level \wedge$
$\qquad\qquad p'.Remake\_Qty = p.ReMake\_Qty$
$\qquad\qquad \bullet$
$\qquad\qquad (l.ProdCode, p')\}$

The *Products* component is a function and function override is used to describe how this component is changed. For each of the products in *lines?*, the record for that product is established as p. A new product record, p', is created, using p as a basis. This new record is identical to p except that the *OnHand* quantity is reduced by the quantity ($l.Qty$) of the product that was ordered. The current record p is replaced by p'. This overriding is repeated for every line on the order.

2. The *Customer* Component

EffectOfTakeOrderOnCustomers

$Customers, Customers' : Customer \twoheadrightarrow CustRec$
$custid? : Customer$
$total! : Money$

$Customers' = Customers \oplus$
$\qquad \{c, c' : CustRec$
$\qquad\qquad |$
$\qquad\qquad c = Customers(custid?) \wedge$
$\qquad\qquad c'.Balance = c.Balance + total! \wedge$
$\qquad\qquad c'.Name = c.Name \wedge$
$\qquad\qquad c'.Address = c.Address \wedge$
$\qquad\qquad c'.Limit = c.Limit$
$\qquad\qquad \bullet$
$\qquad\qquad (custid?, c')\}$

The *Customers* component is also a function. The current version of the customer's record is established as c. A new version, c', of the record is constructed from c except that the *Balance* field is increased by the total value of the order. This new customer record is then used to override the previous one.

3. The *Orders* Component

EffectOfTakeOrderOnOrders

$Orders, Orders' : Order \nrightarrow OrderRec$
$custid? : Customer$
$d? : date$
$lines? : Set\ of\ OrderLine$

$\exists NextOrderId : Order \bullet$
$\qquad NextOrderId \notin dom\ Orders \land$
$\qquad Orders' = Orders \cup$
$\qquad\qquad \{or : OrderRec\ |$
$\qquad\qquad\ or.OrderDate = d? \land$
$\qquad\qquad\ or.Lines = lines? \land$
$\qquad\qquad\ or.CustId = custid?$
$\qquad\qquad \bullet$
$\qquad\qquad (NextOrderId, or)\}$

A new order Id *NextOrderId* is found. This must not currently be in use. A new order record *or* is then constructed from the input supplied. A new pairing is added to the *Orders* function. This pairing maps the new order Id to the new order record.

TakeOrder

$\Delta Rocky$
$custid? : Customer$
$d? : Date$
$lines? : Set\ of\ OrderLine$
$total! : Money$

$custid? \in dom\ Customers$
$\{l : lines? \bullet l.ProdCode\} \subseteq dom\ Products$
$\#lines? = \#\{l : lines? \bullet l.ProdCode\}$
$\forall l : lines? \bullet l.Qty \leq Products(l.ProdCode).Onhand$

$total! = \Sigma l : lines? \bullet l.SoldAt * l.Qty$
$Customers(custid?).Balance + total! \leq Customers(custid?).Limit$

EffectOfTakeOrderOnProducts
EffectOfTakeOrderOnCustomers
EffectOfTakeOrderOnOrders

The schema is to be interpreted as follows.

Case Studies 453

The *TakeOrder* Declaration

The inputs and output have been discussed already.

The *TakeOrder* Predicate

1. $custid? \in dom\ Customers$
   The customer identified as making the order must be a current customer.

2. $\{l : lines? \bullet l.ProdCode\} \subseteq dom\ Products$
   Every product code that appears on an order line must identify one of Rocky's current stock.

3. $\#lines? = \#\{l : lines? \bullet l.ProdCode\}$
   Every line on the order must have a different product code.

4. $\forall l : lines? \bullet l.Qty \leq Products(l.ProdCode).Onhand$
   For every product ordered, there must be enough stock on hand.

5. $total! = \Sigma l : lines? \bullet l.SoldAt * l.Qty$
   The total value of the order is the sum of the product of the sale price and the order quantity over all the products ordered.

6. $Customers(custid?).Balance + total! \leq Customers(custid?).Limit$
   The customer's credit limit, after the order, must still be less than the customer's credit limit.

7. *EffectOfTakeOrderOnProducts*
   EffectOfTakeOrderOnCustomers
   EffectOfTakeOrderOnOrders
   The three state components are changed in the ways described previously.

18.3.5 Making a Request for Production

In this last operation, we will look at specifying a report that lists all the products that have fallen below the relevant re-make level. This corresponds to the `Production Request` which looks like the following.

Production Request

Product	On Hand	Remake Qty	Unit Cost	Total Cost
LTANK	1	2	300	600
GNOME	100	200	2	400
WALLY	10	40	100	4000

454   Chapter 18

ProductionRequest

$\Xi Rocky$
$remake\_list! : Set\ of\ (Product \times N \times N \times Money \times Money)$

$remake\_list! = \{pCode : dom\ Products;\ pRec : ProdRec$

$\qquad |$

$\qquad pRec = Products(pCode)\ \wedge$
$\qquad pRec.OnHand \leq pRec.ReMake\_Level$

$\qquad \bullet$

$\qquad (pCode,$
$\qquad pRec.OnHand,$
$\qquad pRec.ReMake\_Qty,$
$\qquad pRec.Cost,$
$\qquad pRec.ReMake\_Level * pRec.Cost)\}$

The *ProductionRequest* Declaration

1. $\Xi Rocky$
   This is a read-only operation.

2. $remake\_list! : Set\ of\ (Product \times N \times N \times Money \times Money)$
   The list is composed, essentially, of a set of rows. Each row consists of a product code, two numbers, and two money amounts.

The *ProductionRequest* Predicate

Set comprehension is used to define the report.

1. $remake\_list! = \{pCode : dom\ Products;\ pRec : ProdRec$
   The variable *pCode* ranges over *dom Products*, that is, over the set of products currently made by Rocky. The variable *pRec* is a product record, the contents of which are yet to be determined.

2. $|\ pRec = Products(pCode)\ \wedge$
   The variable *pRec* is now established as the product record for the product identified by *pCode*.

3. $pRec.OnHand \leq pRec.ReMake\_Level$
   However, the report only identifies products for which stock has fallen to a level at which manufacture is warranted.

4. $\bullet\ (pCode, pRec.OnHand, \ldots, pRec.ReMake\_Level * pRec.Cost)$
   The details of the report are specified.

18.3.6 The Database

We will use a database with the following structure.

```
        Products           Customers           Orders              OrderDetails
        --------           ---------           ------              ------------
    (*) ProdCode       (*) CustId          (*) OrderId         (*) OrderId
        Desc               Name                OrderDate       (*) ProdCode
        ProdType           Street              CustId              OrderQty
        ListPrice          Town                                    SalePrice
        CostPrice          PostCode
        OnHandQty          Limit
        RemakeLevel        Balance
        RemakeQty
```

The **Products** and **Customers** tables are direct implementations of the corresponding components of the *Rocky* state schema:

$Products = $ **Products**
$Customers = $ **Customers**

The domain of the *Products* function corresponds to the key of the **Products** table:

$dom\ Products = \{p : $ **Products** $\bullet\ p.\text{ProdCode}\}$

or, in SQL terms:

$dom\ Products = $ **Select p.ProdCode From Products p**

The *Orders* component of that schema is represented by the **Orders** and **OrderDetails** tables in conjunction:

$Orders = o : $ **Orders** $\bullet$
$\qquad (o, \{od : $ **OrderDetails** $\mid od.\text{OrderId} = o.\text{OrderId}\ \bullet$
$\qquad\qquad (od.\text{ProdCode}, od.\text{OrderQty}, od.\text{SalePrice})\}\}$

In SQL terms, we have:

$dom\ Orders = $ **Select o.OrderId From Orders o**

We need two further tables to enable us to allocate new customer and new order numbers:

```
        NextCust             NextOrder
        --------             ---------
    (*) NextCustId       (*) NextOrderId
```

The **NextCust** table might be created as follows:

    Create table NextCust (NextCustId integer not null)

One row will be inserted:

    Insert
    Into NextCust
    values(1)

The first customer will be given the number **1** and the **NextCust** table will be updated to contain the number **2**, and so on for every new customer.

18.3.7 Implementing the *AddCustomer* Operation

Suppose we decide to use a data entry screen like that shown in Figure 18.7.

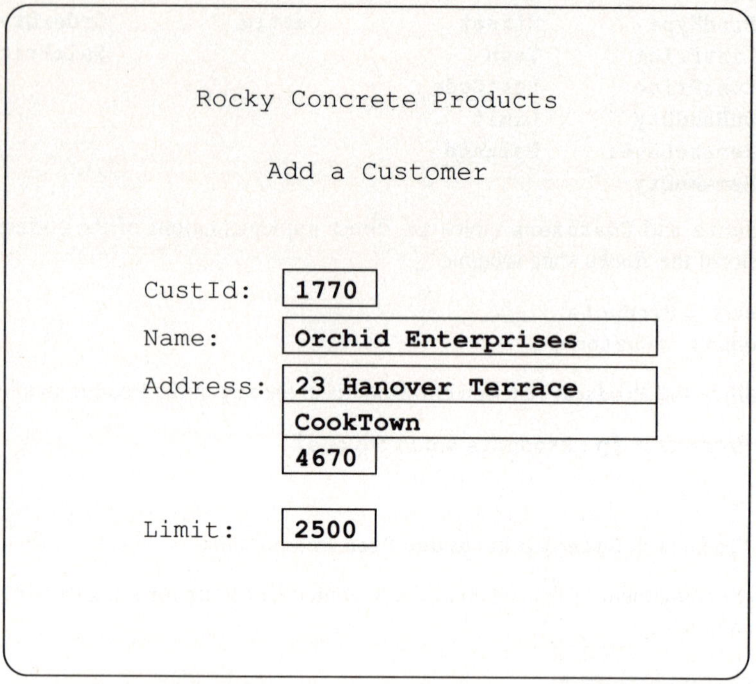

```
            Rocky Concrete Products

               Add a Customer



      CustId:   1770
      Name:     Orchid Enterprises
      Address:  23 Hanover Terrace
                CookTown
                4670

      Limit:    2500
```

Figure 18.7 The *AddCustomer* screen

The form has the following structure:

```
AddCustomerForm ::= CustId + Name + Address + Limit

Address ::= Street + Town + PostCode
```

AddCustomer
Field Usage Table

Field	Usage	Format	Default
CustId	Display	integer	
Name	Mandatory Entry	name	
Street	Mandatory Entry	name	
Town	Mandatory Entry	name	
Postcode	Mandatory Entry	integer	
Limit	Mandatory Entry	integer	

The new customer's Id is supplied by the system; all other fields are to be filled by the user.

Case Studies

	AddCustomer Form Action Table	
Position	**Structure**	**Action**
Start of Form		
	CustId	GetNextId
	+ Name	
	+ Street	
	+ Town	
	+ Postcode	
	+ Limit	
End of Form		AddCustomer

AddCustomer **Form Actions**

GetNextId Action:

1. Extract the next available customer number.

    ```
    Select  NextCustId
    Into    :CustId
    From    NextCust
    ```

2. Update the table to prepare for the next new customer.

    ```
    Update NextCust
    Set NextCustId = NextCustId + 1
    ```

AddCustomer Action:

1. Add a new row to the `Customers` table.

    ```
    Insert
    Into Customers
    values(:CustId,:Name,:Street,:Town,:Postcode,:Limit,
    0)
    ```

    The customer is given a zero current balance.

18.3.8 Implementing the *TakeOrder* Operation

The screen layout for this transaction is shown in Figure 18.8.

This form has the following structure:

```
TakeOrderForm ::=
    OrderId + Date
  + CustId + Name + Address + PostCode
  + {ProdCode + Description + OrderQty + SalePrice + LineTotal}
  + OrderTotal

Address ::= Street + Town
```

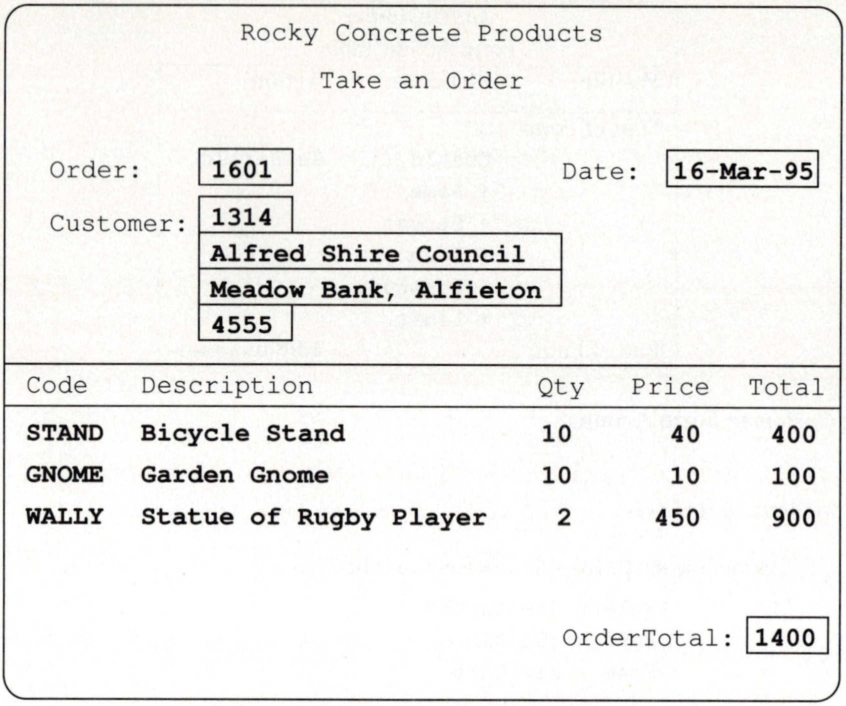

```
            Rocky Concrete Products
                Take an Order


  Order:    │ 1601 │              Date:  │ 16-Mar-95 │
  Customer: │ 1314 │
            │ Alfred Shire Council    │
            │ Meadow Bank, Alfieton   │
            │ 4555 │

  Code    Description              Qty    Price    Total
  STAND   Bicycle Stand             10      40      400
  GNOME   Garden Gnome              10      10      100
  WALLY   Statue of Rugby Player     2     450      900


                               OrderTotal:  │ 1400 │
```

Figure 18.8 The *TakeOrder* screen

Three hidden fields are added. These are shown in italics.

```
TakeOrderForm ::=
    OrderId + Date
  + CustId + Name + Address + PostCode + Balance + Limit
  + {ProdCode + Description + OnHandQty + OrderQty + SalePrice
  + LineTotal}
  + OrderTotal


Address ::= Street + Town
```

These hidden fields are added because, during the processing of an order, we will need to ensure that the customer's credit limit is not exceeded and, for each product ordered, there is enough stock on hand.

Case Studies 459

TakeOrder
Field Usage Table

Field	Usage	Format	Default
`OrderId`	Display	integer	
`Date`	Mandatory Entry	date	
`CustId`	Mandatory Entry	integer	
`Street`	Display	name	
`Town`	Display	name	
`Postcode`	Display	integer	
Balance	Hidden	money	
Limit	Hidden	money	
`ProdCode`	Mandatory Entry	name	
`Description`	Display	name	
OnHandQty	Hidden	integer	
`OrderQty`	Mandatory Entry	integer	
`SalePrice`	Mandatory Entry	money	
`LineTotal`	Display	money	
`OrderTotal`	Display	money	

The sequence of usage is as follows.

- The program will supply the order number.

- The user will supply the order date.

- The user will supply the customer number. The program will check that such a customer exists, and if so, will retrieve their name, address, current balance and credit limit. All but the latter two fields will be displayed on the screen.

- The program will then loop through the body of the order.

    - The user will supply a product code.

    - The program will verify the existence of a product with that code.

    - If one is found then the product description will be displayed.

    - The user will supply the order quantity for that product.

    - The program will check that there is enough on hand.

    - If there is, then the program will ask for the unit sale price for this product. The program will calculate the line total for this product and check that, given this line and all the other lines on the order, the customer has enough credit.

460   Chapter 18

	TakeOrder	
	Form Action Table	
Position	**Structure**	**Action**
Start of Form		
	OrderId	GetNextId
	+ Date	
	+ CustId	CheckCustEtc
	+ Name	
	+ Address	
Start of Body	+ {	SetTotal
Start of Line		
	ProdCode	CheckProd
	+ Description	
	+ OrderQty	CheckEnough
	SalePrice	CheckBalance
	LineTotal	
End of Line		AddLineEtc
End of Body	}	UpdateCust
	+ OrderTotal	
End of Form		

TakeOrder **Form Actions**

- **GetNextId** Action:

    1. Extract the next available order number.

        ```
        Select  NextOrderId
        Into    :OrderId
        From    NextOrder
        ```

    2. Update the table to prepare for the next new order.

        ```
        Update NextOrder
        Set NextOrderId = NextOrderId + 1
        ```

- **CheckCustId** Action:

    1. Retrieve the customer record.

        ```
        Select Name, Street||', '||Town, PostCode,
               Balance, Limit
        Into   :Name, :Address, :PostCode, :Balance, :Limit
        Where  CustId = :CustId
        ```

    If not found then display an error message.

    This condition also satisfies the condition of the operation schema that requires *custid?* ∈ *dom Customers*.

2. Insert an Order (header) record into the database.

```
Insert
Into   Orders
Values(:OrderId, :Date, :CustId)
```

- The **CheckProd** Action:

    1. Retrieve the product record for the product specified.

       ```
       Select Description, OnHandQty
       Into   :Description, :OnHandQty
       From   Products
       Where  ProdCode = :ProdCode
       ```

    If not found then display an error message.

    This condition, since it is applied to every product entered, causes the condition $\{l : lines? \bullet l.ProdCode\} \subseteq dom\ Products$ to be satisfied.

- The **CheckEnough** Action:

    1. Check that there is enough stock on hand.

       ```
       :OrderQty <= :OnHandQty
       ```

    If not found then display an error message.

    This condition, since it is also applied to every product entered, causes the operation schema condition $\forall l : lines? \bullet l.Qty \leq Products(l.prodId).Onhand$ to be satisfied.

- The **CheckBalance** Action:

    1. Calculate the line total.

       ```
       :LineTotal := :OrderQty * :SalePrice
       ```

    2. Check that this line does not take the customer over their credit limit.

       ```
       :OrderTotal + :LineTotal + :Balance <= :Limit
       ```

These two actions cause the condition:

$$Customers(custid?).Balance + total! \leq Customers(custid?).Limit$$

to be satisfied.

- The **AddLineEtc** Action:

This action updates the order total, adds a new line to the database and updates the relevant product record.

   1. Update the order total.

      ```
      :OrderTotal := :OrderTotal + :LineTotal
      ```

   2. Add the order line to the database.

```
              Insert
              Into  OrderDetails
              Values(:OrderId, :ProdCode, :OrderQty, :SalePrice)
```
  This satisfies the *EffectOfTakeOrderOnOrders* condition.

  3. Update the product record.
```
              Update Products
                  Set OnHandQty = OnHandQty - :OrderQty
              Where  ProdCode
```
  This satisfies the *EffectOfTakeOrderOnProducts* condition.

- The `UpdateCust` Action:

  1. Add the order total value to the customer's current balance.
```
              Update Customers
                  Set Balance = Balance + :OrderTotal
              Where  CustId = :CustId
```
  This satisfies the part of the *EffectOfTakeOrderOnCustomers* condition that relates to the body of the order.

Exercises

Q18.1 The League

Suppose the state schema for this case study had been specified somewhat differently.

$$
\begin{array}{|l}
\text{\_\_League_____} \\
Teams : Set\ of\ Team \\
homes : Round \times Team \nrightarrow Score \\
aways : Round \times Team \nrightarrow Score \\
played : Round \times Team \nrightarrow Team \\
\hline
dom\ homes \cup dom\ aways = dom\ played \\
dom\ homes \cap dom\ aways = \{\,\}
\end{array}
$$

The three functions are to be used as follows:

homes What the home teams scored in each round.

$homes(1, Wiseacres) = 12$
$homes(1, Rosewell) = 8$

aways What the away teams scored in each round.

$aways(1, Shinhackers) = 8$
$aways(1, Witsend) = 20$

played Each team's opposition in each round.

$played(1, Wiseacres) = Shinhackers$
$played(1, Shinhackers) = Wiseacres$

a. Respecify the *AddResult* operation using this new schema.
b. Respecify the *ShowTable* operation.
c. The predicate does not mention the relationship between the teams in *Teams* and those in *homes*, *aways* and *played*. What is that relationship?

Q18.2 Rocky Concrete

a. Specify an operation schema *Delivery* that describes what happens when a new batch of product $p?$ arrives from production.
b. Specify an operation schema *Physical* that describes the result of physical inspection of stock that finds that there are actually $s?$ units of product $p?$ out in the yard.

Chapter 18

Additional Cases

The Sporrandangle Valley Water Board

The soils of the Sporrandangle Valley are fertile, but the rainfall is erratic. Fortunately, farmers are able to irrigate their crops from the Sporran River that flows through the valley. This was the way for many years until the late fifties when excessive irrigation by farmers higher up the valley meant that, downstream, the crops failed because of water shortage. The State Government intervened and decided that the most equitable solution was to dam the upper reaches of the river including the famous Sporrandangle Falls. The flow into the river could then be controlled. To pay for the works and to contain any over-watering, they decided to charge farmers for the water (and you can imagine how that suggestion was received). To oversee the situation, the government created the Sporrandangle Valley Water Board.

Water Billing: The Board's water usage accounting system operates on an annual cycle known as the *Water Year*. This runs from July 1 in one year to June 30 in the following. Every farm is allocated a volume of water known as the *water right*. The volume depends on various factors including the size of the farm and its position in the valley (and how well the farmer knows the Board Chairman, perhaps). This water is free of charge. Any water usage in excess of the farm's water right must be paid for. Notification of charges is sent to each farm in the form of a number of periodic, usually monthly, invoices.

The water used by any farm is taken from the river through a number of metered *offtakes* that deliver water specifically to the farm. The volume of water used in the Water Year so far is calculated for each offtake. This calculation is based on the readings taken at the offtake from the start of the Water Year until the present. The volume taken from each offtake is summed to get the total for the farm over the period specified.

Periodic Charges: The Board normally starts sending invoices about the time that water usage starts to exceed the water right. Typically this occurs around November. From then until the end of the Water Year, at approximately monthly intervals, bills are sent out to farmers for any additional water usage. As a rule, readings are taken at the end of a month and invoices are sent out in the middle of the following one.

When the invoice program is run, two dates are supplied, a start date and an end date. The start date is usually the middle of the month prior to the start of the Water Year. The end date is the middle of the month following the last of the water use readings. Charges accruing in the interval defined by the two dates are calculated.

Although it might be thought that calculating usage is merely a matter of subtracting the usage at the start from that of the end, there are two factors that must be taken into account.

1. The meter may have *ticked over*, that is, it may have reached the limit of its measuring capacity and reset itself.

2. There may have been repairs to the meter attached to an offtake, to the extent that the meter may even have been replaced.

A monthly invoice requires the production of the following information.

- the farm number

- the water right for that farm
- the previous usage, that is, the amount of water calculated as used at the time that the previous invoice was produced
- the latest usage

All the readings for the date range specified for the offtake are examined. For each pair of successive readings, any repairs for that offtake in the interval defined by these readings are interspersed.

The *last use* figure for this farm is read out and this latest usage is inserted. This last use figure provides the total water usage for this farm as determined at the end of the previous period. By comparing the previous usage against the latest usage, the periodic charge can be determined.

Meter Tickover: When a meter reaches the limit of its measuring capacity, it ticks over or resets itself, say from **9999** to **0000**. The capacity of the meter depends on its type. This capacity is entered during a repair transaction, and is known as the *maximum reading*. It may vary over time as the meter attached to an offtake may require replacement. At any particular time, an offtake meter's maximum may not have been recorded, in which case, a default of **9999** is used. When examining meter readings, a meter tickover is judged to have occurred if:

1. the water use reading this month is *less* than last month's, or more generally,
2. if one reading is less than the immediately preceding one.

When tickover occurs, water usage is calculated as follows:

$$Water\ Usage = Max\ Reading - Previous\ Reading + 1 + New\ Reading$$

Suppose an offtake has a maximum reading of **9999**. Two successive readings are **9980** and **0010**, so tickover has occurred.

$$Water\ Usage = 9999 - 9980 + 1 + 0010 = 19 + 1 + 10 = 30$$

Repairs: When water usage at an offtake is being calculated, possible meter repairs must be taken into consideration. When a faulty meter is repaired, or even replaced, the following details are recorded:

- the associated offtake
- the date of the repair
- the meter setting *before* the repair
- the meter setting *after* the repair
- an *assessment* of the water unaccounted for due to the fault; this may be a negative figure

The calculation of water usage at an offtake in the period between two successive readings is subject to the following rules:

466   Chapter 18

- **If** there are no repairs in the interval between the readings:
  then

  > The usage is the reading at the end of the period less the usage at the start of the period.

- **If** there *are* repairs in the interval:
  then

  > the usage is the sum of the following:
  >
  > > the difference between the *before* reading for the first repair and the first reading
  > > + the sum of all adjustments made
  > > + the difference between the second reading and the *after* reading for the last repair
  > > + the sum of the differences between successive repairs.

An Example of Repair Accounting

Suppose the following readings had been taken at an offtake, and that certain repairs had been made to the meter at that offtake.

```
Readings                Repairs

Date    Reading         Date    Before   After    Assessment

31/3      60
                        18/4      100      75         2
                        20/4       80     220         5
                        25/4      230     100         4

30/4     120


April Usage = 100 - 60
            + 2 + 5 + 4
            + (80 - 75) + (230 - 220)
            + 120 - 100

            = 40 + 11 + 5 + 10 + 20

            = 86
```

Even though invoices are produced monthly, water usage is always calculated from the beginning of the Water Year. This is done because repairs may not appear in the accounting system in time to be incorporated into the next invoice to be prepared. Even then, the assessment may be disputed. The Board therefore always re-calculates the entire year's usage.

Nuclear Medicine

Nuclear medicine is one of a number of diagnostic services that are available at most medium to large hospitals. It is one of a family of similar services known as medical imaging. Nuclear medicine is an aid that is concerned with *physiology*, that is, the functioning of organs and bones. Other diagnostic aids in medicine, such as cat scans, ultrasound and X-rays are concerned with *anatomy*, that is, the shape or structure of the organs and bones.

The images produced by a nuclear medicine camera are not as striking (in terms of clarity) as those produced by other imaging techniques. However nuclear medicine physicians joke that these other scanning methods would produce equally good pictures of a cadaver! As a practical example, bone infection such as osteomyelitis will show up much earlier on nuclear medicine scans than on others (1 or 2 days as against 2 weeks).

Nuclear medicine exists because different parts of the body tend to process different substances; for example, bones take up calcium, and the liver filters large particles. Advantage is taken of this fact by **labeling** or adding a radioactive nuclide to these carrier substances.

Normally the patient is injected, and after the dose has had time to reach its target the patient is scanned by a special camera. The resulting image is usually produced on X-ray film, although it may also be taken by a Polaroid camera or shown on a screen linked to the computer that interfaces with the camera. Generally, the dose is only taken up by active parts of the body. So, when ordering a bone scan, doctors would be looking at bone growth. Such growth might be a normal part of fracture repair, but it might also be a result of cancer or infection. Some scans, like the bone scan, are looking for active areas, but other scans are looking for a lack of activity.

Nuclear medicine can only hint (however strongly) at why the body is acting in the way it does. Only pathology can accurately determine the cause.

Types of Scan

The most common types of scan done by a nuclear medicine department within a hospital are:

- liver
- bone
- lung
- cardiac
- renal (kidney)

There are other types of scan such as biliary (gall bladder), thyroid and bladder scans; however, we will concentrate on the everyday ones. Some of the relevant features of each of these more common scans are described next.

Liver Scan: Here the liver is being examined with regard to its size, shape and function. The scan might be done because of suspected abscesses or cirrhosis; but such a scan might also be done to check the functioning of a patient known to have cancer. The patient is normally injected 15 to 20 minutes before the scan which lasts about 30 minutes. The scan may be delayed for up to an hour before scanning.

Bone Scan: Bones may be scanned to check for regrowth after trauma or for suspected disease. The patient is injected about two and a half hours prior to the scan although the scan may be delayed for up to four hours. Patients normally come for their injection and then return some time later. The scan takes about 45 minutes.

Lung Scan: These scans are usually done on extremely ill patients who either have cardiac problems or who are in traction after an operation. The doctor is looking for pulmonary emboli (blood clots) that may be in the lung. There are two parts to the scan.

1. Ventilation, where patients breathe a gas labeled with technetium. The patients breathe for about 10 minutes and are then scanned for 20 minutes.

2. After ventilation the patient is injected with a particle that sticks to the lung. A 20-minute scan follows immediately.

By allowing a gap between the two steps, patients can be interleaved. However, it is desirable that patients remain in the department for the minimum possible time.

Cardiac Scan: This kind of scan is done to check the functioning of the patient's heart. It is often done prior to ordering chemotherapy because of the damage such treatment may cause. Patients are injected with a cold (non-radioactive) tin compound which excites the red blood cells. Twenty minutes later some technetium is mixed with the patient's blood. This allows for the detection of blood pooled in the heart and major vessels. It takes an hour to complete.

Renal Scan: This is a differential function scan. It checks for differences in the functioning of the patient's two kidneys. Sometimes it is used before or after transplant. Hypertension can be caused by kidney malfunction or obstruction. Patients are injected directly under the machine. It takes 45 minutes for the complete scan. A blood test is performed alongside this type of scan. A sample is taken every hour for three hours after the injection. For this reason the latest time for injection is 12 noon.

Cameras

There are two rooms used for the scans. Each room has its own camera. Each camera can operate independently, but they may also be linked to a dedicated computer which operates as an extension of the camera. There are two different cameras. Both can handle all the different types of scan. The newer model gives better resolution. The two cameras are:

- the GEEWHIZ1 made by Geelong Electronics

- the ISEEU made by Nuclear Cameras

Although both cameras are capable of all types of scan, there are sufficient differences between cameras and between scans as to make either camera preferable on occasion. In other words, each camera has its own niche. The GEEWHIZ1 is used for fine work such as bone and cardiac scans where there is a need to see greater detail. Patients having these kinds of scans are booked onto the GEEWHIZ1. The rules for booking are roughly as follows:

Scan Type		Camera
Bone	--->	GEEWHIZ1
Cardiac	--->	GEEWHIZ1
Renal	--->	ISEEU
Lung	--->	ISEEU
Livers	--->	either

Even though the two cameras scan at slightly different rates, they are sufficiently close for these differences to be ignored as far as booking is concerned.

Patient Information

The kind of information required by the technologist in order to handle each patient is summarised below:

- type of scan
- name
- address
- phone number
- date of birth
- referring doctor
- drugs used
- hospital UR (unit record) number (if known)

If the patient is an inpatient then the ward number will also be required.

Problems

Things that **do** happen that upset normal operation include:

Camera Failure: When a camera breaks down it is often very difficult for the service engineer to say exactly when it might be working again. This will have an effect upon bookings.

A New Camera: The introduction of another camera may cause problems. It might have significantly faster or slower scanning rates than the current cameras. It might also be preferable for certain types of scan.

CHAPTER 19

Refinement

19.1 Introduction

This chapter is about how we implement our specification, that is, it is about how we turn it into a collection of computer programs operating upon a database. The situation we want to reach is one where we will have two quite distinct pictures *of the same situation*.

We start with one picture, the one provided by the specification. This will be stated or expressed in a language that tries to describe the situation as *we* see it. The other picture is a re-statement of that same situation; but this time the language used is ambivalent. It can be taken as just another way of perceiving the problem, but it can also be thought of as providing instructions to a machine in order for that machine to create an animated equivalent of the original specification. It is a version that is *executable* by the machine. In other words we have made the original problem tractable to information technology.

This use of different forms of language is not restricted to computing. We would give a stranger to town instructions expressed differently from those given to an obvious local asking directions. We would talk to the local in terms of shared knowledge such as familiar streets and landmarks. Conversely, we would talk to the stranger in physical terms – "turn left", "straight ahead for 2 km", "third on the left" and so on.

In this chapter we will take a relatively abstract specification such as shown in Chapter 14 and show how to map that to another specification this time expressed in the relational calculus or tuple oriented set comprehension of Chapter 4. This language is the basis for SQL and it will be assumed that the transformation to SQL is straightforward.

This chapter provides a worked example of how to move, formally, from a specification to its implementation. The technique used is *data refinement*, and here it is used on a database system.

A small situation is described along with some of the events that might impinge upon it. The description or specification is written using the Z notation. The intention is to explain the situation as the user sees it.

That same situation is then recast in terms of tables and the events in terms of operations upon these tables. The language used is, again, Z but now the style is clearly oriented towards SQL. This second specification is intended to be an "executable" equivalent of the original.

How can we be satisfied that the two specifications *are* equivalent? Some discussion is made regarding what we must do in order to demonstrate their equivalence. These rules or requirements are then applied to the case at hand.

19.2 The Abstract Specification

19.2.1 The *class* Situation

We will study a typical educational situation in which a group of people undertake a course of study for a semester. An information system is required. This system, to be written in SQL, will record details of the students enrolled, the assessment set and the marks awarded. It will therefore also need to handle the activities and events that are likely to occur in such an environment. Typically, these events occur when:

- a student enrols in the class;
- an item of assessment is set for the class;
- a student submits work for assessment;
- a student is awarded a mark for some assessment item;
- a mark is amended;
- a student drops out of the class.

We will now develop and describe the classroom situation along the following lines.

- Several different views or observations of the class are made.
- These views are integrated in a **state schema** which provides a *static* picture of the entire situation.
- Each event that may affect the class is described by a separate **operation schema**. These schemas provide a dynamic picture of the class and how it may evolve.

We will refer to this as the **abstract** specification.

A *second* specification is then created. Why? Because the target or implementation language, SQL, has limitations. In particular, it cannot handle the generalised relation that is a major component of the abstract specification. This second specification is intended to be *executable*. The language used is still Z but the style is oriented towards a relational database implementation. We will refer to this as the **concrete** specification. The equivalence of these two specifications will be discussed.

We will begin by modeling the class from three points of view, from that of an individual student who sees only his or her work; from that of the lecturer who sees a set of students; and from a shared viewpoint, that of the assessment set for the subject.

19.2.2 The Individual Student

This view concentrates upon a typical individual student. It contains all that we might wish to know about any student and it can fairly be described as a "student record".

```
                    STUDENT RECORD

        Id:        831
        First:     Stan
        Last:      Zupp

        Item    Submitted     Mark
         1       8th Sep       80
         2      21st Oct       70
         3       1st Nov
```

This particular student has submitted three pieces of work for assessment. The first two of these have been marked; he is still waiting on a mark for the third. Using the above example as a guide, we can introduce some base types:

Type	Interpretation
$[Person]$	the set of all possible students
$[Work]$	all possible items of assessment
$[N]$	numbers such as weightings and marks
$[Name]$	the names of people and things
$[Date]$	the various dates that may arise

The *Date* type will need a number of associated functions and relations that, for example, enable us to say whether one date comes before or after another.

$\_before\_,$
$\_after\_ : Date \leftrightarrow Date$

We can model the student view as a schema record type. This use of the Z schema corresponds to a record type in Pascal or to a group level in COBOL.

$$\begin{array}{|l}
student \\\hline
id : Person \\
first, last : Name \\
sub : Work \nrightarrow Date \\
marks : Work \nrightarrow 0..100 \\
\end{array}$$

Information regarding what work the student has submitted and the marks received is recorded using two separate partial functions *sub* and *marks*.

19.2.3 Assessment

The assessment is a kind of shared view seen by student and lecturer alike. It might appear on a study guide like this:

Item	Title	Due	Weight
1	Programming	10th Sep	25
2	Design	21st Oct	25
3	Final Exam	1st Nov	50

Several items of assessment can be expected. Each item will be identified by a number and have a title, a due date and a weighting relative to other items.

─── $assess$ ─────────────────────────
$title : Work \nrightarrow Name$
$weight : Work \nrightarrow 0..100$
$due : Work \nrightarrow Date$
────────────────
$dom\ weight = dom\ due = dom\ title$
──────────────────────────────────

There are mappings that provide the title, weighting and due date of every item of assessment set for the class.

There will be a schema to handle any changes to the assessment. These will occur while assessment is unfinalized and before any students are enrolled.

─── $\Delta assess$ ──────────────────────
$assess$
$assess'$
──────────────────────────────────

The usual Z conventions for naming such schemas are used. There will also be a "read only" schema to describe inspections of the assessment.

─── $\Xi assess$ ─────────────────────────
$\Delta assess$
────────────────
$title' = title$
$weight' = weight$
$due' = due$
──────────────────────────────────

This leaves the assessment unaltered.

19.2.4 The Lecturer

The lecturer sees the class as a whole – all the students and all the assessment.

```
┌─ class ─────────────────────────────────────────────
│  students : Set of student
│  assess
│  ───────────────────────────────────────────────
│  ∀ s, t : students • s.id = t.id ⇒ s = t
│  ∀ s : students • dom s.sub ⊆ dom title
│  ∀ s : students • dom s.marks ⊆ dom s.sub
└─────────────────────────────────────────────────────
```

This is the abstract state schema for our situation. The three lines of the predicate state that:

1. If two students have the same *id* then they are the same student. More simply, every student has a different *id*.

2. All the work submitted by a student must relate to some item of assessment set for the class.

3. No student can have received a mark for assessment unless he or she has first submitted some work.

The initial state of the classroom will be one where there are no students and no work for assessment has yet been set.

```
┌─ classInitially ────────────────────────────────────
│  class
│  ───────────────────────────────────────────────
│  students = {}
│  title = {}
└─────────────────────────────────────────────────────
```

From the definition of *assess* we can infer that, initially, *weight* and *due* must also be null functions.

19.3 Operations on Student Records

19.3.1 A Student Submits Some Work

In this section we will describe what happens to the class when a student submits some work for assessment.

Refinement

```
┌─ Submit ─────────────────────────────────
│ Δclass
│ Ξassess
│ s? : Person
│ i? : Work
│ d? : Date
│ ─────────────────────────────────────────
│ i? ∈ dom title
│ ¬d? after due(i?)
│ ∃ s : students •
│         s? = s.id
│         i? ∉ dom s.sub
│         ∃ s' : student •
│                 s'.id = s.id
│                 s'.sub = s.sub ∪ {(i?, d?)}
│                 s'.first = s.first
│                 s'.last = s.last
│                 s'.marks = s.marks
│                 students' = students − {s} ∪ {s'}
└──────────────────────────────────────────
```

The intended interpretation is as follows.

The *Submit* Declaration
The submission will cause a change to the class and an inspection of the assessment. The inputs will be $s?$: *Person* the Id of the student making the submission, $i?$: *Work* the item number of the assessment and $d?$: *Date* the date upon which the work was submitted.

The *Submit* Predicate

1. $i? \in dom\ title$
   The item number supplied must identify some item of assessment.
2. $\neg d?\ after\ due(i?)$
   No work will be accepted *after* the due date set for this item of assessment.
3. $\exists s : students \bullet$
   There is a student record s ...
4. $s? = s.id$
   with the same Id as the one supplied ...
5. $i? \notin dom\ s.sub$
   and the student should not have already submitted this item. This line effectively concludes the pre-conditions for the operation.
6. $\exists s' : student \bullet$
   We now start describing how the class changes by introducing a student record s' that will become the new version of the record for student $s?$.
7. $s'.id = s.id$
   First of all, there will be no change to the student's Id.

8. $s'.sub = s.sub \cup \{(i?, d?)\}$
   The submission of work $i?$ on date $d?$ is now recorded by being added to whatever list of submissions the student has already made.
9. $s'.first = s.first$
   $s'.last = s.last$
   There will be no change to the student's name.
10. $s'.marks = s.marks$
    No marks are awarded at this stage, so there is to be no change here.
11. $students' = students - \{s\} \cup \{s'\}$
    The previous version of the student's record is removed and replaced by the new one.

19.3.2 A Student Is Awarded a Mark

―― Award ―――――――――――――――――――――――
$\Delta class$
$\Xi assess$
$s?$: $Person$
$i?$: $Work$
$m?$: $0..100$
―――――――
$\exists s : students \bullet$
$\qquad s? = s.id$
$\qquad i? \in dom\ s.sub$
$\qquad i? \notin dom\ s.marks$
$\qquad \exists s' : student \bullet$
$\qquad\qquad s'.id = s.id$
$\qquad\qquad s'.marks = s.marks \cup \{(i?, m?)\}$
$\qquad\qquad s'.first = s.first$
$\qquad\qquad s'.last = s.last$
$\qquad\qquad s'.sub = s.sub$
$\qquad\qquad students' = students - \{s\} \cup \{s'\}$
―――――――――――――――――――――――――――――――

The intended interpretation is as follows.

The *Award* Declaration
The award will cause a change to the class and an inspection of the assessment. The inputs will be $s?$: *Person* the Id of the student receiving the award, $i?$: *Work* the item number of the assessment, and $m?$: $0..100$ the mark awarded.

The *Award* Predicate

1. $\exists s : students \bullet$
   There is a student record $s \ldots$
2. $s? = s.id$
   with the same Id as the one supplied $\ldots$

3. $i? \in dom\ s.sub$
   and the student must have previously submitted this item ...
4. $i? \notin dom\ s.marks$
   but not yet been awarded a mark.
   This line effectively concludes the preconditions for the operation.
5. $\exists s' : student \bullet$
   We now start describing how the class changes by introducing a student record s' that will become the new version of the record for student $s?$
6. $s'.id = s.id$
   First of all, there will be no change to the student's Id.
7. $s'.marks = s.marks \cup \{(i?, m?)\}$
   The award of a mark $m?$ for work $i?$ is now recorded by being added to whatever list of marks the student has already received.
8. $s'.first = s.first$
   $s'.last = s.last$
   There will be no change to the student's name.
9. $s'.sub = s.sub$
   There is no submission involved in this operation, so there is no change here.
10. $students' = students - \{s\} \cup \{s'\}$
    The old version of the student's record s is removed and replaced by the new version s'.

19.3.3 A Mark is Amended

Occasionally a mark may have to be amended, such as when it was entered incorrectly or when the student makes a case for it.

─── Amend ───────────────────────────────
$\Delta class$
$\Xi assess$
$s? : Person$
$i? : Work$
$m? : 0..100$
─────────
$\exists s : students \bullet$
$\qquad s? = s.id$
$\qquad i? \in dom\ s.marks$
$\qquad \exists s' : student \bullet$
$\qquad\qquad s'.id = s.id$
$\qquad\qquad s'.marks = s.marks \oplus \{(i?, m?)\}$
$\qquad\qquad s'.first = s.first$
$\qquad\qquad s'.last = s.last$
$\qquad\qquad s'.sub = s.sub$
$\qquad\qquad students' = students - \{s\} \cup \{s'\}$
───

The intended interpretation is as follows.

The *Amend* Declaration
The award will cause a change to the class and an inspection of the assessment. The inputs will be $s?$: *Person* the Id of the student receiving the award, $i?$: *Work* the item number of the assessment, and $m?$: 0..100 the new mark.

The *Amend* Predicate

1. $\exists s : students \bullet$
   There is a student record s ...

2. $s? = s.id$
   with the same Id as the one supplied ...

3. $i? \in dom\ s.marks$
   and the student must have previously been awarded a mark.
   This line effectively concludes the pre-conditions for the operation.

4. $\exists s' : student \bullet$
   We now start describing how the class changes by introducing a student record s' that will become the new version of the record for student $s?$

5. $s'.id = s.id$
   First of all, there will be no change to the student's Id.

6. $s'.marks = s.marks \oplus \{(i?, m?)\}$
   The previous mark for work $i?$ is now amended to $m?$.

7. $s'.first = s.first$
   $s'.last = s.last$
   There will be no change to the student's name.

8. $s'.sub = s.sub$
   There is no submission involved in this operation, so there is no change here.

9. $students' = students - \{s\} \cup \{s'\}$
   The old version of the student's record s is replaced by the new version s'.

19.4 The Concrete Specification

We will now re-examine the classroom situation with the intention of constructing an information system from the description just given. The abstract state schema *class* is, effectively, re-specified as a relational database. We will also need to re-specify the abstract operations in equivalent concrete terms, that is, as operations upon the database.

19.4.1 The Tables Used

The database for the classroom will involve three distinct relations or tables in SQL terminology. There will be a relation for students, one for assessment and one for results. A relation, in the database sense, is a set of tuples or records. We will begin by defining three appropriate record types. Each of these types corresponds to an individual tuple of the kind found in the three relations.

- *StRec* – the student record type:

  > **StRec**
  > *Id* : *Person*
  > *First*, *Last* : *Name*

  There will be a relation corresponding to this record type.

  ```
  Students
  -------------------
  Id    First   Last
  -------------------
  831   Stan    Zupp
  :     :       :
  -------------------
  ```

  This relation corresponds to the *id*, *first* and *last* components of the abstract *student* record. Information regarding submission of work and its consequent marking is omitted. SQL cannot handle their set-valued nature.

- *RtRec* – the result record type:

  > **RtRec**
  > *Id* : *Person*
  > *Item* : *Work*
  > *Sub* : *Date*
  > *Mark* : 0..100 | *null*

  The corresponding relation for this record type looks like the following.

  ```
  Results
  ------------------------------
  Id    Item   Sub         Mark
  ------------------------------
  :     :      :           :
  831   1      8th Sep     80
  831   2      21st Oct    70
  831   3      1st Nov     ?
  :     :      :           :
  ------------------------------
  ```

  This relation is used to hold submission and mark information for *every* student in the class. A record is inserted when an item is submitted and updated when the mark is awarded. In the abstract specification, this information was kept as part of each student's individual record and separate from that of other students. To distinguish one student's results from another's we have tagged the result with the student's Id.

Chapter 19

- *AsRec* – the assessment record type:

```
┌─ AsRec ─────────────
│ Item : Work
│ Title : Name
│ Due : Date
│ Weight : 0..100
```

The corresponding relation may be pictured as follows.

```
Assess
-----------------------------------------
Item  Title         Due          Weight
-----------------------------------------
1     Programming   10th Sep     25
2     Design        21st Oct     25
3     Final Exam    1st Nov      50
-----------------------------------------
```

We anticipate having a Class database consisting of these three relations, one for each record type. We can define the database as follows.

```
┌─ Class_DB ─────────────────────────────────
│ Students : Set of StRec
│ Assess : Set of AsRec
│ Results : Set of RtRec
│─────────────────────────────────────────────
│ ∀ S, T : Students • S.Id = T.Id ⇒ S = T
│ ∀ A, B : Assess • A.Item = B.Item ⇒ A = B
│ ∀ R, S : Results • R.Id = S.Id ∧ R.Item = S.Item ⇒ R = S
│
│ {R : Results • R.Id} ⊆ {S : Students • S.Id}
│ {R : Results • R.Item} ⊆ {A : Assess • A.Item}
```

The predicate is divided into two groups of conditions. The first group provides the conditions required of the primary key of each relation. Consider, for example, the first of that group.

$$\forall S, T : Students \bullet S.Id = T.Id \Rightarrow S = T$$

This states that if any two rows in the Students table have the same Id then the two rows will be *entirely* the same; in other words the Id is the primary key.

The second group of conditions provides the referential integrity constraints required of foreign keys. Take the first of that group:

$$\{R : Results \bullet R.Id\} \subseteq \{S : Students \bullet S.Id\}$$

This states that the set of values in the Id column of the Results table must be a subset of those values in the Id column of the Students table. Thus every Id in Results *refers* to an Id in Students.

The natural starting state for the database is to have three empty tables.

$Class_{DB}\,Initially$

$Class_{DB}$

$Students = \{\}$
$Assess = \{\}$
$Results = \{\}$

19.4.2 Mapping Between Representations

We can now define a mapping between the abstract and the concrete versions of the class, that is between *class* and $Class_{DB}$. This mapping is known as the **abstraction schema**. It defines a relationship between the components of the abstract state and those of the concrete one (the database).

Mapping

class
$Class_{DB}$

$students =$
$\quad\quad \{s : student\,|$
$\quad\quad\quad\quad \exists\, S : Students \bullet$
$\quad\quad\quad\quad s.id = S.Id$
$\quad\quad\quad\quad s.last = S.Last$
$\quad\quad\quad\quad s.first = S.First$
$\quad\quad\quad\quad s.sub = \{R : Results | R.Id = S.Id \bullet (R.Item, R.Sub)\}$
$\quad\quad\quad\quad s.marks = \{R : Results | R.Id = S.Id \land R.Mark \neq null$
$\quad\quad\quad\quad\quad \bullet (R.Item, R.Mark)\}$
$\quad\quad \}$
$title = \{A : Assess \bullet (A.Item, A.Title)\}$
$due = \{A : Assess \bullet (A.Item, A.Due)\}$
$weight = \{A : Assess \bullet (A.Item, A.Weight)\}$

The mapping contains four individual mappings, one for each component of the abstract state *class*. Each of these says how an abstract component may be constructed in terms of components of the concrete state, that is, in terms of the database. In particular, the first equation shows how the set of abstract student records may be retrieved from the two separate relations that we are obliged to have at the concrete level.

It is important to be able to make statements about individual students. From the definition of *students* we can say of any individual student s that:

$$\exists S : Students \bullet S.Id = s.id$$
$$S.Last = s.last$$
$$S.First = s.first$$
$$s.sub = \{R : Results \mid R.Id = s.id \bullet (R.Item, R.Sub)\}$$
$$s.marks = \{R : Results \mid R.Id = s.id \land R.Mark \neq null$$
$$\bullet (R.Item, R.Mark)\}$$

Using the above rule for any student s we can construct the *sub* function for that student:

$$s.sub = \{R : Results \mid R.Id = s.id \bullet (R.Item, R.Sub)\}$$

In database terms, the set comprehension on the right-hand side of the equation is a relational calculus expression that corresponds to the SQL statement:

```
Select  R.Item, R.Sub
From    Results R
Where   R.Id = s.id
```

In the abstract specification, two terms have an important role, *dom s.sub* and *dom s.marks*. The first of these, *dom s.sub*, is the set of items of assessment that the student s has submitted. From the definition of *sub* above, we can see that:

$$dom\ s.sub = \{R : Results \mid R.Id = s.id \bullet R.Item\}$$

The second of these terms, *dom s.marks*, is the set of items of work that the student s has submitted and which have received a mark. From the definition of *marks* we can see that:

$$dom\ s.marks = \{R : Results \mid R.Id = s.id \land R.Mark \neq null \bullet R.Item\}$$

If we subtract the two sets then we have the set of items that have been submitted but not yet marked. This set is important for the awarding of a mark. The difference *dom s.sub − dom s.marks*, when expressed in terms of the concrete state as above, has the form:

$$\{t : T \mid P\} - \{t : T \mid P \land \neg Q\}$$

When we consider the set of things of type T that are P, and subtract from it the set of things of type T that are P and not Q, then we are left with the set of things that are both P and Q. In other words, the difference reduces to:

$$\{t : T \mid P \land Q\}$$

Applying this rule to the difference between *dom s.sub* and *s.marks* gives us:

$$\{R : Results \mid R.Id = s.id \land R.Mark = null \bullet R.Item\}$$

19.4.3 The Award Operation Re-specified

We will now re-specify the *Award* operation in terms of the $Class_{DB}$ database rather than the *class* state. This new specification will be deemed *executable* for the following reasons.

- It will operate upon a state defined using data structures available in the implementation language. In this case there is one major type of data structure, the relation or table.
- It will manipulate that data structure using a mixture of set theoretical and relational calculus expressions, mimicking in Z, the implementation language, SQL.

$$
\begin{array}{|l}
\hline
\textit{Award}_{EXE} \\
\Delta\, Class_{DB} \\
s?: Person \\
i?: Work \\
m?: 0..100 \\
\hline
\exists\, R: Results \bullet \\
\quad\quad R.Id = s? \\
\quad\quad R.Item = i? \\
\quad\quad R.Mark = null \\
\quad\quad \exists\, R': RtRec \bullet \\
\quad\quad\quad R'.Id = R.Id \\
\quad\quad\quad R'.Item = R.Item \\
\quad\quad\quad R'.Sub = R.Sub \\
\quad\quad\quad R'.Mark = m? \\
\quad\quad\quad Results' = Results - \{R\} \cup \{R'\} \\
Students' = Students \\
Assess' = Assess \\
\hline
\end{array}
$$

The $Award_{EXE}$ Declaration

1. $\Delta\, Class_{DB}$
   This operation changes the class database.

2. $s?: Person$
   $i?: Work$
   $m?: 0..100$
   These three inputs supply the student, the item and the mark respectively.

The $Award_{EXE}$ Predicate

1. $\exists\, R: Results \bullet$
   There will be a result record R in the *Results* relation ...

2. $R.Id = s?$
   that relates to the student in question ...

3. $R.Item = i?$
   and that also relates to the item of assessment in question ...

4. $R.Mark = null$
   but where the student must not yet have been awarded a mark. This line concludes the pre-conditions for the operation.

5. $\exists R' : RtRec \bullet$
   Here we introduce a result record R' that will represent the state of the result *after* the amendment.

6. $R'.Id = R.Id$
   $R'.Item = R.Item$
   $R'.Sub = R.Sub$
   None of these aspects of the result record are to be changed, naturally.

7. $R'.Mark = m?$
   The student is awarded the mark supplied.

8. $Results' = Results - \{R\} \cup \{R'\}$
   The new set of results is formed by taking the original results, removing the old result record and adding the new one.

9. $Students' = Students$
   $Assess' = Assess$
   Neither of the other relations is affected by this operation.

19.5 A Review

A classroom situation has been modelled. The *class* schema provides a static picture; the *Enrol*, *Award* and *Amend* schemas picture it dynamically.

The state schema is to be replaced by a relational database, and the operations by programs that retrieve from and manipulate that database. However, this replacement is of no concern to the user. The user sits at a machine and imagines that he or she is, for example, carrying out an *Award* operation. This operation may be viewed in terms of its pre-conditions and its post-conditions.

1. The user believes that the *Award* "program" makes checks upon his or her "database" as represented by the *class* state schema. If an error is detected then the error message will be phrased in terms of the operation's inputs and the current state of the *class*.

2. If the pre-conditions are satisfied then the "program" proceeds to update the "database" according to the requirements set out in the post-conditions.

Figure 19.1 shows this interpretation pictorially.

However satisfying this picture may be to the user, it is *not* the way that the programmer sees it. The programmer does not have at his or her disposal a machine that is directly executing or interpreting its conditions as instruction. Nor does he or she have a DBMS that is capable of storing the data structures used to build the schema. The programmer

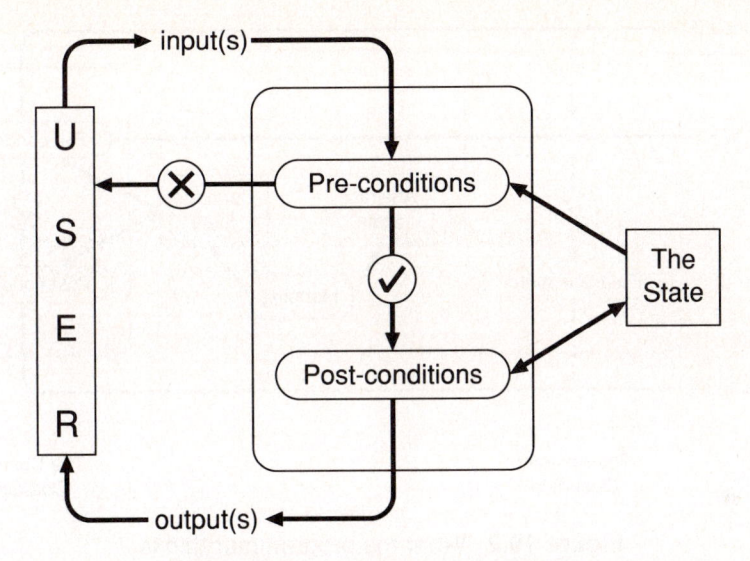

Figure 19.1 What the user thinks

must describe the situation and operations upon it in a way that is genuinely executable, that is, in a way that a machine can obey directly. So he or she must describe changes using operators that the machine can execute upon data structures the machine can support. The programmer must **simulate** the original abstract operation. What does this mean?

- The programmer must disguise his or her presence. No dialog with the user must hint that, when the pre-conditions are being evaluated, it is *not* the user's database that is being examined, but is instead some substitute. Any checks made by the real program upon *its* data structures must somehow correspond to those that the abstract program would have made.

- No traces may be left upon the user's database to suggest other than that the operation affected that database in the way expected. Any changes made by the real program upon *its* data structures must somehow correspond to those that the abstract program would have made.

This process of simulation is shown in Figure 19.2.

19.6 Verification

How can we satisfy ourselves that this re-specification is equivalent to the original? In other words is it a correct *refinement*?

There are conditions relating the concrete and the abstract that must hold true for each operation. The set of conditions to be satisfied will be determined by the nature of the relationship between the concrete and the abstract states. In our case, the relationship is a **total onto function**. The conditions apply only if the mapping is a relationship of that kind.

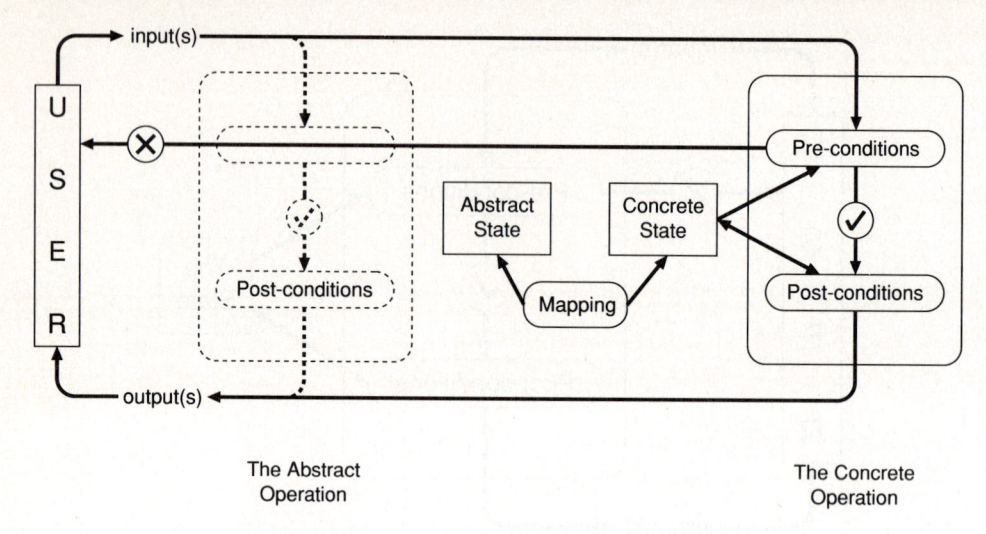

Figure 19.2 What the programmer thinks

Applicability
If the pre-conditions of the abstract operation are met and the abstract and the concrete states are related in the way specified by the mapping schema, then the concrete operation should go ahead; that is, its pre-conditions should also be satisfied.

$\forall\ Cstate;\ Astate;\ x?: X\ \bullet$
$pre\ Aop \land Abs \Rightarrow pre\ Cop$

Correctness
If the pre-conditions are met and the concrete operation is satisfied, then the abstract operation should also be satisfied.

$\forall\ Astate;\ Astate';\ Cstate;\ Cstate'x?: X\ \bullet$
$pre\ Aop \land Abs \land Cop \land Abs' \Rightarrow Aop$

The Initial State
In general, for any situation where we are relating the initial state of some abstract situation to its initial concrete realization, we can say:

$\forall\ Astate;\ Cstate\ \bullet$
$Cinit \land Abs \Rightarrow Ainit$

These rules are presented as they appear in [Spi89a]. When interpreting them for the class situation, and for the award operation, we should make the following substitutions.

Symbol	Representing	Our Situation
$Astate$	the abstract state schema	$class$
$Cstate$	the concrete state schema	$Class_{DB}$
Aop	an abstract operation	$Award$
Cop	the (supposedly) equivalent concrete operation	$Award_{EXE}$
Abs	the abstraction mapping	$Mapping$
Abs'	the abstraction mapping between the after states	$Mapping'$
Cop	a concrete operation	$Award_{EXE}$
$Ainit$	the initial abstract state	$classInitially$
$Cinit$	the initial concrete state	$Class_{DB}\,Initially$

19.7 Verifying the $Award_{EXE}$ Operation

19.7.1 The One-point Rule Revisited

Before applying the rules discussed in the previous section, we should look at one particular inference rule that we will need. This rule is known as the **one-point rule** and it was introduced in Section 12.3.2. The rule allows us to move from a set theoretical expression to a predicate calculus expression and vice versa. It has the following form:

$$\exists x : S \bullet x = t \wedge P \equiv t \in S \wedge P[t/x]$$

S is some set
P is a predicate of some kind
t is a term
$P[t/x]$ is the predicate P with all free occurrences of x replaced by the term t

If there is an object x of type S that satisfies P and t is another name for that object then t is an element of S and P is true of t, and vice-versa.

This rule may be extended to the case where the set S is a generalized relation, that is, a set of records. Suppose that the record type forming the basis for the relation is defined as follows:

```
┌─ T ─────────────────────────────────
│ :
│ att : AttType
│ :
└─────────────────────────────────────
```

It has any number of attributes but we are only interested in the one labelled att which is of type $AttType$. The relation S is declared as:

S : Set of T

The one-point rule is revised to allow for the object in question being part of some record structure.

$$\exists x : S \bullet x.att = t \wedge P \equiv t \in AttType \wedge P[t/x.att]$$

Suppose we have the following set-up:

> **AgeRecord**
> Name : Person
> Age : N

and this record is used to define the relation *Ages*:

> *Ages* : *Set of AgeRecord*

The left-hand side of the equivalence is:

> $\exists\, a : Ages \bullet a.name = Alan \wedge a.Name$ plays tennis

the right-hand size is:

> $Alan \in Person \wedge (a.Name$ plays tennis$)[Alan/a.Name]$

which reduces to:

> $Alan \in Person \wedge Alan$ plays tennis

19.7.2 Applicability

Applying the pre-conditions check to this operation requires us to prove that:

> $\forall\, class;\ Class_{DB};\ s? : Person;\ i? : Work;\ m? : 0..100 \bullet$
> $pre\ Award \wedge Mapping \Rightarrow pre\ Award_{EXE}$

The pre-conditions for the (abstract) Award operation, *pre Award* are:

> $\exists\, s : students \bullet s? = s.id\ \wedge$
> $i? \in dom\ s.sub \wedge i? \notin dom\ s.marks$

Now we can attempt to derive the pre-conditions for the concrete operation.

> $\exists\, s : students \bullet s? = s.id\ \wedge$
> $i? \in dom\ s.sub \wedge i? \notin dom\ s.marks$

(The abstract state invariant says that for all students $dom\ s.marks \subseteq dom\ s.sub$.)

$\Rightarrow \exists\, s : students \bullet s? = s.id\ \wedge$
$i? \in (dom\ s.sub - doms.marks)$

(We can replace the set difference by its equivalent concrete representation as discussed in Section 19.4.2.)

$\Rightarrow \exists\, s : students \bullet s? = s.id\ \wedge$
$i? \in \{R : Results \mid R.Id = s.id \wedge R.Mark = null \bullet R.Item\}$

(The set membership is rephrased using existential quantification. If $t \in R$ then $\exists\, x : R \bullet x = t$. This is a special case of the one-point rule with $P \equiv true$.)

$\Rightarrow \exists s : students \bullet s? = s.id \land$
$\quad \exists R : Results \bullet R.Id = s.id \land R.Mark = null \land R.Item = i?$

(We can now apply the modified one-point rule discussed previously.)

$\Rightarrow s? \in students \land$
$\quad \exists R : Results \bullet R.Id = s? \land R.Mark = null \land R.Item = i?$

(We can eliminate the first conjunct.)

$\Rightarrow \exists R : Results \bullet R.Id = s? \land R.Mark = null \land R.Item = i?$

(Now we have the pre-condition of the concrete operation, that is, $preAward_{EXE}$.)

19.7.3 Correctness

Now we must show that the changes that the concrete operation makes to the concrete state correspond to those that are required to be made to the abstract state.

$\forall class; class'; Class_{DB}; Class'_{DB} \bullet$
$pre\ Award \land Mapping \land Award_{EXE} \land Mapping' \Rightarrow Award$

In this section, we will concentrate our proof on the most significant line of the *Award* operation, which is:

$s'.marks = s.marks \cup \{(i?, m?)\}$

We will attempt to show that the set on left-hand side of this equation is the same as the one on the right-hand side.

$s'.marks$

(This may be replaced by its concrete representation using *Mapping'* the after version of the abstraction schema.)

$= \{t : Results' \mid t.Id = s.id \land t.Mark \neq null \bullet (t.Item, t.Mark)\}$

(The post-condition of the concrete operation $Award_{EXE}$ provides an equation relating *Results'* and *Results*.)

$= \{t : (Results - \{R\} \cup \{R'\}) \mid t.Id = s.id \land t.Mark \neq null \bullet (t.Item, t.Mark)\}$

(The declaration of the set comprehension involves three sets in a set expression $Results - \{R\} \cup \{R'\}$. This may be expanded to three separate pieces of set comprehension.)

$= \{t : Results \mid t.Id = s.Id \land t.Mark \neq null \bullet (t.Item, t.Mark)\}$
$\quad - \{t : \{R\} \mid t.Id = s.id \land t.Mark \neq null \bullet (t.Item, t.Mark)\}$
$\quad \cup \{t : \{R'\} \mid t.Id = s.id \land t.Mark \neq null \bullet (t.Item, t.Mark)\}$

(The first piece is just *s.marks* as defined in the mapping. The second piece reduces to the empty set because $R.Mark = null$ according to $Award_{EXE}$ and so the predicate $t.Mark \neq null$ is not satisfied. The third piece simplifies to a set consisting of one element, the pair $(i?, m?)$. This is because $R'.Id = R.Id$ and $R.Id = s.id$ and $R'.Mark \neq null$ and $R'.Mark = m?$ and $R'.Item = R.Item$ and $R.Item = i?$. All of these come from $Award_{EXE}$.)

$= s.marks - \{\} \cup \{(i?, m?)\}$

(The empty set makes no difference to the set expression and so the line may be further simplified.)

$= s.marks \cup \{(i?, m?)\}$

We have proved the most significant line of the abstract operation:

$s'.marks = s.marks \cup \{(i?, m?)\}$

19.7.4 The Initial State

We require that the initial state of the database corresponds to the initial state of the abstract specification.

$\forall class; Class_{DB} \bullet$
$Class_{DB} Initially \land Mapping \Rightarrow classInitially$

The initial state of the concrete specification, that is, the database, in conjunction with the abstraction mapping must represent a valid initial abstract state. The initial state of the classroom will be one where there are no students and no assessable assignments have yet been set. A set of concrete results gives rise to one set of abstract results.

$Class_{DB} Initially$

$Class_{DB}$

$Students = \{\}$
$Assess = \{\}$
$Results = \{\}$

An empty Students table guarantees that the existential quantification in the retrieval function for *students* can never be satisfied and so the *students* set will be empty which is what we require. An empty Assess table will guarantee that no assessment exists in the abstract state. What about the Results table? The initial state of the database must also conform to the concrete state invariant. Therefore, the referential integrity conditions:

$\{R : Results \bullet R.Id\} \subseteq \{S : Students \bullet s.Id\}$
$\{R : Results \bullet R.Item\} \subseteq \{A : Assess \bullet a.Item\}$

each require that the Results table be empty initially in order to provide referential integrity.

$classInitially$

$class$

$students = \{\}$
$title = \{\}$

19.8 The External Interface

We will now examine how a student may be awarded a mark by an application system using the *Class* database. A simple user interface might look like the following.

```
          The Class Information System

            Award a Mark Operation

        Id:      831

        Item:    3

        Mark:    80




        Msg:    [        ]
```

The screen offers none of the usual feedback that one would expect. It simply allows the user to enter the three values that the operation requires. About the only concession to user-friendliness is a message area at the bottom of the screen.

1. The pre-conditions

    When the lecturer has entered the three inputs required by this operation, he or she will press some kind of **OK** button. The program will then make the following check.

    ```
    Exists (Select *
            From    Results R
            Where   R.Id = s?
            and     R.Item = i?
            and     R.Mark is null)
    ```

    If there exists a row in the **Results** table for the student in question, relating to the item of assessment in question *and* no mark has yet been awarded then the pre-conditions are satisfied. If these conditions are not satisfied then a message will be displayed and the inputs will need to be resupplied.

2. The post-conditions

    If the pre-conditions are met then the program will proceed to change the database.

    ```
    Update Results R
    Set     R.Mark = m?
    Where   R.Id = s?
    and     R.Item = i?
    ```

    The **Mark** column of the appropriate **Result** row will be set to the value supplied.

19.9 Translating the $Award_{EXE}$ Schema into SQL

The SQL statements shown above can be derived in a mechanical fashion from the concrete specification. That specification was designed, after all, to mimic in Z the operations of SQL. In this section we will step through that specification interpreting it in the form of SQL syntax.

- Those lines in the schema involving just R become the pre-conditions.

$$\exists R : Results \bullet$$
$$R.Id = s?$$
$$R.Item = i?$$
$$R.Mark = null$$

They are interpreted as the following SQL condition.

```
Exists (Select *
        From    Results R
        Where   R.Id = s?
        and     R.Item = i?
        and     R.Mark is null)
```

- The line introducing the "after" variable R' merely establishes that an update is occurring. Its type $RtRec$ indicates that the corresponding table **Results** is the one to be updated.

$$\exists R' : RtRec \bullet$$

- Lines involving corresponding components of R and R' that merely equate these components can be ignored from an SQL point of view.

$$R'.Id = R.Id$$
$$R'.Item = R.Item$$
$$R'.Sub = R.Sub$$

- Lines that set an after component, that is some part of R', to some other value should be mapped to the **set** clause of the **update** statement.

$$R'.Mark = m?$$

Thus the above line gives rise to the clause:

```
Set R.Mark = m?
```

- The final line of this group confirms that an update is required:

$$Results' = Results - \{R\} \cup \{R'\}$$

- The rest of the schema lists the database tables that are unaffected by the operation. These lines may safely be ignored.

$$Students' = Students$$
$$Assess' = Assess$$

Although we have formed part of the **update** statement, it remains to calculate its **where** clause, if any. For that we can return to the pre-conditions. There we established the record r that was to be changed and the conditions that it had to satisfy. These conditions can be transferred to the **where** clause. The entire statement becomes as follows:

```
Update Results R
    Set R.Mark = m?
  Where R.Id = s?
    and R.Item = i?
```

19.10 Summary

This chapter has demonstrated the technique of data refinement for a practical database application. We have taken an abstract specification of the class situation and implemented it as a concrete specification. The abstraction schema *Mapping* relates the components of the two specifications by defining the abstract ones in terms of the concrete. A typical operation, the awarding of a mark for some item of assessment submitted by a student, is specified as *Award* for the abstract state *class* and as $Award_{EXE}$ for the concrete state $Class_{DB}$.

The initialization, applicability and correctness rules for *functional* data refinement are used to prove the validity of the concrete representation. In Section 19.9, the concrete operation $Award_{EXE}$ is shown to be a near-SQL statement of the operation.

Appendix A
Further Reading

[Che76]   Chen P.P. (1976). "The Entity-Relationship Model – Toward a Unified View of Data", *ACM Transactions on Database Systems*, 1(1): 9–36. Also reprinted in [Sto88].

[Che80]   Chen P.P. (ed.) (1980). *Entity-Relationship Approach to Systems Analysis and Design*. Amsterdam, Holland: North-Holland.

[Cod70]   Codd E.F. (1970). "A Relational Model of Data for Large Shared Data Banks", *Communications of the ACM*, 13(6): 377–387. Also reprinted in [Sto88].

[Dat89]   Date C.J. (1989). *A Guide to the SQL Standard*, 2nd edn. Reading, Mass., USA: Addison-Wesley.

[Dat90]   Date C.J. (1990). *An Introduction to Database Systems* Vol. 1, 5th edn. Reading, Mass., USA: Addison-Wesley.

[Dav80]   Davenport R.A. (1980). "The Application of Data Analysis – Experience with the Entity-Relationship Approach" in [Che80].

[Dil90]   Diller A. (1990). *Z: An Introduction to Formal Methods*. Chichester, England: John Wiley.

[Dro89]   Dromey R.G. (1989). *Program Derivation: The Development of Programs From Specifications*. Sydney, Australia: Addison-Wesley.

[EN89]   Elmasri R.A. and Navathe S.B. (1989). *Fundamentals of Database Systems*. Redwood, Calif., USA: Benjamin/Cummings.

[EDB89]   Emerson S.L., Darnovsky M. and Bowman J.S. (1989). *The Practical SQL Handbook*. Reading, Mass., USA: Addison-Wesley.

[FZ87]   Folk M.J. and Zoellick B. (1987). *File Structures: A Conceptual Toolkit*. Reading, Mass., USA: Addison-Wesley.

[Gra84]   Gray P.M.D. (1984). *Logic, Algebra and Databases*. Chichester, England: Ellis Horwood.

[Hal90]   Hall A. (1990). "Seven Myths of Formal Methods" *IEEE Software*, September 1990, 11-19.

[Haw90]   Hawryszkiewycz I.T. (1990). *Relational Database Design*. Sydney, Australia: Prentice Hall of Australia.

[Haw91]   Hawryszkiewycz I.T. (1991). *Introduction to Systems Analysis and Design* 2nd edn. Sydney, Australia: Prentice Hall of Australia.

[Hay87]   Hayes I.J. (ed.) (1987). *Specification Case Studies*. London, England: Prentice Hall International.

[Hod77] Hodges W. (1977). *Logic.* Middlesex, England: Penguin Books.

[IBM89] IBM Corporation (1989). *DB2 Version 2: Application Programming and SQL Guide.* San Jose, Calif., USA: IBM Corporation.

[Inc88] Ince D. (1988). *An Introduction to Discrete Mathematics and Formal Systems Specification.* Oxford, England: Oxford University Press.

[Lan88] Lans, R.F. van der (1988). *Introduction to SQL.* Wokingham, England: Addison-Wesley.

[Lip66] Lipschutz S. (1966). *Finite Mathematics.* New York, USA: McGraw-Hill.

[NH89] Nijssen G.M. and Halpin T.A. (1989). *Conceptual Schema and Relational Database Design.* Sydney, Australia: Prentice Hall of Australia.

[Ora86] Oracle Corporation (1986). *SQL Language Reference Manual.* USA: Oracle Corporation.

[Ora89] Oracle Corporation (1989). *Programmers Guide to the Precompilers.* USA: Oracle Corporation.

[Pag80] Page-Jones M. (1980). *The Practical Guide to Structured Systems Design.* New York, USA: Yourdon Press.

[Par80] Parkin A. (1980). *Systems Analysis.* London, England: Edward Arnold.

[PST91] Potter B., Sinclair J. and Till D. (1991). *An Introduction to Formal Specification and Z.* Hemel Hempstead, England: Prentice Hall International.

[PV89] Papazoglou M. and Valder W. (1989). *Relational Database Management.* Hemel Hempstead, England: Prentice Hall International.

[Ric78] Richards T.J. (1978). *The Language of Reason.* Sydney, Australia: Pergamon Press (Australia).

[RTI86] Relational Technology Inc. (1986). Ingres Release 5.0 for VMS Operating System, *Ingres/SQL Reference Manual.* Alamada, Calif., USA: Relational Technology Inc.

[Som89] Sommerville I. (1989). *Software Engineering* 3rd edn. Wokingham, England: Addison-Wesley.

[Spi89a] Spivey J.M. (1989). *The Z Notation: A Reference Manual.* Hemel Hempstead, England: Prentice Hall International.

[Spi89b] Spivey J.M. (1989). "An Introduction to Z and Formal Specifications", *IEE Software Engineering Journal,* 4(1), Jan 1989: 40–50.

[Sto88] Stonebraker M. (ed.) (1988). *Readings in Database Systems.* San Mateo, Calif., USA: Morgan Kaufmann.

[Sup57] Suppes P. (1957). *Introduction to Logic.* Princeton, NJ, USA: Van Nostrand.

[Vos91] Vossen G. (1991). *Data Models, Database Languages and Database Management Systems.* Wokingham, England: Addison-Wesley.

[Whi88] Whittington R.P. (1988). *Database Systems Engineering.* Oxford, England: Oxford University Press.

[WL88]   Woodcock J.C.P. and Loomes M. (1988). *Software Engineering Mathematics*. London, England: Pitman.

[Woo89]   Woodcock J.C.P. (1989). "Structuring Specifications in Z", *IEE Software Engineering Journal*, 4(1), Jan 1989: 51–71.

Chapter 1: Introduction

See [Spi89b] and [Woo89] for tutorial introductions to Z. Also see [Hal90] for a discussion of formal methods.

Chapter 2: Specific Facts

[Hod77, pp 86–168] contains much material relevant to this chapter.

Chapter 3: Sets

See [Lip66, Chapters 5 to 8] and [Dro89, pp 92–108]

Chapter 4: Relations

See [Dat90, Chapters 11 to 15] for an extensive discussion of the relational model. See also [EN89, Chapter 8], [Gra84, Chapters 6, 7 and 8]. Codd [Cod70] is generally credited with making us see the importance of the relational model.

Chapter 5: Introducing SQL

See [Lan88, Chapter 2], [EN89, pp 176–182].

Chapter 6: SQL Retrieval

See [Lan88, Chapter 4], [Dat90, pp 145–156].

Chapter 7: SQL Modularisation

See [Lan88, Chapter 5], [Dat90, pp 156–163] and [EN89, pp 184–194].

Chapter 8: Facts and Relations

[NH89] comprehensively discusses conceptual schema design.

Chapter 9: Uncovering Facts

See [Haw91, Chapter 10] and [Pag80, pp 75 – 8].

Chapter 11: Entity-Relationship Modeling

The paper by Chen [Chen76] started it all. However, the discussion and notation in this chapter is based on [EN89, Chapter 3 and pp 327–34]. See also [Dat90, Chapter 22] and [Par80, Chapter 7].

Chapter 12: Knowledge

[Gra84, Chapters 1 and 2], [PST91, Chapters 2, 4 and 5], [WL88, Chapters 1 to 8], [Inc88, Chapters 3 to 7], [Dro89, Chapter 2 and pp 112-39] and [Dil90, Chapters 1 to 8]. See also [Sup57, Chapters 1, 2, 3 and 8].

Chapter 13: The Knowledge Base

See [Inc88, Chapters 9 and 11], [PST91, Chapter 6], [Som89, Chapter 9], [WL88] and [Woo89].

Chapter 14: From Specification to Implementation

See [Som89, Chapter 9] and [Spi89a, pp 134–5].

Chapter 15: Database Definition in SQL

See [Dat89, Chapters 3, 4, 5 and 9]. For discussion of the internal structure of a relational database, see [PV89, Chapter 6], [Whi88, Chapter 7] and [FZ87].

Chapter 16: Database Manipulation in SQL

See [Dat89, Chapter 8].

Chapter 17: Application Programming

See [Dat89, Chapters 2, 7 and 11].

Chapter 18: Case Studies

See [Hay87] for a number of case studies in the use of Z. See also [WL88, Chapter 9] and [Inc88, Chapter 12].

Chapter 19: Refinement

[PST91, Chapter 9]

Appendix B
SQL Syntax Summary

This appendix contains a summary of what we can say in SQL. This syntax is presented in the form of a dictionary. Each entry in the dictionary describes a grammatical component of SQL. An example of the kind of entry to be found is the **order_clause**.

    order_clause

        ORDER BY *list_of_order_specifications*

This definition says that an **order_clause** may be formed by writing the words **ORDER BY** followed by a list of things called **order_specifications** and an order specification is defined elsewhere in the dictionary.

In the definition of each entry, several notational conventions are followed. These are perhaps best described by example. Here are two related entries.

    order_clause

        ORDER BY *list_of_order_specifications*

    order_specification

        column_name [ASC|DESC]

  or **integer [ASC|DESC]**

The conventions are as follows.

1. Words that we will enter ourselves are written in upper case, such as **ORDER BY**. The names of entries in the dictionary are written in lower case, such as **order_clause** and **order_specification**.

2. A grammatical entry may have several major ways of being phrased, for example, an **order_clause** can only be formed in one way; but an **order_specification** can be formed in two different ways. The second and subsequent alternatives are introduced by an *or*.

3. A vertical bar | is used to separate alternative parts of a statement; **ASC|DESC** indicates that **either ASC or DESC** may be used.

4. Square brackets [ ] are used for optional parts of the statement being defined; **[ASC|DESC]** indicates that **neither** of the enclosed options need be used.

5. An expression such as *list_of_order_specifications* signifies that we should substitute a series of **order_specifications** separated by commas. So an example of an **order_clause** would be **ORDER BY AGE DESC, SEX, 1 ASC**.

SQL Syntax Summary 499

The data objects that SQL allows us to use, such as tables and columns, must all have names. The rules for naming objects are as follows.

1. The first character of the name must be a letter or one of the symbols $, # or @.
2. The other characters may be a letter or a digit or one of the symbols $, #, @ or _.

```
access_right
      ALL
   or [SELECT|INSERT|DELETE|ALTER |INDEX]
   or UPDATE (list_of_column_names)

assignment
      column_name = item

column_definition
      column_name datatype [NOT NULL]

column_name
      A standard SQL name.

condition
      simple_condition
   or ( condition )
   or condition OR condition
   or condition AND condition

comparison
      [< | <= | = | <> | >= | >]

datatype
      CHAR(integer)
   or DATE
   or INTEGER
   or DECIMAL(p[,s])
   or NUMBER
   or NUMBER(p)
   or NUMBER(p,s)

delete_statement
      DELETE
      FROM table_name
      [where_clause]
```

expression

    This may be any kind that matches a datatype.

from_clause

    FROM *list_of_table_name*s

grant_statement

    GRANT *list_of_access_right* s|ALL
    ON table_name
    TO *list_of_user_name*s
    [WITH GRANT OPTION]

group_by_clause

    GROUP BY *list_of_column_name*s

having_clause

    HAVING condition

index_component

    column_name [ASC|DESC]

index_definition_statement

    CREATE [UNIQUE] INDEX index_name
    ON table_name(*list_of_index_component*s)

index_name

    A standard SQL name.

index_removal_statement

    DROP INDEX index_name

insert_statement

    INSERT
    INTO table_name [(*list_of_column_name*s)]
    VALUES (*list_of_constant*s)

  or INSERT
    INTO table_name [(*list_of_column_name*s)]
    select_statement

integer

    A sequence of digits.

SQL Syntax Summary   501

item
    column_name
 or constant
 or expression

order_clause
    ORDER BY *list_of_*order_specification*s*

order_specification
    column_name [ASC|DESC]
 or integer [ASC|DESC]

pattern_string
    A character string literal containing the special characters % or _.

revoke_statement
    REVOKE *list_of_*access_right*s*|ALL
    ON table_name
    FROM *list_of_*user_name*s*

select_clause
    SELECT [ALL|DISTINCT] *list_of_*item*s*
 or SELECT *

select_statement
    select_clause
    from_clause
    [where_clause]
    [group_by_clause [having_clause]]
    [order_clause]

simple_condition
    item comparison item
 or special_condition
 or subquery_condition

special_condition
    item [NOT] BETWEEN item AND item
 or column_name [NOT] LIKE pattern_string
 or column_name [NOT] NULL

subquery

    (select_statement)

subquery_condition

    item [NOT] comparison subquery
  or item [NOT] comparison [ALL|ANY] subquery
  or item [NOT] IN subquery
  or [NOT] EXISTS subquery

table_alteration_statement

    ALTER TABLE table_name
    ADD column_name data_type

table_definition_statement

    CREATE TABLE table_name
    (*list_of_*column_definition*s*)

table_name

    A standard SQL name.

table_removal_statement

    DROP TABLE table_name

update_statement

    UPDATE table_name
    SET *list_of_*assignment*s*
    [where_clause]

user_name

    PUBLIC
  or An SQL name.

view_definition_statement

    CREATE VIEW table_name [(*list_of_*column_name*s*)]
    AS select_statement

view_removal_statement

    DROP VIEW table_name

where_clause

    WHERE condition

Appendix C
The Z Notation

The Structure of a Specification

A specification using the Z notation will be a mixture of formal description and informal narrative – lots of informal narrative – that discusses, interprets and highlights various aspects of the formal part, just as any well written program will include comment to explain the otherwise cryptic nature of the program code. In the description of the syntax that follows, no mention is made of this essential commentary.

The formal part of the specification consists of a number of paragraphs, where a paragraph may take any of the forms shown below.

Paragraph:

      Type Introduction

  or Global Definition

  or Generic Global Definition

  or Schema

  or Abbreviation

Type Introductions

A specification is a description of some world. It identifies the kinds of objects to be found there, how the objects are related and how these relationships may change. When we discuss an object, we must always declare its type, and we must have introduced its type beforehand.

    Type_Introduction:

        [*Symbol*]

    or [*Symbol*, ..., *Symbol*]

We may introduce one or more types together. We do not need to introduce all required types at the same time, but may choose to spread their introduction throughout the specification, subject to the restriction that no type is used before being introduced.

Global Definitions

A global definition introduces one or more variables which may be used subsequently. It has the following form:

| Declaration
|
| Predicate

Symbols such as the arithmetic operators ($+, -, *$, etc.) and relations ($<, \leq, \geq, >$) are global symbols and are introduced as global definitions.

| $\_ + \_ : N \times N \to N$
| ...
|
| ...

However, it is normal to assume that these are provided as part of a standard package of mathematics.

Generic Global Definitions

These are global definitions that may be used with any type. They have the form:

$[X, \ldots, Z]$
| Declaration
|
| Predicate

Typical of these generic symbols are the set operators and relations. We could introduce them as follows.

$[S]$
| $\_ \cup \_ : \text{Set of } S \times \text{Set of } S \to \text{Set of } S$
| ...
|
| ...

Like the arithmetical symbols, however, the set operations are part of the standard mathematics package.

Schemas

A schema is the name given to the box-shape that characterizes the Z notation. It enables us to introduced some objects, to constrain them in some way, and to name that constraint.

Name
| Declaration
|
| Predicate

Schemas may used in a variety of ways. They allow us to describe things statically or dynamically, or to introduce composite record types.

Abbreviations

These allow us to shorten commonly required expressions. The relation and function symbols are examples.

Abbreviation:

    NewSymbol == *Term*
or *Symbol NewInfixSymbol Symbol* == *Term*
or *NewPrefixSymbol Symbol* == *Term*

Terms

A term is an object. It may be an individual object, a set-valued object or a composite object.

Term:

    Symbol
or *Set_Term*
or *Tuple*
or *Symbol Term*
or *Symbol.Term*
or (*Term*)

Tuple:

    (*Term*)
or (*Term*, ..., *Term*)

Sets

There are many ways of describing a set. A symbolic expression that represents a set is called a **set term**.

Set_Term:

    Symbol
or *Set_Extension*
or *Set_Comprehension*

or *Type_Construction*
or *Set_Operation*
or *Special_Set_Operation*
or *Fact_Type*

or (*Set_Term*)
or *Symbol Set_Term*
or *Set_Term Symbol Set_Term*

Set_Extension:

> { }
> or { *Term* }
> or { *Term*, *Term*, ..., *Term* }

Set_Comprehension:

> { *Declaration* }
> or { *Declaration* | *Predicate* }
> or { *Declaration* | *Predicate* • *Term* }
> or { *Declaration* • *Term* }

Type_Construction

> or Set of *Set_Term*
> or *Set_Term* × *Set_Term*

Set_Operation

> or *Set_Term* ∪ *Set_Term*
> or *Set_Term* ∩ *Set_Term*
> or *Set_Term* − *Set_Term*

Special_Set_Operation

> or *Set_Term* ◁ *Set_Term*
> or *Set_Term* ▷ *Set_Term*
> or *Set_Term* ⊕ *Set_Term*
> or dom *Set_Term*
> or ran *Set_Term*

Fact_Type

> or *Set_Term* ↔ *Set_Term*
> or *Set_Term* ↣ *Set_Term*
> or *Set_Term* → *Set_Term*
> or *Set_Term* ↣→ *Set_Term*
> or *Set_Term* ↠ *Set_Term*

Declarations

All objects must be introduced or *declared* before being used in any way. Declarations are required in set comprehension, quantified predicates and in schemas.

Declaration:

> *Basic_Declaration*
> or *Basic_Declaration*; ...; *Basic_Declaration*

Basic_Declaration:

> *Symbol* : *Set_Term*
> or *Symbol*, ..., *Symbol* : *Set_Term*

Although the semicolon has been shown as the separator, a new line may also be used.

Predicates

A predicate is a statement about the universe of discourse. It may be either true or false.

Predicate:

> *Simple_Predicate*
> or *Compound_Predicate*
> or *Quantified_Predicate*

Simple_Predicate:

> *Symbol Term*
> or *Term Symbol Term*
> or *Term* $\in$ *Set_Term*
> or *Term* $=$ *Term*

Compound_Predicate:

> $\neg$*Predicate*
> or *Predicate* $\wedge$ *Predicate*
> or *Predicate* $\vee$ *Predicate*
> or *Predicate* $\Rightarrow$ *Predicate*
> or *Predicate* $\Leftrightarrow$ *Predicate*

Quantified_Predicate:

> $\forall$ *Declaration* • *Predicate*
> or $\exists$ *Declaration* • *Predicate*
> or $\exists!$ *Declaration* • *Predicate*

Symbols

A symbol is merely a recognisable and distinguishable mark of some kind. Most symbols are constructed as identifiers, that is, as sequences of alphabetic characters drawn from the keyboard. However, we may use any means we wish to construct a symbol. The set operations such as $\cup$ and $\cap$ are of this kind.

Appendix D
Selected Answers

Chapter 1

Q1.1 Happenings in the bank. The pre- and post-conditions are matched with the necessary SQL.

    a.   A person *c?* comes into the bank and joins the others.

        1. The person is not among the others.
```
Select  CustId
From    Others
Where   CustId = 'c?'
```
           Continue: if no rows returned.

        2. The person is not in the queue.
```
Select  CustId
From    Queue
Where   CustId = 'c?'
```
           Continue: if no rows returned.

        3. The person is not being served.
```
Select  CustId
From    Busy
Where   CustId = 'c?'
```
           Continue: if no rows returned.

        4. Now add this person to the others.
```
Insert
Into    Others
Values(c?)
```

    b.   A person *c?* leaves the bank.

        1. The person is among the others in the bank.
```
Select  CustId
From    Others
Where   CustId = 'c?'
```
           Continue: if a row was returned.

        2. Take this person out of the others.
```
Delete
From    Others
Where   CustId = 'c?'
```

c. A teller *t?* opens up his or her window.
   1. The teller is not open already.
      ```
      Select  Teller
      From    Open
      Where   Teller = 't?'
      ```
      Continue: if no rows returned.
   2. Add this teller to those open.
      ```
      Insert
      Into    Open
      Values(t?)
      ```
d. A teller *t?* closes down his or her window.
   1. The teller is open.
      ```
      Select  Teller
      From    Open
      Where   Teller = 't?'
      ```
      Continue: if a row is found.
   2. The teller is not busy.
      ```
      Select  Teller
      From    Busy
      Where   Teller = 't?'
      ```
      Continue: if no row is found.
   3. Either: the queue is empty...
      ```
      Select  Place
      From    Queue
      ```
      Go to step 5: if no row is found.
   4. Or: there is another open teller.
      ```
      Select  Teller
      From    Open
      Where   Teller <> 't?'
      ```
      Continue: if a row is found.
   5. Remove the teller from the open ones.
      ```
      Delete
      From    Open
      Where   Teller = 't?'
      ```
e. A customer *c?* joins the queue.
   1. The customer is among the others.
      ```
      Select  CustId
      From    Others
      Where   CustId = 'c?'
      ```
      Continue: if a row is found.
   2. Add the customer to the end of the queue.

```
        Insert
        Into    Queue
        Select  max(Place)+1,'c?'
        From    Queue
     3. Remove the customer from the others.
        Delete
        From    Others
        Where   CustId = 'c?'
  f. A customer c? finishes his or her transaction, and prepares to leave the bank.
     1. The customer is busy.
        Select  CustId
        From    Busy
        Where   CustId = 'c?'
        Continue: if a row is found.
     2. Move the customer out to the others.
        Delete
        From    Busy
        Where   CustId = 'c?'

        Insert
        Into    Others
        Values(c?)
  g. A customer c? leaves the queue to fill out a form.
     1. The customer is in the queue.
        Select  CustId
        From    Queue
        Where   CustId = 'c?'
        Continue: if a row was found.
     2. Move the customer back to the others.
        Insert
        Into    Others
        values(c?)
     3. Rearrange the queue.
        Update Queue
            Set Place = Place-1
            Where Place > (Select Place
                           From    Queue
                           Where   CustId = 'c?')

        Delete
        From    Queue
        Where   CustId = 'c?'
  h. A customer c? leaves the queue to fill out a form but only if not at the front.
```

1. The customer is in the queue.
   ```
   Select  CustId
   From    Queue
   Where   CustId = 'c?'
   ```
   Continue: if a row was found.
2. The customer is not at the front.
   ```
   Select  CustId
   From    Queue
   Where   Place = 1
     and   CustId = 'c?'
   ```
   Continue: if no row was found.
3. Move the customer back to the others.
   ```
   Insert
   Into    Others
   values(c?)
   ```
4. Rearrange the queue.
   ```
   Update Queue
      Set Place = Place-1
     Where Place > (Select Place
                     From   Queue
                     Where  CustId = 'c?')

   Delete
   From    Queue
   Where   CustId = 'c?'
   ```

Q1.2 Extending the bank model – changes to the operations.

a. A person *c?* comes into the bank.
   We will have to check that:
   1. The customer is not among the others.
   2. The customer is not being served.
   3. There is no stand at which the customer is queueing.

   We will then:
   4. Add the customer to the others.

b. No change
c. No change
d. No change
e. We will have to identify the queue that the customer joins.

   c? : *Person*
   s? : *Stand*

f. No change
g. We will need to ensure that only one queue is affected.
h. See previous operation.

Chapter 2

Q2.1 a. relation(s): **likes** and **writes**
        function(s): **age**
        injection(s): **drives**

   b. (1) **drives** is a partial injection; and (2) by inspection.

   c. **likes** and **writes** are used in infix form; the others are used in prefix form.

   d. { Honda, Ford }
       ran drives

   e. { Bill, Sue, Alan }
       dom likes

Q2.2 a. **true**
   b. **false**
   c. **true**
   d. **true**
   e. **false**

Q2.3 a. Bill writes SQL
        = true [Because (Bill,SQL) is in **writes**]
   b. Bill likes Sue
        = true
   c. drives(Sue) = Ford
        = Honda = Ford
        = false
   d. Alan likes Sue
        = false
   e. age(Sue) = 19
        = 19 = 19 [Applying **age** to Sue gives 19]
        = true

Q2.4 a. not true = false
   b. true or false = true
   c. true and false = false
   d. true and true = true

e. not false = true
f. false and false = false
g. not (not true) = not false = true
h. (not false) and (not true) = true and false = false
i. not (false or true) = not true = false
j. true and false = false

Q2.5 a. not (Alan likes Bill)
= not true
= false

b. not (Bill writes SQL)
= not true
= false

c. (Sue likes Bill) and (Bill likes Sue)
= false and true
= false

d. age(Bill) > age(Sue)
= 19 > 19
= false

e. (Sue writes C) and (Sue writes Pascal)
= true and false
= false

f. not(Alan writes FORTRAN) and not(Sue writes FORTRAN)
= not(true) and not(false)
= false and true
= false

g. (drives(Sue)=Honda) or (drives(Bill)=Honda)
= (Honda=Honda) or (Ford=Honda)
= true or false
= true

h. age(Alan) = age(Bill)+5
= 16 = 19+5
= 16 = 24
= false

i. drives(Sue) = drives(Bill)
= Honda = Ford
= false

j. (Bill writes SQL) and (Sue writes SQL)
= true and true
= true

Q2.6 a. Bill is in the range of likes.

b. COBOL is *not* in the range of **writes**.

c. The domain of **writes** is the same as the set of all people.

d. The range of **likes** is the same as the set of all people.

e. All the numbers in the range of **age** are between 13 and 19 inclusive.

Q2.7 a. Bill and Sue
 b. Bill
 c. Bill and Sue
 d. nobody
 e. Sue *and* Bill
 f. Alan
 g. Alan
 h. Sue
 i. Sue, Alan and Bill

Q2.9 a. `cap(QLD)`
 b. `pop(Melbourne)`
 c. `pop(cap(QLD))`
 d. `loc(Cairns)`
 e. `pop(Sydney) - pop(Melbourne)`

Q2.10 a. `pop(cap(NSW)) > pop(cap(QLD))`
 b. `(pop(Sydney)>pop(Melbourne))` and `(pop(Sydney)>pop(Brisbane))`
 c. `pop(Sydney)>(pop(Melbourne)+pop(Brisbane))`
 d. `(cap(SA)=Adelaide) and (cap(TAS)=Hobart)`
 e. `loc(Newcastle)=NSW or loc(Newcastle)=WA`

Chapter 3

Q3.1 a. The members who like Alan: {`Bill, Sue`}.
 b. The languages that Sue writes: {`C, SQL`}.
 c. The ages of the members who write SQL: {`19`}.
 d. The members of Bill's age: {`Bill, Sue`}.
 e. The members who like Alan and whom Alan likes: {`Bill`}.

Q3.2 a. {`m : Member | Alan likes m`}.

Selected answers for Chapter 3   515

   b. $\{m : \text{Member} \mid \text{Alan likes } m \bullet \text{age}(m)\}$.
   c. $\{m : \text{Member} \mid \text{age}(m) > \text{age}(\text{Alan})\}$.
   d. $\{l : \text{Language}; m : \text{Member} \mid \text{age}(m) = \text{age}(\text{Sue}) \text{ and } m \text{ writes } l \bullet l\}$.
   e. $\{m : \text{Member} \mid \text{age}(m) = \text{age}(\text{Sue}) \text{ and } m \text{ likes Sue}\}$.

Q3.3   a. $\{t : \text{Town} \mid \text{loc}(t) = \text{NSW}\}$
   b. $\{t : \text{Town} \mid \text{loc}(t) = \text{NSW} \bullet \text{pop}(t)\}$
   c. $\{s : \text{State} \bullet \text{cap}(s)\}$
   d. $\{t : \text{Town} \mid \text{pop}(t) > \text{pop}(\text{Newcastle})\}$
   e. $\{t : \text{Town} \bullet (t, \text{pop}(t))\}$

Q3.4   a. $\{s : \text{State} \mid \text{pop}(\text{cap}(s)) > 1\,000\,000 \bullet \text{cap}(s)\}$
   b. $\{s : \text{State} \bullet \text{pop}(\text{cap}(s))\}$
   c. $\{t : \text{Town} \mid \text{loc}(t) = \text{loc}(\text{Cairns})\}$
   d. $\{t : \text{Town} \mid \text{cap}(\text{loc}(t)) \neq t\}$
      or
      $\text{Town minus } \{s : \text{State} \bullet \text{cap}(s)\}$
   e. $\{s : \text{State} \bullet (s, \text{count}\{t : \text{Town} \mid \text{loc}(t) = s\})\}$

Q3.5   a. A minus B
      $= \{5, 3, 21, 16\} \text{ minus } \{10, 5, 4\}$
      $= \{3, 21, 16\}$
   b. $\{n : A \mid n > 11\}$
      $= \{n : \{5, 3, 21, 16\} \mid n > 11\}$
      $= \{21, 16\}$
   c. $\text{count}(A) = 4$
   d. $\text{count}(B \text{ minus } A)$
      $= \text{count}(\{10, 5, 4\} \text{minus} \{5, 3, 21, 16\})$
      $= \text{count}(\{10, 4\})$
      $= 2$
   e. $\text{count}(B \text{ minus } B) = \text{count}(\{\}) = 0$
   f. $A \text{ intersect } \{n : (B \text{ union } A) \mid n < 16\}$
      $= \{5, 3, 21, 16\} \text{ intersect } \{n : (\{10, 5, 4\} \text{ union } \{5, 3, 21, 16\}) \mid n < 16\}$
      $= \{5, 3, 21, 16\} \text{ intersect } \{n : \{10, 5, 4, 3, 21, 16\} \mid n < 16\}$
      $= \{5, 3, 21, 16\} \text{ intersect } \{10, 5, 4, 3\}$
      $= \{5, 3\}$
   g. $A \text{ intersect } (B \text{ union } \{n : A \mid n < 16\})$
      $= A \text{ intersect } (B \text{ union } \{5, 3\})$
      $= A \text{ intersect } \{10, 5, 4, 3\}$
      $= \{5, 3\}$

h. count ((A intersect B) union {n : A | n > 16})
= count ({5} union {21})
= count ({5, 21})
= 2

i. {n : B • n − 1}
= {n : {10, 5, 4} • n − 1}
= {9, 4, 3}

j. {n : B | n > 6 • n ∗ (n − 1)}
= {n : {10, 5, 4} | n > 6 • n ∗ (n − 1)}
= {10 ∗ (10 − 1)}
= {90}

Q3.6   a.   {(5, 5)}

b.   {(5, 4), (21, 10), (21, 5), (21, 4), (16, 10), (16, 5), (16, 4)}

c.   {(5, 10), (3, 10), (3, 5), (3, 4)}

d.   {(5, {4}), (3, {}), (21, {10, 5, 4}), (16, {10, 5, 4})}

e.   {(10, {5, 4}), (5, {4}), (4, {})}

f.   { (5,3), (21,5), (21,3), (21,16), (16,5), (16,3) }

g.   { 5, 21, 16 }

h.   { {5,3}, {5,21}, {5,16}, {3,21}, {3,16}, {21,16} }

i.   { {5}, {5,3}, {5,21}, {5,16}, {5,3,21}, {5,21,16}, {5,3,16}, {5,3,21,16} }

j.   {3} – of course

Q3.7   a.   A

b.   A

c.   A

d.   {}

e.   {}

f.   {}

g.   A

Q3.10   a.   Jim
$size = 4$

b.   { Sue, Alan }
$size = 2^4 = 16$

c.   (Sue, Paris)
$size = 4 \ast 3 = 12$

Selected answers for Chapter 3

    d. { (Jim,London), (Jim, Paris), (Alan, Yeppoon) }
$size = 2^{4*3} = 2^{12} = 4096$

    e. ({Sue,Jim,Bob},Yeppoon)
$size = 2^4 * 3 = 16 * 3 = 48$

    f. { {Jim,Alan}, {Alan}, {Alan,Bob,Sue} }
$size = 2^{2^4} = 2^{16} = 32768$ (a famous number in computing)

    g. ({Sue,Bob},{Yeppoon,Paris})
$size = 2^4 * 2^3 = 16 * 8 = 128$

Q3.11
- a. Us
- b. Us x Us
- c. Set of Us
- d. Set of Us
- e. Set of (Us x City)
- f. Us x Us x Us
- g. Set of (Set of Us)
- h. Set of (Us x Set of City)

Q3.12
- a. { {}, {spoon} }
- b. { {}, {fork}, {spoon}, {fork,spoon} }
- c. { {}, { {} }, { {spoon} }, { {}, {spoon} } }
- d. { {} }
- e. { {}, { {} } }

Q3.13
- a. This total function pairs one town with another. The second town is the capital of the state in which the first town is located.

$$\begin{array}{|l}
\text{hascap} : \text{Town} \longrightarrow \text{Town} \\
\hline
\text{hascap} = \{t : \text{Town} \bullet (t, \text{cap}(\text{loc}(t)))\}
\end{array}$$

- b. This function pairs a state with a set of towns, each of which is located there.

$$\begin{array}{|l}
\text{alltowns} : \text{State} \longrightarrow \text{Set of Town} \\
\hline
\text{alltowns} = \{s : \text{State} \bullet (s, \{t : \text{Town} \,|\, \text{loc}(t) = s\})\}
\end{array}$$

- c. This relation states that two towns t and u are in the same location if they are different towns but in the same state.

$$\begin{array}{|l}
\_\text{sameloc}\_ : \text{Town} \longleftrightarrow \text{Town} \\
\hline
\text{sameloc} = \{t, u : \text{Town} \,|\, t \neq u \text{ and } \text{loc}(t) = \text{loc}(u)\}
\end{array}$$

d. This function pairs each town with the set of *other* towns located in the same state.

$$\text{samepop} : \text{Town} \rightarrow \text{Set of Town}$$

$$\text{samepop} = \{t : \text{Town} \bullet (t, \{u : \text{Town} \mid u \neq t \text{ and } \text{loc}(u) = \text{loc}(t)\})\}$$

e. This function pairs each integer with the set of towns that are larger.

$$\text{exceed} : \text{N} \rightarrow \text{Set of Town}$$

$$\text{exceed} = \{n : \text{N} \bullet (n, \{t : \text{Town} \mid \text{pop}(t) > n\})\}$$

Chapter 4

Q4.1 The tables look something like this:

Schools

School_Id	School_Name	Phone	Head_Id
CS	Computing Science	2299	1
AC	Accountancy	8756	4
CH	Chemistry	1869	?

Staff

Staff_Id	Staff_Name	School_Id
1	Prof B.Tree	CS
2	I.Drone	CS
3	L.R.Parser	CS
4	Ms C.R. Double-Entry	AC
5	D.Fraud	AC
6	M.Bezzle	AC
7	P.P.Lounge-Lizard	AC
8	C.A.Quick-Lime	CH
9	A.G.Silver	CH
10	H.H.Esso-Fore	CH

Quals

Staff_Id	Degree	Place	Year
1	BSc	UW	1925
1	PhD	UQ	1928
2	BSc	UQ	1979
2	MSc	UNSW	1984
3	BAppSc	QIT	1987
4	BBus	QIT	1972
4	MBA	UWA	1975
5	BComm	UQ	1995
5	MBA	UCLA	1998
6	BBus	WU	1989
7	BBus	QUT	1989
7	MBA	UQ	1990
8	BSc	UNT	1956
8	PhD	UW	1958
9	BSc	UW	1975
9	MSc	UW	1977
9	PhD	UW	1980
10	BSc	MU	1970
10	PhD	UNT	1974

Q4.2 Academic database analysis

Relation:	Schools	Staff	Quals
Attributes:	4	3	4
Tuples:	3	10	19
Foreign keys:	Head_Id	School_Id	Staff_Id

Q4.3 Resources database analysis

Relation:	Staff	Theaters	Allocation
Attributes:	3	2	4
Tuples:	4	4	7
Foreign keys:	none	none	Theater
			Teacher

Q4.4
No, the null value signifies either that he has no phone *or* that, so far, no-one has been able to record it in the database.

Q4.5
There will be 4 * 7 = 28 tuples in the product. A typical tuple is shown below:

Subject	Enrolled	Theater	Teacher	Teacher	Room	Phone
:	:	:	:	:	:	:
Ballet	25	Cosy	Tripp	Hacker	18	2868
:	:	:	:	:	:	:

Q4.6
The **Allocation** and **Staff** relations share the **Teacher** attribute, and so the join will be based on matching the values there.

Subject	Enrolled	Theater	Teacher	Teacher	Room	Phone
Music	10	Tiny	Drone	Drone	21	2240
Ballet	25	Cosy	Tripp	Tripp	21	2240
TapDancing	35	Cosy	Tripp	Tripp	21	2240
Programming	10	Cramp	Hacker	Hacker	18	2868
Singing	25	Tiny	Drone	Drone	21	2240
Surgery	15	Cramp	Hacker	Hacker	18	2868
Poetry	10	Cramp	Drone	Drone	21	2240

Yes, this is the same as the join of **Staff** and **Allocation**. Even though the appearance of the table may differ, the column headings (attributes) will be the same, as will the basic information contained in the resulting relation.

Q4.7 a. What teachers does Witsend have?
          {Drone, Slack, Tripp, Hacker}

      b. Which teachers have no teaching commitments?
          {Drone, Slack, Tripp, Hacker} minus {Drone, Tripp, Hacker}
          = {Slack}

      c. Which theaters can hold more than 15 students?
          { (Chockers,20), (Cosy,30) }

      d. What subjects are being taught and what is the phone number of that subject's teacher?

      e. Name those subjects and give the enrollments for those subjects with an enrollment at least that of the Ballet class.

Q4.8 a. { s:Staff | s.Teacher = Hacker • s.Phone }

      b. { s:Staff; a:Allocation
            | s.Teacher = a.Teacher and a.Subject = Music
            • s.Room }

      c. { a:Allocation | a.Theater = Cramp • a.Teacher }

      d. { a:Allocation; t:Theaters
            | a.Theater = t.Theater and a.Enrolled > t.Capacity
            • a.Subject }

      e. { s,t:Staff | s.Room = t.Room and s.Teacher = Drone
            and not(t.Teacher = Drone) • t.Teacher}

      f. { t:Theaters • t.Theater }
          minus { a:Allocation • a.Theater }

      g. { t:Theaters | t.Capacity > 25 • t.Theater }

      h. { t,u:Theaters
            | t.Theater = Chockers and u.Capacity > t.Capacity
            • u.Theater }

      i. { a:Allocation; t:Theaters
            | a.Subject = Singing and t.Capacity >= a.Enrolled
            • t.Theater }

      j. { s:Staff; a:Allocation; t:Theaters
            | s.Teacher = a.Teacher and a.Theater = t.Theater
               and a.Enrolled > t.Capacity
            • (s.Teacher, s.Phone) }

Chapter 5

Q5.1 Shinhackers Rugby Club (SQL to English)

      a. Details of all games played in April

b. The names of teams that we have defeated.

c. Details of all games

d. The date of the game and the name of the opposition team for all games played in May which resulted in a draw.

e. The scores of games against the Bellyfloppers or the Kneeknockers

f. The number of games we have won.

g. Our biggest winning margin

h. Details (*) of all games in the order in which they were played (in `Month` order, and within month, in `Day` order).

Q5.2 Shinhackers (English to SQL)

a.
```
Select    count(*), sum(Ours), sum(Theirs)
From      Games
```

b.
```
Select    Team
From      Games
Where     Theirs - 10 >= Ours
```

c.
```
Select    Day, Month, Team, Ours, Theirs
From      Games
Order by  Ours desc
```

d.
```
Select    *
From      Games
Where     Month = 4
and       Day > 15
```

e.
```
Select    distinct Team
From      Games
```

Q5.3 Defining the `Games` table.

```
Create table Games
(Day     integer   not null,
Month    integer   not null,
Team     char(15)  not null,
Ours     integer   not null,
Theirs   integer   not null)
```

Q5.4 Modifications to the database

a.
```
Insert
Into    Games
Values (9,5,'Knuckledusters',6,3)
```

b. ```
Update Games
Set   Theirs = Theirs+5
Where   Day = 14
and   Month = 3
```
c. ```
Delete
From    Games
Where   Team = 'Toecrushers'
```

Q5.5 To ensure that only one result is created for any particular date, we can define an index like the following:

```
Create Unique Index Once_A_Day
on Games(Day, Month)
```

A unique index, like this, will prevent any two rows from having the same day and month.

Chapter 6

Q6.1 The ACADEMIC Database

a. ```
Select   School_Name, Phone
From   Schools
```
b. ```
Select   *
From     Staff
```
c. ```
Select   School_Name
From   Schools
Where   Head_Id is null
```
d. ```
Select    Staff_Name, School_Name
From      Staff, Schools
Where     Staff.School_Id = Schools.School_Id
Order by  Staff_Name
```
e. ```
Select   School_Name, Staff_Name
From   Schools, Staff
Where   Head_Id = Staff_Id
```
f. ```
Select    Staff_Name, Degree, Year
From      Staff, Quals
Where     Staff.Staff_Id = Quals.Staff_Id
Order by  Staff_Name, Year
```
g. ```
Select   count(*)
From   Staff
```
h. ```
Select   min(Year)
From     Quals
```

i. Select   Staff_Id, count(*)
    From   Quals
    Group by Staff_Id

j. Select   School_Id, count(*)
    From   Staff
    Group by School_Id

k. Select   Staff_Id
    From   Quals
    Group by Staff_Id
    Having   count(*) > 1

l. Select   Staff_Id, max(Year) - min(Year)
    From   Quals
    Group by Staff_Id
    Having   count(*) > 1

m. Select   Staff_Id, max(Staff_Name), max(Year)
    From   Staff s, Quals q
    Where   s.Staff_Id = q.Staff_Id
    Group by s.Staff_Id

n. Select   s.Staff_Id
    From   Staff s, Staff t
    Where   s.Staff_Id = t.Staff_Id
    and   s.Year = 1975
    and   t.Year = 1985

o. Select   Staff_Id
    From   Quals
    Where   Degree like 'B%'
    and   Year < 1950

p. Select   Staff_Name
    From   Staff, Quals
    Where   Staff.Staff_Id = Quals.Staff_Id
    and   Degree like 'B%'
    and   Place like '%IT'

Q6.2 Cars and Effect

a. The number of rows in the Cars table.

```
--------
count(*)
--------
      10
--------
```

b. The average distance traveled.

```
---------
avg(Kilo)
---------
   52
---------
```

c. The average distance traveled by cars that have done less than 70 000 kilometers.

```
---------
avg(Kilo)
---------
  47.2
---------
```

d. The minimum sale price of any white car with air-conditioning.

```
---------
min(Sale)
---------
   41
---------
```

e. For each category of air-conditioning (that is, **y** or **n**), give the maximum sale price.

```
------------------
Aircon   max(Sale)
------------------
  n         50
  y         95
------------------
```

f. Group the cars by the distance traveled, then keep any groups that contain more than one car and discard the rest. Show the results in descending order of group size.

```
---------------
Kilo   count(*)
---------------
 50       3
 41       2
 46       2
---------------
```

Since two groups are the same size, they might appear in either order.

Q6.4 Rocky Concrete SQL: Answers to odd-numbered exercises

Simple Queries (SQ)

```
SQ1.   select    cust_name
       from      customers

SQ3.   select    *
       from      customers

SQ5.   select    cust_name, curr_bal
       from      customers
       where     curr_bal > 250

SQ7.   select    *
       from      products
       where     qty_on_hand * list_price > 1000

SQ9.   select    *
       from      customers
       where     post_code between 4000 and 4999
```

Join Queries (JQ)

```
JQ1.   select    p.prod_code, p.description, d.order_price, d.order_qty
       from      products p, order_details d
       where     p.prod_code = d.prod_code
       and       d.order_no = 1234

JQ3.   select    d.order_no, p.prod_code, d.order_price, p.list_price
       from      order_details d, products p
       where     d.prod_code = p.prod_code
       and       d.order_price <> p.list_price

JQ5.   select    p.description, c.cust_name
       from      products p, order_details d, orders o, customers c
       where     p.prod_code = d.prod_code
       and       d.order_no = o.order_no
       and       o.cust_no = c.cust_no
       and       c.town = 'Brisbane'

JQ7.   select    c.cust_name
       from      customers c, orders o, order_details d
       where     c.cust_no = o.cust_no
       and       o.order_no = d.order_no
```

526   Information Modeling

```
            and      d.prod_code = 'GNOME'
            and      o.order_date between 910401 and 910430

    JQ9.    select   p.prod_code, o.order_no, o.order_date, d.order_qty,
                     p.remake_level
            from     products p, order_details d, orders o
            where    p.prod_code = d.prod_code
            and      d.order_no = o.order_no
            and      d.order_qty > p.remake_qty


            Statistical Queries (ST)
            ------------------------

    ST1.    select   sum(order_qty * order_price)
            from     order_details
            where    order_no = 1234

    ST3.    select   max(cr_limit - curr_bal)
            from     customers

    ST5.    select   min(order_date)
            from     orders

    ST7.    select   max(order_qty * order_price)
            from     order_details
            where    prod_code = 'LOO'

    ST9.    select   max(order_qty)
            from     order_details
            where    prod_code = 'MOO'


            Simple Group-by Queries (SG)
            ----------------------------

    SG1.    select   town, count(*)
            from     customers
            group by town
            order by town

    SG3.    select   prod_group, sum(list_price * qty_on_hand)
            from     products
            group by prod_group

    SG5.    select   prod_code, sum(order_price * order_qty)
```

```
        from       order_details
        group by prod_code
        order by 2 desc

SG7.    select     town, avg(cr_limit)
        from       customers
        group by town
        having     avg(cr_limit) > 1000

SG9.    select     order_date, count(*)
        from       orders
        where      order_date between 910601 and 910630
        group by order_date
        order by order_date


        Multi-table Group-by Queries (MG)
        ---------------------------------

MG1.    select     d.prod_code, sum(d.order_qty * d.order_price)
        from       order_details d, orders o
        where      d.order_no = o.order_no
        and        o.order_date between 910501 and 910531
        group by d.prod_code

MG3.    select     o.order_date, sum(d.order_qty * d.order_price)
        from       orders o, order_details d
        where      o.order_no = d.order_no
        and        o.order_date between 910601 and 910630
        group by o.order_date
        having     sum(d.order_qty * d.order_price) > 1000

MG5.    select     c.cust_no, max(c.cust_name), count(*)
        from       customers c, orders o
        where      c.cust_no = o.cust_no
        and        o.order_date between 910501 and 910531
        group by c.cust_no
        order by c.cust_no

MG7.    select     c.cust_no, max(c.cust_name),
                   sum(d.order_qty * d.order_price)
        from       customers c, orders o, order_details d
        where      c.cust_no = o.cust_no
        and        o.order_no = d.order_no
        and        o.order_date between 910101 and 911231
        group by cust_no
```

```
        order by 3 desc

MG9.    select     d.prod_code, count(distinct o.cust_no)
        from       order_details d, orders o
        where      d.order_no = o.order_no
        and        o.order_date between 910601 and 910630
        group by d.prod_code


        Product Queries (PQ)
        --------------------

PQ1.    select     p.cust_no, p.cr_limit, q.cust_no, q.cust_name,
                   q_cr_limit
        from       customers p, customers q
        where      p.cust_no = 2345
        and        p.town = q.town
        and        q.curr_bal > p.curr_bal

PQ3.    select     p.list_price - (cr_limit - curr_bal),
                   (p.list_price-(c.cr_limit-c.curr_bal))*100/p.list_price
        from       products p, customers c
        where      p.prod_code = 'L00'
        and        c.cust_no = 6789
```

Chapter 7

Q7.1 Nested queries on the **People** table

    a.   Who earns the most?

```
            Select    Name
            From      People
            Where     Earns = (Select  max(Earns)
                               From    People)
```

The subquery determines the largest figure in the **Earns** column. The outer query names anybody whose earnings equal that amount.

    b.   Which men earn less than the average male earnings?

```
            Select    Name
            From      People
            Where     Sex = 'm'
            and       Earns < (Select  avg(Earns)
                               From    People
                               Where   Sex = 'm')
```

The subquery determines the average male earnings. The outer query then names the men who earn less than that amount. The test `Sex = 'm'` is required in *both* the inner and the outer query.

c. Who like the same things as Mario?

```
Select    Name
From      People
Where     Likes = (Select Likes
                   From    People
                   Where   Name = 'Mario')
```

This will name Mario as well, becasue he is one of the people who like the thing that Mario likes! To exclude him, we should add an extra condition to the *outer* query: `and Name <> 'Mario'`

d. Who dislike students, politics or SQL?

```
Select   Name, Dislikes
From     People
Where    Dislikes in ('students', 'politics', 'SQL')
```

It's hard to believe that anybody could be offended by these.

e. Which men earn more than all women?

```
Select    Name
From      People
Where     Sex = 'm'
and       Earns > all (Select Earns
                        From    People
                        Where   Sex = 'f')
```

The subquery returns the set of female earnings. The outer query names the men whose earnings exceed *all* the amounts in that set.

f. Which women earn more than at least one man?

```
Select    Name
From      People
Where     Sex = 'f'
and       Earns > any (Select Earns
                        From    People
                        Where   Sex = 'm')
```

The subquery returns the set of male earnings. The outer query names the women whose earnings exceed *any* (at least one) such amount.

g. Which men like things liked by females?

```
Select    Name
From      People
Where     Sex = 'm'
and       Likes in (Select Likes
```

```
                        From    People
                        Where   Sex = 'f')
```

Q7.2   Union queries on the `People` table

    a.   Men and women

```
        Select  'Men', count(*)
        From    People
        Where   Sex = 'm'

        union
        Select  'Women', count(*)
        From    People
        Where   Sex = 'f'
        Order by 2 desc
```

    b.   The young and the decrepit

```
        Select  'young', count(*)
        From    People
        Where   Age < 30

        union
        Select  'middle-aged', count(*)
        From    People
        Where   Age between 30 and 49

        union
        Select  'elderly', count(*)
        From    People
        Where   Age >= 50
```

    c.   Annual accounts

```
        Select  Name, Earns, (0.5 * Earns)/100
        From    People
        Where   Earns < 15000

        union
        Select  Name, Earns, (0.75 * Earns)/100
        From    People
        Where   Earns between 15000 and 29999

        union
        Select  Name, Earns, (1.25 * Earns)/100
        From    People
        Where   Earns >= 30000
```

Q7.3 Views of the `People` table

    a. Only the men:

```
Create view Men as
Select *
From   People
Where  Sex = 'm'
```

    b. Only the rich:

```
Create view Rich(Name, Sex, Income) as
Select Name, Sex, Earns
From   People
Where  Earns > 40000
```

    c. Only the rich men:

```
Create view Rich_Men(Name, Age, Worth) as
Select Name, Age, Earns
From   People
Where  Name in (Select Name
                From    Rich)
  and  Name in (Select Name
                From    Men)
```

or, alternatively:

```
Create view Rich_Men(Name, Age, Worth) as
Select Rich.Name, Men.Age, Rich.Income
From   Rich, Men
Where  Rich.Name = Men.Name
```

Q7.4 Rocky Concrete SQL: Answers to odd-numbered exercises

```
Simple Nested Queries (SN)
--------------------------
```

```
SN1.   select   cust_name
       from     customers
       where    cr_limit = (select  max(cr_limit)
                            from    customers)

SN3.   select   cust_name
       from     customers
       where    cust_no in (select cust_no
                            from   orders
                            where  order_date = (select max(order_date)
                                                 from   orders))
```

532   Information Modeling

```
SN5.   select   prod_code
       from     products
       where    remake_qty * list_price
                = (select max(remake_qty * list_price)
                    from    products)

SN7.   select   cust_name
       from     customers
       where    cust_no
                in (select cust_no
                    from    orders
                    where   order_no
                            in (select order_no
                                from    order_details
                                where   prod_code = 'STANK'
                                and     order_price
                                        = (select max(order_price)
                                            from    order_details
                                            where   prod_code = 'STANK')))

SN9.   select   cust_name
       from     customers
       where    cust_no
                = (select cust_no
                    from    orders
                    where   order_no = (select min(order_no)
                                        from    order_details
                                        where   prod_code = 'GNOME'))


       In Queries (IQ)
       ---------------

IQ1.   select   cust_name, street, town, post_code
       from     customers
       where    cust_no in (select cust_no
                            from    orders
                            where   order_date = 910812)


IQ3.   select   prod_code, description
       from     products
       where    prod_code in (select prod_code
                              from    order_details
                              where   order_no = 1234)
```

```
IQ5.    select    count(*)
        from      orders
        where     order_date between 910401 and 910430
        and       cust_no in (select cust_no
                              from   customers
                              where  town = 'Bundaberg')

IQ7.    select    prod_code
        from      order_details
        where     order_no
                  in (select order_no
                      from   orders
                      where  order_date between 910701
                                              and 910731
                      and    cust_no in (select cust_no
                                         from   customers
                                         where  town = 'Gympie'))

IQ9.    select    cust_name
        from      customers
        where     cust_no not in (select cust_no
                                  from   orders
                                  where  order_date between 910101
                                                          and 911231)
```

Complex Group-by Queries (CG)

```
CG1.    select    prod_code
        from      order_details
        group by  prod_code
        having    sum(order_qty) >= all (select  sum(order_qty)
                                         from    order_details
                                         group by prod_code)

CG3.    select    order_no
        from      order_details
        group by  order_no
        having    count(*) >= all (select   count(*)
                                   from     order_details
                                   group by order_no)
```

```
CG5.    select      *
        from        customers
        where       town = (select    town
                            from      customers
                            group by town
                            having    max(cr_limit)
                                      <= all (select  max(cr_limit)
                                              from    customers
                                              group by town))

CG7.    select      o.order_date
        from        orders o, order_details d
        where       o.order_no = d.order_no
        group by    o.order_date
        having      sum(d.order_qty * d.order_price)
                    >= all (select    sum(e.order_qty * e.order_price)
                            from      orders p, order_details e
                            where     p.order_no = e.order_no
                            group by p.order_date)

CG9.    select      prod_group
        from        products
        group by    prod_group
        having      sum(qty_on_hand * list_price)
                    >= all (select    sum(qty_on_hand * list_price)
                            from      products
                            group by prod_group)




        Correlated Subqueries (CR)
        --------------------------

CR1.    select      p.prod_code, p.description
        from        products p
        where       p.list_price > any (select  order_price
                                        from    order_details
                                        where   prod_code = p.prod_code)

CR3.    select      p.prod_group, p.prod_code, p.description, p.list_price
        from        products p
        where       p.list_price = (select  max(list_price)
                                    from    products
                                    where   prod_group = p.prod_group)
```

Exists Queries (EQ)

```
EQ1.    select   *
        from     orders o
        where    not exists (select *
                             from    customers
                             where   cust_no = o.cust_no)

EQ3.    select   *
        from     order_details d
        where    not exists (select *
                             from    products
                             where   prod_code = d.prod_code)

EQ5.    select   *
        from     customers c
        where    not exists (select *
                             from    orders
                             where   cust_no = c.cust_no)
```

Union Queries (UQ)

```
UQ1.    select   cust_name, street, town, post_code
        from     customers
        where    town = 'Toowoomba'
        union
        select   cust_name, street, town, post_code
        from     customers
        where    town = 'Bundaberg'

UQ3.    select   p.prod_code, max(p.description),
                 sum(d.order_qty * d.order_price)
        from     products p, order_details d
        where    p.prod_code = d.prod_code
        group by p.prod_code
        union
        select   q.prod_code, q.description, 0
        from     products q
        where    not exists (select *
                             from    order_details
                             where   prod_code = q.prod_code)
```

Chapter 8

Q8.1 The Pigs

    a. Yes: there is a uniqueness constraint on the Pig's role in F4.

    b. No: there is no constraint on the Sty's role in F1.

    c. No: there is a constraint on the (Pig/Day) role in F3.

    d. No: the constraint bar crosses both roles on the link between FoodType and DietType.

    e. No: a Pig is only on one DietType, and for any type of diet there is a fixed daily allowance of each FoodType in that diet.

Q8.2 Turning the model into a relational database schema

    a. Record types

Pig Record Type

Fact	Key?	Attribute	References?
F1	(*)	PigNr	
F2		StyNr	
F4		Breed	
		Diet	

Score Record Type

Fact	Key?	Attribute	References?
	(*)	PigNr	Pig Record
	(*)	Date	
F3		Score	

Ingredient Record Type

Fact	Key?	Attribute	References?
	(*)	Food	
	(*)	Diet	
F5		Weight	

    b. Deciding on null values

The `Pig Record` type

F1:	Is every pig kept in a sty?	yes
	Will we always know in what sty?	surely
F2:	Is every pig of some breed?	yes
	Will we always know what breed?	yes
F4:	Is every pig on a diet of some kind?	yes
	Will we always know what kind?	yes

The `Score Record` type

F4:	On every day that a pig is tested will its score be recorded?	yes
	Will we always know its score?	surely

The `Ingredient Record` type

F4:	Will every food type in a diet have its daily allowance?	yes
	Will we always know that daily allowance?	yes

c. The database

```
┌─PigRecord─────────────────
│ PigNr : Pig
│ StyNr : Sty
│ Breed : Breed
│ Diet : DietType
└───────────────────────────
```

```
┌─ScoreRecord───────────────
│ PigNr : Pig
│ Date : Day
│ Score : N
└───────────────────────────
```

```
┌─IngredientRecord──────────
│ Diet : DietType
│ Food : FoodType
│ Weight : N
└───────────────────────────
```

538   Information Modeling

```
┌─ IQ_Database ─────────────────────────────────────────────
│ Pigs : Set of PigRecord
│ Scores : Set of ScoreRecord
│ Ingredients : Set of IngredientRecord
│──────────────────────────────────────────────────────────
│ count Pigs = count {P : Pigs • P.PigNr}
│ count Scores = count {S : Scores • (S.PigNr, S.Date)}
│ count Ingredients = count {I : Ingredients • (I.Diet, I.Food)}
│ {S : Scores • S.PigNr} ⊆ {P : Pigs • P.PigNr}
└──────────────────────────────────────────────────────────
```

Q8.3   The CLUB Model

1. The `likes` relationship

   a. The MEMBER with the first name 'Bill'
      likes
      the MEMBER with the first name 'Sue'

      The MEMBER with the first name 'Sue'
      is liked by
      the MEMBER with the first name 'Bill'

   b. The corresponding conceptual schema diagram for this relationship is as follows:

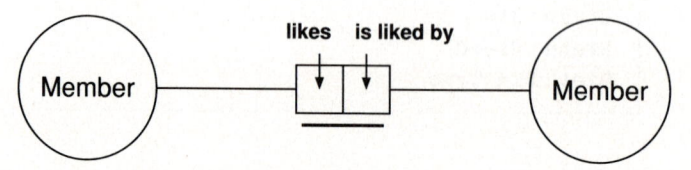

   However, the two **Member** entity types should be merged.

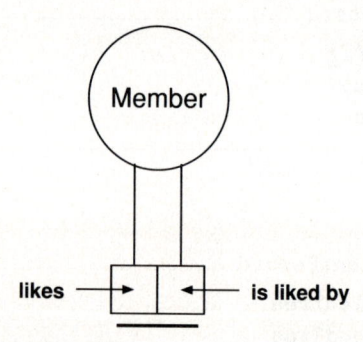

2. The `writes` relationship

   a. The MEMBER with the first name 'Bill'
      writes

the LANGUAGE with the name 'FORTRAN'

The LANGUAGE with the name 'FORTRAN'
is written by
the MEMBER with the first name 'Bill'

  b. The diagram:

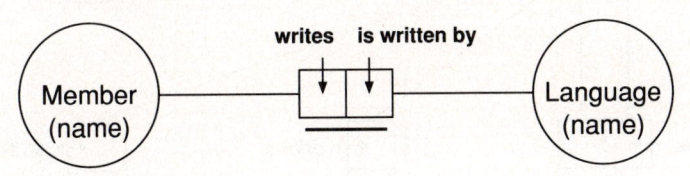

```
                    writes   is written by
   ╭───────╮          ┌──┬──┐          ╭─────────╮
  ( Member  )─────────│▼ │▼ │──────────( Language )
  ( (name)  )         └──┴──┘          (  (name)  )
   ╰───────╯           ────            ╰─────────╯
```

3. The **age** relationship

  a. The MEMBER with the first name 'Bill'
has age
the AGE with the years '19'

The AGE with years '19'
is the age of
the MEMBER with the first name 'Bill'

  b. The diagram:

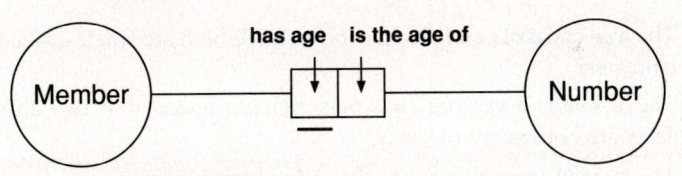

```
                   has age   is the age of
   ╭───────╮          ┌──┬──┐          ╭────────╮
  (  Member )─────────│▼ │▼ │──────────( Number  )
   ╰───────╯          └──┴──┘          ╰────────╯
                       ────
```

4. The **drives** relationship

  a. The MEMBER with the first name 'Sue'
drives
the CARMAKE with the name 'Honda'

The CARMAKE with the name 'Honda'
is driven by
the MEMBER with the first name 'Sue'

  b. The diagram:

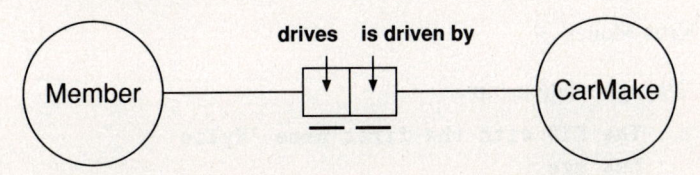

```
                    drives   is driven by
   ╭───────╮          ┌──┬──┐          ╭────────╮
  (  Member )─────────│▼ │▼ │──────────( CarMake )
   ╰───────╯          └──┴──┘          ╰────────╯
                       ────
```

Using only the data given, this is a one-to-one relationship.

540 Information Modeling

Q8.4   a.   Here is the conceptual schema diagram:

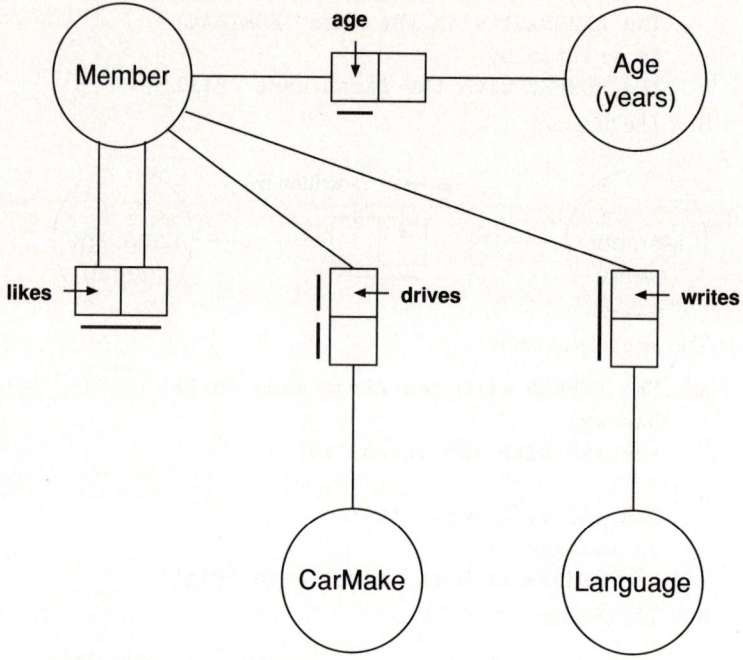

[Conceptual schema diagram with entities Member, Age (years), CarMake, Language connected by relationships: age, likes, drives, writes]

b. The **age** and **drives** facts may be merged; both are single-valued facts about a member.

The **likes** and **writes** facts must remain separated as two different tables. They are both many-to-many.

c. The merged facts give rise to the following table:

```
MemberFacts
--------------------------
Firstname    Age    CarMake
--------------------------
   Bill      19     Ford
   Sue       19     Honda
   Alan      16     ?
--------------------------
```

Q8.5   The KIDs Model

1. The **age** relationship

   a. The KID with the first name 'Kylie'
       has age
       the AGE with years 14

       The AGE with years 14

```
    is the age of
    the KID with the first name 'Kylie'
```
  b. The corresponding conceptual schema diagram for this relationship is as follows:

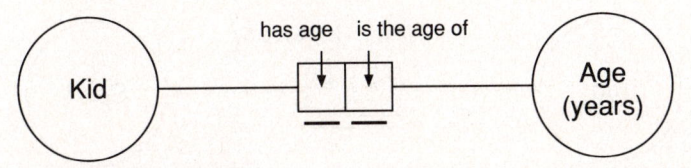

```
                has age   is the age of
      ┌─────┐   ┌───┬───┐            ┌──────┐
      │ Kid │───│ ▼ │ ▼ │────────────│ Age  │
      └─────┘   └─┬─┴─┬─┘            │(years)│
                                     └──────┘
```

2. The **sex** relationship

  a.
```
    The KID with the first name 'Kylie'
    has sex(!)
    the GENDER with the name 'f'

    The GENDER with the name 'f'
    is the sex of
    the KID with the first name 'Kylie'
```
  b. The diagram:

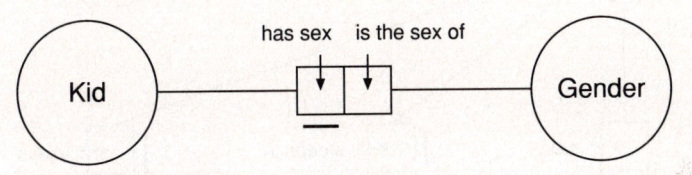

```
                has sex   is the sex of
      ┌─────┐   ┌───┬───┐            ┌────────┐
      │ Kid │───│ ▼ │ ▼ │────────────│ Gender │
      └─────┘   └───┴───┘            └────────┘
```

3. The **age** relationship

  a.
```
    The KID with the first name 'Tim'
    sleeps in
    the ROOM with the name 'back'

    The ROOM with the name 'back'
    is slept in by
    the KID with the first name 'Tim'
```
  b. The diagram:

```
                sleeps in   is slept in by
      ┌─────┐   ┌───┬───┐            ┌──────┐
      │ Kid │───│ ▼ │ ▼ │────────────│ Room │
      └─────┘   └─┬─┴─┬─┘            └──────┘
```

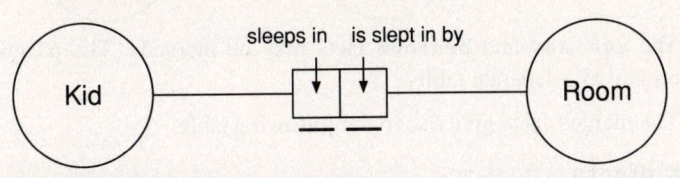

4. The **plays** relationship

  a.
```
    The KID with the first name 'Kylie'
    plays
    the SPORT with the name 'tennis'
```

542   Information Modeling

```
       The SPORT with the name 'tennis'
       is played by
       the KID with the first name 'Kylie'
```
b.   The diagram:

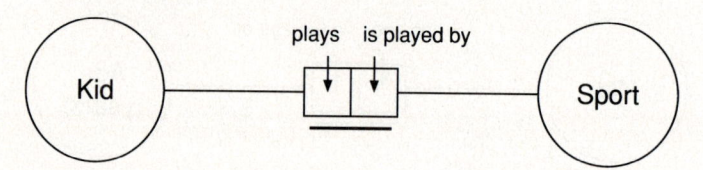

Q8.6   The KIDS model

a.   The conceptual schema:

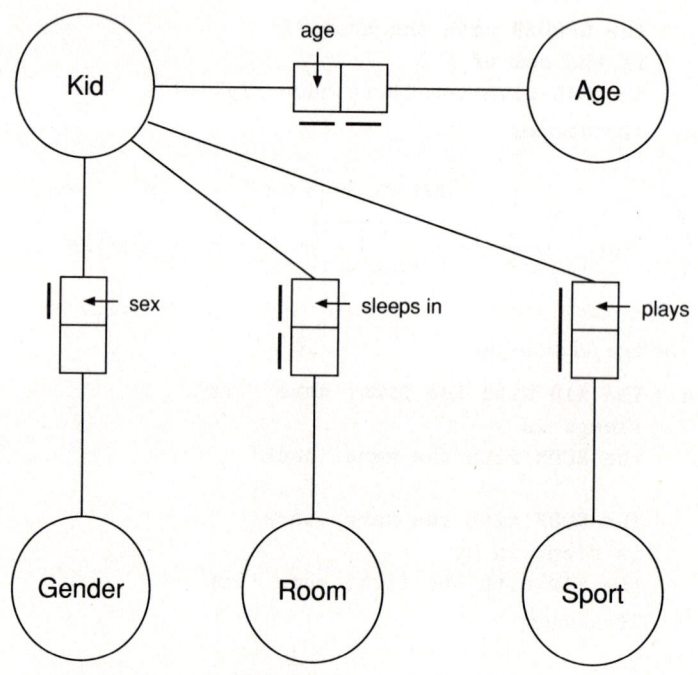

b.   The **age**, **sex** and **bedroom** facts may be merged. The **plays** fact must remain as a separate table.

c.   The merged facts give rise to the following table.

```
KidFacts
---------------------------------------
FirstName    Age    Gender   Room
---------------------------------------
Kylie        14     f        ?
Tim          12     ?        back
```

```
        Matthew      4      m      front
        Emma         8      f      ?
    ----------------------------------------
```

    d.   The **Gender** and **Room** attributes would need to be allowed to contain nulls.

Q8.7 The PARLIAMENT Model

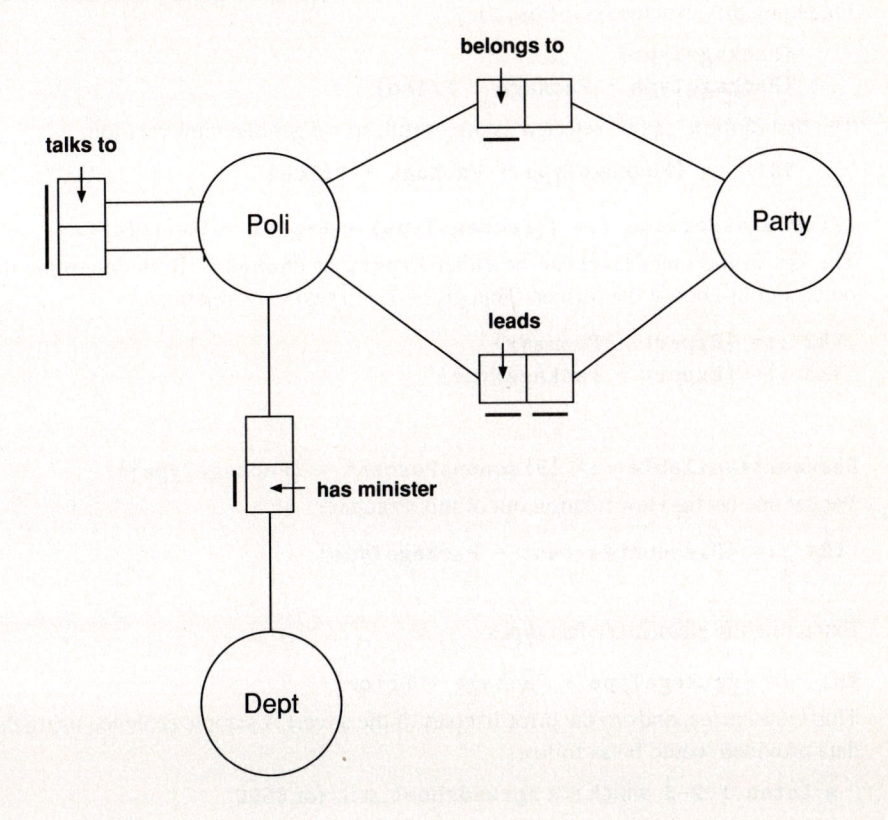

[Diagram: Entities **Poli**, **Party**, **Dept** with relationships "talks to" (Poli to itself), "belongs to" (Poli–Party), "leads" (Poli–Party), "has minister" (Poli–Dept).]

Chapter 9

Q9.1 The Software Softies

    a.   Deriving the view structures

We have been presented with three pictures of the user's world: the first relates to prices, the second to after-sales service, and the third to discounts available on certain categories of software.

```
        Prices ::= {PackageType + {Package + Price}}
```

where `PackageType` means Spreadsheet, Languages and so on and `Package` means Word Perfect and Turbo Pascal, for example.

   `AfterSalesService ::= {{PackageType} + Expert + PhoneNr}`
   `DiscountAvailable ::= {DiscountPercent + {PackageType}}`

b.   Deriving the view relations

 `Prices ::= {PackageType + {Package + Price}}`
Flattening this structure gives rise to:

  `{PackageType}`
  `{PackageType + Package + Price}`

The first of these can be rejected as not useful, so we get one view relation.

  `VR1 ::= {PackageType + Package + Price}`

`AfterSalesService ::= {{PackageType} + Expert + PhoneNr}`
The key in the outer level can be either `Expert` or `PhoneNr`. Both determine the other. Let us choose the former. This gives rise to two view relations.

`VR2 ::= {Expert + PhoneNr}`
`VR3 ::= {Expert + PackageType}`

`DiscountAvailable ::= {DiscountPercent + {PackageType}}`
We get one useful view relation out of this structure.

  `VR4 ::= {DiscountPercent + PackageType}`

c.   Extracting the elementary fact types

`VR1 ::= {PackageType + Package + Price}`
This view corresponds to the price list part of the advert. A sample sentence using the data provided would be as follows:

- `Lotus 1-2-3`, which is a `spreadsheet`, sells for $500.

This can be decomposed into the following simpler sentences.

- `Lotus 1-2-3 spreadsheet package.`
- `Lotus 1-2-3 sells for $500.`

Generalizing them gives rise to two fact types.

  F1.   `Package is a PackageType.`
  F2.   `Package sells for Money.`

`VR2 ::= {Expert + PhoneNr}`
A sample sentence from this view relation would be as follows:

- `Bill Board should be contacted on 228 1165.`

This sentence is binary and so is already irreducible. The corresponding fact type is:

        F3. Expert should be contacted on PhoneNr.

   VR3 ::= {Expert + PackageType}

A sample sentence from this view relation would be as follows:

- Bill Board handles spreadsheet software.

This sentence is binary, like the previous one, and so is also irreducible. The corresponding fact type is:

        F4. Expert handles PackageType.

   VR4 ::= {DiscountPercent + PackageType}

A sample sentence would be as follows:

- A 10% discount is offered on spreadsheet software.

This sentence is binary, like the previous two, and so is also irreducible. The corresponding fact type is:

        F5. DiscountPercent is offered on PackageType.

Summary

- The entity types
  ```
  DiscountPercent
  Expert
  Money
  Package
  PackageType
  PhoneNr
  ```
- The fact types
  ```
  F1. Package is a PackageType.
  F2. Package sells for Money.
  F3. Expert should be contacted on PhoneNr.
  F4. Expert handles PackageType.
  F5. DiscountPercent is offered on PackageType.
  ```

Q9.2 **The Library**

a. Deriving the view structures

   We have been presented with two pictures of the library.

   ```
   OnLoan  ::= {PatronNr + PatronName + {ItemNr + DueDate}}
   Catalog ::= {Title + {Author}
                      + {CopyNr + ItemNr + LoanType}}
   ```

b. Deriving the view relations

   The OnLoan report has a key PatronNr, so flattening gives:

   ```
   VR1 ::= {PatronNr + PatronName}
   ```

VR2 ::= {PatronNr + ItemNr + DueDate}

The `Catalog` has a key **Title**, so flattening gives:

VR3 ::= {Title + Author}
VR4 ::= {Title + CopyNr + ItemNr + LoanType}

c. Extracting the elementary fact types

VR1 ::= {PatronNr + PatronName}
A sample fact is:

- Patron number 899 is called Bill Thompson

This may generalized into:

F1. Patron is called Name

VR2 ::= {PatronNr + ItemNr + DueDate}
A sample fact is:

- Patron number 899 borrowed item 12099 which is due back on 13/08/91.

This may be split into two simpler sentences:

- Patron number 899 borrowed item number 12099.
- Item number 12099 is due back on 13/08/91.

These may be generalized to:

F2. Patron borrowed Item.
F3. Item is due back on Date.

VR3 ::= {Title + Author}
A sample fact is:

- The text entitled "Autumn Leaves" was co-authored by Smith.

This may be generalized to:

F4. Text was co-authored by Author.

VR4 ::= {Title + CopyNr + ItemNr + LoanType}
A sample fact is:

- Copy number 1 of Autumn Leaves is item 45689 and is a 2-week loan item.

The *and* indicates that the sentence may be split – but how? The first sentence is clearly:

- Copy number 1 of Autumn Leaves is item 45689.

and this may be generalized to:

F5. CopyNr of Text is Item.

But what should the other sentence be? It could be either of the following:

- Copy 1 of Autumn Leaves may be lent for 2 weeks.

or Item 45689 may be lent for 2 weeks.

Both are acceptable because copy 1 of Autumn Leaves and item 45689 are the same thing. The word *is* in fact type **F5** indicates this. We have two alternative ways of identifying an item: (1) by item number, and (2) by the copy number and title in conjunction. We will choose the item number – as we have already done in fact types **F2** and **F3**. So we have:

```
F6.   Item may be lent for LoanType.
```

In summary, we have uncovered the following fact types:

```
F1.   Patron is called Name
F2.   Patron borrowed Item.
F3.   Item is due back on Date.
F4.   Text was co-authored by Author.
F5.   CopyNr of Text is Item.
F6.   Item may be lent for LoanType.
```

Chapter 10

Q10.2   Marge and the Cholesterols

Step 1: Uncover the fact types

The compilation album can be defined as follows:

```
BestSpread ::= {TrackInfo}

TrackInfo  ::=

            TrackNr + TrackTitle + Length + {Writer}
            + AlbumTitle + YearReleased + Producer
            + {[ {Musician}+Instrument | Musician+{Instrument} ]}
            + {Musician + RecordCo}
```

We can see the following entity types being represented by the data elements named.

Data element	Associated entity
TrackNr	Track
TrackTitle	Track
Length	Time
Writer	Person
AlbumTitle	Album
YearReleased	Year
Producer	Person
Instrument	Instrument
Musician	Person
RecordCo	RecordCo

548   Information Modeling

There are two alternative representations for the `Track` entity type – `TrackNr` and `TrackTitle`. We choose the former, although that choice is arguable. This means that the `TrackTitle` is banished to a role as a `TrackTitle` entity type. The three roles `Writer`, `Producer` and `Musician` have been merged into a single `Person` entity type. This seems reasonable since someone might play any or all of these roles.

With the `TrackNr` as key, flattening gives us:

```
VR1 ::= {TrackNr + TrackTitle + Length
         + AlbumTitle + YearReleased + Producer}
VR2 ::= {TrackNr + Writer}
XXX ::= {TrackNr + {[{Musician}+Instrument
                    | Musician+{Instrument} ]}}
```

This is not yet a relation because it still contains repeating components. these need to be removed. The repeating component contains an alternative structure. It is either several musicians playing the same (kind of) instrument; or it is a musician playing several different instruments. Either way, the final form is:

```
VR3 ::= {TrackNr + Instrument + Musician}
VR4 ::= {TrackNr + Musician + RecordCo}
```

`VR1 ::= {TrackNr+TrackTitle+Length+AlbumTitle+YearReleased+Producer}`
A sample sentence is:

- Track number 3 is called "Case Tool Cool" and lasts 4 mins 30 secs; it first appeared on the album "Seek Well" which was released in 1985 and produced by Norman D. Butter.

This sentence can be reduced to the following simpler sentences:

- Track number 3 is called "Case Tool Cool".
- Track number 3 lasts 4mins 30secs.
- Track number 3 first appeared on the album "Seek Well".
- The album "Seek Well" was released in 1985.
- Track number 3 was produced by Norman D. Butter.

These may be generalized into the following fact types:

```
F1.  Track is called TrackTitle.
F2.  Track lasts Length.
F3.  Track first appeared on Album.
F4.  Album was first released in Year.
F5.  Track was produced by Person.
```

`VR2 ::= {TrackNr + Writer}`
A sample sentence is:

- Track number 3 was co(written) by Hans Zupp.

which may be generalized to:

F6. Track was (co)written by Person.

VR3 ::= {TrackNr + Instrument + Musician}
A sample sentence is:

- On track number 3, Hans Zupp played drums.

This is an irreducible fact. the general form is:

F7. On Track, Person played Instrument.

VR4 ::= {TrackNr + Musician + RecordCo}
A sample sentence is:

- **On track number 3, Split Reed appears courtesy of ILL WIND records.**

Presumably Split Reed appears courtesy of ILL WIND Records regardless of which track he plays on. We can split this sentence:

- **Split Reed appears courtesy of ILL WIND records.**
- **Split Reed plays on track number 3.**

The second fact is already incorporated in fact type **F7**, and so we need only generalize the first.

- **F8. Person appears courtesy of RecordCo.**

The fact types are summarized as follows:

    F1.   Track is called TrackTitle.
    F2.   Track lasts Length.
    F3.   Track first appeared on Album.
    F4.   Album was first released in Year.
    F5.   Track was produced by Person.
    F6.   Track was (co)written by Person.
    F7.   On Track, Person played Instrument.
    F8.   Person appears courtesy of RecordCo.

Step 2: Look for uniqueness constraints

F1. Track is called TrackTitle.
    Q1.   Is any track known by more than one title?   No
    Q2.   Is any tracktitle the title of more than one track?   No

F2. Track lasts Length.
    Q1.   Does any track last more than one length of time?   No
    Q2.   Is any time the length of more than one track?   Possibly

F3. Track first appeared on Album.
    Q1.   Did any track first appear on more than one album?   No
    Q2.   Was any album the place on which more than one title was first released?   Possibly

F4. Album was first released in Year.
    Q1.   Was any album first released in more than one year?   No
    Q2.   In any year was more than one album released?   Yes

F5. Track was produced by Person.
    Q1.   Was any track produced by more than one person?   No
    Q2.   Did any person produce more than one track?   Possibly

F6. Track was (co)written by Person.
    Q1.   Was any track co(written) by more than one person?   Yes
    Q2.   Did any person co(write) more than one track?   Possibly

F7. On Track, Person played Instrument.
    Q1.   On a given track did any person play more than one instrument?   Yes
    Q2.   On a given track was any instrument played by more than one person?   Yes
    Q3.   Did any person play a given instrument on more than one track?   Possibly

F8. Person appears courtesy of RecordCo.
    Q1.   Does any person appear courtesy of more than one record company?   No
    Q2.   Did any record company permit more than one person to appear on this album?   Possibly

Selected answers for Chapter 10   551

Marge and the Cholesterols Conceptual Schema

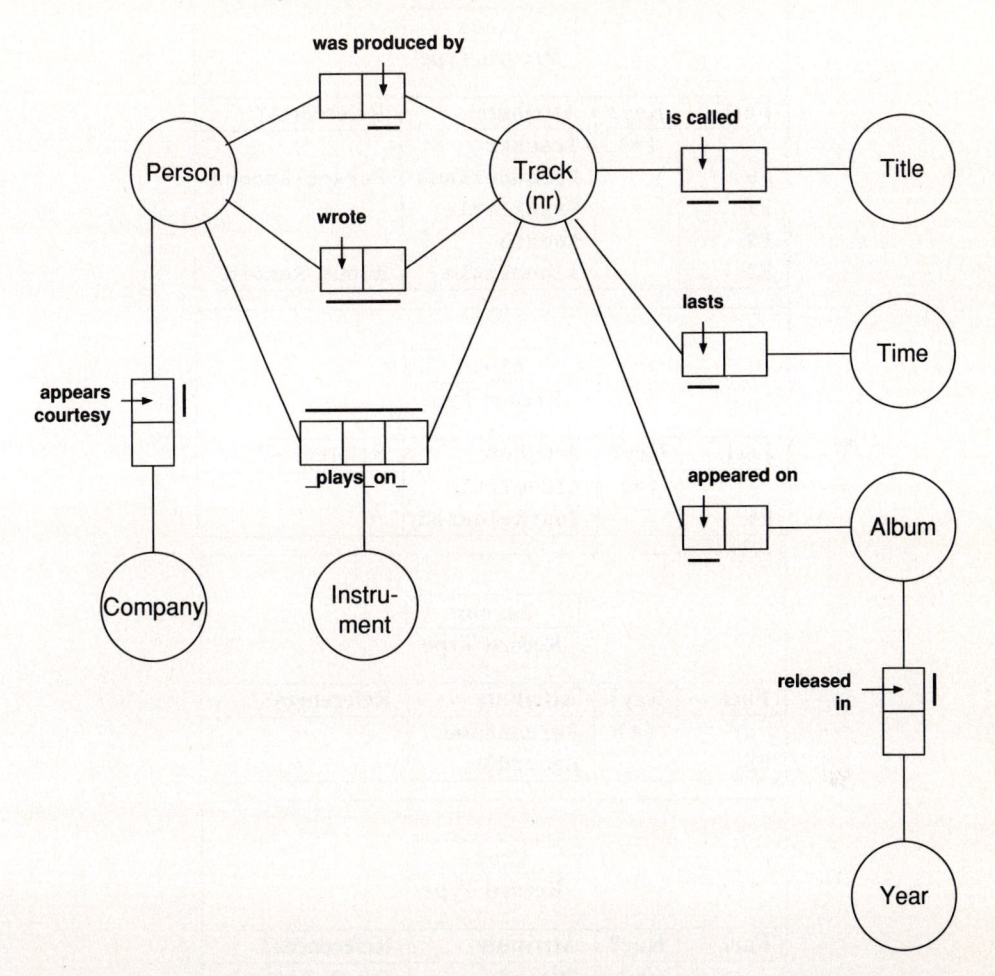

Step 3: Construct record types
The determinants are as follows:

Determinant	Entities	Fact types
Track	Track	F1, F2, F3, F5
Album	Album	F4
Person	Person	F8
Wrote	Track+Person	–
Played	Track+Person+Instrument	–

Track Record Type

Fact	Key?	Attribute	References?
	(*)	TrackNr	
F5		ProducerName	Person Record
F1		TrackTitle	
F2		Length	
F3		AlbumTitle	Album Record

Album Record Type

Fact	Key?	Attribute	References?
	(*)	AlbumTitle	
F4		YearReleased	

Person Record Type

Fact	Key?	Attribute	References?
	(*)	PersonName	
F8		RecordCo	

Wrote Record Type

Fact	Key?	Attribute	References?
	(*)	TrackNr	Track Record
	(*)	PersonName	Person Record

Played Record Type

Fact	Key?	Attribute	References?
	(*)	TrackNr	TrackRecord
	(*)	Musician	Person Record
	(*)	Instrument	

Step 4: Decide which attributes may be null

F1. Track is called TrackTitle.
Every track has a title and we will always know that title.

F2. Track lasts Length.
Every track lasts some length of time and we will always know how long that time is.

F3. Track first appeared on Album.
We will always know on what album a track first appeared.

F4. Album was first released in Year.
We will always know when an album was first released.

F5. Track was produced by Person.
We will always know the producer.

F8. Person appears courtesy of RecordCo.
No, not everybody appears courtesy of some (other) record company. Nulls must be permitted here.

Step 5: Define the database

The SQL `create table` statements might be:

```
Create table Tracks
        (TrackNr        integer(2,0)    not null,
        ProducerName    char(20)        not null,
        TrackTitle      char(20)        not null,
        Length          char(10)        not null,
        AlbumTitle      char(20)        not null,

        Primary key(TrackNr),
        Foreign key(AlbumTitle) references Albums(AlbumTitle))

Create table Albums
        (AlbumTitle     char(20)        not null,
        YearReleased    integer(4,0)    not null,

        Primary key(AlbumTitle))

Create table People
        (PersonName     char(20)        not null,
        RecordCo        char(20),

        Primary key(PersonName))

Create table Wrote
        (TrackNr        integer(2,0)    not null,
        PersonName      char(20)        not null,

        Primary key(TrackNr, PersonName),
        Foreign key(TrackNr) references Tracks(TrackNr),
        Foreign key(PersonName) references People(PersonName))
```

```
Create table Played
        (TrackNr         number(2,0)    not null,
         Musician        char(20)       not null,
         Instrument      char(20)       not null,

         Priamry key(TrackNr, Musician, Instrument),
         Foreign key(TrackNr) references Tracks(TrackNr),
         Foreign key(Musician) references People(PersonName))
```

Step 6: Review the design

Q1. On what album and in what year was track number one released?

```
Select    *
From      Albums
Where     AlbumTitle = (Select AlbumTitle
                        From   Tracks
                        Where  TrackNr = 1)
```

Q2. Who played what on track seven?

```
Select    Musician, Instrument
From      Played
Where     TrackNr = 7
```

Chapter 11

Q11.1 The ROCKY CONCRETE model

    a. Entity types:

Entity type	Identifier
Product	ProdId
Order	OrderNr
Customer	CustomerNr

    b. Relationships:

Relationship	Cardinality
part of	many-to-many (M:N)
made by	one-to-many (1:N)

    c. Database design

1. Entity types

The following record types are introduced for the entity types mentioned above.

Product Record Type

Key?	Attribute	References?
(*)	ProdId	
	ProdType	
	ListPrice	
	CostPrice	
	OnHand	
	ReMakeLevel	
	ReMakeQty	

Order Record Type

Key?	Attribute	References?
(*)	OrderNr	
	OrderDate	

Customer Record Type

Key?	Attribute	References?
(*)	CustNr	
	CustName	
	Address	
	Limit	
	Balance	

3. Dependent entity types

There are none in this model.

3. Many-to-many relationships

There is one in this model – **part of**. We introduce a record type and add the key of the record types associated with the entity types that participate in the relationship – **Product** and **Order**.

OrderLine Record Type

Key?	Attribute	References?
	Qty	
(*)	ProdId	Product Record
(*)	OrderNr	Order Record

4. One-to-many relationships

There is also one of these – made by. The Order entity type is at the N-side of the relationship and so this relationship is implemented by extending the Order record type to include the key of the Customer record type – CustNr.

Order Record Type

Key?	Attribute	References?
(*)	OrderNr	
	OrderDate	
	CustNr	Customer Record

5. One-to-one relationships

There are none.

6. Set-valued attributes

There are none of these either.

The final design

The database consists of four record types – Product, Customer and Order-Line as specified, and the second form of the Order record type.

Chapter 12

Q12.1
- a. $\neg(Bill\ writes\ SQL)$
- b. $(Sue\ likes\ Bill) \wedge (Bill\ likes\ Sue)$
- c. $(Sue\ writes\ C) \wedge (Sue\ writes\ Pascal)$
- d. $\neg(Alan\ writes\ FORTRAN) \wedge \neg(Sue\ writes\ FORTRAN)$
- e. $(drives(Sue) = Honda) \vee (drives(Bill) = Honda)$
- f. $(Bill\ writes\ SQL) \wedge (Sue\ writes\ SQL)$

Q12.2 Simple quantification
- a. $\forall p : Member \bullet p\ likes\ Alan$
- b. $\exists p : Member \bullet p\ likes\ Alan$
- c. $\neg \exists p : Member \bullet p\ likes\ Alan$
- d. $\neg \exists p : Member \bullet age(p) > age(Bill)$
- e. $\neg \exists p : Member \bullet age(p) < age(Sue)$

Selected answers for Chapter 12   557

Q12.3 More complex quantification

   a. $\forall p : Member \bullet drives(p) = Honda \Rightarrow sex(p) = F$
   b. $\forall p : Member \bullet sex(p) = F \Rightarrow drives(p) = Honda$
   c. $\forall p : Member \bullet drives(p) = BMW \Rightarrow p\ writes\ SQL$
   d. $\forall p : Member \bullet p\ writes\ C \Rightarrow drives(p) = BMW$
   e. $\forall p : Member \bullet Alan\ likes\ p \Rightarrow drives(p) = BMW$
   f. $\forall p : Member \bullet Alan\ likes\ p \Rightarrow sex(p) = F$
   g. $\forall l : Lang \bullet Sue\ writes\ l \Rightarrow Alan\ writes\ l$
   h. $\forall p : Member \bullet Bill\ likes\ p \Rightarrow Sue\ likes\ p$
   i. $\forall p : Member \bullet sex(p) = M \Rightarrow p\ writes\ COBOL$
   j. $\exists p : Member \bullet sex(p) = M \wedge p\ writes\ SQL$

Q12.4 Even more complex quantification.

   a. $\forall p : Member \bullet (\exists q : Member \bullet q\ likes\ p)$
   b. $\exists p : Member \bullet p\ writes\ FORTRAN\ \wedge$
      $(\neg \exists q : Member \bullet q\ writes\ FORTRAN \wedge p \neq q)$
      OR
      $\exists ! p : Member \bullet p\ writes\ FORTRAN$
   c. $\exists ! p : Member \bullet age(p) < age(Alan)$
   d. $\forall p : Member \bullet sex(p) = M \Rightarrow \exists q : Member$
      $\bullet sex(q) = F \wedge q\ likes\ p$
   e. $\forall p : Member \bullet sex(p) = F \Rightarrow p \in dom\ drives$
      OR
      $\forall p : Member \bullet sex(p) = F \Rightarrow$
      $\exists c : CarMake \bullet (p, c) \in drives$

Q12.5 Domain subtraction

   a. $\{(Sue, Alan), (Alan, Bill)\}$
   b. $\{(Sue, 19), (Alan, 16)\}$
   c. $\{(Alan, Bill)\}$
   d. $\{(Alan, 16)\}$
   e. $\{(Alan, Bill)\}$
   f. $\{Sue, Alan\}$
   g. $\{Alan\}$
   h. $\{Alan, Bill\}$

Q12.6 Range subtraction

a. $\{(Bill, Sue), (Bill, Alan)(Sue, Alan)\}$
b. $\{(Bill, 19), (Sue, 19)\}$
c. $\{(Alan, 16)\}$
d. $\{(Sue, Honda)\}$
e. $\{(Sue, C), (Sue, SQL), (Bill, SQL)\}$
f. $\{(Bill, FORTRAN), (Alan, FORTRAN)\}$
g. $\{(Bill, M)(Alan, M)\}$
h. $\{Bill, Alan\}$

Q12.7 Function override

a. $\{(Bill, 20), (Sue, 19), (Alan, 16)\}$
b. $\{(Bill, 19), (Sue, 19), (Alan, 16)\}$
c. $\{(Sue, Toyota), (Bill, Ford)\}$
d. $\{(Sue, Toyota), (Bill, Ford), (Alan, Ford)\}$
e. $\{(Bill, 19), (Sue, 19), (Alan, 16)\}$

Q12.13 Writing sequences in set extension form.

a. $\{(1,B), (2,A), (3,T)\}$
b. $\{(1,T), (2,A), (3,B)\}$
c. $\{(1,T), (2,A), (3,T), (4,A)\}$
d. $\{(1,A)\}$
e. $\{(1,A), (2,B), (3,C)\}$
f. $\{\,\}$
g. $\{(1,A)\}$
h. $\{(1,A)\}$

Q12.14 Rewriting sets as sequences.

a. [Q,U,T]
b. [U,Q]
c. [U,N,I]
d. [B,C,A,E]
e. []

Q12.15 Evaluating expressions as simple sequences.

    a.   K

    b.   [U,E,E,N]

    c.   [S,H,O,P]

    d.   [K,E,E,N]

    e.   [B,I,S]

Chapter 13

Q13.1 Process descriptions

    a.   A schema *Successor* which takes an integer and returns the next integer in sequence.

$$\begin{array}{|l}\hline \textit{Successor} \\ \hline in?, out! : N \\ \hline out! = in? + 1 \\ \hline \end{array}$$

    b.   A schema *Max* which takes two integers and returns the larger of the two.

$$\begin{array}{|l}\hline \textit{Max} \\ \hline i?, j? : N \\ max! : N \\ \hline i? > j? \Rightarrow max! = i? \\ \neg(i? > j?) \Rightarrow max! = j? \\ \hline \end{array}$$

    c.   A schema *Largest* which takes a set of integers and returns the largest.

$$\begin{array}{|l}\hline \textit{Largest} \\ \hline in? : \text{Set of } N \\ max! : N \\ \hline \#in? > 0 \\ max! \in in? \\ \neg \exists n : in? - \{max!\} \bullet n > max! \\ \hline \end{array}$$

    d.   A schema *Between* ...

```
┌─ Between ──────────────────────────────
│ hi?, lo? : N
│ b! : N
├────────────────────────────────────────
│ hi? > lo?
│ b! ∈ hi?..lo?
└────────────────────────────────────────
```

Q13.2   Family matters

```
┌─ Family ───────────────────────────────
│ mum, dad : Person
│ children : Set of Person
├────────────────────────────────────────
│ sex(mum) = F
│ sex(dad) = M
│ ∀ c : children • mother(c) = mum ∧ father(c) = dad
│ ∀ c : children • (age(mum) − age(c) ≥ 16) ∧ (age(dad) − age(c) ≥ 16)
│ #children < 16
└────────────────────────────────────────
```

Chapter 14

Q14.1   Pete's TV RENTAL Company

The *RentTV* Declaration

1. $\Delta\,TVRental$
   The operation causes a change to the state of the shop.
2. $t? : TV$
   The TV being rented must be identified.
3. $p? : Person$
   The person renting the TV must also be identified.

The *RentTV* Predicate

1. $t? \in Stock$
   The TV must be one of Peter's.
2. $t? \in Working$
   The TV must be in working order.
3. $t? \notin \text{dom } OnHire$
   But, obviously, it cannot already be out on hire to someone.

Selected answers for Chapter 14

4. $OnHire' = OnHire \cup \{(t?, p?)\}$
   The record of which TV's are on hire and to whom is extended to show that this TV is being hired by this customer.

5. $Stock' = Stock$
   The operation does not affect the overall stock of TV's owned by Peter.

6. $Working' = Working$
   Renting a TV does not miraculously fix a TV nor does it cause one to break down (we hope).

Q14.2 Operation Schemas

a. *NormalReturn* – a TV $t?$, currently out on hire, is returned at the end of its period of contract.

$$
\begin{array}{|l}
\_NormalReturn_____ \\
\Delta TVRental \\
t? : TV \\
\hline
t? \in dom\ OnHire \\
OnHire' = \{t?\} \vartriangleleft OnHire \\
Stock' = Stock \\
Working' = Working
\end{array}
$$

1. The TV must be out on hire.
2. The TV is no longer recorded as being on hire.

b. *BreakDown* – a TV $t?$, currently out on hire, has broken down.

$$
\begin{array}{|l}
\_BreakDown_____ \\
\Delta TVRental \\
t? : TV \\
\hline
t? \in dom\ OnHire \\
t? \in Working \\
Working' = Working - \{t?\} \\
Stock' = Stock \\
OnHire' = OnHire
\end{array}
$$

c. *BigDeal* – a customer $p?$ rents a number of TV's $tvset?$, all of which are in working order of course.

$\underline{\quad BigDeal\quad\quad\quad\quad\quad\quad\quad\quad\quad\quad\quad\quad\quad\quad\quad\quad\quad}$
$\Delta TVRental$
$p?: Person$
$tvset?: Set\ of\ TV$
\
$tvset? \subseteq Working$
$tvset \cap dom\ OnHire = \{\}$
$OnHire' = OnHire \cup \{t : tvset? \bullet (t, p?)\}$
$Stock' = Stock$
$Working' = Working$

d. *Target* – a list *whingers*! of those customers with a faulty TV is to be produced.

$\underline{\quad Target\quad\quad\quad\quad\quad\quad\quad\quad\quad\quad\quad\quad\quad\quad\quad\quad\quad}$
$\Xi TVRental$
$whingers!: Set\ of\ Person$
\
$whingers! = \{t : dom\ OnHire \mid t \notin Working \bullet OnHire(t)\}$

e. *FixIt* – a faulty TV $t?$ is repaired at the customer's home or premises.

$\underline{\quad FixIt\quad\quad\quad\quad\quad\quad\quad\quad\quad\quad\quad\quad\quad\quad\quad\quad\quad}$
$\Delta TVRental$
$t?: TV$
\
$t? \in dom\ OnHire$
$t? \notin Working$
$Working' = Working \cup \{t?\}$
$Stock' = Stock$
$OnHire' = OnHire$

f. *SwitchTV* – a working TV $ok?$, one that is not on hire, is provided in place of a faulty TV $rs?$ that *is* currently on hire.

$\underline{\quad SwitchTV\quad\quad\quad\quad\quad\quad\quad\quad\quad\quad\quad\quad\quad\quad\quad}$
$\Delta TVRental$
$ok?, rs?: TV$
\
$ok? \in Working - dom\ OnHire$
$rs? \in dom\ OnHire - Working$
$OnHire' = (\{rs?\} \triangleleft OnHire) \cup \{(ok?, OnHire(rs?))\}$
$Stock' = Stock$
$Working' = Working$

Q14.3 At the corner shop

    a. How long is the queue?

$$\begin{array}{|l}
\underline{QueueLength} \\
\Xi Shop \\
q! : N \\
\hline
q! = \#queue
\end{array}$$

    b. How many people are there in the shop altogether?

$$\begin{array}{|l}
\underline{HowFull} \\
\Xi Shop \\
c! : N \\
\hline
c! = \#queue + \#shopping
\end{array}$$

    c. Someone, $c?$, enters the shop.

$$\begin{array}{|l}
\underline{Entry} \\
\Delta Shop \\
c? : Person \\
\hline
c? \notin shopping \\
c? \notin ran\ queue \\
shopping' = shopping \cup \{c?\} \\
queue' = queue
\end{array}$$

    d. Someone, $c?$, joins the queue.

$$\begin{array}{|l}
\underline{JoinQueue} \\
\Delta Shop \\
c? : Person \\
\hline
c? \in shopping \\
queue' = queue \frown [c?] \\
shopping' = shopping - \{c?\}
\end{array}$$

e. Someone pays and leaves.

$\boxed{\begin{array}{l}\textit{Pays} \\ \Delta\textit{Shop} \\ \hline \#queue > 0 \\ queue' = tail\ queue \\ shopping' = shopping \end{array}}$

f. Someone, $c?$, leaves the queue.

$\boxed{\begin{array}{l}\textit{JustRemembered} \\ \Delta\textit{Shop} \\ c? : Person \\ \hline \exists f, b : seq\ Person\ \bullet \\ \quad queue = f \frown [c?] \frown b \\ \quad \#f > 0 \\ \quad queue' = f \frown b \\ \quad shopping' = shopping \cup \{c?\} \end{array}}$

The predicate within the *JustRemembered* schema states that:
- There must be two sequences of people f and b.
- The queue must consist of the sequence f followed by the customer who has just remembered followed by the sequence b.
- The sequence f must not be empty (and so the customer must not be at the front of the queue).
- The queue afterwards is formed by joining those customers before and those after our selected customer.
- The customer returns to the set of those still looking.

g. Which customers are still "just looking"?

$\boxed{\begin{array}{l}\textit{JustLooking} \\ \Xi\textit{Shop} \\ c! : Set\ of\ Person \\ \hline c! = shopping \end{array}}$

Q14.6 In the bank

a. Someone comes into the bank.

$$
\begin{array}{|l}
\underline{CustomerEnters} \\
\Delta Bank \\
p? : Person \\
\hline
p? \notin others \\
p? \notin ran\ queue \\
p? \notin ran\ busy \\
others' = others \cup \{p?\} \\
open' = open \\
busy' = busy \\
queue' = queue
\end{array}
$$

b. Someone leaves the bank.

$$
\begin{array}{|l}
\underline{CustomerLeaves} \\
\Delta Bank \\
p? : Person \\
\hline
p? \in others \\
others' = others - \{p?\} \\
open' = open \\
busy' = busy \\
queue' = queue
\end{array}
$$

c. Someone completes a transaction and leaves the teller's window.

$$
\begin{array}{|l}
\underline{CompletesTransaction} \\
\Delta Bank \\
p? : Person \\
\hline
p? \in ran\ busy \\
busy' = busy \rhd \{p?\} \\
others' = others \cup \{p?\} \\
open' = open \\
queue' = queue
\end{array}
$$

Or, alternatively with the teller as input:

┌─ *Completes Transaction* ─────────────────
│ $\Delta Bank$
│ $t?: Teller$
├───
│ $t? \in \text{dom } busy$
│ $busy' = \{t?\} \triangleleft busy$
│ $others' = others \cup \{busy(t?)\}$
│ $open' = open$
│ $queue' = queue$
└───

d. Someone goes from the front of the queue to a teller.

┌─ *NextPlease* ────────────────────────────
│ $\Delta Bank$
│ $t?: Teller$
├───
│ $t \in open$
│ $t? \notin \text{dom } busy$
│ $\#queue > 0$
│ $busy' = busy \cup \{(t?, \text{head } queue)\}$
│ $queue' = \text{tail } queue$
│ $open' = open$
│ $others' = others$
└───

e. A teller opens his or her window.

┌─ *OpensUp* ───────────────────────────────
│ $\Delta Bank$
│ $t?: Teller$
├───
│ $t? \notin open$
│ $open' = open \cup \{t?\}$
│ $busy' = busy$
│ $queue' = queue$
│ $others' = others$
└───

f. A teller closes down, but only if he or she is not handling a customer and only if there is at least one other teller still open.

─ *CloseDown* ─────────────────────
$\Delta Bank$
$t? : Teller$
─────────
$t? \in open$
$t? \notin dom\ busy$
$\#open > 1$
$open' = open - \{t?\}$
$busy' = busy$
$queue' = queue$
$others' = others$
──────────────────────────────

g. Someone joins the queue.

─ *JoinQueue* ─────────────────────
$\Delta Bank$
$p? : Person$
─────────
$p? \in others$
$queue' = queue \frown [p?]$
$others' = others - \{p?\}$
$open' = open$
$busy' = busy$
──────────────────────────────

h. Someone leaves the queue without commencing a transaction.

─ *LeavesQueue* ───────────────────
$\Delta Bank$
$p? : Person$
─────────
$\exists f, b : seq\ Person \bullet$
$\qquad queue = f \frown [p?] \frown b$
$\qquad queue' = f \frown b$
$\qquad others' = others \cup \{p?\}$
$\qquad open' = open$
$\qquad busy' = busy$
──────────────────────────────

Q14.7 Files on floppy

Here is an operation schema that specifies the effect of deleting a file from the disk.

$$
\begin{array}{|l}
\_DeleteFile _____ \\
\Delta Floppy \\
f?: Name \\
\hline
f? \in dom\ FileData \\
FileData' = \{f?\} \triangleleft FileData \\
Used' = Used - \#Filedata(f?) \\
Left' = Left + \#Filedata(f?) \\
\end{array}
$$

The *DeleteFile* Declaration

1. $\Delta Floppy$
   The operation will cause a change to the contents of the floppy.

2. $f? : Name$
   The name of the file to be deleted will be supplied as input.

The *DeleteFile* Predicate

1. $f? \in dom\ FileData$
   There must be a file on disk with the name specified.

2. $FileData' = \{f?\} \triangleleft FileData$
   The file (and its contents) are removed by domain subtraction.

3. $Used' = Used - \#FileData(f?)$
   There is a decrease in the amount of used space on the disk.

4. $Left' = Left + \#FileData(f?)$
   There is a corresponding increase in the space left for new files.

Q14.8 Floppy operations

a. A new file called $f?$ containing data $d?$ is to be created on the disk.

Selected answers for Chapter 14

```
┌─ CreateFile ────────────────────────────────
│ Δ Floppy
│ f? : Name
│ d? : seq Byte
│─────────────────────────────────────────────
│ f? ∉ dom FileData
│ #d? ≤ Left
│ FileData' = FileData ∪ {(f?, d?)}
│ Used' = Used + #d?
│ Left' = Left − #d?
└─────────────────────────────────────────────
```

b. The contents of a file called *from?* are to be copied to a new file to be called *to?*.

```
┌─ CopyFile ──────────────────────────────────
│ Δ Floppy
│ from?, to? : Name
│─────────────────────────────────────────────
│ from? ∈ dom FileData
│ to? ∉ dom FileData
│ #FileData(from?) ≤ Left
│ FileData' = FileData ∪ {(to?, FileData(from?))}
│ Used' = Used + #FileData(from?)
│ Left' = Left − #FileData(from?)
└─────────────────────────────────────────────
```

c. The file currently called *old?* is to be renamed as file *new?*.

```
┌─ RenameFile ────────────────────────────────
│ Δ Floppy
│ old?, new? : Name
│─────────────────────────────────────────────
│ old? ∈ dom FileData
│ new? ∉ dom FileData
│ FileData' = ({old?} ⩤ FileData) ∪ {(new?, FileData(old?))}
│ Used' = used
│ Left' = Left
└─────────────────────────────────────────────
```

d. A list *all!* of all the files on the disk and their sizes is to be output along with the number of files *count!* and the amount of space available *free!*.

570 Information Modeling

Directory

$\Xi Floppy$
$all! : Name \nrightarrow N$
$count!, free! : N$

$all! = \{f : dom\ FileData \bullet (f, \#FileData)f))\}$
$count! = \#all!$
$free! = Left$

---

e. The contents of the file called $f?$ are to be replaced with new data $nd?$.

NewData

$\Delta Floppy$
$f? : Name$
$nd? : seq\ Byte$

$f? \in dom\ FileData$
$\#nd? - \#FileData(f?) \leq Left$
$FileData' = (\{f?\} \triangleleft FileData) \cup \{(f?, nd?)\}$
$Used' = Used + \#nd? - \#FileData(f?)$
$Left = Left' - (\#nd? - \#FileData(f?))$

Chapter 15

Q15.1 Defining the ACADEMIC database.

    a. Creating the tables.

```
Create table Schools
(School_Id      char(2)    not null,
 School_Name    char(30)   not null,
 Phone          char(4)    not null,
 Head_Id        integer)
Create table Staff
(Staff_Id       integer    not null,
 Staff_Name     char(20)   not null,
 School_Id      char(2)    not null)
Create table Quals
(Staff_Id       integer    not null,
 Degree         char(10)   not null,
 Place          char(20)   not null,
 Year           integer    not null)
```

    b. Creating unique indexes.

```
           Create unique index Schools_Key
               on Schools(School_Id)
           Create unique index Staff_Key
               on Staff(Staff_Id)
           Create unique index Quals_Key
               on Quals(Staff_Id, Degree)
```
   c. Creating secondary indexes on foreign keys.
```
           Create index School_Staff
               on Staff(School_Id)
           Create index Staff_Quals
               on Quals(Staff_Id)
```
   Note that the **Head_Id** column of the **Schools** table is also a foreign key, referring to the relevant row in the **Staff** table. A secondary index is not required because there should be only one staff member with the relevant Id and that person's row may be quickly accessed through the **Staff_Key** index.

Q15.2 Creating tables for the ACADEMIC database using the extended syntax.

```
           Create table Schools
           (School_Id       char(2)     not null,
            School_Name     char(30)    not null,
            Phone           char(4)     not null,
            Head_Id         integer,

            Primary key(School_Id),
            Foreign key(Head_Id) references Staff(Staff_Id),
            Unique(School_Name))
           Create table Staff
           (Staff_Id        integer     not null,
            Staff_Name      char(20)    not null,
            School_Id       char(2)     not null,

            Primary key(Staff_Id),
            Foreign key(School_Id) references Schools(School_Id))
           Create table Quals
           (Staff_Id        integer     not null,
            Degree          char(10)    not null,
            Place           char(20)    not null,
            Year            integer     not null,

            Primary key(Staff_Id, Degree),
            Foreign key(Staff_Id) references Staff(Staff_Id))
```

Q15.5 The `Time_24` view

```
Create view Time_24(HH, MM)
   as Select trunc(Minute/60), mod(Minute/60)
      From   Mins
```

Q15.8 GRUMBLERS

```
Select Id, Day, Mth, Year, 'Error 1'
From   Grumblers
Where  Mth in ('Sep', 'Apr', 'Jun', 'Nov')
 and   Day not between 1 and 30
union
Select Id, Day, Mth, Year, 'Error 2'
From   Grumblers
Where  Mth in ('Jan', 'Mar', 'May', 'Jul', 'Aug', 'Oct', 'Dec')
 and   Day not between 1 and 31
union
Select Id, Day, Mth, Year, 'Error 3.1'
From   Grumblers
Where  Mth = 'Feb'
 and   mod(Year,4) <> 0
 and   Day not between 1 and 28
union
Select Id, Day, Mth, Year, 'Error 3.2'
From   Grumblers
Where  Mth = 'Feb'
 and   mod(Year,4) = 0 and (mod(Year,100) <> 0
                             or mod(Year,400) = 0)
 and   Day not between 1 and 29
union
Select Id, Day, Mth, Year, 'Error 3.3'
From   Grumblers
Where  Mth = 'Feb'
 and   (mod(Year,100) = 0 and mod(Year,400) <> 0)
 and   Day not between 1 and 28
```

Q15.9 The Horse Racing Database

a. For each table, identify any foreign keys it contains.

Selected answers for Chapter 15

Table	Foreign Key	Table referenced
Horses	Sire	Horses
	Dam	Horses
Races	Course + Race_Date	Conditions
Results	Course + Race_Date	Conditions
	Race_No + Course + Race_Date	Races
	Horse_Name	Horses

b. Defining the database

```
Create table Horses
(Horse_Name    char(20)       not null,
 Age           number(2,0)    not null,
 Sex           char(10)       not null,
 Sire          char(20),
 Dam           char(20),

 Primary key(Horse_Name),
 Foreign key(Sire) references Horses(Horse_Name),
 Foreign key(Dam)  references Horses(Horse_Name))

Create table Races
(Race_No       number(2,0)    not null,
 Race_Name     char(20)       not null,
 Time          char(5)        not null,
 Length        number(4,0)    not null,
 Course        char(20)       not null,
 Race_Date     number(6,0)    not null,
 Prize_Money   number(6,0)    not null,

 Primary key(Race_No, Course, Race_Date),
 Foreign key(Course, Race_Date)
         references Conditions(Course, Race_Date))

Create table Results
(Course        char(20)       not null,
 Race_Date     number(6,0)    not null,
 Race_No       number(2,0)    not null,
 Gate_No       number(2,0)    not null,
 Handicap      number(2,0)    not null,
 Odds          number(3,1),
 Horse_Name    char(20)       not null,
 Jockey_Name   char(20)       not null,
 Trainer_Name  char(20)       not null,
 Place         number(2,0)    not null,
 Distance      number(4,0)    not null,

 Primary key(Course, Race_Date, Race_No, Place),
```

```
            Foreign key(Course, Race_Date)
                    references Conditions(Course, Race_Date),
            Foreign key(Race_No, Course, Race_Date)
                    references Races(Race_No, Course, Race_Date),
            Foreign key(Horse_Name)
                    references Horses(Horse_Name))
        Create table Conditions
        (Course          char(20)        not null,
         Race_Date       number(6,0)     not null,
         Weather         char(20)        not null,
         Track           char(20)        not null,

         Primary key(Course, Race_Date))
```

    c.   Primary indexes

```
        Create Unique Index Horses_Key
            on Horses(Horse_Name)
        Create Unique Index Races_Key
            on Races(Race_No,Course,Race_Date)
        Create Unique Index Results_Key
            on Results(Course,Race_Date,Race_No,Place)
        Create Unique Index Conditions_Key
            on Conditions(Course,Race_Date)
```

    d.   Secondary indexes for the foreign keys

```
        Create Index Horses_Sired
            on Horses(Sire)
        Create Index Horses_Damed
            on Horses(Dam)
        Create Index Race_Conditions
            on Races(Course,Race_Date)
        Create Index Results_Conditions
            on Results(Course,Race_Date)
        Create Index Race_Results
            on Results(Race_No,Course,Race_Date)
        Create Index Horse_Results
            on Results(Horse_Name)
```

Chapter 16

Q16.1   The ACADEMIC Database

    a.   A new member of staff.

```
Insert
Into   Staff
Values(25, 'J.Muir', 'AC')

Insert
Into   Quals
Values(25, 'BA', 'UFO', 1985)

Insert
Into   Quals
Values(25, 'MBA', 'UBute', 1992)
```

b. The sudden departure of M. Bezzle.

```
Delete
From   Staff
Where Staff_Id = 6

Delete
From   Quals
Where Staff_Id = 6
```

c. The overdue departure of Prof. Tree.

```
Delete
From   Staff
Where Staff_Id = 1

Delete
From   Quals
Where Staff_Id = 1

Update Schools
Set    Head_Id = null
Where  Head_Id = 6
```

d. The doctoring of L. R. Parser.

```
Insert
Into   Quals
Values(?, 'PhD', 'UCC', 1995)
```

e. Maybe chemists don't have solutions after all.

```
Delete
From   Quals
```

576   Information Modeling

```
        Where Staff_Id in (Select Staff_Id
                           From    Staff
                           Where   School_Id = 'CH')

        Delete
        From   Staff
        Where  School_Id = 'CH'

        Delete
        From   Schools
        Where  School_Id = 'CH'
```

Q16.2   The RESOURCE Database

    a.   The Cosy Theater partitioned.

```
        Insert
        Into   Theaters
        Values('Tiddly', 5)

        Insert
        Into   Theaters
        Values("Winks', 25)

        Delete
        From   Theaters
        Where  Theater = 'Cosy'
```

    b.   Knocking rooms together.

```
        Update Theaters T
        Set    Capacity = (Select T.Capacity + Capacity
                           From    Theaters
                           Where   Theater = 'Tiny')
        Where  Theater = 'Cramp'

        Delete
        From   Theaters
        Where  Theater = 'Tiny'
```

    c.   The bureaucratic answer to market forces.

```
        Delete
        From   Allocation A
        Where  Enrolled > (Select Capacity
```

```
                     From   Theaters
                     Where  Theater = A.Theater)
```

d. The effect of late-night showings of Fred Astaire films.

```
Update Allocation
Set    Enrolled = Enrolled + 1
Where  Subject = 'TapDancing'
```

e. Mr Hacker has been trapped by Ms Tripp.

```
Update Allocation
Set    Teacher = 'Hacker'
Where  Teacher = 'Tripp'
```

Q16.3 Political moves.

a. Hooray for Mike!

```
Insert
Into   Members
Values('Mike', 'Labor', 'West Wyalong')
```

b. Duane on the wane.

```
Update Parties
Set    Leader = null
Where  Leader = 'Duane'
```

c. A great honor for Denzil.

```
Update Parties
Set    Leader = 'Denzil'
Where  Party = 'Business'
```

d. Duane and Denzil no longer on speaking terms.

```
Delete
From   TalksTo
Where  Talker = 'Duane'
  and  Listener = 'Denzil'
```

e. Duane is isolated.

578   Information Modeling

```
        Delete
        From  TalksTo
        Where Listener = 'Duane'
```

f. Marge is disgusted.

```
        Delete
        From  Members
        Where Member = 'Marge'

        Delete
        From  TalksTo
        Where Talker = 'Marge'
           or Listener = 'Marge'

        Update Parties
        Set    Leader = null
        Where  Leader = 'Marge'
```

Q16.4 The Supermarket Shuffle

a. Alan comes into the supermarket and joins those people still shopping.

```
        Insert
        Into  Shopping
        Values('Alan')
```

b. Sue joins the end of the queue at checkout C3.

```
        Insert
        Into    Queues
        Select 'Sue', 'C3', max(Place)+1
        From    Queues
        Where   CheckId = 'C3'
```

c. The customer at the front of checkout C2 pays and leaves.

```
        Delete
        From   Queues
        Where  CheckId = 'C2'
          and  Place = 1
```

d. Bob, somewhere in the queue at checkout C1, returns to the aisles.

```
        Update Queues
          Set Place = Place -1
        Where CheckId = (Select CheckId
                         From   Queues
                         Where  CustId = 'Bob')
          and      Place > (Select Place
```

```
          From    Queues
          Where   CustId = 'Bob')
Insert
  Into Shopping
Values('Bob')
```

Index

− (set subtraction) 288, 289, 293, 319
== 297, 299
8, 271, 339
Δ 334
Ξ 339
∩ 287
∪ 267, 287, 288, 292
≡ 41
∃! 272, 324
∃ 271, 272, 324
∀ 275, 324
⇔ 281, 282, 323
⇒ 276, 277, 323
∈ 10, 323
∧ 270, 323
∨ 271, 323
¬ 268, 270, 323
⊕ 294, 295
⌢ 300, 321
⊆ 7, 59, 287, 289
× 62, 82, 248
◁ 293, 294, 295
↦ 26, 36, 269, 320
    defined 297
↠ 29, 36, 269, 320
    defined 298
↔ 21, 36, 268, 320
    defined 297
▷ 294, 295
→ 26, 36, 269, 320
    defined 297
↣ 28, 36, 269, 320
    defined 298
Abbreviations
    defining 297
ACADEMIC database 107, 142, 381, 400
Aggregation 82, 186, 189, 191
    rule 182, 185
Alias
    in SQL 156

And 36, 38, 270
Application
    generator 120, 421
    programming 405
Assess
    relation 92
    table 372
Association 41
Attribute
    domain 81
    naming rules 190
Attributes
    as functions 246
    as products 248
    as sets 248
    compound 248
    in ER modeling 241, 242, 246
    key 93, 191, 360
    naming 260
    non-key 192, 360
    of relationships 246
    or entities? 258
    record type 190
    relation 80
    set-valued 248, 249, 257
    simple 246
    that identify 246, 260
    that measure 260
avg 132
Base
    tables 112
    types 22
Built-in functions
    in SQL 154
Change
    describing 291
COBOL 309, 314
    host language interface 407
Commutation 41
Conceptual schema 189, 221

Index

as rudimentary knowledge-base 311
diagram 170, 182, 183, 187, 188
Conjunction 36, 37, 270
   and 36
   truth table 38
   used with existential quantification 272
Constraints
   entity integrity 191
   foreign key 104
   inclusion dependency 197
   referential integrity 89, 104, 190, 197
   relation key 104, 196
   uniqueness 178
Correlated subqueries 155, 156
`count` 117, 132
`Create index` 114
`Create table` 113
Data modeling 16, 262, 310
Database
   schema 186, 197, 221, 235
Database definition
   formal 197, 234
   in SQL 358
Database design 79, 344, 360
   ER modeling vs fact-based analysis 244
   from an ER model 252
   using ER modeling 241
Database manipulation
   in SQL 386
Database security
   in SQL 397
Databases
   ACADEMIC 107, 142
   RESOURCES 108
   ROCKY CONCRETE 144
   SUBJECT 92
Datatypes
   character strings 365
   date 368
   numbers 363
DBMS 111, 358, 406
   host language interface 407
De Morgan's laws 41, 279

Declaration 6, 60
   syntax 61
Defining
   new partial function symbols 285, 286
   new relation symbols 283
   new total function symbols 283, 285
`Delete` 118
Derived column
   in SQL 137
Determinants 189, 230, 233
Disjunction 36, 38, 271
   or 36
   truth table 39
Documentation
   as knowledge repository 309
dom 7, 22, 287, 288
Domain 7, 22
   attribute 81
   subtraction 293
Domains
   composite 89
   compound 85
   set valued 86, 90
   simple 85
`Drop table` 114
EBNF 204, 341
   and power set 342
   and product set 342
   and state schemas 343
   further abstraction 213
   summary 204
Embedded SQL 120
Entity integrity 191
Entity types 170, 172, 220, 252, 253
   dependent 248, 249, 250, 253
   in ER modeling 241, 242
   integrity 191
   naming 259
   or attributes 258
   or relationships 259
   regular 249
   weak 248, 249, 250
Equivalence 271, 281, 282
   truth table 282
ER diagram

582   Index

    as rudimentary knowledge base 311
ER modeling 241, 262, 344
    and fact-based analysis 244, 261
    attributes 241, 246
    attributes that identify 246
    cardinality of relationships 243
    entity types 241
    many-to-many relationships 245, 247
    one-to-many relationships 243, 244, 245
    one-to-one relationships 246
    relationships 241
Existential quantification 271, 272
    and sets 273
    used with conjunction 272
Exists 156, 157
Fact types 77, 170, 172, 177, 220, 320
    aggregating 182
    extracting 209, 211, 223, 224
    irreducible 183, 184
    many-valued 177, 181
    merging 78, 79, 174, 220
    nested 185, 187
    single-valued 177, 178, 179, 181
    uncovering 222
Fact-based analysis 220, 221, 262
    and ER modeling 261
Facts
    adding new 291
    and relations 170
    general 3, 267
    general, strong 278
    general, weak 278
    modifying 294
    removing 293
    specific 3, 18, 267
First-normal form 86
Foreign key 88, 94, 95, 235
    constraint 104
Forms
    automated 422
    control panel 423
    data fields 424
    filling 421
    office use only 422, 424
    triggered actions 425

From 115, 125, 130
Function
    application 25, 29, 30, 269
    argument 25
    override 294
    symbol ($\rightarrow$) 26
Functions
    age 35
    as sets 64
    defining new symbols 283, 285
    domain 27
    drives 35
    generic 287
    partial 26, 269, 285
    partial function symbol defined 297
    range 27
    sex 35
    total 26, 269, 283
    total function symbol defined 297
General statements
    strong 278
    weak 278
Generic
    functions 287
    relations 287
Grant 119
Group by 133, 136
Having 135
head 300
Host language interface
    assignment 414
    COBOL 407
    cursors 408, 418
    declare section 407, 411
    exception handling 407, 412
    indicator variables 408, 419
    null values 408
    pre-processing 408
    SQL communications area 407, 411
    SQLcode variable 415
Implementation 12, 312, 331, 343, 348, 351, 470
    verification 485
Implication 271, 275, 276, 277
    truth table 277

used with universal quantification 276
In 152, 153
Inclusion dependency 197
Indexes
    advantages and disadvantages 379
    and joins 377
    creating 376
    dropping 380
    in SQL 114, 358, 374
    primary 374
    secondary 376
    unique 374, 375
Infix
    form 33, 34
Injections
    `left` 35
    partial 29, 269
    partial injection symbol defined 298
    `spouse` 35
    total 28, 269
    total injection symbol defined 298
`Insert` 118
Irreducible fact types
    marking uniqueness constraints 185
Join 126, 130
    condition 128, 131
    in SQL 126
    operation 95, 100
    using indexes 377
Key
    attributes 93, 191
Keys
    foreign 88, 94, 95, 235
    primary 235
    relation 85
Knowledge 267, 310
    base 4, 309
    embodied in a specification 312
    embodied in an implementation 312
    forms of expressing 311
    organizational 309, 311
    representation using Z 312
    two forms 309
Many-to-many relationships
    in ER modeling 245, 247, 253

`plays` 35
`speaks` 35
Many-valued fact types 181
`max` 132
Merging
    fact types 174
    single-valued fact types 175, 178
`min` 132
Negation 36, 37, 268, 270
    not 36
    truth table 37
Non-first normal form 86, 406
Not 36, 268, 270
Null values 78, 79, 82, 177, 190, 192, 360
    and nested fact types 194
    disallowing 370
    in SQL 113, 126
    in table alteration 361
    indicator variables 419
    looking for 192, 193, 220, 233
    not in key attributes 194
One-point rule 274, 488, 489
    revisited 487
One-to-many relationships
    `age` 35
    `drives` 35
    in ER modeling 243, 244, 245, 253
    `sex` 35
One-to-one relationships
    in ER modeling 246, 256
    `left` 35
    `spouse` 35
Or 36, 271
`Order by` 116
Partial function 26, 35
    symbol ($\nrightarrow$) 26, 36
Partial injection 29, 35
    symbol ($\rightarrowtail$) 29, 36
Pattern matching
    in SQL 139
Post-conditions 9, 336
Power set 6, 7, 59, 318
    and EBNF 342
    and set-valued attributes 248
    construction 60

operator (*Set of*) 60
Pre-conditions 9, 336
Predicate 6, 19
    substituting in 274
    symbol 20
Predicate calculus 267, 268
    and set theory 274
Prefix
    form 33, 34
Primary key 235
Product
    operation 95, 99
    queries 138
Product set 62, 318
    and EBNF 342
    and compound attributes 248
    construction 62
    operator ($\times$) 62
Project operation 95, 98
Pseudocode 309
Quantification 268, 271
    equivalences 278
    existential 271, 272, 272
    summary 277
    unique 272
    universal 275
Queries
    all 153
    any 153
    group by 133, 136
    in 152
    inner 154
    join 126
    nested 150
    nesting 149
    product 138
Query nesting 149
ran 7, 22, 287
Range 7, 22
    subtraction 294
Record types 83, 190, 220, 221, 252, 345
    attributes 190
    constructing 229
    formal definition 195
    non-key attributes 220
Redundancy 174, 175, 177

Referential integrity 89, 104, 190, 197
    and deletion 394
    and insertion 394
    and update 394
    in SQL 370, 393
Refinement 470, 485
    applicability 486, 488
    correctness 486, 489
    data 470
    initial state 486, 490
    rules 486
Relation
    attribute 80
    definition 84
    key 93
    subset 287
    symbol ($\leftrightarrow$) 21, 36
Relation key
    constraint 104, 196
Relational
    terminology 112
Relational algebra 95, 96
    join 95
    product 95
    project 95
    select 95
Relational calculus 95, 96
    and SQL 96, 492
    summary 101
    syntax 102
Relational database 91, 92
Relational languages 94
Relational model
    general 80, 91
    standard 80, 91
Relational product 128
Relations
    and facts 170
    as sets 63
    binary 77, 171
    defining new symbols 283
    domain 81
    dynamic data object 81
    first-normal form 86
    generic 287, 289
    in computing 81

Index

infix 35, 268
key 85
NF2 86
non-first normal form 86
normalized 86
plays 35
prefix 35, 269
speaks 35
symbol defined 297
Relationship
   objectified 185
   one-to-one 24, 27
Relationships
   attributes of 247
   cardinality of 243
   hierarchical 249, 250
   in ER modeling 241, 242, 243
   naming 259
   or entities 259
   recursive 249, 250
RESOURCES database 108, 381, 400
Results
   relation 92
Results table
   foreign key references 372
Revoke 119
ROCKY CONCRETE database 144
Role
   box 172, 179, 185
Roles
   mandatory 261
   optional 261
Schema
   decoration 333
   inclusion 332
   signature 314
Schema type 83
Schemas
   abstract state 346, 471
   abstraction 481
   conceptual 170, 182, 186, 221, 344
   concrete state 346
   database 186, 197, 221, 235, 345, 351
   developing state 341
   frame 334

in Z 324
mapping 347, 481
operation 9, 331, 334, 344, 351, 434, 449, 471
operation (as transactions) 405
operation (conventions) 10, 334
operation (implementation of) 348, 349
program 349
read-only 339
simulation 485
state 6, 326, 331, 341, 343, 351, 433, 448, 471
state (implementation of) 350
state and database 346, 349
type 83, 326
Z 312
Security
   in SQL 119
Select 115, 125
Select operation 95, 97
Sentence
   assocation 41
   commutation 41
   construction 39
   equivalence 41
   evaluation 40
   phrasing 41
Sentences
   compound 36, 268, 270
   declarative 18, 170
   simple 268
seq 7
Sequences 7, 298, 299, 321
   concatenating 300
   constructing 300
   decomposing 300
   domain 299
   head 300
   operations on 300
   tail 300
Set
   cardinality (size) 8
   comprehension 48, 49, 52, 68, 162, 318
   count 58

extension 48, 49, 68, 162, 317
    `in` 57
    `intersect` 58
    intersection 58, 287
    membership 10, 57
    `minus` 57
    operations 49, 57, 68
    power 59
    product 62
    size 8, 58, 271
    subset 59
    subtraction 57, 288
    terms 68, 317
    theory 267
    `union` 57, 267, 287
Set membership
    in SQL 152
Set theory
    and predicate calculus 274
Sets 48, 317
    and existential quantification 273
Signature 314
Significant set of facts 179
Single-valued fact types 181
Specific facts 172
Specification 309, 312, 331, 351
    abstract 471
    concrete 478
    executable 470
SQL 12, 267, 358
    alias 156
    `all` 154, 155
    `all` queries 153
    `alter table` definition 361
    and relational calculus 492
    `any` 154
    `any` queries 153
    application generators 120
    assignment 414
    `avg` 132
    base tables 112, 162
    `between` 125
    built-in functions 154
    catalog 112
    `check` clause 370, 371
    `close cursor` 418

`commit` 393
communications area 407, 411
correlated subqueries 155, 156, 169
`count` 117, 132
`create index` 114
`create index` definition 376
`create table` 113, 235, 236, 358
`create table` definition 359
`create unique` index 374
`create view` 162, 164, 372, 373
`create view` definition 374, 396
cursors 408, 418
database definition 113, 358
database manipulation 117, 386
database modification 117
database retrieval 115
database security 119
datatypes 362
`declare cursor` definition 419
`delete` 118, 386, 391, 394
`delete` definition 392
`delete` statement 14
derived column 137
`drop index` definition 380
`drop table` 114
`drop table` definition 362
`drop view` definition 374
embedded 120
`exists` 156, 157, 159, 160
`exists` queries 156, 169
`fetch` 418
`fetch` definition 419
foreign key 235, 236
`foreign key` clause 370, 371
`from` 115, 125, 130
`from` clause 13
`grant` 119, 397, 398
`grant` definition 397
`group by` 133, 136
`group by` queries 147, 168
`having` 135
host language interface 120
`in` 153, 155
`in` queries 152, 168
index 114
indexes 358, 374

Index

inner query 153, 155, 156
`insert` 118, 386, 394
`insert` definition 387, 388
`insert` statement 14
interactive 119
`into` clause 414
introduction 111
join 130, 152
join condition 131
join queries 126, 146
`like` 139, 139
`max` 132, 132
modes of usage 406
modularization 149
nesting 149
null value 113
null value detection 126
null values 370
`open cursor` 418
`order by` 116, 160
outer query 155, 156
pattern matching 139
primary indexes 374
primary key 235, 236
`primary key` clause 370, 371
product 127
product queries 138, 148
pseudonym 156
query nesting 149
referential integrity 370, 393
`revoke` 119, 397
`revoke` definition 399
`rollback` 393
secondary indexes 376
`select` 115, 125
`select *` 115, 125
`select` clause 13
`select distinct` 115
`select` statement 13
`set` clause 389
set comprehension 162
set extension 162
set membership 152
simple nesting 151, 167
simple queries 125, 145
`SQLcode` variable 415

statistical queries 132, 146
subquery 150, 151, 152, 153
subquery in `set` clause 389
subquery usage 158
`sum` 132
summary functions 117
system catalog 163
system tables 112
table 114
terminology 112
three retrieval methods 124
transactions 392
`union` 149, 158, 159, 160, 161
`union` queries 169
`union` usage 161
`unique` clause 370, 371
`unique` indexes 374
`update` 118, 386, 394
`update` definition 389
`update` statement 15
using 119
`values` clause 387
view 114, 149, 162
view update 395
view usage 164
views 372
views with the check option 396
whenever clause 413
`where` 115
`where` clause 13
State
    invariant 7, 339, 339, 350
    schema 6, 326
    transition 333
States
    abstract 346
    concrete 346
    initial 341
Statistical queries
    in SQL 132
Students
    relation 92
    table 359, 372
SUBJECT database 92, 124, 371, 372, 393
Subquery 150

Subset 7, 59, 287
    symbol (⊆) 59
sum 132
Summary functions
    avg 132
    count 117, 132
    max 132
    min 132
    sum 132
System
    catalog 112
    tables 112, 113
Systems development
    data-oriented 310
    evolutionary 309
    knowledge-based 310
    process-oriented 310
Tables
    altering 361
    base 358
    creating 359
    dropping 362
    in SQL 114
    virtual 358
tail 300
Telephone heuristic 171
Terms 31, 269
    constant 32, 270
    function application 32, 270
    set 68, 317
    variable 32, 270
Theory 4
Total function
    symbol (→) 26, 36
Total injection 28, 35
    symbol (↣) 28, 36
Transactions
    in SQL 392
    processing 405, 420
Triggers 425, 457, 460
Truth table
    conjunction 38
    disjunction 39
    equivalence 282
    implication 277
    negation 37

Tuple 61, 81, 82
    projection 96
    variable 96
Type
    construction 318
    declaration 21
    introduction 23
    schema 83
Types
    base 22
    record 83
    schema 83
Union
    in SQL 149
Unique quantification 272
Uniqueness constraints 178, 179, 220
    looking for 227
    on irreducible fact types 185
    questions regarding 179, 180
Universal quantification 275
    used with implication 276
Universe of discourse 170, 183, 189
Update 118
Upto function 75, 284
Variable 32
Verification
    of implementation 485
View
    analysis 209
    relations 209
    structures 209
View relations
    deriving 209, 223, 224
View structures
    deriving 209, 223
    flattening 209
Views
    definition in SQL 374
    dropping in SQL 374
    external 91
    in SQL 114, 162, 372
    updating 395
    user 203, 221, 341, 351, 471
Where 115
Z 267, 343
    − 288, 319

Index

∩ 319
∪ 288, 319
∃! 272, 324
∃ 272, 324
∀ 275, 324
⇔ 323
⇒ 323
∈ 323
∧ 323
∨ 323
¬ 323
⊕ 294, 319
⌢ 300, 321
⊆ 289
◁ 293, 319
⇸ 320
⤔ 320
⇹ 320
▷ 294, 319
→ 320
↣ 320
as a knowledge representation language 312
compound predicates 323
conjunction 270
declaration 315
dom 288, 319
equivalence 271, 281
existential quantification 271, 272
fact types 320
head 300
implication 271, 276
introducing types 316
negation 270
notation 6, 267
power set 318
predicate calculus 267, 268
predicates 321, 322
product set 318
quantification 268, 271
quantified predicates 324
ran 319
schema 312, 313, 314
schema signature 314
sequence 321
sequences 298

set comprehension 318
set extension 317
set operations 319
set terms 317
set theory 267
simple predicates 322
special set operations 319
SQL 267
tail 300, 321
terms 269
type construction 318
type introduction 316
unique quantification 272
universal quantification 275